EARLY ENGLISH STAGES

1300 to 1660

Volume One 1300 to 1576

BY THE SAME AUTHOR

Early English Stages 1300–1660:
  Volume II, 1576–1660, Part I
  Volume II, 1576–1660, Part II
  Volume III, Plays and their Makers to 1576

Shakespeare's Dramatic Heritage

Death Watching a Combat; manuscript illuminations

Two illuminations in the MS. of Olivier de la Marche's allegorical poem, *Le Chevalier Délibéré* (*c.* 1485–1490), illustrating Atropos watching a Tournament from a scaffold stage. The Cloth of Estate is crimson edged with gold and the throne is draped with cloth of gold.

(See Notes to Illustrations, p. 391, below.)

EARLY
ENGLISH
STAGES

1300 to 1660

Volume One 1300 to 1576

by
GLYNNE WICKHAM
Head of the Department of Drama, University of Bristol

LONDON AND HENLEY: Routledge & Kegan Paul
NEW YORK: Columbia University Press
1980

First published in 1959
by Routledge & Kegan Paul Ltd
39 Store Street, London WC1E 7DD and
Broadway House, Newtown Road,
Henley-on-Thames, Oxon RG9 1EN
and Columbia University Press
New York
Reprinted 1963 and 1966
2nd edition 1980

Revisions set by Western Printing Services Ltd
and Printed in Great Britain by
Lowe & Brydone Printers Ltd
Thetford, Norfolk

British Library Cataloguing in Publication Data
Wickham, Glynne
Early English stages, 1300 to 1600.—2nd ed.
Vol. 1: 1300 to 1576
1. Theater—England—History
I. Title
792'.0942   PN2585
(RKP) ISBN 0 7100 0276 9
(CUP) ISBN 0 231 09620 8

FOR

GILBERT TALBOT, JACK BECKE
JOHN GOLDINGHAM, LEONARD SOLOMON

and

CHARLES KNAPP
killed in action, 1942–1944

PREFACE
TO THE SECOND EDITION

Twenty years ago when this first volume of *Early English Stages* was originally published, I had thought to try to reverse within the seemingly ample space of two volumes the approach that had prevailed until then towards English dramatic literature of the Middle Ages and the Renaissance, first by viewing the plays of both eras as components of an organically related and expanding whole that reached its zenith during the reign of James I, and secondly by examining the texts of these plays from the standpoint of a theatre artist rather than from that normally offered in books and by teachers to students of English literature.

This idea arose in my mind on returning to Oxford from the Royal Air Force in 1946 when I was already sure that I wished to make a career in civilian life as a director of plays. Even then, however, I suspected that anyone who was fired by this ambition, and who hoped to succeed over the next two or three decades in a profession where the classical repertoire (centred as it was on revivals of Elizabethan and Jacobean plays) was bound to figure largely in his or her directorial commissions, must first come to terms with a paradox: a canon of plays that had unquestionably first been scripted for open stages which had nevertheless in fact been presented for nearly three centuries behind a proscenium arch and against changeable, landscape settings. Which way, then, did the future beckon? Towards perseverance within the restrictive limits of the tired, aristocratic theatrical conventions of stage realism epitomized for us in nineteenth-century Grand Opera and twentieth-century cinematic melodrama? Or towards a recovery of poetic, imaginative freedom through a return to use of theatrical conventions appropriate to open stages?

William Poel, Harley Granville-Barker, Jacques Copeau—even, on occasion, Max Reinhardt—and above all the productions of Shakespeare's plays presented every summer by Robert Atkins in Regents Park and by the Oxford University Dramatic Society in College Gardens had already implanted the suspicion in my mind that the answer must lie in a return to open-stage techniques;

but nowhere, as yet (Nugent Monk's Maddermarket Theatre at Norwich nobly excepted) was there any theatre in Britain, amateur or professional, where such an idea could habitually be put to the test of practice. Accordingly any student who wished to try to prove what is now taken for granted—as well in North America at such centres as Stratford, Ontario; Minneapolis; Stratford, Connecticut; Ashland, Oregon; and in many university community theatres, as in this country by the R.S.C., the National Theatre and every Repertory Company—found himself obliged to re-examine the surviving records of an earlier theatrical tradition that had made Elizabethan and Jacobean actors and playmakers opt for an open, thrust stage. This study thus became the subject of my D.Phil. thesis, reinforced in so far as time and opportunity allowed, with practical experience of stage-productions adopting this convention.

Once launched upon this exploration, the deeper I probed behind the familiar De Witt sketch of the Swan Playhouse and the several reconstructions of the so-called Globe and Fortune Theatres (distinction rarely being made in those days between the first and the second in either case) the more I became aware of a connection that must once have existed between dramatic spectacle and illiteracy; or rather between theatrical spectacle employed to figure abstract concepts in concrete terms for audiences whose tolerance, still less their understanding, of intricate, verbal debate was limited by their lack of formal education, and drama that sought self-consciously to mix profit (or moral instruction) with pleasure (or entertainment) for men and women untrained in clerkly skills. And within that broad context Tournaments, Civic Pageants, Folk Mummings and Court Disguisings, far from being the mere trivia they were so frequently dismissed as being in histories of English drama because seemingly bankrupt of texts of literary importance, now clamoured to be taken into account: so did the specifically religious plays of Roman Catholic inspiration and the Moral Interludes of Reformation polemic that were habitually and contemptuously relegated in schools and universities to the outer perimeters of their syllabuses as too quaint, naive and crude to merit serious study. I therefore chose, both within my doctoral thesis and in terms of the opportunity later afforded to me by the University of Bristol to build my own 'Elizabethan' stage,* to ignore Aristotle and give precedence to spectacle; to allow it, for

---

* This was executed by Richard Southern and opened in 1951.

once, to reveal its own secrets in as dispassionate and disciplined a manner as the surviving historical evidence would permit; and to try to set down on paper the data that this unconventional approach might bring to the surface.

At first I thought two volumes would amply serve the likely results. Much to my own surprise I found this initial estimate of the situation to have been hopelessly optimistic: so, thanks to the generosity of the publishers, those two volumes will ultimately have stretched into four-within-five, Volume II having had to be split into two separate Parts. Thus, in the event, Volume I and Volume II (Parts 1 and 2) sufficed only to contain an historical outline of the development of English stages, stage-conventions and theatre buildings with no more than an occasional glance at particular plays. Volume III has been added, with Volume IV to follow, in the hope that the balance can be redressed with a wholesale re-examination of the drama in the light of the findings set out in Volumes I and II about the actor, his stage and his audience.

Initially I naturally relied heavily upon the work of the past masters—William Fairholt, Albert Feueillerat, Sir Edmund Chambers, Karl Young, Harold Gardiner, Gerald Bentley and my own supervisor, the late Donald Gordon. In more recent years, I have come equally to rely on the exciting findings of younger scholars whose studies, I venture to think, were stimulated at least in part by the publication of the first edition of this volume— V. A. Kolve, David Bevington, Jean Jacquot, Wolfgang Clemen, A. C. Cawley, O. B. Hardison Jr., Richard Axton and David Bergeron: and it is largely as a result of their work, supplemented by the theatrical achievements of such courageous pioneers as Sir Tyrone Guthrie, Sir Bernard Miles, Tanya Moisewitch, E. Martin Browne and the late Robert Speight, that I have felt obliged to re-write both the Introduction and Chapter 4 (Miracle Plays) of this volume when asked to prepare a second edition. No other section has been significantly re-written.* This is not due to sloth, but because, in my own view, despite the mass of supplementary evidence that has appeared in print since 1959, the principal conclusions then reached, expanded by what now appears within the

* Although inclined initially to re-write Chapter VII (Morals and Interludes), I decided that as this Chapter already found its logical extension in up-to-date form within Volume II where staging was concerned and within Volume III where the plays were concerned, and as any re-writing had to be contained within the same number of pages, this was likely to defeat its own purpose.

covers of Volume III (and what will shortly follow in Volume IV) remain generally sound, if only in the sense that they have not yet been seriously disputed or—if that is too strong a phrase—not yet convincingly refuted; but only the present reader can be the true judge of that opinion.

The Bibliography is that of the original edition. Authors and books now cited in the revised Preface, Introduction and Chapter IV are included in the revised Index.

GLYNNE WICKHAM

Department of Drama
University of Bristol
1978

ACKNOWLEDGEMENTS

To Professor Nevill Coghill I owe the first acknowledgement both for awakening my interest in mediaeval studies and for sustained advice and criticism during twelve years of research. I am indebted to my colleagues of Bristol University, Professor Kitto, Professor Beare, Dr. Joseph, Mr. Campbell, Mr. Tester and Mr. Warne, for advice on a variety of linguistic points and to Dr. Merlin Thomas of New College, Oxford, for hospitality and assistance when studying in Paris.

I wish to thank the staff of the Salles des Manuscrits of the Bibliothèque Nationale, Paris, for their advice on likely source material relating to the Tournament and Mme. Raoul of the Musée du Rourre, Avignon, not only for substantial help with the history and language of the Troubadours of Provence, but for putting me on the track of the MS. text and accounts of *Le Mystère des Trois Doms*. To Signor Rossi, Director of the Uffizi Gallery, Florence, a special word of thanks is due for permission to study in the print room when it was still officially closed after the war and for having the Medici tapestries unpacked from their war-time cases for me to view.

In England, I am particularly grateful to Garter King at Arms, Sir Anthony Wagner, for loaning me *College of Arms MS. 1st M.*13 for three months, as well as for much friendly advice about Heraldic matters; to the Keeper of the Corporation of London Records, Mr. Thomas, for bringing the *Bridge House Rentals* to my notice; to the Society of Antiquaries for facilities to inspect the Fairholt Collection in their library; and to the Director and Librarian of the Warburg Institute, as well for the opportunity to roam at liberty among shelves containing the finest collection of books on Pageantry I have encountered anywhere, as for the loan of many rare books.

For assistance in securing photographs for the illustrations I am grateful to the Photographic Service of the Bibliothèque Nationale, Paris, the British Museum, the Victoria and Albert Museum, the Warburg Institute, and the Colston Research Society of Bristol University.

I feel I must also acknowledge the immense assistance I have

xi

ACKNOWLEDGEMENTS

received from eighteenth- and nineteenth-century antiquaries whose facts and figures, salvaged at the cost of much labour from private collections, have often led me directly to the most profitable of original sources and sometimes provided me with reliable information from sources now lost.

To Professor Gordon, my patient supervisor over five years of graduate research, I owe such discipline as I may have managed to impose upon a field of study which has proved to be far wider than ever anticipated. A similar debt of thanks is owing to Mrs. Dora Pym whose care in checking the proofs has saved me from committing many mistakes to print. Lastly, I would like to thank ten successive groups of Degree candidates for teaching me what questions to ask of the subject.

In correcting errors in the first edition I must acknowledge the practical assistance received from Mr. John Allen and from that most courteous friend and critic the late Professor F. P. Wilson.

GLYNNE WICKHAM

Department of Drama
    University of Bristol
        August, 1963

CONTENTS

ILLUSTRATIONS

FIGURES

PLATES

xv

ILLUSTRATIONS

ILLUSTRATIONS

ABBREVIATIONS, CUE-TITLES, SYMBOLS, ETC.

Ant. Rep.　　F. Grose, *The Antiquarian Repertory* (ed. for the Society of Antiquaries), 4 vols., London, 1775; 2nd ed., 4 vols., London, 1807.

Arches of Triumph　　Stephen Harrison, *The arches of triumph erected in honour of K. James I at his maiesties entrance and passage through his honourable citty of London 15. March 1603. invented and published by S. Harrison and graven by W. Kip*, London, 1604, fol.

Chester　　Canon R. H. Morris, *Chester during the Plantagenet and Tudor Periods*, 1893.

CM.　　Enid Welsford, *The Court Masque*, Cambridge, 1927.

Dissertation　　T. Sharp, *A dissertation on the Pageants or dramatic mysteries anciently performed at Coventry*, Coventry, 1825.

EP.　　R. Withington, *English Pageantry, An Historical Outline*, 2 vols., Harvard, 1918–20.

ERD.　　H. Craig, *English Religious Drama*, 1955.

Eliz. Stage　　E. K. Chambers, *The Elizabethan Stage*, 4 vols., Oxford, 1923.

Fishmongers Pageant, 1616　　J. G. Nichols, *The Fishmongers Pageant on Lord Mayor's Day 1616 devised by Anthony Munday*, ed. Nichols, London, 1844, fol.

HEP.　　T. Warton, *A History of English Poetry* (a full reprint—text and notes—of ed. London, 1778–81), London, 1840.

H.O.　　*Household Ordinances, A Collection of Ordinances and Regulations for the Government of the Royal Household* (edited for the Society of Antiquaries), 1790.

MDC.　　F. M. Salter, *Mediaeval Drama in Chester*, Toronto, 1955.

Med. Stage　　E. K. Chambers, *The Mediaeval Stage*, 2 vols., Oxford, 1903.

Mémoires　　Olivier de la Marche, *Les Mémoires* (ed. Henri Beaune et J. d'Arbaumont), 4 vols., Paris, 1883–8.

MP.　　John Lydgate, *Minor Poems*, 2 vols., ed. H. N. MacCracken, E.E.T.S., London, 1934.

P.J.I.　　J. Nichols, *The Progresses, Processions and Magnificent Festivities of King James the First*, 4 vols., London, 1828.

ABBREVIATIONS, CUE-TITLES, SYMBOLS, ETC.

P.Q.E. J. Nichols, *The Progresses and Public Processions of Queen Elizabeth*, 3 vols., London, 1st ed. 1788–1804: 2nd ed. 1823.

Survey John Stow, *The Survey of London*, ed. C. L. Kingsford, 2 vols., Oxford, 1908.

The Tournament N. Denholm-Young, 'The Tournament in the Thirteenth Century', *Studies in Mediaeval History presented to F. M. Powicke*, 1948, pp. 240–68.

THK. A. Favyn, *A Theatre of Honour and Knighthood*, London, 1623.

Works Ben Jonson, *Complete Works*, edited by C. Herford and P. Simpson, 11 vols., 1925–52.

York Records R. Davies, *York Records of the Fifteenth Century*, 1843.

MANUSCRIPTS

BHR. MSS., Guildhall, London: The Bridge House Rentals.

B.M. MS. MSS., British Museum, London.

B.N. MS. MSS., Bibliothèque Nationale, Paris.

Bodl. MS. MSS., Bodleian Library, Oxford.

C.A. MS. MSS., College of Arms, London.

INTRODUCTION

1 *The combined effects of literary criticism and a time lapse of four centuries on our knowledge of Mediaeval Drama*

Tackling a history of the Early English Theatre is like deciding to build a house in a forest. Before any bricks can be laid a clearing must be cut. All undergrowth must be destroyed. Some substantial trees of long standing must be selected to provide shade and character while others must be felled. Given an open space, the house may be sited and building can start. Similarly, a critical assessment of the subject's existing bibliography is an essential prerequisite; partly because of serious neglect and partly because so much of what has been written conflicts with itself. What precisely is known and what imagined? What grounds are there for accepting some of the many contradictory suppositions already in print and for rejecting others? Are there any sources of information, as yet virgin territory, but likely to reward cultivation?

At first sight, it may seem strange that knowledge of English Drama and Theatre during the sixty odd years covered by the reigns of Elizabeth I and James I should be detailed enough to fill a whole library of critical works while that of the preceding six hundred odd years can only fill a few shelves. Yet reasons are not really hard to find. Foremost among them is that a posse of literary giants in the years 1580 to 1640 created between them a stock of plays of sufficient merit and convenient shape to warrant constant revival. This fact has, in turn, given innumerable scholars mental and economic stimuli to write about them. By contrast, the Miracle Plays and other entertainments of the Middle Ages, being anonymous, unwieldy and often lacking in literary merit, have failed to convince actors or theatrical managers that revival would benefit either their reputations or their pockets. Consequently, the study of English drama in the Middle Ages, as opposed to the study of English literature, has gone largely by default.

One curious result of this neglect has been that where common sense tells us that Shakespeare and his contemporaries reaped the harvest of the seed, tilth and growth of preceding centuries, most modern dramatic criticism, with its heavy literary bias, has in fact severed Elizabethan drama from its roots. Marlowe, we have been told, invented the 'tragic flaw' in character; Lyly provided his successors not only with 'models of refinement', but with a treasure house of new 'characters from classical mythology'; while Peele and Greene bequeathed the further delights of an 'ornamental style'. The fact that the tragic flaw in character had for generations accounted for Lucifer's quandary (who, as Shakespeare's Cardinal Wolsey was to reflect, fell 'never to hope again') and the still more significant one that Chaucer, Lydgate and their successors define literary narratives treating of the Fall of Princes from Lucifer onwards *as tragedies* have been largely overlooked. The fact that mythological characters had appeared in the street theatres of the Royal Entries for at least a hundred years before Lyly wrote is never mentioned. Literary judgements of our drama, however, have gained sufficient credence for the many clichés about Elizabethan 'originality' to be firmly established in all popular histories of the theatre.

Unfortunately, the impression thus created, of a true drama bursting upon England in the late sixteenth century with a suddenness as startling as the birth of Venus from the sea, is seemingly corroborated by data of a specifically theatrical kind. Not only does the period see the construction of the first permanent theatre buildings in Europe, but it is then too that actors regain positions in society of sufficient standing for their names to be recorded and remembered. The *Globe*, the *Swan*, Burbage and Alleyn are household words, without precedent but with plenty of successors.

Again, however, it is conveniently forgotten or just not known that John English and his company of actors, for example, were well and frequently rewarded for playing in London and in the provinces in the reigns of Henry VII and Henry VIII, while huge sums of money were spent annually on the staging of plays in countless towns throughout the British Isles, long before London acquired its *Theater* in 1576. Moreover, if the first *Globe* and other Public Theatres in London were regarded as perfect at James I's accession, why within a couple of years was the Court (which included those men of education whom the dramatists termed 'judicious') ready to reject them in favour of a new kind of stagecraft under a proscenium arch?

If these claims for the earlier drama are true—and I shall hope to produce ample evidence to substantiate them—the reader may well ask why such information has not been available hitherto. I have already suggested that the mediaeval drama was not of a kind which readily interests modern actors or managers who hope to profit from revivals. There are other reasons. One of them is that nearly all the English drama of the Middle Ages was either of an occasional nature—Royal Entries, Disguisings and Interludes for instance—or else a living demonstration of Catholic doctrine. Now no occasional drama is likely to be of more than academic interest to audiences for whom the events celebrated or persons honoured lack topical relevance. The Stuart Masks are a case in point. Equally, a country that has first disestablished its Church from Papal hegemony and then fought a Civil War, as much to confirm this disestablishment as for political and economic reasons, is unlikely to seek to preach Roman Catholic dogma from its stages by deliberate revival of pre-Reformation plays—at least until the new order of things has been delivered from all threat of reversal. In other words, not until the nineteenth century was any serious interest again likely to be tolerated in Miracle or Morality Plays.

By then, of course, sufficient time had elapsed for new obstacles to be placed in the way of even the academic interest, obstacles of time's own invention. Not only were manuscripts of the plays great rarities thanks to the literal bonfires of Puritan zeal, but the language and handwriting in which all records of the performances of plays were couched had changed drastically. Italian script had replaced the Court and Chancery hands of the fifteenth century. Vocabulary and syntax had been thoroughly latinized. Consequently, direct access to records became limited to those scholars with time and enthusiasm enough to equip themselves with a knowledge of palaeography and mediaeval French and Latin in addition to old and middle English. It is a daunting prospect. Small wonder then that few have ventured into the archives of our mediaeval dramatic heritage when quicker gains can patently be made by ignoring it.

2 Modern attempts to place Mediaeval Drama in its historical context

(a) Overcoming prejudice

In recent years, largely because of the interaction of scholarship and Shakespearean production initiated by William Poel and Harley Granville-Barker, and propagated by the increasing attention given to play production in schools and universities, especially in America, a realization that the truthful interpretation of all Elizabethan and Jacobean drama is unobtainable without reference to its antecedents has steadily gained ground. H. D. F. Kitto in a notable book comparing the *Oresteia* with *Hamlet** suggests that if we approach Elizabethan tragedy through our own preoccupation with psychology we are in danger of overlooking the fact that the play of Hamlet deals with the total destruction of two whole families. The image created in the public mind by actor-managers and literary critics during the nineteenth century of title roles *et praeterea nihil* has thus steadily been giving place to a much more complex image of a richly peopled society; an hierarchical society where the laws of degree automatically involve the lowliest in the personal tragedy of the highest.†

E. M. Tillyard, L. B. Campbell and Irving Ribner have similarly reminded us that, in the Chronicle Plays, Shakespeare is more directly concerned with universal laws of government than with the idiosyncrasies of individual monarchs and their entourage, however richly peopled his canvases may be: ‡ an idea substantially reinforced by the production of four history plays in sequence at Stratford-on-Avon in 1951. In the Comedies, too, Nevill Coghill has demonstrated the direct line of descent of such diverse plays as *The Comedy of Errors, Measure for Measure* and *The Tempest,*§ from a dramatic formula inherited from the ancient world by men of the Middle Ages and upon which they stamped a Christian ethos before bequeathing it in turn to their successors.

A similar trail back into the past, initiated by William Fairholt and Robert Withington with studies in English Pageantry, ‖ has

* *Form and Meaning in Drama*, 1956.

† See Willard Farnham, *The Mediaeval Heritage of Elizabethan Tragedy*, 1936, and *Shakespeare's Tragic Frontier*, 1950; W. H. Clemen, *The Development of Shakespeare's Imagery*, 1951; H. C. Baker, *The Dignity of Man, studies in the persistence of an idea*, 1947, and *The Wars of Truth*, 1952. Fundamental to all these recent special studies is J. Huizinga's, *The Waning of the Middle Ages, a study of the forms of life, thought and art in France and the Netherlands in the XIVth and XVth centuries*, 1924.

‡ *Shakespeare's History Plays*, 1944. See also, A. P. Rossiter, 'Ambivalence: the dialectic of the histories' in *Talking of Shakespeare*, ed. J. Garrett, 1954; Irving Ribner, *The English History Play in the Age of Shakespeare*. Princeton, 1957 and L. B. Campbell, *Shakespeare's 'Histories', Mirrors of Elizabethan Policy*, San Marino, Calif., 1947.

§ 'The basis of Shakespearean Comedy' in *Essays and Studies*, 1950, ed. G. Rostrevor Hamilton. Also 'Comic Form in "Measure for Measure"' in *Shakespeare Survey* 8, ed. A. Nicholl, Cambridge, 1955.

‖ W. H. Fairholt, *Lord Mayors' Pageants*, London, 1843–4, for Percy Society (2 vols.); R. Withington, *English Pageantry: An Historical Outline*, Harvard, 1918–20 (2 vols.). See also David Bergeron, *English Civic Pageantry, 1558–1642*, London, 1971.

been actively pursued recently by people whose interest is more directly centred on Elizabethan stagecraft. The picture that slowly emerges is of a theatre as ornate and colourful as the one it replaces was spare and drab. Researches into architecture, painting and music, however differently pursued, are arriving at similar conclusions.

All in all, scholarship is teaching us that our ancestors of the Middle Ages, far from being crude, barbarous, illiterate and generally inferior beings, were, on the contrary, civilized. Despite their lack of our cushioned, conveyor-belted and cellophane-wrapped amenities, their world had meaning and purpose: and what is more, they were fully able to make this manifest in all they left behind them. Anyone doubting this of England should visit the tiny Church of St. Mary, Kempley, in north-west Gloucestershire, frescoed throughout by an unknown artist some hundred and fifty years before Giotto was born. Beautifully painted within a splendid overall design, these pictures have now been revealed to view once more after four hundred years' oblivion behind whitewash. Again, we must try to remember that our drama did not originate in an exclusively Gothic setting, but variedly in Romanesque, Saxon and Norman environments. Nothing in creation was too trivial for these artists and craftsmen to depict in their cathedrals and churches: nothing in daily life was too insignificant to find a place. The beauty of shape and form is everywhere apparent, but most notably in the proportions of the buildings themselves, whether seen from within or without. In the glowing colour of their stained glass, in the rich inventiveness of their carving and illumination there survives the testimony of a people aware of the detail of their environment and of their sense of community.

Faced with all this evidence, which any of us can see within a few miles of our own homes, is it not reasonable to suppose that in their drama too these people would be self-aware and articulate? I regard that as a more reasonable starting point of criticism and research, at any rate, than the assumption that they were silly, unbusinesslike people who accepted a theatre of make-do-and-mend because they knew no better. How many of us, for example, could conceive of building a Salisbury Cathedral denied the machinery of modern engineering, let alone achieve it? In making this plea, I do not want to set up our mediaeval ancestors as a race of supermen before whom subsequent men of distinction pale into insignificance; but I do ask that the reader try to rid himself of centuries of deliberately fostered prejudice when approaching what records survive of mediaeval English drama and the stages on which it was originally produced. As is well known, these records are meagre. That is due in part to the normal ravages of time on perishable materials and in part to systematic destruction. Sculpture and stained glass were not the only things that 'Cromwell knocked about a bit'. Anything which served the same purpose, as much of mediaeval drama did, shared the same fate. Far more survives, however, than the general trend of literary criticism allows. The literary critic tends to expect the text of a play, supplemented perhaps by some biographical or social material, to yield *of itself* all the information required to form a judgement. Yet any actor knows very well that that is only half the story. Having wrung sense out of his text by personal study and 'laboursome petition', he must then devise ways of communicating that sense to an audience who must comprehend it at the moment of utterance or not at all. It is a familiar theatrical paradox that for an actor to have the best command of the text's meaning by no means implies his giving the performance that best satisfies the audience. If only more actors had left behind them accounts of their performances we might not fall so easily into the heresy that drama is synonymous with literature: but to the actor, the moment of performance is all: he is rarely interested in making a permanent record of his art. The startlingly successful revival of the York and Chester Cycles of Miracle Plays in 1951, however, and of other Cycles and Moralities since then, has aroused suspicions of a possible misjudgement between literary and dramatic values. But the idea that drama is literature or nothing dies hard: and most faculties of language and literature in our schools and universities seem determined to make a last-ditch stand to defend it. However, there are signs that the opposite view—that no text in the theatre can ever be more than shorthand notes for actors—championed for so long by Gordon Craig, is beginning to bear fruit. This is relevant to the present subject: for acceptance of such a notion has already led some able scholars to source material hitherto ignored because it lacked a text altogether, or, possessing one, lacked distinction. The most succinct expression of this new view known to me is an essay of Professor Agne Beijer's, 'The Study of Theatre History in Universities'.*

The time seems ripe then to make a new assault on the annals of our drama in the Middle Ages: to look for drama and not neces-

* Printed in *Universities and the Theatre*, ed. D. G. James, 1952, pp. 51–61.

sarily literature: conflict, contrast, portrayal of life as lived and honest endeavour to interpret its significance on the count of content: beauty, colour, form, movement, in a word, spectacle, on the count of staging: and value for money or the trouble taken to attend on the part of the audience. This resolution at once raises a large question: where to begin?

(b) *Prescribing bounds for the Period*

The answer to that, I feel sure, depends on where one wants to end: and the fact that we use labels like 'Mediaeval', 'Renaissance', 'Classical', and so on, to denote distinct civilizations is, in this instance, a helpful determinant. Deciding the coverage of such labels is always a somewhat arbitrary matter because invariably personal. Convenience is a major factor. Where the British theatre is concerned, however, it seems to me that this is comparatively easy: or at least much easier than with literature. We can take one of four immediately recognizable physical phenomena as our closing point: the establishment of the first permanent public theatre in London in 1576, the appearance of the first proscenium-arched stage at Court in 1605, the closing of all English theatres by Act of Parliament in 1642, or the triumph of the new style of stagecraft in the public theatres built after 1660. Of these, the event of 1605 seems easily the most significant: for, in my view, the establishment of the proscenium-arched stage containing perspective settings aiming at verisimilitude started a train of events which, in logical sequence, lead us directly to the wholesale realism of the motion-pictures in twentieth-century cinema and television. The old theatre of poetry and visual suggestion was translated, through the agency of the proscenium arch and perspective scenes, into a new one of pictorial realism and prose. By contrast the closure of the theatres in 1642 merely sealed the fate of the open stage of visual suggestion, whether organized loosely for the production of Miracle Plays and occasional drama, or formally as at the *Globe* or *Red Bull*. I am arguing, in fact, that the public theatres of Elizabethan London were the crowning glory of mediaeval experiment and that an explanation of why they capitulated to the new form is the end of my quest in both senses. For the theatre, the Middle Ages end when vitality departs from the open stage. I date this early in the reign of James I; for Ben Jonson is clearly aware of the threat to the drama of words presented by the rising popularity of the drama of pictures when he comes to argue with Inigo Jones:

'O Showes! Showes! Mighty Showes!
The Eloquence of Masques! What need of prose
Or Verse, or Sense t'express Immortall you?
You are the Spectacles of State! Tis true

xxvii

Court Hieroglyphicks! & all Artes affoord
In the mere perspective of an Inch board!
You aske noe more than certeyne politique Eyes,
Eyes than can pierce into the Misteryes
Of many Coulors! read them! & reveale
Mythology there painted on slit deale!
Oh, to make Boardes to speake! There is a taske
Painting & Carpentry are the Soule of Masque.
Pack w(i)th your pedling Poetry to the Stage,
This is the money-gett, Mechanick Age!'*

It is a mistake, I think, to write off this poem of blistering invective as a mere expression of piqued vanity or even as of simple application to a short-lived dramatic genre. Jones, after all, won the day; and it was his pupil and son-in-law, John Webb, who looked after the visual aspects of the first plays presented to the public after the Civil War. There can be little doubt about the fact of change, nor really of its nature. I have already suggested that the cinema had its genesis, not in twentieth-century science, but in seventeenth-century perspective settings. And do not the gradual retirement of the actor from his forestage in the eighteenth and nineteenth centuries, his adoption of historical accuracy in costume and the frantic efforts of the melodramatists (once gas-light and a darkened auditorium became available to them) to provide their audiences with verisimilitude even in shipwrecks, forest fires and earthquakes point logically to just such a conclusion? By the close of the nineteenth century the theatre had acquired the means to offer its audiences a pictorial representation of any natural phenomenon and was slowly forcing the dramatist to provide the actors with 'natural' as opposed to 'rhetorical' speech. All that was lacking was continuity: for the pictorial illusion was always in danger of collapse if the attempt were made to move, in full view of the audience, FROM the shipwreck THROUGH the forest fire TO the earthquake. And here science came to the rescue. Progress in the field of

* 'An Expostulation with Inigo Jones', *Complete Works*, ed. C. Herford and P. Simpson, 10 vols., 1925–50, viii. 403–4.

optics, coinciding with the demands of melodrama, produced the motion picture.†

If this argument strikes the reader as at least plausible—and I do not wish to press for more than that—then I trust he will accept the digression as necessary in order to explain the rather unorthodox coverage which I intend to give to the label 'mediaeval' in terms of theatre history and the consequent arrangement of the subject matter within these volumes. For if we are to understand why the proscenium-arched indoor theatre arrived in this country at the very moment when the techniques of open staging seemed most propitious to our finest dramatists, and swiftly ousted the latter, we must adjust our focal length to take in a wide historical horizon rather than narrow it for microscopic inspection of the year or genre in question.

I hope, therefore, by surveying the drama of the Middle Ages and of the Renaissance as a single entity, to show that the public theatres of the Elizabethan era and their stagecraft were formal organizations for the convenience of professional actors of the heterogeneous scenic units developed over the preceding three centuries; and to suggest that the proscenium-arched indoor stage was introduced into this country to meet the changed taste of a society that was estranging itself from the values that had informed the previous epoch. For the purposes of this volume and its se-quels, therefore, I am bracketing several labels of period coverage —Mediaeval, Early Tudor, English Renaissance and so on— within the single title Early English Stages or, approximately, our Theatre from 1300 to 1660. I have chosen the building of *The Theater* in 1576 as my point of demarcation in dividing Volume I from Volume II. Although the division is in fact both arbitrary and approximate (since Volume I trespasses on occasions beyond that date, and Volume II behind it) it does nevertheless represent a climacteric within the subject: a point towards which everything seems inexorably to move and after which those same things are never quite the same again. A similar demarcation line will divide Volume III from Volume IV where detailed study of the texts of plays and entertainments is concerned.

(c) *Study of the apron stage, the proscenium arch and the use of scenery in conjunction*

Regarding the introduction of the proscenium arch, as I do, as an event as revolutionary in the history of drama as the invention

† See Nicholas Vardac, *Stage to Screen*, Harvard U.P., 1949.

of printing has been in the history of literature, I intend to examine the causes of its advent from the standpoint of records concerning audiences, actors, dramatists and production rather than those concerned with the texts of plays alone. I intend therefore to look at material outside the immediate field of the literary drama itself. And while I shall endeavour not to neglect what communicated itself to the mind aurally, I shall be principally concerned to ascertain how much of what mediaeval audiences regarded as essentially dramatic entertainment reached them visually. Something they must have received visually if we are to account for the triumph of spectacle in the seventeenth century; for if practical experience of the theatre equips the theatre historian at all, it is with the knowledge that audiences will only accept from promoters and dramatists what they have first been prepared to accept. Here we must approach Ben Jonson's attitude with caution, for he was not only a poet and a dramatist, but a scholar and a purist, contemptuous of the multitude's 'grounded judgement'. In his feud with Inigo Jones, he is clearly at one with Aristotle in his attitude to spectacle. The civilized dramatist will use it sparingly: those who use it as an end in itself do so at their peril. In the twentieth-century film, however, as in the late Caroline Masks or nineteenth-century melodrama, this view does not prevail. There, words are no more than an *aide-mémoire* to the spectacle; the text of D'Avenant's 'Salmacida Spolia' being no more a literary classic than the script of Chaplin's 'City Lights' or George Lucas's 'Star Wars'. Similarly, Restoration Heroic Tragedy, which bears so many resemblances to Jacobean Tragedy, seems an anaemic thing when stripped of the spectacle that originally accompanied it. This constant rivalry between the claims of words and spectacle upon audiences and dramatists alike—for 'those who live to please must please to live'—seems to me the most important fact for any historian of the drama to have before him and justifies Mr. W. G. Keith in his assertion, made sixty-five years ago, but still not taken seriously, that the development of scenic decoration 'for good or evil' has shaped our modern theatre.* It is the neglect or sometimes plain ignorance of this fact which, in my opinion, has posed in the advent of the proscenium-arched stage such a conundrum to many historians of the English Drama.

Texts alone, whether mediaeval or Elizabethan, defy solution of the riddle. Stage directions are scanty. Pictorial evidence is hard to come by. Expense accounts create as many problems as they solve.

* *The Builder*, Vol. CVII, 1914, p. 46.

A pointer, however, has long lain to hand in the many 'Entertainments' to the decoration of which Elizabethans and their ancestors gave so much care and cash; jousts and civic welcomes, by land and water; Disguisings and Barriers indoors at night; folk plays, Church Ales and other holiday pastimes. Many of these not only possess a clear dramatic structure, but were expensive and enjoyable enough to warrant careful description by eye-witnesses, as may be judged by a glance through the table of contents to John Nichol's *The Progresses of Queen Elizabeth* (3 vols., London, 1788–1804) and *The Progresses of King James I* (4 vols., London, 1828). The entertainment lay in the drama and the spectacle, with words serving much the same purpose as the narrator's role in a documentary film or radio programme.

Historians of literature, whose sense of scholarship might have overcome a natural disinclination to examine these records, were conveniently relieved of the trouble when Sir Edmund Chambers lent the weight of his authority to the belief that 'a full analysis of all this municipal imagery would be extremely tedious' and that Pageantry could continue to enjoy 'a perhaps merited oblivion'.* In fairness to the historians, however, it must be admitted that many have not only sensed that drama written before the advent of the proscenium-arched stage must have possessed some visual background to rejoice the spectator's eye, but tried to ascertain its nature. If they have failed to reach satisfactory conclusions—by which I mean that they are still arguing†—that may in part be due to a confusion in terminology over the precise meaning of the word 'scenery'. In its modern connotation this word has become dangerously vague: for in one sense we are apt to limit it to mean *'naturalistic settings'*, while in another we employ it to cover the whole range of *'spectacle'*. This done, it is only a short step to equate 'spectacle' and 'naturalistic settings' as the same thing: and once this is permitted, the resulting confusion is sufficient to make any clear reconstruction of the development of scenic background impossible. The reason is not hard to seek. Settings providing an

* In *Malone Society Collections*, III, 1955, ed. F. P. Wilson, Miss Jean Robertson and Professor D. J. Gordon have gone far to redress the balance by transcribing and editing the dramatic records of the London City Companies. The Society's subsequent volumes of *Collections*, IV–IX, are no less helpful in this respect.

† See Leslie Hotson, *The First Night of Twelfth Night*, 1954 and *Shakespeare's Wooden O*, London, 1959: also Irwin Smith's *Shakespeare's Blackfriars Playhouse*, New York, 1964; London, 1966; C. J. Sisson's *The Boar's Head Theatre*, ed. Stanley Wells, London, 1972.

illusion of actuality depend for their effect upon the magical de-
ceptions of perspective drawing. This art was only rediscovered in
Europe during the fifteenth and sixteenth centuries. It is therefore
useless to expect to find in mediaeval and early Renaissance drama
the sort of scenic background employed in our modern theatre. But
we may look for something else: for drama has ever made its
appeal to two of the senses simultaneously—to the ear and to the
eye. If we want to discover just what dramatists provided to satisfy
their audiences' eye prior to the rediscovery of perspective, I think
we had better forget the terms 'scenery' and 'naturalistic settings'
altogether and investigate the wider term 'spectacle': for this word
came into the language long before the others. Here I must risk
being dogmatic and attempt some definitions.

Shakespeare at once comes to our aid with a useful sentence
which might have been written for a lexicographer!

> 'This wide and universal theatre
> Presents more woeful pageants than the scene
> Wherein we play in.'*

The word 'scene' is used here, as defined by Dr. Johnson, for 'The
stage; the theatre of dramatic poetry', as opposed to the theatre of
the world. The earliest definition is Blount's of 1656—'the front or
forepart of a Theatre or Stage, or the partition between the Players
Vestry, and the Stage; a *Comedy* or *Tragedy*, or the division of a
Play into certain parts, viz. first into *Acts*, those again into
Scenes'.† '*Pageants*' Johnson defines as, 'Any show; a spectacle of
entertainment.' '*Spectacle*' he further defines as

'1. A show; a gazing stock; anything exhibited to the view as
    eminently remarkable.
2. Anything perceived by the sight.'

Now whereas the words *pageant* and *spectacle* are known in Middle
English usage,‡ the word *scene* is not recorded in the language before 1540.§ More important still, the word *scenery* is not introduced until 1695 (Dryden). Spelt 'scen*a*ry', it is defined by Dr.
Johnson (in its stage sense) as, 'The disposition and consecution of

* *As You Like It*, II, vii, 136–8.
† T. Blount, *Glossographia* (1st ed., 1656; 2nd ed., 1661) *sub* 'scene'.
‡ O.E.D. *sub* 'pageant' and 'spectacle'.
§ *Ibid.*, *sub* 'scene'.

the scenes of a play.' The word *scenography* was in use by 1645; and in 1656 Blount defines it as 'the model or draught of any work presented with its shadowes, according as the work itself shews, with its dimensions, according to the Rules of prospective.' ‖

From this it should be clear that spectacle is the essential visual element of drama: scenery is merely one form of background to drama which may or may not be spectacle, depending entirely upon the calibre of the artist responsible for its design and construction. I suggest, therefore, that we abandon the fruitless search for naturalistic scenery in drama written before its invention and look instead for spectacle of all sorts both there and under the proscenium arch. There may then be some chance of establishing whether links exist between the two and, within the texts of plays and entertainments, between the verbal figuration of ideas and the simultaneous figuration of them in stage-pictures.

3 Notable books on the subject

(a) Pageantry

The reluctance of historians to take this subject seriously does not, however, imply that it is virgin territory. Several expeditions have been made into it, but all have been of an exploratory rather than a colonizing kind. William Fairholt was the pioneer. Writing in the mid nineteenth century, his work was that of an antiquary and his interest prescribed to civic pageantry, notably the Lord Mayors' Shows.* Robert Withington followed him in 1918 with a much wider work, *English Pageantry*, that embraced all forms of pageantic spectacle which enriched English life during the thirteenth, fourteenth and fifteenth centuries—Royal Entries, Tournaments, and Civic Perambulations. Instead, however, of following it up by analysing the spectacle presented on either the Court or Public Stages of the sixteenth and seventeenth centuries, he pursued his straightforward historical outline of developments in Pageantry up to the present day. He did, however, provide his successors with strong reason to believe that the Stuart Mask was no sudden foreign importation, but constructed on English foundations, all components of which 'were united in the time of Henry VII'.†

In 1954 Miss Jean Robertson and Professor D. J. Gordon, by

‖ Blount, *op. cit.*, *sub* 'Scenography'.
* See p. xxiv (note §) above.
† Withington, *EP*, i, p. 123.

transcribing and editing all the dramatic records of the twelve great Livery Companies of London from the surviving Court Books, Account Books and Apprentice Books, added much detail to the existing general information. Their work was published by the Malone Society in *Collections III*. In France, the *Centre National de la Recherche Scientifique* has, more recently, published a splendid sequence of illustrated studies of particular Royal Entries under the general title of *Les Fêtes de la Renaissance* (ed. J. Jacquot, Paris, 1956 and 1956–60). A. M. Nagler's *Theatre Festivals of the Medici, 1539–1637* (New Haven, 1964, 2nd ed., 1976) is no less helpful in respect of Italy.

Chambers, having pioneered so much else in theatre research 'in the rare intervals of a busy administrative life', may well be forgiven for his attitude to pageantry. Miss Welsford followed up some of Withington's suggestions in her notable book, *The Court Masque*, ‡ but it was not until the early nineteen-forties that a fresh assault was made upon the whole territory. Two books were then published in America, of major importance for everyone interested in Shakespearean or earlier drama: *The Globe Playhouse*, by J. C. Adams, and *From Art to Theatre*, by G. R. Kernodle.* Between them these two books, as much because of their seemingly contradictory conclusions as because of the source material deployed to reach them, obliged anyone who read them to reappraise his or her previous assumptions about Elizabethan and Jacobean theatrical traditions and stage-conventions. The latter investigates in considerable detail the *Tableaux Vivants* of the Middle Ages and early Renaissance both in England and on the continent, seeking to establish features of scenic background common to them all. These he claims to find and assumes that they were not only incorporated into the Court and Public Stages of the sixteenth century but were indeed fundamental to their very design.

(b) *Elizabethan Public Theatres*

'I am convinced', writes Kernodle in his introduction, 'that we must revise many of our ideas about the stage of Shakespeare, the stage of Corneille, the stage of Lope de Vega, and the stage of the Italian court spectacles. Not only can we throw new light on how each one functioned, but we can now explain how each one originated and why each one differed from the others'.†

‡ E. Welsford, *The Court Masque*, Cambridge, 1927.

* Published Cambridge, Mass., 1942, and Chicago, 1944, respectively.

† Kernodle, *op. cit.*, p. 1.

He attributes the failure of earlier authors to arrive at his own conclusions to their neglect of the traditions of visual arts.

'There in the paintings, sculpture, stained glass, tapestries, and *tableaux vivants* were the stage wings, proscenium arches, inner stages, curtains, side doors, upper galleries, heavens, and canopies they were looking for. There the principles of illusion and of symbolism were developed and associated with the types of background that were copied by Italian and by English architects.' ‡

Now such a thesis is not hard to prove if you invent theatre façades to fit the proof. It is all very well, for instance, to visualize an Elizabethan stage with marble columns, inscriptions, classical cornices, etc. But where is the proof? In *The Globe Playhouse* J. C. Adams, in marked contrast (yet with the same material at his disposal), documents passages from Elizabethan and Jacobean drama which seem to demand elaborate scenic background with far more detailed textual reference than Kernodle, but makes no claim to establish the appearance of the interior. On drawing up a scale reconstruction of the Globe based on the figures which Mr. Adams presents, I find the popular conception of an interior resembling the half-timber tan and brown of Tudor houses is still permissible, if unlikely. It is interesting to note that on occasions Mr. Kernodle and Mr. Adams use the same textual evidence. For example both quote the following passage from Heywood's *English Travellers*: *

'What a goodly gate . . . what brave carved posts . . . what goodly fair bay windows . . . what a gallery, how costly ceiled, what painting round about . . . terraced above, and how below supported.'

But whereas Adams simply seeks to show that the Elizabethan stage was a highly flexible instrument, able to suggest any place real or imagined in Heaven, Earth or Hell, Kernodle tries to improve on this statement by forcing evidence from the passage to establish its appearance, which to my view does not exist. Or again, discussing the plays of the Elizabethan amateur William Percy, Mr. Kernodle observes:

'They are all the more interesting to us, therefore, as they indicate how a person familiar with both public and private playhouses

‡ *Ibid.*

* Kernodle, *op. cit.*, p. 134; Adams, *op. cit.*, p. 164.

and, of course, with the street theatres as well, would imagine a scene if his fancy were free.'†

He then proceeds to use Percy's stage directions (although he admits that it is very doubtful whether the plays were ever performed) as evidence of the scenic background in the contemporary professional theatre. Surely such evidence can only amount to what Mr. Kernodle imagines William Percy would imagine?

While, therefore, I accept Mr. Kernodle's conclusion that the spectacle of the sixteenth and seventeenth centuries was drawn in large measure from the conventions of earlier pageantry with the consequent likelihood of an ornate interior, I feel bound to regard the detail of his evidence as hypothesis that still requires proof: for it is clearly possible in all the plays published between 1550 and 1650 to find sufficient evidence, *if picked at random*, to establish almost any hypothesis. Since, however, it is with hypothesis that we must content ourselves where the interiors of Elizabethan Playhouses are concerned (failing the discovery of authentic drawings or the provision of a concordance of stage directions), C. W. Hodges' *The Globe Restored* (1st ed., 1953; 2nd ed., 1968), is probably the best; for this is based not only on a digest of modern scholarship with substantial pictorial supplement, but on practical experience in Bernard Miles' Mermaid Theatre. Once again the result remains an hypothesis: but text and pictures together present the strongest case yet made for a reappraisal of the mediaeval antecedents of Elizabethan Public Playhouses.* This opinion has only been further substantiated by the more recent studies of Richard Hosley, Herbert Berry and D. M. Rowan relating respectively to the Swan, the Boar's Head, and the Cockpit-in-Court.

In this context it seems appropriate to say something about the so-called Private Theatres and other theatres in the provinces (if the word 'theatre' can be admitted) where plays written for the Public Theatres were frequently performed. To take Shakespeare's plays alone for the moment, it is known that some of them were

---

† Kernodle, *op. cit.*, p. 135.

* See also I. A. Shapiro, 'The Bankside Theatres', in *Shakespeare Survey* 1 (1947), pp. 25–37, where he discusses the validity of various views of the theatres; C. W. Hodges, 'Unworthy Scaffolds' in *Shakespeare Survey* 3 (1950), pp. 83–94. For standard works on the subject, see my List of Authorities (pp. 405–13 below) under E. K. Chambers, W. J. Lawrence, C. F. Reynolds, A. H. Thorndike and C. W. Wallace.

written for first performance at Court (where no permanent theatre existed) and for subsequent performance in a Public Theatre. It is known that some plays were performed at both the indoor Black-friars theatre and at the outdoor Globe. It is known that some plays were toured in provincial cities without permanent theatres when outbreaks of plague and other tribulations made it impossible or inadvisable to play in London. It is known that Shakespeare derived a substantial part of his personal income from membership of a syndicate of theatrical management that owned two theatres and actively directed a company of actors.

All this seems to me to have obliged dramatists and actors alike to accustom themselves to a far greater degree of adaptability and improvisation than is ever allowed by those who have hitherto sought to reconstruct the Public Theatres. Suppose we argue, as many have done, that De Witt, in sketching the Swan Theatre, forgot himself and omitted to draw an inner stage, are we to suppose that its presence could be relied on in every other building, metropolitan and provincial, where stage plays were performed? Mr. Leslie Hotson, sensing the likelihood of such difficulties where performances at Court were concerned, has gone so far as to argue that they must have been presented in 'arena-staging'; that is, in conditions resembling a boxing ring.† This theory may well commend itself to those who are anxious to bestow upon the exiguous and expedient arena-stage of modern times the dignity of an historical past, but it too falls into the general error of treating one place of performance in isolation from the others. We must endeavour to remember that despite the novel permanence of some fourteen theatres built in London between 1576 and 1614, conditions of performance resembled the occasional and itinerant ones of the Middle Ages much more closely than the regular and uniform ones of our own times.

Once again, therefore, we are forced to examine the sort of dramatic spectacle that accompanied dramatic entertainments in England and how they were presented to the public before either permanent theatres were built or experiments began in the possibilities of perspective settings. I have indicated that some specific aspects of mediaeval stagecraft have recently received some detailed treatment, notably the Lord Mayors' Shows, Royal Entries, the Court Mask and the early Public Playhouses. Yet no comprehensive survey of early English stages or production methods has

† Hotson, *op. cit.* For a more comprehensive approach to this subject see R. L. Southern, *The Open Stage*, 1952.

so far been attempted. One possible reason for this is the strange neglect of the Miracle Plays.

(c) *Miracle Plays*

Until the start of the Second World War, knowledge of the staging of Miracle Plays, Moralities and Interludes, the normal theatrical fare of the fifteenth and early sixteenth centuries, had depended almost wholly upon the fragmentary gleanings of eighteenth- and nineteenth-century antiquaries and the two attempts to collate them into some sort of coherent pattern made by Chambers in 1903 and Nicoll in 1931.* Karl Young in *The Drama of the Mediaeval Church* (1933, 2 vols.) vastly increased our knowledge of how the plays came to be written. When, after the war, Professor Hardin Craig published *English Religious Drama* (1955) he faithfully re-echoed his own and other writers' former findings: and Grace Frank, in a book which has withstood the test of time far better than Craig's, performed a similar service for religious drama in France.† Yet neither of these works advance our knowledge of staging or production methods.

I have already suggested some cogent reasons to explain the general neglect. There are two more worth stating now. The first is that Chambers, in pioneering a comprehensive view of the mediaeval stage, was sometimes obliged to rely on secondary sources of information which there is now strong reason to suspect as being misleading where not positively false, while others with much less excuse have taken over Chambers' verdicts without checking those sources for themselves. This question is dealt with at length in the first half of Chapter IV.

The second reason stems from the first. It has been generally assumed that the English Miracle Cycles received substantially different staging and production from their continental equivalents. Source material, therefore, of continental origin—and much more survives in Roman Catholic countries than in Protestant England —has been used very gingerly, if at all. Yet we are dealing with conditions in Christendom, a form of internationalism beside which the United Nations or the old League seem sketchy ghosts.

The first scholar to grasp this point and to explore its wide implications was H. C. Gardiner whose *Mysteries' End*, first published in 1946 and subsequently reprinted in 1967, can still be

* E. K. Chambers, *The Mediaeval Stage*, 1903, 2 vols.; A. Nicoll, *Masks, Mimes and Miracles*, 1931.

† G. Frank, *The Mediaeval French Drama*, 1954.

described as the foundation stone of all modern approaches to English mediaeval and renaissance drama. Nine years later Professor F. M. Salter again took up this theme in his four published lectures, *Mediaeval Drama in Chester*. There he said, 'You could have heard the same trope in any of a thousand churches from Dublin to Constantinople in the earlier Middle Ages, just as you could have heard the same Mass, on the same day. The homogeneity of material in the mystery plays is due to the same universal or catholic reason.'*

It seems logical to me therefore to reverse the usual tendency to isolate the English Miracle Plays and to assume instead a common, European basis of stage procedure except where unimpeachable evidence exists to prove English practice exceptional: or, in other words, to approach this drama from the standpoint of a uniform religion: and this I have attempted to do both in Chapter IX and in Volume III. Only after the Reformation did this situation change substantially.

(d) *Foreign source material*

Quite apart from the universal influence of the Church on its own drama during the Middle Ages, Crusades, alliances of sovereign states and the trading of merchandise from the Baltic to the Mediterranean served to keep ways open for the exchange of ideas on all forms of courtly entertainment and civic recreation. Again, therefore, mutual borrowing (where climatic, social and economic conditions warranted) is more to be expected than regarded as exceptional. Indeed, universities came into being to share ideas.

The connection between England and France where drama is concerned is obvious enough in such varied cases as the Anglo-Norman *Jeu d'Adam* of the twelfth century, the Pageants for Henry VI's Coronations in Paris and London in the fifteenth, or in John Heywood's use of French farce in the sixteenth; and similar connections have been remarked on often enough in the wider context of literature and of the fine arts. No less important, however, are those with the Low Countries. That the ideas governing trade symbolism in English Pageantry were drawn from Flemish sources was suggested by Fairholt a hundred years ago. This belief has been corroborated and greatly extended by Kernodle and Hodges in their recent studies of the *landjuweels* and the *Redereyker* stages of the fifteenth and sixteenth centuries. Similarly direct religious, academic and artistic connections may be observed between English

* *MDC*, p. 44.

theatrical enterprises undertaken during the reigns of Henry VII and Henry VIII and those being pursued at that time in both Italian- and German-speaking states.* It is principally from these sources, therefore, that I have chosen to supplement the English material in this present volume.

Mention of the Low Countries at once raises the question of the Spanish connection in the sixteenth century both there and in England. We should not forget that two Tudor sovereigns had Spanish consorts. Unfortunately, I have not myself had time or opportunity to examine any of the material in Spain; nor does much exist by way of commentary in English. However, as N. D. Shergold has shown in *A History of the Spanish Stage* (1967), the Spanish Theatre, like the English and unlike the Italian and French, retained a homogeneous audience until the seventeenth century. This suggests that a serious comparative study of them both would yield important results.

Very different is our knowledge of the Italian theatre at this time and I shall have reason to draw substantially upon it in Volume II. L. B. Campbell's *Scenes and Machines on the English Stage* (1923) and Nicoll's *Stuart Masques and the Renaissance Stage* (1937) between them offer the student a full analysis of the birth and development of perspective scenery in Italy supported by excellent illustrations; and Richard Southern has continued the story of its adoption and subsequent fortunes in the theatre in *Changeable Scenery* (1954). Despite these accounts, however, the idea persists that in England Inigo Jones imported wholesale a ready-made system of scene-changing from Italy for the decoration of the Stuart Masks and that this marks the beginning of the modern theatre. Once again, however, it is the historian's and the critic's convenience which most recommends this theory. In this case, to argue a divorce from past tradition, self-conscious and deliberate, banishes the need to examine the past tradition for likely elements of continuity. The fact, for example, that Ben Jonson, while working with Inigo Jones on the Court Mask, was also working with Shakespeare's company at the first Globe is ignored, or at least not carried beyond a few desultory speculations on the staging of *The Tempest*. Victorian scholars preferred to believe in straight-line progress from the Middle Ages to their own time and, in consequence, attributed the proscenium arch of the modern theatre to

* See S. Anglo, *Spectacle, Pageantry and Early Tudor Policy*, O.U.P., 1969, and Thora Blatt, *The Plays of John Bale*, Copenhagen, 1968.

a process of extension of the 'inner room' of the Elizabethan Public Theatres under Renaissance pressure which swiftly swallowed up the 'apron stage'. In this supposition they were encouraged by the unflattering comparisons made by Restoration critics of the old stages with their own, and by lack of De Witt's sketch of the Swan.

Neither of these approaches is permissible in the light of modern knowledge, for most of which we are indebted to foreigners. A new and much more rational approach is suggested by Helen Leclerc in *Les Origines italiennes de l'architecture théâtrale moderne* (Paris, 1946). The importance of this work lies in its theme: that the size and shape of an auditorium has direct bearing on the form of entertainment presented in it. This should be obvious enough. Yet so far as I am aware it has been consistently ignored by previous writers. In Mlle. Leclerc's words,

'Nous tenterons . . . de lier pour la première fois de façon méthodique, l'évolution des formes architecturales du théâtre à celle des genres dramatiques, en nous efforçant d'expliquer le contenant au moyen du contenu et *vice versa*.'*

She gives as her reason for employing this approach, 'Le théâtre est une projection vivante du texte dans un espace défini par son cadre architectural.' Or, as an actor might express it, the quality and very nature of a performance depend largely upon the relationship established by the actor with his audience, which, in turn, is conditioned by the physical structure of the building that contains them both. Another modern author, S. Wilma Holsboer, in her book *L' Histoire de la mise en scène dans le théâtre français 1600–1657* (Paris, 1933), makes a revealing remark about the development of the French theatre in almost the same terms.

'Ajoutons enfin que, fort probablement, les dimensions des nouvelles scènes et les possibilités restreintes qu'elles offraient pour le déploiement d'un spectacle, ont fait tout autant que les théories pour amener peu à peu les metteurs en scène et les auteurs d'abord à concevoir puis à pratiquer l'unité de lieu.'†

If then, both in France and in Italy, the shape and size of hall in which an entertainment was presented conditioned the form that entertainment took, is it not possible that this may have happened in England too? One of Dudley Carleton's letters points to just such a conclusion: 'The Hall was so much lessened by the works that

* *Op. cit.*, p. 16.
† *Op. cit.*, p. 32.

were in it, so as none could be admitted but men of appearance.'
Add to this the fact that the Lord Chamberlain's White Staff was
often no mere symbol of office but rather a deterrent to 'gate-
crashers' who felt its weight upon their pates and there seems little
doubt that overcrowding at English Court entertainments had, by
the close of the sixteenth century, become an endemic problem.

Another related matter is the appropriateness of the shape and
decoration of the hall to the nature of the entertainment itself; an
aesthetic question which occupied Italian theorists throughout the
sixteenth century and was beginning to exercise English minds by
the end of it.

In both these matters we have to deal with problems of supra-
national application and should in consequence take foreign source
material into account, Italian in particular. Yet, in using it, one
must always be careful to differentiate between the circumstantial
evidence that may well surround the same actual event in several
countries: for in these differences may lie the clue that will
account for the inconsistencies apparent in so many theses already
advanced. For instance, it is arguable that the problem of overcrowding at all European Court entertainments was uniformly
aggravated by the system of simultaneous staging uniformly employed in the drama of the Middle Ages: yet it is most dangerous
to assume that, in consequence, the reasons governing the advent of
the proscenium-arched stage in, say, Italy and England were identical, simply because Inigo Jones learnt its secrets at the hands of
Italian masters. In Italy, as Mlle. Leclerc points out, those responsible for the presentation of drama and the patrons who encouraged
them deliberately divorced dramatic theory from popular art forms.
With the foundation of the Academies, contemporary dramatic
forms were ignored and experiments conducted instead, based on
theories formulated out of earlier Graeco-Roman traditions. In
England, however, no such academies existed: nor was architectural theory sufficiently advanced or appreciated for anyone to
argue with or contradict Inigo Jones. Thus even if the motives for
change in these two countries (or any other) can be shown to have
been identical, the moment and nature of the change is likely to
have been very different.

In this connection it is relevant to remember that even in Italy
the divorce between the old and the new could hardly be effected
overnight. Just as drama itself appeals simultaneously to ear and
eye, any theoretical assessment of drama, whether critical or ex-
perimental, involves a twin approach, aural and visual. Literary

and architectural research, as I have urged throughout this Introduction, have to proceed together. In Renaissance Italy the former
swiftly outpaced the latter and thereby compelled a measure of compromise in stage settings for a time. Nor, in any other country, did
dramatic performances stop, merely to allow architectural and
scenic theorists time to invent new stages to contain them. Everywhere compromise is what we should expect, at least for a while.
Such an attitude will help us to make more sense of the woodcuts
illustrating Renaissance editions of Terence's plays whether of
French, German or Italian origin, than has hitherto been achieved
by regarding them as applicable to all European countries at the
same point in time.* It is the ingredients of the compromise that
should concern us. What existed initially? What was desired? What
considerations, artistic, economic, social, political and climatic,
governed the speed and the degree of change? By handling the
problem in this way, there is some chance of obtaining a coherent
picture of the nature of the change which not only corresponds with
the known results in individual countries, but is consistent with itself within a European frame. And surely, if we admit common
origins for the drama and stagecraft of mediaeval Christendom and
acknowledge common practice in the revolutionized national
theatres of eighteenth-century Europe, no other approach to the
revolution itself is likely to yield more than half-truths, misleading
and self-contradictory?

To summarize, then, the principal uses that I intend to make of
continental source-material in both this volume and its sequels are:

(1) To supplement, particularly with illustrations, the meagre
original English accounts of dramatic spectacle thought by men of
the Middle Ages and early Renaissance to be the appropriate
accompaniment of civic, ecclesiastical and domestic ceremonies devised to celebrate, commemorate or explain the significance of
special occasions.

(2) To help to formulate a clear picture of the effect upon spectacular outdoor entertainments of confining them within a space
limited by walls and a ceiling.

(3) To ascertain how far, if at all, the wholesale substitution of
neo-classic for contemporary popular dramatic forms in the Italian

---

* Significant additions to knowledge have been made here by E. W.
Robbins in *Dramatic Characterization in Printed Commentaries on Terrence
1473–1600*, Urbana (Ill.), 1951.

Renaissance was repeated in England in the early seventeenth century.

Whether using foreign or home-grown material, however, my approach will be the same: one which seeks to discover what a play-goer heard and saw at the performance rather than what he may have read or discussed at home afterwards. After all, in a modern context, ballet is conducted under very similar stage production techniques to those used for stage plays and is thus of equal merit as a source of information about modern stagecraft. Yet normally it is only stage-plays that are published for study at home, choreography being a 'closed book' to all but those who profess it.

4 *Conclusion*

It is my hope that this lengthy introduction will have cleared the ground for a reasonably straightforward narrative within the ensuing chapters, unimpeded by the otherwise inevitable justification for matters of procedure used and the constant cross reference that controversy incorporated in the text necessitates. The latent danger, as I am well aware, is to seem to offer a much smoother solution of problems than the evidence really allows. There are times, however, when these risks must be taken in a subject if knowledge of it is not to be fragmented into articles which, in their increasing punctiliousness, interest a diminishing number of people.

I have accordingly abandoned chronology as a narrative pattern in Volume I, preferring to divide the subject up under a number of dramatic genres, distinguishable enough to us, if overlapping at many points for their begetters and practitioners. The most important of these is an arbitrary division of entertainments into two classes, outdoor and indoor, for these do correspond to what we might broadly call large popular audiences and small select ones: the initial distinction, in fact, between the Public Theatres and the Court and Private Theatres of the seventeenth century. I put this first because I believe that the nature of the audience largely dictates the sort of conditions that will exist within an auditorium: seating arrangements, acting conventions and the nature of the entertainment.

In this volume, therefore, I shall endeavour only to demonstrate how two kinds of theatre took their genesis in mediaeval England —that of worship, appealing to a universal audience; and that of social recreation, appealing to smaller sectional audiences—and how these two theatres of independent origin came to encroach upon one another under religious, political and social pressures to the point where they became virtually indistinguishable. I take this to be the essential stage and dramatic heritage of the Elizabethans.

In Volume II I shall try to assess the artistic significance of this fusion during the Elizabethan era and to show why social and critical pressures sufficed to make it so transitory and illusionary that it could have started to disintegrate early in the next reign, as it in fact did. Together, the two volumes are intended to show how a drama of religious inspiration, universally appreciated, came to be transformed by 1670 into a drama of rationalist philosophy and secular entertainment for fragmentary coteries within that same society, and to be sharply castigated by Jeremy Collier in 1697 for its profanity and immorality.

The principal difficulty throughout has been to preserve a due proportion within so vast a range of subject matter. My task might well have been easier had it been possible to tackle the production of the Miracle Plays within any generally accepted context of their historical development. This, however, has proved impossible, since barriers of prejudice and misconceptions have first had to be removed and a new chronology attempted that takes the startling findings of recent research into account. Where, then, with the Tournament, the Disguising, Moralities and Interludes, I have been able to call a halt by, approximately 1576, the year when the first permanent Public Playhouse was built, with the Miracles and Pageant Theatres of the Streets I have had to pursue the broad outlines of the story for a further thirty odd years. With the Miracles this was necessary if any adequate historical context was to be supplied within which to discuss their staging, and a similarly extended discussion of the Pageants seemed to be an essential supplement to the fragmentary records of the Miracles.

Where theory and criticism are concerned, and their bearing upon the formulation of regular comedy, tragedy and other dramatic genres, I have deferred treatment of virtually all ideas of Italian Renaissance origin for discussion in Volume II, contenting myself in this with an attempt in the last chapter to elucidate what is essentially religious, English and traditional in the Elizabethan stage inheritance. Discussion of plays is relegated to Volumes III and IV.

In Book I of this volume I shall discuss the principal outdoor entertainments of the period 1300–1600, the Tournament, the Royal Entries and other Civic Pageants and, finally, the Miracle Plays—both development and stagecraft. Book II concerns the indoor entertainments—Minstrelsy, the Disguising (subsequently called the Mask) and the Interludes. Book III surveys the interaction of these varied entertainments both on each other and on the general staging principles which open-air and indoor performance respectively suggested. The advent of the proscenium-arched stage with its perspective settings, along with that theorizing in matters of genre which assisted it to oust its rival, can then be discussed in the second volume, properly related to both its own contemporary conditions and its antecedents. The period covered in detail is the fifteenth and sixteenth centuries with overlaps of some fifty years at either end, treated in more general terms.

BOOK ONE

Open-air Entertainments
of the Middle Ages

I

PROLOGUE: MONKISH
DARKNESS

THIS book is primarily concerned with the visual aspect of
English dramatic entertainment during the fourteenth,
fifteenth and sixteenth centuries. If it comes as a surprise to most
of us that there was any stage spectacle during this period, that is
because we were brought up to believe Shakespeare and his contemporaries had to present their plays on sparsely furnished stages
with no front curtain behind which scenery could be erected or
changed, with only signposts and a few odd properties to serve instead. The dramatist—so the supposition goes—had to supplement
this by padding out his text with descriptive verse. If the Elizabethans had to endure so bleak a prospect, how much worse off
were those 'centuries of monkish darkness', the Middle Ages?
Mediaeval drama is thought of exclusively in terms of Mystery and
Morality Plays which are vaguely associated with churches, market-
places and pageant-waggons. These churches of the mind's eye,
moreover, are uniformly and misleadingly Gothic and seldom, if
ever, Romanesque or Norman: in addition, they are not the genuine
article, frescoed from floor to ceiling like S. Francesco at Assisi or
S. Maria Novella at Florence and a-glitter with painted or gilded
images, but neatly whitewashed or stripped to the bare stone by
three centuries of reforming zeal.

It was along such lines that I was taught at school; and from
teaching pupils since, I have learned that most people are similarly
taught today. Yet such suppositions are, literally, preposterous.
They can easily be seen to be so if we stop accepting what the 'concise histories' of the drama tell us (concise, because cribbed from
ampler but now largely outdated histories) and ask a few questions
ourselves.

First, let us take the Miracle Plays. This is a logical thing to do,

3

since far more pictorial evidence concerning their staging has survived than that relating to the interior aspect of Elizabethan or Jacobean Public Theatres. What is more, some of the scenes are represented in colour. All these depict architectural units, usually known as 'mansions', of elaborate design and gorgeously decorated. Where ground-plans alone exist, the idea of an elaborate stage picture is again substantiated by the multiplicity of scenic units set out thereon. Even the stage directions within the literary text often corroborate the pictorial evidence. How, for instance, can stage-managers be dismissed as naïve who could arrange a mass-ascension of fifty people into heaven, or a 'deluge' of five minutes' continuous 'rain'? Yet this was achieved at Mons in 1501.[1] Is the burning at the stake of effigies (substituted in a fraction of a second by a trap mechanism for the former, live actors), stuffed with animal bones and entrails to crackle and smell, so much inferior to the 'realism' achieved in the modern theatre? Or the burning of a temple on the stage as in the Digby play of *St. Mary Magdalen*, or an earthquake as in the Coventry play of the *Destruction of Jerusalem*? Yet faced with all this pictorial and textual evidence, we have been asked to connive at the idea of a dull, brown-timbered and white-plastered *Globe*, *Rose* and *Fortune*.

This hypothesis, for that is all it amounts to, is again contradicted by much of the surviving literary evidence from related sources. Why are the theatres of Shakespeare's day so frequently referred to with such epithets as 'stately', 'gorgeous', 'vain' or 'painted' if writers sought only to describe a façade of virgin white and modest sepia? Or why, to jump back a century or two, should religious plays, when they migrated from their gorgeous, painted churches of origin, have been suddenly divorced from their wonted spectacular environment? Is it not much more likely that their audiences would have insisted that proper substitutes be constructed by those charged with their staging in market places? This would not be difficult, as we can see for ourselves from the reversion in recent years to the painting of tombs with their effigies and canopies which, in effect, bear a remarkable resemblance to the 'mansions' depicted in the illuminations of mediaeval manuscripts. To take another aspect of the plays, what right have we to regard organizers and administrators who were capable of handling casts of between fifty and a hundred actors, budgets totalling several thousands of pounds and audiences comprising thousands of people, as simpletons? If they were, then it is surely quite extraordinary that these audiences (which could as easily contain kings and nobles as apprentices and peasants) should have supported the plays regularly all over Europe for some two hundred years? One further question is relevant. Where, in 1605 and after, did Inigo Jones find the craftsmen and technicians to execute and operate his proscenium-arched, perspective-painted and multi-machined stage for Court Masks, if these spectacular scenic devices were as revolutionary as our history books would have them be? Anyone who has worked in a modern theatre knows well enough that the efficient construction and handling of stage scenery requires skill of a sort that is only acquired after a long and patient apprenticeship. How much more so in days when the lighting was provided by hundreds of candles and rush lights which, if clumsily handled, could easily set the stage on fire. Yet Jones, on his return from Italy, was able to muster, without difficulty, a large stage staff who appear to have given every satisfaction. We forget that the history of indoor production stretches almost as far back as that of open-air production.

There are many other pertinent questions which I could raise, but I trust I have asked enough for my purpose, which is to sow legitimate doubts about the widely-held belief that our English stage of Shakespeare's day and earlier was a dull, simple thing, virtually devoid of decoration to entrance the eye. If I have succeeded at all in doing this, I ought, in decency, to give some reasons which can explain how this belief ever came first to be held, and then propagated: for once that is understood, it becomes much easier to examine all the evidence afresh without prejudice and with the aid of all the new information which research has brought to our knowledge since then.

I may compare what has happened here to a frequent occurrence in crime stories. A misleading clue has led the detective down a false scent to an erroneous conclusion. The misleading clue, in this instance, was most probably the famous Inn Yards. There is no doubt at all that during the reign of Elizabeth I, stage plays were often acted in the courtyards of several London inns. The practice became less frequent after 1576, when more permanent playhouses became available. These Inn Yards bear a close resemblance to the one surviving picture of an Elizabethan Theatre as it appeared to a spectator inside it, at least in point of construction. In both, the actors had to perform on a platform projecting from a rear wall. In both, room for spectators was provided at ground level on three sides of this platform, and in galleries surrounding it at higher levels. Some inns of the period survive to prove this. They are constructed from tarred, timber beams with lath and plaster set between, arabesques, in appearance, of white and sepia. De Witt's representation of the *Swan* theatre is a drawing in ink in the commonplace book of his friend, Van Buchell, though whether sketched on the spot or drawn from memory afterwards, nobody knows. Since the Inn Yards and this drawing of a theatre's interior possess certain structural features in common, it is permissible (and, of course, highly convenient) to assume that they resembled each other in appearance too. The fact that De Witt described the columns supporting the penthouse roof as 'painted in skilful imitation of marble' is ignored; though why these columns should be so ornate and the back wall so plain, it is difficult to comprehend. It is notoriously difficult, however, when clues are few and far between, to abandon a train of thought which one of them has set in action. The sleuth prefers to seek corroboration from almost any source rather than acknowledge an inconsistency which involves jettisoning the case laboriously compiled thus far. Here it is worth remarking that nearly all historians of the theatre to date have been more interested in dramatic literature than in dramatic action, or spectacle. This is important because this very corroboration, albeit of a negative kind, lay to hand in the texts of the surviving plays of the period. Unlike the printed versions of modern plays, stage directions *per se* are scanty; so scanty, indeed, that if one wished to believe that the actors presented the text on a platform equipped only with a few traps and a back wall in which were set a pair of doors, an inner recess and an upper level, it is not impossible to do so. Above all, the proscenium-arched stage of Italian origin which Inigo Jones introduced to the Stuart Court in 1605 and which is amply documented and became public property after 1660, superficially at least bears no resemblance to the stage of De Witt's pen. 'Ergo,' says the detective, 'the case for a sober and well-nigh empty stage is proved.' In the course of the past fifty years, however, research into popular entertainments of a less literary kind—in a word, Pageantry—has opened up a new vista of possibilities (see Introduction, pp. xxxiii–xxxvii). Already G. R. Kernodle, Dr. Richard Southern, C. Walter Hodges and others have begun to apply some of these novel ideas to restoration of the *Globe* and other Elizabethan Public Theatres with startling results.[2] Their most important achievement perhaps is to have disposed once and for all of the long cherished illusion that Burbage, Peter Street and other theatre builders of the later sixteenth century provided the embryo out of which our modern theatre was destined to grow by steady enlargement of some arched 'inner stage'. Instead, they have substituted the idea that the *Globe* theatre and its neighbours were 'principally the repository of a great mediaeval tradition of stage-craft which was not handed on'. This notion, that the Elizabethan theatre represents a climax rather than a beginning, is much easier for us to appreciate (even as a possibility) than it was for the Victorians who were accustomed to think optimistically of straight-line progress from the Dark and Middle Ages through the bigger and better things of their own Bright Ages towards the refulgence of ultimate perfection. Two world wars have taught us to adjust our view of history: to admit that civilizations could conform rather to repeated cyclic patterns of growth, fruition and decay. Viewed in this light, the strong contrasts and apparent inconsistencies of Elizabethan and Jacobean life become more readily acceptable to us than to our forefathers. We can acknowledge at this particular point in time the simultaneous existence of two fundamentally opposite philosophies of life: the traditional, mediaeval and Catholic view alongside the novel, neo-classical and rationalist view: Christendom on the one hand and the individual *per se* on the other. It depends on the sections of society into which our research takes us which view we find uppermost. In Tudor universities and leading schools, neo-classicism is in the ascendant. So is it at Court, where diplomatic contact with Latin countries is most developed. Elsewhere, however, tradition is the stronger force. Merchants and petty officials who aspire to 'better things', like Ben Jonson's Sir Politic and Lady Would-Be, are mocked by the true scholar for their pretensions. It is into this general context that we must place the theatre of Elizabeth I and James I. And once this is done we can perceive at once the admissibility of two theatres as naturally different in kind as evidently different in inspiration.

In these volumes I make no attempt to restore, yet again, the interior aspect of an Elizabethan or Jacobean Public Theatre. I want only to lay before the reader as much of the new, factual material as it has been my good fortune to discover from the sources suggested by Kernodle and others, concerning the spectacular amusements and entertainments of the English people which formed the common heritage of William Shakespeare, Inigo Jones, and the contemporaries whom they served: and to demonstrate from it the sort of theatre that was theirs.

The most astonishing features of this material are, first, its diversity, and next the mass of it which exists, even though much of it is fragmentary and tucked away in obscure corners. For convenience, however, I have imposed certain arbitrary divisions

7

upon these entertainments, though they ought properly to be thought of as inter-related, mere variants of a pastime which mixed profit with pleasure. The best single word to describe all these entertainments, as I have suggested, is Pageantry. Under this general heading, I have singled out for special treatment the Tournament, the Pageant Theatres of the streets, the Disguising. All three are closely inter-related, for all three were the usual accompaniment of a Coronation, although each was organized independently and often on different days.

The facts concerning mediaeval stagecraft which a study of Pageantry reveal are the more valuable when related to what is already known about the staging of Miracle Plays. Taken together they supply us with a picture of stage-decoration and stage-machinery far more elaborate than we have been allowed to visualize hitherto. I make no pretensions here to supplying the reader with a comprehensive history of the staging of Miracle Plays, for that is not my purpose. I wish only to point out what tradition had made available to Burbage, Inigo Jones and others in the matter of scenic background, costumes, stage properties and machinery, when they came to build and equip theatres themselves under Elizabeth I and James I. And for that purpose, a few selected Miracle Plays will serve. Unfortunately it is no longer possible to assume a firm chronology for the development of these plays. Modern research has at least undermined, if it has not fully exploded, most of the general beliefs that have been common currency since the nineteenth century, as I have indicated in my Introduction.* It is becoming increasingly clear that for some four hundred years we have been the dupes of Puritan bigotry where the mediaeval religious stage is concerned. Some attempt must be made therefore to supply a synthesis of this recent work and apply it to the standard assumptions of the textbooks before tackling the stagecraft. This, in effect, means raising a host of further questions. Monkish darkness must itself be questioned. Monks, for example, may legitimately be expected to have had an intimate connection with strictly liturgical plays: but what business had these men, who had so firmly abjured the wicked world, to be concerning themselves with plays performed outside their cloistered retreat? Did they in fact do so? Modern agnosticism has so obscured the difference between a monk and a friar as to make meaningless many of the phrases bandied about in handbooks. We have got to try to understand why religious orders came into existence and what pur-

* pp. xxiii–xxvii & xxxvii–xxxviii.

pose they were created to serve before we can begin to understand why the religious stage flourished at all, let alone discuss its particular forms. Historians have grown so accustomed to generalizing in terms of 'the Church', 'the Clergy', 'layman', 'secular', 'trade-guilds', and so on, that they have ceased to pause and enquire whether such phrases have any meaning when applied to the Middle Ages. How can they then be expected to differentiate between regular and secular clergy in the Middle Ages or appreciate the difference of their functions in that society? So loosely have these words and others like them come to be used, and such are the liberties taken with chronology in a period of some seven hundred years, that ambiguity and confusion have usurped the place of sense and reason in our textbooks. Nor are students in any way assisted to counter this tendency for themselves when they can reach a university to read Arts subjects in apparent ignorance of the meaning of such words as Epiphany or Pentecost and unable to recount the story of Cain and Abel—as in my experience is now common.

In short, four centuries of Protestant prejudice and the disastrously narrowing effects of modern specialist education in literary subjects have combined to relegate mediaeval drama to a cloud-cuckoo land of remote primitivism that has got to be rudely assaulted if the genuine article is to be approached at all. This, in turn, means that after all the facts and figures have been scrutinized century by century and town by town they are not likely in themselves to enlighten us much more than they have done already, except in point of accuracy. For instance, we may come to know more about the detail of the earliest *quem quaeritis* introits for Easter Day in Winchester, Fleury or Augsburg: but until the vital question is asked and answered of WHY the Resurrection and the Virgin Birth formed the nucleus of Christian Drama and not, say, the Crucifixion or the Fall (both seemingly more innately dramatic subjects), progress will be slight. Whatever the risk, an attempt must be made to place the facts and figures within an overall context of developing Christian thought made manifest in religious practice, in social institutions, in architecture and the other arts. To take yet another example: it is useless to go on arguing about the likely impact of the institution of the Feast of Corpus Christi on the drama if we have failed even to enquire why the Feast itself was instituted. Why was it instituted in the early fourteenth century and not in the twelfth or the fifteenth? If we know the answer to that question we may hope to understand how plays came to be associated with it, but not otherwise.

9

One immediate and practical result of trying to approach the particular subject of the mediaeval stage through the general contexts of religion and art is that the possible inter-relationships between one form of dramatic activity and another come to take precedence over the usual isolation into stereotyped, literary genres. Indeed, until the close of the fourteenth century at least, and in many respects throughout the fifteenth century, it will be seen that the methods of presenting Miracle Plays, Pageants in city streets to welcome royal visitors, Tournaments and Disguisings follow a common pattern. Thereafter, particular national characteristics become more noticeable; but so, happily, does documentation of these events. In other words, then, where common practice in matters of staging can be proved to exist in the countries of North-Western Europe, it is worth while profiting from the fact, and using the best documented accounts of each type of entertainment with only small regard to locale.

Of the entertainments we are to examine, the Tournament was the first to acquire an artistic unity of expression. Nor is the reason hard to find. Participation in Tournaments was the exclusive privilege of the Nobility, who, in the early Middle Ages, alone possessed the wealth required for the indulgence of spectacular entertainment. The only rival of consequence was the Church. Development of the Miracle Plays, originating from certain physical accompaniments to the Liturgy during the tenth century, thus runs parallel with that of the Tournament. The Disguising, another speciality of the Nobility, demanded more than mere wealth for its existence. Whereas the Tournament derived from practical necessity, a training ground for battle, the Disguising was a sophisticated means of passing leisure time in stable social conditions. By marked contrast, the Street Pageant Theatres were an essentially bourgeois creation. Their existence, too, was largely dependent upon wealth. The merchant princes, however, who sponsored them, had not acquired enough so to ornament their celebrations until late in the fourteenth century. Thus it comes about that the Disguising and the Street Pageant Theatres derive most of their stagecraft from the Tournament and Miracle Play. The Disguising, however, can make a claim of its own for special treatment. This entertainment alone was staged indoors and by artificial light. Today, when it is far more normal to be entertained indoors than out, this fact ought to strike the stage historian as of especial significance. It should indicate to him that the history of our drama is as much concerned with architecture as with literature; for how else

10

can this reversal of the normal conditions of performance be explained? In other words, information about the building in which a play is staged and the equipment which it contains is quite as relevant as information provided by the play's text.

Tournaments, Street Pageants and Disguisings would have been nothing without audiences. Provision, accordingly, had to be made for their accommodation. Occasionally spectators were left to their own devices. More frequently—and in the case of royal persons invariably—action was taken by the organizers to ensure that seating arrangements were made to suit spectators' social status. Long before Burbage ever dreamed of building his *Theater* or his *Globe*, the Sheriffs of London had caused tiered galleries to be created for the benefit of spectators at Tournaments. Long before Shakespeare's plays or Jonson's Masks were performed at Court, the nobility had been accustomed to attending Disguisings in the Great Hall or Great Chamber of Royal Palaces on Shrove Tuesday or Twelfth Night. What is more, paintings and drawings survive to show us what they saw: and besides these pictures, there is ample descriptive material, eye-witness accounts, orders governing procedure (which apply to spectators as well as performers), instructions to carpenters, masons, tailors and painters, and even their respective bills and receipts.

The overall impression is one of visual splendour, at once rich and delicate, as substantial and ornate as the corresponding decoration of churches, palaces and mansions of the Middle Ages. Naïve these entertainments often were, and simple-minded the audiences who took pleasure in watching them; but so, much later, were many of Shakespeare's groundlings, 'capable of nothing but inexplicable dumb-show and noise', and so, much later still, is much of what is prepared for us on television. Under the Early Tudors the impression gained is one of steadily increasing splendour both in scope and detail. What Tudor Monarchs stripped from the Church and its Festivals they added to their own. Pageantry, in all its aspects, exactly suited the needs of rampant nationalism. Monarch and subjects alike employed it both to impress 'outsiders' and for their own pleasure. In this way, after centuries of trial and error, indoors and out, at its very zenith in the England of Elizabeth I, Pageantry came into the hands of Burbage, Shakespeare, Inigo Jones and the audiences on whose purses they lived: and with it came also that great repository of stagecraft plundered from the Miracle Plays. Together, they were welded into the permanent Public Playhouses of Elizabethan London. Together, and greatly modified by the critical strictures of an élite educated in the revived classical humanism, they were adapted to suit the needs of the private, indoor theatres both at Court and elsewhere.

The following chapters seek to show just what this means in terms of money, bricks, mortar, wood, canvas, cloth, paint and what skilled hands and brains could fashion from them.

II

THE TOURNAMENT

From the Norman Conquest to the Tudor Accession

---

1 *An Historical Outline*

OF the many separate components that Time has welded together to form the literary drama, few have received such
scant attention from historians as the Tournament. This perhaps is
natural; for the Tournament is essentially an affair of action and of
show, not of words. Literary records, however, provide plenty of
information: but before plunging into them and the mass of detail
they afford, it might be as well to obtain a grasp of the salient historical facts which served first to popularize the Tournament and
then to effect its eventual decay. I do not intend here to discuss the
origins of the Tournament or even the derivation of the word. I
shall simply accept the fact that the word 'Tournament' exists,
both in Latin and in Norman French, at the time of the Norman
Conquest of England and take up my tale from there.[1]

These early Tournaments were nothing more than training
exercises for war, as realistic as a modern battle school and as
devoid of glamour.

'For war', Cassiodorus had said, 'is an art. Those who do not train
themselves for it lack all ability in it when the need arises.'[2]

This had been the Roman view; and those responsible for this form
of training in the tenth and eleventh centuries A.D., first in Germany
and then in France and England, accepted the same principle.
Roger of Hovendon, after citing Cassiodorus, continues:

'The athlete who has never suffered a bruise cannot face battle with
real courage: but the athlete who has seen his own blood, whose
teeth have been knocked out; who, overthrown, has felt the full
weight of his opponent on top of him and is still not downcast;

13

who, however often he has fallen, has still risen the more obdurate
—that man goes into battle with a high heart.'[3]

Under these circumstances it takes little imagination to perceive
that these 'peaceful' skirmishes between friends were both dangerous and crude. The pages of Matthew Paris' Chronicle are
littered with the names of noble persons who met untimely death
thereby. It is principally this aspect of Tournaments, although the
vanity and expense also counted, which seems to have aroused the
hostility of the ecclesiastical authorities, and provoked a succession
of Popes into using the most formidable weapons in their armoury
in attempts to stop them: excommunication and the refusal of
Christian burial.[4] Commenting on Tournaments as 'a sort of preparation for wars', Henry of Knighton adds tartly 'notwithstanding Papal prohibitions'.[5] Nevertheless these Papal injunctions
presented kings with an awkward dilemma. If they were to persist
with their 'battle schools' somehow the risk of wholesale slaughter
had to be curtailed. In England, Tournaments were officially
banned until the accession of Richard I. Descriptions of them before
that date therefore have to be sought in foreign records. A full
account of these early and usually lethal Tournaments exists in Jean
d'Erlée's *L'Histoire de Guillaume le Maréchal*, written *c.* 1220,
which describes the life of William Pembroke, the trusted friend of
Henry III and Regent for the first three years of his reign.[5]
Barbarous affairs they must have been when, 'between Pentecost
and Lent they took prisoner one hundred and three knights, to say
nothing of horses and accoutrements'.[6]

Yet, however crude, these 'sparring matches' do contain the
essential spark of drama—strife. Here admittedly there is nothing
more than physical conflict. But onto physical combats it is quite
easy to graft spiritual and idealistic issues. This conception seems
to have occurred at an early date to temporal rulers who, skilled in
casuistry, regarded it as an excellent reply to their ecclesiastical
opponents.[7] If Popes wanted Crusades and Holy Wars, then kings
must have their Tournaments to train for them. Once, however,
the Tournament is regarded as preparation for the fulfilment of an
ideal higher than mere territorial and material aggrandizement, it
is launched upon a path of elaboration that is bound to lead to
eventual decay. Already by 1285, a mere sixty odd years after the
Tournaments described by Jean d'Erlée, we can see the effects of
this elaboration at Chauvenci, a small town in the modern Department of Meuse. It is admittedly a French Tournament and the

record we have of it, *Les Tournois de Chauvenci*, is in the form of a *chanson de geste* by a Frenchman, Jacques Bretex. But he specifically notes the presence of English knights.

'Those men', he says, 'are Englishmen from across the sea. They are much liked. Brave, wise, and noble knights who have come to watch the feast.'[8]

This association of a Tournament with a festive occasion, as we shall see, is no exceptional occurrence; and, in considering the influence of the Tournament upon the drama, is a factor of immense importance. For throughout the Middle Ages the Tournament is second only to religion in uniting responsible men of all nationalities on matters of cultural thought and its artistic expression.* An English knight would go as far afield as Germany or Spain to tourney, taking with him a whole train of Esquires, Pursuivants and Heralds. England, in exchange, extended hospitality to Frenchmen, Spaniards, Flemings, Armenians and Cypriots who journeyed here to try their fortunes in the lists.[9] And as ceremonial grew ever more elaborate during the fourteenth and fifteenth centuries, still men of all nations seemed able to understand it, advancing together and rivalling each other in the splendour of their fêtes.

It appears from recent research that the thirteenth century was the Tournament's crucial formative period both in England and abroad. In England, as I have remarked, Tournaments had been banned until the accession of Richard I.

'This manner of exercise', writes William Lambarde, 'was accompted so dangerous to the persons having to do therein, that sundry Popes had forbidden it by decree, and the Kings of this Realme before King Stephen would not suffer it to be frequented within their land, so that such as for exercise of this feat of Armes were desirous to prove themselves were driven to pass over the seas, and to perform it in some different place in a foreign country.'[10]

Once authorized, however, the English barons needed no urging to indulge in Tournaments whenever they could.[11] Henry III, a monarch with little taste for warlike pursuits, adopted a policy of prohibiting each Tournament as it was arranged; but, like earlier papal prohibitions abroad, his own had small effect. His prime interest being to prevent Tournaments becoming a focus for baronial conspiracy, he was probably satisfied if participants knew that they

---

* On this important subject see J. Huizinga, *The Waning of the Middle Ages*, 1924, Chs. IV–VII.

were both under observation and liable to severe penalties. What matters is that Tournaments were frequently held throughout his long reign: for, in such conditions, experience probably did more than anything else to convince the moving spirits that Tournaments must be regularized. This would suffice to explain the change that overtook them during the reign. By the close of the century conduct had been both regulated and associated with the chivalric ideals of contemporary literature.

An expression of the former is the *Statuta Armorum*, usually assigned to the year 1292. Its provisions were originally drafted as a Petition in 1267.[12] The Petition was aimed primarily against the irresponsible suites of retainers attending on noble combatants who, once one or other of the protagonists appeared to have suffered defeat, fell to blows among themselves and thereby reduced a dignified (if savage) recreation into a serious breach of the peace. The Petition therefore (and later the Statute) forbids such intervention and, as a further precaution, provides that, '. . . no knight or Esquire serving at a Tournament shall bear a Sword pointed, or Dagger pointed, or Staff or Mace, but only a broadsword for tourneying.'[13] These provisions, if enforced, would obviously go far towards reducing the risk of wholesale slaughter.

A second softening influence of no less importance was exercised by the gradual association of actual combats with the ideals of Arthurian chivalry—especially *Round Tables*. A *Round Table* was not itself a form of Tournament. It was essentially a session of knights, a social occasion. 'Jousting' with blunted weapons was merely one, if possibly the most popular, of the games which accompanied it. The models for these Tournaments are to be found in literature even during the early thirteenth century. This practice marks a major advance in the artistic development of the Tournament, for it is adopted ever more frequently and more thoroughly to the end of the Middle Ages.[14]

The Tournaments of the eleventh and twelfth centuries, as we have seen, had been mock battles. Tournaments of the late thirteenth and the fourteenth centuries could fairly claim to be artistic entertainments. While the old mock battle (now better ordered and less dangerous) retained both its usefulness and popularity, the new practice of single combat became increasingly fashionable. This took the name of the *Joust*. Combat between two troops of two or more persons continued to be known as *Tournament*: but the word tournament was also used generically to signify all forms of combat. Thus a knight would issue his challenge under the general title of tournament and would go on to specify the various forms of combat he intended, whether Tournament or Joust.[15] With the passage of time the Joust gradually superseded the Tournament, since single combat proved less dangerous and more demonstrative of individual prowess. As this happened, the Joust began to assume distinct forms of its own. A competitor had the choice of the *Tilt*, which was a Joust on horseback with spears, or the *Barriers*, which was a Joust on foot with swords.* Both these forms were usual in the most elaborate and spectacular of all mediaeval Tournaments—the *Pas d'Armes*. Originally, some suitable spot in open country had been chosen for this, with a narrow defile such as a pass or bridge which the challenger could only get through or over by fighting with the defendant. By the fifteenth century, however, so popular had the *Pas d'Armes* become that it was normal to erect an artificial obstacle, with lists adjacent, in the streets and squares of towns.† Castles, gateways and arches were set up to be defended against all comers, descriptions of which correspond closely with the Pageants erected for Royal Entries and other civic fêtes. Nor would it suffice simply to appear before the *Pas* in armour. A labyrinthine, allegorical fantasy was thought necessary to explain the presence of the knight. This could scarcely have happened without the presence of the ladies: for a lady became, invariably, the central figure of the allegory. The first mention of their attendance in England is at the Kenilworth Round Table of 1279, although little is said of what they did there. At another Round Table, at Nefyn in North Wales (1284), we learn that there was dancing; for the historian notes that the floor collapsed. A more detailed picture is given by Jacques Bretex in his account of the Tournaments at Chauvenci (1285) which, as I have remarked, were attended by English knights. Ladies were present and, doubtless because of this, comparatively formal etiquette governed the proceedings. Music and dancing seem to have played an important part.

'In pavilions, in rooms and in arbours as large as markets, trestle tables were laid out . . . Of the food I'll say no more because it defeats description, so much was there to eat and drink. After eating for a while, the guests devoted themselves to singing. They rose to their feet and removed the tables, trestles and tops. They played flutes, tabors and flageolets and, generally, were as merry as could be. Then the singing began, Madame de Chini first as she was the

* See Fig. 2 (p. 31 below) and Plates II, III and VII. No. 10.
† See Fig. 1 (p. 29 below) and Plates IV and VI. No. 8.

initiator of the feast, its very pivot, a lady of wealth and breeding. After her everyone stepped forward to sing. Curses descend on those that won't join the dances. Nothing could look more delightful than the ladies as they advance, each led forward by the hand by a knight-bachelor. Beautiful it seemed and beautiful, indeed, it was. Let no one try to contradict or gainsay me.'[16]

The presence of ladies as spectators, then, together with the rudimentary etiquette, the music and the dancing which their presence invited and imposed, were probably features of the English Tournament by the end of the thirteenth century. The direct imitation of chivalric literature, which the *Round Tables* of this period indicate, led naturally to the elevation of ladies from the role of mere spectator to that of initiator and presiding genius at the fully developed *Pas d'Armes*. A knight, having invented an allegory involving his lady to explain his presence in arms, designed his method of arrival before the *Pas* to suit his story; and, ever more frequently, this became a symbolic pavilion or pageant car. At sundown all present retired to dinner, and afterwards, to the dancing and the prize-giving when the ladies again dominated the proceedings. Thus we see, in the process of formation, a species of mimed heroic drama, the central action of which was the actual combat. But, as distinct from what happens in literary drama, the outcome of the action was open to chance and therefore more exciting than any play except on its first night. As late as 1559 the final curtain might be a king's death. *

By the sixteenth century, however, deaths in Tournaments were rare. If danger threatened they were usually stopped in time. The object of the tilt, instead of to unhorse the opponent, became to splinter a lance; and with the invention of gunpowder, armour became heavier and more cumbersome in order to be proof against shot. This change, however, did not kill the tilt as one might expect: but it did altogether change the *raison d'être*. Instead of regarding it as a useful exercise for war, men came to think of it in terms of bodily exercise combined with skill. For a short while private tilts became fashionable and a tiltyard a necessary adjunct to a nobleman's dwelling. But this fashion was short-lived: for the two objects of the new styled tilt parted company. By the end of the Tudor period the best form of exercise on horseback was thought to be hunting, while equestrian skill was shown to best advantage

* Henry II of France died of a wound received in a Tournament in Paris, 30th July 1559.

in the *Carrousel* or horse ballet, from both which pursuits the war-like elements of the Tournaments had entirely disappeared. *

The joust on foot lingered longer, though that too was greatly modified and softened. Once the obstacle of the *Pas d'Armes* which had to be defended had been transferred from open country into the streets of a town, space was at a premium. The simplest form of obstacle, if there were no room for an elaborate arch or castle, was a low fence or barrier. Indeed the Barriers could even be removed indoors. And there, by the start of the seventeenth century, in the Great Hall or Chamber of Palaces, we find this relic of the Tournament elaborately 'staged' by Ben Jonson and Inigo Jones in Masks for Barriers: even Shakespeare and Burbage could be called upon and find time to assist, for together they prepared an allegorical 'impresa' for the Earl of Rutland in 1613 in connection with the tilt marking the anniversary of the king's accession, and were paid 43s. each.

So much for historical fact—sufficient, I hope, to show how the Tournament, designed originally as a battle school for war, but always carrying within itself the seed of drama, was forced by circumstances to allow that seed to grow, first as a mere protective measure, then for its own sake, until the child eventually swallowed up its parent. More detailed analysis of this process can extract the many elements of drama which grew out of the Tournament and came to be introduced into the more deliberate forms of dramatic entertainment, the Mommeries and Disguisings on the one hand and the Civic Pageants and Miracle Plays on the other.

2 *The Development of Spectacular Ceremonial*

(a) *The Prestige of English Arms*[17]

An illusion widely held is that England, because an extreme outpost of Europe, has always been a backward country and anything up to a hundred years behind the times in adopting ideas originated by countries bordering on the Mediterranean. A study of the Tournament rapidly dispels such an illusion, at any rate during the Middle Ages, since any country that could keep pace with the complexities of the conventions of chivalry must have perforce been abreast of the cultural and aesthetic tenets of its neighbours.

On the continent the process of softening the Tournament was

* The archaisms of the Elizabethan 'accession' Tournaments and the chivalric revival associated with Prince Henry will be held over for discussion in Volume II.

well advanced by the close of the thirteenth century, as we have seen. England cannot have been far behind; for with Edward I's return from Crusade the English Tournament became a fully fledged social institution 'officially recognized and formally attended by the court'.[18] From that time onwards the reputation of English chivalry, already widely associated with Arthurian romance, advanced steadily until it had earned a place second to none. Writing of the Black Prince's feats of arms in Spain, Froissart records:

'South and North Germans, Flemings and English alike, agreed that the Prince of Wales was the flower of chivalry throughout the world.'[19]

The fame of Edward III for prowess in arms was scarcely less redoubtable; and to England flocked the nobility of Europe to try their fortune in the lists.

In 1331, the King himself and his nobles appeared in the lists dressed as Tartars. In 1342, Edward III gave a Tournament in honour of the Countess of Salisbury.

'He had a grand fete of jousts ordained to be held in mid-August in the great city of London which was advertized overseas by proclamation in Flanders, Hainault, Brabant and in France.'[20]

Alas, no description of these jousts survives. Less than a year later, however, another Tournament was held in London, the account of which is more explicit.

'This year (1343) about Midsummer, there was solemne justs proclaimed by the Lord Robert Morley, which were holden in Smithfeeld, where for challengers came foorth one aparelled like to the pope, bringing with him twelve other in garments like to cardinals.'[21]*

Some form of dressing up now becomes more usual in accounts of English Tournaments and gives a strong fillip to their aesthetic development. In 1374,

'Dame *Alice Perrers* (the kings Concubine) as Lady of the Sunne, rode from the Tower of London, through Cheape, accompanied of

* These jousts followed directly upon a serious fracas with the Papacy. The persistent appointment of foreigners to high office in the English Church had provoked King and Parliament into sending Sir John Shoreditch to Avignon with a sharp note of protest. His mission met with as sharp a rebuff. Is it then just possible that national pride, stung by this affront, turned to satire in revenge?

many Lords and Ladies, every Lady leading a Lord by his horse bridle, till they came into west Smithfield, and then began a great Just, which endured seven dayes after.'[22]

This feature of a procession is frequently repeated afterwards. In 1386, 'every Lord led a Laydyes horse bridle', while in 1391 the ladies again lead the lords, this time by chains of gold. The joust of 1395 'betwixt David Earle of Craford of Scotland, and the Lord Wels of England' was held on London Bridge. The fullest account, however, of English ceremonial is that given in several MSS. for the celebrated jousts between Lord Scales and the Bastard of Burgundy in 1467.[23] This, again, took place in London, and the Queen and her ladies were clearly responsible for initiating it. They presented Lord Scales with a collar which they somehow attached to his thigh when leaving Church. * 'And to the same color was attached and tied a noble floure of Souvenance ennameled and in manner of emprise.' By convention he was in honour bound to accept this as a token of the ladies' favour and prove himself worthy of it by challenging a distinguished opponent to feats of arms. He entrusts this emblem to Chester Herald and instructs him to take it to the Court of Burgundy. There it is touched by the Bastard as a sign of acceptance of the challenge. Chester Herald returns with it to England and reports on the success of his mission. The Bastard duly crosses from Burgundy to England at a time mutually convenient to himself and the English Court. The occasion is marked by the splendour and expense usually associated with official ceremonial. Its detail will be examined later. Here it suffices to remark that the ceremonial itself was clearly understood by (because common to) both Courts. Further proof of this is evident in the presence as referees of more than five Kings of Arms. These duties must therefore have been shared by English and Burgundian Kings of Arms; which justifies the assumption that the ceremonial used in the two countries can scarcely have differed more radically than that used for international boxing or football matches today.†

The prize-giving ceremony which concluded all Tournaments was as elaborate in England as anywhere. This took place of an evening, usually after the second course at dinner.

---

* This acted as a symbol of recognition in the Tournament itself, the favoured knight wearing it in the crest of his heaume or on his lance.

† Specialists interested in procedure should note that this corresponds in detail with that laid down in the MS. textbook for the ordering of Tournaments prepared by René d'Anjou, King of Sicily and Naples and the father of Margaret, Queen to Henry VI of England.[24]

'Then comys foorth a lady by the avise of all the ladyes and Gentil-womans and gevis the diamonde unto the best juster withoute . . . (*her speech*). . . . This shall be doon with the Rubie and with the saufre unto the othir two next the best Justers. This doon than shall the heraude of armys stonde up all an high. And shall sey w^t all an high voice. John hath wele justid, Ric(har)d hath justid bettir and Thomas hath justid best of all.

'Then shall hee that the diamount is geve unto take a lady by the hande and begynne the daunce.'[25] (See Plate X.)

(b) *The Continental* Pas d'Armes

I now turn without further apology to two eye-witness descrip-tions of foreign Tournaments full enough to provide a clear picture of the formula used in the most elaborate type of Tournament evolved in the Middle Ages, the *Pas d'Armes*. To the South of France then and Tarascon. Here in June of 1449 was held the *Pas de la Bergière*, organized by Le Roi René and described by his friend Loys de Beauvau, Seneschal of Anjou.[26] As I am not aware of any full description of this fête in English publications, I will let the poem speak for itself as far as possible.

'At Tarascon, in a very agreeable spot, you will find jousting lists adjoining these delightful surroundings. And at one end everyone will see a gentle shepherdess stationed beneath a tree watching over her flock with all the charming objects that most befit her.

'There you may see two jousting shields attached to a tree: one white, signifying joy, devoid of all other colour*: and the other black, signifying noblesse. These are guarded by two gentle shepherd-squires striving as loyal servants to attain the favour of the shepherdess. For those who may wish to know more, the white shield is for those who are happily in love; the other for those who are not. Each Knight is to go and strike that shield which befits his state.

'Whoever will joust with the shepherds, if he is content both with love and his lady, should approach the black shield fearlessly as an avowed champion and strike it with his baton without risk of reproach: if he is discontented he should strike the white shield.'[27]

---

* This is the usual significance of white in mediaeval colour-symbolism. Black symbolized not only 'melancholie', but Prudence and Constancy as well, which latter qualities may well be understood by the use of the word *noblesse* in this passage. Nobility was normally symbolized by the colour gold. See pp. 46–49 below.

Those then who issued the challenge to attack the *Pas* were dressed as two shepherds; and the object they offered to defend against all comers, supposedly a shepherdess and her sheep, was Jeanne de Laval, René's second wife. For the benefit of spectators, these disguised persons process round the lists accompanied with all the heraldic pomp available before starting the jousts.

'There, you could have seen the shepherdess approach; the leader of the judges on her right and the King of Arms on her left, who were going to adjudicate the contests. Her flock of sheep choose a fold not too far removed from their mistress. All the men are splendidly mounted except the two leading the sheep. . . .

'The shepherdess herself was riding a palfrey most magnificently caparisoned in cloth of gold embroidered with crimson. And her horse was led also by two young men walking at the bridle. They too were of gentle birth and properly disguised in shepherds' clothes.'[28]

It is worth examining this tableau, presented by the defendants at their end of the lists. In the centre is a tree on which are hung the two shields, one on either side of the trunk. At its foot sits the shepherdess.

'The shepherdess had a place especially reserved, as attractive as the mind of man could make it and suitably decorated with trees, flowers and smooth pasture. And there she awaited events.

'The pursuivant hung the two shields on a tree near the shepherdess. . . .

'Her crook was about six foot long, the metal work being fashioned in fine silver. A little barrel at her side for thirst-quenching drink was also made of silver. Besides these she had a little food basket which was very quaint.'[29]

On either side of her were the shepherd-challengers: and behind them their pavilions, fashioned to resemble cottages.

'There was also an attendant for each of the two shields, one guarding the white one, the other guarding the black. At the first encounter between the contestants, one or other rode out from his cottage.'[30]

The romantic element of a *Pas d'Armes* is illustrated by the author's delight in the reward gained by his own prowess: 'In short, having won the baton with the bouquet attached I also received a kiss the which I treasure sweetly.'[31] At sunset all leave the lists and

23

retire to the castle hall to dine. There the prizes are given by the erstwhile shepherdess, Jeanne de Laval, who with the winner leads off the dancing.[32]

The poem is explicit in all things except the root cause of this particular masquerade. Why shepherds? Why a shepherdess? What are shepherds doing fighting anyway? The place to look for answers to these questions should normally be the same for this *Pas d'Armes* as for all others: the preamble to the Heralds' Proclamation announcing the Challenge. Unfortunately no record survives of the Proclamation for this Tournament. But there are plenty of others, and, by taking one as an example, we can obtain a clear enough picture of the general formula employed.

The *Pas d'Armes de la Sauvaige Dame* was held in Ghent in 1469. The Challenger is Claude de Vaudray.[33] Provoked by a lady into convening a Tournament, he cannot rest content with simply jousting on her behalf; but he must needs dramatize the affair and invent an elaborate allegorical fantasy to explain his reasons for holding the Tournament. For this purpose he dubs himself 'Le Compaignon de la Joyeuse Queste' and continues:

'It is true that the said entrepreneur, for his first real adventure, left—albeit not far—the rich Kingdom of Childhood behind him and entered a bleak, tenuous and sterile country called Youth. There he wandered vacantly with nothing more substantial than thoughts, ideas and hopes to occupy him. Imagined adventures alone sustained and strengthened him in these pastures until he came upon the great plain of Happiness, which is situated between the castle of Beauty and the noble mountain of Grace, called High Renown.'[34]

There he meets with a knight called 'Regart' who fights with him *à outrance* (i.e. until the death of one leaves the other undisputed victor) and leaves him for dead. So too he imagines he would have been, but for the opportune arrival of a hermit,

'who, with great difficulty, led him to the hermitage of Good Accord, on the top of the mountain of Grace, where he doctored and cured the Knight.'[35]

There he is visited by the 'dame d'icelle signourie'. La Marche's description of her appearance is too delightful to mutilate by translation:

'Une Dame Sauvaige, couverte naturèlement par toutes les parties de son corps, de cheveux et de long poil, le plus bel et le plus blont que l'on porroit veoir, sans quelque aultre vesture, ayant sur son chief une moult belle couronne de petits rameaulx flouris.'[36]

From this description it may seem reasonable that her charm should suffice to restore him to complete health: and so it was; and in gratitude he offers to perform some feat of arms for her.

In Ghent he fulfils his promise. An elaborate gateway, either erected or dressed for the occasion, with an artificial forest on top, serves for the *Pas*. The 'Dame Sauvaige' is brought to life together with appropriate wild men and wild women in attendance, who, wearing the prizes around their necks, enter through the gate and take their places in the forest-loggia above it.[37]

I have quoted this preamble thus fully because it illustrates so well the conventional formula to which all these *Pas d'Armes* of the fifteenth century conformed. A lady or ladies commission a favoured knight or knights to serve them. This fact is elaborated into a mimed heroic drama. The knight invents a reason to explain his presence in the lists on behalf of the lady. This usually takes the form of an allegory built round the knight and the lady who, together with their servants, assume the dress appropriate to the character in the allegory whom each represents and set it in action against a suitable setting. An English example of the happy connection between the practical and literary exposition of mediaeval chivalry is to be found in the Romance in Chaucer's style, *The Flower and the Leaf*.[38] Since this poem provides a description in English of most of the conventions we have been examining it merits quotation.

'Out of the grove, that I spak of before,[39]
I sy come first, al in their clokes whyte,
A company, that ware, for their delyt,
Chapëlets fresh of okës cereal
Newly spronge, and trumpets (*trumpeters*) they were al.

On every trumpe hanging a brood banere
Of fyn tartarium (*thin silk from Tartary*), were ful
richly bete;
Every trumpet his lordës armës bere;
About their nekkës, with gret perlës set,
Colers brode; for cost they would not lete,
As it would seme; for their scochones (*emblazoned
shields*) echoon
Were set about with many a precious stoon.

25

Their hors-harneys was al whyte also;
And after hem next, in on company,
Cámë kingës of armës, and no mo,
In clokes of whyte cloth of gold, richly;
Chapelets of greene on their hedes on hy,
The crownës that they on their scochones bere
Were set with perlë, ruby, and saphere,[40]

And eek gret diamondës many on;
But al their hors-harneys and other gere
Was in a sute according, everichon,
As ye have herd the forsayd trumpets were;
And, by seeming, they were nothing to lere;
And their gyding (*guiding*) they did so manerly.
And after hem cam a greet company

Of heraudës and pursevauntës eke
Arrayed in clothës of whyt veluët;
And hardily, they were nothing to seke
How they (up)on hem shuld the harneys set;
And every man had on a chapëlet;
Scóchones and eke hors-harneys, indede,
They had in sute (*their master's livery*) of hem that before
   hem yede.

Next after hem, came in armour bright,   }[41]
Al save their hedes, seemely knightës nyne;
And every clasp and nail, as to my sight,
Of their harneys, were of red gold fyne;
With cloth of gold, and furred with ermyne
Were the trappurës of their stedës strong,
Wyde and large, that to the ground did hong;[42]

And every bosse of brydel and peitrel
That they had, was worth, as I would wene,
A thousand pound; and on their hedës, wel
Dressed, were crownës (al) of laurer grene,[43]
The best (y)-mad that ever I had seen;
And every knight had after him ryding
Three henshmen, (up)on him awaiting;

Of whiche the first, upon a short tronchoun,
His lordës helme(t) bar, so richly dight,
That the worst was worth(y) the raunsoun
Of a(ny) king; the second a sheld bright
Bar at his nekke; the thridde bar upright
A mighty spere, ful sharpe (y-)ground and kene;
And every child ware, of leves grene,

A fresh chapelet upon his heres bright;
And clokes whyte, of fyn velvet they ware;
Their stedës trapped and (a)rayed right
Without(en) difference, as their lordës were
And after hem, on many a fresh co(u)rsere,
There came of armed knightës such a rout
That they bespread the largë feld about.

And al they ware(n), after their degrees,
Chapëlets new, made of laurer grene,
Some of oke, and some of other trees;
Some in their handës berë boughës shene,
Some of laurer, and some of okës kene,
Some of hawthorn, and some of woodbind,[44]
And many mo, which I had not in mind.

And so they came, their hors freshly stering
With bloody sownës of hir trompës loud;
Ther sy I many an uncouth disgysing[45]
In the array of these knightës proud;
And at the last, as evenly as they could,
They took their places in-middes of the mede,
And every knight turned his horsè(s) hede

To his felawe, and lightly laid a spere
In the (a)rest, and so justës began
On every part about(en), here and there;
Some brak his spere, some drew down hors and man;
About the feld astray the stedës ran;
And, to behold their rule and governaunce,
I you ensure, it was a greet plesaunce.

And so the justës last an houre and more;
But tho (*they*) that crowned were in laurer grene
Wan the pryse; their dintës were so sore
That ther was non ayenst hem might sustene;
And (than) the justing al was left of clene;
And fro their hors the nine alight anon;
And so did al the remnant everichon.

And forth they yede togider, twain and twain,
That to behold, it was a worldly sight,
Toward the ladies on the grenë plain,
That song and daunced, as I sayd now right.'

This is romantic fiction, but the fragmentary records of actual
jousts in mediaeval England already quoted, if pieced together,

show that the author of this romance had little cause either to depart from or embroider upon familiar fact.

We noted that jousts as opposed to Tournaments were established in England by 1279, that the organizers were disguised in 1331 as Tartars and in 1343 as a Pope and Cardinals, while those whom they challenged were not, and that in 1374 a lady attended the lists in an allegorical role (Alice Perrers as 'Lady of the Sunne'): processions with minstrelsy and Lords on foot leading ladies' horses by decorative bridles were frequent (1366, 1374, 1391, 1395): and finally, that the entire ceremonial, from the presentation of the device of emprise to the eventual giving of the prize, followed continental practice so closely that in the same fête not only could knights of many nationalities take part but even the duties of refereeing could be shared.

Regarding these facts as simultaneous in a single Tournament and associating them with the passage quoted from *The Flower and the Leaf*, we should reasonably expect to see ladies of high birth requesting favoured knights to honour them; an allegory invented round these characters with a lady as the central figure surrounded by knights and attendants assembled in her defence and appropriately disguised, who fight with all comers: at night a banquet with the prize for the champions and the final honour of the first dance with the lady herself: in fact, a typical continental *Pas d'Armes*.

In Tudor times these festive accretions to Tournaments take precedence over the martial elements; and while physical danger still provided excitement, the sensuous pleasure of the spectacle was something to be enjoyed by performers and spectators alike.

In 1501, when Katherine of Aragon arrived in England, Henry VII arranged a series of magnificent tournaments at which the combatants appeared sumptuously attired in the lists which were decorated with trees, a ship, a mountain and huge heraldic beasts.[46] The allegorical preamble drawn from romance literature is still *de rigueur*. In 1511,

'. . . iiij knights borne in the Realme of Ceour Noble (*sic*) whose names followeth, that is to saie, C'eur Loyal (*sic*) vailant desire bone voloyx and Joyeuse Penser, to accomplish certaine feates of Armes which at the instance and desire of the s(ai)d Princesse (*i.e. the Queen*) hath gotten and obtayned of the King . . .'[47]

The required permission was not unnaturally forthcoming since Henry VIII was himself *Coeur Loyal*. At his Coronation two years earlier the allegory had taken a classical twist, Pallas and Diana figuring in it. The lists were then decorated with castles running wine, of which an illustration survives (Fig. 1). As in the fourteenth and fifteenth centuries, Tournaments appear to have been held at the request of particular nobles to celebrate special occasions.

'Noble men . . . remembringe theym selff that auncyent custome of this noble realme of Englond att suche roiall festes to be great a(nd) notable actis of armes . . .'[48]

This extract from the prelude to the account of the Tournament to celebrate Prince Henry's creation as Duke of York in 1494 is

FIG. 1. The Castle called Loyaltie, constructed for a *Pas d'Armes* at the English Court 1524. It is chiefly remarkable for the imposition of Renaissance decorative motifs on a Gothic structure. *

typical. Tournaments, therefore, may be expected to take place in the course of festivities to mark coronations, weddings, the creation of a Prince, or the induction of knights to the principal Chivalric Orders.

The ceremonial itself would also still appear to follow the internationally accepted pattern. Challengers still demand '. . . to answer all commers of what nacion so ever they bee'.[49] For Prince Arthur's wedding we learn that the accompanying Tournament was advertised in Calais and that news of it was sent beforehand to the kings of France and Scotland.[50] Thus, in general, the manner of convening Tournaments clearly follows precedent. Ladies figure

* Pen drawing, B.M. MS. Harl. 69, f. 20b. This is a copy of the original in C.A. MS. M.6, f. 57b. Edward Hall (*Chronicle ed. cit.*, pp. 688–91) gives a detailed description of this *Pas d'Armes* which includes the dimensions of this emblematic castle.

prominently in the proceedings as in earlier times. The Tournaments are said to be held in their honour and for their pleasure: though whether the knight-defenders were more devoted to the service of their ladies in the old chivalric sense than to the service of their own interest is open to doubt. Be that as it may, ladies still continue to dispense the prizes of an evening and lead off the dancing.[51]

I cannot help thinking myself that this traditional association of dancing with tournaments was the magnet which eventually drew them indoors to make an evening entertainment, either in the form of Barriers (as at James I's Court) or as Equestrian Ballets (as in all continental Court Theatres of the late seventeenth century). By then, of course, the Tournament had ceased to contribute ideas towards the development of stage spectacle. Rather did it owe its survival in large measure to the spectacular decoration with which the stage could adorn it.* No one in Tudor England could seriously claim participation in Tournaments to be an essential part of a gentleman's training for his own or his country's defence. Instead, Henry VIII's nobles ask permission to hold a Tournament on the grounds that it will assist '. . . in the eschewing of Idleness the ground of all vice, and to exercise that thing that shall be honorable and to the bodye healthfull and profitable.'[52]

As a creative force, then, the Tournament's services to drama were complete by the time that gunpowder was invented. Nevertheless, by retaining its popularity throughout the sixteenth century, it did much to preserve alive traditional conventions of staging a dramatic spectacle in the open air before an audience in which all ranks of society were represented.

This account suffices, I hope, to give some idea of how Tournaments, developing from simple battle-training into elaborate social recreations, superimposed upon a basis of physical combat the more civilized ornaments of literary associations and spectacular display.

It is in these accretions that our interest principally lies. Who were the participants, the actors? Who watched these performances? What arrangements were made for seating the spectators or at least to provide them with a good view? Who organized the proceedings? These are the questions we ought to ask, for in the answers lies information that bears directly on other dramatic entertainments including those of a literary character.

* Discussion of the late Tudor tiltings and those sponsored by Prince Henry, along with the detailed examination of the indoor Masks at Barriers, is reserved for Volume II.

3 The Stage

The field of a Tournament, or in the present sense 'the stage', was invariably known as the lists. These could be open or closed, a factor that was bound to condition the nature of the auditorium. They were built to a stereotyped pattern and reconstruction is here made easier by the survival of considerable pictorial evidence. 'Open' lists were rectangular, the combatants gaining admission at

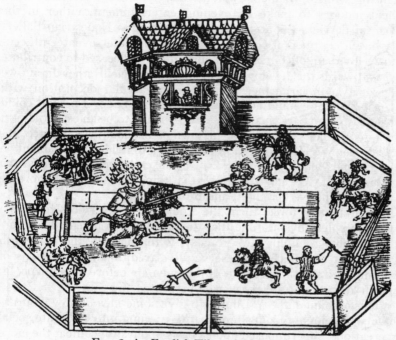

Fig. 2. An English Tiltyard (*c.* 1515).*

either end. Rules were drawn up for their construction some time in the fourteenth century (or even earlier), as we learn from the orders prepared by Thomas, Duke of Gloucester, Constable of England under Richard II:

'The Kynge shall find the feelde to fight in, and the listes shalbe made and devised by the constable; and yt is to be considered, that the listes must be 60 pace long and 40 pace brode, in good ordre . . . , and that the listes be strongly barred abowte, with one

* Pen drawing, B.M. MS. Harl. 69, f. 19. This is a copy of the original in C.A. MS. M.6, f. 56.

dore in the este, another in the weaste. . . . The daye of the bat-
taile, the Kinge shalbe in a state upon a highe skaffolde, and a place
shalbe made for the constable and marshall at the foote of the stears
of the said skaffolde, where they shall sit.'[53]

This was not an invariable rule. Sir John Ferne, in *The Blazon of
Gentrie*, describes the lists erected for Trial by Combat in England,
'which is a place *circular* and *rounde*, compassed in with lowe rayles
or pales of wood, painted with red'.[54] Chaucer also describes a cir-

FIG. 3. One of the Schiedam woodcuts illustrating the original edition of *Le
Chevalier Délibéré* by Olivier de la Marche, 1486. It depicts a combat in closed,
circular lists, with Death in state on a raised stage. (See Frontispiece.)

cular auditorium for a Tournament which he even calls a theatre.
'Round was the shap, in maner of compas, Ful of degrees, the
heighte of sixty pas.'[55] Since the greater part of both pictorial
and descriptive evidence, however, depicts rectangular lists, I think
we may assume that this was the more usual pattern. A compromise
is depicted in the MS. *Le Livre des Tournois* written and illustrated
by René, King of Anjou, one of the Tournament's most enthusiastic
devotees as well as its most accomplished expositor.[56] Here the

Fig. 4. Trial by Combat in England (temp. Hen. VIII).*

* Pen drawing, B.M. M.S Harl. 69, f. 24b. This is a copy of the original and much finer drawing in C.A. MS. M.6, f. 63.

lists are rectangular but closed at the ends with a simple gate in each for admission. René instructs that lists *'doivent être d'un quart plus longues que larges, et de la hauteur d'un homme'*. Further, that the form should be a double rectangle allowing four feet between the two to accommodate servants of the combatants and those appointed by the judges to prevent the crowd from pressing too close. If the Tournament took the form of a *Pas d'Armes*, the object to be defended was set up at one end of open lists.

We shall not be badly wrong, then, in assuming that the stage for these performances, whether circular or rectangular, took the form of an arena at ground level. The auditorium, we might suppose, could correspondingly surround 'closed' lists of either sort, as at the modern cricket or football ground, or flank 'open' lists as at a race course 'straight'. Equally, the auditorium would have to be raised, if the lists were to be of a man's height and the spectators were to command a good view. Lastly, when time, cost and skill were required to construct an auditorium we may well suppose that the provision of places in it was likely to be governed by considerations of social status. All these suppositions are confirmed by the evidence.

4 *The Auditorium*

Actual participation in Tournaments was rigidly confined to gentlemen, an Esquire being the lowest rank that could enter the lists. There seem, however, to have been no restrictions to prevent anyone from watching, provided he neither entered the lists nor usurped positions in the auditorium prepared for his superiors.*

Pictorial records show considerable diversity of arrangement. We must remember that Tournaments were not daily occurrences, but special occasions. So long, therefore, as the 'stage' itself was properly ordered and, in relation to it, the spectators were well placed, the detail of the arrangements could well vary according both to the site chosen and to the scale of the celebrations. Another factor is the hazy knowledge of perspective possessed by the mediaeval artist which may well have led him, on occasions, to omit or distort parts of the auditorium.†

* For general discussion of this subject see J. Strutt, *The Sports and Pastimes of the People of England* (ed. W. Hone, London, 1830), pp. 117, *et seq.*

† The principal sources are these: B.M. MS. Harl. 4379; B.M. MS. Cot. Jul. E. IV; MS. Français 2692. (Bibl. Nat., Paris). See Plates Nos. II–X, and Fig. 4 above. See also the brief explanatory and bibliographical notes, pp. 392–393 below.

What is certain is that the most privileged spectators, among whom we must number the judges and their staff of officers and the ladies in whose honours the combats were staged, were invariably given raised positions near the centre of action. These platforms are called scaffolds or galleries: sometimes they are described as boxes or pavilions. They were built of wood, raised at least six feet off the ground and roofed to afford protection from the weather.*

Stow gives a full account of the seating arrangements for one of King Edward III's Tournaments in the year 1331. It was held in the widest part of Cheapside, the most populous thoroughfare in London, 'the stone pavement being covered with sand, that the horse might not slide, when they strongly set their feete to the ground'. It lasted three days.

'And to the end, the beholders might with the better ease see the same, there was a wooden scaffold erected crosse the streete, like unto a Tower, wherein Queene *Philip*, and many other Ladies, richly attyred, and assembled from all parts of the realme, did stand to behold the Justes: but the higher frame in which the Ladies were placed, brake in sunder, wherby they were with some shame forced to fall downe, by reason wherof the knights and such as were underneath were grievously hurt, wherefore the Queene tooke great care to save the Carpenters from punishment.'[57]

Several facts of importance emerge from this account. First, there was only one set of galleries—'crosse the streete like unto a Tower', allows no other interpretation. Yet these galleries appear to have been double banked: for what else can Stow mean by stating so explicitly that 'the higher frame' gave way? He makes it equally clear that the edifice was built of wood and that the spectators were required to stand. After this disaster a permanent structure, a 'fayre building of stone' was built on the south side of the street, adjacent to St. Mary Bow.[58] It appears, however, to have been the only one of its kind. Even in Smithfield, where quite as many Tournaments were held as in Cheapside, there was no permanent auditorium, let alone one built in stone; for, late into the fifteenth century, calls continue to be made by the King in Council upon the Sheriffs of London to erect spectators' galleries there, charging the cost to the King. Such, for example, was the procedure at the famous jousts already discussed between Lord Scales and the Bastard of

* See Frontispiece and Plate VIII.

Burgundy in 1467: 'The King callyng his counsell to hym, com-aundid his Sherefs of London to make the barrers to be made in Smythfeld . . .' etc. On this occasion at least two sets of galleries were erected, one on either side of the lists.[59] We are told that those on the south side were for the King and the nobility while those on the north side (i.e., facing into the sun) were for the Lord Mayor, Sheriffs, Aldermen and representatives of the City Companies. Similar arrangements existed in Germany where the places allotted to Princes, Judges and Burgomasters were duly in-dicated by their respective coats-of-arms.[60] The pictorial evidence shows segregation of the sexes to have been *de rigueur*. The fact that the scaffolds were primarily erected, 'To thentente that ladyes myght have prospeccyon', probably accounts for their being sump-tuously decorated with stuffs, tapestries and armorial bearings. In *The Castle of Pleasure*, the author, William Nevill, goes so far as to describe the scaffolds as, 'well gargaled galeryes': he also notes their, 'quadrant facyon'. Admittedly this is an allegorical poem; so that these singular details may be accounted for by poetic licence. But Nevill shall speak for himself.

> 'Now goodly Iustes here on they excersyse
> By thactyfnes of many a champyon
> And these well gargaled galeryes they dyd devyse
> To thentente that ladyes myght have prospeccyon
> And to suche as were worthy graunte love and affecyon
> And also whan theyr lust were theyr courage to use
> To daunce amonges them they toke a dyreccyon
> As they myght well and not them selfe abuse
>
> Whan I adverted of these galeryes the quadrant facyon
> Me thought . . .' etc.[61]

Quadrant fashion, too, seems to have been what the illustrator of the famous Beauchamp Tournaments of 1461 was aiming to depict (see Plate VII No. 10).

Quadrant auditorium or otherwise, the general arrangements for accommodating spectators became routine: and so they remained to provide a model for builders of permanent outdoor theatres in the late sixteenth century. Two examples can serve to illustrate the point. The first is taken from the detailed eye-witness description of the Tournaments celebrating Katherine of Aragon's marriage to Prince Arthur in 1501. These were held at the Palace of West-minster in the space between Westminster Hall and the Palace itself. The Herald-historian describes the auditorium as follows:

'. . . and on the southesid of this place there was a stage stronge and substauncially byldid w^t his p(ar)tic(i)on in the Myddis whoes part upon the righthand was apparellid and garnysshid for the King's G(ra)ce and his Lords full pleasauntly w^t hangyngs and Cusshons of golde; and the lougher p(ar)te, uppon the left hond, in like man^r addressed and purveyed for the quene's grace, and all her goodly company of ladies. And annempst this p(ar)tic(i)on there were grees and steyres down to the place of turney for Messangers. . . . In the Northe sid, annempt the stage of the King's, there was another stage, cov^{r}ed with red say, for the May^r of London, the Shrevys, Aldremen, and w(o)rshipfull of the crafts; and in all the circuyte of this feld of werre, by and uppon the wallys, were duble stages very thyk, and many welbyldid and plankyd for the honest and comon people, the which by the great p(ri)ce and coste of the seid comon people were hiryd.'[62]

The siting of the tilt or barrier on an east–west axis was quite deliberate; and the reason, that the combatants should not have to fight with the sun in their eyes. Similarly the best seats are those which face north, that is, away from the sun. These were invariably reserved for the Court. Opposite, facing into the sun, would sit the civic dignitaries. And at either end 'the honest and comon people': some standing. Again, however, one should remember that to them the scaffolds on the south side of the lists contained in the persons of the King, the Queen and their advisers a spectacle as absorbing as the lists themselves. As Olivier de la Marche observed of the Tournament between Lord Scales and the Bastard of Burgundy, the King's scaffold was *'moult beau veoir'*. Bearing these facts in mind, it is difficult to avoid the conclusion that here, by 1501, is an auditorium the design of which anyone wishing to build a public theatre could do worse than follow.

Five years before Burbage in fact built his *Theater* a 'Trial by Combat' was held

'in Tuthill fields, where was prepared one plot of ground one-and-twenty yards square, double-railed for the combat, without the West square, a stage being set up for the judges, representing the court of Common Pleas. All the compass without the lists, was set with scaffolds one above another, for people to stand and behold.'[63]

Burbage and his carpenters could scarcely have invented a better method of seating a large number of spectators assured of a satisfactory view of the performance. This system, as we have seen, had

TOURNAMENT LISTS & AUDITORIUM

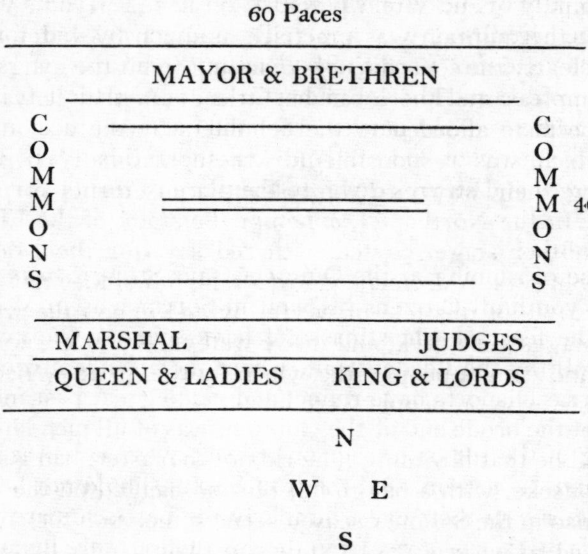

60 Paces

MAYOR & BRETHREN

C
O
M
M
O
N
S

C
O
M
M 40 Paces
O
N
S

MARSHAL   JUDGES

QUEEN & LADIES   KING & LORDS

N

W   E

S

FIG. 5. Ground plan of rectangular, open lists, standardized in shape and size in the reign of Richard II by Thomas, Duke of Gloucester and enforced throughout the fifteenth and early sixteenth centuries. For closed lists, see Figs. 3 & 4, pp. 32 & 33 above.

also for long permitted spectators to be accommodated according to their social rank and the length of their purses. *

5 Popular Imitations

The arrangements for accommodating spectators make it clear that opportunity enough existed for Tournaments to colour the popular mind despite the bar against participating as combatants. Further proof exists in the many popularized imitations like running at the Quintain. The quintain, originally, was nothing more than the trunk of a tree or post for target practice. In the course of time the resemblance of a human figure carved in wood was introduced. The Crusades gave to this figure the likeness of a Turk or Saracen, fully armed with a shield on its left arm and a club to brandish with its right. This figure, although it served the same purpose as a sandbag in modern bayonet practice, was altogether more subtle and lively: for it was set on a pivot so that unless the

* Cf. Fig. 3, p. 32 above with De Witt's sketch of the Swan theatre.

striker hit it correctly he was himself hit by the club as it swung round after him.[64] (See Plate VI. No. 7.)

The tilt at the quintain was practised as much by water as by land, where clearly the consequences of failing to hit the mark were even more unpleasant. There can be little doubt that it was the humorous spectacle afforded to the beholders by the discomfited champion which was responsible for these originally bellicose sports finding their way into the routine amusements of public holidays.

'This exercise of running at the Quinten', says Stow,[65] 'was practised by the youthfull Citizens, as well in Sommer as in Winter, namely, in the feast of Christmasse, I have seene a Quinten set upon Cornehill, by the Leaden Hall, where the attendantes on the Lords of merrie Disports have runne, and made great pastime, for he that hit not the brode end of the Quinten, was of all men laughed to scorne, and he that hit it full, if he rid not the faster, had a sound blowe in his necke, with a bagge full of sand hanged on the other end. I have also in the Sommer season seene some upon the river of Thames rowed in whirries, with staves in their hands, flat at the fore end, running one against another, and for the most part, one, or both overthrowne, and well dowked.'*

In one way or another therefore the Tournament affected the imagination of all ranks of mediaeval society. Its principal features are transferred from battle school to festival and the whole field of heraldic symbolism made common property. In consequence, a tremendous stimulus and organizing force is thereby added to the developing interest in other forms of pageantry, not the least being the possibilities offered by a river.

Quite apart from what was picked up by watching and by imitating at a debased level, the conventions of the Tournament were transmitted to a whole host of craftsmen who would put what they learnt to effect in other directions. Since, in London, the Sheriffs were charged with the responsibility of providing the lists and auditorium, not only they but their workmen too—carpenters, joiners, painters and armourers—must have acquired a detailed

---

* I have myself seen the Water Quintain practised in the Vieux Port at Marseilles and in the small fishing village of Porto Santo Stefano on the west coast of Italy. In the latter, the hill dwellers challenge those of the valley whose headquarters in the main square on the waterfront take the shape of a castle and a ship respectively. Both are made of light timber, canvas and paper. The sport of Running at the Ring is illustrated in Plate V.

knowledge of this pastime reserved for their social superiors. There is a world of difference, however, between doing and watching others do. The Tournament could well generate ideas which commoners could copy and apply elsewhere, but commoners could contribute nothing to its development. As an essentially aristocratic exercise and recreation, its vitality and consequent influence on other forms of entertainment rested with courtiers and their personal retinues. Heralds, minstrels, wardrobe and other household officials were the most directly affected.[66]

The Heralds' duties were legion and their responsibilities exacting. It was their business to proclaim the Tournament at home and abroad; to give notice of it to prospective combatants and inform the local population that would form the audience. The Tournaments of 1501 in honour of Katherine of Aragon, for example, we know to have been advertised in Scotland, France and Calais at least. Local advertisement involved the crying of a proclamation and the posting of bills at prominent assembly points. In London, the Bridge, the Standard in Cheapside, and Westminster were the chosen sites in 1474.[67] The same procedure was observed in Paris in 1493.[68] Manuals on Tournament etiquette tell how the Heralds chose Judges and ordered both precedence and the conduct of the jousting. Finally, it was through them that an outdoor recreation of the daytime was carried indoors and linked to another one in the evening: for it was their function to proclaim the Judges' verdict and thus initiate the prize-giving and subsequent dancing and other revels.* This link between an open air and an indoor entertainment was further reinforced in the persons of the minstrels. They both played the cortège through the streets to the lists and performed during the Tournament itself. The *trouvères* amongst them were expected also to record the day's events in suitable verse: to which happy circumstance we owe most of the accounts of early Tournaments which we possess. In the evening and indoors, they were expected to provide the music for the dancing after the prize-giving.

The household official to whom most responsibility fell was the Controller.† Under Henry VII (again for Katherine of Aragon) we learn from the Minutes of the Privy Council that

'And asfor justes, torneys and suche other Cerymonyes thei be remytted to the said Mr. Comptroller Sergeant of the Kinges armoury.'[69]

* See Plates VII. No. 9 and X.
† See Ch. VIII, pp. 278–280 below.

The earliest abstract supplies a few more details:

'And as for the provision of the scaffoldes and all other thinges belonging to the said justes maist(er) countroll(e)r and Worley have
taken upon theym the charge.'[70]

The 'other thinges belonging' include the decoration of the lists and
auditorium, the advertisement of the Tournament by Heralds' Proclamation and the posting of blazons, the assembly of judges,
minstrels and so on. There is little doubt that the Controller could
safely depute many of these duties to the College of Arms and to
the Wardrobe.

The cost of the lists and auditorium was borne jointly by Court
and Commons. Each paid for their accommodation. At the Tournament of 1501 the scaffolds on the north side of the lists for the
Mayor and 'the worshipfull of the crafts' and the places at either
end for the less exalted, 'by the great p(ri)ce and coste of the seid
comon people were hiryd'.[71] Unfortunately no information has
come my way to throw light on what is meant by 'great p(ri)ce
and coste'; but, whatever the sum, it was probably contributed
from the civic levy raised primarily to meet the cost of the Pageants,
which are discussed in the next chapter.

It is at least clear that if at any time the Tournament should
migrate indoors (where, indeed, we find it under James I, hand-
somely decorated by Ben Jonson and Inigo Jones) the transfer
could be easily effected within the framework of any large, noble
household. Equally, should commoners find anything in the
methods of staging Tournaments which they felt they could usefully apply to other of their own open-air entertainments, channels
for wholesale borrowing existed at all times.

Armed now with what, I hope, is a clear picture of how Tournaments were staged and what people were involved, we can profit-
ably examine the actual staging conventions of these dramatic
spectacles.

6 The Spectacle: Scenic Devices

Knowledge that Tournaments were governed by international
convention makes a wide variety of source material available from
which to examine the allegorical decorative devices that developed
out of the Tournament and were later introduced into entertainments of a more deliberately dramatic sort.

Simplicity is the essence of the story enacted in a fifteenth-century *Pas d'Armes*. For an example, let us return to the *Pas d'Armes de la Sauvaige Dame*.* A young man saved from imagined death by the charm of a strange woman offers to risk his life in arms to prove his gratitude. This offer is accepted; and accompanied by the lady and her attendants he goes to the lists. She watches her servant's prowess and at a banquet afterwards distributes prizes to those who have conducted themselves with most distinction against him; and thus his debt of gratitude is discharged. In practice, only a portion of this story is brought to life—the actual demonstration of his gratitude. The preamble to this deed is told in the form of Proclamation by the Heralds when issuing the challenge. Thus Act I, as it were, is already known to the spectators before they take their places on the scaffolds. But, as the next portion of the story is one of action without verbal explanation, the spectators will need some artificial aid to keep them in mind of it. A single object is provided. An archway. Above the arch is a recess. This recess is in reality a cave surmounted by a wooded mountain. Suddenly the gate of the archway opens and through it the performers enter the lists in procession. Two 'wild-men' first, with trumpets; then two more, leading gaily caparisoned horses by the bridle, on which ride 'wild-ladies' wearing the prizes on their necks. The Heralds present the cortège to the judges. The ladies dismount and climb the stair within the arch which leads to the cave above it from which they view the proceedings. Finally the Knight-entrepreneur arrives and takes up his position before the gate of the arch to defend it against all comers. The procession gives the spectators the chance to become acquainted with the performers. The final grouping at once crystallizes the setting for them and the point arrived at in the action. A knight, the selected champion of the wild ladies, is defending their country for them against all assaults. The assaults begin.

To deduce this from the tableau, three symbols must be accepted. First, that a mountain represents a country: secondly, that the forest on top denotes a remote and wild country: and thirdly, that a gate controls access to that country. Of these the first two are not difficult for the modern mind to accept. And if the 'gate' seems farfetched, it is only so to us: for to the mediaeval mind, in an age of walled cities whose gates were the key to their defence, a better symbol could not have been found.

Before leaving the *Pas d'Armes de la Sauvaige Dame* we should note that even had the organizers wished they could not have

* See pp. 24 and 25 above.

staged a second tableau *on the same spot*. The materials used for the construction of this particular structure are not specified: but it was obviously too solid to move.[72] All of them had to be large, for in the open air, nothing else would serve to focus the attention of the spectators on a single spot. '*A manière d'un bas palais*', is Olivier de la Marche's description of the edifice raised for the '*Pas d'Armes de l'Arbre de Charlemagne*' in 1443. It is built of freestone with a high capital on which are embossed the arms of the defendants. Above the capital are '*images de Dieu, de Nostre Dame et de Madame Saincte Anne*'. In the foreground a fountain played. This '*bas palais*' corresponds with the '*chateau*' of the *Pas d'Armes du Château de la Joyeuse-Garde*[73] and with the English 'Castle'. No single illustration can give an exact picture of this castle structure, since there was virtually no end to the variety of walls, turrets, battlements and vanes that could be used together. These variants are well shown in three French ivory carvings, all of them representing Tournament structures.* The suitability of the castle for this purpose is obvious. In a feudal world the castle was the ultimate stronghold, to lose which was to lose all. Communities clustered round it. Little imagination was needed then for it to represent the city itself, prosperity or safety.

The fountain too acquired several meanings. In an age devoid of taps and water mains, the fountain was literally the source of life and indispensable to hygiene. It was not difficult in consequence to attach to it the significance of fertility, abundance or purity.

In the *Pas d'Armes de l'Arbre d'Or*[74] the principal symbol is the golden tree itself. Chained to it sits a giant at the head of a flight of steps; in front of him a dwarf and a large hour-glass under a pavilion. The tree is possibly the most protean of all symbols. It can stand for fertility. For this purpose the Church used it in the Jesse Window and the designers of street pageants as a device for Royal genealogy. A single tree is as good a symbol for a garden and several trees for a forest. It is not hard from there to equate the forest with the wild, the dangerous and the unknown. The tent or pavilion could also be treated symbolically. In the *Pas d'Armes de la Bergière*, already cited, it serves to represent a shepherd's cottage.† A cave similarly houses the wild lady and her attendants.

In the English Tournaments of 1501 devices to indicate provenance and locale include the tree, the mountain, and add a ship and a chapel.

* See Plate IV and Fig. 1, p. 29 above.   † See pp. 22 *et seq.* above.

On the first day,

'att the uppar ende of the tilte, . . . a certen space beside from the seid tilte, there was a goodly tre enpayntid wt pleasaunt levys, flours, & frute, and sett upp, encompassed, and closed, wt pale rownde abought, undre the which tre uppon railys were hangyd the skochons and shildes.'[75]

William de la Ryvers entered the lists 'in his pavylion, in a goodly shippe borne up wt men, wtin himself ryding in the myddes'. We are told that 'the sides of the ship (*were*) covered wt cloth peynted after the colour or lykenesse of water'.[76] The actual entry was spectacular:

'Forthwt appiered in the gate . . . a goodly shipe, wt all manr of tacklyngs and marin(e)rs in her, the which in the seid appier-au(n)ce made a great and an houge noyse wt s(er)pentyns, and other gun(n)eshote, . . . the v. rehercyd defendours beyng all wtin her, in complete harnes.'[77]

Such a vessel could equally well have accommodated Noah and his family in another context. The Earl of Essex, on the same occasion, entered the lists,

'in a great mountayn of grene wt many raggs (*sic ?rocks*), treis, herbys, stones and m(ar)velous bests upon the sidds, and on the highte of the mountayn there was a goodly yonge lady, in her heer (*sic ?hair*), pleasauntly beseen.'[78]

I assume that this young lady resembled the *Sauvaige Dame* already cited; for we are told that the device was preceded by a wildman carrying 'a sere tre, and a Red Dragon drawing the said Mounteyn'.

This Dragon was probably contrived on the same principle as the other heraldic beasts which appeared on this occasion, notably the lion, the hert and the ibex.

'ev(er)y oon havyng wtin them two men, ther leggs, aloonly apperyng, beyng after the colour and symylitude of the beasts that they were inn.'[79]

The Duke of Buckingham's Chapel Pavilion was decorated with turrets, pinnacles and flags.

The gateway then, the mountain, the castle, the fountain, the ship, the pavilion and trees are the principal emblematic devices to be found in use at Tournaments, together with a variety of heraldic beasts. Several symbols could be used simultaneously.[80] But because the story which the Tournament Tableaux had to tell was simple, the tableaux themselves were simple too. The principal facts alone were stated. Such detail as was necessary was added in dress.

7 *The Spectacle: Costume*

Dress was made to assist narrative in two ways; first, by the adornment of personal attire with objects possessing associated meanings; and secondly, by attributing meanings to the colour or colours of that attire. The purpose of such adornment and specific colouring was simply to assist the spectator in recognizing the person represented. It is easy enough to see why this happened. One man in armour looks very like another, so that in tournaments of the general *mêlée* sort the combatants would be known neither to the spectators nor to each other.[81] Colour was the simplest method of assisting recognition. It remains so on the football field today. By the turn of the thirteenth century more definite means of individual identification had been evolved—usually a personal attribute. Mediaeval stained-glass windows and statuary afford ample evidence of this practice—St. Peter with his keys, St. John with his lamb and so on.

For Christians of the Middle Ages, the meanings of many colours had been standardized by the rules laid down for their use in vestments in 1198; and the process thus begun was continued by those responsible for formulating the codes of Heraldry, due largely to the requirements of the Tournament.[82] Thus colours, besides serving the simple function of distinguishing one armoured combatant from another, could be given additional allegoric significance. Thus black and white are used in the *Pas d'Armes de la Bergière* to symbolize noblesse and joy respectively; contented lovers and hopeful aspirants.*

Identification of the person was further assisted in Tournaments by the wearing of a device surmounting the helmet. In England the first example of which pictorial record survives is the Lion worn by King Richard I. In *Le Livre des Tournois* helmets are depicted with not only birds, animals and fishes as crests but, among other things, a basket of fruit, a wheel, a crown and a pair of wings.

Colours and attributes come together in the coat-of-arms and in livery as signatures of identity, both of the individual and of those

* See p. 22 above.

dependent on him. In the Tournament they are thus employed for purposes of advertisement as well as recognition.[83]

As I have said already, the first steps in codifying the significance of colours and the iconography of portraiture during the Middle Ages were taken by the Church. In doing this, precedent was to hand both in the Old Testament and in classical literature and art. The precedent, however, was followed in principle rather than in detail. Indeed, Christianity was felt to have given new or at least a different significance to certain colours.[84] Red, for example, which in the ancient world had been associated with blood and hence with

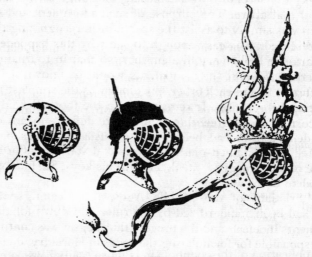

FIG. 6. Diagram illustrating the method of attaching an heraldic crest to an iron jousting helmet. The skull-cap worn over the helmet was made of leather (c. 1450).*

Power, symbolized for the Christian the blood of Christ and therefore Justice and Mercy. Even so, the code was not allowed to develop on a solely Christian basis. Contact during the Crusades with Jewish and Arabic mysteries—especially the properties of mineral ores and precious stones—supplied fresh impetus and added complexity to the process, which must be thought of as one that developed gradually over several centuries.

The following lists taken from College of Arms MS. 1st M16 gives a fair indication of the method adopted for tabulating the colours and emblems in Heraldry:

* Pen drawing in B.N. MS. Français, 2,692.

	Spirits	Virtues	Stones *	Colours
Noble Stones	Angels	A sure messenger	Topaz	Or
	Archangels	Keen and hardy in Battle	Emerald	Vert
	Vertues	Knightly of government	Amethist	Purple
	Powers	Fortunate of Victorie	Margarite	Tawney
	Dominacions	Mighty of Power	Aloys or Sardonix	Sanguine
Glorious Stones	Principalities	Hot of Courage	Ruby	Gewles
	Thrones	Wise and Virtuous in Working	Sapphire	Azure
	Cherubims	Unfaint and durable	Diamond	Sable
	Seraphims	Full doubty and glorious	Carbuncle	Argent

These ideas reached the Elizabethans in the much elaborated form printed in Sir John Ferne's *The Blazon of Gentrie* (London, 1586) and as reproduced here on the next page.

To these it is worth adding, for completeness, the Insignia of Kingship and the Emblems of Nobility, both of which played their part in costuming the drama.

The Insignia of Kingship

Symbol	Meaning
The Ring	Faithfulness
The Bracelet	Good working
The Sceptre	Justice
The Sword	Vengeance
Purple Robes	Reverence
The Diadem	Triumph

The Emblems of Nobility

(1) The Sun	(6) Gold
(2) Fire	(7) The Diamond
(3) The Cedar	(8) The Dolphin
(4) The Rose	(9) The Eagle
(5) Wheat	(10) The Lion

The application of this symbolism is more easily illustrated from the Street Pageants and Disguisings than from the Tournament, as will be seen in the course of ensuing chapters. I need only add here that the Tournament illustrates the existence in the Middle Ages of two sorts of costuming designed to serve separate ends. On the one hand there is costume designed to enable the spectator to identify the performer—coats of arms, crests, livery and so on: and on the other hand there is costume designed to disguise the identity of

* The symbolic significance of jewels is an involved subject and only concerns us in that it affords yet another example of the mediaeval determination to give meanings to physical objects in their quest to interpret the Universe to their fellow men. The diamond, amongst its other supposed properties, 'Kepit þe bones in þe membres hole, so-fere-for þat u schalt not fale of horse ne of oþer best but þat þe bone schal beleue hole.' See *English Mediaeval Lapidaries* (ed. J. Evans & M. S. Sergeantson, for E.E.T.S., London, 1933), p. 83 (The Peterborough Lapidary LIX).

COLOURS

Objects and Properties	Yellow (or)	White (argent)	Vermillion (geules)	Azure	Black (sable)	Green (vert)	Purple
Planets	Sun	Moon	Mars	Jupiter	Saturn	Venus	Mercury
Stones	Topaz and Chrysolith	Marguerit and Pearl	Ruby, Coral, Carbuncle	Saphire	Diamond, Agate, Chelydoin	Emerald	Amethyst, Opal and Hyacinth
Vertues*	Faith and Constancy	Hope and Innocency	Charity and Magnanimity	Justice, Loyalty	Prudence, Constancie	Loyalty in love, courtesy and affability	Temperance, Prudence
Celestial Signs	Lion	Scorpio and Pisces	Aries, Cancer	Taurus and Libra	Capricorn and Aquarius	Gemmini and Virgo	Sagittarius and Pisces
Months	July	October and November	March, June, July	April and September	December and January	May and August	November and February
Days	Sunday	Monday	Tuesday	Thursday	Saturday	Friday	Wednesday
Ages of Man	Young age of Adolescence (14 to 20)	Infancy (1st seven years)	Virility or Man's age (30 to 40)	Puerility (7 to 14)	Decrepit or crooked old age	Lusty green youth (20 to 30)	The age of grey hairs
Flowres	Marygold	Lily and White Rose	Red Rose Gillyflower	Blue Lily	The Aubifaine	All manner of verdures or green things	Violet
Elements	Ayre	Water	Fire	Air	Earth	Water	Water and earth
Seasons	Spring	Autumn	Summer	Spring	Winter	Spring	Winter
Complexions	Sanguine	Flegmatique	Choler	Sanguine	Melancholie	Flegmatique	Flegmatique with some choler
Numbers	1, 2, 3	10, 11	3, 10	4, 9	5, 8	6	7, 12
Mettailes	Gold	Silver	Latten	Copper	Iron, lead	Quicksilver	Tin

* Additional common uses were Joy (white), Power (red) and Purity (blue).

48

the performer from the spectator—Tartars, shepherds, cardinals, 'wild ladies' and so forth. Both of these theatrical conventions were largely pioneered by the Tournament.

Lastly it is worth observing that the colours used in Heraldry were of the most brilliant. Pastel tints cannot be employed with much effect in the open air. The Victorians knew this when planting their gardens with geraniums, calceolarias, lobelias and marguerites. Brilliant colour to the point of gaudiness was the rule: and on the whole a safe one; for the mediaeval decorator could be sure that the sun would eat up most of it to make the result, in practice, much more harmonious than often would appear in description.

8 Conclusion: Tournaments and Dramatic Spectacle

During a period when records of our regular drama offer very little indication of how plays appeared in performance, records of the Tournament supply, by contrast, much information concerning the sort of dramatic spectacle that found favour with mediaeval audiences.

The latter records may be used to supplement the former since Tournaments are essentially dramatic entertainments, not only because they depend for their existence upon a conflict between the performers, but equally upon the co-operation of an audience which was expected to follow the story accounting for the conflict and to identify the performers by interpreting the costume and scenic aids provided. The performance, for such it may be called, at first no more than a crude mock battle, was gradually transformed into an elegant entertainment which conformed to an etiquette as elaborate as its staging. This transformation occurred in all Christian countries over approximately the same period of time, with England having as much to contribute as to receive. It is thus permissible to supplement the sundry records of procedure in one country with those pertaining to another.

A survey of European Tournaments on this basis shows that if the Tournament, always dramatic, was at its noblest during the thirteenth century, it was at its most spectacular during the fourteenth and fifteenth centuries. During this period scenic devices were evolved: at first as a simple means to help audiences to identify person and place; later, as increasing wealth permitted the indulgence of greater display, for their own decorative effect. Throughout the period, however, despite the steady growth in the appeal of their decorative quality, these devices were regarded essentially as symbols. The first step to this end seems to have been the adoption of disguise of the person: this is followed by disguise of the person's immediate environment. 'Popes', 'Tartars', 'wildmen', 'shepherds', and 'foresters' rode the lists; castles were manufactured to adorn them; mountains, cottages, trees, fountains; each could be endowed with a variety of meanings or used in combination with others. Codified by the Church and Heraldry, these devices could be readily interpreted and thus served their intended purpose.

Participation as performer was the exclusive privilege of gentlemen, a fact of some importance in the development of costly spectacle. Participation as spectator was denied to none: a fact of equal importance in determining the taste of audiences; but all spectators had their allotted place in an auditorium graded according to social status. Performers and spectators were brought and held together by Heralds who presented and ordered the spectacle. By the middle of the fifteenth century it is not too much to say that a Tournament had become a mimed heroic drama presented in the open air to a formally organized audience who were kept informed of the drama's significance in part by the Herald-presenter and in part by what they deduced themselves from symbolic costume and scenic background. In conclusion, it should be repeated that outdoor Tournaments concluded with an indoor prizegiving and dancing after dinner, which was to form the basis of the Disguising and later Mask. Importation of the Tournament's scenic devices was also an obvious possibility if and when spectacle should be desired to enhance the indoor evening entertainment. Early Tournaments thus supply the theatre historian with information that concerns not only mediaeval dramatic spectacle and auditoriums but also a secular dramatic form, however rudimentary, which deserves consideration alongside the literary Miracle Plays of the period.

III

PAGEANT THEATRES
OF THE STREETS

*From the Coronation of Richard II (1377)
to the Coronation of James I (1603)*

1 *Their Nature and Purpose*

For many people the word Pageant conjures up visions of a marathon drama in which the notable events of a town's history are re-enacted in a local park for the benefit of the inhabitants and the instruction of summer tourists. Others associate the word with Miracle Plays and decorated waggons. Few people, however, associate the word pageant with mediaeval market crosses, water conduits or gates in city walls. Fewer still think of the two together as sometime theatres. Yet that is what they were, or rather, what they became on important civic occasions, in the later Middle Ages and throughout the Tudor epoch.

The use of these architectural features of major thoroughfares in large towns as stages is something quite distinct from the specially erected platforms raised on barrels or trestles for performances in market squares or other open spaces. The latter were used by mountebanks, professional minstrels or players on public holidays or at other times of regular general assembly. They are familiar enough from many pictures and engravings and are usually known by such names as 'booth theatres', *théâtres de la foire*, or simply 'street theatres'. The addition of the distinctive prefix 'pageant' suggests at least a special occasion and a spectacular display quite out of the ordinary. For us of the twentieth century, therefore, the easiest approach to this unfamiliar subject is probably via the word pageantry: for this is something we still associate with special State or civic functions, with processions and decorated streets, with

51

flags and uniforms, with heraldic blazon and livery, with a sense of occasion, above all with rituals bringing ruler and subject into mystic communion: in fact, all these aspects of British pageantry stretch back in unbroken tradition to the Middle Ages, and the pageant theatres of the streets were simply one aspect of this kind of pageantry; an aspect which flourished until the closing of the Public Theatres and the Civil War jointly damaged it beyond repair. If we are to understand, therefore, what purpose these theatres served and what connection they have with other dramatic activity of the period, it is necessary first to consider briefly how they came into being.

At the root of the matter lies the delicate balance of relationships between ruler and subject in mediaeval Europe, not altogether divorced by time from memories of similar relationships within the Roman Empire expressed in the word 'triumph'. At first, the conception of 'ruler' extends only to the sovereign and that of 'subjects' to those who, dwelling in the capital city, serve to represent the nation. This conception is stretched in the course of time to cover both the citizens of large provincial towns and subsequently to the first citizen or sovereign's representative resident within such cities. The idea of military victory, however, implicit within the Roman triumph is modified in mediaeval Europe by Christian thinking to imply acknowledgement by the subject that the particular ruler is the representative in their midst, chosen by God for their own good as a figurehead and arbiter of justice. His anointment and acclamation at Coronation are indicative of this belief: and, by means of presentation to the citizens of the capital during a procession through the streets, the acclamation is extended to a wider range of subjects than those privileged to attend the service in the Cathedral. Provincial 'Progresses'—i.e. journeys with the specific object of visiting and being seen in cities other than the capital—extend the range still further. It needs little imagination to see that the significance of such events automatically translated them into occasions of rejoicing; equally that events significant of smooth dynastic succession like royal weddings or the birth of an heir were occasions for similar celebrations. Nor does it rule out thanksgiving for military victory of the Roman kind.

Acknowledgement, however, of God's Providence in ordering such matters for the nation's good did not carry with it automatic servility to the sovereign or, later, to the Lord Mayor. Rather did the subject see fit to keep the ruler aware of the responsibilities corresponding with the privilege of office. I cannot illustrate the point more succinctly than by direct quotation from the pageant-text prepared by the citizens of Worcester to greet Henry VII when visiting the city in the year following his Coronation:

'O Henry! moche art thou beholde to us
That thee have reysede by our oune Election.
Be thou therfor merciful and graciouse;
For Mercye pleaseth moost our Affection.
Folow King Henry,* whiche is thy Protection
As welle in Worke as in Sanguinitie.'[1]

It is within these terms of reference that the pageant theatres of the streets developed. The starting point was the physical manifestation of the ruler's person to the subjects assembled within the capital city. This could most conveniently be achieved by a procession through the streets which were lined for the occasion with beholders. I say 'lined' rather than 'thronged' because the fullest discipline that mediaeval civic administration could achieve was enforced on these occasions. The normal procedure was for the City Fathers to ride to a prearranged meeting place outside the city to greet the sovereign and his household officers. Together they would then ride back into the city, where they would find the citizens positioned along the route and disposed according to the rules of the trade guilds, and dressed in the liveries of those guilds. The cortege would then proceed to the Cathedral or City Church for Divine Service. Following this, the sovereign would be escorted to his palace, which, in London, unlike many continental capitals, was never established within the City boundaries. To this day the sovereign remains 'a visitor' to the City of London.

Processional pageantry of this kind was established in London early in the thirteenth century. Before its close, four separate kinds of event are thus celebrated: the visit of a distinguished foreigner (the Emperor Otho in 1207), a royal wedding (Henry III to Eleanor of Provence in 1236), a coronation (Edward I in 1274) and a major military victory (Edward I's defeat of the Scots at Falkirk in 1298).[2] The last of these has an importance of its own since it is also the first, of which record survives, to be accompanied by specifically theatrical attributes. Edward was met by the citizens who each,

'according to their severall trade, made their severall shew, but specially the Fishmongers, which in a solemne Procession passed

---

* i.e. Henry VI. The speaker is an actor representing Henry VI, the martyred champion of the House of Lancaster and Henry VII's great-uncle.

through the Citie, having amongest other Pageants and shews, foure Sturgeons guilt, caried on four horses: then foure Salmons of silver on foure horses, and after them six and fortie armed knights riding on horses, made like Luces of the sea, and then one representing Saint *Magnes*, because it was upon S. Magnes day, with a thousand horsemen . . .' etc.[3]

The trade symbolism that is evident here is a useful reminder that these celebrations were essentially civic affairs. In many respects the development of the street pageant theatres runs parallel with that of the Tournament; but whereas the Tournament was essentially an aristocratic pastime organized and enacted by the nobility, the street pageants, although frequently prepared for Royalty, were essentially bourgeois activities, responsibility for their devising and enactment lying with the municipality in liaison with the ecclesiastical authorities. This suggests a connection with the Church's own liturgical plays, at least at that point in their development when they are severed from the liturgy itself and performed outside the Church's own precincts with the co-operation of the laity.* It is interesting to observe the reaction of these parallel developments in the Tournament and the Miracle Plays upon civic pageantry. Celebrations in London to mark the birth of Edward III in 1313 include the construction by the Fishmongers of a ship, gaily decorated with the heraldic blazons of the English and French royal houses; while Froissart finds himself at a loss for words to describe the splendour of the Black Prince's reception into Bordeaux at the hands of both *'bourgeois et clergiés'*.[4] However, it must suffice for the moment to take note of the probable interaction of dramatic genres both in the fourteenth century and afterwards and, for the sake of clarity, to continue to treat them independently.

Processional pageantry could not develop much further, except as a gazing stock, without a stage for speech. By 1377, at Richard II's coronation, such a stage existed and was used.

'Nor did these great guilds lack a large company of flutes and trumpets: for every guild (*in the procession*) is led by its own trumpeters. Trumpeters had been stationed by the Londoners above the Conduit, as above the tower in the same street, which had been built in the King's honour, to sound a fanfare on his approach. . . . For a kind of castle had been constructed, having four towers, in the upper part of the shopping street called Cheapside: and from two of its sides wine flowed abundantly. In its

* See Ch. IV., pp. 122–3, 132 and 147–9 below.

towers, moreover, four very beautiful maidens had been placed, of about the King's own age and stature and dressed in white garments. There was one in each of the four towers. On the King's approach being sighted, they scattered golden leaves in his path and, on his coming nearer, they showered imitation gold florins onto both him and his horse. When he had arrived in front of the castle, they took gold cups and, filling them with wine at the spouts of the said castle, offered them to him and his retinue. In the top of the castle, and raised above and between its four towers, a golden angel was stationed holding in its hands a golden crown. This angel had been devised with such cunning that, on the King's arrival, it bent down and offered him the crown.'*

The Latin wording does not make altogether clear whether the castle was constructed round, on or adjacent to the water conduit. The fact, however, that wine flowed out of its spouts, together with our knowledge from subsequent pageants that the Great Conduit was itself normally used, inclines me to interpret the siting in this instance as on and around rather than adjacent to the conduit.†

Where did the idea of using the water conduit as a stage originate? Certainly not in the Tournament. It may possibly have been borrowed from the Church, but if so the derivation is very obscure.

* This translation is made from Walsingham's *Historia Anglicana*, ed. H. T. Riley, London, 1863, i, 331, which reads as follows: 'Nec defuit tantae turbae magna vis lituorum et tubarum; nam quaelibet turba seorsim suos tubicines praecedentes habebat, statutique fuerant per Londonienses super Aquaeductum, et super turrim (in eodem foro quae) in honorem Regis facta fuerat, tubicines qui clangerent in adventu Regis. . . . Factum etiam fuerat quoddam castrum habens turres quatuor, in superiori parte Fori venalium, quod "Chepe" nuncupatur; de quo etiam per duas partes vinum defluxit abundanter. In turribus autem ejus quatuor virgines speciosissimae collocatae fuerant, staturae et aetatis regiae, vestibus albis indutae, in qualibet turri una; quae adventanti Regi procul aurea folia in ejus faciem efflaverunt, et propius accedenti, florenos aureos, sed sophisticos, super eum et ejus dextrarium projecerunt. Cum autem ante castellum venisset, ciphos aureos acceperunt, et implentes eos vino ad fistulas dicti castelli, Regi atque Dominis obtulerunt. In summitate castelli, quae ad modum tali inter quatuor turres elevata fuerat, positus erat angelus aureus, tenens auream coronam in manibus, qui tali ingenio factus fuerat, ut adventanti Regi coronam porrigeret inclinando.' This device so impressed William Langland that he used it in the B. Text of his *Piers Plowman*, Prologue, 11. 128–138. See E. T. Donaldson, *Piers Plowman*, Yale, 1949, p. 118.

† See Figs. 7 and 8: also the London road map showing sites of the principal pageant theatres in the fifteenth and sixteenth centuries (Fig. 9, p. 60 below).

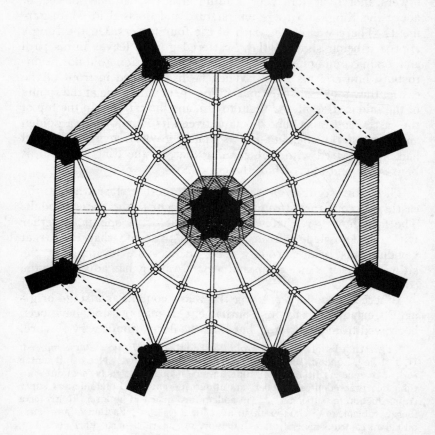

Scale

5   10   15   20 feet

Fɪɢ. 7. Ground plan of the Market Cross (*temp*. Hen. VII) which may still
be seen at Malmesbury, so typical of the edifices adapted to serve as a stage
for Royal Entries and other civic celebrations. The 'acting area', supported
on a vaulted roof, is raised clear of the street by some twelve feet and is
surrounded by a low parapet.

FIG. 8. A sketch from the city walls of the castellated water cistern, or conduit, at Dubrovnik: a typical multi-level, pageant stage, built in 1438.

The first stage used as a street theatre in the present context was the water conduit in Cheapside. According to John Stow this was 'the first Cesterne of leade castellated with stone in the Citty of London . . . which was begunne to bee builded in the yeare 1285. Henry Wales being then Mayor.'[5] A fair interval of time seems to have divided its completion and its first use as a stage. After 1377, however, several other conduits and similar monuments were built in London and taken into service as street theatres for ceremonial processions almost as soon as they were built. This sudden outburst of building activity—in stone at that—which characterizes the close of the fourteenth century came about because the merchant classes were by this time becoming rich enough to rival the great nobles whose wealth was vested in land and who were becoming self-consciously aware that they could express this fact in their style of living. They had the money, too, to impress themselves and their families upon their fellow citizens in the role of public benefactors. One means to such an end was the construction of these flat-topped cisterns in the principal thoroughfares; for the donors might safely reckon on earning the thanks of every householder for whom this simple but vital commodity was thus made more easily accessible. The order and speed with which these conduits were built governs the growth of the street pageant theatres in that they provided the platforms necessary to raise the actors and their setting into easy view of the beholders in the streets. Once this idea had been conceived and translated into action, gateways, market crosses and other architectural units prominently positioned along the processional route could easily be adapted to serve the same end. By 1392, the single pageant 'stage' of 1377 in London had developed to three (one of which was a gate beyond the west wall of the city, better known as Temple Bar). By 1432 the number extended to six. About both of these celebrations I shall have more to say later; but for the present I want to establish what we should understand by the word stage in this context.

First, there can be no doubt that the word stage was used by contemporaries to describe the area on or within which the tableau was positioned and that this stage was raised. An anonymous historian of the fifteenth century in describing the pageant procession of 1392 says that

'betwene seynte Poules (*Cathedral*) and the crosse in chepe (*Cheapside*) (th)ere was made a stage. . . . And an Aungell come a downe from (th)e stage on hye by a vyse (*i.e. a winch*). . . .'[6]

The words, '*super Aquaeductum et super turrim (in eodem foro quae) in honorem Regis facta fuerat*', used by Thomas Walsingham to describe the stage of 1377 are equally categoric.*

The next fact of consequence about this 'stage' is that it never contained more than one tableau. No attempt was made to change the scene. For a change of scene, the procession had to move along the street to the next major monument converted for the occasion into another stage. This use of a number of separate 'stages' for separate 'scenes' inevitably made it hard for the devisers of these celebrations to endow the show as a whole with the coherent logic of consecutive action: for although the journey from one stage to the next amounts in theory to little more than a pause between scenes, the actors (and thus the characters) who have appeared in one 'scene' are marooned on their island stage with no chance to give the subsequent action that continuity which their further presence in it would supply. Actors and authors alike, however, derived a corresponding advantage from this unusual disposition of scenes on independent and isolated stages: for, what was said both verbally and visually in each tableau was addressed directly at the person thus honoured and his retinue. His or her presence before each of the tableaux in turn provided a common link between them all. The effect was inevitably to endow the pageants with a unity of theme instead of the unity usually discernible in plot or through character.† To express the matter in more concrete terms, the separation of the scenes by virtue of the physical apartness of the stages was counterbalanced by the presence before each in turn of the person whom they were designed to honour. This dictated a unified thematic content, presented in the form of a sermon which used a variety of texts to treat appropriate but independent aspects of a single topic. The nature of the occasion governed the nature of the topic, which thus resulted in an illustrated lecture in dramatic form on government and political philosophy.

It follows from what I have been saying that the actors of the street pageant theatres performed to two distinct audiences simultaneously. On the one hand there was the distinguished visitor and his retinue who processed from one stage to the next and thus saw the whole show in its predetermined sequence of scenes. On the other hand there was the much larger audience who could not hope to see more than the tableau nearest to the position where they

---

* See p. 55 above.

† In the Miracle Plays, the Bible narrative: in the Moralities, title roles like Everyman, or Mankind.

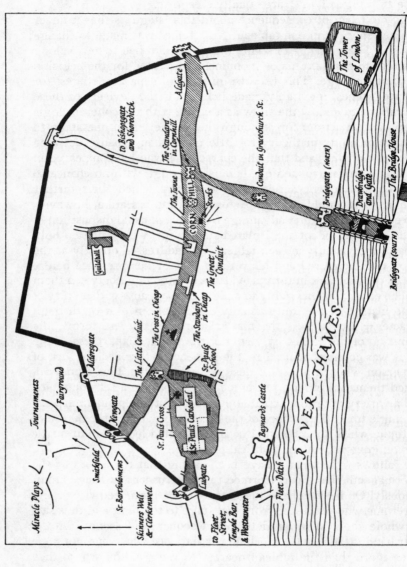

PLAN OF LONDON

Fig. 9. Showing the principal processional routes throughout the City, A.D. 1300–1600 and the principal
stages for civic pageantry.

were themselves stationed. Yet this second audience reaped a com-
pensatory reward which must not be overlooked: the spectacle of
what, to the actors, was the primary audience but which, to the
stationary audience, was an integral part of the show. They thus
participated with the author—at least as observers—in the moral
lecturing of the sovereign and his household. As watchers, these
subjects could assist in putting their ruler in mind of his duties and
responsibilities towards them.

In this context it is scarcely appropriate to talk of an auditorium.
Yet the physical conditions governing the viewing of these spectacles are not without significance as a formative influence on later
theatre building. It is obvious enough that the street, and the
houses which defined it, provided accommodation for the spectators.
What may not be so obvious is the disposition of the spectators
within this accommodation. The best place was the centre of the
street directly facing the tableau. This was reserved for the distinguished visitor and his retinue who, as I have remarked, formed
an integral part of the spectacle as viewed by everyone else. Outside these privileged ranks, the people with 'the best seats' were
those who occupied rooms in adjacent houses with windows overlooking the street. It was from this point of vantage that Henry VII
and his Queen watched Katherine of Aragon's reception into London
in 1501, receiving hospitality from one 'William Geffrey, haberdasher'.[7] When, two years later, their daughter Margaret arrived
in Edinburgh to marry James IV an eye-witness states that 'the
houses and wyndowes war full of lordes, ladyes, gentyl-women and
gentylmen'.[8] Positions of less vantage were the pavements and the
roofs.* The former, known as 'standings', were allotted to members of the Livery Companies.[9] Those for whom no specific provision was made could scale the roofs if they were sufficiently agile
or take back places on the pavements.

Three features in these viewing arrangements stand out as

---

* See Plate XVIII. 'See if the streets and the fronts of the houses be not
stuck with people, and the windows filled with ladies as on the solemn day of
the Pageant.' (Epilogue to *Westward Hoe*, 1605.)

> '. . . Many a time and oft
> Have you climb'd up to walls and battlements,
> To towers and windows, yea, to chimney-tops,
> Your infants in your arms, and there have sat
> The livelong day, with patient expectation,
> To see great Pompey pass the streets of Rome.'

(*Julius Caesar*, I., i., 41.)

recurring with varying degrees of importance in the seating arrangements for subsequent regular drama. The first is the 'open' nature of the stage in relation to the audience: veritable islands in the surrounding sea of spectators.[10] The second is the repetition of that grading of positions for spectators according to social status already remarked on in the auditorium for Tournaments. The third is a peculiar extension of that grading: the placing of the most notable spectator of all in such a dominating position that the others are hard put to determine whether he is a participant like the actors or a member of the audience like themselves. This relationship is of particular consequence to the development of the Court Theatre. *

Before proceeding to analyse the spectacle presented in these pageant theatres of the streets, it may be helpful to summarize this necessarily long examination of what they actually were. In a very special sense they may be said to have been 'national' or 'civic' theatres; theatres that only came into existence on rare occasions of exceptional national or civic importance. Intended both to entertain and to instruct they can truly be called theatres. Their site was the main streets of large towns and their form a sequence of separate tableaux loosely linked by the presence before each in turn of the notable person whose presence the nation or the city wished to celebrate. The nature of their content was a sermon, spectacular and dramatic, the significance of which was specifically directed at the visitor but which the occasion caused author, actors and audience to share alike. In consequence of all these facts, thematic content took precedence over everything else in the construction of both text and spectacle. Where topical subject matter was inevitably of so personal a kind, courtesy, if nothing else, forbade bald statement. Instead, it suggested allegorical treatment. This could be scriptural, historical, mythological or whatever best fitted the occasion and justifies the remarks which Warton made in his *History of English Poetry* and which I quote in full since they appear to have sustained such unwarrantable neglect from subsequent historians of our drama:

'It seems probable, that the PAGEAUNTS, which being shown on civil occasions, derived great part of their decorations and actors

---

* See also Ch. VI, p. 223 and Ch. VII, p. 249 below. In my opinion, this comes in consequence to occasion the curious and gradual substitution of the glittering stalls public of the pre-war opera house for those 'rank stinkards' of groundlings in the yard of the Elizabethan Public Playhouse. The latter, if my hypothesis is true, are now banished from the pavement, but may still climb to the roof.

from historical fact, and consequently made profane characters the subject of public exhibition, dictated ideas of a regular drama much sooner than the MYSTERIES; which being confined to scripture stories, or rather the legendary miracles of sainted martyrs, and the no less ideal personifications of the christian virtues, were not calculated to make so quick and easy a transition to the representations of real life and rational action.'

I believe that Warton guessed correctly. Certainly, the examples of these pageants which I intend to examine now, appear to lead from that of Richard II's reconcilement with the City of London in 1392 in a patently direct line through Tudor Chronicles to plays like *Gorboduc*, *The Misfortunes of Arthur* or *Endymion* with their expositional dumbshows and acutely personal allegory and thus to Shakespeare's History Plays with their thinly veiled sermons on government.

2 Subject Matter of the Pageant Theatres

Sir Edmund Chambers inclined to dismiss the records of civic pageantry as too ephemeral to warrant the tedium of full analysis. Tedious much of it may be. Nevertheless, some attention has been given to these records in recent years. One result is to make anyone who has studied this work suspect that it is this failure to analyse them hitherto which has deprived historians of the theatre and dramatic literature of information in default of which any convincing connection between the ecclesiastical drama of the Middle Ages and the regular drama of Elizabethan times has been hard to establish. For this reason I have listed in an Appendix all the important English Royal Entries together with sources providing descriptions of them.* In the text, therefore, I do not feel bound either to include them all or to treat any of them exhaustively as a special subject. Those which I regard as relevant to this section of the chapter are:

1392   Richard II's reconciliation with the City of London.

1432   Henry VI's entry into London on return from his coronation in Paris.

1486   Henry VII's Provincial Progress to York, Hereford, Worcester and Bristol.

1558   Queen Elizabeth I's Coronation in London.

1603   James VI of Scotland's entry into London for his corona-
–04   tion as James I.†

* See pp. 348–349 below.

† Prepared in 1603 but postponed because of plague till March, 1604.

These Pageants all illustrate especially well some aspect of the subject matter used in these street theatres and the manner in which it was treated.

The Pageant of 1392 is interesting, principally for its occasion. In that year the citizens of London refused a loan to Richard II who, in revenge, deprived the mayor, sheriffs and aldermen of office and removed his Court to York. In York he stayed from

'(th)e feste of seint John Baptiste vn to (th)e feste of cristenmasse next comyng after. And (th)an (th)e Kyng and his counsaille sawe it not so prophitable there as he was atte London.'[11]

In short, London's merchants were powerful enough through their wealth to call his bluff.[12] The King capitulated, returned to London, restored the civic liberties and received a variety of gifts including some money from the 'grateful' citizens. Exactly whose 'triumph', therefore, the pageantry on the King's return to London celebrated is hard to distinguish. This ambivalence is reflected in the descriptive verses written in Latin by Richard Maydiston, and which, in a free prose translation, run as follows:

'Cicero* thought friends worth such great praise because, should they be all removed, even the best of things are worthless. "Be you in Paradise," he says, "be your eye delighted by all it sees; be your ear ravished by all it hears; and still the physical world is immaterial unless you have a friend with whom to share your experience. Lacking a friend to whom you can relate your pleasure, these very pleasures will appear jaded." Hence, Richard, doubly yoked to me both as namesake and by keepsake, so much are you my friend that I am now impelled to relate those celebrations we witnessed of late in Troynovant (i.e. London). And if, in labouring to compose these trifling verses for you I stumble, look mercifully on my labour, I pray, for love should be merciful.

* 'Tullius in laudem tantam sustollit amicos,
Quod licet, his demptis, optima nil valeant:
"Stes," ait, "in coelis, videas ibi quaeque beata,
Hauriat auris in his utraque dulce melos,
Quicquid adhuc sensus poterit tibi pascere quinos
Nil valet acceptum, si nec amicus adest.
Si careas socio, cui sata placentia narres,
Haec eadem senties non placuisse tibi."
Hinc tibi, Ricarde, duplante jugo mihi juncte,
(Nomen et omen habes, sic socius meus es,)
Gaudia visa mihi Trenovantum nuper in urbe,
Actus amicitia, glisco referre modo.
Et licet incultum carmen tibi condere curem,
Parce precor curae, parcere debet amor.

'Take one thousand; add three hundred, then ten times nine plus
two. The sum is what I reckon to have been the date when, six
months after your reconciliation with New Troy—on the 21st day
of August, tidings of great joy reached the city. For the city's
spouse, its King and master, whom evil counsel had estranged, was
welcomed back again. An invidious clique turned the King's wrath
against the city and caused the city's bridegroom to withdraw his
Court and his own presence. But he cannot hate you for long when
the vision of the lover is more beautiful than Paris and all his love
is yours. Add the fact that it is always his wont to have compassion
on those who arouse it: nor is vengeance a quality of the good
King's. All England knows what wrongs and what misfortunes he
has endured since infancy of which he is unavenged. Why else
should he seek to serve God if not to preserve peace and goodwill
among men, and to see that nothing good may perish? Thus he
cherishes the Church and by his control of legislation he guards
against the overthrow of our ancestral heritage. He takes into his
service whatever becomes his person and banishes the ingrate, the
selfish, the base and the cruel. In Christendom he is unrivalled,
knowing, like Solomon, how to govern his Kingdom. Although he
was angry with you for a while, O Troy, his kind face now radiates

M. cape, ter quoque c. deciesque novem, duo junge,
Hunc numerum anni supputo dando notis.
Tunc bis ter Phoebo fuerat soror associata,
Cum bona felici sunt, Nova Troja, tibi.
Mensis ut Augusti ter septima fulsit in orbem
Lux, tibi, Londoniae, rumor amoenus adest.
Namque tuum regem, sponsum, dominumque tuumque,
Quem tibi sustulerat perfida lingua, capis.
Invidiosa cohors regem tibi vertit in iram,
Deseret thalamum sponsus ut ipse suum.
Sed quia totus amor tuus est, et amantis imago
Formosior Paride, nescit odisse diu.
Adde quod in miseros semper solet hic misereri,
Nec habet ultrices rex pius iste manus.
Quot mala, quot mortes tenero sit passus ab aevo,
Quamque sit inultus, Anglia tota videt.
Quid cupit hic servire Deo, nisi semper et esse
Pacificum, laetum, nilque perire bonum?
Sic fovet ecclesiam statuens statuum moderamen,
Sternere ne liceat quod statuere patres.
Effugat ingratos, cupidos, stolidos, truculentos,
Quaeque decent regem haec rapit ipse sibi.
Talis adolescens toto non restat in orbe,
Qui sciat ut Salomon regna tenere sua.
Hic licet accensus foret in te, Troja, parumper,

parental affection. No detractor's tongue could overcome the bride-groom's longing to enter his bridal chamber. He who had deprived you of your accustomed liberties now returns, ready to restore them manyfold.'*

Since no translation yet exists of this remarkable document it is worth devoting further space to some extracts from Maydiston's description of the scene.

The City's preparations for the King's arrival.†

'As the day dawns, the Knight appointed by the King to watch over the City (*i.e. the Mayor*) addresses the citizens. "Prepare yourselves for the arrival of your King that he may plainly see how welcome is his coming. Arrange a procession of the clergy of every church and let each order carry its crosses before it. Let every Craft ensure that it rides out across the river in its own ceremonial livery more grandly than usual. Let the honour of the City be shown in your bearing and rejoice this day—an amnesty will be granted."

'Inspired by these words, the whole community unites in ensuring a gay welcome. The streets are gaily decorated and, in a City sparkling with countless golden cloths, breathe the fragrance of blossoms.

Grata modo facies se docet esse piam.
Non poterat mordax detractans lingua tenere,
Quin cuperet thalamum sponsus adire suum.
Qui libertates solitas tibi dempserat omnes,
Nunc redit, et plures reddere promptus eas.'

* Bodl. MS. E. Museo. 94. Ricardi Maydiston de concordia inter Regem Ric. II et civitatem London, ff. 8b *et seq.*

† 'Urbis custodem miles quem rex ibi signat,
Alloquitur cives sic, rutilante die:
"Regis in occursum vestri vos este parati,
Percipiatque palam quam bene nunc veniat.
Totius ecclesiae fiat processio cleri,
Omnis et ordo suas se ferat ante cruces.
Nulla sit ars urbis, quae non distincta seorsum
Splendidius solito trans vada vadat eques.
Quicquid in urbe probum fuerit promatur, in ista,
Nam gaudete die, pax tribuetur," ait.
His animata loquelis tota cohors sociatur,
Praeparat et cultu se meliore suo.
Ornat et interea se pulchre quaeque platea,
Vestibus auratis urbs micat innumeris.
Floris odoriferi specie fragrante platea,

No house lacks its purple hangings; so that what with gold, purple, brown and other dyed draperies overhead, it seemed that art had painted a new heaven. It is impossible to relate the exertions to which the people had put themselves, the costs they had borne. Why do I delay? The day passes. People hasten from the city to meet the King and his consort. How may I number the number of so numerous a throng as that which flowed thence, thicker than the galaxy! Twenty thousand young men went mounted; but how many went on foot there's no knowing! The Mayor is at the head accompanied by twenty-four Aldermen whom the city elects as its governors: for this City is ruled by them as Rome was ruled by its Senate, while they are themselves responsible to the Mayor, elected by the citizens. They were dressed in their liveries of red and white, distinguished from the rest by their parti-coloured cloaks.

'First, then, rides the Mayor, bearing the keys and the sword of the City, followed by the City Fathers in whose wake come the gaily caparisoned representatives of the Crafts. Each Guild manifestly keeps its own ranks. Here go the silversmiths; there the fishmongers; with them the mercers and vintners, *etc.* . . .'
(*A long list follows.*)

Pendula perque domos purpura nulla deest;
Aurea, coccinea, bissinaque, tinctaque vestis,
Pinxerat hic coelum arte juvante novum.
Quos tulit ante dies istos plebs ista labores,
Quas tulit expensas, os reserare nequit.
Quid moror? ecce dies transit! properatur ab urbe
Regis in occursum conjugis atque suae.
Quis numerare queat numerum turbae numerosae,
Quae velut astra poli densius inde fluit?
Millia viginti juvenes numerantur equestres;
Qui pedibus pergunt, non capit hos numerus.
Custos praecedit, comitantur eumque quater sex,
Quos aldirmannos urbs habet ut proceres.
Jure senatorio urbs his regitur quasi Roma,
Hisque praeest major, quem populus legerit.
His erat ornatus albus color et rubicundus,
Hos partita toga segregat a reliquis.
Clavibus assumptis, urbis gladio quoque, custos
Praecedit proceres, subque sequuntur eum.
Hos sequitur phalerata cohors cujuslibet artis;
Secta docet sortem quaeque tenere suam.
His argentarius, his piscarius, secus illum
Mercibus hic deditus, venditor atque meri.'

. . . .

The citizens go to meet their King.*

'Strike up, citizens! Play now for your King. Look! your King approaches. Strike a fitting note! As the King draws near, so the groups of noblemen draw together. Ah me! The beauty of the sight that meets their eyes you may imagine. While the good King rides up on his white horse (*Barbary?*) the crowd makes way for him that all may have a better view of him. His face and features, springlike in their freshness, are framed in brown curls which look so well beneath his glowing crown. His fiery cloak of cloth of gold, which enfolds such delicate limbs, dazzles the eye. He is as beautiful as Troilus or even Absalom himself and bewitches the senses of all who look at him. Fortunately there is no need to describe his appearance in every detail: for among all Kings he has no fellow. If nature, so liberal in looks, had done more for him, then Venus would have confined him to his chamber for very envy. As he took his place in the midst of the throng in that packed field he was surrounded by the nobles of the kingdom as befitted his state and his queen with her ladies close at hand. Her name is Anne and may she live up to it. Beautiful herself, she stands surrounded by lovely ladies in waiting, and with these Amazons New Troy is without rival. Her dress is embroidered with glittering jewels: from head

* 'Psallite nunc, cives, regi nunc psallite vestro,
En! rex vester adest, psallite quod sapit hic.
Rege propinquante comites glomerantur heriles,
Ha mihi! quam pulchrum cernere credis eos.
Dum niveo resideret equo, se quique retractant,
Ut pateat populo rex pius ipse suo.
Vernula quam facies fulvis redimita capillis,
Comptaque sub serto praeradiante coma!
Fulget et ex auro vestis sua rubra colore,
Quae tenet interius membra venusta nimis.
Iste velut Troilus, velut Absolon ipse decorus,
Captivat sensum respicientis eum.
Non opus est omnem regis describere formam,
Regibus in cunctis non habet ille parem.
Larga decoris ei si plus natura dedisset,
Clauderet hunc thalamis invida forte Venus.
Sistit ut in medias super arva repleta catervas,
Nobilibus regni cingitur, ut decuit.
Nec procul est conjunx regina suis comitata,
Anna sibi nomen, re sit et Anna precor!
Pulchra quidem pulchris stat circumcincta puellis,
Vincit Amazonibus Troja novella sub his.
Sternitur ex gemmis nitidis sparsim sua vestis,

to foot precious stones. Diamonds abound; beryls and carbuncles. Every gem of value adorns her head: that which shines on her glowing brow and those which sparkle on her ears dazzle the eye to prevent an excess of delight.'

Once assembled, and after an address of welcome from the Mayor to which the King replied, the cortège returned to London. On arriving in Cheapside they see before them the Great Conduit decorated for the occasion.

'The Conduit distils red wine instead of the usual water and there is ample for a thousand people to drink. A heavenly host is stationed on the top of it who sing songs with pleasing skill. Gold coins are scattered on all sides by maidens which flutter down like leaves or flowers.'*

Seemingly adjacent to the Conduit is a tower, specially constructed for the occasion.†

'Departing thence, the King moved on to the middle of the street and there he saw a castle: he halted as this greatly impressed him. The whole structure of the tower is suspended on cords, and towers into the sky. A youth and a beautiful girl stand in this tower; he represents an angel: she wears a crown. No one who saw these figures, or so I feel, could doubt that anything under

---

Ad caput a planta nil nisi gemma patet.
Nulla deest adamas, carbunculus, atque beryllus,
Qui lapis est pretii, sternitur inde caput.
Quod nitet in fronte nitida, radiatque per aures,
Verberat obtuitum, ne foret inde satur.'

* 'Stillat aquaeductus Bacchum, nec adest ibi Thetis,
Rubra dat iste liquor pocula mille viris.
Hujus et in tecto steterat coelicus ordo,
Qui canit angelicos arte juvante melos,
Densa velut folia seu flores sic volat aurum,
Undique virginea discutiente manu.'

† 'Itur abhinc mediam dum rex venit usque plateam,
Cernit ibi castrum, stat, stupet hic nimium.
Pendula per funes est fabrica totaque turris,
Aetheris et medium vendicat illa locum
Stant et in hac turri juvenis formosaque virgo,
Hic velut angelus est, haec coronata fuit.
Cerneret has facies quisquis, puto, non dubitaret
Nil fore sub coelo quod sibi plus placeat.

69

heaven might please him more. The King and his Queen draw near and spend much time speculating what this high tower or these youths might signify. Both the youth and the girl descend together from the tower without the aid of any visible steps or ladder. In their descent they were surrounded by clouds and suspended on air—by what machines I know not.'

They then proceed to offer a cup of wine and a crown, thereby repeating the ceremony of the pageant on the same spot fifteen years earlier.* On this occasion, however, the gifts are stated to have been accompanied by a speech. London rejoices to see its King again: that is the substance. It is worth noting that both the *'custos'* of the pageant and the Mayor in his earlier speech of greeting never supply the least hint that London was in the wrong in the initial quarrel or that there was any justification for Richard's arbitrary conduct. They are glad to see him back: they look forward to having their rights restored: but they are well aware that the reason prompting both is that Richard cannot govern without their money. Rather are his present actions in his own best interests and thus fit cause for general rejoicing.

A second pageant stage is erected on the newly built 'Little Conduit' on which the Trinity is presented amidst a crowd of angel musicians and singers. After seeing this, the King and Queen, together with the Mayor and Aldermen, attend a service of thanksgiving in St. Paul's Cathedral. It is shortly after this that the citizens present the pith of their business in its most distinct form—despite a suitably sugared coating for the pill.

On leaving St. Paul's, the whole procession moved towards Westminster via Temple Bar, the city's western outpost, where 'A forest had been erected on the roof of the gate which, representing a wilderness, was populated by all manner of wild beasts.' In the middle of this tableau stood St. John the Baptist pointing with his finger, *agnus et ecce Dei*. The King and Queen were each given an engraved tablet by an angel who 'descended from the high roof' to present them. The scripture given to the King reminded him

---

Rex reginaque tunc astant bene discutientes
Quid velit haec turris alta, vel hi juvenes.
Descendunt ab ea juvenis simul ipsaque virgo,
Nulla fuit scala, nec patuere gradus.
Nubibus inclusi veniunt, et in aethere pendunt,
Quo tamen ingenio nescio, crede mihi.'

(See p. 66, note*, above.)
* See p. 55 above.

that as forgiveness most became Christ on the Cross, so that quality would most become Richard in relations with his subjects. The Queen's tablet told her that as Esther mediated between the wrath of Ahasuerus and his subjects so she too should mediate between the King and the citizens when the need arose.*

The choice of St. John as the governing figure in this tableau is curious. It indicates, to my mind, that the Merchant Taylors Company were responsible; for Richard had himself become an honorary member of that Company in 1385 and in 1392 had granted them their second charter recognizing St. John the Baptist as their patron saint.[13]

This account of the pageants would be incomplete without its sequel. The following morning, the Mayor, Sheriffs and Aldermen visited the King at the Palace of Westminster,

'presentyng hym with ij Basyns of silver and over gilte full of coyned gold sum of xx.m.li. prayng hym of his heigh mercy and Lordship and speciall grace: that they myght have his goode love and libertees and fraunchises like as they have hadde before tymes and bi his lettres and patentes and (th)ir charter confermed. And the Queene and other worthy lordes and ladies felle on knees and bi-sought the Kyng of grace to conferme this: than the Kyng tooke up the Queene and graunted hir all her askyng. And than they (th)anked the Kyng and the Queene and wente home ageyne.'[14]

This sequel to the pageant of 1392 indicates clearly that the civic devisers of these entertainments had a firm didactic intention in mind when preparing them and that they succeeded in expressing it explicitly enough in mime, spectacle and speech for the recipient to understand its significance and take appropriate action. Nearly a hundred years later Henry VII was in Bristol. There (a year after the Battle of Bosworth Field) the legendary founder of the city, King Bremius, addresses him from a pageant stage.

'. . . Bristow is fallen into Decaye,
Irrecuperable, withoute that a due Remedy
By you, ther Herts Hope and Comfort in this Distresse,
Proveded bee, at your Leyser convenyently,
To your Navy and Cloth-making, whereby I gesse
The Wele of this Towne standeth in Sikernesse,
May be maynteigned, as they have bee(n)
In Days hertofor in Prosperitie.'[15]

* In Maydiston's poem, these events are described in lines 358 *et seq.*

71

The Herald-historian adds an illuminating postscript to his account of these shows:

'After Evensonge the King sent for the Mayre and Shrife, and Parte of the best Burges of the Towne, and demaunded theym the Cause of ther Povertie; and they shewde his Grace for the great Losse of Shippes and Goodes that they had loost within 5 Yeres. The King comforted theym, that they shulde sett on/and make new Shippes, and to exercise ther Marchandise as they wer wonte for to doon. And his Grace shulde so helpe theym by dyvers Means like as he shewde unto theym, that the Meyre of the Towne towlde me they harde not this hundred Yeres of noo King so good a Comfort.'[16]

Queen Elizabeth I, on entering London for her coronation in 1558, kept up a running commentary of pithy answers to everything addressed to her from the many stages in the streets. On the Conduit in Gracechurch Street was the pageant called 'The uniting of the two howses of Lancastre and Yorke'. After watching this, and before moving on, she made a short speech promising that she would 'doe her whole endevour for the continuall preservation of concorde, as the pageant did emport'.[17] The fact that Elizabeth fulfilled expectation in being able to interpret the symbolism of this show (as well as all the others) is scarcely less important than that it forms the governing theme of Shakespeare's subsequent history plays: for here on the stage of this street theatre of 1558 stood Henry VII, his wife Elizabeth of York, Henry VIII and Anne Boleyn in person.

The idea of using historical personages to point a moral in the street pageant theatres was of much earlier origin. The first example known to me is Lydgate's pageant for the Entry of Henry VI into London in 1432 after his Paris coronation. On this occasion the Cross in Cheapside had been transformed into a tower.

'garnysshed with the Armys of Englande and of Fraunce this Tower was wonderfull to beholde for there was shewd in Ordre the Tytle which the kynge had unto the Crowne of Frau(n)ce.'[18]

Lydgate describes the Tower as 'a castell bilt off jasper grene'. In front of it stood two green trees, artificially made, and, on the far side of it, a third tree on its own. This third tree 'was made for the sprynge of Jesse wherein was shewyd the Genelogy of our blessyd Lady'. * The other two served a similar purpose, 'one beryng (th)e

* The Town Clerk, John Carpenter, in his account of the proceedings adds the interesting detail, 'repraesentans in ramis (*branches*) per personas vivas.' See note 16 and Plate XVI.

Genelogy of Seynt Edward and that other of Seynt Lowys and garnyshed with Leopardes and Flourdelycz'. Here the biblical and historical application of two particular conventions already remarked in the Tournament—the tree and heraldic blazons—are to be seen conveniently side by side.

The forward move of time brings the historical morality of the street pageant theatres into ever increasing preponderance and clarity. Henry VII encountered it everywhere he went on his Provincial Progress of 1486.

At Bristol *Justice* proclaims darkly that the visiting sovereign had been

> 'Preserved by dyvyne Power certeygn,
> And so hider sentt.'[19]

This somewhat delphic utterance may be swiftly interpreted by reference to the Pageants at York and Worcester. At York *Solomon* 'in his Habite Roiall crownede', was placed, we are told, in a

> 'Pajannt garnyshede with Shippes, and Botes in every
> Side, in Tokenyng of the King's Landing at Milforde Havyn.'[20]

From this symbolic station he addresses Henry:

> 'Moost prudent Prynce of provid Provision,
> Ther premordiall Princes of this Principalitie,
> Hath preparate your Reign, the vii by Succession,
> Remytting this Reame, as right to your Roialtie.'

Not only God, it would seem, but the spirits of earlier Princes are taking an active interest in the fortunes of this Welshman. And *Janitor*, at Worcester, supplies the reason. 'Quis est ille qui venit? so great of Price,' he asks. At first he thought it must be Noah; then Jason.

> 'Or is it Julius with the Triumphe of Victorie
> To whom I say welcome most hertely?' [21]

But it is none of these. Nor is it Abraham, Isaac, Jacob, Joseph, David nor Scipio. No; this is

> '. . . Arture, the very Britain Kyng.
> Welcome Defence to England as a Walle.
> Cadwaladers Blodde lynyally descending,
> Longe hath bee towlde of such a Prince comyng.
> Wherfor Frendes, if that I shal not lye,
> This same is the Fulfiller of the Profecye.' [22]

What prophecy, the reader may ask? And it is as well that he should: for the answer informs much of Tudor literature. Legend had insisted that King Arthur was not dead, but sleeping. In the words of Hall's Chronicle,

'. . . it was by a heavenly voyce reve(a)led to Cadwalader last kyng of Brytons that his stocke and progeny should reigne in this land and beare domynion agayn: where-upo(n) most men were persuaded in their awne opinion that by this heavenly voyce he (*i.e. Henry VII*) was provided and ordeyned longe before to enjoye and obteine this kyngdome, whiche thing kyng Henry the VI did also shewe before.'[23]

When Hall wrote his Chronicle, this theme had already long been in the air. Henry himself had been among the first to grasp its significance when, in 1486, he christened his son and heir Prince Arthur,

'Of whiche name,' and here again I quote Hall, 'Englishemen no more rejoysed then outwarde nacions and foreyne prynces trymbled and quaked, so muche was that name to all nacions terrible and formidable.'[24]

Already by 1486, as noted, the author of the Worcester Pageant had exploited the dramatic possibilities latent in this theme. His example was followed by others, notably in the London Pageants for Prince Arthur's wedding to Katherine of Aragon in 1501, and the theme was swiftly assimilated into the Pageant tradition. Thence it was destined to blossom into a regular Inns of Court Play—*The Misfortunes of Arthur*—and to give precedent for Cranmer's famous prophecy in the closing scene of Shakespeare's *Henry VIII*. I incline to go further and to suggest that Shakespeare took more than a hint in the composing of this speech from the words which Ben Jonson gave to *Genius Urbis* in the pageants for James I's entry into London in 1603.

Prophesying of James, Cranmer says:

> 'Peace, plenty, love, truth, terror,
> That were the servants to this chosen infant, (*i.e. Elizabeth*)
> Shall then be his, and like a vine grow to him:
> Wherever the bright sun of heaven shall shine,
> His honour and the greatness of his name
> Shall be, and make new nations; he shall flourish,
> And, like a mountain cedar, reach his branches
> To all the plains about him.'*

* *Henry VIII*, V, v, 48; and cf. *Macbeth*, IV, i, 86.

Genius Urbis, addressing James from the pageant stage at Fenchurch some ten years earlier:

> 'His country's wonder, hope, love, joy and pride:
> How well doth he become the royal side
> Of this erected and broad-spreading tree,
> Under whose shade may Britain ever be!
> And from this branch may thousand branches more
> Shoot o'er the main, and knit with every shore
> In bonds of marriage, kindred and increase;
> And style this land the navel of their peace.'*

Whether or not the reader cares to regard this similarity as no more than coincidence, the common stock from which both passages stem is exposed in Jonson's description of the costume for Genius Urbis: 'a person attired rich, reverend and antique: his hair long and white, crowned with a wreath of plane-tree, which is said to be *Arbor genialis.*'†

And so the wheel comes full circle back to Lydgate's 'castell bilt of jasper grene' and the trees 'one beryng the Genelogy of Seynt Edward and that other of Seynt Lowys'.‡

Historical morality, however, is by no means the only contribution of these pageant theatres to the themes of regular drama. It is just as easy to spot and then to trace the morality of personal conduct extended to the body politic developing within the pageant theatres for a citizen audience and subsequently handed over to the regular drama.

The Christian basis of this morality and the path of its extension from a code of personal conduct to government of the State is apparent in 1392 where figures taken from the Bible (in this instance Esther and Christ) are used as precepts for the instruction of Richard II and his Queen.

In 1432, Lydgate greatly widens the range of characters employed to inform the young Henry VI of the ethics of kingship. Six pageants were presented on this occasion. The south bank gate of London's Bridge housed the first show and fitly symbolized London's hopes that the new king would fulfil the city's aspirations.[25]

---

* Ben Jonson, 'Part of King James' Entertainment'. *Works*, vii. p. 94.

† *Ibid*, p. 85. The quotations are given here in modern spelling and punctuation.

‡ See Plate XVI and p. 72 above.

'Entryng the Brigge off this noble town,
Ther was a pyler reysed lyke a tour
And ther-on stoode a sturdy champeoun,
Off looke and chere sterne as a lyoun,
His swerde up rered proudely gan manace,
Alle fforeyn enmyes ffrom the Kyng to enchace.

And in deffence of his (e)state ryall
The geaunt wolde abyde eche aventure;
And alle assautes that wern marcyall,
For his sake he proudely wolde endure,
In tokne wheroff he hadde a scripture
On eyther syde declaryng his entent,
Which seyde thus by goode avysement:

"Alle tho (*those*) that ben enemyes to the Kyng,
I shall hem clothe with confusioun,
Make him myhty with vertuous levyng
His mortall foon to oppressen and bere adoun,
And him to encresen as Cristis champioun,
Alle myscheffes ffrom hym to abrigge
With the grace off God at thentryng off the Brigge."

Twoo antelopes stondyng on eytheyr syde
With the armes off Englond and off Fraunce,
In tokenyng that God shall ffor hym provyde,
As he hath tytle by iuste enheritaunce
To regne in pees, plente and plesaunce.'[26]

In short, the young king is told that he has no cause for fear in entering upon his reign while he is sustained by the love and loyalty of his subjects. The second pageant, along with several others, acquaints him with the price of this loyalty or, in other words, what is expected of him in return for the privilege of kingly office.

This pageant was staged in the tower of the drawbridge, richly dressed with hangings of velvet, silk, cloth of gold and tapestry. Representing a moral allegory of the Virtues Nature, Grace and Fortune, it was very elaborate and is carefully expounded. The following quotations show plainly how emphasis shifts from a personal interpretation of the moral to a political interpretation. The virtues are represented as Empresses. The first, Grace—

'. . . gaff him ffirst at his komyng
Twoo riche gifftes, Sciens and Kunnyng;

Nature gaff him eke strenth and ffeyrenesse,
Forto be lovyd and dredde off euery wiht;
Fortune gaff him eke prosperite and richesse,
With this scripture apperyng in theire siht,
To him applyed off verrey dewe riht,
"First undirstonde and joyfully procede
And lange to regne" the scripture seyde in dede.

This ys to mene, who-so undirstonde a-riht,
Thow shalt be (by) Fortune have lange prosperite;
And be Nature thow shalt have strenth and myht,
Forth to procede in lange ffelicite;
And Grace also hath graunted unto the,
Vertuously lange in thy ryall citee,
With septre and croune to regne in equyte.'27

The Virtues were flanked by attendant maidens, seven on each side, who offered further advice. Those on their right, representing the seven Gifts of the Holy Ghost, spoke first.

'God the ffulfille with intelligence
And with a spyryt off goostly sapience.

God sende also unto thy most vaylle
The to preserve ffrom alle hevynesse,
A spyrit off strenth, and off goode counsaylle,
Off konnyng, drede, pite and lownesse.'

The seven virgins on the Empresses' left offered him regalia—

'God the endewe with a croune off glorie,
And with septre off clennesse and pytee,
And with a swerde off myht and victorie,
And with a mantel off prudence cladde thow be,
A shelde off ffeyth fforto defende the,
A helme off helthe wrouht to thy encrees,
Girt with a girdyll off love and parfyte pees.'28

The procession then moved on to Cornhill. At the entrance a pageant-stage presented Dame Sapience attended by the Seven Liberal Sciences to the king in the persons of sages like Aristotle, Euclid and Boethius; while next, on the Conduit in Cornhill, David and Solomon are cited to him by Clemency as precedents for the proper use of authority.

'Honour off kyngys, in every mannys siht,
Of comyn custum lovith equyte and riht.'29

These excerpts illustrate the application of scriptural example to the occasion in question. In three out of the four pageants considered a passage from the Bible appropriate as a text on the subject of government is lifted from its context and embellished and elaborated into a short dramatic sermon of political intention. St. Paul's Epistle to the Ephesians (vi. 11–17), 'Wherefore take unto you the whole armour of God . . .' supplies the basis for the regalia offered to the king by the Virtues; Proverbs (viii. 12–21), 'I wisdom dwell with prudence . . . By me kings reign, etc. . . .' suggests the presence of Sapience and the Liberal Sciences through cultivation of whom wisdom is attained*: and the Judgement of Solomon is familiar enough for there to be no need to press the point further.

The longevity of these ideas is nowhere more startlingly illustrated than in the verbatim repetition of these pageants of the Virtues and of the Liberal Sciences more than a hundred years later at Edward VI's Coronation (Feb. 1546).[30] Elizabeth I was given 'The Seat of Worthy Governance' to study in Cornhill, the Virtues in this instance being Pure Religion, Love of Subjects, Wisdom and Justice, represented as persons treading underfoot the contrary vices. The Conduit in Fleet Street was the stage for a tableau of 'Deborah the Judge and restorer of Israel'.[31] This same Conduit remained faithful to the presentation of scriptural precept at James I's Coronation, this time in the shape of the Four Cardinal Virtues in association with the new king's four kingdoms.†

In short, almost every character that ever appeared as a Virtue or Vice in the cast list of a Morality Play and many biblical figures familiar from the Miracle Plays were presented at one time or another in these pageant theatres of the streets. They were, moreover, as familiar in provincial cities as in London. Linking them all was the conception of Divine Providence taking an active part in the nation's affairs; ready to look kindly on any new beginning or promise of future good, but equally prompt to intervene directly or indirectly where privilege was abused or responsibility shirked.

Henry VII was specifically reminded of this in Worcester, York and Bristol in 1486, not only in the passage quoted concerning 'succession' and 'election',‡ but in the outspoken reactions of

---

* See p. 108 below.

† Thomas Middleton wrote the speech for Zeal, 'the Presenter of this Device', called *Cosmos Neos*.

‡ See p. 53 above.

citizens who are sick of Civil War and its attendant evils.* A Christian, mercantile bourgeoisie expresses its abiding dislike for the gangster and profiteer. Times, say the citizens of Bristol, are troubled and honest labour goes unrewarded.

> 'In moost loving wise now graunte ye
> Some Remedye herin, and He wille quit your Mede,
> That never unrewarded leveth good Dede.'[32]

The citizens of Worcester were of like mind.

> 'If thou serve God in Love and Drede
> Havyng Compassion of them that hath Nede,
> Everlasting Joye shal be thy Mede
> In Heven above wher all Seints dwelle.'[33]

If seeking to complete the triple rhyme for 'dwelle' one would have to look far for a more appropriate couplet than,

> 'Vain world and vanity, farewell.
> Who builds his Heaven on earth is sure of Hell.'

The lines are Thomas Dekker's and are taken from *Old Fortunatus*.†

> 'Judges are termed the Gods on earth,'‡

wrote Webster in his revised version of *Appius & Virginia*. This sentiment, with the order inverted, is expressed of Henry VII in 1501 at Katherine of Aragon's reception into London to marry Prince Arthur. Speaking in the fifth pageant at the Standard in Cheapside, 'the Prelate of the Chirche' says,

> 'The Kyng of Heven is like an erthely Kyng
> That to his Sone preparith a weddyng.
> And right so as our sovereign lord, the Kyng,
> May be resemblid to the Kyng celestial.'[34]

Lest there should be any misunderstanding, God, in the pageant, was costumed to resemble Henry VII. It was this tableau which the monarch chose to watch himself, from William Geffrey's house, as his son and daughter-in-law elect passed below.

The idea of such lofty comparisons was not new to him. In 1486, 'King Bremius' in a pageant at Bristol had described him as

> 'Seint Hider, by the holsome Purviaunce
> Of Almyghty God moost mercifull and gracious,
> To reforme Thyngs that be contrarious
> Unto the Comen Wele, . . .'[35]

* See pp. 71–2 above.
† V, ii, 196.
‡ V, ii, 140.

It needs little imagination, dramatically, to step from passages like that to,

> 'If you deale ill with this distressed boye
> God will revenge poore orphants iniuries,
> If you deale well, as I do hope you will,
> God will defend both you and yours from ill.'[36]

or even,

> 'Haste still pays haste, and leisure answers leisure,
> Like doth quit like, and Measure still for Measure.'

It is only the Christian virtue of Mercy which releases Angelo from his deserts, the harsh penalties of the strict Old Testament Justice which he had pursued so ruthlessly himself. *

Another method of presenting these personal homilies in the pageant theatres was through characters of classical mythology. Jonson, as one might expect, uses them extensively in his text for James I's Entry. Jason and the Golden Fleece appear in London as early as 1522 for the reception of the Emperor Charles V. Ann Boleyn saw Apollo with the Nine Muses on the Conduit in Gracechurch Street and the Judgement of Paris on the Little Conduit in 1533. The Nine Worthies appeared in Coventry as early as 1456. It is not, however, until the latter half of the sixteenth century that the range of mythological characters in the pageants is seriously widened. Their introduction was not helpful to the vitality of the pageant tradition: for although they obviously increased the spectacular possibilities, their use as speakers was limited to compliment rather than to direct instruction. Bacon, in his *Essay on Praise*, illustrates contemporary sentiment on the subject.

'Some praises come of good Wishes, and Respects, which is a Forme due in Civilitie to Kings, and Great Persons, *Laudando praecipere*: when by telling Men, what they are, they represent to them, what they should be.'

This notion finds its most forcible expression in the Court Mask.[37] Nevertheless, the occasional use in England (frequent on the continent) of characters from classical mythology to assist in the delivery of these theatrical homilies on politics, economics and government, provided a precedent for a dramatist who had the ear of the Court to extend their conjoined presence and purpose to regular drama. Rastell, Udall and Peele are cases in point, all of

* See Nevill Coghill's Essay on 'Comic Form in "Measure for Measure",' *Shakespeare Survey* 8 (1955).

whom are known to have devised pageants as well as to have written plays. Rastell and Lyly provided verses for the shows of 1522 for Charles V: Udall co-operated with John Leland in composing the text for Ann Boleyn's Coronation reception in 1533: Peele devised the Lord Mayor's Show for 1585, 1588 and 1591.[38] The commission for these shows, in terms of both financial remuneration and prestige, was sufficient to stimulate competition for the appointment. In the early seventeenth century, Jonson, Dekker, Heywood, Middleton and Webster among major dramatists were all commissioned at one time or another to compose for the street pageant theatres; though in fairness it must be admitted that this work was probably more keenly sought after to stave off a visit to the debtors' prison than for artistic satisfaction comparable with that derived from plays written for a Public Theatre.

3 *Stagecraft*

The positioning of the stage in relation to the audience has already been discussed. The salient points to emerge were that the stage was raised, open to the sky and surrounded on at least three sides by spectators adjacent to it and looking down upon it: that a separate stage was required for the presentation of each scene: and that, in consequence, such unity as governed the whole show lay rather in the theme than in any continuity of plot-line or development of character. Dominating everything was the nature of the occasion celebrated and the relationship between ruler and subject which it illustrated. Thus it is that the spectacle of the street pageant theatres and its attendant stagecraft was subordinated from its inception to meet these requirements.

The fact that clerics, schoolmasters and poets were employed as devisers of the pageants must not lead to our giving an undue literary bias to subsequent assessment. As I have suggested, we should use the word 'pageantry' as the road by which we approach reconstruction and realize in consequence that the primary appeal of these occasional festivities, then as now, was visual. If the 'very important persons' who occupied the best positions in this rudimentary 'auditorium' could be regarded as grounded in Latin and English, the majority of the spectators could not. Elaborate precautions were therefore taken to ensure that the significance of the occasion was visible to all: for, as Volumnia observes to Coriolanus in a more urgent context, 'the eyes of the ignorant' are 'more learned than the ears.'

Ben Jonson is most helpful here: for he is specific and explicit on what he is doing and why. Writing of the visual appearance of his two pageant-arches for James I's Coronation he says:

'Thus farre the complementall part of the first (*pageant-arch*); wherein was not onely labored the expression of state and magnificence (as proper to a triumphall Arch) but the very site, fabricke, strength, policie, dignitie and affections of the Citie were all laid downe to life: The nature and propertie of these Devices being, to present alwaies some one entire bodie, or figure, consisting of distinct members, and each of those expressing it selfe, in the owne active spheare, yet all, with that generall harmonie so connexed, and disposed, as no one little part can be missing to the illustration of the whole: where also is to be noted, that the *Symboles* used, are not, neither ought to be, simply *Hieroglyphickes*, *Emblemes*, or *Impreses*, but a mixed character, partaking somewhat of all, and peculiarly apted to these more magnificent Inventions: wherein, the garments and ensignes deliver the nature of the person, and the word the present office.'[39]

The reader who is patient enough to have construed this erudite sentence will have discerned that there was no doubt in Jonson's mind about the function of the spectacle in the Pageant Theatre: the appropriate and harmonious reinforcement of the spoken speeches in every detail of costume and setting. Dekker, far less troubled in mind by classical precept, expresses the same point of view much more directly. Writing of his own contribution to these same festivities of 1603 he says:

'By this time imag(in)e the Poets (who drawe speaking pictures) and Painters (who make dumbe poesie) had their heads and hands full; the one for native and sweet invention, the other for lively illustration of what the former should devise: both of them emulously contending, but not striving, with proprest and brightest colours of wit and art, to set out the beautie of the great triumphant day.'[40]

For Elizabethans and Jacobeans, then, there can be no doubt but that the spectacle of the Pageant Theatres was something on which great care and ingenuity was lavished because its purpose was to instruct. By 'proprest and brightest colours' Dekker means colours which serve the twin function of both delighting the eye and teaching through it. This use of visual symbols is not unfamiliar to us, but many people today find it very hard to conceive of its extension as an everyday occurrence, into allegory. Jonson is precise on this subject. Of the separate symbols in his pageant—the 'distinct members'—he says:

'These are all the personages, or live figures, whereof only two were speakers (GENIUS and TAMESIS) the rest were mutes. Other dumbe complements there were, as the armes of the king-dome on the one side, with this inscription—

HIS VIREAS
With these maist thou flourish.
On the other side the armes of the citie, with,
HIS VINCAS
With these maist thou conquer.'[41]

Of the extension to the 'entire body' he says:

'This, and the whole frame, was covered with a curtaine of silke, painted like a thicke cloud, and at the approach of the K(*ing*) was instantly to be drawne. The Allegorie being, that those clouds were gathered upon the face of the Citie, through their long want of his most wished sight: but now, as at the rising of the Sunne, all mists were dispersed and fled.'[42]

However hard this kind of invitation to allegorical thinking may be for the modern mind to grasp, it was a matter of long established custom to Jonson's audience and to Dekker's. To confirm the point I will instance only those examples already used to illustrate subject matter.

Regarding the separate visual symbols, Jonson's heraldic arms and mottos are directly paralleled in Lydgate's pageant at the south gate of London Bridge for Henry VI in 1432, where a giant on 'a pyler reysed lyke a tour' was supported by

'Twoo antelopes stondyng on eytheyr syde
With the armes off Englond and off Fraunce,
In tokenyng that God shall ffor hym provyde,
As he hath tytle by iuste enheritaunce.'[43]

Indeed, we can trace the idea back a further hundred years to the ship decorated with heraldic blazon that the Fishmongers built to celebrate the birth of Edward III in 1313.

The symbols extended into a mute allegory are apparent in the pageant theatres erected for Richard II: the mechanical angels in the tower who bent down (or were lowered) to offer him a cup of wine and a crown in 1377 and St. John the Baptist who, in a 'wildnerness' of trees and wild beasts, points to the lamb.

In 1522, when the Emperor Charles V entered London, the island 'set in a silver sea' already cited contained a similar forest,

'where were dyvers bestes goyng abowte the mountayns by vyces (*i.e. winch mechanism*) and dyvers maner off trees herbys and flowres as roses, dayses, gyloflowres, daffadeles and other(s) so craftely made thatt hitt was harde to knowe them from very naturall flowres, and in the mountayns pondys off fressh water w^t fisshe. And att the comyng off the emprowr the bestys dyd move and goo, the fisshes dyd sprynge, the byrdes dyd synge reioysyng (*at*) the comyng of the ij princes the emprowr and the kynges grace (*Henry VIII*). Also ther were ij goodly ymages one in a castell lyke to the emprowr in visage, and the other in an herbar (*arbour*) wyth rosys lyke to the kynges grace with ij swerdys nakyd in ther handys. Which castell, garden, and the ymages dyd Ryse by a Vyce. The ymages dyd beholde eche other, and then cast away ther swerdys by a vyce, and w^t another vyce ioyned eche to other and embrasede eche other in tokennyng off love and pease, whiche don an ymage off the father off hevyn all burnyd golde dyd disclose and appare and move in the topp of the pageant wyth thys scripture wrytyn abowte hym—

'Beati pacifici qui filij dei vocabuntur.

'. . . Also there were ij children in goodly apparell on (*one*) on the one syde which spake englisshe and the other on the other syde which spake frenche salutyng the emprowr and the kynges grace declaryng and poyntyng every thing in the pageannt off the premisses at the tyme and in ordyr accordyng as hitt was done and playede.'*[44]

Here machinery adds primitive animation to a tableau already replete with independent visual symbols and a self-contained allegory.

The list of such illustrations could be drawn out almost limitlessly, so many were thought by contemporaries to be worth recording and have survived. However I must trust to have quoted

* Lest this be thought an isolated exception, I would cite as examples of similarly complex machinery the great astrological pageants for Katherine of Aragon's reception in 1501 (at Cornhill and on the Great Conduit) and the revolving Globe of Cosmos Neos for James I's entry in 1603. There were many others, but these suffice to illustrate the continuity of the tradition either side of the example quoted. See pp. 87, 96, 97 and 99 below.

a sufficiency for it to be obvious that in any such description symbol and allegory are what we should look for, just as they were anticipated by the spectators for whose entertainment and instruction they were prepared.

If this argument is accepted, the way is open to a vast treasurehouse of information about the English mediaeval and Renaissance stage. It is simply a question of knowing what to look for; of banishing our present-day ideas that the exclusive purpose of stage spectacle is to represent; of substituting instead the idea of conventions that, for the beholder, reached beyond the here and now into the realms of imaginative perception. In short, we must look further and deeper than at a photographic image of environment: we must anticipate a whole language of signs and learn to read it. The preceding chapter on Tournaments has, I hope, laid the necessary foundation. In what remains of this chapter I shall attempt to widen the vocabulary of this 'dumbe poesie'.

The stage of action for a Tournament—the lists—was invariably at ground level; a field, a street, even a floor. The stage of the street pageant theatres was as invariably raised above ground level; the flat top of a water conduit, the roof and niches in the vertical face of a gateway or specially constructed arch, or a platform adjacent to these and other monuments temporarily positioned on trestles or barrels. Where too the shape and size of the lists was standardized at an early date, the shape and size of the pageant stages varied widely until very late. Both of these important differences are directly attributable to some practical exigency or other. (See Plate XVII and Figs. 7 and 8, pp. 56, 57 above.)

The Tournament, being essentially a competitive sport, like other sports today, could only be established on an international basis by the introduction of internationally accepted rules: and nowhere are such rules more demanding than in the delineation of the combat area, in this context the acting area. By contrast, the street pageants, being essentially processions punctuated with *tableaux vivants*, were parasitic growths which battened on such monuments as existed along the processional route for the placement of the tableaux. These edifices not only varied in shape and size from country to country but from city to city and over the centuries as taste in architecture changed. The only pressure compelling uniformity of stage appearance was that towards the adoption of triumphal arches specially erected for the occasion. This was motivated by humanist interest in Roman 'triumphs'; but was gradual and countered by the fact that, however desirable on aesthetic grounds, the arch made a poor stage. In England, it was only in 1603 that the archway triumphed to the exclusion of all former rivals. Even then compromise is evident in the final result: for not only were the arches sited in the traditional places but were provided, as often as not, with a projecting platform raised off the ground in the accustomed manner to supplement the 'acting area': or, failing that, with an upper stage within the arch itself. That stage is the right word to use here is clear enough from Dekker's account. Writing of the second pageant-arch erected in Gracechurch Street he says:

'These were the mutes and properties that helpt to furnish out this great Italian theatre (*i.e. erected by and at the cost of the resident Italian merchants*); upon whose stage the sound of no voice was appointed to be heard, but of one.'[45]

Dekker's use of the words 'theatre' and 'stage' is here self-conscious and deliberate. Where the word stage figures in descriptions of earlier pageants it is not directly in the context of the acting area of a theatre, but rather in the sense of a raised platform: *

'Also att the standard in chepe dyd stand a pageant off great hyght rychley garnysshed w^t golde and silver and asure and dyuers setes (and) stages, and in the hyghest stage sate a yong man.'[46]

In the numerous lengthy descriptions of Katherine of Aragon's Progress through London in 1501 the word stage is only used once, and then it is not in the context of any of the pageants but of the arrangements within St. Paul's Cathedral:

'There was enhaunsed a certayne po(siti)on of v or vi grees like a stage, rownde encompasse, covred w^t red say takyd fast w^t gilte nailys, uppon the which the P(ri)nce, P(ri)nces, and mynysters of the sacrement of matrimony might conveniently stond.'[47]

In the normal phraseology of the fourteenth, fifteenth and early sixteenth centuries the word 'pageant' embraces the whole spectacle and the position of the characters is defined by such qualifying phrases as 'on the top of' or 'in the face of which' or 'on both floors'.

The last of these phrases was necessary whenever an 'upper stage' (as we would call it) was used. The idea of distributing the spectacle in the vertical plane came automatically with the employment

* For a rare exception see p. 58 above.

of city gateways as pageant theatres. It was on the 'roof above the gate' that St. John the Baptist's wilderness was situated at Temple Bar in 1392. It was from within the tower of the Drawbridge on London Bridge that the three Empresses and their fourteen attendant maidens addressed Henry VI in Lydgate's pageants of 1432. There again, in 1501, Katherine of Aragon saw

'a tab(er)nacle of two flowres (*floors*) assemblaunt unto tweyne rodelofts, in whoes lougher floure and p(ar)tic(i)on, there was a sete, and w^{t}in the sete a faire yong lady w^t a wheel in hir hand, in liknes of Seint Kathryn, w^t right many virgyns on eu(e)ry side of her; and in the ii^{de} and higher floure and story there was another Lady in likenes of Seint Ursula, w^t her great multitude of virgyns right goodly dressed and arrayed: above the bothe floures there was a pictour of the Trinyté.'[48]

The 'upper stage' remains a regular feature of the pageant theatres throughout the sixteenth century. A notable example at mid-century was the interconnecting, double stage in Cheapside for Edward VI's Coronation in 1546, about which I shall have more to say in connection with stage machinery. Thus the idea of stages in the vertical plane was carried into the seventeenth century where we find Jonson writing of his Fenchurch Arch of 1603:

'The *Scene* presented it selfe in a square and flat upright, like to the side of a Citie: the top thereof, above the Vent, and Crest, adorn'd with houses, towres and steeples, set off in prospective. Upon the battlements, in a great capitall letter, was inscribed, LONDINIUM.'[49]

Dekker in the same series of pageants confined the action of *Cosmos Neos* to an upper stage above the Conduit in Fleet Street. The architect who designed it, Stephen Harrison, says:

'over the Gate, and iust in the midst of the *Building*, (which was spacious and left open) a Globe was seene to move being fild with all the estates that are in the land.'[50]

A similar upper stage was constructed by the Dutch merchants in London for their pageant in Cornhill. It was large enough to hold seventeen people and took the form of 'a spacious square roome, left open, silke curtaines drawne before it; which, upon the approach of his Majestie (*were*) put by'.[51] These pageant stages of the water conduits, crosses and archways, whether double or single tiered, were sometimes equipped with an additional platform projecting out into the street from the basic architectural unit, but

were normally self-contained. Dekker tells us that an acting platform in front of the fourth pageant-arch of 1603 'extended thirtie
foote in length frome the maine building'.[52] I suspect this device,
however, to have been borrowed from the regular theatre.

An exception to everything noted so far is the portable stage.
This becomes a feature of London pageantry in the late sixteenth
century after the inception of the Lord Mayor's Show: but, as far as
I am aware, its use is exclusively confined to this annual festivity.
In 1567 Walter Browne is paid 49 shillings by the Ironmongers
Company 'for porters which carried the pageant, and hogsheads to
rest it on, sundry times'.[53] In 1561, for the Merchant Taylors
Company,

'Evan Davys, porter, agrees to find, with himself, 16 tall and
strong men to bear the pageant at 20d. each, and to see it brought
safely into the house at night.'

In 1602 the Merchant Taylors are still paying 20 porters to carry
their pageant. *

Summarizing this survey of the nature of the pageant stages, before proceeding to consider their facilities, I think we may fairly
conclude that a marked change overtook them within the period
1377 to 1603. Excluding the portable stages of the Lord Mayor's
Show, the authors and producers of these tableaux, who were at
first content to batten on any raised platform that was ready to
hand, came to prefer the triple-gated and triple-level archway to
which a projecting platform at ground level could be added. By
1603, this form of 'theatre' has triumphed to the complete exclusion
of the circular conduit and other irregular stages.

I have already suggested that one pressure towards this end was
Renaissance enthusiasm for the appropriateness of the Roman
triumphal arch. But in England the force of tradition was strong
and nobody responsible for the creation of the pageant-spectacle
would willingly sacrifice popular and well-tried stages for new ones
until they were satisfied that the new stages were as functionally
effective as the old.

* Change seems to have been long overdue. Dekker, describing his
Pageant for the Lord Mayor's Show of 1612, mentions Dolphins and Mer-
maids, 'which are not (after the old procreation) begotten of painted cloath
and broune paper, but are living beasts so queintly disguised like the natural
fishes of purpose to avoyd the trouble and pestering of porters, who
with much noyse and little comliness, are every year most unnecessarily
imployed.'[54] See Vol. II, 1576–1660, Pt. 1, pp. 209–244 for fuller discussion.

The mediaeval 'stage-designer' was faced with the same basic problem that confronts his counterpart today: to provide upon the stage a convincing representation of the Universe as understood by his audience. To the spectator of the Middle Ages the Universe consisted of three separate but interrelated worlds—Heaven, Earth and Hell—all three equally real. Heaven and Hell were interpreted in terms of the known world of Earth. The only differences of importance for the stage-designer were that Heaven lacked all the blemishes of Earth while Hell exaggerated those blemishes to the exclusion of all else. The designer was nevertheless forced to provide for the simultaneous presentation of all three worlds; since Man, whose fortunes any stage show must concern, was himself thought of as on a journey to one or other of them. From Heaven he had come and the dramatist might wish to refer to this past history: on Earth he was now and the dramatist could scarcely avoid concerning himself with the present; ahead lay Heaven again or Hell, and both must be provided for. The need therefore to present Man as on this journey from Heaven through Earth to alternative Salvation or Damnation led naturally to the adoption of a stage-convention which placed Earth as the central stage area with Heaven and Hell either flanking it or situated respectively above and below. The flanking device seems to have been used most frequently in the staging of Miracle and Morality Plays.* Pageants, where lateral space was at a premium, prefer the alternative device.

'In the entre of the citie', reads the House Book of the City of York, 'and first bar (gate) of the same, shalbe craftely conceyvid a place in maner of a heven, of grete joy and Anglicall armony; under the heven shalbe a world desolaite, full of treys and floures. . . .'[55]

On another stage in the same group of Pageants we learn of

'. . . our Lady, commyng from hevin, and welcome the King . . . and y'upon ascend agayne in to heven'.[56]

Since these Pageants are staged by way of celebration, calls upon the designer for reminders of Hell were obviously rare. However, if descents from a world above earth were spectacular, so also were ascents from beneath the earth. The York Pageants just cited tell us that from beneath the 'world desolate'

'. . . shall spryng up a roiall, rich, rede rose, convaide by viace, unto the which rose shall appeyre an other rich white rose, unto

* See Ch. IV, pp. 157–60 below.

whome so being to gedre all othre floures shall bow to and evidently yeve (*give*) suffrantie. . . .'

In considering the conventions indicative of place, I propose to treat first of those used to represent Earth. All devices could be used in several senses, just as a simple narrative could be used allegorically. The significance of the device depended on the plane of the allegory the author desired to stress. Thus a single object could be given a moral, historical and spiritual significance as well as its natural significance in the narrative plane. The three wells at the Great Conduit in Lydgate's Pageants for Henry VI's entry into London are a good example. There, the conduit which supplies the wells is itself the stage. That its jets should be converted into wells is particularly appropriate because of the Mayor's name—John Wells. Instead of the normal water the conduit has been made to feed wine into the wells since this is a festive occasion. These wells, in association with their guardians, *Pity, Grace* and *Mercy*, have a moral significance:

> 'Convenable welles, moste holsom off savour,
> Forto be tasted off every governour.'[57]

Containing wine, they also possess an obvious spiritual significance.

The same scenic devices as appeared in the Tournaments were used in the street pageant theatres with the same regularity. Thus a castle can as easily represent a city as itself, the New Jerusalem as easily as Jerusalem. Ships, trees, mountains and pavilions are all used in this fashion as occasion warrants. I do not propose here to catalogue all the possible variants: so numerous and so ample are the surviving descriptions that they would make up a substantial book in themselves. There are, however, two points worth singling out for attention: first, the fact that these scenic symbols could be used in combination, and, secondly, that the passage of time affects them very little. Names may have changed, but not the objects denoted: for just as Dekker's *Sylvannus* in 1603 is only the traditional *Wildman* under a new name, so his *Fount of Vertue* is really only Lydgate's *Wells of Grace* under another name. For Ann Boleyn's benefit the Fountain was dubbed Helicon. It was there again for Edward VI without a name, but 'garnished with Roses, Juli-flowers, and other kinde of Flowers' and with Grace once more presiding. In every instance wine flowed from the fountain, as the Herald-chronicler on one occasion puts it, 'descending through Pipes into the Street amongst divers Sorts of People, who, . . .

with great Diligence fetched it away'.[58] Even in 1603, when *Detraction* and *Oblivion* did 'their best, with clubs to beate downe the Fount', it still 'ranne wine very plenteously'. To understand the symbolism intended on this occasion we have only to remember that the device was 'called the Fount of Vertue' and that *Detraction* and *Oblivion* were thwarted in their purpose by *'his Maiesties approach'*.[59] (See Plate XIII No. 19.)

The mountain similarly retained its popularity. Labelled Parnassus, it served to seat Apollo and the Muses for Ann Boleyn's reception. For Elizabeth's coronation, two mountains, the one barren, the other green, represented a decayed and a flourishing commonwealth. In 1603 five of them accommodate the senses. As for the Arbour or Garden, we are lucky to have two pictures of early seventeenth-century examples.*[60] In Dekker's 'Hortus Euporice' this is achieved by the spreading of an elaborate vine over and around the main façade. Fruits and flowers grow upon it with the same abundance as in Lydgate's orchard of 1432. Because it is so early an example, this is worth quoting for comparison. Lydgate calls his orchard a 'gracious paradys', and the Grocers Company were clearly responsible for its construction.

'Ther were eke treen, with leves ffresh off hewe,
Alle tyme off year, ffulle off ffruytes lade,
Off colour hevynly, and euery-liche newe,
Orenges, almondis, and the pome-gernade,
Lymons, dates, theire colours ffresh and glade,
Pypyns, quynces, blaunderell to disport,
And the pome-cedre corageous to recomfort;

Eke the ffruytes which more comune be—
Quenynges, peches, costardes and wardouns,
And other meny fful ffayre and ffressh to se;
The pome-water and the gentyll ricardouns;
And ageyns hertes ffor mutygaciouns
Damysyns, which with here taste delyte,
Full grete plente both off blak and white.'[61]

By contrast to this sort of arbour, mountain and fountain, two scenic devices, the Castle and the Ship, so singularly popular in the fourteenth and fifteenth centuries, lose ground in the sixteenth. Ann Boleyn was greeted with 'a tower with foure turretts'; but her

* See Plates XIX and XXVIII No. 40. Also, *Arches of Triumph*, which contains Stephen Harrison's designs for all the Pageants for James I's Coronation. Three of them are reproduced in Vol. II, 1576–1660, Pt. 1, Plate XII, Nos. 15 & 16, and Plate XVII, No. 22.

daughter saw none in London's streets and neither did James I. It might be argued that the castle was absorbed into the arch-façade. Certainly many of these façades are ornamented with the familiar turrets, battlements and pinnacles which formerly surmounted the normal scenic castle: but they bear about as much resemblance to the original structure for Richard II's Coronation as did the Elizabethan manor-house to a fortified stronghold. The ship seems to have shared the fate of the castle: it is seldom seen in sixteenth-century streets except in the Lord Mayor's Shows.

On the other hand, devices employed to represent an interior steadily gain ground in use and diversity. The simplest of them is Arras and other hangings. These were used as much for their functional as for their decorative value. Whether on the stage or in the auditorium such hangings are a splendid aid to good acoustics. They had long been used domestically as curtains. We learn of them being thus employed on the stage at Bruges in 1468 from the eye-witness report of an English Herald. The Pageants, he says, were 'sheued and soubdanly closed w^t cortayns drawynge craftelye'. On the same occasion (the wedding of Edward IV's sister Margaret) a similar effect was achieved in the town of Sluys where the Herald saw

'. . . a Stage made of Tymbyr' warke, . . . cov'de w^t tappettes, and before subtelly corteynyd; with'oute those cortaynez a man gevyng attendance att soche tyme as my lady passid by, and drew the cortayne of the last pageaunte of the iij pageauntes afore reh'sid, and than secretly closed it a gayne, and shewde as lytill' sight as myght be sheued; and soo sodenly from pageaunt to pageaunt.'[62]

Domestically, too, such hangings had been used to screen off particular areas desired for privacy. Instructions to just such purpose are given to Henry VII's Lord Chamberlain supervising arrangements in St. Paul's Cathedral for Katherine of Aragon's wedding:

'And to thentent that the said prince and princesse may have alwayes som place Secretly to resort unto for such casualtees that may fall during the high Masse of the Mariage, It is to be forseen that the prince schal have a trav(er)se seled made and sett on the North side the Quere nere the high Aultre in place convenient with a rennyng curteyn to s(e)rve when nede shalbe so as the Mynstrells aboute the high aultr(e) and those in the vawts shall not (.....?) see what shalbe doon in the said traverse.'[63]

Domestic practice could thus be used on the stage to the same end—namely to represent a private enclosure; more especially an interior. Froissart, describing the Paris Pageants for Isabella of Bavaria in 1389, writes:

'At the *Porte du Chastelet de Paris* there was a castle . . . and on this castle a bed trimmed, prepared and curtained about as richly as if it were the King's bedchamber. And this bed was called the bed of Justice.'[64]

For Katherine of Aragon in 1501, in the first pageant, 'The wallis of the saide . . . lofts were peynted; w^t hangyng courteyns of cloth of tissue, blue and red.'[65] The device holds good for the rest of the century: and in 1603 both Ben Jonson and Dekker use it for the purpose of a 'discovery'. Jonson's, as already quoted, was 'a curtain of silke, painted like a thick cloud', and had an allegorical significance.*

Heaven, as a general rule (like the other uncharted world of Hell), was interpreted in terms of the known world of Earth. Since Heaven was popularly supposed to lie above the blue vault of the sky, sun, moon, stars, clouds and blue sky were the simplest symbols for its representation upon the stage. All that was required for easy identification was some sort of blue superstructure with the signs of the Zodiac set neatly upon it. The earliest record of this practice in pageant theatres is a French one, Isabella of Bavaria's Paris reception of 1389 described by Froissart:

'At the first gate of St. Denis . . . there was a heaven stuck with stars, and within this heaven young children dressed and presented as angels . . .'

The convention is in this instance directly linked to those of Tournaments, for

'. . . this heaven was richly enblazoned with the arms of France and Bavaria, and a golden sun with its beams which was the King's 'device' for the jousting fête.'[66]

Clouds served a double purpose: for not only did they assist identification, but they could be used to conceal the mechanism by which descents or ascents out of or into Heaven were made. Nothing delights or holds the attention of most audiences better than the seemingly magical appearance or disappearance of persons or

* See p. 83 above.

objects: and stage mechanism is only an elaborated conjuring trick. In this respect, mediaeval stage technicians were far more adept than has been allowed hitherto. Indeed, I doubt whether any mechanism which had not already existed on Pageant stages for at least a hundred years had to be provided for the staging of such spectacular Elizabethan plays as Heywood's *Bronze, Silver* or *Golden Age*.

Cloud mechanism had been at the service of the stage designer since 1399 and maybe earlier. In that year Don Martin I was crowned at Saragossa. One of the Pageants on this occasion was a two-level stage representing Heaven and Earth with a cloud passing between them carrying an actor representing an angel.*

It is difficult to say of what materials these early mechanical devices were made or how they operated: but it is quite clear that means were available to permit the heavenly superstructure to open, and for a figure to ascend or descend at will, before the fourteenth century was out. A hundred years later information of a more detailed character comes to our assistance. Not only do we learn the principle upon which the machine was operated, but that its application had been greatly extended. Trees and flowers rise, open and fall as well as clouds; rain, hail and snow are counterfeited; globes turn and figures with them; a dragon appears to fly.

The mechanism in question is undoubtedly a simple winch, windlass or vice. Installed in the roof above a stage or under its floor, it could be turned unseen and the spectators provided with the required surprise. Thus, after a panel or trap had been opened, the mere turning of a winch could make an angel appear to descend from heaven or a flower grow in the desert. A slightly more elaborate winch, employing the principle of the mill wheel, could, when operated, cause globes to turn and even offer the producer a revolving stage! This last device appears to have been available as early as 1414—at least in Spain:

* In 1377 the London Goldsmiths greeted Richard II with a castle erected round and about the Great Conduit in Cheapside: 'In summitate castelli, quae ad modum tali inter quatuor turres elevata fuerat, positus erat angelus aureus, tenens auream coronam in manibus, qui tali ingenio factus fuerat, ut adventanti Regi coronam porrigeret inclinando.' This device was repeated for him on the same spot in 1392. See pp. 55, 70 above. In 1389, Parisians decorated the second gate of St. Denis to represent a heaven. 'Et ad ce que la royne passa, dedens sa littière, dessoubs la porte, le paradis s'ouvry, et deux angèles yssirent hors en eulx avalant et tenoient en leurs mains une très-riche couronne d'or garnie de pierres précieuses, et la mirent et assirent les deux angèles moult doucement sur le chief de la royne en chantant tels vers.'

'A castle of marble had been built, in the central tower of which there was a dwarf. . . . The tower formed the centre of a gyrating wheel on which were four maidens. . . .'*

By 1481, when Isabella la Católica was received at Barcelona it was possible to greet her with 'an allegorical representation of Saint Eulalia furnished with three spheres turning the one against the other'.† By 1514, when Mary Tudor was married to the King of France in Paris, she saw 'a rose bush . . . out of which there projected a stem carrying a red rosebud which grew upwards towards the throne of honour . . .' This throne was positioned on an upper stage and a lily grew in front of it,

'and the lily descended from above midway to the ground (*i.e. the lower stage*). Then, lily and rosebud ascended together up to the said throne where the said rosebud opened to reveal within itself a little girl gorgeously dressed who spoke . . .'‡

This device was neither new nor exclusively French, its double having been used in York in 1486; but I quote it here because a picture happens to survive of this tableau. The MS. containing it is illustrated with other illuminations particular to this occasion but typical of all the pageant stages discussed in this chapter.§

In England descents from above were practicable before the end of the fourteenth century. The York Pageants of 1486 describe both ascents and descents from overhead and an ascent by machine from under the floor.‖

Another simple winch mechanism employed in these York Pageants was used to make hail. The City Fathers order

'hailestones to be maid by viace falling on the lordes and othre commyng ne before the King, hailestones to be made by craftes of cumfettes'.

* 'se construzó un castillo de madera, en cuyo torreón central había un niño, . . . El torreón era el centro de un disco giratorio en el cual iban cuatro doncellas. . . . Adémas en los cuatro ángulos del castillo había otras tantas torres. . . .'67

† 'representacion alegórica de Santa Eulalia en la cual había tres ciclos girando el uno contra el otro.'

‡ '. . . avoit ung buisson de rosiers . . . du quel buisson sailloit une tige ou estoit ung bouton dung rosier vermeil qui montoit iusques au throne d'honneur (i.e. the upper stage in front of which grew a lily) et le lis descendoit du hault iusques à my voye. Puis montoyent ensemble iusq(ue)s audit throsne où ledit bouton sespanouytsoit et se montroit dedans icelluy bouton une pucelle pompeusement accoustrée disant ce qui sensuit.'68

§ See Plates XIII–XV and accompanying Notes.

‖ See pp. 89 and 90 above.

In the Pageant of Our Lady they order that on her ascension 'schall it snow by craft to be made of waffrons in maner of snow'. In yet another, 'a convenient thing divisid whereby . . . it schall raine rose water'.[69] The hailstones and snow were clearly sweets and biscuits. The rose-water rain was probably a form of fumigation to protect noble nostrils from loyal but noisome 'stinkards'. Evidence is available from the accounts for the Pageant on London Bridge in 1464 for the Coronation of Edward IV's Queen, Elizabeth Woodville: 'And for fumigation in front of the drawbridge at the Queen's approach 3/4d.'

We get another glimpse of the sort of machinery employed on these tableaux stages in one of the Bristol Pageants of 1486:

'an Olifaunte, with a Castell on his bakk, curiously wrought. The Resurrection of our Lorde in the highest Tower of the same, with certeyne Imagerye smytyng Bellis, and al went by Veights merveolously wele done.'[70]

But it is in the operation of globes and spheres that the heaviest demands were made upon the mechanic's ingenuity. The Pageant of the Sun in Katherine of Aragon's reception, besides demonstrating the complexity of such machines, serves as a summary of all devices used in representing Heaven on the Mediaeval Pageant Stage. I will therefore quote it in full.

'And from this pagent of the mone in Cornell they proceded in their seid former ordre, and raise unto the IIIIth pagent, which was in Chepesid, betwene the great conducte and the Standard; the which was corneryd w[t] IIII great posts, two before and II behynde. Upon the II former posts, a red dragon upon oon of them, and on the tother a whight hert w[t] a crowne of gold abowte his neke, and a cheyne of golden lynkys comyng from the crown: The other II bests on the other posts, the oon of them a rede lyon rampand, the other a whight grehound. And in the face of this pagent there was a whele (*wheel*), wonderfully wrought w[t] clowds abowght the compasse outward, and undre thys whele was there a scochon of whight, w[t] Seint George's crosse and a rede swerd, and in the II lower corners II astronomers, oon w[t] a tyrangell, and the other w[t] a quadrat, havyng their speculation to the bodies above. Upon the upper part, above directe, was the father of Heven, and on the two corners besid him II Anglis, w[t] trumpetts, and armys upon them bothe; the oon of them havyng a scripture w(ri)tten "Laudate Dom̄ de celis;" the other his scriptor aunsweryng, "laudate Dn̄ in excellis.'' Ov(e)r the father there was meny Angels, havyng scriptours of te Deum, and tibi omnes, etc. W^t in the meddell of this great whele there was a chare, and w^{t}in the chare a P(ri)nce stondyng* full richely beseene: benethe his chare there was IIII great sterres, (*stars*) like IIII wheles, runyng very swyft(l)y; and betwene the II former sterres the centour of erthe. In the brede of this whele ther were meny dyv(e)r figures sum of berys (*bears*), sume lyons, sum hors, sume wormys, sume fisshis, sum mermeyds, sume bullis, sume virgyns, sume naked men, sume ramys stikked full of sterrys, as they be appropred and namyd in bokys of astronomy havyng lynys, sume red, sume whight, deducte from iche sterre, planet, and/Signe, and after the aspect that naturally iche (*each*) of them hath unto other. In the brede of this whele were III armyd Knights, the which, as they wolde, ascendid, tornyd this whele very swyftly all the season of the comyng of this P(ri)nces. The highte of this pagent was goodly wrought w^t penacles, and lanternys holow, w^t wyndowes many and craftyly wrought, and empayntid and gilte full costeously bothe w^{t}in and w^{t}out; and this was named the sp(h)ere of the sunne, appropriat to the P(ri)nce of Englond, shewyng (and) declaryng his fatall disposic(i)on and desteny.'[71]

Recurring throughout these descriptions is the persistent distribution of two or three acting levels deployed in the vertical plane: and the reason for it is obvious enough in that it facilitates the use of spectacular machinery. Its effectiveness sufficed to preserve this vertical distribution of the acting levels throughout the sixteenth century despite the gradual change over from irregular stages to the uniformity of triumphal arches in 1603. As Ann Boleyn's cortège moved up-river from Greenwich to the Tower in 1533, the spectators were treated to the spectacle of 'a great red dragon continually moving and Casting wildfire'. From the roof of a Pageant near Leadenhall a falcon descended to a tree,

'all white, and set upon the root, and incontinently came downe an

---

* B.M. MS. Cot. Vit. A. XVI adds: '. . . Arthure, clene armed, in his Golden Chaire. And in the compas of the firmament wer iij yong stripelinges of the age of xij or xiij yeres, clene armed, the which went evir by a vice toward the chare of Arthur, but they neuer passed a certeyn height' (f. 191b). A passage in MS. Guildhall 3313 concerning this same Pageant proves beyond doubt that these effects were carefully predetermined. It refers to the 'armyd Knights' and describes them as 'iij childyr clene armyd which by a vyse ascendid by a determyned heygth toward the chare of arthur' (f. 32). In this account, the word *volvell* is used to describe the machine.

angell with great melodie, and set a close crowne of golde on the faulcon's head.'[72]

Besides demonstrating the continued use of machines, these two devices prove that animal symbolism was as popular as ever. *

With machines, as with all else in sixteenth-century pageantry, novelty may be found in names but not in method. Edward VI may have seen Jason and the Golden Fleece: but the Bull and Serpent guardians of the Fleece cast 'out of their Mouthes flaming Fire', like the Dragon before them. In another pageant,

'. . . representing the State of King Edward the Confessor . . . there lay a Lyon of Gold, which moved his head by Vices'.[73]

Yet another device prepared for him by the machinists is quite as elaborate as anything demanded of them by Elizabethan dramatists. It is virtually a mechanical allegory of the legend 'The king is dead! Long live the King!' and should be enough in itself to banish any idea of machinery in Elizabethan theatres being derived from the Mask.

'And at the End of the (*Great*) Conduit . . . thear was a double Scaffold one above the other, which was hung with Cloath of Gold and Silke, besides rich Arras. There was also devised under the uper Scaffold, an Element or Heaven, with the Sunn, Starrs and Clowdes very naturally. From this Clowde there spread abroad another lesser Cloud of white Sarsenet, fringed with Silke powdered with Starrs and Beames of Gold, out of the which there descended a Phenix downe to the neither (*lower*) Scaffold, where settling herselfe upon a Mount, there spread forth Roses white and red, Julliflowers and Hoithorne Bowes. After that the said Phenix was there a little, there approached a Lyon of Gold crowned, makeing Semblance of Amyty unto the Bird, moveing his Head sundry Tymes, between the which Familiarity, as it seemed, there came forth a young Lyon that had a Crowne Emperiall brought from Heaven above, as by two Angells, wich they sett upon his Head. Then the old Lyon and the Phenix vanished away, leaving the young Lyon, being crowned, alone.'[74]

The only device which these busy machinists seem to have been unable to squeeze into this pageant is their revolving mechanism.

* The Red Dragon of Cadwalader was adopted by Henry VII as Duke of Richmond on landing at Milford Haven. Under it he fought the battle of Bosworth Field which brought the house of Tudor to the throne (see pp. 73–74 above). The falcon was Ann Boleyn's personal signet. See p. 105 below.

Their skill in this respect, however, had not been forgotten. In 1579, when James VI was crowned in Edinburgh, they had ready

'a curious globe, that opnit artificallie as the King came by, wharin was a young boy that discendit craftelie, presenting the Keyis of the toun to his Majestie'.[75]

Nor had Ben Jonson any need to *invent* artificial spheres for his Masks. Before he came to write any of them he had co-operated with the designers of the Fleet Street Pageant for James I which, in its upper stage, contained

'a Globe (*which*) was seene to move being fild with all the estates that are in the land; And this Engine was turned about by foure persons, representing the foure *Elements* . . . who were placed so queintly, that the Globe seemed to have his motion even on the Crownes of their heads.'[76]

The technical methods used to operate this machinery and fashion these devices were as traditional as the devices themselves. The capstan-winches called 'Viaces' or 'Vices' turned the Globes and raised or lowered figures: while the customary materials went to the making of the images and animals. Bishop Hall says of his congregation:

'I fear that some of you are like the Pageants of your great solemnities wherein there is the show of a solid, whether of a Lion, or Elephant, or Unicorne, but if they be looked into, there is nothing but cloth and sticks and wyre.'[77] (See Plate XVIII).

He might well have added paint to his list; for paint, dye, and gold and silver leaf were used on a lavish scale. One has grown used to thinking of Elizabethan theatres as drab in appearance; their decoration confined to the arabesques of timber beams on white plaster: and, since they were the first theatres, to thinking of mediaeval performances as similarly drab. This seems to me as gross a misconception as to suppose that Gothic cathedrals were designed as the monochrome piles of natural stone they appear to-day. Yet so widely accepted has that idea become that the restoration of colour even on so limited a scale as that at Gloucester was enough to launch an acrimonious correspondence in *The Times*. Mediaeval pageant-stages were every bit as richly painted as the roofs, tombs and altar-screens of mediaeval churches.

Here is a list of coloured materials used for the decoration of a single pageant-stage in the Coronation festivities for Queen

Elizabeth Woodville, 1464. I quote from the material I had the good fortune to find in the Bridge House Rentals at Guildhall.

Coloured Paper

5½ Dozen Gold Paper . . .	6/–
1½ Dozen Red Paper . . .	2/–
19 Leaves of Red Paper . . .	3/–
4 Leaves of Green Paper . . .	3/–
1 Ream of White Paper . . .	2/6
1 Ream of Black Paper . . .	1/3

Coloured Buckram

2 Pieces of Buckram . .	10/6
1 Piece of Red Buckram . . .	2/6
1 Piece of Purple Buckram . .	3/4
2½ Yards of Purple Buckram . .	1/8

Gold and Silver

2 Gross Tinfoil	8/–
1 Gross Tinfoil	3/–
600 Party Gold . . .	16/–
300 Party Gold . . .	8/–
200 Party Silver . . .	1/8

Paint

1 lb. Vermillion . . .	1/3
½ lb. Indigo . . .	7d.
1 lb. Verdigris . . .	1/2
6 lb. White Lead . .	9d.
6 lb. Red Lead . . .	9d.
18 lb. Black Chalk . .	3/–

The list also includes paint brushes and pots for mixing paints. *

Unfortunately the Keeper of the Bridge House Accounts did not include a description of the finished result. But we do possess a description of the Pageant which was rigged on the same spot, namely the South Gate of London Bridge, when Katherine of Aragon passed through London thirty-seven years later. The pageant presented St. Catherine, St. Ursula and the Trinity one above the other.

'The wallis of the saide flours or lofts,' we are told, 'were peynted . . . and a p(ret)ty space before this pagent were II great posts set,

* See Appendix B, p. 326 below.

enpeynted w^t the thré estriche fethers roses red, and portcullys, and on ev(er)y of them a red lyon rampand, holdyng a vane enpeynted w^t the armys of Englond; and all the hoole worke corvȳn of tymbre, gilte, and peynted w^t golde, byse, and asur.'

Some degree of realism was aimed at, when required, as we learn from the description of the second of this same set of pageants:

'. . . w^{t}in a manys highte from the stone work were batilments of tymber cov(e)red and leyed ov(e)r w^t canvas empeynted like frestone and whight lyme, so that the semys of the stone were p(er)ceyved like as mortur or sement had ben betwene.'[78]

Timber, canvas, paper and paint then—the very materials still used by the scenic artists of today—were all used in the decorations of mediaeval pageant stages.[79]

Inextricably bound up with painting is of course the use of heraldic devices borrowed from the Tournament. For instance, to anyone familiar with the armorial bearings of the House of Tudor, the following devices as well as possessing a decorative value would tell a tale in themselves:

'And in ev(er)y batilment, and voyde of batilment, in ordour and c(o)urse were sett certeyn bagḡs (*badges*); furst, a red rose and a whight in his mydds, with a crowne upon the hight, of gold: the secunde was thre garters of blew, w^t this poysie in Frenche ritten, "Hony soit que malé pens", inviround, and in his mydds, on his hight, a crown̄ of gold. The thurd was a flowrd luce of golde. The IIII^{te} was the portcullys of gold, and II cheynes hangyng on iche sid, and on the height of the portcullys a crowne of golde: And sum part also were clowds, w^t beamys of golde; the grounde as it were th'ayre, blew. In other plac(e)s whight herts: In some other, pekokks displayed.'[80]

This conventionalized employment of paint, giving to colour its own significance within the ensemble as well as a decorative function, survives the sixteenth century in pageantry. Ben Jonson, for instance, says of his 'Temple of Janus', for James I's Entry that 'The walls and gates of this Temple were brasse; the Pillars silver, their *Capitals* and Bases gold.' This visual reference to the return of the Golden Age is made specific by 'Genius Urbis', who says of the new king that he is a bringer of peace,

'And doth (in all his present acts) restore
That first pure world, made of the better ore'.[81]

Frequently this visual imagery, or 'dumbe poesie' as Dekker so picturesquely names it, had to work overtime: for many of the characters who figure in the pageant-tableaux were mutes. Sometimes these mutes were live actors, but more often they were what were known then as Images. We would call them statues. Their presence was required partly to complete the allegorical significance of the tableau as a whole and partly because they added to the spectacular effect of its appearance. Of the former, Jonson's 'Temple of Janus' offers an excellent example. After listing their names and describing their appearances he says: 'This is the dumbe argument of the frame. . . . The speaking part was performed, as within the temple. . . .'* Of the latter kind, examples (especially angels) may be seen on the apex of pinnacles and turrets of many mediaeval tombs, reredoses or picture frames. Yet on pageant structures of similar shape it would clearly have been asking too much of actors to balance on such precarious positions for any length of time. This I think explains why we hear of 'certeyne Imagerye smytyng Bellis' or, 'an image of our Lady holding in figure a little child' and so on. The 1464 Pageant accounts in the Bridge House Rentals tell us much about the manufacture of these images:

'And for rods of hazel bought for making images 4d. . . . And for eight pairs of gloves bought for the hands of eight images 9d. And for one pound of flock wool bought for stuffing the said gloves 1½d. And for six kerchiefs of "pleasaunce" bought for the apparel of six images of women 8s. 8d. . . . And for a thousand pins bought and used in fixing the clothes on the images 14d. . . . And to William Parys and Richard Westmyll, tailors, preparing and making clothes for diverse images . . . for 3½ days, 6s.'†

From this one may deduce that the making of the Images was a skilled job. They were constructed on a frame of hazel switches, and tailored clothes were attached to the frames with pins. Gloves stuffed with wool served as hands, while some of the coloured paper, buckram and paint mentioned elsewhere in the accounts was probably used to fashion the headgear and faces. No less prominent on pageant-stages were expository texts, or 'scriptures' as Lydgate calls them. These were sometimes in Latin and sometimes in French or English. The choice of language seems to have depended largely on the source of the text: even so it would be difficult to prescribe any definite rules. Familiar texts from the Bible or Psalter were rendered in Latin: moral mottos and occas-

* See also p. 83 above.　　　　　　　　　† See Appendix B.

102

ional ballads in Latin, French or English. The intention was clearly to supply the literate part of the audience with the easiest of all clues to an interpretation of the allegory. The convention was frequently employed in illuminating manuscripts and in stained-glass windows to indicate persons or place. Even Ben Jonson is prepared to bestow labels and mottoes in liberal profusion on his pageant arches, provided that they were written in Latin.

The 1464 pageant account in the Bridge House Rentals are again informative about the expository texts:

'And to John Genycote for writing and limning six ballads delivered to the Queen at her approach—3s. And to John Thompson for writing the said six ballads on tablets fixed to the pageant on the bridge—8d.'*

That the same number of ballads was presented to the Queen as was set on boards upon the stage leads me to suppose that those given to the Queen were in fact copies of those on the pageants and were intended to form a souvenir. If this were a regular practice it would at once explain why so many pageant texts have come down to us intact.[82]

Costume in the Pageant Theatres

Stage costume seems in general to have been kept in harmony with stage settings: that is to say, the unknown was interpreted in terms of the known. But no matter whether the intention was to dress mortal men or supernatural beings, the costume chosen formed an integral part of the spectacle and was subject to the same guiding principles. Costume was designed to assist recognition of the characters rather than to disguise the actors representing them, and, at the same time to delight the eye both in terms of the materials and colours used and in the context of the tapestries, heavens, wildernesses and other stage decorations. Such evidence as I have gathered leads me to believe that, with the possible exception of representatives of both foreign and ancient founder races, contemporary costume was used to dress all historical characters including figures from Biblical history.

The persons whom it was sought to represent can be grouped in three categories: mortal beings, supernatural beings, either heavenly or hellish, and what Warton calls 'the ideal personifications of the Christian Virtues'—not forgetting the Vices. For a foundation, contemporary costume served all three groups. The

* See Appendix B.

variants superimposed upon this foundation consisted of well-known attributes either worn or carried and the use of specific colours. Perhaps the best example of these devices in action is the normal costume for a king. The style of a stage-king's dress is contemporary whether he be David, Solomon, Ethelbert or Henry VII. That he is a king, as opposed to a subject, is signified by his wearing of a crown. If he were represented in bed, the crown would still be worn and not a night-cap.* Almost as certainly the colour of his robe or cloak will be crimson-purple.

This use of particular attributes to assist recognition derives from the use of decorative *heaumes* and blazons in the Tournament, of which it is merely an extension. The coat-of-arms figures frequently in pageants. As early as 1389, this device was used in Paris to help Isabella of Bavaria identify those knights represented in a pageant-tableau who had taken part in the famous *Pas Salhadin.*† When we find the Kings of France, Spain and England thus represented with their scutcheons in the London Pageants of 1501 for Katherine of Aragon, we may be confident that the audience had little difficulty in recognizing them. [84]

If kings could wear crowns and carry orbs or sceptres, the Saints and Fathers could just as well be equipped with some token associated with their story. As St. Peter carried keys, St. Christopher a child and St. John a lamb in the statuary and stained glass of countless cathedrals and churches, so St. George could place a foot on his dragon in the Hereford Pageant of 1486 and St. Catherine could lean on her wheel in the first of the 1501 Pageants: [85] nor was it difficult to find similar symbols with which to aid identification of the various Virtues and Vices (Plates XIV-XX). In the Paris Pageants of 1498 for Louis XII, *Liberalité* held a Cornucopia and *Puissance* was equipped with a sword. [86] So too, for Margaret Tudor in Edinburgh in 1503, Justice was presented, '. . . holdynge in hyr right Haunde a Swerde all naked, etc.'[87] This convention was over an hundred years old then; for in one of the 1389 Paris Pageants we hear of children guarding the seat of Justice,

'very richly ornamented with chaplets of gold, holding naked swords in their hands . . . which signify that they wish to guard the Hert and the bed of Justice'. [88]

* See Ch. IV, p. 173, note †, below.

† 'Et là estoient par personnages tous les seigneurs de nom, qui jadis au Pas Salhadin furent, et armoiés de leurs armes, ainsi que pour le temps d'adont ils amoient. Et ung petit ensus (*above*) de euls estoit par personnage le roy de France et autour de luy les douze Pers de France, et tous armoiés de leurs armes.'[83]

The Hert (*Cerf*) here represented France. This use of animals, or rather human beings dressed as animals after the fashion of the pantomime horse, to represent the State, is yet another extension of the original Tournament identification device. In the same 'Pageant of Justice' just quoted we learn that

'Out of these trees there issued a whyte Herte and went to the bedde of Justyce and out of the other part of the wood there issued a Lyon and an Egle properlye, and fresshlye approched the Herte.'*

The Lion and the Antelope were similarly used in London Pageants for Henry V and Henry VI.[89] The Lion Rampant, Red Dragon and White Greyhound figure in all Pageants for Katherine of Aragon. The Red Dragon was the emblem chosen by Henry VII to remind his subjects of his Welsh connections and Cadwalader's prophecy. Ann Boleyn was represented by her own signet, the falcon: and if animals could be used in this way, so could flowers, as the mechanical roses and lilies already cited go to show. Livery, a device with a similar origin, could be put to similar use. In the York Pageants of 1486, for instance,

'. . . y' shalbe in that castell citizins which . . . shall appeir in clothing of white and greyne, shewing y' trueth and hertly affection unto the Kinge'.[90]

That these colours were those of the King's livery we know from a passage in the account of Katherine of Aragon's passage through London where it is described as

'Clothing of Large Jaketts of Samase whytt and grene goodly embrowdred bothe on ther brestys before and also on their bakkys behynde . . .' etc.[91]

The wearing of livery combines both a particular attribute and colour symbolism. The latter we know to have been used in Lydgate's pageants of 1432. In the pageant on the drawbridge of the three Empresses, the seven virgins on their right, representing the seven gifts of the Holy Ghost, were 'outward figured by vii doves white'. They were dressed in 'Bawdrykes all off saffir hew'.† The seven Virtues on the Empresses' left were 'Alle cladde in white, in tokne of clennesse'.[92]

---

* The syntax of this passage in the original is exceptionally difficult to follow. The translation given here is Berners (London, 1545), II. clxxix.

† In the *Fall of Princes*, Lydgate says of Delilah that
    'She wered colour(e)s of many heue
    In stede of bleu, which stedfast is and cleene' Bk I. line 6, 445.

The chronicler of Louis XII's entry into Paris provides a useful list of colours in use at the turn of the fifteenth century. At the Porte St. Denis, against a blue ground of hangings, grew a seven-branched lily; in the seven flowers of which sat seven Virtues; *Humanité* dressed in grey, *Richesse* in yellow, *Fidelité* in pearl-white, *Puissance* in red, *Liberalité* in white and *Noblesse* in violet. The Presenter was clad in scarlet. *Noblesse*, in the Pageants for Katherine of Aragon, was dressed as a knight; *Virtue* as a bishop; *Honour*, 'Full plesantly beseen in purpill velvett'. [93]

A figure prominent in all pageants was the angel. One could desire more information than exists concerning the garb of angelic hosts: but what survives, convinces me that the same conventions were used for their representation on the stage as we see in countless mediaeval paintings. We constantly hear of 'Singing Childerne. Some arrayde like Angells, and others like vyrgyns' [94]—or words to that effect. I am myself inclined to believe that the only difference between these stage angels and virgins was the ownership of a pair of wings. Boys usually played the parts of both.* They were vested in some sort of gown. In Newcastle in 1503,

'At the Bryge Ende, apon the Gatt war many Chyldren revested of Surpeliz, syngynge mellodyously Hympnes, and *oth*(e)r Instruments of many Sortes.' [95]

Some justice was done to their figures by the wearing of a girdle. In Bristol in 1486 there was a 'Pageant of many Mayden Childern richely besene with Girdells, Beds (*sic—Beads?*) and *Ouches*'. [96] It is clear from this that the wearing of jewellery was also permissible. The Bridge House Rentals testify to nine pence having been spent on three pounds of flax bought and used in the likeness of hair for the angels and virgins. Another ten pence was spent in the purchase of one ounce of saffron used for dyeing the flax to make hair for the angels and children.† So far, then, I think we may reckon on something after the fashion of a surplice, drawn in at the waist by a girdle and a wig of long golden hair surmounted with a fillet as the usual costume for virgins and angels. In addition, the angels possessed—what the boys in the roles of simple maidens must have coveted greatly—wings. Raphael, in the third Pageant presented to Katherine of Aragon, 'with his goldyn & glyteryng wyngis & ffedyrs of many & sundry colours', clearly made an impression on the mind of one witness. [97] In the Bridge House Rentals

* This question is discussed fully in Chapter VII.
† See Appendix B.

there is an item in the 1464 Pageant Accounts for 1/9d. spent in the purchase of 900 peacocks' feathers for making these angels' wings. These feathers were presumably bound to hazel frames with pack-thread and wax; which items were provided in considerable quantities.* On the same premise that Hell figured rarely in the pageants, because they were ceremonies of rejoicing, descriptions of costumes for devils are rare. I include one illustration (Plate XXI) of a Dutch seventeenth-century pageant in which they do appear.

The sixteenth century is not notable for change in English pageant costume, any more than it is in the other aspects of stage-spectacle. In Fleet Street for Ann Boleyn in 1533,

'Upon the conduit was a tower with foure turretts, and in every turrett stood one of the cardinal vertues with their tokens and properties, which had severall speeches.'98

The Herald who provides the account of Edward VI's Coronation describes some of these 'tokens and properties':

'*Regallity* having a Regall (Sceptre) in his Hand,
Justice   having a Sword
Truth   having a Book, and
Mercy   having a little Curtane.'99

But it is Dekker, describing the Fleet Street Pageant of 1603, who settles the point:

'Having tolde you that her name was Justice,' he says, 'I hope you will not put me to describe what properties she held in her hands, sithence every painted cloath can informe you.'100

He is equally explicit about the continued usage of traditional colour symbolism. *Virtue*, in the same Pageant, was dressed in white; *Envy*, in black; 'the foure cardinall vertues . . . in habiliments fitting to their natures'. The *Senses*, in another Pageant, were similarly 'appareled in roabes of distinct cullours, proper to their natures'. *Fame*'s costume was light blue with eyes and tongues on it and a pair of gold wings attached. Jonson's 'Soteria' or Safety was 'a Damsel in carnation, the colour signifying cheer and life'. *Vigilance* was dressed 'in yellow, a sable mantle, seeded with waking eyes, and a silver fringe'. *Gladness* 'was suited in green, a mantle of divers colours, embroidered with all variety of flowers'.

---

* See Appendix B. Gabriel, in The Annunciation by Jan Van Eyck, has wings of peacock's feathers: reproduced by J. Huizinga, *op. cit.*, p. 260.

Several colours could be used in combination to present several aspects of a character's nature. Thus Jonson dressed Divine Wisdom

'all in white, a blue mantle seeded with stars, a crown of stars on her head. Her garments figured truth, innocence, and cleanness. She was always looking up: in her one hand she sustained a dove, in the other a serpent: the last to shew her subtilty, the first her simplicity.'

The justification given for this symbolic figuration is none other than the scriptural text used by Lydgate one hundred and seventy years earlier to explain his own Dame Sapience, *per me reges regnant.** These descriptions show that the lavish symbolic costumes of the contemporary Mask were not the exclusive property of courtiers but could be appreciated, at least in a Street Theatre, by a popular civic audience. Dekker, so much less sensitive to classical precept than Jonson, is just as scrupulous in observing appropriateness of detail. Describing Peace in these same pageants, he says:

'EIRENE. She was richly attired, her upper garment of carnation hanging loose, a robe of white under it powdered with starres, and girt to her; her hair of a bright colour, long, and hanging at her back, but interwoven with white ribbands and jewels; her browes were encompast with a wreath compounded of the olive, the lawrell, and the date tree. In one hand she held a Caduces, or Mercurie's rod, the God of Eloquence; in the other ripe ears of corne gilded; on her lap sate a dove; all these being ensignes and furnitures of Peace.'

I have suggested that contemporary fashion formed the basis of all costuming in the pageant theatres throughout their history. I must now qualify that opinion with a pair of exceptions. One concerns nationality; the other, historical detail.

In the Paris Pageants for Louis XII in 1498, 'Humanité' wore '. . . en sa teste une grande perruque, à deux bosses, couverte de fermillets d'or & pierrerie, *en la façon du temps passé*'.[101] This corresponds with 'iiii or sage p(er)sonys after the auncyent fachion arayed s(o)m(e) w^t m(ar)velous hoods: and sum̄ w^t hatts: and their robys sett full of perlys and were semblaunt unto the p(ro)phetts'[102] in the London Pageants of 1501. What this *façon du temps passé* or *auncyent fachion* might imply I cannot say with any certainty. If these phrases are considered in a strictly dramatic

* See p. 78 above.

context, they could well refer to the conventions of costuming liturgical plays, the 'oldest' and most 'ancient' of dramas in France or England. However, in a wider context, the simplest explanation would be that these characters wore the elaborate headgear and neck-to-foot robes which, though still remembered by the elderly, were no longer fashionable. One is nevertheless warned against discounting all possibility of a sense of period in stage costume during the Middle Ages. Like the use of live birds and rabbits in stage settings, it would seem to argue that some sort of visual realism was demanded by audiences and granted by designers when sufficiently decorative or sensational.[103] This problem was no doubt aggravated in the sixteenth century by the advent of newcomers from classical mythology. At Norwich, Queen Elizabeth I saw 'Mercury' dressed

'. . . in blew Satin lined with cloth of gold, his garmentes cutte and slashed on the finest manner, a peaked hatte of the same coloure, as though it should cutte and seuer the wind asunder, and on the same a payre of wings, and wings on his heeles lykewise.'[104]

In 1603, Jonson's 'Genius Urbis' was 'a person attired rich, reverend, and antique'. Liberty was dressed in white, 'somewhat antique, but loose and free'! Safety wore 'an antique helm'.

The second exception to the rule of contemporary fashion may derive from the same source. This is an apparent insistence upon the detail of national characteristics in dress. For Edward VI eight French trumpeters played their instruments 'after the Fashion of their Country', while Queen Elizabeth, at Norwich, saw

'. . . an excellent Boy, wel and gallantly decked, in a lo(n)g white roabe of Taffeta, a Crimson Skarfe wrought with gold, folded on the Turkishe fashion aboute his browes, and a gay Garlande of fine floures on his head.'[105]

All this elaborate spectacle could not have been achieved without great cost and considerable organization. I propose to hold over that question for discussion in Chapter VIII, where it may be better handled in conjunction with the arrangements for financing and executing all other forms of mediaeval entertainment. One further question, however, does cry out to be asked and answered here and now. How did audiences react to these costly shows? It is usually assumed, on the strength of the disparaging way they seem to be treated in the texts of Whetstone's *Promos and Cassandra* and in Shakespeare's *Love's Labour's Lost*, or *A Midsummer Night's*

Dream, and from the equally disparaging attitude displayed by professional dramatists to that perennial pageanteer, Anthony Munday, that they must have been too simple, too tedious and too clumsily executed to receive the approbation of the audiences on whose patronage Elizabethan Court and Public Theatres flourished.[106] Personally, I do not think Whetstome intended his 'Royal Entry' as a burlesque, nor that his audience regarded it as such. All descriptions of Royal Entries read as something trivial until their symbolic and allegorical significance is appreciated—a fact which in large measure accounts for their neglect by so many historians. The true mood of the passage is provided in *Phallax*'s lament:

> "A syr, heare is short knowledge, to entertayne a Kyng.
> . . . Yea, at a dayes warning."

Neither is Shakespeare, in *Love's Labour's Lost*, burlesquing a Royal Entry, nor even a Lord Mayor's Show. The lamentable entertainment provided by Holofernes is much more akin to one of those hastily contrived provincial entertainments for a sovereign on a Progress in which Churchyard specialized:

'The Thurseday in the morning, my Lorde Chamberlaine gave me warning yᵉ Queenes highnesse woulde ride abroade in the after noone, and he commaunded me to be ready dutifully to presente hir with some Shewe.'[107]

Again, short notice is the crux of the matter. He did his best with a Show of Nymphs which, in the event, had to be abandoned because of a thunderstorm. He admits that he and his cast looking like 'drowned Rattes' afforded more entertainment than anything in the show he had prepared could have done.

The mechanicals' show in *A Midsummer Night's Dream*, though likened by Theseus to a Royal Entry, is a regular play performed by amateurs. As such it is scorned by the rude courtiers and may be better compared with an amateur performance today of some recent West End or Broadway success.*

The gibes at Anthony Munday from professional dramatists may equally be explained by their jealousy. For it should be remembered that they too wrote pageant texts, often in competition, and that the successful competitor received a handsome reward. In 1617 Middleton received £282 for his labours from the Grocers Company. Munday and Dekker, who were his unsuccessful competitors, received £5 and £4 respectively.[108] Munday happened to please

* See Ch. VII, p. 235 below.

his merchant patrons more frequently than his rivals, all of whom were struggling for a livelihood in an age when the writer's profession was a hazardous one.

I believe that Bishop Hall accurately assessed contemporary audiences' opinion of the Street Theatres in describing them as 'The Pageants of your great solemnities'. This at any rate accords better than disparagement with the money spent on them and the distinguished company of dramatists who devised them.

'Tryumphs,' says Dekker, 'are the most choice and daintiest fruit that spring from peace and abundance; Love begets them; and much cost brings them forth.'[109]

That is a dramatist's opinion. The same pageant-dramatist assesses the taste of his audience. In 1603 he wrote:

'The multitude is now to be our audience, whose heads will miserably run a wool-gathering if we doo but offer to breake them with hard words.'[110]

This implies that his audience preferred simple words—how well Shakespeare appreciated this—and spectacle. The only qualification I should add is that he may here be thrusting at his collaborator, Jonson, to whose work he gives the scantiest recognition. But even so Jonson in his account, and he ignores Dekker altogether, substantiates the point. He says that the pageants are

'so to be presented, as upon the view, they might, without cloud, or obscuritie, declare themselves to the sharpe and learned: And for the multitude, no doubt but their grounded iudgements did gaze, said it was fine, and were satisfied.'[111]

Indeed, from whatever angle we approach the pageant theatres of the streets—purpose, characters, stages, scenic background, cost or costume—the same startling constant emerges: that the mediaeval and Tudor 'multitude' were consistently addicted to spectacle. Still more significant, professional dramatists of the regular Elizabethan and Jacobean theatres, as begetters of these pageants were made aware both of this popular hunger for spectacle and of the means to oblige their patrons in this respect.

IV

MIRACLE PLAYS

---

1 Death by Execution or from Natural Causes?

'The texts contain some very quaint stage directions which
well show the primitive nature of the scenic arrangements.'
S. W. CLARKE, *The Miracle Play in England*, 1900

FOLLOWING directly upon what has been said about the staging
of Tournaments and the Royal Entries, this representative
Victorian sentiment about mediaeval stagecraft is, I trust, so
patently in conflict with the evidence of these parallel sources as to
seem misconceived. Yet the idea has died so hard that it is far from
extinct today. Since it stems from similar critical assumptions
about the plays and their history,* there is little chance of writing
comprehensibly about their staging without first providing a more
rational context for its study.

As a starting point, a second quotation will indicate the direction
in which modern criticism has been moving:

'The power which was really working for the ultimate extinction of
the religious stage was none other than the Crown itself, whose
motives were the extirpation of the old customs and practices
under the cry of "superstition and idolatry".' (H. C. Gardiner,
S.J., *Mysteries' End*, 1946; reprinted 1967, p. 77.)

Nobody has ever seriously questioned the fact that performance of
the Miracle Cycles in England petered out during the latter half of
the sixteenth century; for, indeed, the surviving evidence supplies
no reason to do so. The reasons chosen to explain this fact, however, must colour our whole assessment of both the plays and their
staging. If we regard the plays as having outgrown their strength,
then it follows logically enough that Elizabethan plays and stagecraft were a great improvement upon them. The sequel is to conclude that plays, acting and production were alike 'primitive'.
Simple chronology seems to substantiate such an argument,

* See Introduction, pp. xxxviii–xxxix above.

especially in the light of the subsequent splendours of Restoration stage spectacle.

The idea, however, that possibly the plays did not die a natural death, but were deliberately extirpated, must cause us to think again. Nor is this idea just a casual hypothesis. It corresponds altogether too accurately with the mysterious disappearance of all but a fraction of the many texts known to have existed, and also with the long-established knowledge that other artistic manifestations of Catholic doctrine—statues, frescoes, stained glass—were defaced, despoiled or removed at precisely this time.* There is also the evidence of those plays written after 1530 that adopt a militant, Protestant, theological stance, and that set out to identify vice in all its aspects with Roman Catholicism.†

If we suppose that this idea can be substantiated, what follows? First, it would seem that far from having outgrown its strength, the Miracle stage was still vigorous enough to warrant official intervention to suppress it. A vigorous religious stage, in turn, suggests direct comparison with the conventions of the sixteenth-century Tournaments and Royal Entries already examined. This done, it becomes both possible and reasonable to consider the stagecraft of Tournaments, Royal Entries, the Miracle Cycles and the Elizabethan Public Theatre as so many different manifestations of a single homogeneous tradition of stage spectacle, acting and production: and all these aspects of dramatic art are likely to have affected the writer, to some extent, in the actual construction of his plays. The net outcome of these speculations, if proved to be correct, is nothing short of a total revaluation of the Elizabethan and Jacobean Drama in terms of early English stages, which will take many years and many books to complete.

Where the Miracle Plays are concerned, the evidence prompting reassessment of the long-established critical tenets is of two kinds. There is first the astonishing success of recent revivals of the Cycles, starting with E. Martin Browne's production of the York plays in Canon Purvis' translation for the Festival of Britain in 1951. Popular enthusiasm has warranted regular revivals, while

* 'In the first year of Edward VI there were certain commissioners appointed to deface all such ornaments as were left in the parish churches at Durham undefaced in the former visitation. The commissioners were Dr. Harvey and Dr. Whitby. Dr. Harvey called for the said shrine (of Corpus Xp'i); and when it was brought before him he did tread upon it with his feet, and broke it all to pieces, with diverse other ornaments pertaining to the church.' See R. Davies' *York Records of the XVth Century*, 1843, p. 260.

† See *Early English Stages* (*EES*), III, pp. 76–8, 97–8, 208ff. and 228ff.

Chester has similarly staged its own plays on several occasions.

The warm support given to these revivals has since warranted professional production of the Wakefield (Towneley) Cycle at the Mermaid Theatre in London: *Ludus Coventriae* has been presented in Tewkesbury Abbey and at both Coventry and Lincoln; and the Cornish Cycle has been revived in its entirety in its original earthwork 'round' at Piran, near Perranporth. * Chester's plays have even reached the television screen and York's plays have been seen in the streets of Toronto. Such support contrasts so strangely with the words 'primitive', 'naive', 'crude' and other such patronizing epithets of traditional critical evaluation, that modern minds are now keenly awake to the idea that they may have been misinformed.

The second sort of evidence is of a less speculative kind: records, of fifteenth- and sixteenth-century provenance, discovered or newly analysed by scholars since the first edition of this volume was published twenty years ago. These include the systematic transcription and publication of provincial records in the *Malone Society Collections*, VII, VIII and IX (Kent, Lincolnshire, and Dorset and Suffolk respectively); Eleanor Prosser's *Drama and Religion in the English Mystery Plays* (Stanford U.P., 1961), V. A. Kolve's *The Play Called 'Corpus Christi'* (Stanford U.P., 1966), O. B. Hardison Jr.'s *Christian Rite and Christian Drama in the Middle Ages* (Johns Hopkins Press, 1965), Richard Axton's *European Drama of the Early Middle Ages* (U. Pittsburgh P., 1975), and a remarkable number of shorter essays either edited collectively or published singly as articles in a variety of journals. The sad but inescapable truth that emerges from all this research is that divines and academics in the early seventeenth century, upon whom posterity depended for its records, chose to follow their government's iconoclastic lead.[1] Successive Protestant governments in the late sixteenth century, seeing in the plays and the large assemblies which their performance attracted a constant reminder of earlier habits of thinking, together with ideal opportunities for violent demonstrations, determined to suppress them. In this endeavour, they were aided and abetted from pulpits, lecture rooms and books by a smear campaign of great ingenuity and thoroughness.†

* Presented by the Drama Department of Bristol University directed by Dr. Neville Denny, 1969; for photographs, see *New Theatre Magazine*, Vol. 9, No. 3 (summer 1969).

† See *EES*, II (1), Chs. III and IV.

In 1568, for example, the Dean of York, who was a member of the Queen's Commission for Ecclesiastical Causes in the North, answered the Corporation's request for permission to perform the Creed Play as follows:

'As I find so manie things that I muche like because of th' antiquities, so I see manie things that I cannot allow because they be disagreeinge from the sinceritie of the gospell, . . . mine advise shuld be that it shuld not be plaied, for thoghe it was plawsible to (?10) yeares agoe, and wold now also of the ignorant sort be well liked, yet now in the happie time of the gospell, I knowe the learned will mislike it, and how the state will beare it, I know not.'[2]

Dean Hutton's attitude may seem equivocal, but his intention is clear: to avoid incurring the popular odium of a direct refusal, and yet achieve refusal by hinting darkly at dire penalties in store for those who might rashly take it upon themselves to sponsor a performance.*

That the implied threat was not an idle one may be judged by the cases of Mr. Hankey and Sir John Savage, Mayors of Chester in 1572 and 1575 respectively. Both of these gentlemen were summoned before the Privy Council to explain their conduct in permitting performances of the Cycle at Whitsun. Savage's offence was the more heinous of the two, since he allowed the production under his Mayoralty in the face of direct instructions to the contrary from the Archbishop of York and the Lord President of the North. It took a whole year for him to clear himself, and then only as a result of the Corporation accepting corporate responsibility for an action which they had deemed to be 'to the comon wealthe and benefite and proffitte of the saide citie'.[3]

In the face of such danger, however, it was clearly becoming very difficult for anyone in authority to risk yielding to popular pressure and allow performances. By 1576, the Government's agents, having thus effectively undermined the will of local authorities, felt strong enough to come out in their true colours. In that year the Diocesan Court of High Commission at York revealed their attitude to the citizens of Wakefield in no uncertain terms. Permission is granted for the performance of their Cycle provided that

'in the said playe no pageant be used or set furthe wherin the

---

* In 1572 Archbishop Grindal, after a performance of the York Paternoster Play, demanded to read it. He impounded it and never returned it.

Ma(jest)ye of God the Father, God the Sonne, or God the Holie Ghoste or the administration of either the Sacrementes of baptisme or of the Lordes Supper be counterfeyted or represented, or anythinge plaied which tende to the maintenaunce of superstition and idolatrie or which be contrarie to the lawes of God or of the realme.'[4]

In other words, the Cycle is censored out of existence.

Other methods of indirect suppression, of calculated strangulation, had been employed insidiously and effectively over the preceding forty years. The dissolution of the monasteries in 1539 provided grounds for the destruction, along with other books in their libraries, of all dramatized lives of the saints and of the Virgin.[5] Another means of attack was the encouragement of a rival drama, calculated to ridicule the old. Thomas Cromwell and Cranmer saw to it that men like John Bale (later to become Bishop of Ossory), who were busily engaged in the writing of Protestant polemics in dramatic form, got a wide hearing. In *Kyng Johan*, a violent attack on the Papacy and all things Roman, Bale associates his title-role quite unmistakably with Henry VIII and the Pope as unmistakably with Anti-Christ.[*] It is the more remarkable, therefore, to find the following lines put into John's mouth:

> 'Than for Englondes cawse I wyll be sumewhat playne.
> Yt is yow, Clargy, that hathe her in dysdayne:
> With yowr Latyne howrs, serymonyes, and popetly playes.'[†]

In other words, we must recognize that the drama of the sixteenth century was adult enough to reflect in detail the quickly shifting religious and political issues of the day. As one of the most inflammatory instruments of propaganda known to the age, it invited the attention of the lords temporal as well as its traditional controllers, the lords spiritual.

Bale himself, under Cromwell's patronage,[7] seems to have revised the normal Miracle Cycle on Protestant lines: but it was through the Morality Play and the Interlude rather than the Miracles that the drama could best be used for political and religious polemic. Detailed treatment of this subject is therefore postponed for discussion in Chapter VII, and in Chapters VIII and IX of Vol. III.

[*] See *EES*, III, pp. 228–9.

[†] *Kyng Johan*, lines 413–15. In all probability this play was performed in Cranmer's house at Christmas 1538/39.[6] See pp. 238–40 below.

It suffices to say here that it is in a context of Protestant controversy, as I read the evidence, that we ought to consider the disappearance of the Miracle Plays in England.

The religious stage, far from being too crude and naïve in its technique to command the continued allegiance of the populace in face of competition from the new drama of Renaissance origin, was at the summit of its powers. Trade guilds responsible for play production amalgamate: not, as has hitherto been argued, because they were losing interest in the plays, but because the staging of them was becoming ever more spectacular and costly.[8] The fact that every performance was a living representation of Catholic dogma may not have been a matter of much consequence to their audiences, but it could not fail to concern a government occupied with the political consequences of the breach with Rome. Had these plays been effete and in decline, the Government need not have taken any action: yet the evidence of recent research shows that successive governments from 1535 to 1575 first undermined the Catholic stage by ridicule, censorship and threats and ultimately directly forbade its continuance. * These calculated and consistently repressive measures can only have been undertaken because nothing short of them would serve to wean performers and spectators away from the plays. This, in its turn, can only mean that on grounds of civic pride, financial gain and spectacular entertainment the Miracle Plays commanded the allegiance of the populace to the very end. In short, the builders of the Public Playhouses of Elizabethan England were the direct heirs of a fully developed tradition of stagecraft and not novices in their profession as they have so often been represented. As stated, when James Burbage was preparing to open the *The Theater* in 1576, Sir John Savage, Mayor of Chester, was also in London, and busy defending himself before the Privy Council for permitting a performance of the Cycle on the grounds that this was in the best interests of the citizens.†

Scarcely less important is the corollary that executive control of the Miracle Plays need only have passed from the Church to the Municipality when there was no longer a single Catholic Church to sponsor them. Henry VIII's break with Rome, acknowledgement of him as Supreme Head of the Church in England in 1531 and the

* The Marian reaction (1553–58) was too brief for any effective counter measures to be taken. See *EES*, II (1), Chs. I–IV.

† It is in the year *The Theater* was built, 1576, that the Wakefield plays are censored out of existence. See p. 116 above.

dissolution of the monasteries in 1539, created just these circumstances.

These deductions, if permissible, are of such consequence to the whole history of English drama and theatre that they must now be applied in some detail to the currently accepted history of the Miracle Plays.

2 *The Case for an Overhaul of Accepted Judgements*

The new perspective, then, within which we view the story of the Miracle Cycles, is, briefly, this. For political reasons, arising from the Disestablishment of the Roman Church in England, the plays were suppressed in the reign of Queen Elizabeth I. They were suppressed, at the height of their dramatic achievement, by the Government working through the Reformed Church and in the face of determined opposition from the participants who, either from natural conservatism or commercial interest or both together, favoured their continuance. The opponents of suppression, however, were in a fatally weak position. They lacked, above all, the weight of any traditional authority for exercising control over the text, since this had only recently passed into their hands. Until the period 1530–1540 it had rested with the monasteries and cathedral chapters, working, as often as not, indirectly through the secular clergy.[9] The monasteries were silenced by dissolution and it is to be assumed that control passed then to the municipalities who, up to that time, had only exercised jurisdiction over conditions of performance and attendance. But even then their control of the text must have been in doubt; for on what other grounds could members of the Ecclesiastical Commission in Elizabeth's reign claim the right to censor and eventually suppress? Archbishop Grindal and Dean Hutton were able to discharge their duties in suppressing 'idolaterous' and 'superstitious' plays in York and Chester just because they could argue that responsibility for the texts of religious plays continued to be, as it had always been, the Church's prerogative. This view was never challenged by the municipalities in their long and sustained fight to preserve the plays.[10]

This reversal of standard judgements on the decline and death of the Miracle Cycles obliges us to revise our ideas about control of the plays, their literary form, translation from Latin into English and their migration from Church to precincts. This involves revision of our interpretation of the terms 'secular' and 'secularized' as applied to the plays. Until the middle of this century historians supposed that the transition from 'religious' to 'secular' was strictly marked by the transference of performances of liturgical plays* from inside a church to its immediate precincts, and that the process of 'secularization' proceeded in direct proportion with the distance away from the church that performances were given.† As a sequel, it was supposed that it was this change of the locale of the performance which marks the change in literary form—liturgical plays or groups of plays, to Miracle Cycles. Again, this change, in its turn, is usually taken to imply simultaneous translation from Latin into the vernacular.[11]

Since it was known that plays were performed outside churches before the end of the thirteenth century, any 'tradition' that established the start of the surviving Cycles in the early years of the fourteenth century passed muster without any serious testing of its accuracy.‡ Misleadingly for historians of drama, such a tradition exists in respect of the Chester Cycle. What no one until the middle of the present century had ever questioned was the genesis of this tradition. Whether it derives from pre- or post-Reformation sources, and whether these sources are likely to have been amicable or hostile to performances, no one had tried to distinguish. On the strength of its existence, however, events at York, Wakefield, Coventry and elsewhere were forced to follow a similar supposed pattern without any supporting evidence of substance. It happened to be easier to reach broad generalizations within a very complicated subject by making everything else conform to the Chester tradition than to question the validity of the tradition itself.[12] Once, however, we concede that the Church, whether Roman Catholic or Reformed, controlled the plays' destiny to the very

---

* Plays, that is, which were still linked to specific church services. See p. 161 below.

† Hardin Craig appears to entertain some doubts on the matter, since he seems to contradict himself on it: 'They were liturgical and they became secular; this fact is obvious and needs no proof' (*English Religious Drama*, O.U.P., 1955, p. 83). 'The materials out of which these amplifications were composed were to the minds of medieval people authoritative, sacred, and dramatically interesting. They were religious and not secular' (*ibid.*, p. 158).

‡ See Chambers, *Med. Stage*, ii, pp. 348–56 and 407–9. Chambers does probe the tradition indeed at almost every point. Unfortunately he relied, when doing so, on transcripts of documents by Canon R. H. Morris which have since been shown to be, in places, very inaccurate and generally misleading. See pp. 133–6 below.

end, the grounds on which these long-accepted suppositions have been based are exposed as being both flimsy and improbable.

By way of illustration, we may start with transference of performances from the interior of a church to its precincts. This can now be seen as a natural extension of an approved liturgical practice. The plays were not 'ejected by the Church', but guided there on grounds of convenience. Still as nearly liturgical as when they were first divorced from the Mass and presented as an extension of Matins or Vespers, they clearly do not become 'secular' merely by virtue of the change of locale: nor, for that matter, simply because laymen are invited to assist by acting some parts in a rigorously prescribed text. Such suppositions only begin to have some justification if, simultaneously with outdoor migration, the plays are translated from the liturgical Latin into the secular vernacular: but in fact they were not. A full hundred years separates the first recorded instance of an outdoor performance (Beverley, c. 1220) and even the old attribution of vernacular plays to Chester.*

This careless attitude to chronology is equally pronounced and equally mischievous where the association of the plays with first the Guilds and, secondly, the Festival of Corpus Christi, is concerned.

'In the well-ordered life of the Middle Ages it would have been surprising if the religious plays, after leaving the Church, had not come under the control of some other authority. In fact they were taken over by the Trade Guilds. . . . They became linked, too, to one particular day in the Church calendar . . . Corpus Christi Day.' (*Oxford Companion to the Theatre*, 1st, 2nd and 3rd editions.)†

This statement is typical. The author has apparently not thought it at all odd that the plays having 'passed from the control of the Church to that of the Guilds' (i.e. become secular) should then 'become linked' with a Church Festival, a novelty at that. This argument is about as coherent as saying that responsibility for the inauguration of Feast Days passed out of the Church's control into the hands of the Guilds who, wishing to perform plays in July, told the Church to establish a new Festival for the purpose. Both are preposterous. If anybody linked the plays with the Festival of

* What is more, no text of a Miracle Play *in English* survives of earlier date than the first quarter of the fifteenth century.[13]
† *sub* England.

Corpus Christi it could only have been the Church itself which controlled both its plays and its feast. The word 'control' is itself all too ambiguous. Controlled what? The plays' text or the performance? Even in our own times plays were controlled by two authorities working simultaneously. Until 1968 the Lord Chamberlain controlled the text and therefore the dramatist: the Corporation, through its Police and Fire Regulations, still controls the conditions of performance. In the Middle Ages, so long as performances were *restricted to consecrated ground*, the Church possessed unchallenged authority over its plays. Once, however, performances extended beyond these limits, the King, or his representative, had a right to say how, when and where they were to be conducted: for the distinction between *The King's Peace* and *The Peace of God* was real and carried with it judicial powers over property and persons. *
The crux of the matter is that since the Church had good reason both for fostering lay interest in performances of its plays and in celebrating its festival, there was also a likelihood that the two might coalesce in due season, especially if we think of the Church as itself divided into regular and secular clergy: but there was no good reason why plays should be linked to the festival either immediately or automatically.

The Festival of Corpus Christi, established in 1311, was accepted throughout England by 1318.† The basis of the celebrations was a procession of priests and laymen which had for its object the honouring of the Host by carrying it ceremonially from the principal church in the city, around its streets and back again. Beyond that, nothing was defined in any detail or decreed for universal acceptance. Far then, from assuming an immediate and automatic conjunction of the plays to this Festival—plays in English at that—we should surely question how plays ever became attached to a procession, a form of celebration so antipathetic to their performance. Equally relevant is the question of what purpose this new Feast was designed to serve. Knowledge of the form the Feast took is not likely to help us much in finding connections between it and dramatic performances unless we are also aware of what basic spiritual need its begetters hoped it would meet. My own answer is that establishment of the Feast marks a peak in the campaign of the rapidly expanding orders of friars, aided and abetted by the parish clerks, to inject the relevance of Christian

* See p. 203 below.
† See pp. 130–3 below.

worship into secular life. That, however, is a point of view which is argued at much greater length in Volume III.* Here I wish only to analyse the known facts afresh and to pursue the problem of how stationary performances could be satisfactorily related to a procession.†

If this question is asked, as it should be, there is no answer forthcoming from what the surviving evidence tells us about Miracle Plays.[14] There is, however, another source of information which, if neglected hitherto, is still very useful. It was at exactly this time, at the start of the fourteenth century, that Pageantry first became associated with civic ridings. Can this be just coincidence? Or is it possibly an instance of parallel development such as we have seen between the Royal Entries and Tournaments, and shall see again when we come to consider Mummings and Disguisings? From the survey of the Pageant Theatres in Chapter III three facts emerged of immediate relevance here. First, quite early in the fourteenth century, the devisers of processional, civic celebrations incorporated spectacular scenic items in their perambulations, as a matter of course. The Fishmongers of London turned out in 1298 'w* solempne processyon' carrying huge, gilded sturgeons, silver salmon and sea horses, also an image of St. Magnus. The saint's presence is explained as a token of thanksgiving for Edward I's victory at Falkirk. 'And this they dyd on St. Magnus Day in honour of the Kyngis Victorye.' In 1313, the Fishmongers similarly celebrated the birth of Edward III by carrying a ship in the procession.‡

The second point to notice is that these ridings, although organized by the Corporation, were really ordered assemblies of individual guilds and that these guilds adopted appropriate visual symbols to ensure that the nature of their 'craft', 'mystery' or occupation be demonstrated to the spectators.

---

* See Ch. VIII.

† The fact that procession and plays did *not* dovetail harmoniously is illustrated in part by the Chester preference for Whitsun as the regular time of performance, and in part by the familiar wrangle on the subject in 1426 in York, when the 'Very religious father, *William Melton*, of the order of the *friars minors*', successfully urged that the performance of the plays should be transferred from the Feast to the Vigil. Performances seem to have reverted to the day itself, however, shortly afterwards. See Sharp's *Dissertation*, pp. 133–5, and Siegfried Wenzel, 'An Early Reference to a Corpus Christi Play', *Journal of Modern Philology*, Vol. 74, No. 4, May 1977, pp. 390–4.

‡ See Ch. III, pp. 53 and 54 above.

Thirdly, it is not until 1377, the year of Richard II's Coronation, that these processions change their nature. It is in that year, for the first time, that a stage is used for a mimetic performance. It is not without interest that this performance and the more elaborate one of 1392 are both given in Latin: vernacular speech was not used in Royal Entries until the start of the fifteenth century.*

These observations provoke a number of further questions about the conventional history of the Miracle Cycles. Why, for instance, should the same guilds, responsible for both civic and ecclesiastical processions, have regarded and treated one as different from the other? Processional Pageantry in civic celebrations is clearly of earlier origin than the Corpus Christi riding: yet we are asked to believe that the Chester Cycle at least (called Corpus Christi Plays in all early records) was translated into English and performed in 1327–28, while in civic perambulations no such performances are given at all until fifty years later and no performances in English for a further forty years: a difference of ninety years in all. This question is the more pertinent if the dates of the first factual references to the Miracle Cycles (as opposed to recollected traditions) are taken into account: Beverley 1377, York 1378, Coventry 1392, Chester 1422. The coincidence of the Beverley date with that for the first recorded mimetic performance in a Royal Entry is too good to be true, and I don't propose to force any argument from it: but the general coincidence of the two sets of dates is a matter which one would be foolish to ignore. Indeed they seem to me to provide sufficient framework on which to reconstruct a history of the Miracle Cycles very different from that accepted hitherto.

3 Suggestions leading to a new Chronology

(a) Migration from within the Church

I will first outline my presumptive chronology in the baldest possible terms and then proceed to amplify it. My hope is that the reader will thereby find it easier to pick his way through an argument which, in the nature of the subject, cannot be reduced to simple terms without replacing the old confusions, complexities and contradictions it is designed to remove by new ones just as misleading.

The starting point is the development of the introit-play within the liturgy of the Catholic Church growing slowly and naturally

---

* *Ibid.*, pp. 55–58 and 70 *et seq.*

over some three whole centuries (*c.* 950–1250). The expanding scale of the narrative enacted provoked a proportionate expansion both in the number of persons needed to act it and in the ground-area required for its performance, but no change in either purpose or language, both of which remained devotional. For the actors, however, this modest expansion brought with it a change of major consequence for the future, since provision had to be made for distinguishing Christian characters from non-Christian ones, and thus differentiating the good (*honestus*) and decorous behaviour of the former from the bad (*inhonestus*) and indecorous behaviour of the latter: the touchstone proved to be the figure of Herod in the *Officium Stellae.* *

This steady extension of the original activity ensured a general similarity in text and production techniques, since all were directly controlled by the single, universal Church; but it admitted a wide variety of local differences because of geographical isolation and in-different communications between the widespread administrative centres of that universal Church.[15] There is no reason to anticipate a uniform exodus of plays from churches; and, lacking any evidence of a Papal Decree commanding it, we may assume that the Church had its own reasons for promoting the migration, as also for deciding to enlist secular clergy to participate in religious plays. In some places where there was no monastery (as, for example, Beverley) the secular clergy (at Beverley, canons of the Collegiate Church) probably handled all plays both inside and outside the Minster itself. Elsewhere, with the arrival of the preaching friars in England during the first half of the thirteenth century, there is clear evidence of a growing desire, matched with positive action, to translate devotional exercises into forceful instruments of instruction.†

This change, dictated by a growing awareness that re-enactment of historical events within liturgical ritual invited responses more appropriate to a play (*ludus*) presented in a theatre (*teatrum; amphi-teatrum*) than to a sacred Office (*Ordo; Officium*) conducted in the sanctuary of a Church, took place piecemeal during the thirteenth century. If, however, the Church had by then decided to rationalize this situation and to legitimize its continuance by adding a new didactic dimension to dramatic representations that had originally been authorized for strictly devotional ends—and here a growing concern with repentance and the salvation or damnation of

* See *EES*, III, pp. 158, 175–6 and 181–4.
† See *EES*, III, Ch. VI.

individual souls supplies the strongest of reasons for this shift of direction—the corresponding shift in physical environment must have created new problems of a strictly technical kind for the actors: these involved acoustics, optics, climate and seasonal weather.[16]

Once this is recognized, we have to ask ourselves whether the bishops found themselves obliged to answer these problems without any precedents to guide them, or whether, in the event, advice was forthcoming from secular quarters where similar problems had already been faced and answered. The evidence that recent research has brought to light suggests powerfully that just such an alternative source of information did exist: our knowledge of it is still incomplete, but scholars today are at least more critically aware than were their predecessors of the directions in which to turn to find it.

Two such sources have been discussed in the preceding chapters of this book—Tournaments and Civic Pageantry—but there are others. These include those traditional dramatic games, collectively known as 'folk-drama', which continued to be organized and conducted within the context of Christian Calendar Festivals such as Plough Plays, May Games, Midsummer Watches and Mummings; the monologues that enlivened the sermons of the preaching friars and the fabliaux of the trouvères; and perhaps most important of all, the artistic enterprises of a dramatic character undertaken by the students of Europe's newly established universities. The normal environments of all these activities were, respectively, village greens and city streets, the churchyard and the market crosses, and the halls and refectories of colleges, castles and monasteries.

It was these backcloths that provided the settings for such plays as the quasi-liturgical *Anti-Christus* from Tegernsee (*c.* 1160) with its abstract personifications and its battle-scenes; the Anglo-Norman *Ordo Representacionis Adae* (or *Jeu d'Adam*) and *La Sainte Resurrection* (*c.* 1150), both of which were scripted in the vernacular rather than in Latin; the Play of the Resurrection at Beverley (1220) staged in the Minster yard and Saints' Plays in London (*c.* 1180); the plays of Hilarius, Jean Bodel, Rutebeuf and Adam de la Halle (spanning the years 1125–1285); the fragmentary English *Interludium de Clerico et Puella*, a domestic farce (*c.* 1300) and the satirical play directed against profiteering among the leather-workers of Exeter banned by Bishop Grandisson in 1352.*

* On these plays see *EES*, III, Ch. VIII, pp. 31–4, 178–86 and 264–6.

None of these plays in point of date and character—still less all of them collectively—allows the old hypothesis of the systematic growth, coalescence and translation transforming Latin liturgical music-dramas into spoken vernacular cycles to stand: rather does each of them in its own particular way proclaim the existence of a sturdy tradition of dramatic performances conducted during the twelfth and thirteenth centuries *outside* the basilica and for non-liturgical, if still festive, purposes. Yet in all of them the Church played an important role, and in some instances a controlling one.

If this reasoning is accepted, it becomes obvious that we must reverse traditional judgements inherited from the nineteenth century and earlier about 'growth', 'coalescence' and 'secularization' of liturgical music-dramas and view those developments in religious drama particular to the twelfth and thirteenth centuries not as a virtual abandonment by the Church of its own plays to the laiety, but rather as progressive adaptations by the Church to its own ends of those principles of secular stagecraft that answered its own needs.

In the verbal currency of twentieth-century agnosticism, 'The Church' is doubtless an adequate word with which to label anything and everything of ecclesiastical provenance. Indiscriminate use of it, however, in the context of Miracle Plays breeds confusion at every turn. By processes of generalizing and over-simplifying, historians have assumed that if 'The Church' was not responsible for production of the plays, then laymen were. The flaw here is that the distinction which existed in the thirteenth and fourteenth centuries between regular and secular clergy has been forgotten —and with serious consequences to all subsequent arguments about conditions governing performances. We must remember that between the extremes of cloistered devotion represented by the regular monastic orders under vows on the one hand and the layman (whether lord temporal, merchant or peasant) on the other there intervened two types of clergy having affinities with both extremes. There were the regular orders of friars whom Jusserand described as 'microbes' infecting the stationary part of the community with new ideas and whom Trevelyan terms, just as aptly, 'religious roundsmen'.* Secondly, there was 'the army of unbeneficed priests, deacons and clerks in holy orders who were scattered about the country, in every variety of employment, often under no control beyond that of their lay employers'.†

* See *English Social History*, 1942, pp. 40–55.
† *Ibid.*, p. 51.

Here was a source through which advanced ideas of continental origin about performances of the plays could percolate all England. Here was the first source to which the monastic city churches would turn if they needed to supplement their own numbers to perform the plays. Here too were men already as closely identified with industry and commerce as they were with religion. Such a one indeed, was 'Jolyf Absolon' who played the part of Herod 'on a scaffold hye': a parish-clerk of Oxford. *

Taking these factors into account, then, I think we may assume that the transition from clerical to lay production of the plays was not necessarily an abrupt one. Rather was it likely to have been smooth and gradual, with the friars and the secular clergy as the active intermediaries:† for the craft guilds, although commercial institutions controlling the hierarchy of labour, themselves had a religious basis. So accustomed are we to a state of mind which regards all work as an odious necessity, to be reduced to a minimum, that a mentality which regarded toil as itself a devotional exercise, a return of thanks to the Creator for the endowments of skill and bodily health, is well-nigh inconceivable. Yet that was the unquestioned view of the guilds, all of which existed in the service of a Patron Saint as well as for the better conduct of trade and the regulation of employment.[17] We talk about the Merchant Taylors Company and mean a group of businessmen. Mediaeval members of that Company thought of themselves as the Fraternity of St. John the Baptist, under whose patronage they worked and to whom they prayed. A guild chapel was *de rigueur* and also the provision of funds to pay a priest to serve its users.[18]

In these circumstances it is surely arguing against all reason to assume that there should have been any fundamental conflict of opinion about either the purpose or nature of the liturgical plays between the monastic begetters of them, the secular clergy who were first called upon to assist, and the lay brethren of the craft-fraternities who eventually assumed responsibility for financing and producing them. The point at issue is simply that in the Middle Ages a layman's attitude to something of ecclesiastical origin and purpose was not, *a priori*, secular. The steady growth of religious plays from the tenth to the thirteenth century testifies to their popularity: and that, in my view, is adequate reason for the monas-

* Chaucer, *Miller's Tale*, lines 1–200. Chaucer does not say whether Absolon acted in Latin or in English: but his Latinity is scarcely to be doubted. See pp. 143–4 below.

† See Ch. VIII, pp. 293–4, Ch. IX, p. 313 below.

tic churches, first to seek assistance from the secular clergy and then, at a later date, to extend the invitation to the guilds who would be more than ready to accept. Collaboration was a natural gesture within the fabric of mediaeval society.

The evidence points to this process beginning some time before any question of the existence of Miracle Cycles in English or Corpus Christi plays arises: that is, well before 1311.[19] Extension to incorporate the craft guilds could hardly happen before vernacular texts replaced the Latin ones. *

The Church favoured the plays developing along these lines for at least three reasons. From their inception they had been regarded as a form of worship, sometimes as praise, at other times as thanksgiving or intercession.[20] Scarcely less important, their popularity served as an encouragement to greater devotion. Thirdly, performance served to inform and educate. The guilds were ready to accept the invitation to assist when it came, since production of the plays, by virtue of pleasing God and the Saints, could not be anything but meritorious.† For individual members there was the additional good reason of enjoyment.

Another lesson which the Church had to learn in the course of legitimizing performances of religious plays outside the basilica was how best to accommodate the texts and stage-conventions to their changed environment. Anyone with practical knowledge of the theatre knows that an open-air performance raises problems of acoustics, optics and temperature. Sound waves travel in concentric circles outwards from the point of origin and continue to do so until they are finally assimilated into absorbent surfaces. Some surfaces, far from absorbing, reflect. Of all materials, wood, stone, glass and water reflect most sharply, giving what is known accordingly as 'a sharp acoustic'. This will produce reverberation and echo, dependent on the respective distances between the point of origin of the sound, the reflecting surface or surfaces and the receiving instrument. Absorbent surfaces, on the other hand, quickly swallow up and smother sound giving, by contrast, 'a dead acoustic'. Draperies, perforated or broken surfaces, and groups of people absorb sound in this way; and so does the earth's atmosphere itself, depending on the degree of relative humidity. Thus, reduced to its simplest dimensions, the acoustic problem involved in the change of locale for performances from inside a church to outside is the substitution of a dead acoustic for a sharp one. Since

* See pp. 142–6 below.
† See Ch. VIII, pp. 293–5 below.

audibility is a factor of prime concern to any audience, we should anticipate that some changes in the technical management of the plays would be introduced (if only by trial and error) to provide a satisfactory open-air acoustic. It will suffice here to cite only the most obvious of such inevitable changes, the relaxing of obligatory chanting in favour of spoken dialogue.* Circumstances external to the text accompany another aspect of the change of locale from an interior to an exterior environment, the optics of stage performance. Inside a church the walls of the building circumscribe the playing space and serve to focus the attention of spectators upon it. In the open air there is no such ready-made control of spatial proportions. Any that exist, either laterally, vertically, or in depth, are superimposed by the producer, partly in his choice of site and partly in such structural alterations within it as he may choose to make.

We see these principles, both optical and acoustic, at work in Cornwall, where amphitheatres provided a solution to both kinds of problem. Spectators sitting round the circumference of a circle, as at some Tournaments, were provided with both the best general acoustic and a good view of a concentrated acting area. Nor, if the MS. which contains the stage plan for the production of *The Castle of Perseverance* is to be believed, was this method of dealing with them confined to the extreme south-west.†

There remain the problems created by the impact of the seasons upon the plays, the hazards of rain and frost. In England both are normally more real and of longer likely duration than in latitudes further south. Neither performers nor spectators are willing to submit voluntarily to either of these discomforts. Open-air performances are accordingly restricted to the summer months in England, and organizers, if they are wise, will do what they can to protect both their audience and their actors' costumes from thunderstorms or intermittent drizzle.

Granted this simple premise, it follows that any decision to present liturgical plays outside the church must have carried with it the likelihood of consequent dislocation of many of them from their

---

* It is worth observing that when Latin ceased to be chanted it would become far more noticeably Latin and unintelligible to an audience not skilled in that tongue, which fact would of itself promote pressure for its translation into English.

† Richard Southern, in *The Mediaeval Theatre in the Round*, argues this case very persuasively. The 1969 revival of the Cornish Cycle finally settled the point.

appropriate Red Letter Days in the Christian Calendar. April and May are risky months as far as English weather is concerned, but the Christian Calendar was very obliging in its provision of summer Festivals, if 'fixed' Saints' Days are added to the major 'floating' Feasts of Ascension, Pentecost (or Whitsun) and Trinity Sunday.[*] At the start of the fourteenth century yet another summer festival was added to the Calendar to celebrate the miracle of Eucharistic Redemption—the Feast of Corpus Christi— prescribed for the first Thursday following Trinity Sunday. Although promulgated by Pope Urban IV in 1264, formal observance of it was delayed for nearly fifty years until it was made effective by his successor, Clement V, at the Council of Vienne in 1311.[21] According to the annals of the Monastery Church of St. Peter of Gloucester, now Gloucester Cathedral, the Feast was established 'generaliter . . . per totam ecclesiam anglicanum' by 1318.[22] And this, I think, brings us very close to the ultimate reason for the growth of religious plays presented in secular environments during the thirteenth and fourteenth centuries; for what these plays shared in common with the long debate surrounding the establishment of this new Festival was an evangelistic concern with the need for repentance to obtain salvation while time permitted it. As Hardin Craig pointed out in *English Religious Drama* (1955), the establishment of the Corpus Christi plays in England was 'a conscious and deliberate community act. Why,' he asks, 'should such an establishment have been suggested by the Festival of Corpus Christi?' His answer to this question supplies good reason for regarding the Festival as the possibly coincidental, but effective, catalysis which, before the close of the fourteenth century, opinion in many places was seeking in order to resolve the future of the plays:

'The service of Corpus Christi is theologically and ritualistically a consummation of the entire plan of salvation, and the grand cycle of religious themes from the Fall of Adam to the Ascension of the Saviour and the Passion-play theme as developed at Easter were an objectivization of the same grand theme. It epitomized schematically and sometimes imperfectly, but nevertheless adequately, the service of the liturgical year.'[23]

The long discussions about the desirability of the Festival which

[*] St. Anne's Day, the Nativity of St. John the Baptist and St. Peter's Day are the most important: 26th July, 24th June and 29th June respectively. See *EES*, III, Appendix B for a full table of major Feast Days.

preceded its eventual establishment on the grounds of bringing all Christians, priests and laymen, face to face with the cosmic nature of Christian doctrine, point logically enough to a likely association with the plays, since the plays provided a unique and ready made opportunity for laymen to participate actively in this great act of faith. V. A. Kolve in his detailed examination in *The Play Called 'Corpus Christi'* (1966) of the Papal Bulls that established the new Feast carried Craig's surmise to the point of proof. Neither of these scholars, however, claimed that we must therefore assume that the Cycles came automatically to be composed and performed simultaneously with the inauguration of the Feast. Indeed, there was no obvious point within the liturgy of Corpus Christi calling for presentation of plays: moreover, no standard form of observance, beyond the institution of a procession, was ever authorized. A Parisian Council reacted to the new Feast as follows: 'As to the solemn procession . . . we prescribe nothing at present and leave all concerning it to the devotion of the clergy and the people.' This latitude of interpretation within a specific frame, allowing local enterprise and invention ample liberty to supply the appropriate detail, is paralleled in the development of Royal Entries. As we have seen, not only did the uniformity of the triumphal arch fail to supersede the original heterogeneous stages of London streets until 1603, but never were any hard-and-fast rules established, applicable in London and the provinces or in any single city, concerning the scale or detail of the reception.[24] Only the riding itself conformed to a standard pattern. The detail of the reception within that formula was left to the municipality to organize according to its financial and other resources.

What is certain about any ceremonial procession in the Middle Ages is that a strict order of precedence was observed. As an example, I have already quoted Richard Maydiston's account of Richard II's reception into London in 1377.* From our standpoint, what is important is that each guild rode in the procession as a corporate body: and, not content with displaying its identity by the wearing of livery, carried with it manufactured symbols of trade and dedication. If this could happen by 1298 in a civic riding, what would be more natural than to adapt the custom to suit a devotional riding instituted some twenty years later?

My suggestion is that it was in fact in this way that the trade

* The ceremonial and its antiquity are fully discussed by Withington, *English Pageantry*, I, pp. 11–43. In Chester, this applied with equal force to the various orders of clergy resident in the city. See Morris, *Chester*, p. 146.

guilds first became associated with particular devotional plays. If the Fishmongers in 1313 could carry a large ship in procession with them to greet Queen Isabella, why should the Shipwrights of Newcastle or the Water Drawers of Chester not carry Noah's Ark with them, at first simply painted on a banner and then as a three-dimensional model, when riding at Corpus Christi shortly afterwards? The carrying of a symbol of this kind, appropriate both to the craft concerned and its devotional duty on the day in question, simply adds to the pageantry of the occasion and in no way obliges performance of a text. Needless to say, sooner or later someone, more especially the Parish Clerks, was certain to suggest that this be done: and, where the civic ridings of the Royal Entries are concerned, this suggestion was made, put into practice by 1377, and adopted generally.[25] Discounting, for the moment, the mischievous Chester 'tradition', we have no firm evidence to prove that plays were regularly acted on Corpus Christi Day before that year: we know that the practice probably began a little earlier and spread widely after it, giving to the plays the name of the Feast. We know also that once this had happened it became necessary to safeguard the procession from seeming an anticlimax.

Once this hypothesis can be entertained there is every reason to believe that the whole subsequent story of the staging of Corpus Christi plays alias Miracle Cycles, may be traced in the parallel development of the Royal Entry and the Lord Mayor's Show. The major obstacle to entertaining it is the four-hundred-year-old Chester tradition. Since this is so, I must now devote a little space to recapitulate the very effective manner in which Professor Salter has demolished it and throw in some bricks of my own. This involves jumping forward in time by some two hundred odd years to discuss documents of sixteenth-century provenance.

(b) *Refutation of the Chester 'Tradition'*

The validity of the Chester tradition that Corpus Christi plays (in this context, a Miracle Cycle) were first translated into English and acted in 1327–28 rests on the post-Reformation Banns of 1600 for a performance which does not seem to have taken place; the Proclamation of a performance of the plays in 1575 which, in the event, proved to be the last presentation recorded; and sundry other documents of *subsequent* origin.[26] The most important is a description of the method of performance written some thirty-five years after the last recorded performance. Let us first be clear what is meant by 'Banns' and 'Proclamation'. Both of them are, in a sense, police documents: that is to say, they are primarily concerned with the conduct of performances. The Proclamation, as one might expect, is a form of advertisement. After announcing and justifying a forthcoming performance, it concludes: '*Wherefore* maister maier in the Kyngez name straitly chargeth and commandeth . . .' etc.—the remaining remarks being directed at the prospective audience who are told to behave peaceably on pain of imprisonment.

The Banns, by contrast, are intended primarily to instruct the performers in the whys and wherefores of their task. Transcriptions of all the relevant copies of the Proclamation and the Banns are given in Appendix D.

One may presume that both documents were read aloud with fitting ceremonial prior to every intended performance: and that, in consequence, both followed a set formula which would only be altered or modified when there was some special reason for a change in the ordering of events. What is important to us is that, in the troubled times following the dissolution of the monasteries, no document could reflect more sensitively the changed circumstances of performance. It is the greater pity therefore that scholars have relied for so long on transcripts of them from Corporation archives made by Canon R. H. Morris in 1894, which have recently been shown to be very inaccurate and misleading.* One result has been to give far more weight than is justifiable to the evidence of the Banns of 1600. The following extract is the passage in question.

(1)

Reverende Lordes and ladyes all,
That at this tyme here, assembled bee,
by this message understande you shall,
That some tymes there was mayor of this Citie
Sir John Arnway, Knyght, who most worthilye
contented hym selfe to sett out in playe
The devise of one done Rondall, moonke of Chester abbe.

* The blunt truth is that Chambers incorporated these transcripts in his *Med. Stage* without checking them and everyone else has followed suit since, until F. M. Salter read the originals for himself and noticed the discrepancies. See also G. R. Owst, *Literature and Pulpit in Mediaeval England*, pp. 475 and 476.

(2)

This moonke—moonkelike in Scriptures well seene,
in storyes travilled with the beste sort—
In pagentes set fourth apparently to all eyne
the old and newe testament with liuelye comforth,
Interminglinge therewith onely, to make sporte,
some thinge, not warranted by any writt,
which to gladd the hearers, he woulde men take yt.

(3)

This matter he Abbrevited into playes twenty foure;
and every playe of the matter gaue but a taste,
leavinge for better learninge the Scircumstance to accomplishe,
for all his proceedinges may appeare to be in haste,
yet all-together unprofitable his labour he did not waste.
For at this daye and ever he deserveth the fame
which all monkes deserves, professinge that name.

(4)

These Storyes of the Testament at this tyme, you knowe,
in A common Englishe tongue neuer read nor harde;
yet thereof in these pagentes to make open shewe,
This moonke and moonke was nothing Afreayde
with feare of hanginge, brenninge or Cuttinge off heade,
to sett out that all maye disserne and see,
and parte good be lefte (?), beleeve you mee.

(5)

As in this Citie divers yeares the haue bene set out,
soe at this tyme of penticoste, called whitsontyde,
Allthough to all the Citie followe labour and coste,
yet god giuinge leave, that tyme shall you in playe,
ffor three dayes together, begynninge one mondaye,
see these pagentes played to the beste of theire skill,
wher to supply all wantes, shalbe noe wantes of good will.

(6)

As all that shall see them, shall most welcome be,
soe all that here them, wee most humble praye
not to compare this matter or Storie
with the age or tyme wherin we presentlye staye,
but in the tyme of Ignorance wherin we did straye;
then doe I compare that this land throughout
non had the like nor the like dose sett out.

(7)

If the same be likeinge to the comons all,
then our desier is to satisfie—for that is all our game—
yf noe matter or shewe therof speciall
doe not please, but misslike the most of the trayne,
goe backe I saye to the firste tyme againe,
then shall you finde: the fyne witt, at this day aboundinge,
at that day and that age had verye small beinge.

(8)

Condempne not our matter where grosse wordes you here,
which ymporte at this day small sence or understandinge,
as sometyme 'postie,' 'lewtie,' 'in good manner,' or 'in feare'
with such like wilbe uttered in there speeches speakeing,
at this tyme those speeches carried good likeninge,
tho at this tyme you take them spoken at that tyme,
as well matter as wordes, then is all well and fyne.

(9)

This worthy knyghte Arnway, then mayor of this Citie,
this order toke, as declare to you I shall:
that by twentye fower occupations, artes, craftes or misterie,
these pagente(s) shulde be played after breeffe rehearsal,
for everye pagente A carriage to be provyded withall,
in which sorte we porpose this whitsontyde
our pageante into three partes to devyde. *

Less faith might have been placed in this record than actually
was, if closer attention had been paid to the earlier Banns for the
Cycle and the Proclamation of it which also survive.

Professor Salter has shown that in 1532 it was found necessary
to delete certain words and phrases from the Proclamation and to
undertake further revision in 1540. The deletions and corrections
stand under the signature of William Newhall, Clerk of the
Pentice (Town Hall) of Chester, who took office in 1532.[27]

The points of major consequence arising from the Proclamations
are:

---

* The last three lines are clearly ambiguous and have been misinterpreted
by historians to mean that each guild had its own waggon, whereas in fact
waggons were shared. The consequences to an understanding of production
methods are as serious as those which derive from accepting the stanzas
about Higden at their face value. See pp. 171 and 296 below.

A. That of 1532:

    (i) It contains no mention whatsoever of Randle Higden.

    (ii) It attributes translation of the plays to Sir Henry Francis 'monk of this monastery'.

    (iii) Certain words and phrases referring to Papal Bulls and Indulgences in respect of the audience are deleted.

B. That of 1540:

    (iv) The word 'dissolved' is inserted following monastery and the word 'sometyme' before it.

C. That of post-1540:

    (v) All reference both to Sir Henry Francis and the Pope is expurgated.[28]

These changes and their sequence indicate clearly enough the context in which the alterations were made, the Reformation. In 1531 Henry VIII was acknowledged as the Supreme Head of the Church in England and a year later Newhall adapts the Proclamation to conform with the change by deleting all reference to Papal control over the conduct of the audience. In 1539 the monastery was dissolved, leaving the Mayor, the Town Clerk and the Corporation in sole charge of the arrangements for performances of the plays. The fact of the dissolution is noted: and all remaining suggestions of Papist connections are subsequently deleted.

The rest of the story may be traced through a comparison of the pre- and post-Reformation Banns.[29] Higden's name does not figure in the former any more than it does in any of the Proclamations. Sir John Arnway, however, appears consistently in all the Proclamations and both sets of Banns.*

The sensible conclusion reached by Professor Salter is that the Corporation took over responsibility for the plays from the monastery sometime between 1530 and 1540. Commercially it was in the City's interest to ensure the continuance of performances; but, with charges of heresy abroad and with fines, imprisonment and even the death penalty attaching to it, continuance was only feasible at the price of expurgating the Roman Catholic origins and nature of the Cycle. Accordingly, all references to Papal sanction and interest were deleted, involving the disappearance of Henry Francis from the picture. A substitute for Francis was found in Randle

---

* Although there are two versions, one of these has been tampered with in the same way as the early Proclamation, i.e. certain passages have been deleted in the pre-Reformation copy. Strictly speaking, therefore, we have three copies. See pp. 133–5 above and pp. 346–7 below.

Higden, author of *Polychronicon*, Chester's most renowned man of letters, and consequently an appropriate 'author' of the plays. For good measure, Higden is reported as being if not a Lollard, at least as good a Protestant as it was possible for a monk to have been. *

Higden and Francis were as near contemporaries as made no difference to the Tudor mind. Higden who, according to the tradition, wrote or translated the Cycle *c.* 1328, died in 1364: Francis was senior monk at Chester Abbey in 1377 and 1382, and was made Papal Chaplain in 1389. To our minds, however, this small difference of fifty years or so is of great importance in its consequences: for if we restore authorship to Francis as the early Proclamations testify before they were tampered with, it brings the initiation of the Chester Cycle into line with our records of the other Cycles.

There remains the problem of Sir John Arnway's position in the tangle. Whether associated with Higden or Francis (and his name is the only constant) he seems an anachronistic figure since he died in 1278.[30] Professor Salter thinks Arnway's name may have been linked to the plays as a first step towards taking the credit for them away from Francis. I do not wish to be of contrary mind, yet I confess to not being satisfied about this particular step in the argument†—especially since a better alternative exists.

I have said earlier that the word 'control' must be used cautiously, as it is ambiguous in the context of plays. Control of the text is often in independent hands from control of the conditions of performance. I suggest now that Arnway's name came into the tradition quite rightfully as the first person representing civic authority in Chester to take performance of religious plays out of the context of a strictly ecclesiastical festival and to place them within that of a civic occasion of major importance. If so, the Church had reason to be grateful for the wider audience and instructional opportunity attendant on such recognition, while the citizens had equal reason for gratitude, since it opened the way to co-operation with the Church in the production of religious plays which was, in time, to lead to their active participation and great commercial advantage.

I am aware that what I have suggested about Arnway's place in the tradition is largely guesswork. In putting it forward, however,

* A cue had been provided earlier by Bishop Bale, author of the violent Protestant polemical drama, *Kyng Johan*. See p. 116 above: also p. 239 below.

† If his name is a Reformation invention, why does it figure in both the pre-Reformation Proclamation and Banns *before* they were tampered with?

for serious consideration I have some evidence which, if it does not amount to factual proof, is at least corroborative. None of it is new. It has been in print for a long while, but it has not been used.

If, for the time being, we try to forget all preconceived ideas of the development of the plays derived from an approach through texts and consider instead the substantial, but hitherto unnoticed evidence of conditions governing Festivals in Chester, some surprising facts emerge.

The most important, by far, is that a Midsummer Fair was established in Chester, long before Corpus Christi was ever thought of, probably indeed before dramatic tropes were ever interpolated into the liturgy. This Fair and market was held in the week of 24th June, the Nativity of St. John the Baptist, and was known in the district as St. Werburgh's Fair. It took this name, as so many English Fairs still do, from its topographical situation. In short, the Chester Midsummer Fair was held annually on ground owned by the Benedictine convent of St. Werburgh: the great open space before the Abbey Gates.[31] It was precisely on this spot, in the fifteenth and sixteenth centuries, that the plays of the Chester Cycle were not only proclaimed, but given their first performance every year.

The obvious inference is that, contrary to all previous argument, in Chester at least, the trade guilds' vested interest in a Midsummer association with the Church *preceded* the Church's interest in the guilds as possible executants of its plays. The frequent bickering over the government of the Fair came to a head in 1288, when the matter was taken to arbitration. The award made on that occasion (which survives in B.M. MS. Harl. 2148, f. 28) is significant to our purpose: for in it, although the Abbot successfully maintained his claim for jurisdiction over the Fair, he conceded certain rights to the citizens.[32] The date of this settlement lies within ten years of that now established for Sir John Arnway's death. Despite further bickering, this settlement held good for the next 220 years. In 1509 an appeal was made by the citizens against the Abbot and an award made substantially curtailing his powers, notably his jurisdiction over St. Werburgh's Fair. This proved binding until the monastery was itself swept away in the general dissolution of 1539.[33]

The history of the Midsummer Fair confirms the view that the shift of power from ecclesiastical to civic authority in Chester was very slow and gradual: also that the Abbey did not lightly surrender its prerogatives. This, however, is not all that the story of the Fair can tell us. There is the vital matter of date to be considered, in relation to Liturgical Feasts. Since Easter is a movable Feast, Whitsun, Trinity Sunday and the adjoining Festival of Corpus Christi are also movable and vary, with Easter, over a span of five weeks. If Easter falls at its earliest or at its latest, 21st March or 25th April, this is what happens to the other Feasts.

EASTER	WHITSUN	TRINITY SUNDAY	CORPUS CHRISTI
March 24	May 12	May 19	May 23
April 25	June 13	June 20	June 24

It will be seen that Corpus Christi could occasionally coincide with the Nativity of St. John the Baptist, a fixed Festival in the Calendar (24th June and Midsummer) which in Chester was the date of St. Werburgh's Fair. Whitsun would then fall some ten days earlier. In general, however, Corpus Christi Day was more likely to precede Midsummer Day by at least a fortnight, with Whitsun two weeks earlier still.

The question arises, therefore, why the plays are associated with the liturgical festivals of Whitsun and Corpus Christi and not with the Midsummer Fair.* If, as has been generally assumed, the guilds took over responsibility for the plays as soon as they acquired cyclic proportions (at the start of the fourteenth century), why did these same guilds not choose to produce the plays in association with their own Midsummer Fair and market? A ready made audience from the City and County Palatine was then assured. Moreover, since the Abbot held jurisdiction over the fairground itself—the area before the Abbey Gates where the plays were actually proclaimed and played at Whitsun—a more appropriate place, as well as time, could hardly have been found. Yet throughout the lengthy and detailed records of the controversy about the Fair between 1093 and 1509, the many Charters and Plea Rolls are uniformly silent on the subject of the plays.

The common-sense conclusion is that the guilds had no say in the matter. In other words, responsibility for choosing the most appropriate occasion for performances rested with the clergy: and in their choice they expressed their own interest in liturgical appropriateness. The sixteenth-century Proclamations and Banns, both pre- and post-Reformation, confirm this supposition in general and

* After the Reformation and the suppression of the Cycle, Midsummer Day replaced Whitsun quickly as the holiday marked with dramatic activity. One or two of the old cyclic plays were even transferred to it.[34]

suggest in particular that initiative in the matter lay with the Abbot.

It remains to consider whether ecclesiastical responsibility stopped there, and if so, when it was thus curtailed. I have already argued that it is a mistake to regard the allocation of responsibility as a straight choice between monks and laymen. The division of the clergy into regular and secular orders, with the further division of the regular clergy into orders of monks and of friars, is an important one in any mediaeval context and a vital one here. Before we accept the standard assumption that the guilds were called in because the monastic clergy were numerically inadequate to tackle a full Cycle of plays, we might put the matter to a simple test, and enquire how many clergy actually were resident in say, Chester.

We know that *c.* 1250 the number of Benedictine monks at St. Werburgh's was increased to forty.[35] We also know that, at the dissolution, there were in addition seven Grey Friars, five Black Friars, and ten Carmelite, or White, Friars; while, at the Collegiate Church of St. John there were seven canons, four vicars, and a clerk under their Dean.[36] This makes a total of seventy-four resident regular clergy excluding the nuns of St. Mary's Priory. If we add to this figure the secular clergy (priests, deacons, and clerks) who can scarcely have numbered less than thirty, we have an overall total of at least a hundred. I know from the practical exercise of producing the Passion and Resurrection Plays from the *Ludus Coventriae* and the whole Cornish Cycle that both can be mounted comfortably with a cast of about fifty actors. On the premise then that in Arnway's mayoralty at least a hundred clergy were resident in Chester, there is no reason to suppose that the Abbey could not play the Cycle without enlisting laymen from the craft guilds.

The evidence usually cited for dating cyclic performance of the plays and the consequent enlistment of lay assistance is Giuliano da Cividale's account of performances at Cividale in 1298 and 1303. It is in Latin and quoted in full by Chambers in a footnote.[37] I can only assume that subsequent historians have accepted Chambers' opinion without troubling to translate the passage into English: for although it provides the fullest evidence of cyclic performance, it equally proves that lay assistance was not required.

'In the year of Our Lord 1298 on the 25th of May, that is to say on Whitsunday and on the two following days, plays on the Life of Christ—the Passion, Resurrection, Ascension, Descent of the Holy Spirit and the coming of Christ to Judgement—were performed in the Court[a] of our Lord Archbishop of Austria, honorably and praiseworthily, by the Clergy of the area. . . .[b]

'In the year 1303 a performance was given by the Clergy or by the Chapter of the Diocese,[c] or rather, performances as follows: first, the play of the Creation of our first parents; then that of the Annunciation to the Blessed Virgin, that of the Nativity and many others, that of the Passion and Resurrection, of the Ascension and Pentecost, that of Antichrist and others,[d] and lastly that of Christ's coming to Judgement. And the above said plays were presented solemnly in the Court of our Lord Archbishop on Whitsunday and on the two following days, in the presence of the reverend Lord Ottobono, Archbishop of Aquileia, the Lord Jacobus Bishop of La Guardia, and the Lord Ottonelli (*? of Cividale*), and many other great men of the region and of the town of Friuli, the seventeenth day of May.'*

This account substantiates five points of cardinal importance to the present argument.

The performances at Cividale were (1) cyclic; (2) at Whitsun; (3) by the clergy; (4) in the *curia* of the Archbishop; and (5) made notable by the number and status of the spectators.

If the clergy could achieve a Whitsun performance of a full Cycle without lay assistance and could present it in a single place at Cividale, why should it have been otherwise at Chester? It seems to me improper to argue that Arnway's name enters the Chester story because he either instituted lay participation in the performances or gave permission for them to be presented at several

---

* Anno domini Mcclxxxxviii die vii exeunte Maio, videlicet in die Pentecostes et in aliis duobus sequentibus diebus, facta fuit Repraesentatio Ludi .Christi, videlicet Passionis, Resurrectionis, Ascensionis, Adventus Spiritus Sancti, Adventus Christi ad iudicium, in curia[a] Domini Patriarchae Austriae civitatis, honorifice et laudabiliter, per Clerum civitatensems[b] . . .

Anno Mccciii facta fuit per Clerum, sive per Capitulum civitatense,[c] Repraesentatio: sive factae fuerunt Repraesentationes infra scriptae: In primis, de Creatione primorum parentum; deinde de Annunciatione Beatae Virginis, de Partu et aliis multis, et de Passione et Resurrectione, Ascensione et Adventu Spiritus Sancti, et de Antichristo et aliis,[d] et demum de Adventu Christi ad iudicium. Et predicta facta fuerunt solemniter in curia domini Patriarchae in festo Pentecostes cum aliis duobus diebus sequentibus, praesente r.d. Ottobono patriarcha aquileiensi d. Jacobo q.d. Ottonelli de Civitate episcopo concordiensi, et aliis multis nobilibus de civitatibus et castris Foroiulii, die xv exeunte Maio.' *Cronaca Friulana* of Giuliano da Cividale.

stations in the city when there is no proof of either and when the collateral evidence argues uniformly against it. As we have seen, there were clergy enough in Chester to tackle a Cycle; performance of the Cycle in the fifteenth and sixteenth centuries was linked with Whitsun and not with the Midsummer Fair; and, unless the plays had been translated into English before the fourteenth century began (and no one has ever suggested this), laymen could hardly have been used as actors. A more legitimate explanation, therefore, is that Arnway took the initiative, possibly in collaboration with the vigorous Abbot Simon, in making Whitsun into an occasion for the performance of a group of plays outside St. Werburgh's Abbey:* that in Chester, as at Cividale, while performances continued to be given on ground over which the Abbot's Court was supreme, the Mayor attended with 'aliis multis nobilibus' from the City and County Palatine. The resulting influx of visitors would not only involve *The King's Peace*, as opposed to *The Peace of God* governing Sundays and Festivals like Whitsun, but bring to the citizens substantial commercial benefits. Viewed in this light, the plays, if repeated as an annual event—although in Latin and by the clergy—would come to be thought of by the citizens as comparable with the Midsummer Fair in the benefits accruing from increased trade: and Arnway, as the initiator of this new civic event, well worthy of a place in the annals.

(c) *From Whitsun to Corpus Christi and from Latin into English*

If it can now be granted that in England, around the turn of the thirteenth into the fourteenth century, a group of religious plays could be performed during the summer Festival of Pentecost by the local clergy and that this event was regarded as something of exceptional civic importance, then I think we have a firm base from which to examine the remaining problems.

The standard assumptions that the institution of the Feast of Corpus Christi itself provoked the playing of the Cycle in England and that the clergy were numerically inadequate to tackle it can only be maintained in flat defiance of the evidence just discussed.

In trying to find alternative answers which accord better with the facts, we can at least narrow down the period to an approximate span of a hundred years: from Arnway's death in 1278 to the

---

* In doing this he would not have encouraged anything more radical than what had already taken place at Beverley half a century earlier: see pp. 124–5 above.

first known record of Corpus Christi Plays, Beverley, 1377, and York, 1378. If we accept the Gloucester date of 1318 for the general observance of Corpus Christi Day as a major Festival, the period is narrowed further to some sixty years; in human terms, approximately two generations. At the start of it, there is good reason to think that performance of a full cycle in Latin could be given in any English city where sufficient clergy were resident from which to cast it as easily as at Cividale: at the end of it, that, in Chester at least, permission had been obtained from the Pope to translate the Latin plays into English, while at York the laity possibly had a share in the production.[38]*

With the twin problems reduced to within this comparatively narrow time-span (1318–1378), it is tempting to seek solutions that are dogmatic and universal. To do this, however, would I think be the one sure way to fail: for we must bear in mind that not only was the form of celebrating the new Feast of Corpus Christi left largely to local enterprise, but that the period in question was one of social revolution, marked in the middle by the ravages of the Black Death and, at the end, by the early Protestantism of Wyclif's Lollards, and the Peasants' Revolt. These three upheavals in the national life militated against conformity and affected the clergy as closely as the laity. Moreover, we know for certain that vernacular plays, both secular and religious, were being acted in England during this period.

An example will suffice to illustrate the point. It is known that special guilds were formed, 'religious and social rather than industrial in character', charged with the management of the Corpus Christi procession and known as Corpus Christi Guilds.[39] A guild of this sort at Cambridge, c. 1350, was responsible for a *Ludus Filiorum Israelis*.[40] In the light of this fact, it is tempting to suppose that the Corpus Christi Guilds were everywhere the intermediary between clerical and lay production of the Cycles and, consequently, between Latin and vernacular performances. Corpus Christi Day, after all, fell only ten days after Whitsun and it could be argued on theological grounds that the plays, as a Cycle, were more appropriate to this new summer feast than to Whitsun.

---

* The word 'anciently' in the York records is the crux here. I think we should guard against interpreting it as 'for hundreds of years'. Substituting a mediaeval for a modern historical perspective, such a phrase could as easily mean 'a generation ago', 'in my father's or grandfather's memory', i.e. twenty to thirty years. See Ch. III, p. 108 above.

Furthermore, records from Lincoln and Ipswich make it clear that the secular clergy and not the regular clergy determined the conduct and actions of such guilds.[41] As parish priests and clerks (in both senses of the word) they were men of the world having close professional ties with the craft guilds. Through this channel, if anywhere, fusion could easily take place. Yet against this we must set the knowledge that at York no Corpus Christi Guild was officially founded until 1408, long after the records testify to the existence of a Corpus Christi Cycle associated with the craft guilds and a Paternoster play in English.

The source of the latter information is especially interesting. It occurs in the *De Officio Pastorali* of John Wyclif, written in 1378: 'herfore freris hav taught in England the Paternoster in English tunge as men seyen in the pleye of Yorke.'[42] Factually, this is the earliest reference to a religious play in English. The year coincides closely with Sir Henry Francis' voyage from Chester to Rome and the start of records of performances of miracle plays by craft guilds elsewhere in England.

The most reasonable hypothesis is that English playmakers followed French example in first inserting occasional French (and possibly English) verses into the Latin texts, 'as decorative touches, extrinsic rather than intrinsic, probably intended to sharpen the attention of the audience.'* Any such process was certain to be accelerated by the social upheavals of the years 1350–1380. The case against deliberate and wholesale *translation* from Latin directly into English is strengthened by a strange linguistic dichotomy. While we know that it was only after the first onslaught of the Black Death (1348) that English took the place of French as the language of educated society,[43] English had just as certainly been the language in which preachers had cemented every aspect of daily life to Christian theology in their sermons for a full hundred years before the Black Death.†

This phenomenon seems scarcely to have been noticed by historians of dramatic literature. Yet its existence should surely raise the question of whether the plays ever were directly translated: that is to say, played in Latin one day and in a literal English translation the next. It is, of course, the mischievous Chester Banns of 1600 which have led historians to accept this idea without serious question.

* G. Frank, *The Mediaeval French Drama*, 1954, p. 57.
† See *EES*, III, Ch. VI.

These Storyes of the Testament at this tyme, you knowe,
in A common Englishe tongue neuer read nor harde;
yet thereof in these pagentes to make open shewe,
This moonke and moonke (*sic*) was nothing Afreayde
with feare of hanginge, brenninge (*burning*) or Cutting off heade,
to sett out that all maye disserne and see,
and parte good be lefte (?), beleeve you mee.

This is a flat lie. The Testament, New and Old, had been *preached* in English from countless pulpits in churches and in churchyards for generations before Higden was born. * And why should Higden have feared being burnt for heresy in 1327? This penalty was not placed on the Statute Book till 1401. William Sawtré was burnt in that year, being the first known victim. If we return to the Pre-Reformation Banns and Proclamation, the smell of Smithfield, which permeates those of 1600, is notably lacking. We are simply told that Sir Henry Francis 'devised and made' these plays representing 'diverse stories of the bible'. There is no mention of translation.

I suggest therefore that the idea of direct translation is a mistaken one. It was invented in a vain attempt to give plays, which had already landed two Mayors of Chester in serious trouble, the semblance of being forerunners of the Reformation and, thus, to make performance of them possible in 1600. Students of English, therefore, would be well advised to abandon the tack of 'translation' and to turn their enquiries about the origin of the plays in other directions. In the present state of factual knowledge the most profitable course to pursue would seem to be the possibility of parallel development of the English sermon and the religious play in English in the fourteenth century alongside of the already substantial Latin cyclic drama. For, granted an *alternative* vernacular drama, closely modelled on the liturgical Latin drama but not a literal translation of it, and written by ubiquitous friars rather than by officiating priests, a path out of the labyrinth becomes clear.† It

---

* In England, indeed, where the golden age of vernacular religious drama coincides, so far as existing records suggest, with the golden age of vernacular preaching, the parallels between them are far too numerous and arresting to be mistaken for mere coincidences . . . overwhelming similarities in the actual handling of the matter, the details of certain characters and topics, the very texture and language. . . .' (G. R. Owst, *Literature and Pulpit*, p. 485.) See also pp. 213 *et seq.* concerning the preaching of satire and complaint in the thirteenth century.[44]

† See Ch. IX, pp. 316–17 below.

would not only explain why, despite local variants, the surviving cycles have so much in common, but also provide the circumstances through which the religious stage of liturgical origin could become intimately associated both with the Feast of Corpus Christi, and with laymen during the fourteenth century.

Turning our attention now to these latter matters, it is important not to overlook the fourfold pressures on the traditional fabric of English society occasioned by the growth of cities and a wealthy bourgeois audience, the Black Death and the incipient Protestantism of such men as John Ball and John Wyclif, and, finally, the Peasants' Revolt of 1381.[45] I do not wish to argue any direct connection between these events and the development of the Corpus Christi plays; but, as a social environment for the dual transition from Latin to the vernacular and from clerical to lay performance, years of such startling social violence and change are important as being hostile to pattern and conformity of any sort. In such a context, any institution that was not deeply rooted in tradition—and the Festival of Corpus Christi was then but a novice on probation —would certainly be affected in proportion to the degree of pressure exercised within the local area.

There can be no doubt that the creation of the new Feast of Corpus Christi exercised a gravitational force of exceptional magnitude upon existing religious plays or Cycles of plays would not, in time, have come to take the name of Feast as they did. Yet we still have to account for the fact that in some cases other summer Feast Days—St. Mark's Day at Beverley, St. Anne's Day at Lincoln, and Whitsun at Chester—took precedence over Corpus Christi as the major annual Festival associated with play production.[46]

Where the admittance of laymen as actors is concerned, it is unlikely that the Black Death of 1348 affected all areas identically. In some places the clergy may have particularly suffered its ravages, in others they may have escaped lightly. Was it possibly as an act of thanksgiving for being alive that the Cambridge Corpus Christi Guild performed the *Ludus Filiorum Israelis* in 1350? The *Exodus* was a much allegorized event, and the happy issue out of affliction which it betokened would supply an obvious motive to present it dramatically, to celebrate the slackening of the terrors of the plague in England. This was certainly the case with the *Mystère des Trois Doms* at Romans in 1509.* In Cambridge, as also

_____
* See p. 302 below.

in Oxford, of all places in the country, clergy enough were likely to have survived to perform groups of such plays or even a full cycle. In other cities or areas, the clergy may well have been faced with a choice of discontinuing the plays or calling on laymen to help them. And what are we to make of the satirical play prepared for performance in Exeter on a Sunday in August 1352 attacking the leather-workers for the over-pricing of their products which the Bishop sought to ban under threat of excommunication? Why the Bishop? Why excommunication? Why not the Mayor? And why not threats of fines and imprisonment?* The point at issue is that in a social upheaval of this kind, with its varying repercussions, may lie an explanation of the correspondingly varied calendar-dates with which performances are associated in different cities, of the lack of universal standard, conditions of performance, of the clergy surrendering a hitherto exclusive prerogative to laymen in some places but not in others. When all is said and done, it is this variety which confronts us in the records of the fourteenth century: and no explanation of a specific change in one place is wholly adequate that does not take into account the patent absence of such change elsewhere.

This argument applies with particular force to the question of how the craft guilds came to be responsible for performing and paying for the Cycles in most Northern and Midland cities, but not in Southern England. The parallel available to us of the development of the civic ridings for Royal Entries at least supplies a pointer to the answer.†

Since the distinguishing feature of the Corpus Christi celebrations was a procession‡ of the most formal kind, it is reasonable to suppose that the livery companies would carry with them not only the obligatory 'lights' or torches and banners, but more material symbols of their calling, as they were wont to do at civic celebrations. What could be more appropriate to the occasion than banners depicting a scriptural scene with which the craft guild had professional affinities? At York, for the Corpus Christi festival of 1397, the Chamberlain's Accounts include two items which strongly support this contention.

---

* See *EES*, III, Appendix C.
† See pp. 122–3 and 132 above.
‡ See pp. 130 and 131 above. Also R. Davies, *York Records in the Fifteenth Century*, 1893, Appendix.

'Et pro vexillo novo cum apparatu, xijs ijd.
Et pro pictura pagine, ijs.'*[47]

And if the symbol was on a banner, why not three-dimensionally as
a model on a small, portable rostrum or platform? Known as
'tabernacles' (sometimes as pageants), these portable shrines
figure often enough in Churchwardens' Accounts whenever porters
have to be paid to carry them or when carpenters, painters and
materials are needed to repair them. A convenient example of
banners, shrines and actors listed collectively in the context of
Corpus Christi festivities is supplied by Sherborne in Dorset
during the years 1511–48. Thus:

'1511   It(em) payed for the beryng of the Shrene on Corpus
           (Christi) day and drynk   v^d

1524/5   It(em) payd ffor halffe a yerde off bocoram to the
           banners   ij^d

1543   It(e)m paid to Henry Clarke for pynnes for the
           pleyer(e)s at Corpus (Christi) day   j^d

1548   It(e)m the bokes of corpus (Christi) play.'
           (*Malone Society Collections*, IX, 1971 (1977), 3–7).

Whether in terms of banners or, subsequently, in terms of shrines,
time alone is needed for association of biblical incident with particular guilds—for example, Noah with shipwrights, the Magi with
the Goldsmiths, or the Paradise Garden with the Grocers—to become accepted as customary: and once thus attached, it is an easy
step for the guilds to claim as 'their own' a particular scene or story
when called upon by the clergy to participate in the performance of
the plays. If they offered to pay the costs in order to secure 'their
scene', the claim would be hard to resist. What is more, the manner in which this association between guilds and scriptural scenes
had come about would suffice for the resulting plays to be called
Corpus Christi plays, whether actually acted on that Feast Day or
on some other summer Festival preferred for reasons of local convenience. Such a state of affairs, if not vouched for by factual proof

---

*   'And for a new banner with furnishings, 12/2d.
                    And for the pageant picture, 2/–.'
Cf. the Festival of the Palio at Siena, where the word *palio* (= banner) is
now used to describe a horse-race. The banner, invariably depicting a
religious subject, is still carried in the procession which precedes the race
and forms the cherished prize. Not only that, but each competing city-guild
or ward carries banners with distinctive emblems.

at every point, at least corresponds with the situation which confronts us in the surviving records of the later fourteenth, fifteenth and sixteenth centuries.

Traditional celebrations of this kind have a habit of growing more spectacular (and costly) as the years go by. This process is amply borne out by the guild records of the fifteenth and sixteenth centuries. The Banns to the cycles show how additional stories were added, and the Companies' account rolls tell how the expenses rose, forcing crafts to join together in presenting the plays if costs were to be met without involving excessive hardship.[48] From Wyclif's day onwards there were doubtless always 'Protestant' elements within the craft guilds as elsewhere who disapproved of what Bale was later to call 'popetly plays', but so long as performance of them drew vast crowds of country folk into the cities to see them and to spend their money, the plays would be firmly entrenched. The essential point is that the Elizabethan stage did not owe its greatness to having superseded something effete and unwanted, but rather to the fact that the religious stage had bequeathed it an audience trained in the conventions of a magnificent stage-craft.

During a span of some six hundred years (c. 975–1575), from the issue of the *Concordia Regularis* until the English Church decided to suppress its own child, the stages of growth are reasonably clear. Liturgical music-drama rooted in the principal liturgical Offices of the Church expanded to its own natural limits by the middle of the twelfth century when all those miracles specifically commemorated within the Calendar had been adorned with mimetic reincarnations of these events as acts of witness to reinforce faith in the truth of their occurrence. Slowly, as the Church became aware of the theatrical quality of some of the representations—more especially the extended *Officium Stellae*—it chose to rationalize this situation by permitting religious plays to multiply and expand on condition that any such addition to existing Offices was recognized as a play, *ludus*; that it was presented in the nave, a hall or in the open air and not in the sanctuary; and that it should be doctrinally directed to edify the ignorant or to exhort sinners to repent. Given this new teaching instrument and this new code of conduct, the majority of bishops in the course of the thirteenth century were ready to countenance new plays, whether in Latin or in the vernacular, just as they countenanced the activities of the newly established Mendicant Orders, as allies in their own battle to sustain faith and to combat vice and heresy.

149

The institution of the new Feast of Corpus Christi early in the fourteenth century, approximating in the date of its annual celebration to midsummer, served to gather this rapidly developing dramatic activity within the community around a single focal point—the Feast itself when all work ceased in order that thought might be concentrated on the redemptive power of the Eucharist—rather than to precipitate sudden and wholesale translation of the Latin Vulgate into vernacular plays, or of long sequences of existing Latin plays into an English cycle. Nevertheless help was sought from secular quarters in resolving the new and specifically theatrical problems of optics, acoustics and weather conditions, a move which opened to question whether judicial control of the performances rested with the ecclesiastical or civil courts, and whether a Festival that attracted large and distinguished audiences more nearly resembled a major civic occasion than a religious ceremony.

From the moment that the Feast was first celebrated, laymen, banded into representative professional groups, were invited to participate in the great procession distinguishing this new Festival, and to associate themselves with an appropriate scriptural incident which could be depicted and displayed on a banner. Wealthy guilds improved upon this by substituting a model of their scene for the simple painted banner. The next logical step was to substitute, if permitted, a *tableau vivant* for a *tableau mort*, and to create new guilds with special responsibilities for the conduct of the Feast in a particular diocese or parish: and we may assume this permission to have been readily granted where Corpus Christi Guilds or trade guilds were prepared to contribute practical skills and meet the financial costs. This change served only to enhance the popularity of the plays which, in turn, expanded the narrative content further and made it desirable to find a principle of selection: in England this became typological appropriateness.* Despite occasional dislocation and redistribution occasioned by changes in the trading fortunes of particular guilds, success attended these developments throughout the fifteenth century. Indeed, the plays were continuing to expand during the sixteenth, when the Reformation effected a schism between the two controlling interests, gown and town, which called it all to a halt.

This story has been reconstructed largely in terms of Chester; but, being Catholic and mediaeval, it can fairly be claimed as universal, and applied to England with variants appropriate to parti-

* See *EES*, III, pp. 41–3 and 83–7.

cular localities. And, granted this new chronology, it becomes possible to say something about the decoration and stage management of the English religious drama which may do its technicians a little more justice than they have received in the past.

4 Stages and Stage-conventions

I have tried to open to question some of the assumptions that have governed standard histories of mediaeval dramatic literature for so long, because they have played havoc with all attempts to re-construct not only the mediaeval stage and its conventions, but also those of Shakespeare and his contemporaries. To assume, for ex-ample, that the Miracle Cycles died of senility and decadence in-volves supposing that the Elizabethan stage was a novel product, born mysteriously out of the genius of the new age: and, since factual information is so scanty, many people naturally conclude that the quotation cited at the start of this chapter is a fair judge-ment on mediaeval stage craft. Agnosticism has also taken a share in colouring the popular view of the religious stage of the Middle Ages:

'Angels went up to heaven and came down by real ladders, and the gloomy portal called Hell's-mouth was contrived to open and shut. Black, blue and red devils came out to claim the damned, while a clanging of unseen pots and pans signified the discord that pre-vailed within.'*

Such is the contempt for angels, devils, heaven and hell engen-dered in the reader by this author that it is something of a surprise to discover that he is a canon of the Church of England. Yet, with only occasional lapses, this attitude to the mediaeval stage has been propagated and sustained ever since the Rev. David Rogers and Sir William Dugdale wrote respectively of the performances in Chester and Coventry. People who know nothing else of the mediaeval stage are conversant with their descriptions of pageant-carts (whether on four wheels or six) 'like a house with ii rowmes', the upper one for playing in and the lower one for changing.† The astonishing thing is that historians can calmly accept the notion of these cumbersome waggons, presumably some 15 to 20 feet high,

---

* Canon Maynard Smith, *Pre-Reformation England*, 1938, p. 146, cit. by G. M. Trevelyan, *English Social History*, 1942, p. 89.

† See pp. 170–6 below.

in the same breath that they tell us about the extreme narrowness of mediaeval streets. It is difficult to credit them with ever having paused to imagine what they are talking about. Had they done so, perhaps the fact that there are almost as many records of performances of miracle plays in England on fixed stages as there are of perambulatory ones would not have been so flagrantly overlooked or concealed. And what, one may ask, was Herod doing raging 'in the street' also? Was this a quite exceptional occurrence? Were the actors normally confined to their converted tumbrils? If so, how for example was the Chester 'Last Judgement', with Heaven, Earth and Hell for setting and a cast of more than twenty actors, accommodated, let alone performed?

When questions of this sort are neither asked nor answered it is hardly surprising that no one has seen fit to credit mediaeval actors and technicians with a mental age of more than seven. Quaint, primitive, naive, childish, simple: we are told they were all of this. Yet they were men and women like ourselves, who built cathedrals, stained glass, painted frescoes, illuminated manuscripts, wove tapestry, composed music, all of a design and taste and skill in execution which are envied and admired today. Why, then, in their theatre should they have been so cretinous and inept as to deserve the patronizing and at times contemptuous epithets so liberally bestowed on them by posterity?

I choose to give them credit for knowing what they were doing and why—at least until it can be proved that they did not. And the odds against this are heavy: for an audience is here involved that came back year after year to see the same plays, and not only in one place but independently in virtually every great city in the kingdom. To write off the stage-craft as quaint and naive is to dispose similarly of the audience. In one sense, of course, description of mediaeval stage equipment as 'primitive' is entirely justified. The machinery, by our standards, was elementary. The hydraulic lifts and other electrically-operated means of 'changing scenes' of the modern theatre were undreamt of: but they were also unneeded. In other words, the machinery that did exist, and the use made of it, was adequate to the particular, dramatic illusion sought for by its creators. If we are to do anything like justice to the mediaeval stage and, consequently, to understand Shakespeare's, we must exercise a little humility and try to comprehend something of the nature of that dramatic illusion.

The most concise symbol to represent the nature of theatrical illusion in our own theatre is the photograph. By an elaborate series of subterfuges we have endeavoured to present on our stages for the past hundred and fifty years an impression of verisimilitude. Painters skilled in *trompe d'œil* techniques have tried to present to audiences not only every brick in a wall as a real brick, but the wall itself in relation to other walls and other physical objects as it appears in actual life. Actors smoke, drink and fidget in countless ways in an endeavour to appear as life-like as possible. Dramatists provide them with staccato prose dialogue which passes for every-day speech—at least during the performance.

Yet, for all its skill and frequent artistry this realist technique is in constant danger of being exposed as the fraud it really is. We all of us know the oil lamp which, when adjusted by the maid, suddenly bathes the opposite side of the stage in light; those mysterious cracks, vertical and parallel round the sitting-room walls; the trunk of the oak tree which appears to be more sensitive to the winds of heaven than its leaves.

If we try to relate mediaeval stage conventions to this sort of stage illusion, it inevitably appears quaint: a 2 × 3 inch charcoal sketch compared to a 20 × 30 foot canvas in oils. We must instead make sufficient effort of imagination to conceive of a possible alternative to this form of theatrical illusion. There are several pointers to its nature. The first is that the texts of mediaeval plays are invariably in verse—a highly artificial form of speech and as unlike talk in actual life as maybe. Nevertheless, the characters who use this strange language succeed in revealing themselves as effectively to us as do characters of our own drama, using staccato prose. Noah's wife, young Isaac, and Sir Pilate of the Chester Cycle, for example, are no less recognizably human in terms of what they say than Mrs. Tanqueray, Lord Windermere or even Jimmy Porter. The latter group are of course punctilious in the accuracy of their observations on time, date or distance, where the former are scandalously lax; but they pay a heavy price for it. Where Mrs. Noah can leave her village, board the Ark, drift on the ocean and land on Mount Ararat, Ibsen's Nora, Shaw's Candida and Pinero's Mrs. Tanqueray are virtual prisoners in their drawing-rooms.*

This little example suffices to indicate a second difference in the nature of the stage illusion: a difference in the relative values placed upon the here and now. Where the conventions of verisimilitude arbitrarily focus attention upon the present, the mediaeval theatre functioned in terms of conventions which left the dramatist

* It is only fair to add that had Mrs. Tanqueray not strayed into bachelor chambers in Act I, there could have been no play.

and the spectator free to regard the present as no more than a starting point. The briefest glance at any form of pictorial art in the period illustrates and confirms this idea. From Cimabue and Giotto to Rubens and Rembrandt costume and scene, irrespective of period are normally those known to the painter. Immediately a 'Visit of the Magi' or 'Last Supper' is painted in 'historical' as opposed to 'modern' dress it is dated: it is placed in the context of the past and, to that extent, loses its relevance to the present.[49] Four centuries of steady advance in scientific, geographical and archaeological knowledge have given us an historical perspective unknown to the Middle Ages. Possibly the price of this knowledge is the feeling of loneliness and isolation which characterizes so much of modern thought and which is reflected in our drama by an almost exclusive concentration upon the immediate present. By contrast, mediaeval thinking is characterized by a sense of community, not only in the here and now, but in relation to time-past and to time-future. The cosmic drama of the Miracle Cycles is the theatrical reflection of this thinking.

A consequence of this basic difference of approach to dramatic composition, perhaps the most important, is that where, in our drama, the ego of the individual is, *per se*, the often exclusive subject matter treated, in mediaeval drama the individual is only likely to be of consequence if his story possesses some significance for the community. Troilus and Cressida matter as individuals because they are symbols of constancy and faithlessness respectively, and therefore have a relevance to humanity outside their own time.

It will be seen at once that to the dramatist interested in significance, the private thoughts and feelings of the individual are of little value compared to the result of those thoughts and feelings. The former are passive states: the latter, actions; and in consequence, the former only become significant in terms of the latter. Whatever else, therefore, this theatre denies the dramatist, it must give him room and means for wide and varied action. Thus, in the Chester Goldsmiths' play of *The Slaying of the Innocents*, the stage is required to serve simultaneously for three separate actions in three separate places: Herod's palace, Bethlehem, and Mary and Joseph's flight. These actions are so arranged for their interrelated significance to become apparent. While the soldiers are killing the children in Bethlehem, one of the women returns with her murdered child to Herod* and says:

*Stage direction, *Tunc ibit ad herodem*, line 392, *Chester Plays*, ed. Diemling for E.E.T.S., 1893, pp. 186–205.

'Loe! lord, loke and see!
the child that thou toke to me,
men of thy owne meny (*household*)
have sleyn it, here the bene.

HERODES (*irabit*)
fye, hore, fye! god geve thee pyne!
why didst thou not say that Child was myne?'

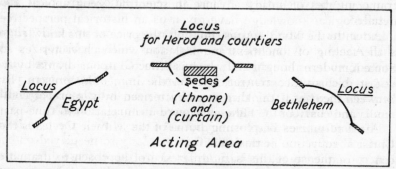

FIG. 10. Plan illustrating the disposition of scenic *loca* in the Chester Gold-smiths' play of *The Slaying of the Innocents* as indicated in the text and stage directions.

FIG. 11. Richard III enthroned under a cloth of estate: A formalized interior representing an audience chamber, drawn by an English Herald, temp. Hen. VIII (*c.* 1515).*

* Pen drawing in B.M., MS. *Harl.*, 69 f. 25, of an original pen drawing in C.A. MS. 6, f. 63b.

155

Thus Herod can be shown to be 'hoist with his own petard' while his intended victim escaped to Egypt, as the audience have just seen in the previous sequence of the play.

In the first of the two Passion Plays of the *Ludus Coventriae* a similar telescoping of dramatic action may be observed to point the double irony latent in the conduct of Judas Iscariot. The Council of Jews, at which the bargain for thirty pieces of silver is struck, is presented simultaneously with the Last Supper: and Judas is shown trafficking between them.* The stage directions are clear and detailed.

After the Demon's and St. John's Prologue, we are told: 'Here shall Annas show himself in his stage dressed like a bishop. . . .'† Some forty lines later:'. . . in the meantime Caiaphas sheweth himself in his scaffold arrayed like Annas. . . .' Messengers pass between them and they then meet in or near 'a little oratory with stools and cushions . . . like as it were a council house.'

After fifty lines of plotting between these two, there follows Christ's entry into Jerusalem. This is a long scene played on the centre of the stage. It is interrupted by these stage-directions: 'Here comyth Simon out of his house to welcome Christ', and

'Here Christ enteryth into the house with his disciples and eats the paschal lamb; and, in the meantime the council house before said shall suddenly unclose shewing the bishops priests and jews sitting in their orders of Estate like as it were a convocation.'

One further stage direction, some 270 lines later, makes the picture complete:

'. . . then shall the place where Christ is in shall suddenly unclose round about showing Christ sitting at the table and his disciples each in their degree. . . .'

We have here a large open space or acting area with stages or houses adjacent to it. Some are small like those for Annas, Caiaphas and Simon. Others are large enough to accommodate some ten to twenty people. The latter are equipped with curtains which can be swiftly drawn open to present a startling 'discovery', or closed to obliterate that area from significance to the action.

It is between these two 'houses', the council chamber and the

* Lines 514–670.

† This and the ensuing quotations are translated from the fifteenth-century East Midland dialect. For the original see *Ludus Coventriae*, ed. K. S. Block for E.E.T.S., 1922, from B.M. MS. Cot. Vesp. D. viii.

upper room, that Judas traffics during the action of the last supper. *

This Passion Play, which Professor Hardin Craig successfully demonstrated as belonging to Lincoln,[50] demands in its later scenes 'the mount of Olivet' and, near it, 'a place like to a Park' for Gethsemane. What are these scenic units if not those of which we have descriptions in Tournaments and civic pageants?

The first stage direction of the second Passion Play in the *Ludus Coventriae* provides us with a graphic description of the whole scene in action. I quote this verbatim, as written:

'What tyme þat processyon is enteyrd into þe place and þe herowdys taken his schaffalde and pylat and annas and cayphas here (*their*) schaffaldys Also þan come þer An exposytour in doctorys wede þus seyng.'

Of many possible instances, I have chosen these from the Chester Cycle and the *Ludus Coventriae*, since the one was certainly written for a movable stage and the other, as certainly, for a fixed one.[51] It is not therefore the type of stage that matters, but the convention: and the understanding of that hinges on our realizing that it is a Christian world with which we are dealing. Where, nowadays, any-one may think his guess as good as the next man's concerning the why and wherefore of mortal existence, in the Middle Ages a single thought pattern served for all. Deviation from this pattern was heresy, and heresy was a punishable offence. The Protestant conscience has always revolted from this aspect of Catholicism, but never with force enough to be effective during those centuries when the conventions of the mediaeval stage were growing to maturity. The fundamental conventions of stage action, therefore, accepted by dramatists, actors and audience alike, were designed to interpret a Christian universe through dramatic narrative. Once grown to maturity, they commanded allegiance in the theatre long after Henry VIII's break with Rome and served the drama of Pro-testant polemic as sturdily as its Roman Catholic predecessor. For Shakespeare, Jonson and Marlowe, Drake's voyage round the world may have confirmed the speculations of Copernicus, but no ad-justment had yet been made to bring stage conventions into line. The universe represented on the stage of *The Globe*, *The Theater*, the 'Rounds' of St. Just and Perran, or the pageant carts of York and Chester, was essentially still that of the Easter morning introit —*Quem quaeritis in sepulchro, O Christicolae?*—a human world which had put Christ to death, a Hell which he had harrowed and a Heaven

* e.g. 'here judas goth in sotylly wher-as he cam fro' (*ed. cit.*, line 657).

to which he was shortly to ascend. No dramatist concerning himself either with the teaching of the Bible from the stage, or with the ethics of human conduct, could do so on a stage which did not make provision for spirit worlds, both wicked and beatific, in addition to the material world of everyday events: for the world of here and now only acquired significance in relation to the two other worlds of all eternity. From Heaven Lucifer had been cast to Hell. From Hell he came to the new creation, Earth, to encompass 'man's first disobedience'. To Hell went Anima Christi to redeem Adam and Eve, the patriarchs and the prophets.[52] To Heaven Christ ascended and from there judged the whole human race at Doomsday. It was the obligation to present this cosmic picture that governed the construction of mediaeval and Elizabethan stages, the theatrical illusion aimed at in them, and the detail of the stage conventions employed to this end. The form which they took was governed, in turn, by the manner in which this cosmic drama came into being.

It was not born whole. It evolved, piecemeal and, at first, unself-consciously. The liturgical representation of the Easter sepulchre, the Christmas crib, or the Epiphany star, was not a photographic likeness of any of those things, because officiating priests within the sanctuary and choir of churches had neither desire nor intention to represent them as an actuality confined within the present moment. Rather was it desired to present them as past facts of abiding significance: and, in these terms of reference, a symbol is more efficacious than an exact copy. Put another way, sepulchre or crib served their purpose so long as they concentrated attention upon the liturgy and assisted understanding of it by identifying the location of the action. They were not intended to be appreciated for themselves and occupy the spectators' attention to the exclusion of other, more important things

We see this principle at work in the sepulchre constructed from books on the altar or in such ceremonies as the *Ordo Deposito Crucis*.[53] In a dramatic ceremony, however, any serious expansion of narrative carries with it the likelihood of multiplicity of place: and an audience will quickly become confused if locale is not clearly differentiated. Even so differentiation is not representation. Where multiplicity of place is concerned a corresponding multiplicity of symbol will meet the case, provided the symbols are not too small to be seen or too obscure to be interpreted. These provisos, however, create a pressure towards realism or, rather, towards the use of contemporary idiom. With swift intelligibility as the criterion, the deviser of the symbol must take the audience into account, judging what will serve, not by his own intellectual accomplishment, but by the capacity of the audience to understand. The key to this is knowledge by association. Symbols, or *figurae*, drawn from the day to day routine in the local environment would be immediately comprehensible to a mediaeval audience, where symbols drawn from book learning or extensive global travel would not.[54]

> 'And I also, without bost,
> though the kinge of Scotis and all his host
> were here, I set not by their bost,
> to dryve them downe bydeene (*together*)
>
> I slue ten thousand upon a day
> of kempes (*champions*) in their best aray,
> there was not one escaped away
> my swoard it was so keene.'

Thus speaks Sir Grimball Launcher Depe to Sir Waradrake, the two soldiers whom Herod commissions to slaughter the Innocents of Bethlehem in the Chester play.* The anachronisms in nomenclature and geography may well strike us as very quaint, but to the audience for whom they were written the realism and pertinence of the scene rested in the use of these very anachronisms. The 'dale or downe' over which these soldiers travel are the Pennines,† and 'the Kinge of Scotis and all his host' a formidable foe known at first hand to citizens of Chester, alive and dead. The language is that of the pulpit, the occupants of which had had years of experience in finding words to make their message comprehensible to illiterate auditors. Before dismissing this drama and its conventions therefore as crude and naive, we might well ask ourselves in what respects it is inferior to a drama which is faithfully realistic in all externals, but devoid of significance to the reality of daily living.

The fortunate survival of St. Ethelwold's *Concordia Regularis* (c. 965–975) and the Sarum Breviary tells not only what the earliest of these conventions were, but illustrates the context within which they were first introduced.[55] By the twelfth century, the narrative represented was of sufficient length and complexity for multiple symbols of place to be needed.[56] The area in which the symbol was set was appropriately described as a *locus* or *lieu*—in English, a place. If the 'place' was an inhabited one, it could as well

---

* *Chester Cycle, ed. cit.*, p. 194.
† *Ibid.*, p. 188, line 51. See p. 170 below.

be known as *domus, aedes,* or 'mansion', a place belonging to some-one and therefore a 'home'. The nature of this 'home' could vary greatly. At times a simple chair (*sedes*) would suffice. At others, a more complicated structure might be required. If, for example, it was a point of consequence in the narrative that access to and from a person was controlled, then the simple *sedes* would need to be screened by a gate or curtain. The principle, however, remains the same: to present the bare, visual essentials for identity and recognition.[57]

The extension of 'a place' from singular to plural may be conceived as having happened lengthwise down the church from the sanctuary through the choir into the nave, possibly including the side aisles, but not the transepts. The area of open ground which the *loca* or *domus* flanked was known, very appropriately, as the *platea* (literally, broad way, or street) which corresponds, in theatrical jargon, with the 'acting area'.*[58] These two concepts, *platea* or acting area, and *loca* or symbols for the identification of place, are the basis of all mediaeval stagecraft and of the Public and Private Theatres of Elizabethan England.

I have urged elsewhere that a theatre is only itself when stage and auditorium are thought of in conjunction. If, then, the *loca* and *platea* of the religious stage covered the full length of a church in the late twelfth century, where was the audience? Chambers ventures two suggestions: 'The people crowded to watch in the side aisles.' 'The (spectators) probably crowded upon barriers between the *sedes*.'[59] No one else appears to have considered the problem.

Chambers' view is the only possible one if we confine enquiry to the ground plan of a church: but if we think, for a change, of the internal elevation, other possibilities emerge. In a church of any size, there is first the triforium and then, above that, the clerestory, often associated with another gallery. From these two arcades surrounding the church internally, not only is the view of action below better than at ground level, but the acoustic is superior. I would hazard a guess that the conception of yards for 'groundlings' and galleries and private rooms for those of higher degree, so familiar to us in Elizabethan theatres, finds its genesis in the architecture of the cathedral church. This idea is not as speculative as it seems, for it not only corresponds with the distribution of seats in Great

* Acting area for us is almost synonymous with 'stage'. If we make this equation in considering the mediaeval theatre, we must be careful not to make 'stage' synonymous with 'raised platform'. See pp. 170–5 below. Also Southern, *The Mediaeval Theatre in the Round*, Ch. I.

Halls or Chambers for subsequent indoor performances* and with those for Tournaments,† but is illustrated in a remarkable picture of the Cathedral at Laon in 1566.[60] (See Fig. 12, p. 162.) Two years earlier Queen Elizabeth I saw a Plautus comedy acted in the Chapel of King's College, Cambridge, in similar circumstances. ‡

The migration of religious plays from churches to other environments was not of itself a change of so revolutionary a character as wholly to abnegate the stage-conventions which had come into existence to service liturgical music-drama. Rather was the pattern already established within the walls of churches simply transferred out of doors and there either modified or clarified as need arose with help from the secular clergy and, occasionally, from laymen.§ Only in cases of gross abuses, such as those which characterized the Feast of Fools, were serious efforts made to suppress dramatic additions to worship.[61] Lacking factual evidence to the contrary, the assumption must be that the plays were universally given performance on a single *platea* either flanked, backed or ringed with *loca* as local topography suggested. Such fragmentary evidence as survives from the thirteenth century indicates that local conditions encouraged considerable diversity rather than uniformity in the time and place of performance.[62] Old forms coexisted with new. Churchyards, open spaces before abbey gates or great west doors presented new problems to performers as, doubtless, did the refectory, hall and *curia* of the lords spiritual; but solution of them could usually be found by direct reference to the conditions still governing performances that continued to be given within churches, on the spot or near by.[63]

In one respect, however, there was a vital difference. Public performance in holiday time and divorced from the ritual of worship could only enhance the entertainment value latent within the very fact of self-conscious representation. The effect of this upon the text of plays is clear enough: but that is not the end of the matter. The visual appearance of the performance, without betraying the principles on which it was based, was likely to become more frankly decorative and elaborate. Any move towards more spectacular presentation would bring the clerical performers up against technical problems which lay artisans were better equipped to solve than they.

* See Ch. VI, pp. 214, 222 and 223 and Ch. VII, pp. 248–51 below.
† See Ch. II, 31–8 above.
‡ See Ch. VII, pp. 248–9 below.
§ On the question of changed acoustics, see pp. 128–9 above.

Fig. 12. A stage erected in front of the roodscreen in the Cathedral at Laon (N. France), *1566*, for ceremonies connected with the exorcism of devils from a woman possessed. The roodscreen itself, together with the triforium and clerestory, serve to accommodate spectators. The original engraving forms an illustration to Jean Boulaese, *Manuel de Victoire du Corps de Dieu sur l'Esprit Malin*, printed in 16mo, Paris, 1575. The alphabet on the engraving is a key to the sequence of rituals employed in the exorcism which are fully explained in the text, pp. 7–15. See note to Plate XXV, No. 37, below.

If, by the start of the fourteenth century, performance of the plays warranted recognition as a major civic event, it is likely that they were already becoming spectacular. This need not mean more than that the *loca* served a decorative purpose in their own right alongside of their strict function: but it does mark the start of those production costs which were destined to rise to a point where it required the weight of a city council in full session to decide how to meet them. In this connection it is notable that in those places where the clergy retained exclusive 'performing rights' the plays succumbed to attack much more quickly than in those where the craft guilds came to exercise a controlling voice.[64]

When, after 1377, records begin of what these expenses both amounted to and were occasioned by, it is in the account books of craft guilds that we find them. I have already supplied a conjectural reconstruction of how these guilds became associated with the Corpus Christi Day celebrations and, consequently, with scriptural scenes.* Here I need only repeat that the step from two-dimensional depiction on a banner to three-dimensional representation in action is a natural one and becomes an easy one if the transition is smoothed by promise of financial backing.

There is evidence that, in London at least, the intrusion of 'inexpert persons' upon clerical preserves was resented. In 1378 the choristers of St. Paul's, who protested to Richard II, are careful to state that they had been themselves 'at great expense' with their own preparations for public performance at Christmas.[65] If St. Paul's Choir School was in the habit of playing 'the history of the Old and New Testament', so was the Guild of Parish Clerks (St. Nicholas' Guild). They seem to have presented a Cycle fairly regularly from 1384 onwards and always at Clerkenwell (sometimes referred to as Skinners Well).† Their audience included Richard II, Henry IV and probably Henry V and Henry VI. These plays were clearly performed in the classic French manner, that is to say on a single *platea* with adjoining *loca*. There is no mention in the records of any assistance from the London craft guilds or of pageant waggons. As a rule the performances were given over some four or five days: but that given in 1411 'lasted vii dayes contynually; and there were the most parte of the lordes and gentylles of Yngland'.

---

* See pp. 147–8 above.

† St. Bartholomew's Priory was close at hand and Chambers thinks the plays may have been associated with Bartholomew Fair (*Med. Stage*, ii., 381). See pp. 138, 139 above and Fig. 9, p. 60 above.

For the performance of 1409 we know that the court watched from specially constructed timber scaffolds.[66] What we do not know is how these scaffolds were arranged. Here, however, what has already been said about Tournaments may fill the gap.* A link exists in the provision of scaffolds for the Court. Tournament auditoriums took their shape from the lists and were normally rectangular: but for Trial by Combat they could be circular. That which Chaucer called a theatre was 'Round . . . in maner of compas, ful of degrees, the heighte of sixty pas'. Without wishing to press this analogy too far, it is notable that the only other auditorium for open-air performances of Miracle Plays on a fixed stage of which we have documented evidence is that for the Cornish Cycle and this was circular. The earth-work amphitheatres at St. Just and Perran survive to give us some indication of their appearance.†

For the civic pageants at Katherine of Aragon's reception into London in 1501, Hall gives a most tantalizing description of the 'auditorium':

'I passe over also the fyne engrayned clothes, the costly furres of the citizens, standynge on skaffoldes, rayled from Gracechurche to Paules. . . . I will not molest you w^t rehersying the ryche arras, the costly tapestry, the fyne clothes bothe of golde and silver, the curious velvettes, the beautiful sattens, nor the pleasaunte sylkes which did hange in every strete where she passed, the wyne y^t ranne continually out of the conduytes, the graveling and rayling of ye stretes nedeth not to be remembered.[67] (See Fig. 9, p. 60 above.)

Clearly Hall wished both to save himself time and effort and to avoid boring contemporary readers with unnecessary description of what was already familiar. But his laconic remarks are adequate, in conjunction with the other fragments of evidence listed above, to warrant a glance across the channel at an auditorium erected for a Miracle Play in Provence in 1509. The play was the *Mystère des Trois Doms*; it was performed in Romans in May of that year; the MS. account book for the production has survived, along with the

---

* See Ch. II, pp. 31–8 above.
† The famous sketch in the Macro MS. of *The Castle of Perseverance* also depicts a circular stage. If Prof. Hardin Craig's attribution to Lincoln is accepted, where a Miracle Cycle also received stationary performance, the sketch becomes still more interesting. See also *EES*, II (1), Fig. 9, p. 167.

full text of the play.* Arrangements for the audience follow those normal for Tournaments (see Fig. 19, p. 306 below).

Spectators were accommodated in the open air on raised scaffolds, the nature of the accommodation being determined by social and financial status. Scaffolds were constructed in tiers rising away from the stage to loggias at the back. There were 84 of these loggias each provided with a lock and key.[68] Five of them were reserved for the *commissaires* who organized this performance and for other responsible officials and their friends. The show lasted three days and the 79 loggias open to the public were each let at 3 florins per day. The scaffold room was sold '*par personnaige soit grant ou petit*' at 1 sol for the first two days and ½ sol on the third. Here is the table of receipts:

27th, 28th and 29th May 1509.

79 loggias at 3 florins per day	237 fl:	—
27th May 1509 scaffold room at 1 sol per person	153 fl:	— 4 sols
28 May 1509 scaffold room at 1 sol per person	130 fl:	— —
29th May 1509 scaffold room at ½ sol per person	160 fl:	7 sols
TOTAL	680 fl:	11 sols.[69]

At 12 sols to the florin one can easily calculate the number of spectators. On the first day the scaffolds held an audience of 1,840 people; on the second day 1,560 and, with 24 persons to the florin on the third day, 3,847. Supposing the loggias to have each held six persons we may add a further 500 to 600 spectators each day. It is especially interesting that the organizers should have been sufficiently alarmed about receipts to risk cutting the cost of admission by half on the third day: and how well they were justified.

The stage which this audience faced was laid out on the normal ground plan: a *platea* with adjacent mansions. The most remarkable feature was three large towers which were used to represent three continents, three countries or three towns. This is paralleled by the use of scaffolds in the MS. ground-plans of the Cornish plays.

* P. E. Giraud transcribed this MS. and printed it in an edition limited to 20 copies in 1848. A copy is in the Fairholt Collection of the Society of Antiquaries' Library in London. The play itself was edited by M. Giraud and printed in 1887. The edition was limited to 200 copies. See G. Cohen, *Histoire de la Mise en scène*, 1906, 2nd ed., 1926, *sub* Romans (Drôme).

At Romans, for the *Mystère des Trois Doms* the carpenters started work on 30th December 1508, four and a half months before the performance. The materials include wood, iron, paper, gold and silver leaf, pigments and oil, tools and brushes. Clothes and wigs were provided for those characters requiring more than the normal dresses of contemporary fashion. For example, wings are provided for angels at a cost of 6 sols: wigs for 8 florins 9 sols. Proserpine's costume is particularly intriguing. She was given a gown of black frizzy cloth lined with green and a wig of cows' tails.*

Apart from the striking similarity between the materials used for the staging of this Miracle and those used in Street Pageants, the most interesting feature of the former is the information provided about machines, their operation, and the technicians who operated them. A certain François Trévenot was invited over from neighbouring Annonay and appointed to supervise the construction and painting of all the scenic devices.[70] He and his apprentice worked on the spectacle for four and a half months. To make the machines, the *commissaires* engaged Amien Grégoire, a local steelwright, and Jean Rozier, a clockmaker, also from Annonay.[71] Possibly Trévenot and Rozier were accustomed to work together in the theatres of the region. Trévenot evidently designed the machines. Grégoire and Rozier then set to work to construct them.

I give three representative entries from a list replete with detail, to indicate the sort of machinery used, its size and the use to which it was put in a mediaeval Miracle Play.

'Pay . . . Amien Grégoire for several iron fittings for the towers and turrets and other machines for the said devices . . . 5 florins 6 sous. Pay Amien Grégoire for 6 long, strong bars for the great winch and three belts for the three angels with the linch pins for their descent from heaven, which weighed altogether 39 lb: and for this he was given the sum of . . . 3 florins 3 sous. Pay . . . Grégoire for two large bolts, weighing three pounds, for making Hell mouth open: in all . . . 3 sous.'[72]

The usual pulleys, cords, weights and levers all figure in these accounts. These machines are so similar to those of the street

* These materials should be compared with those listed and printed by T. Sharp (*op. cit.*,) and F. M. Salter (*op. cit.*,) from the Coventry and Chester craft-guild accounts. I print a further selection of the Romans' expenses in conjunction with those for one of the street pageants in London in 1486. See Appendix F.

pageant theatres that we may reasonably argue that the steel-wright and clocksmith* co-operated with the designer-painter in the Pageants as well as in the Miracles to construct and operate them.†

Here is the balance sheet of the *Mystère des Trois Doms* at Romans:

A. DEBIT 1. Composition.

M. le Chanoine Pra (author)	255 fl:		
M. Chevalet (co-author)	27 fl:	5s.	9d.
Copyists (including materials)	18 fl:	3s.	

2. Auditorium and Stage.

The theatre	645 fl:	7s.	
Settings	655 fl:	1s.	5d.
Music	90 fl:		
Sundries	45 fl:	7s.	
TOTAL	1737 fl:	0s.	2d.

B. CREDIT

Admission receipts	680 fl:	11s.	9d.
Sale of materials afterwards	57 fl:	9s.	6d.
TOTAL	738 fl:	1s.	3d.

C. BALANCE A deficit of 998 florins 10 sols 1d.

That is to say—in today's money‡ a sum of approximately ten thousand pounds sterling of which seven thousand six hundred is attributable to the spectacle.[73] Whatever else this may represent it can by no stretch of the imagination be described as 'primitive' or 'quaint'.

The expenses of the craft guilds at Coventry and Chester and elsewhere, fragmentary though they are, bear out those from

---

* A similar connection between Clocksmith and Miracle Play may still be observed in Venice. In the middle of the face of the clock on the tower in St. Mark's Square is a large statue of a Madonna and Child. Machinery was attached in 1499 to enable the Three Magi to circle past the Virgin, taking off their crowns and bowing as they passed. See Plate XX.

† See Ch. III, pp. 93–100 above.

‡ I base my translation into contemporary English money on M. Giraud's own figure of 70 French francs in 1848 to the florin and twelve sols to the florin of 1509.

Romans and elsewhere in France.[74] Perhaps the best direct comparison, however, that can be made is not in terms of monies, but with the stage directions of the Digby plays of Mary Magdalen. These are English plays dating from approximately 1480 and clearly designed for presentation on a fixed stage.[75] Their editor, F. J. Furnivall, writing in 1896, says of the stagecraft:

'How all the scenes of the Temple, the burning of the Idols, the Shipman and his Ship, the rock on the island where the Queen of Marcylle was left, etc., were managed, I can't tell. . . . But make-believe will do wonders.'[76]

It is to be hoped that the reader, in the light of the foregoing chapters, will not have to resort to make-believe today. The scenic units are those which had been in use at Tournaments and Civic Pageants for over a hundred years. Moreover they had been in use for almost as long indoors, as we shall see.* From these sources we know not only what they looked like and what they cost to construct, but the materials from which they were made. Comparison of the stage directions with those in the Passion Plays of the *Ludus Coventriae* and the *Mystère des Trois Doms* tells us how these *loca* were set out in relation to one another.

Besides Mary's 'castell or maudleyn', Mundus' Pavilion ('my tent'), the rock ('tunc remigat a montem'), the ship ('tunc navis venit In placeam') and other familiar devices, there are some interesting novelties. Satan enters 'In a stage and Hell ondyrneth the stage': one mansion represents a tavern: Lazarus is said to be buried 'In his monument' as Christ is later too.[77] The King of Marcylle falls sick and 'goth to bed in hast, and Mary goth into an olde logge (*lodge*) without the gate'. Machinery is much in evidence. 'Here xall comme a clowd frome hevene, and sett þe tempyl one a fyer', and later, 'Here xall to (*two*) angylles desend In-to wyldyrness: and other to xall bring an olbe (*alb*), opynly aperyng a-loft In þe clowddes.'[78]

This kind of *mise-en-scène* was by no means unique; for a single fixed acting area with, presumably, a single, organized auditorium, was adopted as the most convenient method of presenting Miracle Plays in many places throughout the British Isles ranging from far off Aberdeen and Kilkenny to Shrewsbury, Lincoln and Chelmsford.[79] Performances were also still being given in churches in the late fifteenth and early sixteenth centuries at Lincoln, Leicester,

* See Ch. VI, pp. 216 *et seq.*, below.

Leconfield and Halstead, while plays were frequently performed in other indoor settings.[80]

The point to which I have been leading so laboriously is this. To assume that the stage conventions of the Miracle Plays were invented to suit the conditions of perambulatory staging in York, Chester or Coventry and have no further relevance once that form of presentation ceases to be employed, is a patent fallacy. On the contrary, the use of pageant waggons and the repetition of performances at several 'stations' is only a particular manifestation of a universal stagecraft, the conventions of which possess a common origin and retain their similarity in principle however they are presented to audiences. It is impossible to state dogmatically that one either was or is superior to the other without detailed knowledge of what persuaded a given community to adopt a given method. Rather must we credit them with common sense in having appraised what suited them best, making due allowance for such contributing factors as local rivalries, revenues, manpower and terrain.

The factors which could most readily have suggested perambulatory presentation are, first, a marked reduction of expense in the provision of an auditorium, secondly the prevention of traffic congestion of the sort which a single large stage and auditorium erected in a central thoroughfare could easily engender and, thirdly, organizational convenience where many, already self-contained, groups of people are each contributing a separate part of the whole show.

Opinion may well differ on the adequacy of these reasons, but thinking of this sort at least provides more natural grounds for explaining the choice of this curious (and almost unique) method of performance than that usually offered in terms of the Corpus Christi Procession. If the latter had provoked perambulatory performance, why was it not adopted everywhere in the British Isles? The furthest that I think we can go is to suppose that this Procession, together with the other forms of civic riding described in Chapter III, made it possible to think of splitting up the audience into several distinct groups and of bringing the performance to each group in turn. This method of presentation, considered from the standpoint of its technical implications, involves the provision of a separate acting area for each audience, but does not necessitate the duplication of the *loca*. These can be put bodily on wheels and brought either individually or together to each acting area in turn.

What did this acting area consist of? One possibility is that a raised platform was erected at each 'station', of the same height off

169

the ground as the carts carrying the various *loca*. Another is that a raised acting area was itself transportable and accompanied the *loca* as an 'extension piece' for attachment to it, once both were in an open place and clear of narrow streets. A third is that the *loca* themselves were extended in size sufficiently to combine *domus* and acting area within a single transportable unit. A fourth is that ground level formed the acting area and that access to and from the *domus* on wheels was made possible by steps or ladders carried on the cart for that purpose.

The only description of a performance we possess is David Rogers' notorious account of pageant carts at Chester.* He was certainly a hostile witness, probably not an eye-witness, but is someone nevertheless whose testimony cannot be simply dismissed, since the plays he describes had at least been performed in his father's lifetime if not in his own. As far as the acting area is concerned, in his account it was the floor of the pageant cart, neither more nor less. The stage directions in the surviving texts, if they do not confirm this view, certainly do not contradict it. Only one stage direction states specifically that the street was to be used, and that occurs in the Coventry plays.[82]

If we are to advance at all on this information it can only be by speculation in terms of internal or parallel evidence. Of this there are three primary sources:

1. Sober assessment of what the text for each pageant demands by way of *loca*, machinery, and number of performers.
2. Comparison of expenses incurred with the prices paid for other constructional and decorative work in the same years.
3. Application of the evidence available from other open-air theatres of the period, notably Tournaments and the street-pageant-theatres (concerning the actual shape, size and appearance of the apparatus used and of its function) to the Miracle stage.

Professor Salter has already employed the first two methods in respect of the Chester plays and guild expense-accounts to very profitable result.[83] I intend therefore simply to summarize his conclusions here and carry them as far forward as I may in terms of the third method.

* The reliability of his account is fully discussed by F. M. Salter, *MDC*, pp. 54–8 and also by Hardin Craig, *ERD*, pp. 123 and 124. It is corroborated up to a point, by Sir William Dugdale's description of the waggons in Coventry.[81]

At Chester there were considerably fewer Pageants* than there were plays. This discrepancy is resolved by knowledge that guilds agreed to share a pageant-waggon. This was possible where the guilds in question were not performing on the same day and where the *loca* presented on the Pageant could meet the needs of several plays. For example, the Painters, the Coopers and the Skinners shared a Pageant. The Painters were responsible for Play no. 7, that of the Shepherds, performed on the first day. The Coopers played the Flagellation at the close of the second day and the Skinners the Resurrection at the start of the third day. Common to all three is the need for a hill. 'On this hill I hold me here,' says the shepherd Gartius (line 217). It represents the area 'from comelie Conway unto Clyde' (line 5) whence the shepherds are summoned by the angel to go to Bethlehem.

The Coopers were originally responsible for the Flagellation: but this play, in the Banns of 1600, is merged with the Ironmongers' play of the Passion. After the merger it is clear that the hill was the 'montem Calvariae' of the stage direction in line 384. Before the merger it is not obvious what the hill was used for, but its existence may have played its part in suggesting that the plays be merged. In the Skinners' play of the Resurrection, the hill served for Christ's tomb.

Besides the hill, two other scenic objects were carried in this same cart. The Painters' play requires a stable, and 'heaven' in which both angels and the star can appear.† The Skinners' play similarly requires practicable heavens for the Resurrection: also a *sedes* for Pilate which can serve in the Coopers' play as a '*Cathedra*'. Both the hill and the stable-cum-throne-room must have been substantial structures, if only because of the associated machinery. A roof is here clearly essential despite David Rogers' assertion that the pageants were 'open on the tope'. Faced with this data—a cart on which is mounted both a substantial hill and a small house with a roof on it deep enough to conceal angels and the winches that controlled their appearance 'in heaven'—any actor's first reaction is bound to be, 'What space is left for acting in?' The answer can only be, 'Very little'. A second and equally pertinent question is, 'How can an audience see the action?'

The Coventry records offer two possible solutions. Mention is

* I use the term here and henceforth with a capital P to denote the vehicle and the *loca* carried on it.

† Line 310, '. . . et apparebit stells': line 334, 'Tunc respiciens firmamentum . . .'; line 474, 'Et apparebit angelus . . .'. See Plate XXI, No. 28.

frequently made in the guild accounts of scaffolds in association with the pageant. In 1584 the Cappers paid 8d. 'ffor mendynge of the skaffolds' and 2s. 6d. 'ffor our partes at the settenge and driving off the pagyn and skaffoldes'. The same items cost the Mercers (who presented a new play that year) 4s. 4d. and 5s. 4d. respectively.[84] These charges are very heavy if we reckon that a day's wage varied between 1d. for an unskilled labourer and 4d. for a skilled craftsman.[85] What then could these scaffoldes (i.e. platforms) have been if not an additional acting area set adjacent to and level with the cart carrying the *loca*? This arrangement would provide ample playing space with good clear sight-lines. On rare occasions, for special dramatic effect an actor could come still further 'downstage'—i.e. on to street level.

Sharp in his *Dissertation on the Coventry Mysteries* noticed these scaffolds, but supposed that they were used to accommodate spectators. I see no reason to believe this. He bases his assumption on a passage in Rogers' account of the Chester plays,

'to see w(hi)ch playes was great resort, and also scafoldes and stages made in the streetes in those places where they determined to play theire pagiantes.'[86]

That scaffolds were erected or 'made' for spectators at the appointed playing places accords with our knowledge of other mediaeval auditoriums: but the scaffolds paid for and maintained by the crafts were on wheels.[87] One such vehicle associated with a pageant-cart makes sense. A plurality of them associated with 'great resorte' of spectators makes none. We have only to ask ourselves what happened to the spectators when one craft moved on, taking its scaffolds with it, to appreciate the impossibility of Sharp's interpretation. The alternative is that these scaffolds were the precursors of the Elizabethan 'apron stage', or, looked at another way, the equivalent of the spacious *platea* of the fixed Miracle stage.

Attribution of the scaffolds to this purpose raises the question of how the audience was catered for. The factual evidence is scanty, but there is enough to provide an answer that is not wholly guesswork. Distinguished citizens and visitors were accommodated in the manner usual at civic pageants: * in private rooms of the houses overlooking the various stations ordained for performance. At Chester the Mayor and his brethren watched from the windows and

* It was from the house of one, 'William Geffrey, haberdasher', that Henry VII watched one of the Pageants for Katherine of Aragon in London (1501). See Ch. III, p. 61 above.

galleries of the Town Hall. Queen Margaret watched the Coventry plays from the house of Richard Wodes the Grocer.* At York, the Priory of Holy Trinity in Mickel Gate was chosen to accommodate Richard II and his retainers.[88] It is from York too that we get an idea of how less notable spectators were accommodated. There, the Corporation decided at what places the plays were to be performed, by leasing 'performing rights' to the highest bidder. A citizen, therefore, who was prepared to pay a substantial sum to the Corporation could have the plays performed before or near his house and presumably recover the money by creating scaffolds round the playing area, on which he would then sell places. The Corporation leased eleven of the sites in Henry VIII's reign for 43s. which in modern money corresponds to about £4,000.[89] The money involved is substantial enough, when production costs are added, for this system to compare favourably from a business standpoint with that of the single stage and auditorium instanced at Romans.†

We are now in a position to visualize the general appearance of a play in performance. The audience, on raised platforms and at street level, according to status, saw before them an open stage the size of a large cart, boarded about and backed with several scenic units set on a second cart. These scenic units were ornate in themselves, as we can tell from the cost of the materials used in the construction and decoration: also, substantial enough to contain machinery for special effects. This picture is simple to visualize, but the doing so must prompt us to ask where the actors concealed themselves when not on the stage or in the *loca*. According to Rogers the Pageants

'weare a big scafolde w(i)th ii rowmes, a higher and a lower, upon 4 wheeles. In the lower they apparelled themselves, and in the higher rowme they played.'[90]

Now we know that Rogers was mistaken in saying that they were 'all open on the tope'. Might he not also have been mistaken in distributing the '2 rowmes' vertically? One room might well be described as 'higher' in the sense of 'beyond' another or 'lower' room. I do not myself believe Rogers intended this interpretation, but what I take to be an error on his part, itself suggests the probable distribution of the rooms in actuality. Instead of trying to imagine a waggon so tall as to be top heavy, we should visualize a waggon of more normal proportions split horizontally across the

---

* See Coventry Leet Book, *ed. cit.*, i, 300; also *EES*, III, pp. 51–3.
† On the general subject of finance see Ch. VIII below.

173

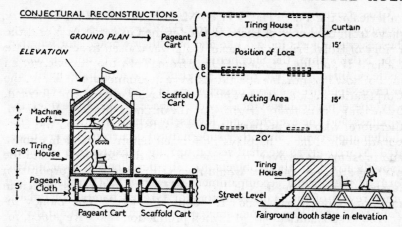

FIG. 13. Conjectural ground plan and elevation of Pageant Waggons as they appear to have been arranged at Coventry. One cart carrying the scenic *loca* is positioned beside a second cart carrying only a scaffold. A raised *platea*, or 'acting area', is thus offered which can itself be extended to include 'the street also'. The dimensions are based on those of the 'Carriage House' of the Tailors' Company in Chester given by Salter (*MDC*, p. 62) and amplified in Plates XIX, No. 25; XXI, No. 28; XXVI, No. 39 and Frontispiece. See also L. J. Morrissey, 'English Pageant-Wagons', *Eighteenth Century Studies*, vol. 9 (spring 1976), No. 3, pp. 355–74.

middle, the forward part serving to accommodate the *loca* and the back part screened off as a 'green room', dressing-room or 'tiring house'. A cart of this kind at least corresponds to the booth-theatres of fair grounds depicted in several early sixteenth-century paintings and drawings.* On this stage actors would have room to move and be seen: God in white or Imperial crimson, fur, and crowned:† high priests in bishops' copes, albs and mitres;‡ merchants and peasants in everyday garments of the period; angels and demons, winged, wigged and masked.§ We can see them all in stained glass, in frescoes and in tapestry today where they were depicted by the mediaeval artist-craftsman going about their daily business against a background of decorative 'cloths' and a variety of scenic *loca*.

* See Plates XXI, No. 28 and XXVI, No. 39.

† Sharp, *op. cit.*, pp. 69 and 26. In Canterbury Cathedral there is a window representing the Three Kings being warned 'in a dream' not to return to Herod. They are depicted fast asleep in bed, wearing their crowns.

‡ Sharp, *op. cit.*, pp. 27, 28; also p. 156 above.

§ Sharp, pp. 56 *et seq.*, 71; Nicoll, *Masks, Mimes and Miracles*, pp. 189–92.

Cross reference to the street pageant theatres of important civic occasions and to Tournaments of the *Pas d'Armes* sort tells us what these scenic objects looked like and how they worked: for whether it be Noah's ship, the Shepherds' hill, Simeon's temple, Emmaus castle, Galilee fountain, the trees in Eden, pavilion judgement seat or cave-sepulchre we have descriptions of them all. We even know why these particular symbols were chosen.* We have met the windlass and the weights and levers by which ascents, descents, sudden appearances and other supernatural occurrences were operated. Moreover, as we shall see on turning our attention to the indoor theatre,† all these objects are fully described in their mobile form as the normal accompaniment to *entremets*, Disguisings and other revels of the Hall, Refectory or Great Chamber of Palaces from 1377 until Inigo Jones started to experiment with a different system in 1604–5. What confirms and strengthens the picture, taking it out of the realms of mere speculation, is that, in whichever of these contexts, the actual materials used are the same and cost the same, the men employed on the construction work are paid the same wages, the finished product is the same;‡ and the reason for all this similarity of detail is simply that the Middle Ages possessed an orthodoxy of outlook upon fundamentals. To them the universe was not a Tower of Babel, but something simple enough in essence to be interpreted to all in terms of human experience and divine grace. If actors hold the mirror up to nature, their stage must be the world. This is indeed what the acting area represented. It took a local habitation and a name from the *sedes*, *domus*, *aedes*, *locus* or 'mansions' in use at the time, Jerusalem, Bethany, Pilate's house, Gethsemane.

This convention enabled the dramatist to present the history of the world as a single, coherent, stage narrative. He relied on his carpenters', his painters' and his actors' powers to evoke images for his spectators which they would recollect and associate with landscapes, streets, and interiors and people of their own acquaintance. It was thus real, not in the sense of photographic accuracy to the original, but to life as they knew it and lived it. Significance and parable were everywhere apparent to the audience wherever story, incident, or action touched something in their own experience. The language in which the story was told was simple and direct, yet always artificial because in verse.

* See Ch. VII, pp. 232, 233 below.
† See Ch. VI, pp. 21, 220 below.
‡ See Appendix F.

Verse was easier to memorize than prose, but it served a more important purpose than that. It enabled the dialogue itself, through poetic images, to suggest an environment which the *loca* (in themselves no more than decorative visual symbols) served to confirm and reinforce. Instead of having to change the identity of the stage by bringing the action to a standstill and changing the 'scenery' mounted on it, the dramatist could reckon on the spectators assuming the scene to have changed immediately an alternative symbol of place (i.e. another 'mansion') was brought into physical use and linked to the narrative with appropriate visual imagery: conventions, in fact, which hold good to this day in the Far East. By the simple expedient of first aligning on the edge of the acting area remotest from the spectators such symbols of place, status and time as would be needed in the action—Heaven, a 'paradise' of clouds and stars out of which angels could descend; Hell, a yawning chasm of grisly teeth belching smoke and fireworks; Eden, a hill and a tree; Herod's palace, a canopied throne *—and then employing these symbols either singly or in combination, the action could move at the pace directed by the painter and the engineer. The acting area remained constant, whether these 'mansions' were laid out behind it, round it, or were brought to it one by one on carts. It then took its identity—street, garden, audience-chamber, and so on—from the 'mansion' employed by the actors at any given moment. Those not in use became frozen, as it were, continuing to serve a decorative, but not a topographical purpose.

This, broadly speaking, was the style of theatre which James Burbage, Shakespeare and Henslowe inherited. Where the open-air Public Theatres were concerned, theirs differed from their predecessors' in that they were permanent: but the conventions which they incorporated and formalized were copied directly from those still in frequent use at Tournaments, Civic Pageants and Miracle Plays. Their auditorium and box-office structure had similar prototypes.

A Note on Music and Acting

The place of music in mediaeval stage production is a subject in itself. I have felt obliged to omit it rather than compress my narrative still further to include a sketch which could not do it justice: discussion of it is deferred to Chapter VI of Volume III.

* See Fig. 11, p. 155 above, and Ch. VII, pp. 243–7 below.

BOOK TWO

Indoor Entertainments of the Middle Ages

V

INDOOR THEATRES AND
ENTERTAINERS

T HE next two chapters must necessarily be somewhat discursive since most of the subject matter is unfamiliar and interpretation of it open to debate. It will perhaps be helpful, therefore, to preface them with a brief chapter of introduction.

It is generally assumed that the English Theatre migrated indoors at the Restoration, spurred thither by the spectacular success of the Jacobean and Caroline Court Mask. This belief, while inoffensive in itself, is an over-simplified generalization: and it is in this compression that trouble starts; for, just as frequently, the Mask itself is taken to be a Jacobean invention, attributable to the originality of Ben Jonson and Inigo Jones. On this assumption, it seems to follow logically that the history of the English Theatre up to the accession of James I is concerned exclusively with performances under an open sky.

In the next two chapters I hope to redress the balance: to show that the obvious difference in product between Jacobean Court and Public Theatres derives from an equally evident difference in the composition of the audience: and that the differences in taste between the two audiences was formulated, not through any sudden awakening to Humanism, but gradually, from the days of Richard II to those of Elizabeth I.

It is easier to make this adjustment if we consider for a moment the position of the Private Theatres in Elizabethan and Jacobean England. Clearly, these theatres were neither public nor exclusive to the Court. Admission prices precluded the presence of the rankest 'stinkards' accustomed to occupying penny and twopenny room at the Public Theatres, while wealthy merchants and their wives, who lacked the social entrée to performances in the banqueting halls of the Court palaces, were regular patrons. Yet apart from the vital

179

fact that these Private Theatres were situated *within* other buildings, very little is known about them. In short, lack of evidence has made these indoor theatres seem of small account compared to the public ones: yet their known existence and popularity ought to suggest to the historian that they developed out of at least as extensive a tradition of use as their more familiar companions.

I am going to argue that alongside of the open-air performance of Miracle Plays and Moralities, entertainments of a primarily secular kind were regularly given indoors and at night before both the nobility and the merchant bourgeoisie from the end of the fourteenth century onwards. Further, that the formulating of a regular drama, usually ascribed to the mid sixteenth century, can be antedated by at least a hundred years in origin: and that these entertainments, both in their texts and in their staging, developed naturally into those offered in the Court and Private Theatres of Elizabethan times, neither of them owing very much to the alternative Public Theatres. Indeed, the probability is, as I read the evidence, that the Public Theatres of the late sixteenth century drew many of their conventions from the Court and Private Theatres. If so, we are half way to an explanation of why the latter should have triumphed to the exclusion of the Public Theatres in the late seventeenth century.

In dividing this subject matter into three parts (the present chapter, one on Mummings and Disguisings and Masks and the third one on Moral Plays and Interludes), I am probably creating greater distinctions than existed for their contemporaries; but, since they appear to have derived from different sources, the division is convenient. Central to all three chapters, however, is the work of John Lydgate, a figure almost totally neglected in the annals of the English drama, yet one who in my opinion must receive the credit for imposing rudimentary form upon the heterogeneous secular entertainments of the minstrel troupes.* This form, once supplied, was embroidered on extensively, but never seriously changed until the Civil War put paid to the Stuart Mask.

The pointers to this conclusion have long awaited anyone who chose to follow their direction. First, Ben Jonson says that the Mask of his own day—and as both a writer of Masks and a Grammarian, no one had better reason to know than he—was formerly called Disguising.[1] A century before he started his collaboration with Inigo Jones, the Privy Purse Accounts of Henry VII's Court record frequent payments for Disguisings indoors and at night. Nearly a

* See Plate XXV, No. 37.

hundred years earlier than that, Lydgate is writing poems which he calls 'the devyce of desguysing' or 'as in a disguising'. Some of these are alternatively billed 'in wyse of mommers desguysed' or 'for a mumyng'. They are written either for the Court or for the Mayor and Aldermen and, although printed as *Minor Poems* and called Mummings by the editor,* are undoubtedly entertainments for presentation indoors and at night. The date is *c.* 1430. If we wish to pursue this path still further back in time, we have to do so under the title 'Mumming'. This will take us at least into the reign of Richard II and maybe earlier still. A glance across the Channel to the French Court confirms both the pattern and the chronology. The starting point of the enquiry must be the constitution and activities of the minstrel troupes; for, as early as the beginning of the fourteenth century, they had become firmly established in all European countries as the recognized entertainers of the lords temporal and spiritual.

Landowners of the fourteenth century who were willing to maintain a private troupe of minstrels or to hire one from a neighbour for occasional festivities could expect an evening's entertainment not dissimilar to the vaudeville or variety bill of our own times. Acrobats, musicians whose appeal lay as much in instrumental virtuosity as in musicianship, jugglers, masters of performing animals, comedians and conjurors provided staple fare: but, unlike the modern music hall, the troupe was led by a poet whose recitations were quite as popular as the skills of his dependent buffoons, gymnasts and instrumentalists. The reason for the troupe taking this form must be sought in Provence: for it was there, in the eleventh and twelfth centuries, that the Northern tradition of serious entertainment represented by the recited sagas of the gleeman and scôp fused with the Southern tradition of lighter amusements represented by the antics of the mime and pantomime: and it was there that a new language was fashioned which Southern and Western Europe were ready to accept as a vehicle for story telling. [2] Southerners, who had for long thought the art of narrative recitation buried with the Greek and Roman poets, were thus encouraged by Northern invaders (whose language was considered as barbarous as it was unintelligible) to look at the present and at the future for source material. Those who experimented in the writing of this new poetry were called *trouvères* and the success of their pioneer efforts, as far as European literature is concerned, was to

* H. N. MacCracken, *The Minor Poems of John Lydgate*, ed. for E.E.T.S., 1934, 2 vols. See Vol. II, pp. 668–701.

be as revolutionary as the invention of printing four hundred years later: for the trouvères managed to convince educated society in South-Western Europe that a modern language was as suitable for composition as the ancient ones.[3] Their verses conveyed stories in a familiar tongue, intelligible to the ladies as well as to the men. Recital of these verses thus rapidly became a popular form of courtly entertainment. Any tendency there might have been for this new form of entertainment to remain localized was dispelled by the advent of the Crusades. The latter, by bringing men together from all over Christendom, not only assured to the new literature a far wider hearing than it might otherwise have obtained, but themselves inspired tales of chivalry and romance which provided its poets with a quantity of themes certain to be enjoyed by the newly acquired audience.* These tales, whether of Godfrey of Boulogne and the Conquest of Jerusalem or of Jason and the Golden Fleece, were told in terms of contemporary ideals and contemporary manners. Thus, from the start, they were treated with the same disregard for historical, archaeological and topographical exactitude as the Miracle Plays which were developing alongside of them in the liturgy of the Church. Significance counted for more than fact and, as time went on, the original tales were embellished with every literary fiction which fancy could invent to decorate them. They were known as 'chansons de geste' and either simply recited or, more probably, chanted to the accompaniment of some musical instrument.[4]

In England, we find our Lords spiritual and temporal being entertained with such 'gestes' on the principal feast days during the fourteenth century. At Winchester, when the bishop visited his priory of St. Swithin in 1338, he was entertained with one of these.[5]

'A certain minstrel called Herbert recited "the song of Colbrond" and especially "the Geste of Queen Emma acquitted by Ordeal by Fire", in the prior's hall.'†

* It is for this reason that Richard I comes to be so closely associated with the trouvères. As a result of his distinguished part in the Crusades he became a typical hero-subject for their romances. Other English warriors of similar distinction were Bevis of Southampton and Guy of Warwick. Their deeds were originally sung in French but were in time translated into English. The tales of ancient chivalry—of Arthur, of Alexander and of the Trojan war—were resurrected for treatment in the same fashion and found as wide an audience.

† 'Et cantabat Joculator Quidam nomine Herebertus CANTICUM Col brondi, necnon Gestum Emmae reginae a judicio ignis liberatae, in aula prioris.'

That this practice was habitual is clear from the following lines of
William of Nassyngton's translation of *A Treatise on the Trinity*[6]:

> 'I warn yow frust at the begynnyng,
> That I will make na vayn carpynge,
> Of dedes of armys, ne of amours,
> As dus mynstralles and jeestours
> That makys carpyng in many a place
> Of Octovyane and Isambrase
> And of many other jeestes,
> And namly when you come to festys.
> Ne of the lyfe of Buys of Hamptoun,
> That was a knyght of grett renown;
> Ne of Sir Guye of Warwyke', etc.

The 'mynstralles' and 'jeestours'* who made these recitals were
the gentlemen-leaders of these troupes, the trouvères. The practice
was deemed respectable enough for it to be recommended in the
Founder's Statutes for the two St. Mary Colleges at Winchester and
Oxford as a fit pastime for scholars on a winter evening.†

Entertainment in a lighter vein was provided by other members
of the troupe which he led: the *joculatores, mimes, histriones, cithar-
izates* and *lusores*, that is to say, 'variety artists' and 'musicians'.

A reasonable idea of their activities, many of them simple not to
say banal, may be gleaned from *Piers Plowman*:

> 'I am a mynstral' quod that man, 'my name is *Activa-vita*:
> Alle ydel ich hatye, for actyf is my name.
> A wafrere (*i.e. a confectioner*) wil ye wite and serve many lordes,
> And fewe robes I fonge (*get*), or furred gounes.
> Couthe I lye to do (*make*) men laughe, thanne lacchen I shulde
> Other mantel or money, amonges lordes mynstralles.
> Ac for I can noither tabre, ne trompe, ne telle none gestes,
> Farten, fythelen, at festes, ne harpen,
> Iape ne Iogly, ne gentlych pype,
> Ne noyther sailly ne saute, ne synge with the gyterne,
> I have none gode gyftes, of these grete lordes.' [7]

Some of these minstrels took up residence in the more rapidly

---

* i.e. singers of gestes, not jesters.

† The Statutes of New College Oxford, Rubric CXVIII: 'Quando ob dei,
reverentiam aut suae matris vel alterius sancti cujuscumque, tempore yemali
ignis in aula sociis ministratur; tunc scholaribus et sociis post tempus prandii
aut cenai, liceat gracia recreationis, in aula, in Cantilenis et aliis solaciis
honestis, moram facere condecentem; et Poemata, regnorum Chronicas, et
mundi hujus Mirabilia, ac cetera que statum clericalem condecorant, seriosius
pertractare.' See also the Statutes of Winchester College, Rubric XIV.

expanding townships * but the majority continued to live a nomadic existence depending for their livelihood on the patronage of the nobility. This was more precarious than is generally imagined. The popular belief, that a troubadour had only to sing without the castle walls for the drawbridge to be lowered to receive him, is romantic fantasy. The entrée to noble houses proved very hard to come by. The password was reputation: and only when reputation had earned a knighthood was free entry guaranteed. The trouvère alone among the troupe was likely to attain to this distinction and even he rarely passed beyond the status of Esquire. The other members of the troupe were his social inferiors and dependent upon him for the opportunity to earn a livelihood. This tended to keep minstrel troupes together; and it was probably the fear of the competition which break-away groups might present that best accounts for the constant preoccupation of the trouvères themselves with means of preserving and improving their own social status. [10]

At what precise date these nomadic groups of professional entertainers became closely enough associated with a particular noble to warrant their using his name as a label under which to travel, it is difficult to say. Warton thought it 'not improbable' that many of the greater monasteries kept minstrels of their own as early as 1180. [11] Durham Priory, a century later, certainly acted as host to named groups of minstrels. Payments were made in 1278 to *Menestrallo Regis Scociae* and *Menestrallo de Novo Castro*, in 1302 to *Histrionibus Domini Regis* and, in 1330, to *Citharistae d'ni Roberti de Horneclyff*. [12] In the fourteenth century the number of troupes enjoying private patronage is very extensive. [13] What they performed and how they performed are matters still open to debate. However, in advancing an hypothesis by way of answer to these problems we may start from firm ground on at least two counts. First, we know that in Langland's and Chaucer's lifetime, no minstrel was embarrassed by a shortage of noble patrons. Secondly, that in this same period (*c.* 1350–1400), if minstrels sought this patronage they were unlikely to obtain it except as members of a

* There they could hope to earn a livelihood under the patronage of merchant-princes on important civic occasions. Such, probably, were the 'tanta histrionum varietas', whom Matthew Paris observes to have graced the marriage festivities of Henry III in the streets of London in 1236. [8] By the late fourteenth century at any rate they must have been firmly established in towns, as is demonstrated by an ordonnance of Guillaume Clermont, Provost of Paris, dated 14th September 1395, which shows a special quarter of that city to have been theirs. [9] On Minstrel Guilds see *Med. Stage*, ii. App. F, pp. 258–262.

reputably organized troupe. Account Rolls speak of payments to these troupes whom the clerks describe under the Latin words *lusores*, *mimes* and *histriones*. All these words can be legitimately translated as meaning actors: and this is where difficulty starts: for where, in the twentieth century, we automatically associate the word actors with ensemble playing, no such association was necessarily present in the minds of fourteenth-century scribes. Rather must we ask ourselves whether these actors ever performed plays written in dialogue or even mimed a co-ordinated scenario. *
Unfortunately, evidence surviving from the fourteenth century, taken on its own, will not provide an answer. Nothing prevents us, however, from taking fifteenth-century records in conjunction with it. If we do this and work backwards from evidence of co-ordinated, ensemble performances, a coherent pattern of development emerges. There is also something else to be considered, the Miracle Plays. For convenience of treatment, I have pigeon-holed subjects into separate chapters which in point of historical time and development were certainly interrelated. Discussion of the indoor theatre, therefore, should not be so exclusive as to overlook the example which the rapidly developing Miracle Plays presented to the minstrel troupes. Both these troupes and their audiences were aware of the techniques of ensemble playing and the pleasure to be gained from watching it. In the Miracles, as we have seen, the nucleus on which all else was built was chanted narrative in dialogue form. A similar nucleus for dramatic development lay to hand for the minstrels in the 'gestes' of their own trouvères, should they wish to use it. At least in France, these stories were in fact being represented dramatically before the end of the fourteenth century.† A further parallel may be observed between the Miracle Plays and secular dramatic performances in the manner by which visual representation of the narrative nucleus was first realized. Where the Bible stories that formed the plots of the Miracles were familiar to the faithful in frescoes, paintings and stained glass before they ever saw them presented three-dimensionally on stages, the subject matter of the 'chansons de gestes' was made equally familiar to the lords spiritual and temporal in the tapestries and wall paintings of their halls and chambers. These tapestries made a strong impression on the popular mind, so strong indeed that

* Chambers is probably right in saying that 'the term *ludi* must not be pressed' and Nicoll probably no less right in suggesting that these *ludi* may have been 'amateur revels'.

† See Ch. VI, pp. 213–216 below. See also *CM*, p. 45, n. 1.

even in the late fifteenth century they could themselves provide subject matter for a 'geste'. I quote here from Bradshaw's *Holy Lyfe of Saynt Werburge*. At a feast given by King Ulpher, says the poet, to celebrate the marriage of his daughter Werburgh,

> 'Clothes of golde and arras, were hanged in the hall,
> Depaynted with pyctures, and hystoryes manyfolde.'[14]

On one side of the hall the tapestries represented scenes from the Old and New Testaments.

> 'Upon the other syde, of the hall sette were
> Noble auncyent storyes, & how the stronge Sampson
> Subdued his enemyes, by his myghty power;
> Of Hector of Troy, slayne by fals treason,
> Of noble Arthur, kynge of this regyon;
> With many other mo, whiche it is to longe
> Playnly to expresse, this tyme you amonge.'[15]

Relevant, however, as both the narrative nucleus and its first visual representation are to subsequent three-dimensional enactment, there is another factor to be considered which is still more important: the nature of the occasion out of which both take their being. Just as the recitals of scripture and its representation through the visual arts, from which the Miracles developed, have their origin in worship, so the chansons de geste and their representation in tapestry and painting, from which all Courtly Plays and Masks developed, have their origin in feasting and social recreation. Whether it be the sumptuous Masks of the Caroline Court or the *ludi domini regis* of Edward III that we have to consider, the occasions, if nothing else, are common to both. These are of two kinds: the long public holidays celebrating the principal festivals of the Christian year and the special festivities dictated by such notable events as coronations, weddings, the coming-of-age of a prince, a state visit or the installation of an abbot or a mayor.[16] Indoor entertainments at night therefore may be expected both with the regularity of the Miracle Plays at Calendar Festivals and, in addition, at those special occasions which provoked such celebrations as Tournaments or Royal Entries. No matter what the occasion, however, Festival is the key-note and, where social recreation is concerned as opposed to official ceremonial, its basic form will be music and dance.[17] In these pastimes the amateur no less than the professional could participate either separately or in conjunction. Froissart describes a banquet which Edward III held at Eltham in 1364 where 'The young Lord de Couci (who was later to marry Edward's eldest daughter, Isabella) danced and sang splendidly when his turn came.'[18] When, in 1640, Charles I and Henrietta Maria together with members of their Court danced in the last of the Court Masks, *Salmacida Spolia*, the difference lay not in the nature of the entertainment but in the additional spectacle, organization and literary sophistication superimposed by professional entertainers upon the simple amateur attainments professed by Edward III and his Court. It is probably foolish to attempt to be dogmatic in differentiating between professional and amateur contributions to the development of indoor courtly entertainment and more helpful to remember that the minstrels, as household servants, could as often render service by co-operating with their masters as by providing entertainment of an exclusively professional kind. At one extreme, therefore, the minstrels might be asked to provide nothing beyond instrumentalists for singing and dancing organized by their masters: at the other extreme they might be expected to provide a stage play for their masters to watch. Once these two extremes become realities, disintegration of the minstrel troupe as originally constituted seems a likely sequel, a division into musicians and players. By the start of the sixteenth century this has happened.

The evidence I have to present shows that the amateurs poached upon the minstrels' preserves extensively in the development of singing and dancing into a co-ordinated, ensemble entertainment: that the dominating position of trouvère was fatally undermined once the recital of narrative passed from his exclusive control to that of his retinue, whether as mimes or as speakers of dialogue: and that dance and dialogue become inextricably intermixed.*

Clear pointers in this direction are the entertainments already examined. The Royal Entries of 1377 and 1392 in London demonstrate the possibility of living tableaux decorated with artificial scenic background, machinery and speech. The Tournaments sponsored by Edward III in 1331 and 1343 involved disguise of the person as a means to allegorical ends; and, in Round Tables, a link with Romance literature had been established. More important still, this festivity of the daytime and open air was already linked through the persons of ladies and in the ceremony of prize giving to the social recreations of the evening and indoor feasting. The

---

* His function as a chronicler is taken over by the Herald whose fortunes were in the ascendant. The College of Arms received its charter in 1483. See p. 208, note ‡ below.

proximity of this link is well illustrated by certain entries in the Royal Wardrobe Accounts for 1347, 1348 and 1388.[19]

Edward III kept the Christmas of 1347 at Guildford. The Wardrobe supplied:

xx
iiij. iiij (28 ? 84) buckram tunics of diverse colours
42 masks of which 14 were female faces, 14 faces of bearded men and 14 angels' heads with silver haloes
28 headdresses of which 14 were in the form of legs upside down with shoes on,* 14 in the shape of mountains with, ?tunnels in them, ?rabbits on them†
14 painted cloaks
14 ?dragons' ?serpents' heads
14 white tunics
14 peacocks' heads with wings
14 tunics painted like peacocks' tails
14 swans' heads with wings
14 tunics of linen thread painted
14 tunics, painted, with silver and gold stars on them.

In 1348, the Feast of the Nativity was kept at Otford and that of the Epiphany at Merton. For the former the Wardrobe supplied:

12 men's heads, each surmounted with a lion's head
12 men's heads, each surmounted with an elephant's head
12 men's heads, with bats' wings
12 wildmen's heads
17 girls' heads
14 tunics of red worsted lined inside with gold
14 tunics of green worsted.

At Merton new costumes were required which included

13 dragons-head masks, 13 masks of crowned men, black buckram and English linen cloth.

These items are entered on all three occasions under the heading *Et ad faciendum ludos Regis*. Whether we accept these costumes as having been required for Tournaments or evening revels depends on how we translate *ludos*. The literal translation is 'games': but even in our own time that word is ambiguous and requires the

* The Latin reads, *Crestes cum tibiis revasatis et calciatis.*
† *crestes cum montibus et cuniculis.* See Fig. 6, p. 46 above, and Plate XXII, No. 31.

epithet 'athletic' or 'party' before it to make the sense clear. Does the word stand here for *hastiludia* (jousting), *ludi* (plays or revels) or both in a general sense? I do not think it greatly matters, but evidence exists to support either contention.

The close relationship between the tunics, mantles and head-dresses suggests that the costumes were the garments normally worn over armour for jousting. King Réné's MS. *Le Livre des Tournois* depicts a wide range of headdresses resembling those listed and actually includes one 'with legs upside down'.[20] The crest set above the helmet, as may be seen, is usually a three-dimensional representation of a motif in the knight's coat-armour. Recurrence of the numbers 12 to 14 is also significant in this context, for it was as 'one aparelled like to the Pope, bringing with him twelve other in garments like to cardinals' that Lord Robert Morley held jousts in London in 1343.[21] That, however, was 'about Mid-summer': these entries are for the midwinter season.

Against these arguments may be set the fact that if cloaks, tunics and crests formed part of a knight's normal equipment to be worn over armour, masks did not. The visor on the helmet could be worn up or down but was made to serve a functional not a decora-tive purpose. Just as singular is the specific dating of the Wardrobe entries: *ad festum Natalis domini* (twice) and *in festo Epiphaniae*. Tournaments were not linked to regular Calendar Festivals and were not usually undertaken during winter months on account of the weather.* The dates then, together with the inclusion in the lists of masks to disguise the face rather than visors to protect it, seem to contradict the idea that these costumes were required for Tournaments, or at least to suggest that some of them were wanted for indoor, evening revels. The uniformity of the costumes suggests further that the revels took some form of corporate en-tertainment involving groups of people rather than individual turns. If we now enquire what form it actually took, evidence sur-vives from other sources that may supply the answer. It is of three kinds. First, there is the old custom of Mumming (quite distinct from the Mummers' Play). Secondly, there is the *entremet* of the French Court. Descriptions of both survive from the last quarter of the fourteenth century. Lastly there are John Lydgate's texts of the early fifteenth century which he entitles 'momyngs', 'disguisings' and 'ballades'. He uses these words loosely, indeed in what seems

* It is of course possible that the jousting took place indoors 'at barriers'. The earliest example of this known to me in North-western Europe is 1378 and that in France. See Ch. VI, p. 215 below: See also *CM*, pp. 42–47.

a deliberately alternative sense; and it is from his texts that I think we may see the heterogeneous revels examined so far fusing into the homogeneous dramatic forms destined to blossom into the Interlude and the Mask. In short, they mark the end of minstrelsy and the beginning of secular drama in England.

VI

MUMMINGS AND DIS-GUISINGS

ARLY in the reign of Henry VI (1422–1461), John Lydgate,
monk from the Benedictine Abbey of Bury St. Edmund's and
the leading poet of his day, devised a number of dramatic entertainments with written texts which are neither plays nor Masks. They
were presented either to the Court or to the Mayor of London at
important Calendar Festivals. What they were and how they came
to take the form they did must now be our concern.

The title of one of them reads as follows*:

'A lettre made in wyse of balade by Ledegate Daun Johan, of a
mommynge, whiche the goldesmythes of the Cite of London
mommed in right fresshe and costele welych (*manner?*) desguysing
to theyre Mayre Eestfeld, upon Candelmasse day at nyght, afffter
souper; brought and presented un to the Mayre by an heraude
(*herald*) cleped Fortune.'[1]

That this was an indoor, evening entertainment can hardly be
doubted. Up to a point, the title is also specific about the nature of
the entertainment. A herald, called Fortune, brings a letter in verse
to the Mayor which serves to introduce, describe and explain a rehearsed charade presented by the Goldsmiths' Company for his
amusement. Charade is an inadequate word to translate *mommynge*,
and so is dumb-show, since both have associated overtones not
necessarily implicit in *mommynge* or, in modern spelling, mumming.
Nevertheless, it is at least clear that the Goldsmiths *mommed*
something: that is, they performed or caused to be performed an
entertainment involving actors in costume.

* 'th' and 'gh' have been substituted for the original þ and ȝ in all quotations from the Lydgate texts.

191

Such suppositions are confirmed by Lydgate's title for another, similar poem written for the Mercers of London in:

'A lettre made in wyse of balade by Daun Johan, brought by a poursuyaunt (*pursuivant*) in wyse of mommers desguysed to fore the Mayre of London, Eestfeld, upon the twelffethe night of Cristmasse, ordeyned ryallych by the worthy merciers, citeseyns of London.'[2]

Again, a herald presents a verse letter to the Mayor introducing 'mommers desguysed' (i.e. actors in costume) to the Mayor. The difficulty which faces anyone trying to construe these titles is that the ensuing text in both cases is a simple, narrative poem from which dialogue is absent. Lacking dialogue, how can these texts, despite their titles, be legitimately considered as dramatic entertainments?

An answer is supplied in the title of a third entertainment which reads:

'The devyse of a desguysing to fore the gret estates of this lande, thane being at London, made by Lidegate, Daun Johan, the Munk of Bury. of Dame Fortune, Dame Prudence, Dame Rightwysnesse and Dame Fortitudo. beholdthe, for it is moral, plesaunt and notable. Loo, first komethe in Dame Fortune.'[3]

The final exhortation to watch, combined with the direct introduction of the first actor, removes any lingering suspicion that these texts may only be curious poems and not dramas at all. Moreover, in this instance, the poem is interspersed with rubrics announcing the entry of other actors:

(Line 138) 'Nowe komethe here the first lady of the foure . . .'
(Line 172) 'Nowe shewethe hir heer the secounde lady . . .'
(Line 220) 'Loo, heer komethe in nowe the thridde lady . . .'
(Line 281) 'And theos edoone, komethe inne the feorthe lady . . .'

These ladies are described in the text, but do not speak themselves. The inference, therefore, is that both this text and the other two represent dramatic entertainments in which the actors were silent, but were presented to the audience by someone who introduced them and interpreted their actions. This supposition not only accords with the facts, but also corresponds with Lydgate's own use of the words 'mummers' and 'mumming': for, although the root meaning of those words is obscure, 'mum' has always been synonymous with silence.[4] In his titles Lydgate also identifies two of the presenters, a herald for the Goldsmiths and a pursuivant for

the Mercers: and it so happens that he has himself left us a long
description of just such an entertainment:

'And whilom thus was halwed the memorie
Of tragedies, as bokis make mynde,
When thei wer rad or songyn, as I fynde,
In the theatre ther was a smal auter (*i.e. altar*)
Amyddes set, that was half circuler,
Whiche in-to the Est of custom was directe;
Up-on the whiche a pulpet was erecte,
And ther-in stod an aw(n)cien poete,
For to reherse by rethorikes swete
The noble dedis, that wer historial,
Of kynges, princes for a memorial,
And of thes olde, worthi Emperours
The grete, emprises eke of conquerours,
And how thei gat in Martis highe honour
The laurer grene for fyn of her labour,
The palme of knyghthod disservid by (old) date,
Of Parchas made hem passyn in-to fate.
And after that, with chere and face pale,
With stile enclyned* gan to turne his tale,
And for to synge, after al her loos, †
Ful mortally the stroke of Atropos,
And telle also, for al her worthihede,
The sodeyn brekyng of her lives threde:
How pitously thei made her mortal ende
Thorugh fals Fortune, that at the world wil schende, ‡
And howe the fyn of al her worthines
Endid in sorwe and (in) highe tristesse,
By compassyng of fraude or fals treasoun
By sodeyn mordre or vengaunce or poysoun,
Or conspiringe of fretyng fals envye,
How unwarly§ (that) thei dide dye;
And how her renoun and her highe fame
Was of hatrede sodeynly made lame;
And how her honour drowe un-to decline;
And the meschef of her unhappy fyne;
And how Fortune was to hem unswete—
Al this was tolde and rad of the poete.
And whil that he in the pulpit stood,
With dedly face al devoide of blood,

* i.e. with a changed manner of expression.
† *Loos*, renown.
‡ *Schende*, ruin.
§ *Unwarly*, without warning.

Singinge his dites, with muses al to-rent,
Amydde the theatre schrowdid in a tent,
Ther cam out men gastful of her cheris,
Disfigurid her facis with viseris,
Pleying by signes in the peples sight,
That the poete songen hath on hight;
So that ther was no maner discordaunce
Atwen his dites and her contenaunce:
For lik as he aloft(e) dide expresse
Wordes of Ioye or of hevynes,
Meving and cher,* bynethe of hem pleying,
From point to point was alwey answering—
Now trist, now glad, now hevy, and (now) light,
And face chaunged with a sodeyn sight,
So craftily thei koude hem transfigure,
Conformyng hem to the chaunt(e)plure,†
Now to synge and sodeinly to wepe,
So wel thei koude her observaunces kepe;
And this was doon in April and in May,
Whan blosmys new, bothe on busche and hay,
And flouris fresche gynne for to springe;
And the briddis in the wode synge
With lust supprised of the somer sonne,
Whan the(se) pleies in Troye wer begonne,
And in theatre halowed and y-holde.
And thus the ryyt (of) tragedies olde,
Priamus the worthi kyng began.
Of this mater no more telle I can.'5

This passage occurs in *The Troy Book* and is entitled: 'of a Thea-
teyre stondynge in the princypale paleys of Troye declarenge the
falle of Prynces and othere'. Many historians have noted this passage and promptly dismissed it as a typical mediaeval misconception of the classical stage.6 The relationship, however, between this
passage and the construction of some of Lydgate's own poems is
far too close to be dismissed as mere coincidence. In fact, it has been
consistently overlooked. Rather must we remember the legend of
British descent from the Trojans and the serious attempt in the early
fifteenth century to rename London New Troy7: and add to this the
mediaeval habit of describing what was unknown or unfamiliar in
terms of the familiar and known without regard to historical,
archaeological or typographical accuracy. This Trojan theatre

* i.e. 'gesture and expression'.
† i.e. 'alternating joy and sorrow'.

then, misconceived as it may be as a reconstruction of Roman, Greek or Trojan practice, may still portray quite accurately the London indoor 'theatre', c. 1430, for which Lydgate wrote. What he is describing is a Mumming or Disguising.

'Loo here begynnethe a balade made by daun John Lidegate at Eltham in Cristmasse, for a momyng tofore the Kyng and the Qwene',

or

The devyse of a momyng to fore the Kyng Henry the Sixst, being in his Castell of Wyndesore, the fest of his Crystmasse holding 'there. . . .' [8]

Three other poems by Lydgate come within this category: one for the King 'holding his noble feest of Cristmasse in the Castel of Hertford', one for 'the Shirreves of London, acompanyed with theire bretherne upon Mayes daye at Busshopes wod, at an honurable dyner', and another 'at the request of a werthy citeseyn of London' called *Bycorne and Chychevache*. [9]

In the light of this, it would be pleasant to be able to say that all eight poems were mummings presented as their author directs in his *Troy Book* and pass on to other matters. Unfortunately, analysis of the actual texts forbids such simple treatment of the subject: for even a casual reading of them reveals striking differences of structure, while two of them contain passages in *oratio recta* for more than one speaker, the Hertford poem and *Bycorne and Chychevache*. These differences can, I think, be explained; but any attempt to do so involves analysis of all eight poems. An abstract in table form, printed on the next page, yields some useful factual information, the most significant point to emerge from which is that the word 'Disguising' does not appear in the title of any of the entertainments which culminate in the presenting of gifts. That practice seems to be associated with Mumming. It accords, too, with what we know about the use of the words 'Mumming' and 'Disguising' before and after the ten-year period within which these texts were written. From the mid fifteenth century onwards, the word 'Mumming' is scarcely ever used to describe a courtly entertainment. The word 'Disguising' on the other hand is regularly used in this sense from then until it is superseded, as Bacon and Jonson inform us, by the word 'Mask' in the early sixteenth century. Thus, in 1489, a herald notes in his diary: 'This Cristmass I saw no Disgysyngs and but right few Pleys.' Two years earlier he had written:

Abstract of dramatic poems written by John Lydgate between 1425 and 1485.

Poem	Descriptive Title	Occasion of Performance	Audience	Presenter	Characters	Special Features
Bishopswood	Ballad	May Day At dyner	Sheriffs of London and Aldermen	A pursuivant	Flora, Ver.	Gifts presented
Eltham	Ballad for a mumming	Christmas	The King and Queen	(Unnamed)	Bacchus, Juno, Ceres Merchants	Gifts presented
Goldsmiths	Ballad of a mumming	Candlemass Day at night after supper	The Mayor of London	A Herald called Fortune	Levites	Gifts presented Levites sing
Mercers	Ballad for mummers disguised	Twelfth Night	The Mayor of London	A pursuivant	Merchants	Mechanical ships used
Windsor	Device of a Mumming	Feast of Christmas	The King and Court	(Unnamed)	King Clovis, St. Clotilda, St. Remigius, a hermit and, possibly, God	Gifts presented Dumb show follows spoken exposition
London	Disguising	New Year's Eve?	Great estates	(Unnamed)	Fortune and four, named Virtues	Dumb show accompanies spoken exposition
Hertford	Disguising	New Year's Eve	King and Court	(Unnamed)	Six, named peasants and their wives. Unnamed Presenter. Unnamed arbiter	Three speakers including expositor
Bycorne and Chychevache	Mumming Disguising	—	? Worthy citizens of London	A Poet	Bycorne, Chychevache, young man, old man, a woman	Speakers

'And on Newres Day at Nyght ther was a goodly Disgysyng, and also this Cristmass ther wer many and dyvers Playes.'[10] Disguisings, then, of which we hear nothing before 1425, had not only become recognized and regular courtly diversions within the next sixty years, but were quite distinct enough in form to warrant distinguishing from plays.

Before 1425, the word mumming occurs frequently enough and, significantly, in the context of prohibition as often as not. This poses a riddle. One full description of a Mumming survives: at Kennington, where Richard II was spending Christmas in 1377. In 1405 the records of Royal and Mayoral prohibitions start.* Yet between 1425 and 1435 Lydgate is still entertaining both the King and the Mayor of London with Mummings.

The Mumming at Kennington is described by John Stow in his *Survey of London*.† It was 'made by the Citizens for the disport of the yong prince *Richard* . . . in the feast of Christmas'. A cortège of 130 citizens rode in disguise through the streets of London. Their way was lit by torches and they were accompanied upon it by minstrels playing various instruments. Nothing is said in this account about the streets being decorated: but elsewhere Stow says that it was customary to do so. 'Against the feast of Christmas, every mans house, as also their parish churches were decked with holme, Ivie, Bayes, and what soever the season of the yeare aforded to be greene: The conduits and Standardes in the streetes were likewise garnished.'[11] Twenty-four pairs, 'in the likenes and habite of Esquires' headed the procession wearing gowns of red cloth and 'comely visors on their faces'. They were followed by forty-eight Knights similarly attired. Next, 'one richly arrayed like an Emperour, and after him some distance, one stately tyred like a Pope, whom followed 24 Cardinals'. It was as Popes and Cardinals, we should remember, that King Edward III's knights had ridden through London to joust thirty-four years earlier.[12] The rear was brought up by 'eight or tenne with black visors not amiable, as if they had beene Legates from some forrain Princes'.[13] Arrived at Kennington, the procession dismounted and went into the hall to greet the young prince, 'whome the said mummers did salute: shewing by a paire of dice upon the table their desire to play with the Prince'. This phrase is important: for it seems to indicate clearly

* See pp. 202–205 below.

† Ed. C. L. Kingsford, 2 vols, 1908, i, 96. For reprints of the full text see Enid Welsford, *CM*, pp. 39, 40; R. Withington, *EP*, i, pp. 104–6; Chambers, *Med. Stage*, i, 394.

enough that the mummers retained their proverbial silence on this occasion, indicating the purpose of their mission by mime. The dice were loaded so that the Prince might win a 'boule of gold, a cup of gold, and a ring of gold', which the mummers had brought with them. Gold rings were won with equal simplicity by the Prince's mother and other noble hosts. Music and dancing followed: but it would appear that the Royal Party and the mummers danced on separate sides of the Hall.

Miss Enid Welsford, discussing mummings in *The Court Masque* (1927), regards this as a sophisticated version of a custom with a long past:[14] for although the root meaning of the word 'mumming' is uncertain, much is known about what it meant during the early Middle Ages. Mumming was the prerogative of those without claim to noble birth and, in all probability, a direct survival of Celto-Teutonic or Graeco-Roman religious rituals. It took the form of a processional visitation: and while the visitors assumed disguises they did this to conceal their identity, not as professional actors. In short, as a sophisticated entertainment in the fourteenth century, it was both amateur and occasional: and it is highly unlikely that the participants were consciously aware of the history or origin of the customs they were perpetuating and embellishing.* The importance of the mumming, then as now, lay in its being the only form of nocturnal, indoor entertainment of which we have any knowledge that involved a coherent group of people, working corporately to a predesigned end. As such, it could scarcely avoid becoming the nucleus around which the self-conscious, artistic energies of the nobility would coalesce; a magnet, drawing to itself the heterogeneous amateur and professional pastimes of earlier social recreation. If the seasonal giving of gifts was the original object of mumming, Stow's account shows that this had already fused with an equally important social recreation, dancing.† Indeed, as between the giving of gifts and dancing it is difficult to distinguish which is potentially the more important socially.

* The intimate relationship between dancing and Tournaments, where the evening prize-giving led automatically into dancing, has already been discussed. See Ch. II, pp. 17, 22 and 27–30 above.

† It is difficult for us, however, not to be conscious of the echoes of pagan customs which Stow's description evokes. Masked persons parading through the streets, often wholly disguised as animals, remind one of tribal sacrifices to propitiate the dead: the entry of the procession into houses not their own recalls the inversion of social status associated with the Roman Saturnalia: the playing of a game of dice called 'mumchance' reminds one that the pagan winter feasts were seasons for prognostication as well as propitiation.

Stow's account, so remarkable in its detail, is curiously silent on one aspect of a mumming: the significance of the disguise adopted by the mummers. Perhaps none was intended. This seems doubtful, however, when we remember the similar, disguised processions associated with Tournaments. The disguises adopted on those occasions had a clear allegorical significance which was interpreted to the spectators by the Heralds.* In Stow's account there is no counterpart to the Herald: but one is to be found some forty years later in the Lydgate mummings. A glance at the table on p. 196 reveals that the four texts associated with the giving of gifts are all directly introduced. In one case, Eltham, the Presenter is unnamed, but in the other three he is specified as a Herald. His function is to introduce the silent gift-bearers, the mummers, to the intended recipients of the gifts and to the audience at large. In addition, since the bearers are disguised to represent persons other than themselves, the Herald-Presenter acts as an interpreter of both the disguise and the allegory to which it is related.

Two examples will serve to illustrate the pattern and the method, the Mummings at Bishopswood and at Eltham, a bourgeois and a royal occasion respectively. A pursuivant presents the former. The presenter of the latter is not named.

Miss Welsford, in her discussion of the Lydgate texts, ignores the Bishopswood one and sums up that at Eltham as

'an explanatory speech introducing some mummers who, in the person of Bacchus, Juno and Ceres, brought wine, wheat and oil to the sovereigns as a token of peace, plenty and gladness'.[15]

If this is so, then Ver, Flora and the Muses are the mummers presented in the Bishopswood ballad. Yet in neither text is there any evidence that human beings impersonated these deities. The construction of both pieces is identical almost to the phrases and words used. In both, characters of Roman mythology are said to be gracing the feast with their interest. In both, these characters express this interest in practical fashion by sending material gifts in token of spiritual blessings. The Eltham ballad starts as follows:

> 'Bacchus, which is god of the glade vyne,
> Juno and Ceres . . .
> Sende nowe theyre gifftes un-to Your Magestee:
> Wyne, whete and oyle by marchandes that here be,
> Weeche represent un-to Youre Hye Noblesse
> Pees with youre lieges, plente and gladnesse.'[16]

* See Ch. II, p. 40 above.

The Bishopswood ballad begins thus:

> 'Mighty Flourra, goddes of fresshe floures,
> . . . .
> Un-to thestates wheoche that nowe sitte here
> Hathe Veere doune sent hir owen doughter dere,'

and concludes thus:

> 'Wher-fore to alle estates here present
> . . . .
> May is nowe comen to fore yow of entent
> To bringe yowe alle to ioye and freshnesse. . . .'17

The key to interpretation rests in the Eltham specification that
Bacchus, Juno and Ceres

> 'Sende nowe theyre gifftes un-to Your Magestee
> Wyne, whete and oyle by marchandes that here be.'

Who are these merchants if not the mummers? The merchants, too,
provide a direct link with the traditional mumming—the arrival of
strangers, at a house not their own, who offer gifts and then depart.
The visitation is explained in terms of a diplomatic mission and the
mummers thereby absorbed into an allegory appropriate to the
occasion. For May Day at Bishopswood they represent emissaries
from the Goddesses of Spring and Flowers: for Christmas at Eltham, ambassadors from a God and Goddesses whose goodwill is
necessary to mortal survival. These allegories, expounded by the
Presenter, have displaced the former, clumsy device of loaded dice
as the means through which the gifts change hands.

Two other Mummings take exactly this form, the Goldsmiths
and the Mercers. The Goldsmiths employ 'an heraude, cleped Fortune', to present a group of Levites, emissaries from King David
and the ten tribes of Israel, with a present for the Mayor.

> 'That worthy David, which that sloughe Golye,
> . . . .
> With twelve trybus is comen to this citee,
> Brought royal gyfftes, kingly him taquyte,
> The noble Mayre to seen and to vysyte.'

These gifts, we are told, are

> '. . . bothe hevenly and moral,
> Apperteyning un-to good gouvernaunce
> Un-to the Mayre for to doo plesaunce.'

200

They take the practical shape of

'The arke of God, bright as the sonne beeme.'[18]

I think we may reasonably suppose the ark to have been a specimen of the Goldsmiths' art, thus linking the trade-symbolism noticed in the street pageants to the mumming. Moral allegory is attached in the simple device of the ark's contents:

'A wrytt with-inn shal un-to you declare
And in effect pleynly specefye,
Where yee shal punysshe and where as yee shal spare
And howe that Mercy shal Rygour modefye.'

The ark is presented to the Mayor by mummers dressed as Levites. There is no dialogue: but the Levites are told by the Herald-Presenter to sing.

Mayor Eastfield was similarly entertained by the Mercers' Company, who also disguised their Presenter as a Herald. Miss Welsford finds the meaning of this text obscure. The syntax is certainly very difficult to follow: but the meaning seems clear enough—a mumming which takes the form of a visit from Oriental Merchants.[19]

The pursuivant first explains his presence. He has been sent by Jupiter from the Far East. He has crossed the Euphrates and, via Egypt and Morocco, has come by ship to England. The splendid fishing grounds he has just seen and the angle of the Pole Star convinced him that he 'was not far frome Londones toune'. He next explains his purpose which is to introduce to the Mayor

'Certein estates, wheche purveye and provyde (i.e. Mercers) . . .
. . . or that they firther flitte.'

Lydgate used this occasion for an extraordinary display of erudition: but, despite the welter of ill-digested classical mythology, the audience were not denied the customary trade-symbolism and scriptural and moral allegory. The Mercers, disguised as Orientals (possibly the familiar Turks and Tartars of earlier Tournaments), enter the hall in three ships, a device which the Fishmongers had first employed in a street-pageant a century earlier. * The first ship, which let down nets and drew nothing, had written on it: GRANDE TRAVAYLE: NULLE AVAYLE. The second ship bore the inscription:

'Taunt haut e bas que homme soyt,
Touz ioures regracyer dieux doyt.'

* See Ch. III, p. 54 above.

The third ship which let down nets and drew a full draught had written on it: GRANDE PEYNE: GRANDE GAYNE. There can surely be little doubt but that these three ships represent an allegory of the miraculous draught of fishes taken from the Gospels and applied to the Mercers' profession.[20] This seems a reasonable assumption recommended as much by its simplicity as by its correspondence with the facts of the Goldsmiths' mumming.

The conclusion that may be drawn from considering the four texts discussed above is, briefly, that between 1377 and 1427 or thereabouts, the traditional folk-mumming (already on the road to sophistication) changed its nature to the extent of dropping the dice-game of 'mumchance' and substituting an explanatory allegory expounded by a Presenter. The mummers, true to their name, remained silent and may be thought of as actors only in so far as they adopted disguise to change their identity. They are essentially citizens, justified by the season of the year and the festive customs traditionally associated with it, in adopting this disguise. At Kennington, they are 'citizens . . . in the likeness of Esquires . . . Knights . . . an Emperour . . . a Pope . . . Cardinals' and 'eight or ten with black visors'. In two of Lydgate's mummings the citizens are specified as being Goldsmiths and Mercers who are disguised as Levites and Oriental Merchants respectively.

Mention has been made of the prohibitions of such mummings which exist to perplex the historian. What can explain the existence of these prohibitions simultaneously with the known continuance of mummings? The answer may well lie in the foregoing remarks about the citizen-actor participants: for, clearly, mumming was a custom open to abuse at several points. Large assemblies of people in festive mood can quickly become riots: disguise offers a convenient anonymity to professional agitators: and, as host to unknown and uninvited guests, the house-owner translates his dwelling into public property for the duration of the visit.*

According to some Chronicles, a Mumming was used to attempt the seizure of Henry IV in 1400. In 1414 Sir John Oldcastle was accused of a similar offence. The risk of sedition and breaches of the peace, therefore, could well supply one good reason for the suppression of mummings; unruly behaviour in the streets and in the Hall or Chamber, another.

* Some Scots, familiar with the age-old custom of 'first footing', can confirm from contemporary experience that such abuses are not unknown today.

In 1418 the Mayor and Aldermen of London

'chargen on the Kynges byhalf, and this Cite, that no manere persone, of what astate, degre, or condicioun that evere he be, duryng
this holy tyme of Cristemes be so hardy in eny wyse to walk by
nyght in any manere mommyng, pleyes, enterludes, or eny other
disgisynges with eny feynyd berdis, peynted visers, diffourmyd or
colourid visages in eny wyse. . . .'[21]

In the preceding year 'mummyng' alone is specifically forbidden.
In 1479 the Mayor and Sheriff of Bristol

'chargen and commanden on the Kyng our souverain lordis behalf
that no maner of personne of what degree or condicion that they be
of at no time this Christmas goo a mommyng with close visageds
nor go aftir curfewe rong at St. Nichollas withoute lighte in their
handes, that is to say sconce light, lanterne light, candel light or
torche light, and that they goo in no wyse with wepyn defensibly
araied wherbye the Kinges peas may in any manor wise be broken
or hurt and that upon peyn of prysonment and makyng fyne and
raunsom to the Kyng.'[22]

Further prohibitions, dating from the years on either side of the
examples given, show that the same official attitude of disapproval
was here adopted towards undue licence and excess by the civic
authorities as by the ecclesiastical authorities where the Feast of
Fools was concerned. In other words, it was the rowdy, uncon-
trolled, free-to-all-comers character of the 'mumming' which occasioned alarm and gave rise to censure and restriction. A quiet
mumming, organized under responsible leadership among friends,
was another matter. Provided it was conducted in an orderly manner there was no need for the eye of authority to notice it. A century earlier identical methods had been adopted by the King to
control Tournaments. Henry III's prohibitions which, if judged by
their frequency, were quite ineffectual, nevertheless succeeded in
their object: to prevent breaches of the peace and the possibility of
subsequent rebellion. Tournaments continued to be held, becoming
ever less dangerous, less boisterous but more artistic in aim and
execution.*

This comparison seems a fair analogy in terms of which to
explain the change that so evidently overtook the custom of
mumming during the fifteenth century.† As the Tournament, in

* See Ch. II, p. 15 above.
† Cf. The Church's attitude to the Feast of Fools.[23]

transforming its *raison d'être* from that of battle-school to a display
of individual courage and skill, lost much of its elemental vitality,
so did the mumming. The surprise and spontaneity of the original
visitation from weird strangers, so evocative of the Roman Saturnalia, gave place to the more refined pleasure of a mock-visitation
from disguised friends. The parallel with the Tournament may be
extended even to nomenclature. With refinement, new forms of
combat are introduced with new names, Joust, Tilt, Barriers. Yet
all remain combats and therefore forms of Tournament. So the
mock visitation of friends disguised as strangers becomes a 'balad
for momers disguised' and thus Disguising *tout simple*: yet both remain forms of mumming, differing from the prototype in the
degree of orderliness and sophistication with which they are
conducted.

If this reasoning is logical, then those texts of Lydgate's in
which the word 'Mumming' is dropped in favour of 'Disguising'
ought to differ from those called Mummings, recognizably and
along these lines. In fact they do. There are two of them; that at
Hertford for the King and Court and that at London for 'the gret
estates of this lande'.[24] In neither case is the prime object of the
entertainment to present gifts. Rather is it to debate a moral problem. At Hertford the problem is the perennial conflict between hus-
band and wife for command in the home. At London it is the equally
omnipresent question of how to combat the fickleness of Fortune.
The method in both instances is to present first the protagonist,
then the antagonist and finally a resolution. At Hertford this was
achieved as follows.

A Presenter, speaking in verse, supplicates to the King on behalf of six peasant-husbands:

> 'Of entent comen, fallen on ther kne,
> For to compleyne unto Yuoure Magestee
> Upon the mescheef of gret adversytee,
> Upon the trouble and the cruweltee
> Which that they have endured in theyre lyves
> By the felnesse (*ferocity*) of theyre fierce wyves.'

Their individual wrongs are listed and the King is asked to judge
in their favour. In reply, one of the wives, acting as spokesman for
all six, pleads for judgement on their side:

> 'Humbelly byseching nowe at oon worde
> Unto oure Liege and Moost Soverein Lord
> Us to defende of his regall(*it*)ye
> And of his grace susteenen oure partye.'

A third speaker, the King's advocate, pronounces judgement by deferring sentence,

> 'Til ther beo(n) made examynacyoun
> Of other partye, and inquysicion'

—and enjoining a truce, in the form of maintenance of the *status quo*, for the year to come.

The method at London differs only in that the prerogative of speech is retained by the Presenter. First he introduces Dame Fortune to the audience and reminds them of her fickleness. Then he introduces four Ladies, the Virtues, and describes their respective potentialities. Finally, he exhorts the audience to resolve their dilemma by cultivating these Ladies' company.

> 'Frome Fortune yee may thane go free,
> Boothe alwey in hert and thought.'

Fortune is then banished from the Hall and the Ladies are invited to sing,

> 'With al youre hoole hert entiere
> Some nuwe songe aboute the fuyre.'

In this entertainment almost the only link with the traditional folk mumming is the silence of the disguised actors. In the entertainment at Hertford even this is jettisoned. Indeed, it is hard to distinguish in some respects from the regular comedy of the following century.

Two other texts remain to be considered: *Bycorne and Chychevache* and the *Mumming at Windsor*.[25] Of the former, it must here suffice to say that this text may be an instruction order in verse to a painter or weaver; it may be the 'devyse' of a disguising: or it may be both. If it is the text of a Disguising, then it is the one which approaches nearest to a play. There is no dialogue, but the argument, which has marked affinities with the Hertford text, is presented through six characters speaking in turn. The Windsor text is a thorn in the flesh; for, although conforming structurally to the pattern of a Disguising—no visitation by strangers, no presentation of gifts, but a dramatized debate—it is called a Mumming. If, for the present, we may shelve this difficulty in the title, the construction and the theme are simple to follow.* A poet recites to the boy-king, Henry VI, a fable of how he comes to bear the blazon of the *fleur de lys* in his coat armour and concludes by telling him that

---

* I hope to resolve this difficulty of title eventually, but at the moment I have no answer which I would be prepared to defend with much vigour.

this same story is about to be acted for him. There is no mention of persons coming to dice or to offer gifts. The story is told in simple language without embellishment—not unlike a good fairy tale—and ends with these words:

> 'Nowe, Royal Braunche, O Blood of Saint LOWYS,
> So lyke it nowe to Thy Magnyfycence,
> That the story of the flour delys
> May here be shewed in thyne heghe presence,
> And that thy noble, royal Excellence
> Lyst to supporte, here sitting in thy see,
> Right as it fell this myracle to see.'

From the story, it seems that St. Clotilda, King Clovis, St. Remigius and the hermit must all have appeared in order to enact the dumbshow; and possibly God as well. Miss Welsford regards this piece as related to the religious drama. I think it is possibly more accurate to reverse the emphasis and say that this piece demonstrates the harnessing of conventions borrowed from the religious drama to Court entertainment, which, as I have remarked, had its origin in social recreation and not in worship.[26]

Before proceeding to consider the manner in which this entertainment and the others we have reviewed were actually staged, it would perhaps be as well to try to assess what conclusions we may legitimately reach about their nature.

Whatever problems are left unresolved, at least it seems possible to detect a clear line of development within Courtly entertainment during the fourteenth and fifteenth centuries. At the start of this period we have evidence to warrant the assumption that the Court was a stable enough institution to possess both leisure for social recreation and the means to obtain it: and that these conditions extended to the larger monastic and noble houses all over the country. This social recreation was provided of an evening in part by the amateur pastimes of singing and dancing, in part by the diversions provided by paid troupes of minstrels, either maintained or hired, and in part by customs of long, traditional usage. Some of these derived from pre-Christian origins, the chief among which was mumming. By the close of the fourteenth century, two outdoor recreations had developed far enough to become potential sources for borrowing: the secular Tournament and the religious Miracle Cycles. The Tournament, although less closely linked to the literary narrative of Romance poetry than the Miracle Plays to Holy Writ, was nevertheless directly associated with indoor evening entertainments through the ceremony of prize-giving. The street pageant theatres of Royal Entries, too, were showing that it was possible to present an allegory of political intention in terms of dramatic spectacle. In these, as in the Miracle Plays, actors pointed story and moral alike in direct speech.

At the start of the fifteenth century, therefore, or perhaps even earlier, it was possible for anyone, given opportunity and encouragement, to weave these several strands into a co-ordinated and artistic dramatic entertainment, at once revealing its diverse points of origin and yet distinctively itself. A person who enjoyed such patronage, if not necessarily the first, was John Lydgate. As a monk and close friend of the Chaucer family, he was a man of letters moving in important social circles. He was thus thoroughly familiar with Romance poetry, with Corpus Christi Plays, and with the conventions of both the Royal Entry and Heraldry.[27] The nucleus which Lydgate seized upon to fashion his sophisticated entertainments was the mumming. Borrowing allegories from romance and scriptural sources, he gave this folk-custom, involving disguise of the person, a literary frame. From the Miracle Plays and Street Pageants he borrowed the idea of speaking actors, if he did not have them closer to hand among the minstrels already. From the Tournament he borrowed the Herald to present his characters and to explain their new significance. By these means the ritual accompanying the giving of presents at appropriate seasons of the year is translated into a literary debate enacted before an audience. Little seems to be left in common between the two except the disguise and the seasonal occasion which, in my view, explains a gradual shift of emphasis in title: Mumming . . . Ballad for or of a mumming . . . Device of a Mumming . . . Ballad or Device for mummers disguised . . . Disguising. Mumming, when all is said and done, is clearly a quite inept title for an entertainment in which the participants speak.

The subsequent history of the Disguising shows that the connection with the Mumming is preserved in the seasonal occasion, the disguise of the participants and the dancing which formed the culmination of the entertainment. In 1377 at Kennington 'ye prince and ye lordes dansed on ye one syde, and ye mummers on ye other a great while'. Not until 1512 is this division healed. In that year, for the first time the participants, 'after the maner of Italie', take their partners from among the audience:[28] and from then on the Italian title, *maschere* or Mask, for this titillating flirtation between disguised performers and the members of the audience, gradually comes to be substituted for the traditional English word 'Disguising'. *

Before this second change of title occurred, Henry VII married his eldest son Prince Arthur to Katherine of Aragon, and the occasion was marked with Disguisings on the same lavish scale as the Tournaments and Civic Pageants of 1501 already examined.† They were held in Westminster Hall and at the Palace of Richmond, and detailed accounts of them survive from the pen of an eye-witness. ‡

It is worth quoting one of these at length to show both how the structure of the entertainment resembles Lydgate's Disguisings and how startlingly spectacular the early Tudor version was.

The first of them was presented in Westminster Hall.

'Upon the Friday at nyght . . . when the Kyng and the Quene hade takyn their noble seats undre their clothis of Estate . . . then began and entrid this moost goodly and pleasaunt disguysing, conveyed and shewed by iii pagens p(ro)per and subtil: of whom the furst was a castell, . . . sett uppon certain whelys, and drawen into the seid hall of iiii‌ᵒʳ great bestis wᵗ cheynys of gold.'

The beasts in question were two lions (one gold, one silver), a hart and an ibex. There were two men inside each who drew the castle-waggon from the end of the hall to its halting place before the throne.

'There were wᵗin this Castell, disguysid, viii goodly and fresshe ladies, lokyng owt of the wyndowes of the same; and in the iiiiᵒʳ corners of the castell were iiiiᵒʳ toretts . . . in the which of evry of these torretts was a litil childe, apparellid like a mayden; and so all they iiiiᵒʳ children syngyng till they came bifore the King's Mageste, where when hit hade comyn, conveyed and sett himself sumwhat owt of the weye, toward the oon sid of the halle.

---

* In addition to the novelty of performers choosing dancing partners from the audience, a particularly distinctive costume of Italian design came to be adopted by the maskers. See p. 218 *et seq.*, below. Even so, it is unwise to seek to be too dogmatic in the matter of definitions. Mummings and Tournaments continue to be loosely associated with both the Disguising and the Mask. Trying to draw hard-and-fast lines between what is a 'borrowing', what is 'an original invention' and what is 'an archaic survival' in Tudor entertainments tends to create more confusion than it sets out to resolve.

† See Ch. II, pp. 43, 44 above.

‡ An attendant Herald, the author of C.A. MS., 1st M13. He says his narrative contains 'truly and without fable the very geste and forme of the matter.' See p. 187 above.

'The secunde pagent was a shippe in like wise sett upon whelys, w^{t}out any leders (*ladders*) in sight, in right goodly apparell, havyng her mastys, toppys, saylys, her taclyng, and all other app(ur)ten-(au)ns necessary unto a semely vessell, as though it hade been saylyng in the see; . . . till they cam byfore the kynge, sumwhat beside the castell. At the which tyme, the masters of the Shippe and their company in their counten(au)ns, spechis and demeano^r usid and behavyd them silf after the man^r and guyse of Marynours. And there (*they*) cast their ankkers. In the which shipp(e) there was a goodly and a faire lady, in her apparell like unto the P(ri)ncess of Hispayne. Owte and from the seid shippe descendid down by a ledder two weelbeseen and goodly p(er)sons, callyng themsilf Hope and Desire, passyng toward the rehersid castell, w^t their baners in maner and forme as ambassadours from Knights of the Mownte of Love unto the ladies w^{t}in the castell . . . for th'en-tente to ateigne the favouris of the seid ladies p(re)sent; The seid ladies gave their final answere of utt(e)rly refuse and knowledge of any such company . . . The two seid ambassadours, therw(ith) takyng great displeasure, shewed the seid ladies that the Knights wolde for this unkyend refusall make bataill . . .

'Incontynent cam in the thirde pagent, in liknes of a great hill . . . in whom were enclosid viii goodly Knights w^t ther ban(ers) spred and displaied . . . they toke their stondyng upon the other sid of the shipp(e) . . . they alited from the seid mount . . . and hastely spede them to the rehersed castell, which they forthw(ith) asaultid so and in such wise that the ladies, yeldyng themselvys, descendid from the seid castell. The knights (were) right freshly disguysed and the ladies also, iiij^{or} of them afte(r) th'englissh fachyon and th'other iiii^{or} afte(r) the man(ner) of hispayne . . . and dauncyd togyders dyv(er)s and many goodly daunces.'[29] (See Plate XXIV and Fig. 15, p. 223 below.)

This eye-witness account could scarcely be more detailed and categoric. For good measure, the Herald-chronicler tells us that the pageant cars were removed during the dance, after which the dancers themselves departed. The spectators then took the floor, their dances being led by Prince Arthur and Lady Cecil. Lest we carry away too sober a picture of this entertainment, the Herald adds that the Duke of York (later, Henry VIII) 'p(er)ceyvyng himself to be encombred w(ith) his clothis sodenly cast of(f) his gowne and dauncyd in his jaket'.[30]

This happy postscript perhaps reveals for us more vividly than anything else could the true nature of these evening entertainments. They are truly secular in that they were designed to accompany feasting as an enjoyable social recreation. This enjoyment, however, was never far removed from ceremonial rituals. The simple, allegoric compliment latent in this and similar entertainments and its obvious affinities with the *Pas d'Armes* and Heraldry testify to that. * The formality of the one is softened to permit the informality of the other, and the whole consequently forms a basis for the mixing of professional and amateur talent in pleasing harmony. Minstrels, gentlemen and ladies could meet on an equal footing, as the pages of Hall's Chronicle bear eloquent witness throughout the reign of Henry VIII, while tailors, carpenters and painters laboured to give to their sophisticated revels 'a local habitation and a name'. Presiding over them all, by virtue of his authority in the Hall or Great Chamber respectively, was the Steward of the Household or the Lord Chamberlain.[31]

Once the antiquity of the latter gentleman's office is appreciated, in so far as it related to control of the ordering of indoor performances, together with the responsibility the office carries for a dexterous balancing of informality within the bounds of traditional etiquette, it becomes possible to speak intelligently about staging conditions at Court and in other noble houses during the Middle Ages.

The mediaeval feast usually began in daylight and was continued by torchlight if necessary into the hours of darkness. By modern standards the menus would appear to tax even the sturdiest digestion past endurance. Yet the meal was conducted in a leisurely fashion with long pauses between courses. It was during these intervals between courses that the minstrel troupe was expected to perform.[32]

From earliest times it had been normal to give time, thought and money to the decoration of the banqueting hall. The earliest English example of painted walls that I have encountered is Westminster Hall in 1272 against Edward I's Coronation.† Hangings of rich materials and tapestry enjoyed great popularity, possibly as much because of the additional warmth and better acoustic which their presence afforded as for their decorative value.

---

* It should be noticed that the castle, ship, mountain and animals described in this Disguising all appeared in the Tournaments held during the celebrations. For other examples, see Welsford, *CM.*, pp. 123–126.

† 'It magna aula & parva dealbate (*sic*) sūt de novo & depicte. ita qđ oculi infra illas intanciū & tantum pulc¹ tudīem (*sic*) intuenciū plenio deliciis & gaudio repleatʳ.[33]

These paintings and tapestries very often represented the stories already familiar from the verse chronicles and romances recited by the trouvères. As I have pointed out, with the example of the liturgical plays already to hand, a pressure existed to fuse these recitals and visual representations into an active narrative. A mid-way point between the two is the static but three-dimensional 'subtilty'.

Subtilties were fashioned out of sugar and, as table decorations, were a tribute by the chef to the person in whose honour the feast was being held or to the occasion being celebrated. A subtilty might therefore be defined as a symbolic device in coloured sugar corresponding, in its attraction, to an elaborate wedding cake. Several could be presented at a single feast, it being usual for one to be brought in between each course. The example which I cite here is one of those which Lydgate provided for Henry VI's Coronation banquet:

('The iij^d course sueth; that is to say:—Blaunde Surrey poudrid w(i)t(h) quatrefoilis gilt. Venyson restid. Egrettes. Curlewe. Cokkes. Plover. Quailis. Snytes. Grete birdes. Larkes. Carpe. Crabbe. Lech of iij colours. A colde bakemete like a shelde quarterly redde and white, set w(i)t(h) loseng(es) and gilt, and floures of borage. Fritour crispes. A sotelte of Our Lady sitting and hir Childe in hir lappe, and she holdyng in hir hand a crowne and Seint George knelyng on that oo side and Seint Denyse on that other side, p(re)sentyng the Kyng, knelyng, to Our Lady, w(i)t(h) this reason folowyng;)

> O blessid Lady, Cristes moder dere,
> And thou Seint George, th(a)t callid art hir knight;
> Holy Seint Denyse, O martir moost entier;
> The sixt Henry here p(re)sent in your sight,
> Shewith of g(ra)ce on hym your hevenly light,
> His tendre yougth with v(er)tue doth avaunce,
> Bore by discent and by title of right
> Justly to reigne in England and in F(ra)unce.'³⁴

Mere prettiness was clearly not enough: the subtilty had to be appropriate to the occasion and its significance, like that of the tableaux in the streets, interpreted by means of a 'scripture'. *

* The Herald, describing the Queen's Coronation banquet in 1487, writes: '. . . A Soteltie w^t writing of balads, whiche as yett I have not' (B.M. MS. Cot. Jul. B. XII f. 40b). Like every other form of mediaeval entertainment which we have discussed, the custom of preparing subtilties at feasts was

At a mediaeval feast, then, in the tapestries which adorned the walls and in the subtilties which decorated the table, we have a series of *tableaux morts* (if the phrase be allowed) which only require live actors to transform them into the *tableaux vivants* with which we are already familiar in the Tournament and the Pageants of the streets.

This notion seems to have occurred to the organizers of feasts at the turn of the fourteenth century into the fifteenth, perhaps even earlier. Chaucer at any rate had witnessed a number of these seemingly miraculous incarnations. His observations are set out in the *Frankleyn's Tale* at the point where Aurelius confides his sickness of heart to his brother, a young clerk. This clerk remembers having seen a book of magic belonging to a fellow student at Orleans which he thinks might help to cure him. Recollecting this book,

> 'Anon for joye his herte gan to daunce,
> And to him-self he seyde prively;
> "My brother shal be warisshed (*cured*) hastily;
> For I am siker (*sure*) that ther be sciences,
> By whiche men make diverse apparences
> Swiche as thise subtile tregetoures pleye."
> For ofte at festes have I wel herd seye,
> That tregetours, with-inne an halle large,
> Have maad come in a water and a barge,
> And in the halle rowen up and doun. *
> Somtyme hath semed come a grim leoun; †
> And somtyme floures springe as in a mede; ‡
> Somtyme a vyne, and grapes whyte and rede; §
> Somtyme a castel, al of lym and stoon; ||
> And whan hem lyked, voyded it anoon,
> Thus seemed it to every mannes sights.'[35]

This passage is of considerable interest; for not only does all

international. At Henry VI's Paris coronation we are told that the day's festivities concluded with a banquet—'Auqel disner furent presentez quatre entremets devant la table: c'est sçavoir, le premier d'un image de nostre Dame', and 'un petit Roy couronné emprés: le second fut une fleur de lys courõnée d'or tenue de deux Anges: le tiers une Dame and un paon, and le quart une Dame & un Cinge.' (Monstrelet, *Chroniques*, ed. Metayer, Paris, 1595, ii, 78.)

* For a later factual example in England see p. 209 above.
† Cf., p. 208 above.
‡ Cf., p. 218 below.
§ *Ibid*.
|| Cf., pp. 214–215 below, and p. 208 above.

this spectacle figure in the confections of chefs, in Tournaments and in the Pageant Theatres, but Chaucer attributes the indoor employment of these familiar devices to the Jongleurs. It would be rash to accept this statement, which after all occurs in a romance, as evidence of fact; but happily a considerable body of factual evidence exists to substantiate it.

One of the first feasts to have been decorated by scenic structures of the sort described by Chaucer was that given by Charles V of France to entertain the Emperor Charles IV in 1378.*

Christine de Pisan tells that on that occasion two entremets or pageants were presented, showing how Godfrey of Boulogne conquered Jerusalem. One of them, representing

'the city, large and splendid, made of wood and painted with the scutcheons and armes of the Saracens (very well executed), was brought in front of the Dais. Next came the ship with Godfrey on board: and then the assault began and the city was taken which was very enjoyable to watch.'† (See Plate XXIV.)

In this connection it is worth remarking that the inventory of Charles V's household goods taken seven years earlier includes a tapestry of this very subject.[36]

In 1389 Charles VI of France married Isabella of Bavaria. We have already discussed the Pageants provided for her entertainment.[37] The feast which followed is no less interesting. Froissart, in describing it, gives a detailed account of how the scenic devices were constructed and of how they were employed. The description commences with the arrangements made for the lay-out of the Hall and the seating of the guests. This is the earliest account of an indoor auditorium that survives and therefore deserves notice. Here a diagram can save a lot of verbiage. (See Fig. 14, p. 214 below.)

'In the middle of the banqueting hall was a castle built on a square frame, forty foot high and twenty foot square. It had four towers, one on each corner, and another, higher tower placed in

---

* On this feast see L. H. Loomis, "Secular Dramatics and Chaucer's 'Tregetoures'", *Speculum*, Vol. XXXIII (April, 1958) No. 2, pp. 242–255.

† 'Deux entremés y ot: l'un, comme Godefroy de Buillon conquist Jherusalem, laquelle histoire ramentevoir estoit pertinent pour exemples donner a telz princes; estoit la cité grande et belle, de bois painte à panonceaulx et armes des Sarrazins, moult bienfaicte, qui fu menée devant le doiz; et puis la nef où Godefroy de Buillon estoit; et puis l'assault comencié et la cité prise: qui fu bonne chose à veoir.'[38]

the middle. The castle itself represented the City of Troy, and the central tower the Palace of Ilion. Pennons flying from it bore the arms of the Trojans, notably those of King Priam, his proud son Hector and his children as well as those of the other kings and

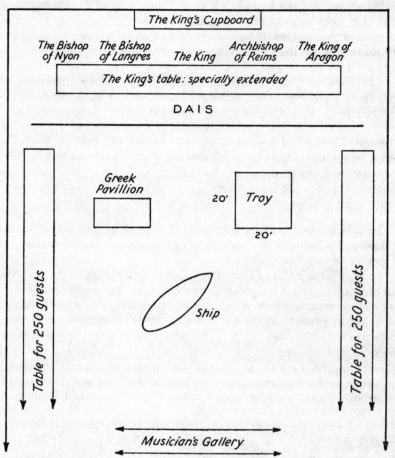

FIG. 14. Ground Plan of the 'Entremet' of 1389 at the French Court, reconstructed from Froissart's description of the scene.

princes besieged in Troy with them. And this castle moved on four wheels, subtly concealed within.

'Mounted on a similar vehicle, in which the means of motion could not be detected, was a pavilion carrying those Grecian Kings and others who long ago laid siege to Troy. There was also,

214

as if by way of reinforcement, a ship, splendidly made, which could easily contain a hundred soldiers. All three—castle, pavilion and ship—moved by the art and ingenuity of these wheels.

'A great assault was made by those in both the ship and the pavilion against the castle, whose occupants stoutly withstood it. But the sport could not be sustained for long on account of the number of spectators who were suffocated with heat and thoroughly discomforted by the crush.'*

The King himself intervened to put a stop to the show. Two centuries later we shall hear much more about this problem of overcrowding. Before commenting however on this elaborate and ill-fated spectacle it is worth considering the equally extraordinary entertainment of three nights later. This feast was held in the King's palace at St. Pol. After dinner,

'. . . the King sitting at table, . . . and a great assembly of ladies, there entered the room, which was large and spacious (and newly built for the feast), two Knights on horseback fully armed for jousting.'†

These French entertainments of the late fourteenth century are

---

* 'Au milieu du palais avoit ung chastelet ouvré et charpenté en quarrure de quarante piés de hault et de vingt piés de long et de vingt piés de large et, avoit quatre tours sur les quatre quartiers, et une tour plus haulte assés ou milieu du chastel, et estoit figuré le chastel pour la cité de Troye la Grant, et la tour du mylieu pour le palais de Ylion, et là estoient en pennons les armes des Troiens, telles que du roy Priant, du preu Hector son fils et de des enffans, et aussi des roys et des princes qui furent enclos dedens Troye avoec euls. Et aloit ce chastel sur quatre roes qui tournoient par dedens moult soubtillement, et vindrent ce chastel requerre et assaillir autres gens d'un lés qui estoient en ung pavillon lequel pareillement aloit sur roes couvertement et soubtillement; car on ne veoit riens du mouvement, et là estoient les armoieries des roys de Grèce et d'ailleurs, qui mirent jadis le siége devant Troye. Ancoires y avoit, sicomme en leur ayde, une nef très-proprement faitte où bien povoient cent hommes d'armes, et tout par l'art et engien des roes se mouvoient ces trois choses, le chastel, le nef et le pavillon. Et eut de ceulx de la nef et du pavillon grant assault d'un lés à ceulx du chastel, et de ceulx du chastel aux dessusdis grant deffense. Mais l'esbatement ne peult longuement durer pour la cause de la grant presse de gens qui les advironnoient, et là eut des gens pour la challeur eschauffés et par presse moult mesaisiés.' (Froissart, *Chroniques, ed. cit.*, XIV, 15.)

† '. . ., le roy séant à table, (la duchesse de Berry, ..., la contesse de Saint Pol, la dame de Coucy) et grant foison de dames, entrèrent en la salle qui estoit ample et large (celle qui estoit faitte nouvellement pour la feste) deux chevalliers montés aux chevauls, armés de toutes pièces pour la jouste.' (Froissart, *Chroniques, ed. cit.*, XIV, 24.)

not only important because they happen to be the first of which record survives, but because the design to which they conform is fundamental for the next two hundred years, first to the Disguising and then to the Mask. The multiple scenic structures employed in the representation of the siege of Jerusalem and the siege of Troy are of the same type as those used in Balthassar Beaujoyeux's *Ballet Comique de la Royne*, of 1582, or any Mask of the Tudor Court. The jousting at St. Pol in the new banqueting hall is seen to be flourishing still in the *Combat à la Barrière* at Nancy, in 1627 for Jacques Callot to record in a superb set of engravings: while, almost as late, in Jacobean England, Ben Jonson is writing Prologues for the protagonists in similar indoor Combats at Barriers. *

It is unfortunate that no English example of an entertainment employing these scenic devices survives from the fourteenth century. Nevertheless Chaucer was clearly aware of them: he could even have been present at the French feast of 1377/8, since he was then on his way from London to Milan: and the Duke of Ireland actually was present.

In the early fifteenth century, however, scenic devices were certainly used in Lydgate's Mumming for the Mercers and probably in both the Mumming at Windsor and the Mumming at London.

The Mercers made an entry in three ships. The Windsor text seems to demand a 'heaven', a hermitage (probably the usual cave in a hill) and a church. In the Mumming at London Dame Fortune is said to inhabit

> '. . . an halle
> Departed (*i.e. divided into two*) and wonder desguysee.
> Frome that oon syde, yee may see,
> Ceryously wrought, for the noones,
> Of golde, of syluer and of stones.
> Whos richesse may not be tolde.
> But that other syde of that hoolde
> Is ebylt in ougly wyse,
> And ruynous, for to devyse.'[39]

The lady's fickleness is thus fitly symbolized visually in the contradictory nature of her dwelling.

What Chaucer and Lydgate hint at is amply confirmed in the latter part of the fifteenth century by both the eyewitness testimony of attendant-heralds and the Privy Purse accounts.[40]

* See Plates XXVII and XXVIII: also Vol. II, 1576–1660, Pt. 1., Plates XX–XXII.

Here for example are some representative payments made for entertainments between January 1495 and January 1496:

i.	i.	95.	To Scot the fole for a rewarde, 6s. 8d.
4.	i.	95.	To the Frenshe pleyers in rewarde, £2.
13.	ii.	95.	Jaks Haute in full payment of his bille for his disguysings £13.10. 6d.
20.	ii.	95.	To the Queen of France ministrels £30.
2.	xi.	95.	To a woman that singeth with a fidell, 2s.
23.	xii.	95.	To Jakes Haute for the disguysing, £10.
28.	xii.	95.	To two pleyes in the Hall, £1. 6. 8.
10.	i.	96.	To Ryngeley, lorde of misrule, in rewarde £2.
24.	i.	96.	To Jakes Haute in full payment for the disguysing to Estermes £6. 17. 6.[41]

Apart from the 'Queen of France ministrels', whose reward possibly included journey money, the disguisings are the most costly items in the list and strikingly more expensive than plays. The reason for this lies in the corresponding emphasis on the respective spectacle and text. The Disguising was, by its very nature, occasional: the spectators' pleasure rested largely in the surprise of the entry: and, being in principle an amateur charade, there was never any question of it being included in a repertoire for commercial advantage. Thus, in the sixteenth century, the Disguising remains much more closely related to Tournaments than to either the Miracle Play or the Interlude.

For Katherine of Aragon's wedding in 1501 the scenic devices for the Disguisings included the familiar ship, castle, tabernacle, arbour and mountain. The ship, tabernacle and mountain had adorned the lists only a few days earlier.[42] For 1511, at Westminster,

'iiij Knights borne in the Realme of Ceour Noble, whose names followeth, that is to saie C'eur Loyal, Valiant Desire, Bone Voloyx and Joyouse Penser . . . at the instance and desire . . .'[43]

of the Queen obtain permission for a Tournament which duly takes place under the title of *Les quater Chevalers de la forrest salvigne*. This was a regular *Pas d'Armes* with a magnificent scenic forest, drawn by heraldic beasts. In the evening, after the jousting, the King and the Queen and the Ambassadors 'came into the White Hall, within the sayde Pallays, whiche was hanged rychely, the Hall was scafolded and rayled on all partes'.[44]

An interlude was presented by 'the gentlemen of his chapell' and songs and dances followed. 'Then was there a device or a pageau(n)t upo(n) wheles brought in.' It was screened from the view of the spectators. 'Then a great cloth of Arras that did hang before the same pageau(n)t was taken awaye, and the pageaunt brought more nere.' It represented a garden and in it there sat Coeur Loyal and his companions of the earlier jousts. Lest there should be any mistake, 'every persone had his name in letters of massy gold'.

Closely as these pageant vehicles for Tournament and Disguising are related they were not one and the same. That for the former was 'made like a forest with rockes, hilles and dales, with divers sundrie trees, floures', etc., and was large enough to contain a castle in the middle. Hall tells us that 'all the trees, herbes and floures, of the same forrest were made of grene Velvet, greene Damaske, and silke of divers colours, Satyn and Sercenet'. The garden or arbour for the Disguising consisted of, 'trees of Hathorne, Eglantynes, Rosiers, Vines and other pleasaunt floures of divers colours with Gillofers and other herbes all made of Satyn, damaske, silke, silver and gold, accordingly as the natural trees, herbes, or floures ought to be'.

This intimate relationship between not only the pageant cars themselves but the actual materials from which they were fashioned is not without significance to the Wardrobe Accounts of Edward III's reign discussed in Chapter V.*

Within a year of the Jousts of the *Chevalers de la forrest salvigne*, in 1512 to be exact, Hall writes in his *Chronicle:*

'On the daie of the Epiphanie at night, the kyng with a xi. other were disguised, after the maner of Italie, called a maske, a thyng not seen afore in Englande, thei were appareled in garmentes long and brode, wrought all with gold, with visers and cappes of gold . . . these Maskers came in, . . . and desired the ladies to daunce, some were content, and some that knewe the fashion of it refused, because it was not a thyng commonly seen. And after thei daunced and commoned together, as the fashion of the Maske is, thei tooke their leave and departed.'[45]

The whole sense of this passage directs that the novelty lay in part in the particular garments worn and in part in the dancing with the audience—one partner masked and the other not. That the Mask was not a new dramatic genre imported from Italy is clearly discernible from comparison of post-1512 examples with earlier Disguisings. Just as in Lydgate's hands the Mumming both was and was not a mumming as depicted by men of Chaucer's day, so

* See Ch. V, pp. 188–189 above.

the Mask of Henry VIII's reign both was and was not the Disguising of Henry VII's. They were one and the same except in small points. First, the disguised mummers chose dancing partners from the audience instead of exclusively from their own ranks. Secondly, they wore special masking cloaks and vizors. Both these novelties were of Italian origin, and thought to be *risqué* enough to provoke comment when first introduced. The essential sameness, however, of the general structure of the entertainment can be easily illustrated from the show given to the French ambassadors by Henry VIII at Greenwich in 1527.[46]

'When the kyng and the quene, were set under their clothes of estate which were rich and goodly, and the ambassadours set on the righte side of the chambre, then entred a person clothed in cloth of golde, and over that a mantell of blew silke, full of eyes of golde, and over his hed a cap of gold with a garland of Laurell set with beries of fyne gold.'

This person was clearly the Presenter and comparable with Lydgate's heralds.*

'This person made a solempne Oracio(n), in the Latin tongue, declaryng what Ioye was to the people of both the realmes of England and Fraunce.'

Thus the entertainment is specifically related to the occasion it celebrates, as of old.

'. . . and when he had doen, then entred eight (?*boys*) of the kynges Chappel with a song and brought with theim one richly appareled: and in likewise at the other side, entred eight other of the saied Chappel bryngyng with them another persone, likewise appareled.'

This entry to song of the characters presented is proper to the old Disguising. However, they proceed to explain their presence in dialogue:

'These two persones plaied a dialog theffect whereof was whether riches were better the(n) love, and when they could not agre upon a conclusion, eche called in thre knightes, all armed.'

Instead of a third person intervening to give judgement, as in Lydgate's Mumming at Hertford,† the quarrel is made the excuse for jousts at barriers:

* See p. 199 above.
† See p. 204 above.

219

'Thre of them woulde have entred the gate of the Arche in the middel of the chambre, and the other iii resisted, and sode(n)ly betwene the six knightes, out of the Arche fell doune a bar all gilte, at the whiche barre the six knightes fought a fair battail, and then thei were departed, and so went out of the place.'

This combat appears to have been inconclusive, for the debate is ultimately resolved in the traditional manner.

'Then came in an olde man with a silver be(a)rd, and he concluded that love and riches, both be necessarie for princes (that is to saie) by love to be obeied and served, and with riches to rewarde his lovers and frendes, and with this conclusion the dialogue ended.'

Where, however, in Lydgate's time dancing would have followed immediately, the entertainment is now extended to include scenic spectacle as a further prelude to it:

'The(n) at yᵉ nether ende, by lettyng doune of a courtaine, apered a goodly mou(n)t, walled with towers and vamures (*ramparts*) al gilt . . . all the mount was set ful . . . of roses and pomgranates as though they grewe: on this rocke sat eight Lordes . . . and then they sodenly descended from the mounte and toke ladyes, and dau(n)ced divers daunces.'*

The Lords' entry was followed by a Ladies' entry:

'The(n) out of a cave issued out the ladie Mary doughter to the kyng and with her seven ladies, . . .: these eight Ladies daunced with eight Lordes of the mount.'

At this point the formal Disguising is translated into the new Mask:

'And as thei daunced, sodenly entred sixe personages, appareled in cloth of silver and blacke tinsell satin, and whodes on their heddes . . . and these persones had visers with sylver be(a)rdes, so that they were not knowne: these Maskers tooke Ladies and daunsed lustely about the place.'

This served as a cue to the King and the Viscount de Tourraine who

'. . . were conveighed out of the place into a chambre thereby, and there quicklie they ii and six other in maskyng apparel of cloth of gold and purple tinsel sattin, greate, lo(n)g, and large, after the Venicians fashio(n), and over them great robes, and there faces were visard wᵗ beardes of gold: then with minstrelsie these viii

* This curtain was probably painted by Hans Holbein. See J. S. Brewer, *Letters and Papers of the Reign of Henry VIII*, iv, Nos. 3097 and 3104.

noble personages entred and daunsed long with the ladies, and when they had daunsed there fill, then the quene plucked of the kynges visar, and so did the Ladies the visars of the other Lordes, and then all were knowe(n).'

Henry gave his own masking robes, 'which were very riche,' to his French guest. Hall concludes his description in a prose worthy of Shakespeare:

'Then the kyng, quene and the ambassadours, returned to the banket chamber, where thei found a banket ready set on the borde, of so many and marveilous dishes, that it was wonder to se(.) Then the kyng sat doune and there was joy, myrth and melody: and after that all was doen the kyng and all other went to rest, for the night was spent, and the day even at the breakyng.'

This description has a double interest. First, it conveniently presents a Double Mask in association with its progenitors the Disguising and the Tournament. Secondly, it shows us that speeches of the kind Lydgate offered in the Mumming (more properly, Disguising) at Hertford are still customary. It is unfortunate that, among the many detailed accounts of Tudor Disguisings and Masks that have survived, none incorporate the spoken text.

At the reception for Katherine of Aragon, the Herald's account of the first of the three Disguisings establishes the existence of a text, but does not provide it: 'The masters of the Shippe,' we are told, 'and their company in their counten(au)ns spechis and demeano^r usid and behavyd themsilf aftir the man^r and guyse of Marynours.' When they approached the ladies, 'the seid ladies gave their final answere of utt(e)rly refuse and knowledge of any such company. . . . The two seid ambassadours, therw^t takyng great displeasure shewed the seid ladies . . .' etc.[47]

The obvious deduction is that the text had become an excuse for the spectacle, the music and the dancing which it served to introduce. Only at the end of the century, when poets of outstanding originality and ability came to take an interest in the devising of these texts, was there any chance of redressing the balance.

If the descriptions of Tudor Disguisings are to be credited, the fascination of the spectacle lay in its surprise and ingenuity. This is understandable enough when the actors and spectators are friends and acquaintances who are ultimately to join hands and dance together. Indeed it is principally to allow dancing that the scenic units are on wheels, and removable, therefore, when the floor space is required. Another consequence is that, unlike the open-air theatres discussed, the indoor theatre was socially exclusive. Those privileged to participate and to watch were synonymous with those who held the *entrée* to the King's Hall or Great Chamber.* This ensured a high minimum standard of literacy but, thereby, did as much to divorce these entertainments from popular standards. The Hall was more usually employed during the fifteenth century: the Great Chamber in the sixteenth century.[48] This fact accounts for much of the difficulty in deciding how these entertainments were organized, since a performance in the Hall came under the aegis of the King's Steward, while a performance in the Great Chamber was the Chamberlain's responsibility.[49] However, whether the performance was in the Hall or in the Great Chamber the lay-out was the same. On the dais at the upper end sat the King and Queen, together with their friends and intimate servants. At the opposite end, above the entrance doors was a gallery for the musicians. 'The Trompetters,' writes John Younge describing the Betrothal of Margaret Tudor and James IV of Scotland in 1502, stood, 'on the Leds at the Chamber End'.[50]

At this end too the special stage was probably erected for the Officers of Arms, when needed for indoor Jousting or for a prize-giving. Down either side of the Hall or Chamber scaffolds were erected to seat the other spectators. On Twelfth Night 1494, according to Stow, the King entertained the

'. . . Maior of London, and his brethren the Aldermen, with other commoners in great number, and after dinner dubbing the Maior knight, caused him with his brethren to stay and behold the disguisings and other disports, in the night following shewed in the great hall (*i.e. Westminster Hall*), which was richly hanged with Arras, and staged about on both sides.'[51]

On the 30th December 1519,

'. . . at the castle of Noseroy (in France) in a ground-floor room were lists framed with cloth for jousting on the floor. About five dozen torches had been lit in this hall at eight o'clock at night. There are the Judges on a scaffold hung about with arras as is normal in such circumstances: and near to this scaffold is another, equally well furnished, whither came the Princess of Orange accompanied by several ladies and young girls.'[52]

* Spinelli, in his account of the entertainment at Greenwich (1527) notes that, "those to whom admission was granted" were seated in the third tier, "they being few". Brewer, *Reign of Hen. VIII*, ii. 152.

The central floor space was thus left vacant for the performance. Despite differences from the outdoor Tournament and Street Pageant in these vital respects, however, the stage and auditorium of indoor entertainments at Court resembled them as theatres of direct address. Devised to celebrate a particular event or in honour of a particular person intimately connected with it, they could not escape being projected at the audience in general and at that person in particular.

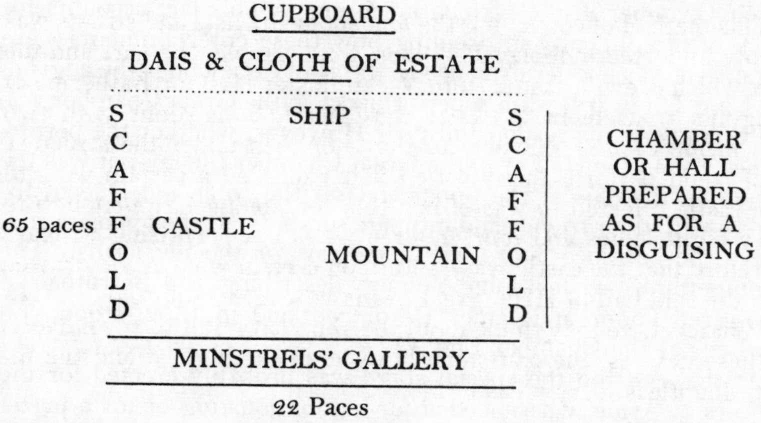

CUPBOARD

DAIS & CLOTH OF ESTATE

....

S	SHIP	S		
C		C	CHAMBER	
A		A	OR HALL	
F		F	PREPARED	
65 paces F	CASTLE	F	AS FOR A	
O	MOUNTAIN	O	DISGUISING	
L		L		
D		D		

MINSTRELS' GALLERY

22 Paces

Fig. 15. Ground plan of the seating and scenic arrangements for one of the Disguisings at Westminster, 1501, reconstructed from the eye-witness description of an attendant Herald. See Plates XXII, No. 32, and XXIII, No. 33.

Since the Disguising had been from its inception a mere preliminary to the ultimate union of performers and spectators in the evening's dancing, the practical feature of adequate floor space for it counted for more than anything else in determining the design of the auditorium for indoor entertainments. It also ruled that scenic *loca*, if used, should be mobile.

In effecting this, the designers seem to have borrowed from the outdoor Tournament and Miracle Cycle (Midlands and North Country) rather than from the Civic Pageants. It was in 1374 that Edward III escorting Dame Alice Perrers as 'Lady of the Sun' rode through London to joust: in 1397 that Richard II saw the Miracle plays at York.* At a tournament in 1501,

'. . . anoon cam owte . . . for the defendeours, Guyllam de la Ryvers . . . in a goodly shippe borne up w^t men, w^{t}in himself

* See Ch. II, 20 above, and Ch. IV, pp. 163, 164 above.

223

ryding in the myddes;' . . . 'and the sides of the ship covered w^t cloth peynted after the colour or lykeness of water.'[53]

A few days later, when the same animals were used, we hear of

'. . . a goodly char . . . drawyn w^t foure m(a)rvellous bests . . . ev(er)y oon havyng w^t in them two men, ther leggs, aloonly apperyng, beyng after the colour and symylitude of the beasts that they were inn.'

This method of conveying the *loca* about the lists and streets was simply imported indoors. The lions, for example, the hart and the ibex which drew 'a castell' into Westminster Hall for Katherine of Aragon's amusement in 1501, were heraldic creations with two men inside each.[54] But neither they nor men under the structure itself could perform this function if it exceeded a certain weight. The castle referred to was of just this sort, being large enough to carry eight ladies and four children. It is not surprising to learn therefore that the castle was, 'sett upon certain whelys and drawen into the seid hall of IIII^{or} great bestis w^t cheynys of gold.'

Whatever we may think about the simplicity, not to say naïveté, of these devices, the craftsmanship was of the highest and the result, doubtless, very pleasing.

'The secunde pagent was a shippe in like wise sett uppon whelys, w^{t}out any leders in sight, in right goodly apparell, havyng her mastys, toppys, saylys, her taclyng, and all other app(ur)ten-(au)ns necessary unto a semely vessell, as though it hade been saylyng in the see.'[55]

Alternatively, as a week later, again in Westminster Hall,

'In the lougher ende . . . were disclosed and brought into sight II mervelous mounts or mounteyns, right cunȳngly p(ra)ctised and made: the oon of them of color grene, planted full of fresshe trees, sume of them like olyffs, sume orangs, sume laurells, genaps (*i.e. junipers*) vir trees, dyvers and many faire and plas(a)unt erbys, flouris and frute, that great delite it was to beholde.'[56]

This was in England, not in Italy, we might remember, and the date 1501.

The need for artificial light, as I have suggested, provoked an additional problem. General lighting was the responsibility of household officials who ensured that there were 'lights in the hall afture the quantite of the hall'.[57]

Mediaeval stage-designers were not so unimaginative as to ignore the inherent spectacular effects made possible by artificial light. Not only did torch-bearers accompany pageants into the hall,[58] but pageant devices were invented which owed their special attraction to the use of lights:

'Therew^t cam in a goodly pagent made rounde, aft(e)r the fachyon of a lanterne, cast owte w^t many p(ro)pre and goodly wyndowes fenestred w^t fyne lawne, wherein were more than an hundred great lights; in the which lanterne were XII goodly ladies disguysid. . . . This lantern was made of so fyn stuf, and so many lights in hit, that these ladies might p(er)fectly appiere and be known thorugh the seid lanterne.'[59]

In the reigns of Edward VI, Mary and Elizabeth there is a discernible change in the tone of Disguisings-cum-Masks. The themes from Romance allegory of the fifteenth century tend to be replaced by the near mythological allegory of the Renaissance, a change which finds its parallel in the pageant theatres of the streets.* But there is a tedious similarity in the devices used to present it. In 1560 it is the rock, the fountain, the castle and the arbour which are wheeled into the Banqueting Hall for the young Elizabeth's delectation.[60] For Samuel Daniel's *Vision of Twelve Goddesses* in 1603 the scenic units remain, the 'cave' of sleep, the 'temple' of Peace and the monotonously persistent 'mountain'.[61]

Despite this seeming lassitude, the cost of these entertainments rose startlingly from the modest £13 paid to Jaques Haute by Henry VII in 1495 to the £400 or more that was usual in Elizabeth's reign. We catch a glimpse of the reason in a letter from Edward VI's Lord of Misrule to the Master of the Revels:

'It seemeth unto us as towching the Apparell of our Counseilloures you have mistaken ye persons that sholde were them as Si(r) Robert Stafforde and Thom(as) Wyndeham with other gentlemen that stande also apon their reputacion and wolde not be seen in London so torchebererlyke disgysed for asmoche as they ar worthe or hope to be worthe.'[62]

If personal vanity stimulated a taste for extravagance on the part of the actors, so did the introduction of classical mythological characters on that of the audience. These Deities, after all, owed much of their popularity to their supposed control of the senses.

* See Ch. III, pp. 80, 81 above: also Vol. II, 1576–1660, Pt. 1, pp. 280–299.

Venus, Mars or Vulcan were tame creations if not visibly more glamorous in person and attire than normal mortals:

'Hereat Proteus, Amphitrite and Thamesis, with their attendants, the Nymphs and Tritons, went unto the rock, and then the Prince and the seven Knights issued forth of the rock, in a very stately mask, very richly attired, and gallantly provided of all things meet for the performance of so great an enterprise.'[63]

Thus did the gentlemen of Gray's Inn deck themselves up at Shrovetide 1594. The important phrase is 'all things meet'—for in them lay the expense. From here it is but a short step to appropriateness and so to verisimilitude: '*Il faut apprendre des Poetes et des Anciens Autheurs . . . ce qui est propre des Dieux pour ces representations.*'[64]

This sort of reasoning, once accepted, spells death to the multiple stage with its conventions of visual aids drawn from the local environment in setting and costume. The significance of the event to the present must eventually give precedence to exactitude and accuracy in chronology and representation. However, the lack of painters and architects of calibre in Tudor England effectively prevented this progression from making any serious headway in the sixteenth century. Neither the Gods and their attendants of the Gray's Inn Mask, nor the rock which they miraculously clove asunder, differ substantially from the *Chevalers de la forrest salvigne*, the Knights of the Mount of Love or the Trojan princes and their assailants and their respective scenic cars.

Development of indoor scenic spectacle therefore, during the sixteenth century, rests rather in the development of the fanciful and the exotic latent within inherited conventions than in any serious or original departure from them. Virtually without exception they are those of the Tournament, the Civic Pageants and the Miracle Plays, put on wheels, set up indoors and presented at night by the light of many torches in an auditorium fundamentally the same as that presided over by Richard II or Charles V of France.

Why this 'standstill' should have characterized the English Court or indoor theatre in the sixteenth century is a fascinating question. Some scholars have found it easier to ignore its existence until Inigo Jones came to Court than attempt an explanation. Others have attributed it variously to Elizabeth's reputed parsimony, the longevity of the Miracle tradition and to lack of interest in the theatre by writers of consequence in the mid sixteenth century.

Possibly the most significant single factor, however, is the absence of any original and dynamic architects, painters or sculptors in England between the departure of Torrigiano, Holbein and Claude from the scene in Henry VIII's reign and the emergence of Inigo Jones, Rubens and Vandyck in that of James I. Elizabethan domestic architecture is reactionary, depending on traditional perpendicular as a frame within which to set ill-assorted Renaissance decorative motifs.* The same is true of house furnishings. The stainers of glass, the weavers of tapestry, the painters in fresco or on panel seem either to have 'gone stale' on their crafts, or to have lacked any sympathy with Italian enthusiasm for the classical style in the fine arts. Truly, this is the province of the art historian, but a matter of such vital concern to dramatic art must become the theatre historian's as well. Here, I cannot do more than suggest that the patent lack of any creative spirit in the fine arts in England in the sixteenth century may be due to the antithesis between the spirit guiding the Reformation and the classical ideal fostered in Renaissance art. Both have a rationalist basis, but they part company where the senses are concerned. The matter is best illustrated dramatically in Ben Jonson's *Bartholomew Fair* and *The Alchemist*. There, Zeal-of-the-land-Busy, Ananias and Tribulation are so avidly pulling things down in this enlightened 'time of the gospel', that they have no room for 'quick comedy refined' or, indeed, for any aspect of that other enlightenment which Jonson himself championed into English life in partnership with Inigo Jones.

Another factor helping to explain this curious hibernation of Renaissance ideas in English visual art between 1530 and 1600 is the lack of any instrument corresponding to the Italian Academies, through which scholastic opinion could be organized and propagated effectively. It is organic to the nature of drama to move at the speed at which its audience is ready to go: and it is clear from the minority voices raised in protest—Edwards, Sackville, Sydney, Fulke-Greville, Jonson—that the majority, for patriotic or other reasons, were happier in the well-charted sea of Gothic convention than in the strange waters of Renaissance experiment.

This question must be taken fully into account before assuming, as some historians do, that the physical appearance of the English theatre of Shakespeare's time can be easily revealed by reference to the contemporary, visual arts.[65] Leadership into the new theatrical

* See Nicholas Pevsner, *The Englishness of English Art*, 1956. See also Vol. II, 1576–1660, Pt. 1, Ch. II, 'Reformation and Renaissance,' especially pp. 25–30.

worlds discovered by Serlio, Palladio and Scamozzi came, in the seventeenth century, from the Court amateurs, not from the merchant bourgoisie of the Public Theatres, and it was from the ranks of the widely travelled and well read Court amateurs that it would have come in the sixteenth century had the audience been ready to follow it. If then their own stage, that of the Tudor Mask, remained essentially that of the Yorkist and Lancastrian Disguising, we have no reason to expect anything else in the popular theatre, whether public or private. This does not mean that the latter was drab and colourless: only that its design and its spectacle was in essence still Gothic.

VII

MORALS AND INTERLUDES

1 Morality Plays

IF the Disguising deserves its place in this narrative by virtue of
its importance to the history of theatre architecture and stage
design, the Moral Play and Interlude owe their inclusion to a
similar importance to the history of acting in England. In this
sense, both are crucibles into which varied but distinguishable ingredients were poured, and out of which emerged the professional
theatre and actor as we know them.

This startling generalization can be clearly and easily substantiated from the surviving evidence, but only if the confusion surrounding the genre and nomenclature of those mediaeval plays
which are not Miracle Cycles and not either Disguisings or regular
Comedies and Tragedies is first dispelled. *

I have endeavoured to show that there were two basic and dis-
tinctly independent sources of dramatic entertainment in mediaeval
England: worship and social recreation. The Tournament, the
Civic Pageants and the Disguising are all examples of the latter.
Even if the subject matter is often serious and sometimes specific-
ally religious,† the occasion for all three is a secular festivity. The
Miracle Cycle, on the other hand, however dramatic and entertain-
ing, was and remains essentially a shared devotional experience. ‡

We are faced with the knowledge that in the fifteenth century
and probably both before and after, there existed in England a considerable variety of plays that were not Miracle Cycles, in that
they did not attempt to represent the history of the world from its

---

* Most of this confusion is directly due to the strongly flowing tide of
modern secularism that has already drowned so much (not only knowledge
but even desire for it) of the pre-Reformation liturgical practice in particular
and of clerical literature in general.
† See Ch. III, Pageants for Richard II, Henry VI, and Katherine of Aragon.
‡ See Ch. IV, pp. 112–18 above.

Creation to Doomsday, but are nevertheless as essentially devotional essays of as specifically Christian a kind as the Miracles: the Creed and Paternoster plays at York, the Croxton play of the Sacrament, the so-called Digby plays of St. Paul and Mary Magdalen,* and other plays like the *Castle of Perseverance* or *Everyman*.

Despite very evident differences, as much between themselves as between them and the Miracles, these plays have at least one common factor. They are in some way directly related to Christian worship. If we want to know how they are related to one another the logical process of enquiry ought to begin in seeking possible sources of drama within Christian worship. It has been generally assumed that there was only one: the *Quem quaeritis* introit of the Mass for Easter Sunday. This is not true, as has long been on record.[1] Yet the implications of this fact have been fairly consistently overlooked. The Easter introit, with its parallel at Christmas, is undoubtedly the source of that part of the Miracle Cycles which, in its story, concerns the New Testament. This liturgical drama, however, only became cyclic when the Old Testament narrative was added to it: and the source of that was not an introit at all, but a *lectio* or reading.† The *lectio* that was first developed dramatically appears to have been the *Sermo contra Iudaeos, Paganos et Arianos de Symbolo*, normally known as the *Prophetae*.[2]

The passage in this *lectio* chosen for dramatization was that in which the Jews are told to call upon their Prophets to bear witness to the coming of Christ. In England we have the testimony of the Sarum Breviary to show that this *lectio* was prescribed for use at Matins on the Fourth Sunday in Advent.[3] If used dramatically, this *lectio*, by virtue of the subject matter, must be epical in effect: a series of incidents, a variety of characters, and only a loose connection between them in the form of a common theme. From the viewpoint of dramatic structure what is important here is the precedence of theme over plot and character. This is the feature, strongly developed, which distinguishes the fifteenth-century Morality Play from the Miracle Cycle.

That the liturgical plays of New Testament content were divorced from Mass and transferred to Matins, adjacent to the *Te*

* See Ch. IV, p. 168 above.

† Lections or readings formed part of the Christian liturgy from the very earliest times. They were taken either directly from the Old and New Testaments or from commentaries by the Christian Fathers upon the scriptures. The subject is fully discussed by Dom. Gregory Dix in *The Shape of the Liturgy*, 1946.

Deum, is generally well known. What, however, seems to have escaped attention is the significance of this association with the *Te Deum*: for it is not only a general song of praise—

'We praise thee, O God: we acknowledge thee to be the Lord.
All the earth doth worship thee: the Father everlasting.'

—but a particularized one as well.

'The goodly fellowship of the Prophets: praise thee.'

Here surely is a direct link with the *Prophetae*? And if with that 'goodly fellowship', why not also with those who flank them in the *Te Deum*, 'The glorious company of the Apostles' and 'The noble army of Martyrs'? The fact that the *Te Deum* is appended to both the Digby play of St. Mary Magdalen and the Croxton *Sacrament* may be coincidental.[4] So also may be the association of the Apostles with the Creed play at York and the fact that it is the Apostles' Creed and neither the Athanasian nor Nicene Creed, which is ordered for normal use at Matins. Nevertheless the coincidence is enough in itself to have suggested the development of dramas associated with the Apostles and Martyrs along the same lines as the *lectio* relating to the Prophets.[5] Fragmentary evidence relating to the Paternoster plays at York, Beverley and Lincoln suggest that these too were similarly constructed and concerned the example of certain Saints and Martyrs associated with the seven clauses of the Lord's Prayer in combating the Seven Deadly Sins.[6]

If this premise is granted, it becomes possible to distinguish easily enough between Miracle Cycles, Saint Plays and Moralities and their respective development in terms of the *lectio*. The life of one or more Saints or Martyrs, even if suggested by the *lectio*, had a more useful dramatic model in the Miracle Cycle than in the homily. Its didacticism lay in the example offered by the life or lives represented and hence in the story and characters of the drama. Where theme took precedence over either or both of these elements, however, a more useful model lay to hand in a third liturgical source not yet mentioned; the one vernacular item in the liturgy, the sermon.* Now where it is proper for a sermon to be

---

* In the early Church the preaching of the Sermon was the strict prerogative of the bishop and usually took the form of an exposition of, or commentary upon, the scriptures. The importance attached to these early sermons may be judged by the fact that they came to be used as *lectiones*. In the Middle Ages, however, the right to preach had been extended to priests, deacons and friars. The range of subject matter discussed in sermons was thus correspondingly wider. See G. R. Owst, *Preaching in Mediaeval England*, 1927.

concerned with the exposition of doctrine, this exposition usually
has a direct application to daily life. The sermon is the one place in
any Church service for topical comment or, in other words, for the
direct application of doctrine to human conduct. This, in dramatic
form, is what the Morality Play consists of, aiming 'rather at
ethical cultivation than the stabilizing of faith'.[7] The form, common to both, is the allegorical *exemplum*.

The idea governing the *exemplum* of the mediaeval sermon is
best paralleled, in modern parlance, by the Cautionary Tale. The
most popular kind was

'the moralized anecdote, whether historically true or fictitious,
drawn from sources both ancient and contemporary, secular as well
as religious'.[8]

This is the all-important link between Holy Writ and secular
'geste' which, where dramatic narrative is concerned, allows the
interaction of one form upon another until all are fused into a drama
that remains essentially religious in tone however secular in its
outward characteristics.

The *exemplum* is the initial *figure* around which the preacher embroidered his sermon. He received direct scriptural sanction for this
embroidery in Christ's preaching by parable.[9] Thus a preacher may
take for his *figure*, 'a ship on the sea'. The sea is equated with the
world and the ship with Faith, the Church, or Man himself.[10]

The extension of this idea to scenic units accompanying dramatic
narrative is apparent in Lydgate's Mercers' Mumming where the
miraculous draught of fishes is presented. * Indeed, the popularity
of all the usual stage symbols—castle, mountain, fountain, tree—
derives from the same source. It is thus no coincidence that where
the virtue of 'Perseverance' is concerned in a dramatic narrative it
is associated with a 'castle'. The tendency to identify the topic of
the sermon with the illustration chosen by the preacher spread
naturally from objects to people. Whole hierarchies of Virtues and
Vices become personified and imprinted upon the popular mind as
inhabitants of the respective Courts of Heaven and Hell. These
courtiers, impersonated by actors and set to war with one another,
can provide as many dramas as there are sermons.[11] Since introit,
lectio or reading, and sermon all form part of the normal offices of
Christian worship, it is natural that dramas developed from these
sources should have interacted upon one another. It explains, for
example, how the Expositor, Nuntius, Prologue and other 'inter-

* See Ch. VI, pp. 200–202 above.

preters' are present in some vernacular Miracle Plays but never in the liturgical plays out of which they grew.[12] Here is a clear instance of the sermon-based Morality affecting the Miracle Cycle. Where the *lectio* is the point of origin, a play may lean either towards the liturgical Miracle or towards the ethical sermon. In Saint plays, for example, where plot and character-drawing are important, the influence of the Miracle is strongly evident.[13] By contrast, in dramas like the Creed or Paternoster play, where the long, episodic and didactic narrative finds dramatic unity in theme, the sermon comes to exercise a dominant influence. Similarly, where the sermon is the point of origin, raids could be made upon the Miracle Cycles or any of the *lectio* derivatives, if useful to the dramatic exposition of the allegory. *

The most obvious example of this interaction at work, at least in the fifteenth century, is to be seen in the street Pageant Theatres of great civic occasions. Prophets, Martyrs and Apostles, Abstract Virtues and Vices, mingle easily and on the same stage with Biblical characters. Choice and inclusion depend there on appropriateness to the occasion. If the occasion suggested employment of a thinly veiled political theme, the devisers had little scruple in adding characters drawn from 'modern' or, at any rate, 'comparatively recent' history.†

Once this general perspective of dramatic genre is appreciated, the physical conditions of staging offer no particular difficulty. The stage-craft governing the lengthy plays deriving from either *lectio* or sermon is copied directly from that originated in the Miracle Cycles to which, in point of textual construction, they are related. Thus a Morality like *The Castle of Perseverance*, which is designed for a fixed stage, and auditorium, resembles the Cornish cycle in its stage conventions, as may be quickly seen by comparing the MS. ground plans of the stages for both of them. ‡ The Creed and Paternoster plays were often given perambulatory performance like the Miracle Cycles at York or Chester. Again proof is available: for the Creed play at York was substituted every tenth year for the Corpus Christi plays.[14] The Cycle of St. Anne plays[15] and other long histories of saints and martyrs could equally well be

* Since the same clerks were often working as both authors and actors, preachers and priests, it is foolish to try to categorize any of these dramas too precisely: for the overlap and interaction between the genres started within their minds.

† See Ch. III, pp. 62, 63 and 71–81 above.

‡ See Edwin Morris' *The Ancient Cornish Drama*, 2 vols., 1859, and Dr. Richard Southern's *The Mediaeval Theatre in the Round*, 1957.

performed in either of these ways, the choice hingeing, as with the Miracle Cycles, on local factors—terrain, ecclesiastical and municipal relations, and so on. The question of how Moral Plays and even Miracle Plays came to be extended in their subject matter into plays of polital polemic can be more conveniently handled in Volume II. In this Volume however something more must be said about the impact upon these plays of the professional minstrel troupe, the *lusores*, *histriones*, or 'Players of Interludes.'

2 *Interludes*

Where the full-length Morality Play, by virtue of its ecclesiastical origin, was likely to receive performance in much the same conditions as the Miracle Cycles or *lectio*-type plays, the Interlude was essentially an indoor entertainment for festive, social occasions. It differs from the Disguising in that it was a play and not a sophisticated Mumming or prelude to dancing. In so far as we are obliged to translate the word from its original Latin sense into a vernacular one, the Interlude was a play in dialogue presented between, or in pauses between, parts of a whole evening's festivities or revels. The fact that it was a play automatically presumes dialogue between actors. Thus the Interlude differs from the sophisticated Mumming, where a speaker introduces disguised mimes and also from the Cyclic dramas (whether developed from the introit or the *lectio*) where the text in dialogue was so long as to require a full day for performance. Beyond that, however, there was no restriction on the form or the subject matter of the Interlude. A self-contained play with a plot drawn from the Bible— Abraham and Isaac, for example; an ethical debate between personified Vices and Virtues harking from the sermon—for instance, the well-known *Everyman*; a farcical treatment of some domestic issue like Lydgate's *Bycorne and Chychevache*, or Heywood's *The Foure PP*; or a dramatized version of an incident from Chronicle or Romance like Godfrey of Boulogne's conquest of Jerusalem, could all aptly be described as Interludes, provided that they were acted in dialogue and were short enough to fit the place appointed during the evening revels.* In short, the essential distinguishing features

* Shakespeare, very obligingly, gives us a thumbnail critical note on the Interlude and its sources in *A Midsummer Night's Dream*, V, 1. 32–82.
>
> 'THESEUS   . . . Is there no play,
>   To ease the anguish of a torturing hour?
>   Call Philostrate. . . .
>   *Philostrate gives Theseus a paper.*

of the Interlude are dialogue and the prescribed limits which Shakespeare was later to define as 'what may be digested in a play'. I see no good reason to depart from Chambers' neat verdict that an Interlude was a *ludus* in dialogue: but, since this admits something as cumbrous as a full Miracle Cycle, I think the factor of time limit deriving from the connection with the banquet, which has been stressed by other historians, is equally important.[16] For here, in effect, we have the first real fusion of the previously independent stages of religious and social origin. Both gained something new. The stage of social recreation acquired dialogue. The religious stage acquired the assistance of a section of the minstrel troupe, *lusores* and *histriones*, in English, professional actors.

The consequences to both theatres cannot have been dreamed of at the time of this fusion, which we may date as having occurred in the reign of Henry VI.* The impact of professional actors upon the religious stage was destined to translate it into a permanent Public Theatre: that of dialogue upon the social revels of the nobility to transform harmless and formless jollification into artistic, polemical plays. Neither of the two was to lose contact with its primal sources. Even in Stuart times the Public Theatre, in the loose construction of its plays (so strongly didactic in tone, mixing scenes of gravity with those of farce, and drawing for its characters upon the contemporary environment) was faithful to the Miracle Cycles, *lectio*-type plays and sermon-based Moralities. The Court

> THESEUS (reads)
> > The battle with the Centaurs, to be sung
> > By an Athenian eunuch to the harp?—
> > We'll none of that: that have I told my love,
> > In glory of my kinsman Hercules.
> [*He might have added, 'It is an all too familiar geste.'*]
> > (reads) The riot of the tipsy Bacchanals,
> > Tearing the Thracian singer in their rage?
> > That is an old device; and it was play'd
> > When I from Thebes came last a conqueror.
> [*As a pageant in the streets? Was it there that he saw 'great clerks . . . shiver and look pale'?* (See lines 92–104.)]
> > (reads) The thrice three Muses, mourning for the death
> > Of Learning, late deceas'd in beggary?
> > That is some satire keen and critical,
> > Not sorting with a nuptial ceremony.
> [*A religious or political polemic?*]
> > (reads) A tedious brief scene of young Pyramus
> > And his love Thisby; very tragical mirth ?
> > . . . I will hear that play.'

* See Ch. VI, pp. 205–207 above.

Theatre remained equally loyal to its antecedents: in the elaborate Mask, to dancing and to spectacular disguise; in the play, to direct address and to the general appropriateness of theme to the occasion celebrated. The important distinguishing feature between the Miracle Cycle and the long, open-air Morality is the precedence in the latter of theme over plot. Dramatically, one is a narrative, the other an argument. Development of the Miracle Cycle therefore could take place in elaboration of narrative, in character portrayal, and in the enrichment of both aural texture and visual spectacle. The latter was also possible in the Morality; but, in point of narrative and character, development could only be slight. In these respects *The Castle of Perseverance* and Skelton's *Magnificence* do not differ noticeably from one another, although separated in date of composition by more than a hundred years.[17] The Morality's potential, as opposed to that of the Miracle Cycle, lay in the variety of possible arguments which the form could contain. Discussion of the state of a man's soul could easily be extended to the state of the body politic, and from there to discussion in allegorical terms of the relationship of sovereign to subject, of Church to State, of one nation to another. The dilemma of Shakespeare's Prince Hal, when faced with a choice between the pleasures of life with Falstaff in East Cheap and the responsibilities of life with the Chief Justice and Parliament in Westminster, is essentially that of Humanum Genus in *The Castle of Perseverance*, even if, with Falstaff, our sympathies find themselves ambivalent. Responsibility for tailoring these discussions into a shape of convenient length for professional actors to handle rests with the players of Interludes in the service of the King and other noble patrons. Pilfer dialogue as they might from the religious stage, they had to adapt it both to suit the restricted time-schedule of the evening revels and to conform with the tastes of an exclusive, literate and sophisticated audience. The resulting Interlude of the fifteenth century served to weld, therefore, the dramatic occasionalia of the Early Middle Ages into the regular, professional drama of the Tudor epoch.

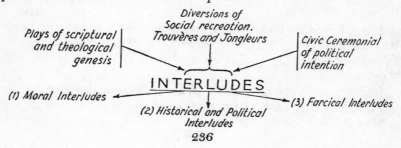

It is from these three resultants (never wholly self-contained), under the combined influences of Renaissance and Reformation thinking that the Chronicle Play and the regular comedy and tragedy of the Elizabethan theatre derive.[18] Discovery and progress in drama is akin to that in science. The old is swallowed up in the development of the new and every step forward is the result of sympathic collaboration between the genius and his traditional apparatus.

The immediate effect of this fusion was to gear the moral content of the play very closely to the occasion chosen for writing and performing it. If therefore we find many such Interludes boring to read today we must make allowance for their possessing a topicality for the audience then which is lost on us. For example, Hall describes a play at Gray's Inn at Christmas 1526/27, which illustrates well what the audience expected to find under the surface of the story and behind the costumes of the actors:

'. . . the effecte of the plaie was, that lord governance was ruled by dissipacion and negligence, by whose misgovernance and evill order, lady Publike wele was put from governance: which caused Rumor Populi, Inward grudge, and disdain of wanton sovereignetie to rise with great multitude, to expell negligence and dissipacion and to restore Publik welth again to her estate, which was so done.'[19]

Although written in 1526 'by master Jhon Roo serjant at the law.xx.yere past, and long before the Cardinall (*Wolsey*) had any aucthoritie',[20] this thematic synopsis of Hall's could have served just as well for Bale's *Kyng Johan* or Shakespeare's *Richard II*. Hall tells us further that the play

'. . . was highly praised of all menne, savying of the Cardinall, whiche imagined that the plaie had been divised of hym (*i.e. about him*), and in a greate furie sent for the said master Roo, and toke from hym his Coyfe (*collar of office*) and sent hym to the Flete (*prison*), and after he sent for the yong gentlemen, that plaied in the plaie, and them highly rebuked and thretened. . . .'

Here then is precedent for Queen Elizabeth I to exclaim 'I am Richard the Second' in the context of a performance of Shakespeare's Chronicle, and for Hamlet to use a play to 'catch the conscience of the King'.

Hall conveniently supplies us with the reverse side of the same coin in describing another Interlude one year later. Following the sack of Rome in 1527, the French and English governments were ready to patch up old grievances in order to meet the threat from the Emperor, whose armies had taken prisoner both the Pope and the French king's children. On the night of Sunday 10th November, before King Henry VIII and the French Ambassadors,

'there was played before them by children in the Latin tongue in maner of Tragedy, the effect wherof was that yᵉ pope was in captivitie and the church brought under the foote, wherfore S. Peter appeared and put the Cardinal in authoritie to bryng the Pope to his libertie and to set up the church againe, and so the Cardinall made intercession to the kinges of England and of Fraunce, that they tooke part together, and by their meanes the pope was delivered. Then in came the Frenche kynges children and complayned to the Cardinal how the Emperor kept them as hostages and would not come to no reasonable point with their father, wherfore thei desired yᵉ Cardinal to helpe for their deliverau(n)ce which wrought so with the kyng his master and the French kyng that he brought the Emperor to a peace, and caused the two yong princes to be delivered. At this play wisemen smiled and thought that it sounded more glorious to the Cardinal th(a)n true to the matter in dede.'[21]

These two instances suffice to show how easy and how natural it would be within a year or so, to adapt the Interlude as a weapon of war in the religious controversy stemming from Henry VIII's break with Rome. As such it was used not only for propaganda in support of the Reformation, but to attack its great, popular rivals, the Miracle Cycle and other lengthy religious plays of Catholic doctrine.[22] This change in the tone, if not the character, of the Interlude is foreshadowed in another of Hall's comments on Court entertainments. In 1531, when the divorce proceedings between Henry and Katherine of Aragon were nearing their climax, Christmas was celebrated at Greenwich,

'. . . with great solempnitie, but all men sayde that there was no myrthe in that Christemas because the Queene and the Ladies were absent.'[23]

Another pointer in this direction was the dedication in 1538 of the violently Protestant German drama *Pammachius* by Thomas Kirchmayer to Archbishop Cranmer.* It was in Cranmer's house

---

* This was acted at Christ's College, Cambridge, in 1545, causing grave concern to Bishop Gardiner who was then Chancellor of the University. The correspondence on the subject between him and the Master of Christ's, Dr. Matthew (later Archbishop) Parker has survived. It is printed by J. Lamb in *Collection of Documents from Corpus Christi College, Cambridge*, 1838.

that Bishop Bale's equally violent *Kyng Johan* was first performed, a fact of no small importance when we consider that Bale's patron at that time was none other than the Lord Chancellor, Thomas Cromwell. These two powerful men, in whom rested the prime responsibility for the suppression of the monasteries and the translation of the Catholic liturgies from Latin into English, seized upon the more flexible Interlude as an alternative form for religious drama, through which to bring the traditional religious stage into contempt and disrepute. *Pammachius* itself, in point of form, is a traditional Antichrist play: but the Antichrist in question is unmistakably the Pope.[24]

This is the true starting point of the war against the Theatre.* The battle fought out in London in the 1590s is only a fresh outbreak of something of much earlier origin and so fundamental to English life as to have had repercussions ever since.

The example of anti-Papal dramatic polemic set in Germany and the Low Countries, introduced into England by Cromwell and Cranmer and grafted to the moral Interlude, was not confined to Court circles. It spread swiftly into the provinces and got so out of hand that measures had to be taken to control it.

Thomas Wylley, for instance, Vicar of Yoxford in Suffolk, wrote to Cromwell requesting assistance.

'The most part of the prystes of Suff(olk)', he says, 'wyll not resyve me ynto ther chyrchys to preche, but have dysdaynyd me ever synns I made a play agaynst the popys counseleurs, Error, Colle Clogger of Conseyens, and Incredulyte.'[25]

He intimates that he is writing other such plays. From far-off Scotland Sir David Lyndsay's *Ane Satyre of the Thre Estatis* created a similar stir.[26] The scale and nature of it can be judged by the fact that a number of repressive measures were taken in the last years of Henry's reign to bring such plays and their actors under control; Proclamations, Injunctions and, finally, an Act of Parliament in 1543.[27] That Statute enacted that no one should 'play in interludes', or otherwise bring into contempt the doctrine of the Church of Rome. Even before that, however, severe disciplinary action had been deemed necessary. An interlude player was burned at the stake at Salisbury in 1539, and in London the Keeper of the Carpenters' Hall was arraigned 'for procuring an interlude to be openly played wherein priests were railed on and called Knaves'.[28]

* See p. 240 below. This subject is treated in detail in Vol. II 1576–1660, Pt. 1, Chs. II–IV.

That these were not isolated exceptions is manifest enough from Bale's heart-cry in exile:

'None leave ye unvexed and untrobled—no, not so much as the poore minstrels, and players of enterludes, but ye are doing with them. So long as they played lyes, and sange baudy songes, blasphemed God, and corrupted men's consciences, ye never blamed them, but were verye well contented. But sens (*since*) they persuaded the people to worship theyr Lorde God aryght . . . ye never were pleased with them.'[29]

The Act was repealed in the first year of Edward VI and Bale returned to England in the same year (1547).[30] The war raged on until the Act of Uniformity, passed in 1559, brought the end in sight not only of polemical Interludes, but also of the Miracle Cycles, *lectio*-plays and Catholic Moralities. The relationship, however, between the polemical plays and the Government was still close: for in the same year the Duke of Feria writes to Philip of Spain about a play defamatory to Philip and Mary and Cardinal Pole, saying:

'I knew that a member of her Council (*Elizabeth's*) had given the argument to construct these comedies, which is true, for Cecil gave them, as indeed she partly admitted to me.'[31]

A habit of some thirty years' duration is not something that can be automatically stopped by simple injunctions to the contrary. An appetite had been whetted among actors and audiences for plays as exciting in their topical controversy as in their stimulating consequences. The stage had undoubtedly gained tremendously in the range of subject matter which, as a result, it could now treat; but it had done so at the price of giving mortal offence to many members of its audience, whether Catholic or Protestant in religious persuasion. Within a decade or so of Elizabeth's accession therefore, the war between creeds which the stage had fostered and exacerbated imperceptibly changed direction and became a war against the stage itself.* The price of survival was reform. To rely on the rabble of pleasure seekers was to invite the animosity of zealous Protestants. To seek the assistance of the aristocracy and liberal-minded merchants meant going a long way to meet their tastes. Both of these pressures led naturally to the exploitation of less controversial subject matter, a more refined handling of it and the security of a permanent home in which to present it.

* See Vol. II, 1576–1660, Pt. 1, pp. 106–121.

Once again the Interlude mapped the new direction: for the Statute of 1543 already cited was not aimed at theatrical performances in general. Provision was made to except from penalty performances intended for

'the rebuking and reproaching of vices and the setting forth of virtue; so always the said songs, plays, or interludes meddle not with the interpretations of Scripture.'[32]

In other words, if the stage could entertain without giving offence, it was welcome to pursue its accustomed function in Society. Those able to take advantage of these conditions were the professional comedians who could present farces on simple domestic themes and the choirmasters and other scholars who had been taking an interest in the Latin drama of Italian origin before things Italian began to become unfashionable as a result of the break with Rome. That these plays can properly be classed as Interludes we know from Ben Jonson:

'Is't not a fine sight, to see all our children made interluders? Do we pay our money for this? We send them to learn their grammar and their Terence, and they learn their play-books.'[33]

It was, of course, as a means of teaching spoken Latin that Nicholas Udall compiled his *Floures of Latine Speaking* for the scholars of Eton in 1533–4, culled from the plays of Terence. Plautus and Horace became equally well known. Terence's *Phormio* was acted by the boys of St. Paul's School at Court in 1528 and from then on such performances become frequent.[34] The practice was adopted in many of the Colleges at Oxford and Cambridge* shortly afterwards.[35] This activity led directly to translation and adaptation of rediscovered classical plays, comedies only to start with but, after 1560, tragedies as well.

The fact that most of these translations and adaptations of academic origin were presented at Court assured them of a greater influence than they would normally have had in their rightful environment of school or college hall: for it brought them and their authors to the notice of professional actors. Thus a play which had served its turn in the school hall or the Great Chamber at Court could, if it had been well received, reach a wider audience at the hands of professional actors both in London and in the provinces.

If the actors profited from contact with the schoolmasters in this

* Aristophanes' *Plutus* was performed in Greek at St. John's College, Cambridge, in 1536.

way, the schoolmasters learnt as much from the actors in another. The minstrel troupe provided them with subject matter from the trouvères' Romances and the jongleurs' farcical mimicry from which to make new and specifically English Interludes within the limits suggested by the classical models. Henry Medwall, chaplain to Cardinal Morton; John Redford master of St. Paul's choir school, and John Rightwise, master of the boys' school; Nicholas Udall, headmaster first of Eton and then of Westminster School; John Rastell, printer and son-in-law of Sir Thomas More; Thomas Ingeland and William Stevenson at Cambridge; and Thomas Watson and Nicholas Grimald at Oxford, are all to be thought of in this context. So may John Heywood.[36] To bring the wheel back full circle, it may be added that the stage direction which concludes the Croxton *Play of the Sacrament*,[37] 'IX may play yt at ease', is almost equally applicable to all the Interludes, whether farcical, moral or polemical, which we have been considering in the past few pages.* A small, compact cast-list is not usually a matter of much concern either to adult amateur dramatic groups or to school-masters or university companies, but it is of major consequence when actors' livelihoods depend on the receipts. This hard financial fact is of equal relevance to the question of the visual spectacle. Professional actors, even in the employment of a generous patron, had not the resources to deploy on costumes and scenic units which Courtly amateurs lavished on their Tournaments and Disguisings and which the City Fathers of wealthy towns extracted in taxes from their citizens to finance their civic rejoicings. The obligation to travel their plays acted as a further brake upon any tendency to scenic elaboration.

However scanty the surviving evidence and whatever may be in doubt about the staging of Interludes, ubiquity of performance is a characteristic shared in common with other mediaeval entertainments. As the sermon-type and *lectio*-type plays of the field, quarry or market-place came indoors to form the short, moral Interlude, so the farcical Interlude of the Court banquet migrated out of doors to the streets, inns and village greens.[38] As the Miracle play and Saint play came into the Guildhall or Great Chamber to form the scriptural Interlude, so the polemical Interlude of the Reformist politicians moved into the churches.[39] Even the classical Interlude with its comparatively narrow audience-appeal was a traveller between one hall and another.

* See Appendix G, pp. 353–354 below: Also Vol. II, 1576–1660, Pt. 1, pp. 196–202.

In these circumstances there can be no serious doubt but that the staging of Interludes was governed by the traditional mediaeval concepts of a *platea* and adjacent *domus*. Within that framework, however, the Interlude did serve to modify if not change certain stage conventions. First, plays with a cast list which could be as small as four characters and rarely exceeded ten did not require an acting area of the proportions needed to accommodate the Miracle Cycles or Tournaments. Secondly, since the Interlude was a self-contained play and did not terminate in the mixing of actors and spectators in formal dances, there was not the same obligation to keep the floor space clear of spectators as was necessary with Disguisings or Barriers. Thirdly, in plays where argument took precedence over narrative and where the playing time was by definition brief, the number of *loca* or 'houses' adjacent to the acting area was not likely to be large. Thus from almost every standpoint, the stage used by the players of Interludes was likely to have reflected the compactness of both the plays themselves and the companies that performed them. Some slight further pressure in this direction may have been exercised in academic quarters by an interest in Italian experiments based on Vitruvius' *De Architectura*: but it cannot have penetrated far in Tudor times, or Inigo Jones' revolutionary methods of staging would have been antedated by half a century, which they clearly were not. The most convincing general testimony to the simplicity of Interlude stagecraft is twofold: absence, in the stage directions of surviving examples, of any regular call for elaborate machinery and *loca* of the kind noticed in the Miracle Cycles or open-air Moralities, together with the small cost in comparison to that for Disguisings as revealed in the Privy Purse accounts.

In Henry VII's reign, plays at Court rarely cost more than £1 or £2, while Disguisings usually cost between £10 and £20*. It is the multiple of difference, rather than the numerical margin, that counts here. In our money, the difference may be expressed by a ratio of something like £50 to £500. Another factor of consequence here is that the money spent on a play is usually entered in the accounts as 'for a rewarde' or 'in rewarde', where the money for Disguisings is 'in full payment of the bill' or 'in full payment of reckonings' or simply 'in payment for'. The inference is clear. The money spent on plays was largely in the form of wages, the actors meeting their own production costs. That these were not very

---

* See Ch. VI, p. 217 above.

heavy is indicated by the setting for the play about liberation of the Pope and the French king's sons already quoted*:

'After supper was done, the kyng led the ambassadors into the great chamber of disguisinges, and in the ende of thesame chamber was a fou(n)taine, and on the one side was a Hawthorne tree all of silke with white flowers, and on the other side of the fountaine was a Mulbery tree ful of fayre beryes all silke. On the toppe of the Hawthorne was the armes of England compassed with the coller of the garter of S. Mychel, and in the toppe of the Moulberie tree sto(o)de the armes of Fraunce within a garter. This fountaine was all of white Marble graven and chased, and the bases of thesame were balles of golde supported by rampyng beastes wounde in leves of golde. In the first worke were gargylles of gold fiersly faced with spoutes running. The second receit (*recepticle*) of this fou(n)taine was environed with wynged serpentes all of golde whiche gryped the second receite of the fountain, and on the somit or toppe of the same was a fayre lady out of whose brestes ran aboundantly water of merveilous delicious saver. About this fou(n)taine were benches of Rosemary fretted in braydes layde on gold, all the sydes sette with roses in braunches as they wer growyng about this fountaine. On the benches sat viii fair ladies in straung attier and so richely appareled in cloth of gold embrodered and cut over silver, that I cannot expresse the connyng workema(n)ship therof. Then when the kyng and quene were set, there was played before them by children in the Latin tongue in maner of Tragedy . . .', etc.[40]

At a casual glance it might seem as if these elaborate and expensive scenic units formed the spectacle for the ensuing Interlude. In a sense it did, but that was quite fortuitous. The two trees symbolize the occasion: the admission of the King of France to the Order of the Garter and of Henry VIII to the French Order of St. Michael. The fountain is the emblem of amity between them. The Interlude concerning the deliverance of the Pope and the French princes from the Emperor's hands is appropriate to the occasion, but is not dependent on the visual emblems provided. They come into their own *after* the Interlude.

'When the play was done', says Hall, 'four companies of Maskers . . . entered with noyse of mynstrelsie and toke the ladies that sat about the fountaine and dau(n)sed with them very lustely'.

This description illustrates vividly why the margin of cost between play and Disguising differed so widely.

* See pp. 237 and 238 above and Fig. 16 opposite.

Presumably, scenic units of this kind, demanding as much artistry as money to make, could be used again and again with only minor modifications. There is little evidence to prove this, but there are

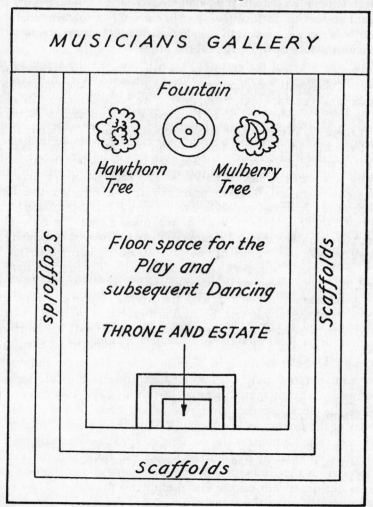

Fig. 16. Plan showing the seating and scenic arrangements for Cardinal Wolsey's Interlude and Disguising of 1527 for Henry VIII and the French Ambassadors at Greenwich. Cf. Plate XXVIII, Nos. 41 and 42.

several indications pointing to such practice. First, the emblematic devices required were comparatively few, appearing and re-appearing with regularity in descriptions of indoor revels both in

England and on the continent from 1378 onwards. Secondly, Hall comments in shocked surprise when on one occasion (1511)

'the rude people ranne to the pagent, and rent tare and spoyled the pagent so that the lord Stuard nor the head officers could not cause them to abstaine, excepte they shoulde have foughten and drawen bloode, and so was this pagent broken.'[41]

After 1545, when Sir Thomas Cawarden was put in charge of the Revels Office with headquarters in the dissolved Convent of the Blackfriars costumes and scenic gear were housed there.* In 1546 for the Shrovetide Revels of Edward VI, a 'mount' was taken from there to Westminster and returned again. If Collier is to be trusted, 'the apparel and furniture for the revels and masks at Court were kept at Warwick Inn' before Blackfriars became the headquarters of the Revels Office.[42] The practice of constructing stage equipment on the assumption that it was intended for a long life certainly survived the sixteenth century. On 6th July 1564, the play of *Old Tobit* was played in the open air at Lincoln. This dramatic narrative of Old Testament history (the text of which has not survived) was admittedly not an Interlude; but neither can it be described as a Miracle Cycle or a Morality. Bearing the date in mind, this play might well be compared to the Coventry *Destruction of Jerusalem*, which replaced the normal Cycle in 1584. An inventory of the 'properties' belonging to the play of *Tobit* has survived, and these are said to have been either 'lying at Mr Norton's house, in the tenure of Wm. Smart' or 'remaining in St. Swithin's Church'. They were:

First, Hell mouth, with a nether chap.
Item, a prison with a covering.
Item, Sarah's chambre.
Item, a tomb with a covering.
Item, the city of Jerusalem, with towers and pinacles.
Item, the city of Rages, with towers and pinnacles.
Item, the city of Nineveh.
Item, the King's palace of Nineveh.
Item, Old Tobye's house.
Item, the Israelite's house and the neighbour's house.
Item, the King's palace at Laches.
Item, a firmament, with a fiery cloud and a double cloud.†

* See Ch. VIII, pp. 275–278 below.
† See Plate XXVII. See also Vol. II, 1576–1660, Pt. 1, pp. 206 *et seq.*, Fig. 14, p. 220, and Plates XVI & XX.

The custodian of the last item was Thomas Fulbeck, Alderman.*

Thirty-four years later, this practice of storing 'mansions' against future use is still normal enough for Henslowe to note in an 'Enventary' of all the 'properties for my Lord Admeralles men', three items identical with those on the *Tobit* list and others besides:

> '*Item*, j rocke, j cage, j tombe, j Hell mought.
> *Item*, j tome of Guido, j tome of Dido, j bedsteade.
> *Item*, viij lances, j payer of stayers for Fayeton.
> *Item*, ij marchepanes, & the sittie of Rome.'[43]

The reasonable conclusion is that elaborate and expensive items prepared for festivities were stored against possible use on a subsequent occasion in the same way that the craft-guilds' pageant-carts were stored in special pageant-houses at Coventry, York and Chester.[44] If this was so, the players of Interludes could supplement their own equipment where necessary, when plays were presented without any other form of accompanying entertainment, at no serious additional cost.[45]

On the other hand, it does seem that when plays were performed as an exclusive evening's entertainment, slightly different conditions prevailed in the arrangement of the hall than when they only formed one of several diversions.

The most important of these was the provision of a raised stage. From the middle of the sixteenth century onwards this item figures in the accounts of plays at Oxford and Cambridge colleges. There is no direct evidence of a raised stage at Court before 1560, while many Interludes indicate in their dialogue a close physical proximity between actors and spectators.[46] There are, however, two practical reasons for not playing on floor level. The first is that it prohibits the use of any trap mechanism. Secondly, if the floor space usually reserved for dancing is fully occupied by spectators it becomes necessary to raise the actors into their view.

At the Universities both these conditions applied. There was no Mask or Disguising to accompany plays and, accordingly, no reason to keep the floor empty except at the sides of the hall. Machinery too seems to have been of a rather novel and exceptional kind if Sir John Dee could be accused of using magic to effect a flying machine in a performance of Aristophanes' *Pax* in 1546.[47] A trapdoor to Hell and subterranean thunder were required at Oxford in 1566 for a performance of *Progne*.[48]

---

* See Sharp, *Dissertation*, p. 62; also Ch. VIII, pp. 295–297 and 301–302 below.

The performances which graced Elizabeth's first Progress to Cambridge in 1564 and to Oxford in 1566 are remarkable from any point of view and deserve closer attention than they have hitherto received.[49] At Cambridge, no one seems to have thought it at all extraordinary or inappropriate that a Plautus comedy should be performed in King's College Chapel on a Sunday night. The play was the *Aulularia*.

'For the hearing and playing whereof, was made, by her Highnes surveyor and at her own cost, in the body of the Church (*i.e. the nave*), a great stage containing the breadth of the church from one side to the other, that the chappels might serve for houses. In the length it ran two of the lower chappels full, with the pillars on a side.'[50]

This first-hand description clearly represents an adaptation of the Chapel to make it conform to standard practice in the matter of

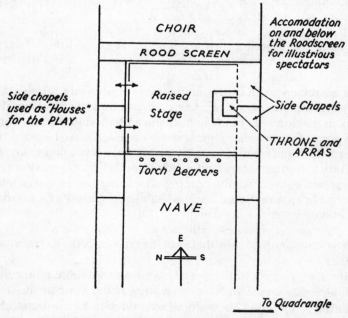

FIG. 17. Ground Plan of the stage and seating arrangements for Plautus' *Aulularia* in the Chapel of King's College, Cambridge, 1564. (Reconstruction.)

stagecraft. The fundamental requirements, as we have come to expect, are an acting area, place or *platea* which is here provided by

248

a raised stage 40 ft. × 40 ft., and *loca*, mansions or houses with which to bestow an identity upon the acting area. Two 'houses' are needed in the *Aulularia* and these are provided by the side-chapels, thus obviating the need to construct them. I think we may take this to be a direct reversion to type, the chapels having served that same function in the liturgical drama, thereby begetting the convention itself.

No less interesting are the seating arrangements: 'Upon the south-wall was hanged a cloth of state, with the appurtenances and half-pace (*i.e. raised dais*) for her Majesty.'

This means that the 'houses' of the play were the two chapels on the north side of the nave and at the eastern end of it.

'In the rood-loft, another stage for ladies and gentlewomen to stand on. And the two lower tables under the said rood-loft, were greatly enlarged and rayled for the choyce officers of the Court.'

Here, then, we have the gallery on top of the roodscreen used as an auditorium for distinguished spectators, as illustrated in the picture of the exorcism at Laon two years later, with a lower gallery constructed immediately below. (See Fig. 12, p. 160 above.)

'When all things were ready for the plays, the Lord Chamberlayn with Mr. Secretary came in; bringing a multitude of the guard with them, having every man in his hand a torch-staff, for the lights of the play (for no other lights were occupied); and would not suffer any to stand upon the stage, save a very few upon the north side. And the guard stood upon the ground, by the stage side, holding their lights. From the quire doore unto the stage was made as 'twere a bridge rayled on both sides; for the Queen's Grace to go to the stage.'[51]

This account is so lucid that we may picture the scene quite easily.

On the eastern side of the raised stage was a double gallery for important spectators. Opposite, standing on the floor of the nave were the guard holding their great wax torches to illuminate the performance. On the north side of the stage were the two chapels serving as 'houses' for the actors, while on the south side, opposite, was the seat set on a raised dais and under a canopy for the Queen herself and her immediate entourage. With everything thus formally arranged,

'At last her Highness came, with certain Lords, Ladies, and Gentle-women: all the Pensioners going on both sides, with torch staves . . . and so took her seat, and heard the play fully.'

It may be objected that such stage arrangements gave only the Queen a perfect view of the action: but the same may be said of the tableaux of the Royal Entries. The answer is that this was fully in-tended and other spectators were as interested in seeing the Queen as the play. Proof is forthcoming from the arrangements made next day in St. Mary's Church for the long programme of ora-torical disputations which were given on 'a great and ample stage' that had been specially constructed

'. . . from the wall of the Belfrey-head unto the Chancell. In the east end (i.e. of the stage) was made a spacious and high room for the Queen's Majestie. Which was, by her own servants, richly hanged with arras and cloth of state, and all other necessaries, with a cushion to lean upon. *All the disputations were driven to that part of the stage.*

'And because both the sides were little enough (i.e. inadequate) for the Lords and Ladys, new stages were devised for the Doctors, upon both the sides, fixed to the side posts; being some space above those who sat upon the forms, and yet lower than the rayls of the higher stages.'[52]

The italics in this quotation are mine. A more vividly explicit phrase could hardly have been penned. Direct address was a tradi-tional stage convention: and, while the whole auditory was to some extent addressed, the degree of directness was geared firmly to social status.

The descriptions of the Queen's visit to Oxford two years later, (1566) are just as detailed, but that giving the fullest account of the plays is in Latin.[53] Here, unfortunately, the Latin tongue proves to be just as ambiguous a language as any other. The major points in dispute are (i) the position of the stage and the Queen's dais and (ii) the appearance of the scenic arrangements.

This being so, I give the full Latin text together with transla-tion, commentary and diagrammatic reconstruction in Appendix H. What matters here is that the general arrangements for both players and spectators followed those made at Cambridge, and that however the Latin is translated the detail of the arrange-ments at Oxford shows an improvement on those at Cambridge in every respect. Greater attention was paid to the comfort of the spectators, who sat on scaffolds constructed round the walls instead of standing. Undergraduates were admitted and, because of the superior lighting arrangements, that part of the floor space unoccupied by the stage was available to less illustrious spectators who, at Cambridge, had not been admitted. There was no makeshift in the matter of scenic houses. These were specially constructed, placed on the sides of the stage (where they would least interrupt the spectators' view of the action) and were consciously designed (in conjunction with the transformation of the walls and ceiling of the hall itself) to resemble the glory of antiquity. Finally, extraordinary pains had been taken to provide the Queen with complete privacy between her lodging and her seat on the stage.

Much more important, however, than the usual spirit of friendly rivalry between the universities, so evident here, is the basic similarity in Englishness of the theatrical arrangements at King's and Christ Church. In the magnificent Gothic environment of the former, the play presented is a classical Latin comedy, while at the latter, Richard Edwards' *Palamon and Arcyte*—a direct link between Chaucer and *The Two Noble Kinsmen* sometimes attributed to Shakespeare—is presented in a setting as nearly classical in appearance as the devisers could conceive. Once this contrast is allowed for, the actual technique of presentation on both occasions remains solid, traditional, English. *

It has been argued that these performances were conducted in conscious imitation of Vitruvian and Serlian precept.† Some knowledge of Italian Renaissance stage practice is to be expected in the Universities, but I doubt whether it extended in practice much beyond the substitution of classical for Gothic decorative detail on a scene that was still typically English, Gothic and Christian in fundamental concept. Why else should a double plural be used—*magnifica palatia aedesque apparatissimae*—to describe the setting, if not to indicate the normal mansions? What may well have been novel in these *aedes*, or houses, is a rounded Roman arch instead of a pointed Gothic one; Corinthian pillars and capitals instead of perpendicular ones; and so on. In short, we may legitimately visualize a difference in the physical appearance of the scene as marked as

---

* See Ch. VI, pp. 212–224 above.

† 'It is also to be remarked that the whole arrangement of the hall must have been similar to that indicated by Serlio as the Vitruvian arrangement adapted to the rectangular hall.' (L. B. Campbell, *Scenes and Machines on the English Stage*, 1923, pp. 90 and 91.) For an alternative commentary, see F. S. Boas, *University Drama in the Tudor Age*, 1914, pp. 98 *et seq.* See also Vol. II, 1576–1660, Pt. 1. pp. 262–275.

that between the triumphal arches erected in London in 1501 for Katherine of Aragon and those erected in 1603 for James I: but just as this difference is superficial, relating only to decorative detail, so the staging of these neo-classical plays is essentially that of the normal English Interlude.

This impression is confirmed by what we know of early performances of neo-classical tragedy given by the gentlemen of Gray's Inn between 1560 and 1590.[54] Thomas Hughes' *The Misfortunes of Arthur*, performed at Greenwich in 1588, is a fair example. The stage directions require 'Mordred's house', 'Arthur's house', 'the Cloister', and a trap through which the furies may rise.[55]

These neo-classical performances, whether of Plautus himself, anglicized versions like *Ralph Roister Doister*, or native inventions in the classical manner like Richard Edwards' *Damon and Pythias*,[56] were all presented by amateurs and for special occasions. One can hardly claim, therefore, that they represent the main stream of English dramatic development during the sixteenth century. Nevertheless one may legitimately make deductions from them which do improve our knowledge of the direction of the main stream. In the first place, the stagecraft employed does not depart materially either from that governing the lavishly spectacular Disguisings-cum-Masks or from that used by the itinerant and more modestly endowed 'players of interludes'. Secondly, since this supposition is amply confirmed by both the descriptive and structural evidence, one may confidently assert that these neo-classical adventures served to awaken both amateur Maskers and professional acting troupes to a range of dramatic and theatrical possibilities that might not otherwise have become apparent for a long time.

Since the sovereign and the principal Court officers were the usual recipients of these novelties, it stands to reason that satisfaction obtained *at the time* (and this is the fact of most importance about the placement of the throne on the stage itself) and expressed in conversation afterwards penetrated English society by eye-witness report and verbal testimony alike. In other words, the Interlude was launched by this means upon its final metamorphosis: at the hands of the poets, painters, musicians and dancers of the Court into the stately Mask and thence to opera and ballet: at the hands of the professional actors and dramatists into the five-act stage play of the Public and Private Theatres.* Both of these developments were translated from possibilities into events by the presence at Court or in the Courtly retinue on Provincial Progresses of the

* These matters will be treated fully in Volume III.

professional players of interludes whose status and economy told them that in these directions lay their best chance of a secure livelihood in the years ahead. Thus, as intermediaries between the *avant-garde* theorists, now to be numbered among the swelling ranks of potential dramatists, and the traditional tastes of conservative, popular audiences, they were destined to play a crucial part in making the Elizabethan and Jacobean drama what it was. Their ability to rise to this occasion and make of it the triumphant success that they did in the face of grave political and social difficulties must be attributed in very large measure to the trust reposed in them and their own wealth of inherited experience. As the direct successors of the *minestralles*, *lusores* and *joculatores*, they were equipped with knowledge of how to retain the patronage of noble masters, clerical and lay, and of how to fend for themselves without the assistance of an organized police force among an unruly peasantry in festive mood. Their knowledge of how to adapt their wares to suit an infinite variety of shop window in church, guildhall, banquet chamber, village green, quarry, market square or fairground supplied them with that special combination of tact and determination that alone enables actors to earn a lucrative livelihood despite constant criticism to the effect that their labours are both offensive to 'the judicious' and 'caviare to the general'. Their status and economy in mediaeval society must therefore be our next concern.

BOOK THREE

Dramatic Theory and Practice in the Middle Ages

VIII

PLAYERS AND COMMERCE

To tell the story of actors and acting, audiences and critics, in mediaeval England in a concise and intelligible manner is impossible without risking generalizations of a kind that may give disproportionate weight to some evidence at the expense of other sources. I have decided to take this risk, partly because it eased my task in handling other subjects already discussed within this volume to isolate that of acting for independent treatment, and partly because it seems to me to be unrealistic to try to discuss theory and criticism in the theatre in divorce from the actor's economy.

Since, however, the evidence consists of a multitude of fragments, scattered through rather more than a thousand years, yet linking Elizabethan England with ancient Rome via the Courts and countryside of mediaeval Christendom, there is little hope of ordering it within a coherent narrative at all without the aid of some preliminary pattern imposed by way of introduction.

The pattern that I am about to put forward to introduce the next two chapters relates to the evidence, in that the evidence has provided the material out of which to create the pattern. Thus, while I am anxious that the reader should not mistake what is no more than a suggested pattern for a proven one, my intention in employing it is to start putting the evidence to work on a tentative basis instead of letting it continue to amass incoherently in silence, simply because it happens to be fragmentary and exceptionally widely scattered.

1 Introductory Pattern

Acting, like the ability to sing or use the hands to draw and model, is an instinctive talent which every child exploits and then, in adolescence, either abandons or develops. Since, however, it is through this mimetic talent that each and everyone of us acquires the knowledge of how to comport ourselves in society, from the simple handling of a knife and fork to the infinitely subtle demonstrations (or screenings) of our emotions, the relationship between both an actor and his audience and a spectator and actors is very much closer than that between other artists and their public. The modern cult of 'star' personality, the eagerness of amateurs, who would not dream of exhibiting a drawing or playing an instrument in public, to display themselves before an audience in major dramatic roles, and the readiness of businessmen or scientists to discuss stage-plays, films and television-drama with the air of informed critics, all illustrate this point.

It is necessary to stress this lest the artificial division of chapter headings between 'actors' and 'audiences' appears to be a real one. Rather are they one and the same; for no actor gets much satisfaction from performing to an empty house and an audience denied the actors promised to it is liable to feel disappointed and even to become abusive. However, there are two other factors, commerce and criticism, which exert pressures upon the single theatrical unit of actors and audience and have the effect of appearing to split it into two independent parts. The actor who chooses to earn his living by his talent can rarely afford to take the initiative in matters of critical theory, while the critics and theorists of the audience usually have to wait a long time before their ideas are put into practice. In other words, the need to earn a living makes the actor chary of doing anything which he suspects his audience *as a whole* is not yet ready to accept, while the theorist has to find sufficient support for his ideas if they are to become acceptable to the actor. These pressures, although ever present in the theatre, vary considerably from age to age in relation to each other. The net effect, however, where practical experiment is concerned, is to ensure that this rests in the hands of amateurs. In the sense that communities can exist and survive without the services of the professional actor, he is a parasite upon society, only able to turn his talent to remunerative ends when possessed of a commodity which society wishes to buy. A community therefore has first to discover that it needs the commodity: the professional actor can then exploit the need. Because the talent is instinctive and shared in varying degree between actor and audience, the need never dies. The sense of need, however, can vary enormously. Broadly speaking it varies proportionately with the nature of society. In a strongly rationalist and materialistic age it will hardly seem to exist except as a frivolous diversion. The process of propagating the sense of need to the point where exploitation of it is remunerative enough to become a profession is thus occasional and, consequently, amateur. This argument seems to me to be fundamental to any understanding of the mediaeval and Renaissance stage.

Where dramatic texts are concerned, the principle may be seen at work in the gradual extension of subject matter from religious instruction to political discussion and eventually to neo-classical ideas of elegant recreation. The moving spirits in this sequence of change, *qua* dramatists, are, first the missionary priesthood, followed by the clerical administrators of the establishment, followed in turn by the scholars conducting the schools and universities. The executants, similarly, are first the officiating priests; next those people with whom they work in close association—secular clergy, schoolboys in their care and, by extension, laymen; and finally, as control of education itself passes from clerical to secular hands in Tudor times, the schoolboys and university wits.

Drama, however, is not simply a matter of words: music, dance and spectacle are other elements all of which are open to development in appropriate circumstances. If they exist in their own right as independent social recreations and if a tradition of amateur acting exists or is established adjacent to them, they will coalesce in varying proportions depending on the circumstances which bring about the coalescence. It can even be argued that dance and song in worship are the ultimate origins of all drama. If this is true, the twin locations propitious to the development of drama within the fabric of mediaeval society are obvious: the antiphonal liturgies of the Christian Church, and the social intercourse between the sexes in many forms of recreation.* Although at first glance these two locations appear to be contrasted to the point of contradiction, they possess a common factor which reconciles them: for clearly both reflect aspects of the life of any society which are fundamental to its survival. It is through the music and dancing of social recreation that the sexes overcome the differences made evident by their functions in the round of daily life and meet as equals on common ground. The probability is that from this occasional social intercourse will spring the more permanent relationship of man and wife, and the survival of the individual in his heirs will be assured. Religious worship is similarly a form of self-assurance: that life is the master of death and that the master Creator thus

---

* The spontaneous *joie de vivre* from which social recreations spring is as surely a form of praise and thanksgiving as the more formal expressions in ecclesiastical ceremonial.

assumed has a purpose for human beings which it is possible for them to interpret and to forward. For these quite different, but equally powerful, reasons religion and social recreation attract assemblies of people which from the actor's standpoint, as already indicated, is the first, essential condition for obtaining a livelihood from his talent.

In mediaeval society, religion by uniting people of high and low degree located an audience universal to Christendom which was open to exploitation by actors if, by their talent, they could help to reveal the particular pattern of Creation which Christianity asserted. Being hierarchical in form, however, mediaeval society could not offer, within terms of social recreation, a similarly universal audience. Here, power and wealth served to create a variety of potential audiences faithfully reflecting the hierarchical orders of society. For our purposes, the important dividing line is that running between yeoman and esquire, for it distinguished broadly speaking between leaders and led. In England, the distinction holds through the formative years of the nascent drama and corresponds therefore with other differences more sharply marked in, say, the twelfth century than in, say, the fifteenth: between literacy and illiteracy, for example, between wealth and poverty, between thinkers and toilers. Drama stemming from social recreation therefore was likely to be much more limited in its audience appeal (because created for coteries) than that stemming from religion. Yet, as regards the actor, it was the top segment of the limited audiences of social recreation that could offer him the best prospects of secure employment rather than the universal audience of Christian worship. Viewing the audience from this standpoint, the pattern of the professional actor's fortunes that emerges shows him at the outset to be struggling for survival in the early Middle Ages in the only stronghold remaining to him, at European Courts and in similarly constituted noble houses whether of lords temporal or spiritual. It is there and there only that anyone has time or inclination to employ him regularly. Elsewhere he runs the risk of arrest as a vagabond and, by inference, a criminal. During the early missionary activity of the Church in North-Western Europe (c. 300–800 A.D.) he was directly open to attack from the Church. And for as long as memories lingered of the actor's behaviour in Rome and his all too close associations with the suppressed cults of primitive religion, he stood no chance of being offered the universal audience that was preparing to receive the drama of re-enacted scripture. His only hope, therefore, of improving his position was to work downwards through the hierarchy of his environment in an attempt to persuade others that his commodity was sufficiently worth having to be worth paying for. This, in fact, he did. Having earned his retention in the houses of those whose wealth lay in land, he came to acquire the interest of a new race of patrons: those whose wealth lay in merchandize and who, by the late fourteenth century, were in a position to rival the landowners and even to hold the Court to ransom.* With them behind him, he was able to compete with the Church for the favours of the popular audience hitherto served exclusively by talented amateurs. Finally, with the advent of the Reformation, he was able to launch a frontal attack through the politically sponsored play of religious polemic. The success of this attack assured him, in Elizabethan times, of mastery of both audiences: his own exclusive Courtly coterie and the great popular audience prepared for him by the amateur religious stage.

This sequence of development reinforces a point made earlier in this chapter: that the actor's need to earn a living from his talent obliges him first to seek to enlarge his audience and then to keep it. The temptation is always to cling to the largest numerical section of that audience. The price of yielding is to lose touch with the swifter-thinking minority, who get bored and desert to something new even if amateur. In the period under discussion this means that the professional actor's quest for centuries was to obtain control of the popular audience and, having succeeded, to retain it as long as he could. The history of European drama suggests that periods of equilibrium come to the professional actor and dramatist when, together, they can claim the allegiance of a cross-section of society, but they are brief. By clinging to the numerically larger base of that audience, dramatist and actor are soon forced to provide for what is becoming old-fashioned in taste and consequently to lose touch with *avant-garde* theorists of the critical minority. In the sixteenth century, the professional actors obtained their long-sought-after popular audience in the reign of Queen Elizabeth I and began to lose the intelligentsia almost simultaneously. In practical terms this may best be expressed in the success attendant upon Inigo Jones's experiments in perspective settings under a proscenium arch: for it is a singular and all too frequently unnoticed fact that Jones, a painter and architect, and his Court Amateurs (the lord and lady maskers) were able to set their ideas up in competition with the leading professional actors and managers of the day and beat them at their own game. It was the amateur stage of

* See Ch. III, pp. 64–71 above.

the Court Mask and not the professional stage of the contemporary Public Theatre which Restoration England accepted as its official stage. Put another way, while Jones is in Italy studying the practical implications of the theory preached by Sir Philip Sydney, Ben Jonson or Francis Bacon, Henslowe, in London, is still buying rocks, tombs and a hell-mouth for 'stinkards' with 'grounded-judgements'*: and those who think with their grandfathers seldom live with the sons.

2 Amateur and Professional Acting in the Middle Ages

The ambivalence of the Church's attitude to the stage, between the translation of Christianity from a force in the world to a world force in the fourth century A.D. and the establishment of the Anglican régime under Elizabeth I, is nowhere more marked than in its attitude to actors. The reason is obvious, since it is from the person of the actor, *qua* mime, and not in either the dramatic text or the theatre building, that drama and theatre take their being.

The professional actors of the Roman Empire had only themselves to blame for incurring the hostility of Christians. Roman drama, although presented in well-ordered and elaborate theatres and amphitheatres, had degenerated of its own accord: vaudeville of a crude, vulgar and egocentric kind had displaced regular tragedy and comedy long before the Emperor Constantine embraced the Christian faith.[1] It was thus principally these actors who incurred the indignant protests of the established Church and not the theatre as an institution or the regular drama as a form of social criticism.[2] These mimes were doubly offensive because so many of their activities served to keep alive in converts' minds memories of rites associated with tribal religions.[3] In short, inside the frontiers of the late Roman Empire the dramatic activity associated with primitive religions and with social recreation were often indistinguishable. Thus, those responsible for the missionary work of the new religion had little option in their own interest but to attack the theatre of social recreation whenever opportunity arose: for in no other way could it establish itself in favour of its rivals.

Once this viewpoint is understood, the Church's attitude to drama throughout the Middle Ages can be seen to be at least consistent. Historians seem to have been very reluctant to face the paradox of how a Church could thunder abuse at actors down the

* See Ch. VII, p. 247 above.

centuries and yet permit a drama within its own most sacred Offices. It is explicable, however, once the intimate connection is appreciated between the professional actors, social recreation and the primitive religions of the late Roman Empire.

In a society whose life and habits are geared to the agricultural year holidays cannot be taken at will, nor can the natural division between the light of day and the dark of night be easily or regularly defied. Social recreation thus comes to be closely associated with seasonal festivals. Christianity was launched upon communities with such widely different climates as those of Greece and Spain on the one hand and those of Poland and Belgium on the other, all of which possessed individual religions, festivals and recreational customs appropriate to the seasonal periods presented by climate. Without substituting an industrial for an agricultural society, Christianity could not alter this. It could only attempt to give a new significance to the old festivals and even to those associated customs which their adherents would not abandon.[4]

Observance of Christmas, for example, spread east and west from Rome, reaching England late in the sixth century.[5] Very near to it in date were the feasts, subsequently established, of St. Stephen (26th Dec.), St. John (27th Dec.), Holy Innocents (28th Dec.), Circumcision (1st Jan.) and Epiphany (6th Jan.). Together they make up a period of twelve days, which corresponded closely to the winter solstice and, by extension, to the many folk rituals and customs attendant upon this deadest time of the year. Solemn as were the new Christian Feasts, it is natural that their gravity should have been rivalled if not eclipsed by the frivolity of the agricultural Festivals of a preceding era.[6] It is within this context that the Feasts of Fools, of the Boy Bishop, and of the Lord of Misrule grew up. It is for this reason that Twelfth Night is better known than the Eve of the Epiphany despite correspondence of date. It is for this reason that in most continental countries gifts are still exchanged, not on Christmas Day, but on New Year's Day.

In terms of the earlier argument, that it is at such times of organized festivity that actors can most readily find audiences, it will be seen that those Christians responsible for ecclesiastical discipline had small chance of being anything but critical in their attitude to actors whose performances directly stimulated the taste for the more profane aspects of such festivals. The precarious balance established over the centuries between the old festivals and the Christian interpretation of them was always in danger of being

upset and the prime movers in this direction were very likely to be
the actors. As the perennial begetters of laughter, the temptation
ever before them was to draw the line below the belt and above the
knees or to satirize and burlesque the established order.

By the thirteenth century the Church had learnt to look facts in
the face. Sir Edmund Chambers has summed up the position as
follows:

'The Church has never been good at altering its formularies to
suit altered conditions. But it has generally been good at practical
compromises. And in the case of minstrelsy, a practical compromise, rough enough, was easily arrived at.

'The effective conscience of the thirteenth-century Church had
clearly come to recognize degrees in the ethical status of minstrels. . . . The profession of an *histrio*, St. Thomas Aquinas de-
clares, is by no means in itself unlawful. It was ordained for the
reasonable solace of humanity, and the *histrio* who exercised it at a
fitting time and in a fitting manner is not on that account to be regarded as a sinner.'[7]

This doctrine is preached in England by Thomas de Cobham,
Bishop of Salisbury in 1313.[8] On the other hand the preachers
offered no quarter to the *histrio* who exercised his talent at an un-
suitable time and in an ill-fitting manner. As Dr. Owst has shown,
in the minds of serious preachers of the fourteenth and fifteenth
centuries,

'A massed array of jesters, jugglers, minstrels, heralds, revellers,
witches, dancing-women, prostitutes, and even miracle-players
were leading a careless world to the Devil and the crack of
Doom.'[9]

This state of affairs accords closely with the known status of the
minstrel troupe, as pictured in Chapter V above. The *mimes*, *histriones* and *joculatores* escape censure, and direr penalties attaching
to their brands of entertainment, by banding themselves together
under the socially respectable trouvères. The trouvères maintain
themselves and their profession through the quality of the entertainment provided by their troupes. As a working arrangement,
though open to complaint and abuse from many quarters, it satisfied the consciences of all concerned from the thirteenth century to
the fifteenth. We may therefore say with some approximation to
truth that the profession of actor, in the sense of vaudeville artist,
survived the vicissitudes accompanying the change over from

Roman to Holy Roman Empire, from paganism to Christianity: and, in the form of the minstrel troupe of jongleurs led by a trouvère in the employment first of the lords spiritual and temporal and subsequently of the new-rich merchant-princes, it awaited the day when it could perform as an ensemble instead of as so many individual 'turns'. In the meantime so long as members of the troupe obeyed the rules, they were well rewarded with the material blessings of this world, in kind and in cash. The stern Dominican preacher John Bromyard compares them to lap-dogs on this account, who 'get rich food and presents' or 'gifts of robes'.[10] Their cry of 'largess' is never ending. There, then, in the halls of honour and renown we must leave them for the moment and consider the amateurs: since it was the experiments of the amateurs, in dialogue, narrative and impersonation on the one hand and in chivalry, polemic and dance on the other, which gave the professional actors the cue to change their métier from vaudeville comedians to players of interludes.

The Church was able to square its own collective conscience about acting in its midst, partly since the initial liturgical plays were unselfconscious demonstrations of the significance of certain scriptural events and therefore not acting in the strict sense of the word, and partly because these representations were conducted, at most, once a year and by priests, not mimes.[11] No less important, the Church, as I have pointed out, never objected to drama and theatre itself, even in Roman times, but only to aspects of social behaviour with which the 'theatre' of the fourth century was inextricably connected. With paganism crushed and the professional actors under control, it was possible to consider organized drama on its own merits again. A drama, therefore, which patently strengthened the faith of the illiterate masses by assisting them to acquire the rudiments of scriptural history and of doctrine was not to be scorned or compared with the *spectacula* of an earlier pagan epoch.[12] By this reasoning, a liturgical ceremony, unselfconsciously dramatic, came to be translated into conscious personification for the purpose of enacting the narrative of scripture. This inescapably involved the admission of both acting and drama as legitimate activities. And this the Church faced squarely. The detachment of the liturgical dramas from Mass in the eleventh century and their placement in Matins admits as much. Nevertheless, the acting remained both clerical and occasional, that is to say, amateur. The drama remained devotional and didactic.

So easy is it to be wise after the event, that the Church of the tenth and eleventh centuries cannot fairly have been blamed by that of a later time for not having foreseen that this innocent beginning could not retain its natal purity for long. Drama does not entertain by instructing: by entertaining it can teach. And the fact that these actors were amateurs, clerks at that, could not prevent them from discovering this for themselves.* The better able these actors became at capturing and holding the attention of their audience the more nearly did they come both to resemble the disreputable mimes and to incur the disapproval of their more ascetic-minded brethren. A thriving tradition of Miracle Plays can therefore coexist with repeated denouncements of those who acted them and fairly represent the state of opinion on the subject in the Church. The result is that any action taken following such denouncements was both local and temporary. Nor was there any logical reason why this kind of acting, and to this end, should not spread in time from clerks to laymen.

In this way a tradition of playwriting and ensemble playing came to be established in England by amateurs while the professional actors persisted in an assortment of variety turns, as an accompaniment to or as an interlude between the formal dancing of their masters. In this way a tradition of scenic representation and costume iconography of Christian inspiration grew up in the liturgical drama of scriptural origin, which was rapidly taken over by the amateur participants in chivalric tournaments associated with Romance literature and the Mummings and Disguisings that often accompanied prize-giving. In this way, on important civic occasions, city streets were translated into classrooms for lessons in politics, with a moral hammered home through the actors' words, through the scenic tableaux and through the complimentary inscriptions of the pageant theatres. All in all, this was the inheritance bequeathed by the amateurs of the twelfth, thirteenth and fourteenth centuries to the professionals of the fifteenth.

In order to make my point forcefully I have perhaps been unfair to the professional actors in stressing the uncreative nature of their activities in comparison with the amateurs. The balance may be adjusted somewhat by stressing now the versatility and technical accomplishment of the mediaeval professional actor in comparison to that of his amateur brethren. The professional's passport to membership of a minstrel troupe and his sole guarantee of retention was his virtuosity whether as dancer, acrobat, musician, reciter of gestes, juggler or clown. So extraordinary was his skill in

* See Ch. IX, pp. 312–313 below.

his chosen mode or modes of entertaining, that it was common to think of him in company with magicians. It was as 'subtile tregetoures' that Chaucer saw them or, again,

'Ther saugh I pleyen jogelours
Magiciens and tregetours.'[13]

There is a general tendency to think of the minstrel troupe as numerically large, but it is hard to confirm this idea from surviving records. What the evidence does seem to justify is the supposition that in the fourteenth and fifteenth centuries there was a very large number of small troupes with a corporate identity who were at least as active in the provinces as at Court. For instance, at Selby Abbey in 1398, it is to *iiij ministrallis* of the Duke of Northumberland that the fee of 3s. 4d. is given; 6s. 8d. to *iiij ministrallis domini Northfaolkie*.[14] In the latter part of the fifteenth century the story of the expense accounts is still much the same. In 1466, 2s. is given by Winchester College to *iiij*[s] *interludentibus et J. Meke citharistae*, and in the following year 2s. in *datis iiij*[or] *mimis dom. de Arundell*.[15] In 1457, Shrewsbury Corporation reward four of the Duke of York's minstrels and four of the Duke of Exeter's.[16] Nevertheless, there is a noticeable difference between the payments made in the thirteenth and fourteenth centuries and those made in the fifteenth and sixteenth. In the former it is more usual to reward the single minstrel or the pair than any substantially larger group. In the latter, rewards to single minstrels are rare by comparison with those to groups. The numbers of these groups are seldom referred to. At Selby in 1479, the entry reads:

'In rewards *histrionibus ducis Gloucestrie*   vjs viijd.'[17]

In 1500:

'Item datum *histrionibus Henrici Pyrcy*   ijs
Item datum *histrionibus domini Regis*   vjs viijd.'

Winchester College paid '*xij*[d] *dat. ministrallis dom. episcopi*' and '*v*[s] *vijd Dat. lusoribus de civitate Winton*.'[18] We know, however, that in Henry VII's household provision was made for a company of six actors, which in his son's reign was extended to eight. The former figure is confirmed by the records of Shrewsbury Corporation. Under the year 1483, there is the entry: '*Soluta pro quodam regardo dato sex histrionibus domini Regis pro honestate villae*.'[19] These six actors of Richard III are in all probability the '*histrionibus ducis Gloucestriae*' of 1479 already referred to as being paid 6s. 8d. by Selby Abbey. And if this is so, the *histrion*[es] *domini*

Regis hoc anno, also at Selby c. 1450, were probably a troupe of actors too, as opposed to minstrels.[20]

As explained in Chapter V, it is very difficult to distinguish accurately between vaudeville artists and ensemble players where the nomenclature of mediaeval account rolls is concerned. Nevertheless, if we add to the data just supplied from the newly discovered Selby records the fact that at Shrewsbury the word *histriones* replaces the word *ministralli* in the records *c.* 1480 and that the visitors to Winchester in 1466 are described as *interludentes*, it becomes possible to make some helpful deductions.

In the first place we may be quite sure that groups of minstrels had taken to ensemble playing by the mid fifteenth century. For myself, I would not be surprised by any subsequent discovery of evidence which showed that this had started in the first half of the century.* For the present, however, we must be guided by the facts set out above and the knowledge that Lydgate, who occupied himself with every known form of dramatic or quasi-dramatic activity in the early fifteenth century, neither attempted an interlude nor wrote for professional actors.

What seems to have happened is that the minstrel troupe of the fourteenth century changed its nature in the fifteenth. The change is most noticeable in the fortunes of the trouvère. As the primary source of 'modern' literary narrative, his function came to be eclipsed in the fourteenth century by the rising fortunes of both the literary-minded clerk and the herald, the one as a writer of fiction, the other as a recorder of fact.[21] This blow to the authority of the leader of the troupe coincided with the growing popularity of ensemble playing among amateurs. At Selby, for example, in 1398 local clerks entertained the Abbot with a play, probably a miracle. The French *entremets* of 1378 and 1389 followed by Lydgate's Disguisings tell the same story. If we consider this knowledge in conjunction with the fact that, by the end of the fifteenth century, the word 'minstrels' is used specifically to denote musicians as opposed to actors, it seems clear that the old minstrel troupe gradually readjusted itself to changed circumstances. The picture that emerges—substantiated by fact in the Tudor household—is of a realignment according to talent and function: troupes of musicians, troupes of players and single specialist entertainers of whom the most notable was the fool or jester.† All of them continue to be licensed by the patronage of a particular household under whose

* See Ch. V, p. 185 above.
† See Plate XXIII, No. 34.

name they travel. I do not think it has been realized quite how widespread were these troupes of actors. Virtually every noble household of distinction came to number among its retainers a small company of actors just as it had previously kept a minstrel troupe. The transition from 'variety artists' to 'players of interludes' was thus both gradual and universal.

Another inference that may be legitimately read from the account rolls is that these small acting companies were very well informed about the dates of the year when they would find a welcome in particular places and were doubtless possessed of itineraries, like the minstrels before them, which made sufficient geographical and financial sense to be described by the modern term 'circuit'. The data they had to work on in preparing these circuits was simple and effective. The Feasts of the Christian year were regulated by the Calendar, became steadily more numerous and were generally observed as holidays. With virtually every important institution in the country under the direct patronage of a particular saint, special holiday celebrations were observed by these institutions on the appropriate Calendar Day. Thus, for example, where the days marking the birth and death of St. German might pass virtually unnoticed in the country as a whole, at Selby Abbey they were regularly observed as major feasts because St. German was the Abbey's patron.[22] Actors could therefore expect *in advance* to be made welcome there on those days. Broadly speaking, their practice was to be on call in their patron's household at the great holidays, the twelve days of Christmas, Shrovetide and Easter, and to travel on the most lucrative, preordained route through the countryside during the rest of the year. In castles and abbeys reputation was doubtless the key to admission for these *lusores, ludentes, histriones, mimes, interludentes* and 'pleyers' as it had been for the trouvère and his jongleurs before them. In towns, the actors presented their credentials to the Mayor, gave their first performance in his presence in the Guildhall and subsequent ones at his discretion.[23] It is on this basis, under Elizabeth I, that we find James Burbage touring the provinces in 1577–8, a year after he had built *The Theater*.

The Treasurer's Accounts in the city archives at Bristol contain the following entries:

'1st quarter. 3rd week.

It(e)m p(ai)d to my L(or)d of Leycesters players at the end of their play in the Geldhall before Mr. Mayor and the

Aldermen and for lyngks to geve light in the evenyng(.) the play was called Myngo—the sum of xxij^s'[24]

And two weeks later:

'. . . mending the borde in the geld hall and dores there, after my L(ord) of Leycesters players who had leave to play there. . . .'[25]

In 1593 it is Edward Alleyn who writes from Bristol to his wife in plague-stricken London:

'now good mouse J haue no newse to send you but this thatt we haue all ou^r helth for w(hi)ch the lord be praysed(.) J reseved yor letter att bristo(*l*) by richard couley for the wich J thank you(.) J haue sent you by this berer Thomas popes kinsman my whit wascote (*white waistcoat*) because it is a trobell to me to cary it(.) reseave it w^t this letter And lay it up for me till J com(.) if you send any mor letters send to me by the cariers of shrowsbery (*Shrewsbury*) or to west chester (*Chester*) or to york to be keptt till my Lord stranges players com(.) and thus sweett hartt w^t my harty comenda(tions) to all o(u)r frends J sess (*cease*) from bristo this wensday after saint Jam(*e*)s his day being redy to begin the playe of hary of cornwall . . .', etc.[26]

And so the wheel swings. Shrewsbury, Chester and York— cities, where the amateurs had for centuries provided the dramatic fare that fashioned the stage conventions which Burbage and Alleyn were to make their own, with their pride and joy crushed by reformist zeal—opened their gates to triumphant and now unrivalled professionals.

Before leaving the subject of actors and acting to consider the actors' economy, something must be said about a third group who are quite distinct from the clerical and courtly amateurs and the professional minstrels, namely, the choristers and schoolboys. These youngsters appear to have been employed as actors from very early days.* *Diversis pueris ludentibus* figure in the Durham Priory accounts in 1416.[27] They do not, however, figure very often. It is in the street pageant theatres of civic welcomes that they are most frequently used. *Juvenes* and *virgines* are constantly mentioned in descriptions and accounts from the fourteenth century onwards. By 1501 they are called 'childyr'. As often as not they came

---

* The first mention of them, specifically as actors, known to me is the complaint of the choristers of St. Paul's about competition from 'inexpert' players of miracles in 1378. See Ch. IV, p. 163 above.

from local church choirs and were rehearsed by responsible clerks. In 1464 for the London Coronation of Queen Elizabeth Woodville, Roger, Clerk of St. Magnus Church, sang with his boys. Holme, a precentor, on the same occasion was paid 3s. 4d.

'for himself & his boys singing at the door of our chapel on the bridge at the Queen's coming. And to Salamon Batell for his labour in form and manner of St. Elizabeth addressing the Queen at the drawbridge—20d. And to Edmund Herte being there in the role of Mary Cleophas—20d.'[28]

In Disguisings, too, children were employed. At Richmond in 1501, for instance, a large throne was drawn into the hall by

'ii mermaydes, o(ne) off them a ma(n) mermayde, th'oth(er) a woman; the man in harnesse from the wa(i)st uppewards; and in ev(er)y off the sayde m(er)mayds a chylde of the chapell, syngyng ryght swetly, and w(i)th g(rea)t armony.'[29]

The story of the boy companies in Tudor England is too familiar to need discussion here. Nor is there any justification for discussing the village amateurs whose St. George Plays, Robin Hood Plays or May King Games brought in some small change for their private use in much the same way that carol singers or makers of a Guy raise funds today.[30]

A last small point worth mentioning is the position of women in relation to the mediaeval stage. It is often said that women made their first appearance on the British stage in 1660. Baldly stated this is not true: if true at all, it means only that, from then onwards, in professional companies, female parts were regularly played by women. The active connection of ladies with the drama begins with the Tournament, where they not only initiate the whole proceedings but also preside over the allegorical disguises adopted, the evening prize-giving and the subsequent revels. They are active participants in the disguisings and later masks. Nor were they banned from the religious stage. In Harleian MS. 2104 in the British Museum there is a list of the guilds responsible for performing the Chester Cycle in the late fifteenth century.* The play of the Assumption of the Virgin is there assigned to 'Ye Wyfves of ye town'.* They assisted with this same scene in the London Lord Mayor's Show for 1523, which was attended by the King of Denmark, and were paid for their pains:

* Fol. 4: see Plate XXIII, No. 33. Also Appendix D, p. 346 below.

'It(em) to Gleyns daughter for thassumpcion & Child(es) eldest daughter for Saynt Ursula & vj virgens w^t bothe nyghts aft(er) viiij apece. S(u)ma. v^s iiij^d.' *

Amongst the professional minstrels women also had a role to play, usually as dancers. Thus, although it is generally true that female parts were played by boys or young men in the Middle Ages and in Tudor times, women could and did perform both as amateurs and professionals in so far as society would allow them to.† My own surmise is that as women were not usually given any training in the art of oratory it was normally found that men and boys were more reliable performers than women. The pitch and resonance of their voices compared to a woman's is also an important factor where performance in echoing churches or halls or in the open air is concerned. This surmise gains in credibility if we reflect that when the change was made after the Restoration, it was in the context of small, indoor theatres with a seating capacity of about four to five hundred people.

To sum up, acting in mediaeval England as a leisure-time activity was permitted to all and popular with all: so popular indeed that it often distracted people from more serious and worthy occupations which devotionally minded clerics and commercially minded merchants agreed should claim their attention instead. Acting as a profession, therefore, was admitted as a legitimate service to the community provided it was strictly regulated. In theory women were allowed to perform as well as men within these regulations, but they had to be able to compete with boys and men in 'theatres', which put them vocally at a severe disadvantage if they were to perform in fact. And just as women had to compete with men, professionals had to compete with amateurs to obtain the favour of audiences. For a long while the dice were very heavily loaded in favour of the amateurs, since the Miracle Plays were financed, in part at least, by a levy. How long this would have lasted in England it is hard to judge had not the Government intervened and, by suppressing the major manifestation of the popular amateur stage, left the field open to the many small companies of professionals. By amalgamation among themselves and by reorganizing the conditions under which they played, they were able

* Malone Soc., *Collections III*, p. 14. Other named girls appeared in the Pageant of the Lady Mary for the Lord Mayor's Show in 1534 and again received 8d. each (*ibid.*, p. 24).

† I know of no decree either ecclesiastical or civic which specifically forbade women to act. This subject is discussed at greater length in Vol. II.

to take full advantage of the change. As the great amateur companies of the provinces fall victims to the Reformation, so the major professional companies based on London replace them in popular esteem. Amateur creativeness deserts both its religious basis and the provinces, now left dependent on touring metropolitan companies, and devotes itself to the narrow confines of the stage of social recreation in the purlieus of the Court. The detailed amplification of this story can more properly be handled in Volume II.

3 Production, Management and Presentation

Perhaps the most notable feature to emerge from the foregoing pages concerning actors and acting is the marked difference in public attitude to the theatre as an organized institution then and now. We incline to think of our theatre as an independent body that provides entertainment for a comparatively small minority of the population who attend because it serves to fill leisure-time and to offer a smattering of 'culture' or material for 'small-talk'. By contrast, the theatre of the Middle Ages was inextricably tied to religion, politics and technology, and regulated by a far more restricted timetable.

The simple economy of the agricultural year in peasant communities and the superimposition upon it of the Christian Calendar determined the organization of the medieval theatre and governed its methods. In the first place, performances in daylight were both easier and less costly to organize than any attempted after nightfall. A further restriction of nature upon the time of performance was the effect of climate and season.

An agricultural community usually has greater leisure, however, in the dead months of the year (November–February) than in the lively ones (March–October). The period of greatest leisure therefore corresponded with that when daylight was shortest and open-air production most difficult. Performances in winter, however, while desirable in terms of the leisure to attend them, could only become regular features of life if conducted indoors and by artificial light. Since the Holy Days of the Christian Calendar tended to conform with the long-established holidays of the agricultural year one may reasonably expect to find lengthy performances for large audiences organized in the open air and restricted to the summer, with performances in winter restricted to an interior environment, unless of very brief duration.

Bearing these facts in mind it is easy to see how Christmas, Shrovetide, Whitsun and Midsummer (St. John the Baptist) come to take precedence over all other festive seasons as occasions for dramatic entertainment: and further, why the popular theatre focuses upon the summer festivals and the courtly theatre upon the winter ones. Large halls, money to pay for fuel and illumination and a staff in attendance are all prerequisites for any successful defiance of nature for turning night into day and snowy fields or streets into a festive theatre. What is important here is that the audience by performing this miracle has the right to call the tune. The actors are its servants who must please to live. Granted an assembly of people on the other hand who have come or been drawn together fortuitously and by external circumstance, the actor has a much freer hand. In so far as he can be both heard and seen, the livelihood he draws from his talent will depend largely upon his ability to attract and maintain the attention of the assembled crowd.

Thus, if the cardinal factor governing the actor's economy in mediaeval society is the leisure-time occasion when performance was practicable, it will be quickly seen that a second factor of scarcely less importance was the provision of the auditorium.

The indoor theatre of social recreation became feasible in Britain when wealth, geared to social prestige, made large and spacious halls regularly available. Another drama, however, that deriving from worship, preceded it into existence already equipped with a suitably spacious auditorium. The actors were clergy who could accordingly control their time, place and type of performance regardless of the seasons for so long as they could claim the allegiance of their audience of worshippers. It was in these circumstances that the liturgical drama evolved during the eleventh and twelfth centuries.

Once, however, the actor-clergy transferred their drama from the precincts of their own auditorium, and began to infringe upon others provided under the King's Peace, they became subject to control from without. If the representative of the King's Peace (usually the Mayor in English towns) was himself an employer of artisan labour or a merchant in business, the commercial interests which he represented were likely to affect the conditions of performance and possibly the drama itself. The most probable point of impingement was the auditorium, since this had to be organized and paid for by someone.

This same discipline applied to professional actors seeking to tap the large audiences brought together by fairs and other public festivities in towns or villages: for membership of a troupe under noble patronage did not automatically rid them of the obligation to obtain permission from the owner to use the auditorium and to subscribe to his rules. Nevertheless, the more sure of themselves they became in their hold over this audience the more urgent did the pressure become to own their auditorium themselves or, at least, to lease it on a long-term basis.

The third factor of consequence is the audience itself: what it will pay in time, money or both, to see. Here actor and theorist seldom see eye to eye. The manager intervenes at this point as intermediary. His duty is to safeguard the livelihood of his actors: his skill is to determine the mean between the theorists' wishes and the popular demand. His presence only becomes a necessity when actors are banded into large enough troupes for small errors in financial judgement to prejudice the survival of the company and when ownership of an auditorium puts the onus of choosing the repertoire in the company's exclusive hands.

In considering the mediaeval theatre, therefore, we may exclude the person of the manager from our discussion of the actor's economy, for it is not until Elizabeth's accession that he becomes a figure of any consequence. Instead, we must concentrate attention upon the actor's patrons, the men, that is, who employed him to perform; and the means devised for meeting the production costs, whether by direct subsidy, indirect levy, or from receipts. *

The logical starting point of such an enquiry in the hierarchical society of mediaeval and Tudor England is the Court.

(a) *Revels at Court*

Since Sir Edmund Chambers wrote his *Notes on the History of the Revels Office under the Tudors* (1906), little has been added to our knowledge of the organization responsible for the presentation of entertainments at Tudor Courts. In effect this means that very little is known prior to 1545. In that year, on the 11th March, a permanent Master of the Revels joined the ranks of Household Officials surrounding the person of the Sovereign.[31] Before that, what knowledge we possess rests largely on hypothesis, if only because no one seems to have followed—at least in this direction— where Sir Edmund dared to tread. His statement therefore that the Revels Office existed on a temporary basis at least as early as 1494 has gone unchallenged.[32] It is founded on a passage in B.M. MS. Harl. 642 (ff. 209b–210) concerning the articles ordained for the

* Appendices B, C, F and G are all directly related to this subject.

regulation of Henry VII's Household drawn up in that year which I quote in the reading to be found in the transcript printed in *Household Ordonnances*, a Miscellany of Ordonnances and Registers published by the Society of Antiquaries in 1790: 'As for the sitting in the King's Great Chamber. . . . and if the master of the revells be there, he may sit with the chapleyns or with the esquires or gentlemen ushers. . . .'[33] A very similar passage occurs in another Miscellany of Household Ordonnances of the same period printed in the *Antiquarian Repertory*. Comparison shows that both are printed transcripts of the same Ordonnance but with a difference in the latter which quite transforms the significance of the whole passage. Here follows what I am convinced is the correct reading:

'For the sittinge in the Kyng's gret Chambre. . . . And if the master of the jewelles be there in p'sens, he may sit w^t the Chambreleyn or squyeres, or w^t gentillmen uschers. . .'[34]

This reading seems the better of the two on practically every count. In the first place it derives from a MS. written by a gentleman usher in the service of Henry VII for the instruction of his successor in office,* where the former is a late copy as both the hand and the spelling testify. Considered, too, in the light of what we know of the organization of the Chamber and of what Sir Edmund himself has to say about the Master of the Jewels, who in his opinion was synonymous with the Treasurer of the Chamber until the posts were divided in 1483,[35] it seems a better reading. The fact that the offending phrase was first omitted in the Harleian MS. and then inserted above the main text advises caution. But perhaps the most forceful argument of all for rejection of the word 'revells' is that the Harleian MS. does in point of fact read 'jewelles' and not 'revelles'.

* The version from 'Ceremonies and Services at Court' in *Ant. Rep.* (2nd ed., i, pp. 296–341) gives the contents of an MS. which, in 1726, was possessed by Peter Le Neve, Norroy King at Arms. Le Neve describes his MS. as the instructions of an Esquire or Gentleman Usher in the service of Henry VII to his successor in office, and bases his attribution on internal evidence (see especially the footnote to p. 296 and pp. 312, 314 and 340). If this attribution is accepted and the *Ant. Rep.* transcript is collated with that in *H.O.*, then clearly the MS. Le Neve worked from was itself a transcript of Hen. VII's original Household Regulations, rearranged and interpolated with personal observations. I have been unable to trace Le Neve's MS. myself: but I suggest that both this MS. and *B.M. MS. Harl. 642* were transcribed from the same source—now lost—Le Neve's providing both the earlier and more reliable version of this passage.

Prior to 1545, then, there was no officially recognized or established office of Revels. In seeking to discover how the many entertainments at Court were organized perhaps the best basis of enquiry is a document of 1573 found by Sir Edmund Chambers among Lord Burleigh's papers and published by him in his *Notes on the History of the Revels Office under the Tudors*:

'The Office of the Revelles, as it shoulde seeme by reporte, hath in tymes past bene in that order, That the prince beinge disposed to pastyme would at one tyme appoynte one persone, at sometyme an other, suche as for creditte, pleasaunte witte and habilitye in learnynge he thought meete to be the master of the Revelles for that tyme, to sett fourthe such devises as might be most agreable to the princes expectation. The workes beinge fynyshed, It is thought that the princes Tayler havinge the oversight of the Workemanshippe brought in the Bill of charges and was payed for it, whereupon is gathered that John Houlte yeoman of the Revelles used to say Concerninge allowaunce of charges in the office of the Revelles "it hathe bene but a Taylers Bill".'[36]

This report testifies to the sovereign being the person upon whose authority preparations could be set afoot for a royal entertainment: equally, that he did not normally organize it himself, but deputed his authority to someone 'suche as for creditte, pleasaunte witte and habilitye in learnynge he thought meete'. The terms of reference suggest a person both educated and intimately known to the sovereign. Such a person we might reasonably expect to find in any of the important Household posts. Of these, the Marshal, the Steward, the Chamberlain and the Treasurer were by tradition the most dignified. But at the close of the fifteenth century, the posts of Controller, Secretary and Lord Privy Seal were gaining in importance thanks to the executive power entrusted to them by Henry VII. Fox, for example, as Henry's Lord Privy Seal, and Wolsey who succeeded him, wielded more power than any other official at Court: and it is Fox whom Bacon, in his *History of King Henry VII*, describes as

'. . . . not onely a grave *Councellor* for Warre or Peace, but also a good *Master* of *Ceremonies*, and anything else that was fit for the *Active* part, belonging to the service of *Court*, or *State* of a great King.'[37]

Bacon actually attributes the arrangements for Katherine of Aragon's reception to Fox. Another official whose fortunes rose with those of the Privy Seal was the Secretary. Fox himself had graduated from Secretary to Privy Seal.[38] Both officials, besides discharging their duties at Court like the Marshal, Steward or Chamberlain, were useful in the conduct of relations outside the Court. It was through the Secretary that Court business was transacted with the Mayor and Corporation of London. He was thus the liaison officer between Court and City in the preparation of Royal Entries.[39] Nor should it be forgotten that it was from Secretary Cecil that the Elizabethan players learnt how best to offend the Spanish Ambassador.* Something must therefore be said about these important Household officers if their part in the initiation and control of courtly revels is to be understood.

Sir Edmund Chambers has related the changing fortunes of the Marshal, Steward, Chamberlain and Treasurer in the first volume of his *Elizabethan Stage*,[40] and I do not propose to do more than summarize his conclusions here. The medieval Household, broadly speaking, was divided for administrative purposes into three major departments, namely the Courtyard, over which ruled the Marshal, the Hall, for which the Steward was responsible, and the Chamber or inner sanctum governed by the Chamberlain. Finance was in the charge of the Treasurer and the Controller who dealt with all expenditure not met directly by the Exchequer. These two offices, after a temporary eclipse, recovered importance during the fifteenth century. The Chamberlain and Steward suffered no diminution of their authority. The Marshal on the other hand, as political and social conditions made for more spacious domestic living, suffered a severe decline. Nevertheless, we might reasonably expect that all these great officers of the Household were responsible in some measure for the Court's entertainment since they controlled the principal auditoriums available for revels at Court. The Marshal, exercising control over the horses, conveyances and armoury of the Household, could scarcely escape association with Tournaments. The Steward and Chamberlain were likely to be similarly involved with Disguisings, ultimate responsibility for their execution depending on whether they were held in the Hall or Chamber. Control over auditoriums outside the Court itself was exercised by either the Bishop or the Mayor of the area and, as already stated, if the Court was to be involved in the entertainment, liaison officers existed in the Secretary and Privy Seal. The Treasurer and Controller of the Household, controlling domestic finance as they did, were bound to be connected with

* See Ch. VII, p. 240 above.

all forms of entertainment that had to be paid for from royal funds.

This picture, based on presumption, is confirmed in considerable detail by factual record dating from the last quarter of the fifteenth century forward.

(b) *Tournaments, Disguisings and Plays*

The Tournament, in all its formative period and through most of the years it was contributing actively to the development of English theatrical convention, was under the control of the Marshal. In the fifteenth century, however, his loss of functional prestige virtually severed his connection with Court entertainment. He still exercised control, at least nominally, over the Heralds as he continues to do today[41]: but he had lost control over the Stable, being replaced in that capacity by a Master of the Horse. The Armoury, too, by the sixteenth century was under its own Master, supervised by the Chamberlain rather than the Marshal. The Household Orders of Edward IV, set out in the *Liber Niger*, convince me that notwithstanding the Marshal's intimate connection with early Tournaments, he was not likely to be deeply involved in arrangements for Tudor entertainments.[42]

The Steward, on the other hand, took over, with the Controller as his deputy, not only some measure of control over the Heralds, but also the accommodation at feasts and the vital matter of precedence.[43] The Controller too becomes largely responsible for the arrangements for Tournaments, including the preparation of the auditorium.[44] We hear explicitly of the Chamberlain's responsibility for Disguisings, much about the many minor officials in his department,[45] and that the Secretary exercised a general supervision over one and all, responsible himself only to the Privy Seal. *
Within these terms of reference and once the King's permission had been obtained, the labour of converting Tournaments from pledges between a knight and his lady into an accomplished fact was divided. The performers looked to their own interests: arrangements for spectators they transferred from their own shoulders to those of the Privy Council, who in turn left the execution of the details to the Controller and the Heralds.† In 1501, on the occasion of the Tournaments to celebrate Katherine of Aragon's

---

* See Ch. II, p. 40 above, where the question of cost is also discussed.

† See p. 283 below.

marriage to Prince Arthur, music was sufficiently important to be entrusted to a special official:

'And th'ordering and guyding of the said Trompettes and Mynistrells for the tyme of the ffest is comitted to Thomas Lovell yoman huissher of the Kings Chamber.'[46]

These trumpeters and minstrels had to perform not only at the Tournament but at the Disguisings and at the wedding ceremony in St. Paul's, where they were positioned 'aboute the high aultr̄' and 'in the vawts'. A sound of quite a different order required at the Tournament was the roar of guns. This was to accompany the entry of knight-defenders in their ships,

'wᵗ all man(ne)r of tacklyngs and marin(e)rs in her, the which in the seid appierau(n)ce made a great and an houge noyse wᵗ s(e)rpentyns,* and other guneshote.'[47]

The Armoury probably looked to this.

Having charged responsible officials with these various duties, the Controller had little else to see to himself beyond the erection and decoration of the auditorium. This has been discussed in Chapter II already.† The cost of the latter was met from the Privy Purse. An entry for 7th May 1492 read: 'At Shene. To the clerk of the werkes for making of the Lystes at Shene, . . . £24. 2.10.'[48]

If staged indoors and at night a Tournament, in the form of Barriers, was probably organized on much the same lines as a Disguising. Ultimate responsibility for this, as for all else, rested with the King's Council: but again deputies were chosen to supervise the actual execution. It seems probable, however, that the King and the Privy Seal exercised a stronger personal influence here than on either Pageants or outdoor Tournaments. This is only natural if one considers the structural formula for a Disguising. Not only were the entries made by courtiers, but in the dancing which formed its climax the sovereign himself and his family were likely to take an active part. The document of 1573 outlining the early organization of the Revels Office is, by itself, very ambiguous: but the following facts help to remove that ambiguity.

In the earliest abstract of the Council's proposals for Katherine of Aragon's reception there occurs the following passage:

'Itm̄ Jaques Hault and William Pawne to be appo(inted) to (him to) devyse and p(re)parre disguisings and som Moresques afte(r) the

---

* A kind of cannon. See *O.E.D.*, *sub* Serpentine (2).

† See pp. 40 and 41 above.

best maner they can wherof they shal have warnyng by my lord Chamberlayn.'[49]

In the face of so straightforward a statement of the position, most problems would solve themselves if we only knew something of Jaques Hault and William Pawne. I have searched far and wide for information about their dramatic activity, but with small success. Hault's name appears in the accounts of the Privy Purse between December 1494 and June 1501, always as a recipient of money for his share in Disguisings, except under the 30th August 1497 when he was paid £10 'for the tenes playe'.[50] During the years 1499 to 1503 payments for Disguisings are also made to John Atkynson. Atkynson was a senior official in the Wardrobe, and it is significant that Hault's name is only mentioned as being responsible for the Disguisings for Katherine of Aragon in the earliest of the abstracts, namely that prepared in 1499. May we perhaps deduce that Hault was still in office when preparations for Katherine's arrival were first undertaken and had been succeeded by Atkynson when they were put into effect in the autumn of 1501? Admittedly the evidence is slender; but in view of the Privy Purse accounts, Atkynson's undoubted connection with the Wardrobe, Jaques Hault's commission and the quip of the later John Houlte, 'yeoman of the Revelles', about his office in former days, there are good grounds for believing that the document of 1573 is accurate in attributing 'the oversight of the workemanshippe' to 'the princes Taylor', and that he 'brought in the Bill of charges and was paid for it'.[51]

William Pawne, Jaques Hault's associate in the 1499 commission, figures nowhere in the Privy Purse payments for revels. In March 1501, we know he was Master of the Works in the town of Calais. The inference is that, by the start of the sixteenth century, responsibility for the spectacle of a Disguising lay with the King's Wardrobe and his Office of Works. The wording of the Commission—'devyse and p(re)parre disguisings and som Moresques'—admits of a wider interpretation than mere execution of the spectacle. I would hazard the guess that the Secretary or Privy Seal (having received a hint from the sovereign about the theme likely to give him pleasure), conveyed this information to the Wardrobe and Works, letting them interpret it as they thought fit. *

---

* Included in the scenic arrangements would be such additional seating accommodation as might be required and also, in the late sixteenth century,

The preparations in hand, it was left to the Steward or Chamberlain to supervise arrangements for the performance itself. Here we are greatly assisted by the survival of the advice given by one of Henry VII's Gentlemen Ushers to his successor.[52] It would seem as if he were quoting from his personal experience and the reminiscences of his predecessor, since custom as early as that under Henry IV is cited. The Usher's advice is based on the 'Articles ordained by Henry VII for the regulation of his Household' of December 1494.[53] First, general procedure:

'The Day of Estate in the Great Chamber. . . . and whether the King keepe the hall or great chamber, all is one; save onely the steward and the marshalle doe the King service in the hall, and the chamberlaine and ushers doe in the chamber.'[54]

We are next informed of the arrangements against the need of a deputy:

'Item, in the absence of the chamberlaine, the usher shall have the same power to command in like manner, alsoe, it is right necessarie for the chamberlaine and ushers to have ever in remembrance all the highe festival dayes in the yeare. . . . what is longing to their office.'[55]

The usher expands this last phrase considerably and adds:

'As ffor the disguysinge, it longithe not to your office, but that ye wot welle it muste be redy under the clothe of estat, quyschins (*cushions*) and siche things y^t be necessary, lights in the hall afture the quantite of the hall and youre discrecion rowme enough for them. If it be in the gret chambre, the dissgisinge then is your office, to se quyschins redy laide for the Kinge, undir the clothe of estat, or els at the King's pleasure, on the cupbord, if the King will lene thereat.'[56]

He concludes:

'Syre one thinge; I vsed alway, and I wold counselle you, yf my lord chambreleyene were p'sent, I neuer did no gret thinge in myne office but by his avice, whiche was to me sufficient discharge.'[57]

It was through the Lord Chamberlain, as we have seen, that the

the provision of a raised stage for the actors if that were necessary. See Queen Elizabeth's visit to Cambridge (1564), Oxford (1566), Ch. VII, pp. 248–252 above and Appendix H.

Wardrobe and the Office of Works were warned of the preparations to be set in hand.* Both were essentially construction departments. Cloth was ordered and made up into costumes by the Wardrobe: scenic units were constructed and painted by the Office of Works together with any special scaffolds required to accommodate spectators around the walls adjacent to the dance floor.†

In the case of plays there is no reason to anticipate any serious difference in organization since the auditorium was the same and accordingly governed by the same officials and deputies.‡ Not having any evidence as to what in fact provoked the decision to create a Revels Office in 1545, we can only surmise the probable reasons for its advent. By far the most likely is a determination to bring the dispersed and often delegated responsibilities of a multitude of officials into line with other specialist departments of the Household with a view to obtaining greater efficiency and eliminating waste.

A second potent pressure to the same end was the rapidly expanding variety of available entertainments that could be obtained from sources outside the Court itself, notably plays performed by schoolboys and by the acting companies maintained by the nobility. A command to play at Court was, by the mid sixteenth century, becoming a matter of importance to the acting companies as a trade mark with which to entice the wider audience of both London and the provinces to support their performances.

A third possible contributing factor—and the coincidence of date is important here—is the desirability of a closer censorship of the themes and texts of plays and masks.§ Responsibility in this rested squarely with the Secretary and the Chamberlain: but their task could be materially eased by the existence of a centralized Revels Office under a Master whose whole-time job it was to sift applications to perform at Court, co-ordinate the work of several interested departments (for whom tasks connected with the Revels were only an occasional interruption of normal duty), and generally ensure

* See p. 281 above.

† See Ch. VII, p. 248 above. See also Vol. II, 1576–1660, Pt. 1, pp. 280 et seq.

‡ See Ch. VII, p. 249 above.

§ No evidence is known to me which would show that the Master's authority extended any serious distance beyond London. On Progresses the entertainments given to Queen Elizabeth indoors and out were written by authors 'approved' by the Lord Chamberlain and the Secretary who were themselves on the spot to supervise arrangements for performance.

the highest possible standards befitting a Court on display before an envious, suspicious and keenly critical world.

(c) *The Street Pageant Theatres*

The conduct of Royal Entries was just as clearly and carefully organized, but the officials charged with regulating them were different, as was the allocation of responsibility for executing them. The fullest records which I have encountered relate to the reception accorded by Londoners to Katherine of Aragon in 1501, and to Elizabeth Woodville, Queen to Edward IV, in 1464; and by provincial cities to various sovereigns in the fifteenth century. By far the most important of these is the Entry of Katherine of Aragon since, in this instance, documents have survived which record the preparations for the reception as well as descriptions of the reception itself. These abstracts are of varying dates and in varying hands. One, however, is definitely annotated in Fox's own hand.[58] This corroborates Bacon's assertion that 'The chiefe man that tooke the care was *Bishop* Fox; . . . a good *Master* of Ceremonies'.[59] Another, not in Fox's hand, is in the College of Arms: and there are others.[60] This, in view of the fact that Heralds are charged with certain functions and that the authors instruct that 'Rob(*er*)t Suthwell & S(*i*)r William Vampage' are to be issued with copies† makes it seem that the normal procedure was for some central authority to draft an abstract and then ensure that copies reached all responsible officials mentioned in it. Since Fox was Privy Seal this central authority was in all probability the Privy Council of which the King's Chamberlain, Steward, Treasurer, Controller and Secretary were all members. This body sorted out which of the proposed arrangements fell within their own particular domain and then, fortified with a copy of the full programme, saw to it that their subordinates discharged whatever was committed to their office. Such a system would ensure both an accurate expression of the Sovereign's wishes, and close liaison between the heads of the

---

† 'Item the Byshop of Duresme (*i.e. Fox; since this can be dated as 1499*), hath taken upon him to make an abstracte oute of this pᵣsente booke of everie mans charge as it is comprised in the same. And the same abstracte devided into severall Articles as the matter toucheth everie man aparte to deliver in writinge to Mr. Secretarie wᶜh shall inclose the Articles severallye in as manie Lⁿres as ther shalbe articles and the same directe and cause to bee sent to such p̄sons as bee named in the heads of the said Articles desiringe them by the said letters to doe p̄forme for their partes as is expressed in the same Articles.' (B.M. MS. Cot. Vit. C. XI, f. 126.) See p. 285, note * below.

departments concerned. It is to the Secretary that arrangements for the Princess's reception in the City of London are entrusted.[61] The cortège escorting her is to assemble in St. George's Fields under the direction of Fox himself (translated between 1499 and 1501 from Durham to Winchester) and Sir John Risley.[62]

This procedure sounds very much like dictation from the Court to the City.* Yet it is obvious from the subject matter of the Pageant welcomes from 1392 onwards that 'dictation' was confined to procedure, the actual content and responsibility for execution resting with the city, whose right to devise and implement the street pageants within their city was almost certainly regarded as one of the civic liberties. This view is substantiated by a curious entry in the Great Chronicle of London which clearly states the City's standpoint rather than the Court's. It refers to the seventh of the pageants in 1501, erected outside St. Paul's.

'. . . a pagend standyng at the west dore of pawlys the whych was ordeynyd & dyvysid by the Kyngis Commaundment the Cityzens thereof noo thyng made of counsayll. But in (th)e ende sir Reynold Bray & othir of the kyngis counsayll had of the Chambyrlayn ffor the charge of the same C. li.'[63]

This passage indicates that the City jealously guarded the privilege of organizing its own pageants; but it shows too that the King, or the Privy Council acting for him, had an interest in their conduct. It also forecasts the battle that was later to develop concerning the right to censor and even ban dramatic performances within the City. Similar procedure was adopted in the Provinces. At York in 1486 we learn from the City's *House Book* that 'the Maier, his breder Aldermen, and othre of the Common Counesell of the Citie', after invoking the good offices of the Archbishop, themselves prepared the reception which greeted Henry VII.†

Reverting to the London preparations for Katherine of Aragon's reception we learn that in 1499 the City Recorder, together with Robert Cate, Chawny, Colet, Martyn, Rede, Shaa and Wood were

'appoyntid to have con(ver)cac(i)on from tyme to tyme w^t the

* A minute from the Privy Council proceedings reads: 'Item, that the maiͬ citezens, and craftes of London attende upon the said p⁻ncesse, at the Crosse in the Chepe, ayenst her comyng to the Citie, in suche maner and suche solempnitie, and w^t suche pagentes and Cerymonye as thei have devised for th'onoͬ of the Citie, and of the fest, wherof their shalbe adv⁻tised by the lord Bergevenny.' (B.M. MS. Cot. Vesp. C. XIV, f. 95b.)

† For similar arrangements in Bristol, see Ch. III, p. 72 above.

kynges com̄yssioners (*i.e. Lord Bergevenny and the Secretary*) touchyng preparacion to be made for receyvyng of the prynces that by Gods g(r)a(ce) shall coym̄ oute of Spayne.'[64]

Of this list of City representatives, John Shaa, Goldsmith, was later to be knighted and, in 1501, supervised the actual reception as Lord Mayor.[65] Responsibility for the various pageants along the processional route was delegated to the Livery Companies.

'The Story on the Bridge
   Xr̄ofer Eliot Goldsmyth
   Willm̄ Marymer Salter
The Story on the grete Conduct & (th)e pagent y^r (*there*)
   Robt Weston M(er)c(er) (*who died and was replaced by his son John*)
   Thomas Howdew Taill(er)
The Conduct in Cornhull
   Aungell dom̄ Groc(er) (*who was replaced by William Butteler, Grocer*)
   John Mane Vynter
The Standard in the Chepe
   John Holdew drap(er)
   John Palmer ffisshmong(er)
The litell Conduct in Chepe
   John pasmere Skynner
   Henr(y) Iby Sherman
The second Stacion atte conduct in Gracechirch Strete
   Thomas Billesdon Hab(er)dassher
   Ric(hard) Grey Ire(n)monger.'[66]

The considerable variations in the scribe's wording of the charge with which these persons are entrusted warn one against literal interpretation. It seems to me most reasonable to suppose that they were severally charged with the engagement and supervision of the artificers required to erect the pageants authorized by the Court of Aldermen. Just such an arrangement seems to be attested to by an entry in the Bridge House Rentals concerning a payment of money to the Warden of London Bridge, Christopher Eliot*:

* Regarding the Warden's function, see pp. 297 *et seq.* below. There is no direct evidence as to the authorship of the text; but the following extract from a contemporary MS. is not without interest: 'As ffor the Ressauynge off a Quene, and her Crownacion . . . And at the Touyr gate the meyre and the worschipfulle men of the cete of London to mete hir in yr̄ best arraye, goinge on ffoot ij and ij togedure, till they come to

'. . . Cxxijl viijs vd . . . to the said Cristopher and Edward the xixth day of September the xixth yere of King Henry VIIth by the maire and Aldermen as in money expendyd and paid for the new making of a pagente set upon London bridge in th'entre of the lady princes of Spayne and as of record in the Courte of the said Maire and Aldermen plainely doth appere & sic sm̄ illa.'67

The 'official channels' through which a civic welcome was organized thus become clearer. At the head was the King in Council. The sovereign's wishes were represented by the Privy Seal who appointed a sub-committee under the chairmanship of the Secretary to treat with the City Council concerned. The Court of Common Council—composed of the Mayor, Sheriffs, Aldermen and Common Councillors—sought the views of this sub-committee or commission, but preserved to itself the right of organizing the city's welcome. After settling an appropriate theme for the reception, either this Council or the Court of Aldermen would proceed to consider the sites on which to erect the illustrative pageants and commit their execution to suitable dignitaries from the City Companies. Two were appointed to each, presumably an officer and his deputy. It was then left to them to engage the workmen, collect the materials, finance the works, engage the actors and ensure that everything was ready for the appointed day and hour. *

Westm̄r : And at the condit in Cornylle ther must be ordined a sight wᵗ angelles singinge, and freche balettes yᵉon in latene, engliche, and ffrenche, *mad by the wyseste docturs of this realme* (the italics are mine); and the condyt in Chepe in the same wyse; and the condit must ryn bothe red wyn and whit wyne; and the crosse in Chepe muste be araid in yᵉ most rialle wyse that myght be thought; and the condit next Poules in the same wyse; And whedur she go furthe at Newgat or Lidgatt, it must be in the like wyse & so goinge furthe till she come to Westm̄r hall . . .' Printed by F. Grose, *Ant. Rep.* (*ed. cit.*), i, 303.

* The Bridge House Rentals for 1464 give us a detailed picture of these activities on one of the traditional pageant sites that I think we may reasonably regard as typical. Remembering the dimensions of these pageant structures, it is scarcely surprising to find masons and carpenters employed. On the Bridge Pageant of 1464 we hear of 'carpentars & alioꝛs oparioꝛs and sᵛientes pontis'. Similarly, for the 1501 Pageants on the same spot, 'for expencis upon Masons and Carpenters the day of the entre of the lady princes for their watche and delygente attendaunce geven by theym unto the same xjs iijd.' Besides them, there were painters to be engaged, tailors to make costumes, cofferers, and sign-writers. A host of tradesmen had to be tackled about the supply of nails, brackets, coal, pails, candles and pins. In 1464 William Westram, Grocer, supplied 12 lbs. of glue; William Brown, Grocer, supplied 19 sheets of red paper; and Richard Syffe, Mercer, 96 ells of 'Siltwych'. Nor was an adequate supply of beer forgotten.68

This pattern, reconstructed from the records relating to the years 1499–1501, is further reinforced by those concerning the welcome of James I in his new capital a hundred years later: for it was again the City Fathers, in 1603, that undertook the organization of the Pageants and commissioned Dekker, Middleton and Jonson to write them. Stephen Harrison's tribute to the Lord Mayor,

'the right worshipfull the Aldermen his Brethren, and to those Worshipfull Commoners elected Committies, for the Managing of this Businesse'[69]

is especially useful in confirming the findings on the organization of earlier days:

'And thus much you shall understand, that no manner of person whatsoever, did disburse any part towards the charge of these five *Triumphes*, but onely the meere Citizens being all free-men; heretofore the charge being borne by fifteenes and the Chamber of London (as may appeare by auncient precidents) but now it was leavied amongst the Companies. The other two *Arch's* erected by Merchant-Strangers (viz. the *Italians* and *Dutchmen*) were only their owne particular charge.

'The Citty elected 16. Committies to whom the managing of the whole businesse was absolutely referred: of which number 4 were Aldermen, the other 12. Commoners, viz. one out of each of the 12. Companies. Other Committies were also appointed as overseers and surveyors of the worke.'[70]

What these Committees did was to organize a show, as far as texts, characters, actors and costume were concerned at least, but little different from their predecessors of a hundred years earlier. The question of finance remains to be considered. If the London Bridge Pageant can be regarded as typical, then it would seem that the Court of Aldermen's two representatives saw to the payment of all tradesmen and participants whom they engaged to prepare the pageant for which they were respectively responsible. This was no small sum. The Pageant on the Bridge in 1464 cost £21 14s. 6½d.* This had probably been used before, for in 1501 we know that £122 8s. 5d. was paid 'for the new making of a pagente set upon London Bridge'.

The lower cost in 1464 can be explained in terms of a curious reference to three loads of 'stuffurs' carted from Guildhall. If we

* See Appendix B.

suppose that the main structural items had been stored in Guildhall since the last 'entry' and only needed to be re-erected and touched up in 1464, we may then reasonably assume that it was the construction of a new frame and façade which rocketed the cost in 1501.[71] A further check on the average cost of a new Pageant is supplied by the figure given for the seventh of those in 1501, which the City chronicler is at pains to point out was none of the City's doing. 'In (th)e Ende', to use his own phrase which conveys so vivid a picture of protracted wrangling, 'Sir Reynold Bray and othir of the Kyngis counsayll had of the Chambyrlayn ffor the charge of the same C. Li'.[72] Thus I think we may safely reckon the average cost at approximately £120 for each Pageant.

The Court of Aldermen's representatives, having duly paid the bills personally incurred, were themselves reimbursed later by the Court of Common Council. The Councillors obtained the money to make these repayments by taxing the citizens over whom they ruled:

'It is agreed that John Hert', reads the City Journal of the year 1500, 'shall receyve alle suche sommes of money as shalbe brought to hym by the Collecto(r)s of ev(er)y Warde of the Citee of and for the XVme & ½XV^me late graunted by auctorite of the Counsell for the Receyvyng of the Lady Kath(er)yn.'[73]

The King himself paid for his Royal Box. An entry under 20th November 1501 in the Privy Purse Accounts reads: 'To Whiting for the Kinges standing in Chepside £6.13.4.'[74]

If we reach forward a hundred years to the start of the seventeenth century it is clear that the cost of financing these shows had risen sharply. The Corporation of London's Finance Committee estimated the total cost of solemnizing James I's coronation at £2,500[75] and the cost of the Pageants at £400, and set about raising a levy to cover it from the City Companies.[76] For the Pageants, each was asked for a sum which varied proportionately with their respective resources, ranging between £37 8s. 9d. asked of the Merchant Taylors and 4s. asked of the Minstrels. The estimate, however, proved sadly insufficient. A simple mathematical sum enables us to judge by how much. The Coopers' contribution was originally assessed at £5 16s. 8d. Two later demands were made, each for another £2 16s. 0d. Similarly the Pewterers' original contribution of £5 was later raised by demands for £2 8s. 0d. on two separate occasions. In both instances the ratio of the original estimate to the combined subsequent levies is as 25:24. Applying this ratio to the original, overall estimate of £400, we find the total actual cost to have been £784—a very considerable sum in the money of that time—which goes far to explain contemporary indignation about the vanity of painted theatres.

I think I may best summarize the conclusions to be drawn from all this by laying before the reader an abstract, as it were, of the necessary preparations for a State Occasion under the first of the Tudors.

Arrangements had to be set in action several months before the time ordained for the celebrations. Responsibility was deputed by the sovereign to his council, of whom the Privy Seal was the moving spirit. Civic Pageants, a Tournament and Disguisings were the time-honoured entertainments which had to be prepared. A sub-committee was set up to treat with the City Fathers about the Civic Pageants. These Pageants presented a politico-historico-moral allegory in some six scenes; were both spectacular and costly; were entrusted to responsible merchants to organize and by them to a variety of craftsmen to construct; were paid for from a capital levy and were presented to an audience representing a cross section of society. Arrangements for the Tournament were put into the hands of the Steward and Controller of the King's Household who, leaving their fellow-courtiers to look after their own interests, saw to the construction and decoration of the lists and auditorium. The performers, after discussion with the ladies, obtained their sovereign's assent to the enactment of some neo-chivalric theme in the lists and then invoked the aid of the College of Arms together with the Wardrobe, the Armoury and the Office of Works to organize and execute the spectacle for them. The Controller arranged for the construction of a draped and painted auditorium open to the sky and surrounding the stage area, approximating in shape and size to an Elizabethan theatre, to seat an audience again representing a cross section of the community placed according to social and financial status. The Council had still to prepare for the Disguisings. These it delegated to the Chamberlain who, advised by the Privy Seal, if not the Sovereign himself, as to likely themes, instructed his deputy, one of the Gentlemen Ushers, and left him with all the hard work. His task was lightened, however, by the appropriation of both costumes and scenic devices from the preceding Tournaments, any additional requirements being met by the Wardrobe and the Office of Works. The performers, all courtiers and numbering ladies in their ranks, as in Tournaments, fended for themselves: but arrangements for seating, indoors and by artificial light, the exclusive and literate audience on three sides of the stage, rested with the Usher. Nor was there any material difference in the arrangements for Interludes.

In short, the organization of these entertainments evolved with the demands of the entertainments themselves. Whatever proved to be successful was absorbed into a tradition which, despite the two centuries separating Richard II's Coronation from James I's, remained organically intact.

(d) *Town and Country Revels*

In mediaeval and Tudor society, if the sovereign were on Progress the provincial city or country mansion of temporary domicile at once became the Court and the procedures usual in London were superimposed on the new environment as far as local conditions allowed.

In the absence of the Court, responsibility for public order, and consequently for the discipline governing stage performances, rested with the Bishop in his Chapter, the Lord in his Manor and the Mayor in his Guildhall.

It is the latter that concerns us most, and we should not be surprised to find that the organization and management of the Miracle Cycles and other civic plays was conducted along much the same lines as the actual execution of the street pageants. The Coventry Leet Book, for example, treats of both in much the same terms.[77] An obvious and outstanding difference is that the Secretary or Privy Seal would not normally have any direct connection with the conduct of the Miracles.* Nevertheless, as I have argued in Chapter IV, a parallel exists in the control of the text, at the least, exercised by the Church directly through the local Prior, Abbot, Bishop, or indirectly through the Guild Priest.

If we may take Chester's Sir John Arnway as the first Mayor to become actively involved in the problems of administering the Miracle Plays, it is not until the last quarter of the fourteenth century that we have any factual evidence of the actual detail of management either there or in other cities. After 1377, when records do start, it is clear that the real burden of organizing these vast annual undertakings fell on the Aldermen rather than on the

---

* It should not be forgotten, however, that it was the Privy Council, of which they were important members, that in the sixteenth century intervened to suppress the Miracles. See Ch. IV, pp. 114–18 above.

Mayor himself. He took the blame if anything went wrong, as is dramatically apparent from the cases of Mr. Hankey and Sir John Savage in Chester in 1575: but even Sir John exculpated himself by invoking the corporate responsibility of the Mayor in Council.* It is the Leet in Coventry, when the costs of the plays are being redistributed in 1494, that is to be corporately responsible for the changes:

'Therfore hit is ordeyned be (*by*) this present lete that the Mair & viij of his Counceill have auctorite to call all the seid Craftes & other that be not charged to the forseid Charges and them to adjoyn to such Craftes as be overcharged with the forseid pagantes, uppon peynes be (*by*) hym & his seid Counceill to be sette.'[78]

In proceeding to consider the delegation of responsibility for the actual execution of the shows and for the maintenance of discipline and standards in performance it must constantly be borne in mind that we are here dealing with procedures in independent municipalities and over a period of more than two hundred years. Some evidence therefore from, say, York may not apply to, say, Lincoln; or, if true of both, may be so in one city throughout the period, but in the other only during the fourteenth century or not until the sixteenth. That caution given, I think there is enough evidence to warrant an attempt at establishing the general outline of procedure governing the production of the plays.

The persons of most importance are these:

   (i) The Mayor
  (ii) The Aldermen
 (iii) The Wardens of the Craft Guilds
 (iv) The Master Craftsmen (employers)
  (v) The Journeymen (employees).

Tabulated similarly, the principal functions with which they were concerned are these:

   (i) Finance
  (ii) Discipline and efficiency
 (iii) Provision of the requisite personnel
 (iv) Provision of raw materials
  (v) Construction work and maintenance.

* See Ch. IV, p. 115 above. A copy of the Certificate through which Sir John eventually exculpated himself is preserved in the archivist's office at Chester Town Hall.

By and large, the five divisions of person given above correspond with the five divisions of function. *

(i) THE MAYOR: FINANCE. As far as the Church was concerned, the principal attraction of permitting the City to represent scripture in the streets was economic.† The secular clergy and, above all, the Friars had permeated every aspect of civic life by virtue of their clerical talents. Their initiative in stressing the humanity of Christ, by dramatic representation of his life in city streets, could hardly be repressed if coupled with a promise from their masters of the financial means with which to accomplish it. The bargain was a good one from both standpoints, ecclesiastical and civic. The plays attracted wide attention, brought many visitors to the city and consequently swelled the profits of artisans and shopkeepers alike. The city's advantage is thus obvious enough. What is often forgotten is that the city's obligation did not end with the performance of the plays: it stretched to include the maintenance of a guild chapel, plate and jewels with which to furnish it and a priest to take charge of it.

'It(em) Wher as the Company, felship, & Craft of Cardemakers & Sadelers of this Citie meny yeires & of longe continuance have hadd & yet have the chief rule, gov(er)naunce, rep(air)yng & meyntenau(n)ce as well of a Chappell w(ith)in the p(ar)ishe churche of seynt Michelles in the seid Citie, named Seynt Thomas Chappell, & of the ornamentes Juelles & lightes of the same, (As also of a pagiaunt w(ith) the pagiaunt house & pleyng geire w(ith) other app(ur)ten(aun)ces & app(ar)elles belongyng to the same pagiaunt). . . ', etc.[79]

Thus reads an Order of the Coventry Leet in 1531, a mere year before Henry VIII's break with Rome. The order goes on to specify:

'The Meyntenaunce & rep(ar)acion wherof haithe been & yeirelie is to the greit charge, cost, & expenses of the seid company & crafte. . . .'

The constant references to charges in other cities for chapel, priest, and lights (i.e. wax candles) substantiate the quotations above. They serve to indicate too how inevitable it was that suppression of the plays must accompany the Reformation, since it was

* See pp. 284–289 above for the management of the street pageants.

† For an alternative, less material and more spiritual view see Ch. IX, pp. 313–315 below.

certainly through the guild chapel in the person of its priest that the Church exercised its control over the play texts.

The Mayor's duty in finding the money to meet these heavy costs, only part of which were occasioned by the plays, was to ensure that the financial burden was equitably distributed among the citizens. It was to this end that the Order in Leet of 1531 from which I have quoted was made by Mayor Richard Rice:

'. . . the seid company & crafte, beyng now but a fewe p(er)sones in nomber & havyng but smale eyde of eny other Craft for the same. So that ther seid Charge is, & like to be, more ponderouse & chargeable to theme then they may convenyentlie bere or susteyn in shorte tyme to come oneles (*unless*) p(ro)vision for a remedy may be spedilie hadd.'

The Mayor's answer is to attach to the Companies of Cardmakers and Sadelers: '. . . the company, feliship, & Craft of Capp(er)s w(ith) in this Citie, now beyng in nomber meny welthy & honest p(er)sons.' The solution in this instance was an easy one; for the Cappers had already 'maide dyv(er)s tymes sute and request unto the Meire' for this privilege. This should finally dispose of any lingering idea that the frequent amalgamation of guilds in the fifteenth and sixteenth centuries betokens any decline in the popularity of the plays. Whether in Chester, York or Coventry (and probably elsewhere) amalgamation and reallocation was simply the means normally used by Mayors to meet a recurrent financial problem, caused by the encroachment of one trade upon another as fashions changed with time.[80] As the fortunes of one guild declined over the years and another rose, so action had to be taken to ensure that the religious and economic life of the city did not suffer. One aspect of this was the production of the plays. The strongest testimony to the common sense of this practical solution adopted is the growth and continuance of the Cycles over two hundred years of virtually annual performance.

With minor variants from place to place and from year to year, the actual means of raising the money was everywhere the same. Ownership of a chapel and a pageant was regarded as possibly the major distinction which a company could aspire to in civic life. For this privilege it was prepared to pay. The contribution was geared to means assessed and agreed in common council under the Mayor's guidance. Employers contributed more than employees. At Beverley Master Barbers were required to pay two shillings and a pound of wax each on joining the Company and a further two shillings for each apprentice engaged (1414). If convicted of insulting an Alderman, a further 1s. 8d. became due.[81] At Chester the Smiths' Company levied 2s. 4d. from each guildsman annually and about 1d. a head from their journeymen (1554).[82] At York the journeymen usually paid 2d. or 3d. A further sharp distinction in liability was made between native citizens and outsiders, 'foreigners'. The latter's contribution was rated at as much as double the former's. The Glovers of York, c. 1476, levied 'of a denysen ijd., and of a straunger iiijd.'[83]

These levies, known in York as 'Pageant silver' and at Coventry as 'Pageant-pence', provided the basic capital with which to finance production. Further money was made available through a fund raised by fining delinquents *, from collections in the guild chapel†and from certain related ground rents.

In York at least, the monies thus raised were divided between two separate funds: a general purpose one administered by the Corporation and a specific guild fund administered by each guild itself. A similar arrangement almost certainly existed in other cities.[84]

(ii) THE ALDERMEN: DISCIPLINE AND EFFICIENCY. Mayoral responsibility for the permission or directive to produce plays on the one hand, and the autonomy permitted to guilds in the ordering of their own affairs on the other, necessitated smooth liaison between the corporation and the guilds. The officials who could most readily fulfil this function were the Aldermen and the Wardens of the Companies. Since, at times, these offices could be held by the same person it is dangerous to attempt a dogmatic differentiation of responsibility. At Beverley, for example, the Companies were directly represented on the town council by the Aldermen. In London, Aldermen were elected from the Wardens of the Livery Companies, but to represent wards of the City rather than the interests of the Companies.

The Aldermen, by their deliberations in the Mayor's Court, decided the means whereby discipline and efficiency in production were obtained. This they did by a number of simple but vital measures. First, it was by their consent that a company desirous to own a pageant or to perform was allowed to do so. Secondly, this consent given, they tried to ensure that it should not be regarded as something lightly gained, by imposing heavy fines on defaulters. At Coventry, in 1461, it is decreed that, if a pageant is not

---

* See p. 296 below.

† 'And upon Seynt Thomas day ... shall also offere yeirelie ev(er)y of theme id. at the high Masse seid in the Chappell ...' (Coventry Leet Book, ii, 709).

exhibited, it shall be 'uppon the peyn of Cs (£5) to be raised of iiij maisters of the Craftes that so offend'.[85] Remembering that all members of the company were taxed for the exhibition of the pageant, a better method of ensuring that the pageant was played could hardly have been devised. In Beverley this method had been adopted as early as 1392 when the Smiths were fined 40s. for failing to present their play. By the sixteenth century it had extended to bad performances. The Painters were fined 2s. in 1520,

'because their play of *The Three Kings of Colleyn* (Cologne) was badly and confusedly played, in contempt of the whole community, before many strangers.'[86]

In addition to revenue from such fines, corporations received a substantial income from leasing their property in connection with plays, partly in the form of ground-rent for the buildings in which the pageant carts and scaffolds were housed when not in use, and partly from the direct lease of areas in the city under their control which were to be used for performances. * The latter was standard practice in York. There is no proof known to me that it was adopted elsewhere. Nevertheless, the otherwise extraordinary fact that there should be no reference whatever to money received by the companies from spectators in Chester and Coventry could be easily explained if the York practice had been generally adopted. Whatever the answer here, it is certain that the practice of charging ground-rent for the pageant-houses was universal wherever perambulatory staging was used. In Chester the charge varied between 4d. and 8d., in York from 4d. to 1s. In Lincoln 4d. was the normal charge, but there was one exception: 'Noy schippe. 12d.'[87]

It is high time that more use was made of this information than has been hitherto. As Professor Salter has shown, the number of Chester companies owning a pageant and a house to store it in did not correspond with the number of guilds presenting plays. The clear inference is that the vehicle was shared,† and that our further knowledge of production techniques will largely depend on

---

* In Henry VIII's reign, at York, charges varied between 2s. 4d. and 6s. 5d. for each site, the total revenue from this source amounting to £2 3s. 0d. (R. Davies, *York Records*, p. 241.)

† See Ch. IV, p. 171 above. Preserved in the Chester archives are two very important documents: the memorandum of agreement, dated 1531, whereby the Goldsmiths and Masons are to use the carriage of the Vintners and Dyers for their play; the account roll of the City Treasurers showing receipts from the Drapers and Mercers for their carriage houses in Watergate Street, dated 1556.

the data that can be made available concerning ownership of the pageant vehicles and storage houses. In my own view, the grouping of other guilds around the wealthy owner of a pageant house and waggon in Coventry discussed above* and also in York suggests a similar arrangement in those cities.

(iii) THE WARDENS (OR MASTERS) OF THE CRAFTS AND PROVISION OF THE REQUISITE PERSONNEL. Responsibility for executing the Orders agreed in the Mayor's Court fell on the Wardens, Masters or Keepers of the Companies. This is logical enough, since they held the money raised by the levy on the guildsmen and journeymen of the Craft. The Coventry Order in Leet of 1531 concerning the Cappers, Cardmakers and Saddlers is succinct on this point:

'. . . the ov(er)pluse of the seid money of the seid revenues p(ro)ffittes and money shalbe bestowed and put in a box w(ith) two lockes & two keyes(,) the on (one) key to remeyne w(i)h the M(aist)ers of the Craft of Cardmakers & Sadelers, And the other Key to remeyn w(it)h the Maisters of the Craft of Capp(er)s, savelie (safely) to keip the seid money in the seid box untill they have nede to bestow it upon the seid Charges or otherwise, as they shall thynk convenyent; and the seid box to remeyn in the seid Chappell fastoned w(it)h a cheyne.'[88]

From this strong-box they paid all those people whose services in the construction and maintenance of pageant house, pageant vehicle, costume properties and play texts warranted reward. Its contents also served to defray the many costs incurred by the actors themselves both in rehearsal and performance, which included large sums on food and drink.

(iv) MASTER CRAFTSMEN: RAW MATERIALS. The tasks of actually engaging the actors and technicians and of arranging for rehearsals was often farmed out to a specialist or specialists. In York these were known as Pageant Masters.† They held office for several years, as might be expected where the same text with only minor modifications was repeated annually. At Beverley, in 1391, John of Arras of the Rope-makers' Company agreed to take charge of the play of the Fall for the rest of his life.[89] In Coventry, we find much

* See pp. 293–294 above. In 1548 the Cappers received 3s. 4d. from the Whittawers Company for the 'Hyer of our pageand' (Sharp, *Dissertation*, p. 48).

† It may be that in York the Pageant Masters were responsible for some of the duties I have attributed, in general to the Wardens of the Companies. It was certainly their task to raise the guild levy or pageant silver. See L. T. Smith, *York Mysteries*, p. xxxviii.

the same system working. In 1454 it was agreed by the Smiths that 'Thom(a)s Colclow* skyn(e)r ffro this day forth shall have (th)e Rewle of (th)e pajannt unto (th)e end of xij yers next folowing.' His duties are clearly outlined.† He is to find the actors and everything else except the cloths, which were draped round the pageant carts to hide the wheels, and the rushes, which were strewn on the stage. These items are the responsibility of 'the keepers of the craft' (i.e. the equivalent of the Wardens). Further, he is to dine with the keepers in Whitsun week when he will be paid. The play duly performed, he is to return the prompt-copy to the Master of the Company on the Sunday following Corpus Christi and all the costumes in as good condition as when he took receipt of them.

In this way the producer is briefed in his task. I find it interesting that Colclow is described as a Skinner by trade. Yet he is employed by the Smiths. This implies, to me, theatrical professionalism at an early date, for this same trend is apparent at York in a record of 1476. An order in Council there decrees that four of the 'most connyng discrete and able players within this Citie' are to audition all applicants for parts. Moreover they are to ensure that 'he or they so plaing plaie not overe twise (th)e saide day, upon payne of xls. . . .'[90]

The audition committee in this instance has its terms of reference limited to 'the plaiers . . . thrughoute all (th)e artificers'. The liberty given by Coventry guilds, however, to Colclow and others would not preclude the employment of professional actors.‡ It

---

* In 1481 a similar agreement was reached with Sewall and Reignald.

† '. . . he for to find (th)e pleyers and all (tha)t longeth (ther)to all (th)e seide t(i)me save (th)e kep(pers) of the craft shall let bring forth (th)e pajant and find Clo(th)ys (tha)t gon abowte (th)e pajant and find Russhes (the)rto and ev(er)y wytson-weke who (tha)t be kep(per)s of (th)e crafte shall dyne w(it)h Colclow and ev(er)y mast(e)r ley down iiijd. and Colclow shall have yerely ffor his labor xlvjs viijd. and he to bring to (th)e mast(e)r on sonday next aft(e)r corp(u)s c(risti)i day (th)e originall (*i.e. prompt-copy*) & ffech his vij nobulles and Colclow must bring in at (th)e lat(te)r end of (th)e t(i)mes all (th)e garme(n)ts (tha)t longen to (th)e pajent as good as (th)ey wer delyv(er)ed to hym.' (Smiths Company Ordinance, Monday before Palm Sunday, 31 Henry VI, cited by Sharp, *Dissertation*, p. 15.)

‡ Professor Salter thinks that the sum of 3s. 4d. given by the Smiths of Chester to Symeon is large enough to indicate that a professional actor was engaged. I doubt this on the evidence which he advances. Nevertheless, remembering that 6s. 8d. was the invariable sum total of the reward given to the King's players at Selby Abbey (and normally elsewhere) in the late fifteenth and early sixteenth centuries, when that sum is given to a single actor—as it is in Coventry in 1584—the contention is clearly worth considering.[91]

would seem that this system of contracting was still operating, in Coventry at least, in the latter half of the sixteenth century. In 1591, the Drapers' Company contracted with Thomas Massye to provide their play and players. He received forty shillings for his pains. In earlier years he had provided materials for the Smiths, the Cappers and the Mercers; and in 1603 he was to land up in prison for attempting to revive the then suppressed plays.[92] Another figure of no less importance, if not actually one of the contractors, was Robert Croo. He not only redacted the surviving *Shearman and Taylors'* Pageant and *Weavers'* Pageant and provided the Drapers with 'the boke' for their pageant, but wrote a play called *The Golden Fleece* for the Cappers. In addition he played the part of God in the Drapers' Pageant of Doomsday in 1560, the book of which he provided three years earlier. That same year he was also paid 'for mendyng the devells cottes'. Four years earlier he had been paid 'for makyng iij worldys' and two years later 'for a hat for the pharysye'.[93] There was thus hardly any aspect of the production with which he and his like were not familiar.

The security of tenure in their office which the pageant contractors enjoyed must have had many practical advantages. These men were clearly engaged because they were expert in their job and, what is perhaps more important where committees are so much in evidence, they had full authority for the artistic direction. It is in terms of this firm control and continuity of tradition that the rehearsal schedule is best approached.

At Chester, three rehearsals and a dress-rehearsal ('generall rehearse') sufficed for the Coopers' Company in their play of the Resurrection in 1574. In Coventry, it could be as little as two and as much as five. In 1490 it is clear that the rehearsals were held in Easter and in Whitsun weeks (giving the actors adequate time to memorize their parts) and that they took place in front of the respective Companies in the morning at breakfast-time.[94] At York, in 1483, when the ostlers were responsible for playing the Coronation of the Virgin, an eight-year contract was given to four men to 'bryng furth yerly' this pageant and to see to its 'reparell' or maintenance.[95] Since this play was one of the most spectacular in the Cycle, it is to be presumed that a production team is here involved. A possible member of this team was the man who, at Coventry, is described as 'the dresser of the Pagent'. The word 'dresser' is not to be equated here with 'costumier': rather was the dresser the stage manager. The dresser of the Cappers' Company was also the mechanic, since he is paid 'for dressynge the pageand

and kepynge the wynde (*windlass*)'. He was also paid for 'color-ynge the bysshoppes hodes'.[96] If the producer and the dresser were two of the team of four men appointed at York, the other two probably took charge of the costumes and the police and commis-sariat arrangements. Their duties included the provision of as many as twelve men to 'drive' the pageant (i.e. to transport it from the pageant-house through the streets and back again); drink to the drivers; rooms for and food at rehearsals; food and drink between playing stations; and 'Jaked men' (i.e. men in armour) 'about the pagent,' presumably to guard it from unruly members of the audience who might damage it.*[97] Although many points of detail about these contractors and those to whom they delegated part or parts of their function are lacking, a general pattern emerges which is clear enough. The Mayor gave orders through his Court for the pageants to be displayed. Either directly through the Aldermen of that Court, or indirectly through the Wardens of the Companies responsible to the Aldermen, the necessary capital funds were raised for production. The artistic and administrative direction was then farmed out to specialists on a long-term basis and chosen for their reputation regardless of whether they were members of the Company or not. Given this liberty of direction, the contractors could call on the whole city to aid them in their task.

(v) THE JOURNEYMEN: CONSTRUCTION AND MAINTENANCE. One of the major props supporting the idea that the production of the Miracle Cycles was naive and amateur (in the derogatory sense of that word) is that each company relied on its own members to present its play. There is no justification in fact for this hypo-thesis. The evidence points in the opposite direction. At York, for example, it was stipulated that no actor could perform in more than two plays. The clear inferences of the order are that the actors were chosen for their ability and that the same man could act for at least one other Company beside his own and possibly for two Companies neither of which was his own. Similarly with the scenic units, costumes and properties; since the contractor was never obliged to find these within the Company with whom he contracted, but was obliged rather to give the Company the best value possible

---

* On the function of similar police-stewards called Stytelers, see Richard Southern, *The Mediaeval Theatre in the Round*, 1957, pp. 81–90. A carpenter was sometimes in attendance with the dresser, possibly to repair any damage done on the spot. (See Sharp, *Dissertation*, p. 49, note t.)

for its subscription money, he turned naturally to the other Companies who were specialist-purveyors of the wares in demand; to the Glovers for gloves; to the Drapers for cloth; to the Smiths for machinery or the Painters for painting. * Consequently, every member of the community was likely to be called upon to assist according to his particular ability to help. The result will be the best that the City can corporately provide—a very much better best than any one Company could hope to offer if restricted to its own resources. It only remains to add that the pride taken by the Company in its achievement is duly reflected in the order to its members to attend on the pageant during performance of the play. [99]

In conducting this enquiry into the production of the Miracle Plays I have not attempted an imaginative, generalized reconstruction of the overall procedure, since I think this is likely to iron out the many local differences between what occurred in one city and in another, which is itself a factor of sufficient importance to preserve. For example, there is evidence from Lincoln that, in 1483, the play of the Assumption of the Virgin was not handled by the Mayor and Crafts at all, but by the Dean and Chapter. This play took its place in the St. Anne's Day Cycle, but was presented in the nave of the Cathedral and paid for by voluntary subscription. [100] Where authorship is concerned, variety is also apparent. We have seen something of the labours of the ubiquitous Robert Croo in Coventry. The Governors of Beverley engaged a Dominican friar, Master Thomas Bynham, to compose the Banns for their Cycle and paid him 6s. 8d. In 1521, in Lincoln, the Mayor turns to the Headmaster of the Grammar School, a Mr. Dighton, to assist with preparation of the Cycle. Coventry likewise, in 1584 commissions 'Mr. Smythe of Oxford' to write the new play of *The Destruction of Jerusalem*. [101] The situation is open to further variants in cities where another play was recurrently substituted for the Miracle Cycle, as the Creed play at York or the Paternoster play at Beverley and Lincoln. In this event the normal procedure was adapted to meet the new circumstances. At Beverley, in 1469, the Paternoster play was divided into eight sections, groups of four or

---

* The Smiths of Chester, for example, engaged Sir Randall Barnes, a minor canon and choir master of the Cathedral, and his choristers to sing in their Pageant of the Purification (1554), while the Smiths of Coventry bought, for 2s. 1d. 'Assadyn (tinsel), silver paper and gold paper, gold foyle and grene (?copper) ffoyle' for Herod's crown (1499). The Coventry Cappers paid 7s. 8d. 'for reprasyons (repairs) of the pagyand, tymber nayles and iren': and 33s. 4d. 'to Horseley the paynter'—an enormous sum in those days. [98]

five crafts were assigned to each, and it was played at seven stations. An Alderman was put in charge of each pageant.[102] A century later, in this same town, the 'Scholemeister' had his own company of players, though what he did with them we do not know.

These examples must suffice to demonstrate the dangers of trying to simplify the organization governing the performance of Miracle Plays in England into a single pattern. If further evidence is wanted it may be found in the similar variations from place to place within a single country, that pertains to French, German and Italian sacred plays in the Middle Ages. For the reader, however, who yearns for something of the vitality which inspired these productions and which the dry narrative of factual analysis precludes, I have added in a Postscript an exceptionally detailed account of the preparations for a single play. I have placed this in a Postscript rather than within this chapter, partly because it is a French example and partly because there is less chance of what is only a single specimen being mistaken for the general rule. On the other hand, since this record has probably survived because suppression of religious plays in France was not accompanied by ruthless destruction, it can be assumed that similarly detailed records were frequently kept in England until the commissioners of the Reformed Church set out upon their iconoclastic Progresses.

POSTSCRIPT

A French Play*

At the town of Romans in Provence on the 4th July 1508, representatives of the Chapter of St. Bernard and the Municipality met together to decide how best to celebrate deliverance from ten years of recurrent epidemics of plague. On that occasion they agreed that an appropriate act of thanksgiving would be to present a play that retold the story of the town's patron saints, *Les Trois*

* Although seemingly unknown to French theatre historians *Le Mystère des Trois Doms* is one of the best documented religious plays to have survived to us. The MS. of the text, preserved in the Civic Library at Lyons, is on paper in a single volume measuring 350 mm. × 260 mm. and includes a Latin Prologue, a French Epilogue and a list of all the parts and the people who played them. The entire MS. is in the hand of a local judge, Loys Perrier, who himself acted the part of the Governor of Vienne.

The MS. Account Book, preserved in the Bibliothèque Nationale in Paris, also forms a single book, bound in 4⁰ and is throughout in the hand of Jean Chonet treasurer to the town council. See Ch. IV, pp. 164 and 166 above.

Martyrs, Sévérin, Exupère et Félicien. They agreed further that the labour of production and the burden of cost should be shared between the town and the chapter.

To this end, nine *commissaires* were appointed as overseers: four representing the town, three on behalf of the Chapter of St. Bernard and two for the Chapel of St. Maurice. The Franciscans offered the courtyard of their convent for the performance together with some money to set up a capital fund out of which to finance production. In the latter point their example was followed by others. On this sound footing the *commissaires,* to whom all organizational responsibility had been delegated, set about their task.

Their first act was to appoint an author: and this onerous task was entrusted to Canon Pra of Grenoble, who enjoyed a reputation in the area for the writing of texts for street pageants amongst other things. He was provided with a secretary and it was agreed that both should be paid. By mid August Pra had something ready —considering the time, probably not more than the plot outline— which he read to the committee. Its members were evidently dissatisfied, for a day later they invited '*M. Chevallet, fatiste on poète de Vienne*' to become co-author. Chevallet refused and gave his reason—'*pource qu'il ne volist pas besoigner avec le chanoine Pra*'. Poor Pra! However, he worked on until the script was completed in February, submitting himself meanwhile to the indignity of routine readings before the *commissaires* and to revising his draft in the light of their comments. When the script was ready, three notaries were engaged to make copies. But Pra's humiliation was not yet complete, as we shall see.

In December, a start was made on the physical preparations. Even by our standards, this seems a large time-allowance for preparations when the date of performances was fixed for late May, a full six months ahead: but these *commissaires* were men of as much forethought as despatch. As producer (*maître du jeu* or *meneur*) they appointed M. Sanche of Dijon; as designer, M. François Trévenot of neighbouring Annonay. Under their guidance work started on the stage and auditorium in the yard of the Franciscan convent on 30th December. By this time it was becoming necessary to dip substantially into the capital fund provided from public subscription. The carpenters, for example, needed an advance of 412 florins for their labours in the courtyard. Trévenot was being paid at the rate of four florins a month. To assist him with machines and other technical matters Trévenot engaged Amien Grégoire, a local smith (i.e. an ironfounder), and Jean Rozier, a clocksmith from his own town of Annonay.

The stage which these men were commissioned to erect was to measure thirty-six yards long by eighteen yards wide and to be raised some four feet off the ground. It was to be boarded round about so that spectators could not see anything beneath the stage. The auditorium was to be similarly constructed of wood on the arc of a semicircle and to be gently raked away from the stage, culminating in a row of boxes on the outer edge. The stage was to be provided with a low trellis on the three sides nearest the audience and the boxes were to be provided with lattice-work grills to prevent small children from falling out. Nine large scenic units were constructed for use on the stage, including Heaven and Hell. The other 'mansions' had to represent three separate localities on the three days of performance respectively. Part of the stage area within the convent courtyard was covered with an awning, presumably to protect the mansions against the effect of heavy rain.

Before all this work was finished rehearsals began. The first was arranged for 18th March, a bare month after Pra had completed the text. The notaries who were employed to copy the actors' parts must have found it a busy month, as the cast comprised 86 characters. No parts were doubled and all ranks of society were called upon, regardless of social status, to fill them. Between 18th March and 29th April seven rehearsals at least were held, i.e. approximately one per week. They took place at the town hall and refreshments were provided. With the exception of the more singular characters like Lucifer or Proserpine, the actors seem to have been expected to provide their own costumes.

Only small provision appears to have been made for music. Trumpets, tambourines, and an organ were required, but nothing more is mentioned in the accounts. The organ had to be installed in Heaven and this task fell to Trévenot. He had been busy in the meantime collecting pigments of every imaginable colour, olive and nut oil to mix with them, pig-bristle brushes, earthenware and wooden mixing bowls, coloured paper, tinfoil, pins, cloth, saltpetre, wood and canvas. Whatever he could not obtain on the spot he acquired from neighbouring towns, whither messengers were despatched regardless of expense.

At long last, on 7th May, ten months since the project had been originally set in hand, arrangements were made for the *'monstre'*, or public parade of the cast in costume. This extraordinary procession, which took place three weeks before the performance, was clearly intended as advance publicity and not unlike the 'riding of the Banns' in England.

It was at this point that the *commissaires* decided that something must be done to strengthen the text and that Pra was incapable of doing it: for, a week later, one of the actors, Etienne Combez des Coppes, was sent to Vienne to tackle Chevallet once again. He carried with him instructions from the *commissaires* that the passage of the text relating to the 'Four Tyrants' was to be rewritten. At the price of a substantial bribe and several good meals, and after four days of negotiation, he returned successfully from his mission. It is in character with Etienne's vocation that he got his own part altered too.

Whitsun that year fell during the last days of May. That was the season scheduled from the outset for performance, and it duly took place on the three days arranged for it, but not, however, without a dress rehearsal and some last-minute alarms and excursions. It will surprise no one who has had any practical experience of production that the worst of these was the discovery that the running time was far in excess of that anticipated. It will equally encourage many who are worried by this problem today, when texts appear sacrosanct, that these mediaeval 'simpletons' (who spent eleven months and five thousand pounds on mounting a Miracle Play of three days' duration) resorted to the simplest of all expedients. They cut the text to fit the time allowed.

The ground plan on the next page is reconstructed from the text and accounts. Details of the budget I have already supplied in Chapter IV.

I have devoted space to this particular example of the production techniques of the religious stage in France because it is virtually unknown: but there are others almost as detailed—notably from Metz, Mons, Valenciennes and Paris—which have been thoroughly worked over by French historians. It seems to me that as great an advance in our knowledge of the medieval religious stage can be made through a comparative study of French and English practice as has been made in the field of the Royal Entries by comparative study of practice in England and the Low Countries. *

It is not generally realized, for example, that the perambulatory technique of staging Miracle Plays in England at York and Chester is paralleled in France: that a close resemblance in stagecraft exists between the stationary Valenciennes Passion Play and the *Ludus Coventriae* (which we must now attribute to Lincoln), between the

* See Introduction, pp. xxxiii and xxix–xl above.

Mystère des Trois Doms or the Metz *Jeu de Ste. Katherine* and the Digby play of *Mary Magdalen*. Even the unusual Cornish 'round' has its French equivalent.

Nor is the parallel confined to general resemblances. Women appear on the French religious stage as they do at Chester.* The English pageant-master has his double in the French *maître du jeu*. The same stage machinery—clouds, trapdoors, conflagrations—is operated similarly on both sides of the Channel: audiences are

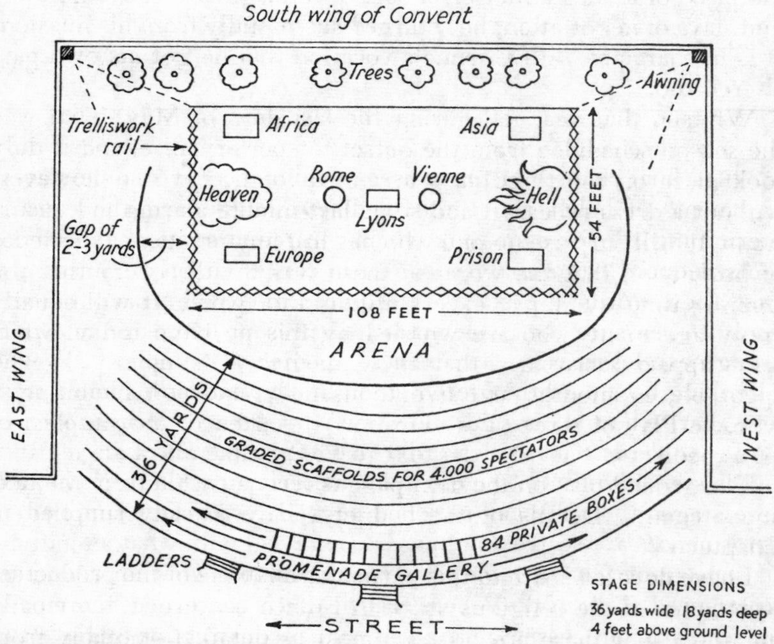

South wing of Convent

Trees — Awning

Trelliswork rail → Africa   Asia

Heaven   Rome   Vienne   Hell

Gap of 2-3 yards   Lyons

Europe   Prison

54 FEET

108 FEET

ARENA

EAST WING   WEST WING

36 YARDS

GRADED SCAFFOLDS FOR 4,000 SPECTATORS

84 PRIVATE BOXES

LADDERS   PROMENADE GALLERY

STREET

STAGE DIMENSIONS
36 yards wide 18 yards deep
4 feet above ground level

FIG. 18. Ground Plan of the Stage and Auditorium for the *Mystère des Trois Doms*, erected in the Courtyard of the Franciscan Convent in Romans, 1509. (Reconstructed from the text and account book; see pp. 164–167 and above.)

assembled and disciplined, production costs paid for and plays initiated by much the same means. These are simply random instances which I have noticed myself. Where, then, a serious comparative study would be most useful is in supplying the detail of this stagecraft and thereby remedying, in part, the loss of so much specifically English source material in the course of the Puritan Revolution.

* See pp. 271 and 272 above.

IX

EPILOGUE: AUDIENCES
AND CRITICS

THIS final chapter of the present volume contains some statements of belief about the mediaeval stage and the causes determining the forms it took which contradict some of the arguments deduced from analysis of fact in earlier chapters. Since this is so, a few words of preface are required to explain this paradox, if only to reassure the reader that it is present by design and not through carelessness or perversity.

Looking back over the preceding eight chapters of this book, it is clear that, when all is said and done, the distance that one may journey towards reconstruction by factual procedures of a scientific kind is strictly limited: for the audience that gave these plays and these stages their life has perished beyond recall. Descriptions of performances are scarce and in any case reveal only what an individual spectator felt *after the performance* and not what an audience experienced *at the time*. Where the theatre is concerned, therefore, the scholarly processes of analysis and reconstruction serve as a necessary discipline towards defining the path to truth, but in themselves they never are that truth nor can they reveal it. At some point on the path, truth has to be sighted and recognized for what it is. To do this one must resort to the imagination, to a process of the spirit rather than of the intellect, at its cheapest a guess, at its best a vision.

Where fact ceases of itself to be much use, where the arrangement and rearrangement of it fails as a process to yield results, is in answering the final question. 'What did men of the Middle Ages aspire to in their drama?' Churchmen, statesmen, scholars, artists, craftsmen all took a vivid interest in it. On it they lavished their energy, their skills, their wealth and their time. But why? If scholarship side-steps this issue it lays itself open to a charge of pedantry: its object is strangled by its means.

In these concluding pages the arguments advanced are not substantiated by the same factual detail as in preceding chapters, since it is not my purpose in this volume to establish them with proof. Rather is it to stimulate thinking about an alternative approach to the subject which I intend to deploy fully in Volume II. My aim, therefore, changes from an attempt to reconstruct what occurred and why it occurred in that way, to an endeavour to discover why it occurred at all. And with it the procedure adopted changes too. Objective analysis gives place to speculation. I have given my reasons for thinking this necessary. The reader who disagrees can always close the book here if he prefers to speculate for himself. The reader who perseveres to the end, however, will find in these pages my present, personal convictions about the development of our early theatre and drama. Since these convictions often go beyond what is warranted by the limited evidence available, and at times even contradict the conclusions suggested by factual evidenc: alone, they are isolated here to be the more recognizable for what they are. For myself, however, they take precedence, since I can much more readily trust the explanation of the effect that springs from an understanding of the cause than any explanation of the cause that rests exclusively upon deductions from the effect; especially when the effect can be known by *us* only imperfectly.

How, then, is one to approach this audience that has been dead for so long and has left so little criticism behind it? At first sight it would seem extremely difficult to establish any contact at all. Yet, on reflection, perhaps this deficiency is, if not positively helpful, at least no serious drawback: for, very frequently, dramatic theory and criticism bear so little relation to the practical realities of the theatre that study of them can as easily confuse the historian as assist him. In our time, for example, official dramatic criticism has much more to do with newspaper sales than with the theatre, the personality of the columnist being of greater interest to readers than play, dramatist or actor. These last have become the ammunition enabling him to fire off noisy pistols around and about a theatre which is dying and renewing itself independently from his attention. Similarly, where theory is concerned in a country or an age that lacks an established theatre, such theory and critical precepts as may exist usually bear a closer relation to the practice of a neighbour country or a former age than to its own: yet no matter how 'admirable' that other theory is, or was, practical expediency, directed by both present circumstance and philosophical conviction, will transmute it into something very different.

The mediaeval theatre grew up under the shadow of its Greek and Roman forbears and it was to this past that it turned for enlightenment and instruction with increasing vigour from the twelfth century to the sixteenth: yet it could never be the same, because the fabric of society was Christian and not pantheistic. The *Teatro Olimpico* built by Palladio and Scamozzi between 1580 and 1585, which still stands at Vicenza, illustrates the point admirably. Here is a conscious imitation of Roman example, painstakingly reconstructed as a result of some hundred years of scholarly research. Beautiful and perfect in itself, it is unique: but there were no bidders for replicas because, in terms of its function, it failed to meet the needs of the day. The five-arched palace façade with receding streets under those arches neither fitted the multi-locational narrative demands of the religious stage nor enabled the architect-painters to 'change the scene' as adequately as they felt they could, given time and money to experiment further. Thus the *Teatro Olimpico* stands as a silent and beautiful monument to theorists who failed to take the measure of both their artist-craftsmen and their audience.

The concern for unities of time, place and action motivating the construction of that theatre meant little to English popular audiences of the time who had grown up in the tradition of the multi-actional drama of the Christian Church and the burning topicality of Reformation polemic. Indeed this indifference to the niceties of form was to be the despair of Sir Philip Sydney, Ben Jonson and their friends of neo-classical persuasion in the early seventeenth century. Jonson, we know, found allies in the architect-painters of the day, most notably in Inigo Jones whose inspiration was Palladian. Shakespeare, however, was either too ignorant or too shrewd to try to compete for the favours of audiences in terms of neo-classical novelty. * Thereby he saved himself the humiliation of a 'show-down' with the painters of the kind that was so to vex poor Ben.[1]

The point of discussing this Jacobean problem here is to show that, in England, problems of theory and criticism provoked by

* Shakespeare's only play on the neo-classical model is *The Merry Wives of Windsor*. Although a marked increase of spectacular quality is noticeable in the late plays, he never wrote a Mask which, as a member of the King's Men, he might more reasonably have been expected to do than Jonson.

Italian interest in the classical theatre were of little or no consequence to the audiences who attended mediaeval and Tudor plays. We may therefore clear our minds of such thinking and concentrate instead upon Christian thinking which so clearly governed the universe represented on the mediaeval stage. From this universe the deities of pagan mythology had been firmly exiled before drama was admitted, and were only allowed to return piecemeal and on sufferance. In other words, this drama was not founded on any inherited or preconceived rationalist theory, but was generated spontaneously from some inner urge demanding expression. In grappling with this problem therefore, and attempting to discover what exactly was this compulsive logic, there is no alternative but to start *ab initio*; to look behind the facts and figures and seek in religion and in art the cause which can account for their taking the form they did.

The unique distinction of drama as an Art is that it appeals to eye and ear simultaneously. The emotions of the recipient are open to assault through two senses at once and, as his emotional temperature rises, the auditor-spectator has the focal length of his imagination steadily enlarged to a point where the mind may perceive truth, meaning, reality, unobtainable by processes of the intellect alone.

It is in this obscure realm that we must grope for some explanation of why the Christian Church gave birth to a drama in the heart of its liturgies. If my premise is accepted, however, it is here in general and in the most sacred rite of all in particular, the Mass, that we might most naturally expect it to appear: for what is religion if not the search for truth, meaning, reality, through the gifts of imaginative perception and faith? At least religion and art have this search and these means of search in common. It is also surely reasonable for the historian, who knows for hard fact that it was the Easter miracle of the Resurrection and the Christmas miracle of Virgin Birth which were first personified in dialogued action, to ask *why* this should have been so. In the fact that these mysteries were made manifest, while seemingly more dramatic events (notably the Crucifixion) were not, must lie at least a pointer to the nature and purpose of the earliest Christian drama. The vital question must be asked: was it a drama at all at the moment of its inception? Or was it simply an attempt to make visible by personification the miracles that form the gateway to faith? My answer is that the birth of Christian drama was a by-product of Christian religion; but it was an immaculate birth, wholly unselfconscious, a materialization out of the forms of worship and the atmosphere in which it was conducted. The genesis of this drama from within the forms of worship has been studied closely and often, but the inevitability of its birth from within the atmosphere of that worship has only been hinted at. Thus only half the story is known and recorded. The other half must be sought in Art.

Historians have noted the steady elaboration of the Christian liturgies between the fifth and tenth centuries. They have discussed the advent of antiphonal singing, of mimetic gesture and ornate vestments. They have debated why, when and where impersonation began: but, mysteriously, they seem to have omitted architecture from their calculations. Yet if the Parthenon on the Athenian Acropolis expresses the harmony and simplicity of the Hellenic spirit, if the Coliseum and other amphitheatres testify to the functional and material mindedness of Imperial Rome, then Europe's cathedrals—Romanesque and Norman, Gothic and Perpendicular —are the stone epitaphs of the aspiration and achievement of the Dark and Middle Ages. In St. Albans, Durham, Salisbury and Winchester these memorials survive as keys to this spirit that we seek. We have nothing in England to compare with the Byzantine magnificence of Constantinople or the Romanesque splendour of the churches of Ravenna, yet the little tri-apsidal Church of St. Andrew at Stogursey in Somerset survives as a ghost of something which once was universal when our drama began: nor is Tewkesbury Abbey so far removed from it in feeling. I think it is the early Christian basilicas and the Romanesque churches which succeeded them—building, decoration and liturgy together—that hold the key to the mystery. There everything was designed to concentrate attention upon the open altar, the table bearing the symbols of Christ's sacrifice, brooded over by a portrait of God in Majesty ten times the size of any human being; no gloom; no screen; no division of clergy from congregation except in the allocation of places. (See Plate XXXII, No. 51.)

To the early Christians the Real Presence was something allowed for in the architecture of God's House, whether within the intimate circle of the fourth-century Church of St. Michael in Perugia or under the vast dome of St. Sophia in Byzantium. Naves of churches grew longer, but still the Real Presence lingered in the sanctuary for the eye of faith to see, between the altar symbols and the mosaic image. As the time span between Christ of the Gospels and the business of daily living lengthened, so this

Presence became less distinct, less tangible, geographically more remote. All the while, the determination to preserve it grew. Art, ever more in antiphon and trope, in fresco and stained glass, in stone and alabaster, was called on to preserve it, until, in drama, the last step was taken and the Presence revealed to believers through man himself, breathing, walking, talking and living again the sacred story.

This called for no premeditated theory, no regular criticism, for it was spontaneous and urgent. It blossomed at Easter, Christmas, Whitsun and Ascension, the Festivals of joyful news, of Resurrection and Redemption, of *Gloria in excelsis Deo* and *Alleluia*. But, spotless as was its birth, it tarnished quickly. Being man-made it was man-tainted. Man's inadequacy, man's ineptitude, man's incapacity to resist the vulgar swiftly proved that the ideal could not be sustained. Drama, from being a means to realizing the Real Presence, became a debatable asset.

The shock of this discovery, in England at least, had repercussions through centuries to come. The first material result was to deflect the constant search for the Real Presence upwards. Towers soared skywards and spires after them. In supporting arches, curves gave place to points. God was sought above men's heads, pure, remote and in consort with Angels. Below, in crypt and dungeon, lay the mouth of Hell and, beyond it, the domains of Lucifer, whose constant stratagems prevented man's earthly being from attaining the celestial perfection his soul aspired to. The anguish of this situation had long ago been expressed by St. Paul in his letter to the Romans: *For what I would, that do I not; but what I hate that I do.* The fact that man was 'carnal, sold under sin' was realized anew and found its most cogent expression in the story of the Fall. Where in the mind's eye Gabriel with lily and song had announced the glad tidings of Christ's divinity, now Michael, standing with flaming sword at the gate of Paradise, bore witness to the depravity of Man. To many, the only answer to this dilemma lay in retirement to the cloister or the enclosed garden. In retreat to this seclusion, where the world could be abjured, lay some hope that the earlier vision could be approached again and even realized. To others, however, monasticism was an answer of escape since at best it only solved the problem for the individual, not for mankind—save in so far as the escaper occupied himself in continual prayer for those from whom he had escaped. And to such men Christ's Church was universal, as much concerned with congregations as with those in orders and under vows, as much with the defeat of Satan in the World as with renouncing him in private. The year one thousand had come and gone, but the world had not come to an end. Judgement had been postponed and God's creation granted a further respite in which to work its own salvation.

It was into this disturbed climate of mental readjustment that St. Francis was born in Assisi, St. Dominic in Caleruega in Old Castile.[2] These men, together with the legions whom their example had impressed into service, set out to preach the message of salvation to those who spent their days in the fields, in the shops, in the market places and the mansions of temporal government. The novelty of their message lay in the accent placed on the Humanity of Christ. The God whom they preached was one acquainted with suffering through the pain of Christ on the Cross and through the grief of the Mother at its foot, the paradox of Man revealed at his noblest when reviled by Man at his worst. With this vision to the front of his mind, each and every individual was possessed of the means of attaining salvation despite the temptations, accidents and premeditated evils his mortality was heir to in the world. God in Man could triumph over the devil in Man, the Good Angel over the Bad. If, in drama, personification of the Mysteries of the Incarnation and Resurrection had failed in its prime object because the agent was human, the mimetic talent in man could just as easily be harnessed to this new quest in the market place and with a better chance of success. No less important, other means than drama existed for bringing home the truth of this message to troubled mankind. It is in this context, I think, that we must approach the establishment of the Feast of Corpus Christi in 1313. I see it as an attempt, inspired by the example of the Friars, to inject the very liturgy itself into the environment of daily living.* If I am correct in this surmise, then the link between the Feast and the plays, which historians have sought for so long, is no longer missing: for both were designed to serve the same end and could consequently join forces without difficulty if circumstances were propitious. If this idea be thought startling, there is surely nothing more extraordinary in the Host being carried ceremonially out of the Sanctuary and into the streets and squares of a town than in the attempt by mortal men to make visible the miracle of the Resurrection by personifying it in the Sanctuary? Yet what else can the presence of the Host in the market place signify if not the determination that the former should sanctify the latter? And is not this also the *purpose* of re-enacting the Crucifixion in and through the commercial

* See Ch. IV, pp. 121, 125–31 above and *ERD*, p. 133.

heart of civic life? Granted similarity of inspiration and objective, therefore, Festival and performance could coalesce when and where desirable. At this point, calendar date, season and climate intervene. All three combine to create a pressure towards coalescence. An equally solid counter-pressure of course exists in the conflict between the processional nature of the Festival and the requirements of a dramatic performance in point of both time and place. Yet here, it seems to me, lies the real importance of that liberty of action in determining the detail of the celebration of Corpus Christi specifically granted by the Papacy to every diocese in Christendom. This allowed local conditions to become the determining factor, suggesting coalescence in some places while militating against it in others.

The long-cherished notion that the story of our drama may be traced by some straight-line process involving gradual but increasing 'secularization' as it progressed from choir to nave, from nave to churchyard, from churchyard to market place and from market place to theatre seems to me therefore as contrary to fact as it is difficult to substantiate. Rather must we admit the likelihood of two dramas of single Christian origin but of independent motivation: the drama of the Real Presence within the liturgy and the imitative drama of Christ's Humanity in the world outside. The one is a drama of adoration, praise and thanksgiving: the other is a drama of humour, suffering and violence, of laughter and sorrow. Where the former remains ritualistic, the latter carries within it the germs of tragedy and comedy.

Let us then try to rid ourselves of the notion of a sacred drama made profane by the steady encroachment of worldly things upon it. Let us recognize instead the deliberate challenge that was issued to a secular world by the injection into it of a sacred drama, which, far from taking acceptance for granted, assaulted the emotions with sufficient intensity to cause an explosion in the imagination: an explosion that would result in perception of the path to salvation prepared by divine grace.

This mode of thinking, as it seems to me, resolves most of the major difficulties and question marks in the surviving factual evidence which, viewed from a material, mundane and scientific standpoint, have so far defied explanation and continue to do so. Failure through these means is almost inevitable, since the giving of priority to names, dates, places and events injects a self-consciousness of thinking and approach into their begetters which they probably did not possess. Worse still, as a process of investigation it leaves room for the investigator to imbue the factual data with motivating opinion that is actually peculiar to him and to his age; and to omit from consideration modes of thinking that in fact governed events at the time.

Factually, five hundred years separate us from the fifteenth century, and it may well be objected that no one can know now what was thought then. Such reasoning, however, is sterile; for it translates study of the past into pedantry by denying it the right to inform us why people behaved as fact tells us that they did. Moreover, the reasoning is false, since a society's religion, philosophy and art can inform us what it thought. And, in the drama of the Middle Ages, all three are present for those with eyes to see and ears to hear.

The liturgical drama of the Church interior seems clearly to have had its origin in thankfulness for the miracles of Christ's Nativity and Resurrection. Dramatically, however, thanks for these two mysteries cannot develop very far, no matter how often the thanks are reiterated. Concern for man's inadequacy, on the other hand, and the means of his redemption lends itself dramatically to limitless development. It not only appeals directly to the whole community, but by the force of its initial impact and the variety of possible subsequent treatments, can hold the attention of that audience for generations. First, it supplies a theme of consequence and interest concerning every individual, regardless of status in society. Secondly, representation of Christ's Passion (as anyone who has seen a performance of the relevant Miracle Plays knows well) substantially surpasses in violence, horror and pity anything presented in *The Spanish Tragedy*, *King Lear* or *The Duchess of Malfi*. Thirdly, the final Judgement, with eternal Damnation or Salvation awaiting Pope, Emperor, Queen, merchant, lawyer, priest and labourer, provides an alternative ending, idyllic or tragic, which the individual has both will and means to determine for himself. Within this framework, the scope for development of particular stories, individual characters and special problems is vast. It is precisely in terms of such a framework that mediaeval drama could stand comparison with the breath-taking splendour of Gothic cathedrals. Anyone, therefore, who is inclined to dismiss it as naive should first reflect that, being cosmic, it would have had a place for him.

The dramatic potential of this structure deserves attention. If a play, to be a work of art, must have the 'beginning', 'middle' and 'end' claimed for it by Aristotle—a situation and relationships translated by some particular event or action into something altogether different—then the Fall of Lucifer and the Last Judgement are clearly the 'beginning' and 'end' of this cosmic Christian drama. It is not so easy to recognize the 'middle'. Theologically, the centre or core of Christianity is the double mystery of the Nativity and Resurrection, since acceptance of these miracles is the gateway to belief. Dramatically, however, the centre or 'middle' is the Crucifixion: for this is the climactic event after which relationships, and the situation arising from them, can never be quite as they were before. The Resurrection, the appearances before the disciples, the Ascension, the gift of tongues and the Judgement are all conditional upon it; while the stories of the Fall and the Nativity, however interesting in themselves, take on their full meaning only in terms of the Crucifixion. Liturgically, the truth of this contention seems to be implicit in the fact that it was and is commemoration of the Last Supper that forms the Church's central sacrament. So long therefore, as presentation of the Crucifixion was shirked, the liturgical drama of the sanctuary, choir, or even nave, could not develop far. Once, however, the central, dramatic oblation was firmly and deliberately re-enacted for audiences, whether in churchyard, meadow, market place or cathedral nave, the possibilities of development were legion: for herein lay the means to translate dramatic protasis into dramatic apodosis.[3] Not only was a Christian cosmic drama attainable, but its pattern could be imitated countless times in terms of man in the universe, microcosms for the macrocosm.

On these grounds I am forced to conclude that the liturgical drama of the churches is most unlikely to have developed *into* the secularized drama of the streets, as historians have repeatedly told us it did and as analysis of surviving evidence (taken by itself and isolated from the past, from religion and from art) would even now seem to indicate. A much more likely conjecture would appear to me to be that original plays of the Fall, Crucifixion and Judgement were presented out of doors during the thirteenth century at the insistence of friars or like-minded priests and clerks, who were determined to bring the relevance of Christ's sacrifice to bewildered mankind in the market place: and that these new plays attracted to themselves such other dramatic narrative as had been formulated within the worship of the Church, the techniques of which were openly copied: for these plays of man's inadequacy and the means to redemption possessed the dramatic dynamic (in the form of the

Passion Play) on which development hinged and which the liturgical drama lacked. In other words, as Passion, Fall, Antichrist and Judgement plays expanded, they absorbed the old liturgical sequences which had developed around the Nativity and the Resurrection and so became linked to one another in a complete cycle. Where, too, the latter were inevitably Latin dramas, the former could as appropriately be conceived in the vernacular as in Latin. Where 'translation' is concerned, therefore, I incline towards the following, presumptive chronology: *

(i) Dramas of the period 975 A.D.–1220/25 were conceived and written exclusively in Latin.

(ii) Plays of the Fall, Crucifixion, Antichrist and Judgement written between 1225 and 1350 were conceived alternatively in Latin or the vernacular with a marked tendency to prefer the vernacular after 1300.

(iii) Old, liturgical dramas of the Nativity and Resurrection were either adapted or translated into the vernacular after 1300.

(iv) A full, vernacular cycle was a possibility at any time after 1350.

There are other features of the archetypal pattern thus created which warrant attention. Perhaps the most important is that alternative verdicts of Salvation or Damnation are meted out in the Judgement play. Provision had thus been made (unselfconsciously of course) for either an idyllic or a tragic ending. It will be seen that as soon, therefore, as the pattern came to be copied at microcosmic level, this alternative close would open the way to a comic or tragic resolution of dramatic conflict. It would then only require a consciousness of literary genre to become established within educated society for comedy and tragedy to re-emerge from oblivion as recognized dramatic forms. Another important feature of the archetypal pattern is the distinctiveness of the three parts within the whole: Creation and Fall, redemptive sacrifice, and

* In support of this conjectural chronology I would instance the characterization of the Virgin in the fully developed, vernacular Cycles. Treatment of her, despite the vernacular, is far less 'human' than that of all the other leading characters. This seems to me to find its explanation in the fact that she is the principal figure of both the Easter and Christmas *Quem Quaeritis*, and of the liturgical *Planctus*. Her own story is only developed in itself in very late additions to the Cycle, and this probably only comes about through fusion with groups of plays about the Life of the Virgin of independent origin as in the *Ludus Coventriae*. (See Craig, *ERD*, pp. 239–280.)

alternative resolution of salvation through repentance and forgiveness, or damnation through wilful rejection of the chance offered.

Presupposing a slow dawning in literary consciousness of the dramatic potential of this pattern, it follows that these parts would be more quickly imitated than the whole and equally that the parts and microcosmic copies of them would be more readily assimilated than the grand design itself. The central part, the redemptive sacrifice, offered a quantity of particularized parallels in the lives of the Apostles and early Christians who imitated Christ in suffering a cruel and unjust martyrdom for their beliefs. I have argued elsewhere that the narrative source for such plays was the *lectio* in one or other of the Church's liturgies.* That, however, does not invalidate my present contention that the dramatic pattern which such narrative was moulded to resemble was that of the Passion Play.

If the dramatic 'middle' of the dominant pattern could thus be reproduced and multiplied in isolation, so could both the 'end' and the 'beginning', if rather less easily and obviously. The 'end' of the macrocosmic cycle was the general Doom; the particularized parallel was the individual balance sheet that each and every human being brought with him from the world to Death's door. This bill of reckoning, represented dramatically as a struggle between sin and righteousness, good counsel and bad, virtue and vice, is essentially the plot and theme of every Morality Play. Again, though the sermon† probably directed thought away from the abstract concept of Doomsday towards the frighteningly specific one of each mortal coming in turn before a judgement seat flanked by celestial bliss and hell's fiery portals to the left and right or above and below, the cyclic plays of the Last Judgement and its immediate antecedents provided the actual pattern for dramatizing this subject. The persistence and vividness with which hell-fire was preached from the pulpit in the fourteenth and fifteenth centuries to a world that, despite knowledge of Christ's redemptive sacrifice, seemed determined to destroy itself in the indulgence of evil and frivolity, is illustrated with equal frequency and force in countless lurid depictions of the final Doom, in stone above the west doors of churches and in fresco above their rood screens. (See Plate **XXXII**, No. 52.)

There is a note of hysteria in this preaching and in this art, as if despair lay hauntingly behind its urgency. Was the God whose

* See Ch. VII, p. 230 above.
† See Ch. VII, pp. 231–233 above.

presence had once seemed so real, who in his house of Byzantine or Romanesque design had seemed near enough to come into view at any moment, who in his darker, more lofty Gothic house had still seemed comfortably within earshot, was this God deserting his Creation in disgust? The prospect of a second disillusionment on this scale seems to me to have stolen unawares upon the religious conscience of the fifteenth century and to have provoked a terror in its heart and soul which expressed itself partly in morbid concern with Death and sensationalism, partly in paralysis of the will to reveal the truth by further effort.

A sure sign of the existence of such hysteria is the inability to recognize the borderline that divides the grim and pitiful from the absurd and ludicrous. This weakness strikes me as being implicit in many aspects of fifteenth-century life and art in North-Western Europe, from the 'decorated' style in architecture to the extravagancies of fashion in dress. It is as apparent dramatically in the absurdly elaborate allegories of chivalric Tournaments as in the deportment of the Devils in the texts of those Miracle Plays that have survived to us. It may even have been obvious to the Reformers of the sixteenth century whose cold clear-headedness told them that such things must be swept away if religion was to survive at all.*

That this degeneracy within religious drama of the fifteenth century which, in England, denied it further creativeness did not emasculate the drama altogether, is a major cause of wonder. I attribute it to the potential latent within the third component part of the archetypal pattern: the Fall. In one sense this part of the whole was the least rewarding of the three, in that, unlike the other two, it did not reverberate with immediate scriptural or didactic echoes which could be accorded a parallel treatment. Yet, in another sense, it possessed greater generative power than either of them, since any microcosmic application of the story must inevitably concern man's shortcomings and inadequacy rather than his dreams. In human terms, it provides the prospective dramatist with a basis of observable fact instead of intuitive speculation. Moreover, any weakening of faith in the legitimacy of man's dreams, or the likelihood of their fulfilment, must inevitably rebound with great force on to this consciousness of his initial depravity. In other words, granted the existence of a macrocosmic religious drama, any loosening of the motive force that spurred it

* See John Bale's letter on religious plays written from exile in 1544 and quoted Ch. VII, p. 240 above: also J. Huizinga, *The Waning of the Middle Ages*, Chs. XV–XIX.

into being is likely to transfer itself proportionately to the creation of a microcosmic drama of similar design: that is to say, a drama that contents itself with explaining man's inhumanity to man instead of attempting to justify God's ways to Man. The pattern will remain Christian as also the ethos: but the subject matter will become much more mortal than divine.

Before this could happen, however, the Fall, as a prototype itself, had to catch up the leeway lost to both the Passion in Saint Plays and the Judgement in Morality Plays. The start which these latter components of the cycle, considered as dramatic prototypes, had upon the Fall, was very considerable, if one may judge by the surviving religious, artistic and factual records. The Fall, however, came into its own as the drama of social recreation matured. One may see the two beginning to affect one another in the literary Romances of the fourteenth and fifteenth centuries. Lydgate, in his *Fall of Princes*, prefaces his tales of the fall of notable historical and mythological figures in the pre-Christian world like Julius Caesar and Alexander, Priam and Jason, with those of Lucifer and Adam. What is more, he both describes these stories as tragedies and tells us that he inherited this sense of genre from Chaucer. *

The step from here to the portrayal of a Dr. Faustus who is damned,† or a Cardinal Wolsey who 'falls like Lucifer never to hope again', is not such a very large one.

Lydgate himself, indeed, when writing his *Troy Book*, felt able to define both tragedy and comedy, at least in regard to literary narrative:

> 'And first also, I rede, (th)at in Troye
> Wer song and rad lusty fresche comedies,
> And o(th)er dites (th)at called be tragedies.
> And to declare, schortly in sentence,
> Of bo(th)e two (th)e final difference:
> A comedie hath in his gynnyng,
> At prime face, a maner compleynyng
> And afterward endeth in gladnes;
> And it (th)e dedis only doth expres
> Of swiche as ben in povert plounged lowe;
> But tragidie, who so list to knowe,
> It begynneth in prosperite,

* 'My maistir Chaucer, with his fresh comedies,
  Is ded, allas, cheeff poete off Breteyne,
  That whilom made ful piteous tragedies;
  The fall of pryncis he did also compleyne.' 4

† 'Chorus: Faustus is gone: regard his hellish fall' (V, iv, 222).

And endeth ever in adversite;
And it also doth (th)e conquest trete
Of riche kynges and of lordys grete,
Of my(gh)ty men and olde conquerou(ri)s,
Whiche by fraude of Fortunys schowris
Ben overcast & whelmed from her glorie.'[5]

These definitions do not depart very far from those familiar to
Seneca, Terence, Plautus and Horace. The link between these men
and Dante, Chaucer and Lydgate was provided by Latin Gram-
marians and monastic scholars down the ten intervening centuries.
I do not, however, feel obliged to trace this in every detail, since I
have already established (in Chapter VI) that Lydgate speaks of
this 'theatre standing in Troy' in terms of his own practical experience as a dramatist. By then, theory had begun its journey back
from books to theatre.[6] If, therefore, the theatre of social recreation in the mid fifteenth century, with its amateur Disguisings, its
professional Interludes, its chivalric physical combats, its political
pageantry and its appreciation of literary genre, did not amount to
a regular drama by our standards, it was nevertheless fully equipped
to assimilate to its own use the three major components of the
religious drama. These came to it in a form suitably abridged to
meet the requirements of a small group of professional actors in the
brief interludes between courses at Feasts or other amateur revels.
The chances, however, of their remaining unaltered in this new
environment for very long were clearly small. Since the purpose of
admitting them within the scope of social revels at all was primarily
to obtain variety of recreation, frequent repetition was likely to
lead to boredom in the audience and to consequent rejection. That
they were not rejected argues that they were adapted to provide
variety. It was in this context then, the revels of social recreation, that the story of the Fall came into its own as a dramatic
pattern for the treatment of subject-matter within the little world
of man. Thus, by the sixteenth century, all three microcosmic
components were ready to be forged together again. This might
well not have happened had the macrocosmic archetype faded from
view: but in England (as also in Spain) it did not. With minor
changes and modifications the great Miracle Cycles continued to
be performed year by year in many places and attracted large
assemblies of spectators. The Tudor dramatist of social recreation,
therefore, had ever before him this grandiose dramatic *exemplum*
the whole as well as the parts. As new sources of dramatic narrative were lifted off the new printing presses, as audiences developed

new interests in modern history and classical antiquity, as critics began to formulate theories of genre and composition, as acting companies grew in number and experience, the dramatist also could experiment. All these novelties could be welded into his work to fashion of it something noticeably fresh and adventurous. Yet all the while this work however new, human and topical, could only have seemed an inferior product, when measured against the structural grandeur and harmony of the Miracle Cycles, still being performed and with which it therefore had to stand comparison— a toy sword matched against a soldier's. Here, it is vital to remember that the Cycles were not suppressed till between 1570 and 1600. *

By the middle of Elizabeth's reign, however, notable advances were being made towards welding the now uniformly developed components of this new, microcosmic drama into a unified parallel to the complete, macrocosmic predecessor that was being slowly strangled. This forging process could be regarded as accomplished when in comedy, the adversity occasioned by human folly, strategy or simple inadequacy was translated into prosperity and happiness by love, mercy and forgiveness: when, in tragedy, the prosperity or equanimity exchanged through fate or human error for adversity or a sick conscience was so tempered by pain, violence and grief as to reveal the nature of the self, merit and desert that had sheltered unknowingly behind it.

The metal through which this welding was achieved was the Chronicle Play, with characters derived from the Street Pageants, plot structure from sequences of Miracle Plays, theme from the Morality Play and brevity from the professional Interlude. Detailed discussion of this welding process and its principal products, tragedy and comedy of Christian inspiration, must introduce the second volume of this survey of early English stages, *New Stages for Old*. It will then be seen that the metal chosen was not proof against corrosive acid, an inevitable price for letting fallen Man dominate the subject matter. When matched against metal of neo-classic forging it chipped and dented. In the lists of Civil War it snapped. Splinters and useless haft were preserved and, as befitted an epic product, received a State Funeral by Royal Patent at the hands of Davenant and Dryden.

* See Ch. IV, pp. 112–18 above: also Vol. II, 1576–1660, Pt. I, pp. 80–83.

APPENDIX A

A list of colours and their properties *temp*. Ed. III in
College of Arms MS. 1st M. 16 in a treatise entitled
'Enseignemens Notablez aulx poursuivans'

Fol. 2

A demande le poursivaunt de son blason darmez, Je te respons quil te
fault scavoir quantez couleurs sont dont fait armez, et enquelle maniere.

E p̄mier est asur et est compare a lellement du ciel ou
de lair dont le ciel est soustenuz, et signifie loyaulte.
Et en pierrerie le saphir qui sont troys choses pures
& nettez & signifie hoṁe sanguin.
e ij^me gullez qui signifie vaillance & feu, Et en
pierrerie signifie le Ruby & signifie hoṁe colerique.
e iij^me sable qui signifie dueil et la terre, et en
pierrerie le dyamāt & signifie hoṁe merencolique.
e iiij^me sinable qui signifie herbes & arbres, et
empierrerie lesmeraude & signifie en homme amour & courtoisie.
e. vme est poupre qui signifie Richesse et la(*mu*)st (*amethyst*) en
pierrerie latu, et signifie habundance de largesse.
e p̄mier metal est or qui signifie noblesse & le soleil
et en pierrerie escarboucle & signifie haultesse en bon vouloir.
e second est argent qui signifie humilite & l'eau, et
en pierrerie la perle et signifie hoṁe fleumatique.

In this same MS. the young pursuivant under instruction is told that
Heralds are to Kings as Angels are to God, namely Messengers (fol. 4b).

See Ch. II, pp 46–48 above.

APPENDIX B

Corporation Records of the City of London

An extract from the Bridge House Rentals, Vol. III (being the Annual Accounts of the Bridgemasters during the years 1460–1484 written in MS. on vellum), fols. 94b–95. This extract comprises the portion of the accounts for the year 1464 relating to expenses incurred in preparing the pageant on London Bridge (South Bank Gate & Drawbridge), for the reception of Elizabeth Woodville at her coronation.

The Latin is printed here in the exact form of the MS. with translation into modern English given approximately line for line below.

All contractions in the MS. are represented by the symbol ⎺: the end of each line in the MS. by the symbol /.

Fol. 94b

Expn̄ fact ad coronāc Regine
Expenses incurred at the Coronation of the Queen

Et in denar̄ solut̄ Janitori Prioratus beate mariē
And in sums paid to the doorkeeper of the priory of blessed Mary

de Overey in Suthwerk p suo /labore & attendencia
of Overy in Southwark for his labour and attention

in āprendo portam dōc Prioratus temporib₃ noctʳnis
in opening the door of the said Priory at night time

pro passaḡ/carpentars & alioꝝ opariors & s̄vientes pontis
for the passage of the carpenters & other workmen & servants of the
          bridge

pdc̄o inde transien̄s ad ōpa de parte/ occidentl̄i
crossing thence to the work on the western side

eiusdc̄o pontis pro hoc anno p̄ut allocatt̄ fuit in annīs p̄cedents
of the said bridge as has been allowed in preceding years.

Et Thome Ostrich̄ p̄ ij l̄b Osode-iiis iiijd. Et eidem̄ pro
And to Thomas Ostrich for two pounds of 'osode' 3/4
                    And to the same for

v dūs & de gold papʳ p̄ q dōs/xiiijd,—vjs.
five & a half dozen of gold paper, price of each dozen 14d,—6s.

Et eidm̄ p̄ i dōs de Cinopre pap^r ijs.
And to the same for one & half dozen of red paper, 2s.

Et eidm̄ p̄ i pees de Redbokeram/ijs vid.
And to the same for a piece of red buckram 2s. 6d.

Et eidm̄ p̄ ij gross tynfoile viijs.
And the same for two gross of tinfoil 8/-

Et Willō Broun̄ Grocer p̄ xix foliis/de Cinop^r pap^r &
And to William Brown Grocer for nineteen leaves of red paper &

iiij foliis papīrs virīd—3s. Et eidm̄ p̄ iij l̄b
four leaves of green paper 3/-. And to the same for three pounds

Geñall xijd. Et pro/i l̄b vermelōn—xvd. Et pro dē l̄b
of general 12d. And for one pound of vermilion 15d. And for half a

ynde vij d. Et pro i lb verdgrece—xiiijd. Et/p̄
pound of indigo 7d. And for one pound of verdigris 14d. And for

vj l̄b White lede-ixd. Et p̄ vj l̄b redlede-ixd.
six pounds of White lead 9d. And for six pounds of redlead 9d.

Et pro i grōss tynfoille iijs. Et Willō Tange pro ij
And for one gross of tinfoil 3/-. And to William Tange for two

scaynes de pakthrede—xiiijd. Et pro ij scayles de small
skeins of packthread 14d. And for two 'scayles' of small

pakthrede/-xijd. Et pro dī dos de Count̄fete mystell-vjd.
packthread 12d. And for half a dozen counterfeit mystell 6d.

Et p̄ i reme de papiro albo—ijs. vjd. /Et pro i reme
And for one ream of white paper 2s. 6d. And for one ream of

papīr nigr̄-xvd. Et R̄ic Syffe mercer p̄ iiij ^{xx} xvj ell
black paper 15d. And to Richard Syffe mercer for ninety-six ells

de Siltwych̄/po cuiusl̄t ell iiijd½-xxxvjs. Et eidm̄ pro
of Siltwyche, price of each ell 4½d. 36s. And to the same for

ij peces de Bokeram xs vjd. Et pro i/pece de bokeram p^{r}pul
two pieces of buckram 10s. 6d. And for one piece of purple buckram.

iijs iiiid. Et pro ij virḡ & dī de purpull bokeram-xxd.
3s. 4d. And for two yards and a half of purple buckram 20d.

Et/Alano Newmañ p̄ CCC party gold C ad ijs viiid-viiis.
And to Alan Newman for 300 'Party Gold' at 2s. 8d. a hundred. 8s.

Et pro CC silver-xxd. Et Joh̄i Abraham pro vj^c party gold, xvjs.
And for 200 silver, 20d. And to John Abraham for 600 party gold, 16s.

Et Simō Turno͏ʳ pro iij pailes ixd & ij bollis viijd lign̄-xvijd/
And to Simon Turnour for three pails 9d. & two wooden bowls 8d,—17d.

Et Willō Westram Groc̄ pro xij l̄b Glew qua̅l l̄b ad ijd½–ijs vid
And to William Westram Grocer for twelve pounds of glue at 2½d. a
pound. 2s. 6d.

Et p̄/Red Wax ij l̄b xvjd. Et p̄ iiij l̄b moty—1½d.
And for red wax two pounds 16d. And for four pounds of 'moty' 1½d.

Et pro blak chalke xviij l̄b—iijs / Et Roche alem i
And for black chalk, eighteen pounds, 3s. And 'Roche' (red?) alum one

qrtr̄—ijd. Et i unce de Safurn̄ pro tinctur͏ᵒ lin̄
quarter, 2d.. And one ounce of Saffron used for dying the flax

expn in factur̄ crini/p̄ anglis & puellis—xd
to make the hair for the angels and children 10d.

Et p̄ ollis̄ & discis terra empt̄ pro pictorib̄s—xxd
And for pots and dishes of earth bought for the painters 20d.

Et/pro Brusshes & Crinib̄s porcum̄ empt̄ pro eisdm̄ pictorib̄s—xxijd.
And for Brushes and pig's bristles bought for the same painters 22d.

Et pro ixᶜ plumis pauonu/ p̄ alis anglor̄s inde fiend̄s—xxid
And for nine hundred peacock's feathers for making the angel's wings
21d.

For florrey empt̄ iijs iiijd. Et pro virgis de corulo/empt̄
And for 'florrey' bought 3s. 4d. And for rods of hazel bought.

pro Imaginib̄s inde fiend̄s—iiijd. Et pro acub̄s empte—iis.
for making images 4d. And for needles bought, 2s.

Et pro iij l̄b linū empt̄ & expn̄/ in silitudine crinis̄ anglor̄s
And for three pounds of flax bought & used in the likeness of hair for
the angels.

& virginis̄—ixd. Et p̄ di l̄b brasell empt̄—xxd.
& virgins 9d. And for half a pound of brasil bought 20d.

Et pro i/lagena de pynke yelow empt̄ ijs viijd.
And for one gallon of pink yellow bought 2s. 8d.

Et p̄ iiij p̄vis shevers empt̄—iid. Et pro filo/albo & blodie
And for four small shevers bought 2d. And for thread white and red

empt̄ iiijd. Et pro viij parib̄s cirothecit̄s empt̄ pro
bought 4d. And for eight pairs of gloves bought for

signe manū viij ymagē /—ixd. Et pro i lb flokkes empt̄ pro
the hands of eight figures. 9d. And for one pound of flock bought for

obstupācē dict̄ cirothecīts 1½d. Et pro vi kerchyfs/de
stuffing the said gloves 1½d. And for six kerchiefs of

plesaunce empt̄ p̄ apparatu vj ymaginš muliebr̄s—viijs viijd.
'pleasaunce' bought for the apparel of six figures of women 8s. 8d.

Et pro ffrenge ijd./ Et p̄ farina empt̄ pro factur̄ paste
And for 'Frenge' 2d. And for flour bought for making paste

p̄ pictores—xiijd. Et pro iiij l̄b candelor̄s expn̄/p̄
for the painters 13d. And for four pounds of candles used for

opar̄ tempe noct˙no—iiijd½. Et pro iiij paribs forpic̄
working at night time 4½d. And for four pairs of scissors

empt̄ pro pictoribs̄ viijd. Et/pro Cole empt̄ xiijd.
bought for the painters 8d. And for Coal bought 13d.

Et p̄ p̄ m̄ pynnes empt̄ & expn̄ in fixur̄ vestmentt̄ ymaginš/xiiijd.
And for a thousand pins bought & used in fixing the clothes on the
    figures 14d.

Et pro i kilderkyn cervis̄ expn̄ p̄ opar˙ˢ
And for one kilderkin of ale used among the workers

infra domū pontis opant̄ in factur̄ ordinac̄/posn̄ sup̄
within the bridge house working in making the announcement placed
    upon

pontem erga aduentū Regine ad Coronacoēm suam—xxd.
the bridge against the arrival of the Queen for her coronation 20d.

Et pro m̄¹ iij half/peny naill̄—xvd. Et pro x m̄¹ & ½ de
And for one thousand three half penny nails 15d. And for ten & a half

Braket—iijs vjd. Et pro m̄¹ m̄¹ m̄¹ Cardenaill̄ / —xd.
thousand brackets 3s. 6d. And for three thousand card nails 10d.

Et pro m¹ patyn naill̄—vd. Et pro Crinibs̄ porcum empt̄ p̄
And for a thousand patyn nails 5d. And for hogshair bought for

brusshes inde fiend̄ occupat̄ p̄ pictores viiid. Et p̄ lyne empt̄—vid.
brushes used by the painters 8d. And for line bought 6d.

Et pro Wyre empt̄ & occupat̄ in eisdm̄ /opibs̄—iiis.
And for wire bought and used in the same work 3s.

Et pro cariage iij lode v̄terrs stuffurs a Guyhalda
And for the carriage of three loads of old material from Guildhall

londoñ usque̅ domu̅ pontis/ixd.
London to the bridge house 9d.

Et Willo Love p̄ una diem Thome Malmayn p̄ vj dies coferers
And to William Love for one day, Thomas Malmayn for six days,
cofferers

opānt in opībs p̄ᵣ dic̄t utrusque/eor̄ p̄ diem, viijd.—iiijs viijd.
working in the aforesaid work to each of them per day 8d.—4s. 8d.

Et Willō Martyn p̄ duos dies & Thome Crulle iij dies/
And to William Martyn for two days & Thomas Crulle for three days

secum opānt in fixur̄ pañu linerum ad ordinac̄oems p̄ᵣdct
working with him in fixing the linen cloth for the aforesaid announce-
ments

utrusqe p̄ diem vjd—ijs vjd.
each at 6d. per day, 2s. 6d.

Fol. 95

Et Joh̄i Brendwode p̄ ix dies Joh̄i Hornton p̄ viij dies
And to John Brendwode for nine days, to John Hornton for eight days

Joh̄i Thompson p̄ viij dies & d̄e/Martius Cokke & Rob̄te Coupe
to John Thompson for eight and a half days, to Martin Cokke
and to Robert Couper

p̄ viij dies steyn̄es opānt in opībs p̄ᵣdic̄t oml̄t eor̄ p̄ d̄ie/xijd—xljs. vjd.
for eight days, stainers, working in the said works every one of
them 12d. per day—41s. 6d.

Et Henrᵒ Poterich̄ & Joh̄i Warthow secum opānt
And to Henry Poterich & to John Warthow working with him

in eisdm̄ opībs per/ix dies utrusqe p̄ diem vjd—ixs.
in the same works for 9 days, each of them at 6d. per day—9s.

Et Thome Wodeward opānt in eisdm̄ opībs p̄ v/ dies & d̄e
And to Thomas Wodeward working in the same works for 5½ days

capient̄ p̄ diem viijd—iijs viijd. Et Joh̄i Aleyn opānt
receiving 8d. a day—3s. 8d. And to John Aleyn working

in eisdm̄ opībs p̄ /vj dies capient̄ p̄ diem vd—iis vid.
in the same works for 6 days receiving 5d. a day—2s. 6d.

328

Et d̄to Johī Horntōn pro ii s̄vient suis secum/opān̄t
And to the said John Horton for two of his men working with him

in opībs̄ pʳdict per viij dies capient pro eis p̄ diem xijd——
in the aforesaid works for 8 days receiving on their behalf 12d. per day

viijs. Et Johī/Brendwode pro s̄vient suo secum opān̄t
8s. And to John Brendwode for his man working with him

p̄ ix dies capient̄ p̄ diem iijd–ijs iijd. Et / Johī Thompson
For 9 days receiving 3d. a day—2s. 3d. And to John Thompson

p̄ s̄vient suo secum opān̄t p̄ vii dies ad iijd ꝑ diem—xxjd.
for his man working with him for 7 days at 3d. a day—21d.

Et/Willō Parys & Riċ Westmyll sissoribs̄ opān̄t in aptur̄ &
And to William Parys & Richard Westmyll, tailors, working at the
       preparing &

factur̄ vestamentors̄ p̄ div̄sis/Imaginibs̄ ordināt pro aduentu
making of clothes for diverse Images provided for the coming of

Regine ad Staplas pontis & ad pontem traxibilem per/tres dies & dē
the Queen to the Staple of the Bridge & to the drawbridge for 3½ days

—vjs. Et Johī Genycote p̄ scripta & lymnyng vj balads
—6s. And to John Genycote for writing & limning six ballads

porrect̄ /Regine in aduent suo-iijs. Et Johī Thompson
delivered to the Queen at her approach—3s. And to John Thompson

pro scriptur̄a dict̄ vi balads sup̄ tabulas / fix ad paginas
for writing the said 6 ballads on tablets fixed to the pagent

apud pontem—viijd. Et in denarˢ soln̄t p̄ expn̄ dictors̄ opars̄
on the bridge—8d. And in sums paid for the expenses of the said
       workmen.

p̄ ips̄ /expendit in tenemente brasineo vocat the croun
by themselves incurred in the alehouse called the Crown

iuxta portam domus pontis tempē factur̄/ordinacios̄ pʳ dc̄s—xlvjs xd.
adjacent to the gate of the bridgehouse when making the said announce-
       ments—46s. 10d.

Et in denarˢ soln̄t Radulpho Brangthwayte p̄
And in sums paid to Rudolf Brangthwaite for

conducc̄es / appar̄at anglors̄—vs. Et Johī Raby pro
the hire of clothes for the angels—5s. And to John Raby for

figura spt sto p̄ ipus prostīt & occupāt
a figure of the holy spirit by himself suppplied & used

in/ordinacos p^rdict ac pro labore & attendēc p̄
in the said preparations both for his work & attendance by

ipus impēns—xxd. Et Petro Johnson/pro camā ab
himself given—20d. And to Peter Johnson for a

ipo condūct apud Staplas pontis pro Clīcs ibm̄
room hired from him at the Staple of the bridge for clerks there

exisēnt & cantānt in aduentu Regine—vjs viijd./
being & singing at the Queen's approach 6s. 8d.

Et Rogers ———— Clīco ecclīs St. Magni pro se &
And Rogers ——— Clerk of the Church of St. Magnus for himself &

pūis suis ibm̄ cantantib̄s etc. ac pro lavās/vj albārs & vj amīs
his boys singing there etc., & for washing 6 albs & 6 amices

—viis iid. Et in expn eorsdm̄ ibm̄—iijs vijd.
—7s. 2d. And in the expenses of the same there 3s. 7d.

Et Robto/Clīco ecclīs St̄. Georgii ibm̄ recipiente
And to Robert Clerk of the Church of St. Gregory welcoming

Reginam in pagine in signe & vice St̄i Pauli /—xxd.
the Queen there on a stage in the form & manner of St. Paul—20d.

Et magistro societatis Clīcor̄s pro se & xxv p̄sonis cantante
And to the master of the Society of Clerks for him & 25 persons singing

apud pontem/traxibilem in aduēnt Regine pro dīct magr̄o
at the drawbridge at the Queen's approach, for the said master

xijd & p̄ quolt alliors xxv, viijd/—xviijs iiijd.
12d. & for each of the other twenty-five, 8d.—18s. 4d.

Et in expn eorsdm̄ ibm̄ vs vijd. Et—Holme cantatori
And for the expenses of the same therein 5s. 7d. And to—Holme,
precentor

pro/se & pūis suis cantantib̄s apud nostrum capelle
for himself & his boys singing at the door of our chapel

sup̄ pontē in aduentu Regine—iijs iiijd./Et Salamon Batell
on the bridge at the Queen's coming 3s. 4d. And to Salamon Batell

pro labore suo vice & loco Sti Elizabeth loquent Regine
for his labour in form & manner of St. Elizabeth addressing the Queen

ad ponte/trax—xxd. Et Edmude Herte ibm existent
at the drawbridge—20d. And to Edmund Herte being there

loco Marie Cleophe—xxd/Et pro fumigacoe fact apud pontem
in the role of Mary Cleophas—20d. And for fumigation done at the

trax in Aduentu Regine iijs iiijd. Et pro cariage/xlv
drawbridge at the Queen's approach 3s. 4d. And for the carriage of 45

lodes arene spars sup pontem trax erga aduentu Regine p
loads of sand sprinkled on the drawbridge against the Queen's coming,
    for

qualt lode,—iiijd,—xvs. Et Stephe Betcock Johi Holme
each load 4d. 15s. And to Stephen Betcock, John Holme

Roge Payn Thome Osemond Johi William Willo/Burton
Roger Payne, Thomas Osemond John William, William Burton

Willo Exhurst carpentars opant in factur opus ligneum
William Exhurst, carpenters working in the making of the woodwork

pro ordinacos prdict/cuilt eors p xij dies capeint
for the said preparations each of them for 12 days receiving

p diem vijd,—xlixs. Et Johi Chambre iijs vjdp /sex dies
7d. a day. 49s. And to John Chamber 3s. 6d. for six days

Willo Crosby ijs iiijd p iiij dies & Johi Newynton ijs iiijd
To William Crosby 2s. 4d. for 4 days & to John Newington 2s. 4d.

p iiij dies cuilt eors p diem vijd/Et Nichoas Carpent iiijs
for 4 days each one of them 7d. a day. And to Nicholas Carpenter 4s.

p xij dies ad iiijd p diem secum opant in eisdm opibs
for 12 days at 4d. per day working with him in the same works

—xijs. ijd.
12s. 2d.

Sm xxjli xiiijs d

vj½.

1431–1432

Et ludentibus coram domino Abbate in festo Natalis domini	xijd

c. 1450

Et tribus histrionibus eodem festo (*St. Germain*) hoc anno	iijs.
Et histrionibus domini Regis hoc anno	vjs. viijd.
Et cuidam histrioni hoc anno	vjd.
Et cuidam histrioni ad festum Natalis (Dom)ini in eodem festo hoc anno	ijs.
Et histrionibus Ducis Eboraci	iijs. iiijd.

1479–1480

In rewardo dato ludentibus coram domino Abbate et convento in festo Innocentum	ijs.
In rewardo dato histrionibus Johannis Conyers militis	xijd.
In rewardo dato histrionibus domini Jacobi Tyrell	viijd.
In rewardo histrionibus Domini Scroop	xijd.
In rewardo trium (*sic*) histrionibus	xijd.
In rewardo histrionibus ducis Gloucestrie	vjs. viijd.
In rewardo dato uni histrioni domini Regis per se venienti hoc anno	xxd.
In rewardo dato histrionibus supervenientibus ad festum sancti Germani prope ad vincula	iijs. viijd.
In rewardo dato histrionibus domini Regis	vjs. viijd.
In rewardo dato histrionibus Comitis Northumbrie	vs.
In rewardo dato histrionibus supervenientibus in festo depositionis sancti Germani	vjs. viijd.

1480

Item histrioni ducis Gloucestrie	ijs.
Item histrionibus ville Beverlaci	xxd.

pre-1483

Item hominibus ludentibus in festo sancti Stephani	xxd.
Item datum histrioni ducis Gloucestrie	xxd.

1431–1432

And to the players before the lord Abbot at the feast of the Nativity
of the Lord .... 12d.

c. 1450

And to three players at the same feast this year (i.e. of St. Germain
to whom Selby Abbey was dedicated) .... 3s.

And to the players of our lord the King this year .... 6s. 8d.

And to a certain player this year .... 6d.

And to a certain player at the feast of the Nativity of the Lord at
the same feast this year .... 2s.

And to the players of the Duke of York this year .... 3s. 4d.

1479–1480

In reward given to the players before the lord Abbot and convent
at the feast of the Innocents .... 2s.

In reward given to the players of Sir John Conyers .... 12d.

In reward given to the players of Sir James Tyrell .... 8d.

In reward given to the players of Lord Scrope .... 12d.

In reward to three players .... 12d.

In reward to the players of the Duke of Gloucester .... 6s. 8d.

In reward given to a player of the lord King coming himself this
year .... 20d.

In reward given to the players coming over at the feast of St.
Germain near (the feast of St. Peter) in chains .... 3s. 8d.

In reward given to the players of the lord King .... 6s. 8d.

In reward given to the players of the Earl of Northumberland .... 5s.

In reward given to the players coming over at the feast of the deposition of St. Germain .... 6s. 8d.

1480

Item to a player of the Duke of Gloucester .... 2s.

Item to the players of the town of Beverley .... 20d.

pre-1483

Item to men playing at the feast of St. Stephen .... 20d.

Item given to a player of the Duke of Gloucester .... 20d.

Item histrionibus domine Fitzhugh	ijs.
Item histrioni Johannis Salvayne militis	vjd.
Item histrioni eiusdem domini	viijd.
Item tribus histrionibus Ducis Gloucestrie, domini Fitzhugh and domini Lovell	xvjd.
Item histrionibus comitis Westmorland	ijd.
Item datum histrionibus in festo Transitionis sancti Germani	vijs.
Item histrionibus domini nostri Regis	vjs. viijd.
In rewardo dato histrionibus domini Principis videlicet tumblers hoc anno	ijs.
Item histrionibus domine Fitzhugh	xxd.
Item histrionibus Willelmi Eure militis	xijd.
Item histrionibus Edwardi Hastynges militis	xijd.
Item histrionibus ducis Gloucestrie	vjs. viijd.
Item histrionibus in festo deposicionis sancti Germani	iijs.
Item histrionibus Jacobi Jaryngton militis	viijd.

post-1483

Et cuidam histrioni ludenti coram domino Abbate hoc anno	xxd.
Et diversis histrionibus in festo sancti Germani hoc anno	viijd.
Et histrionibus Ducisse Norff'	iijs. iiijd.
Et histrionibus in festo deposicionis sancti Germani hoc anno	iijs.

c. 1496

In rewardo dato ludatoribus beate Marie Eboraci hoc anno	xvjd.
In rewardo dato Thome Wortlay histrioni hoc anno	viijd.
In rewardo dato ludentibus in aula domini in festo sancti Stephani hoc anno	xvjd.
In rewardo dato ludatoribus in festo dedicacionis hoc anno	xijd.
In rewardo dato histrioni episcopi Carlientis hoc anno	vjd.
In rewardo dato uni histrioni vocatur Henry hoc anno	xvjd.
In rewardo dato histrioni Thome Dercy militis hoc anno	viijd.
In rewardo dato histrionibus in Transitu sancti Germani hoc anno	iiijs.
In rewardo dato histrionibus domini Regis hoc anno	vjs. viijd.
In rewardo dato histrionibus in festo deposicionis sancti Germani hoc anno	iijs. vjd.

c. 1500

In rewardo dato ij histrionibus	xvjd.
Item histrionibus domini Principis	iijs. iiijd.
Item datum histrionibus comitis Northumbrie ludentibus	vjs.

334

Item to the players of Lord Fitzhugh	2s.	
Item to a player of Sir John Salvayne		6d.
Item to a player of the same lord (i.e. the Duke of Gloucester)		8d.
Item to 3 players of the Duke of Gloucester, Lord Fitzhugh and Lord Lovell		16d.
Item to players of the Earl of Westmorland	2s.	
Item to the players at the feast of the transition of St. Germain	7s.	
Item to the players of our lord the King	6s.	8d.
In reward given to the players of our lord the Prince that is tumblers this year	2s.	
Item to the players of Lord Fitzhugh		20d.
Item to the players of Sir William Eure		12d.
Item to the players of Sir Edward Hastynges		12d.
Item to the players of the Duke of Gloucester	6s.	8d.
Item to the players at the feast of the deposition of St. Germain	4s.	0d.
Item to the players of Sir James Haryngton		8d.

post-1483 (damaged)

And to a certain player playing before the lord Abbot this year		20d.
And to various players at the feast of St. Germain this year	6s.	8d.
And to the players of the Duchess of Norfolk	3s.	4d.
And to the players at the feast of the deposition of St. Germain this year	3s.	

c. 1496

In reward given to the players of (the abbey of) the Blessed Mary of York this year		16d.
In reward given to Thomas Wortlay a player this year		8d.
In reward given to the players in the lord's hall at the feast of St. Stephen this year		16d.
In reward given to the players at the feast of the dedication this year		12d.
In reward given to a player of the bishop of Carlisle this year		6d.
In reward given to a player called Henry this year		16d.
In reward given to the players of Sir Thomas Dercy		8d.
In reward given to the players at the transition of St. Germain this year	4s.	
In reward given to the players of the King this year	6s.	8d.
In reward given to the players at the feast of the deposition of St. Germain this year	4s.	6d.

c. 1500

In reward given to 2 players		16d.
Item to the players of the lord Prince	3s.	4d.
Item given to the players of the Earl of Northumberland	6s.	

335

Item datum diversis hominibus ludentibus in festo cruceficionis
domini   iijs. iiijd.
Item datum histrionibus Henrici Pyrcy   ijs.
Item datum histrionibus domini Regis   vjs. viijd.
Item datum hominibus ludentibus infra monasterium per manus
fratris Thome Cawod   xvjd.
Item datum hominibus ludentibus coram domino   ijs.
Item datum Willelmo Bull histrioni   viijd.
Item datum histrionibus in festo Transitionis sancti Germani   vs. ijd.
Item datum histrionibus in festo deposicionis sancti Germani   iijs. iiijd.

1527–1528

Et de xxd. datis quinque puros ludentibus coram domino in die Nativitatis
domini

Et de ijs. datis in regardo v homines ludat' de Eboraco in die sancti Stephani

Et de ijs. datis quinque puros de le Cle (Che?) in monasterio beate Marie de
Eboraci ludentos coram domino abbate in vigelia sancti Mauri abbatis

Et de xijd. datis iij^{or} hominibus de Ricall ludatoribus coram domino abbate in
die dominica post festum convercionis sancti Pauli

Et de vjs. viijd. datis vj hominibus ludat' domini Regis in die sancti Jacobi
Apostoli

Et de vjs. viijd. datis iij^{or} sistrionibus domini Regis viij˙ die Augusti

1531–1532

Et primo de ijs. iijd. datis in regardo vij^{tem} histrionibus in die sancti Germani
hoc anno

Et de viijd. datis histrioni in die Natalis domini hoc anno

Et de viijd. datis duobus histrionibus feria iij cia ebdomade pasche hoc anno

Et de xijd. datis iij histrionibus de Doncastre hoc anno

Et de xijd. datis iij^{bus} histrionibus de Eboraco in die Apostolorum Philippi et
Jacobi hoc anno

Et de xvjd datis iij^{or} histrionibus apud Eboracum sexto die Junii hoc anno

Et de xxd. datis Ortharedo domini Peyrcy citharizanti coram domino Abbate
in transitu sancti Germani hoc anno

Et de xvjd. datis iij^{or} aliis histrionibus eodem die

Et de vis. datis lusoribus Comitis de Darby in octava beate Marie hoc anno

Et de vs. datis lusoribus Ducis Richmondie in vigilia sancti Bartholomei hoc
anno

Et de vjs viijd. datis histrionibus domini Regis ij^{do} die Septembris hoc anno

Item given to various men playing at the feast of the Crucifixion of the Lord	3s.	4d.
Item given to the players of Henry Pyrcy	2s.	
Item given to the players of the lord King	6s.	8d.
Item given to men playing within the abbey by the hands of brother Thomas Cawod		16d.
Item given to men playing before the lord (Abbot)	2s.	
Item given to William Bull, a player		8d.
Item given to the players at the feast of the transition of St. Germain	5s.	5s.
Item given to the players at the feast of the deposition of St. Germain	3s.	4d.

1527–1528

And for 20d. given to five boys playing before the lord (Abbot) on the day of the Nativity of the Lord

And for 2s. given in reward to 5 men players from York on St. Stephen's day

And for 2s. given to 5 boys (of the choir?) of the monastery of the Blessed Mary of York playing before the lord Abbot on the vigil of St. Maurus abbot.

And for 12d. given to 4 men of Ricall playing before the lord Abbot on the Sunday after the feast of the conversion of St. Paul

And for 6s. 8d. given to 6 men players of the lord King on the day of St. James apostle

And for 6s. 8d. given to 4 players of the lord King on the 8th August.

1531–1532

And first for 2s. 4d. given in reward to 7 players on St. Germain's day this year

And for 8d. given to a player on the day of the Nativity of the Lord this year

And for 8d. given to two players at the festival of the 3rd week of Easter this year

And for 12d. given to 3 players of Doncaster this year

And for 12d. given to 3 players from York on the day of the apostles Philip and James this year

And for 16d. given to 4 players at York on the 6th June this year

And for 20d. to Orthared of Lord Percy harping before the lord Abbot at the transition of St. Germain this year

And for 16d. given to 4 other players on the same day

And for 5s. given to the players of the Earl of Derby in the Octave of the Blessed Mary this year

And for 5s. given to the players of the Duke of Richmond on the vigil of St. Bartholomew this year

And for 6s. 8d. given to the players of the lord King on 2nd September this year

Et de xxd. datis quinque lusoribus de Houdeyn ludentibus coram domino
Abbate in die Sanctorum Innocentum hoc anno.

Et de xxd. datis quinque histrionibus eodem tempore

Et de iijd datis Thome Gresby ludenti coram domino Abbate in die sancti
Johannis evangeliste hoc anno

Et de ijs. datis quinque lusoribus de Ledys ludentibus coram Domino Abbate
hoc anno

Et de iijd datis uni histrioni eodem tempore

Et de xxd datis quinque viris ludentibus coram domino Abbate in die Circum-
cisionis domini hoc anno

These records were discovered by the present Archivist at County Hall,
Beverley, Mr. Higson, and were first printed in his transcription with a short
introduction by me under the title of 'Players at Selby Abbey, Yorks., 1431–
1532', in *Theatre Notebook*, Vol. XII, No. 2, Jan., 1958, pp. 46–53.

And for 20d. given to five players of Howden playing before the lord Abbot on the day of the Holy Innocents this year

For 20d. given to five players at the same time

And for 4d. given to Thomas Gresby playing before the lord Abbot on the day of St. John evangelist this year

And for 2s. given to five players of Leeds playing before the lord Abbot this year

For 4d. given to a player at the same time

And for 20d. given to five men playing before the lord Abbot on the day of the Circumcision of the Lord this year.

APPENDIX D

Transcripts, newly made for this book, of the MS. Proclamations
and Banns of the Chester Plays

A. The Proclamation in the 'Book Containing Fragments of Assembly
   Orders', Chester Town Hall

Note on the transcript. I reproduce the document line for line with the
original. Professor Salter's transcript in *MDC*, pp. 33, 34, is headed 'the
document exactly as I saw it, except that the contractions and abbrevia-
tions are silently expanded'. However, since the expansions are not indicated, since some contractions are not expanded, and since some letters
are supplied which are missing in the MS., I have thought it desirable to
make a fresh transcript which reproduces the MS. in a manner that is both
intelligible and as nearly accurate as print allows. All contractions in the
original are expanded here in brackets, thus (   ). The MS. is badly torn.
I have therefore indicated such tears with brackets, thus [   ]. Where, in
my opinion, the tear has not caused the disappearance of a word or words
from the original, the brackets are left empty; where a word or words
appear to be missing, the brackets contain a number, thus [1]. The
number within the bracket is repeated at the foot of the page and against
it are the readings from transcripts B and C and from Professor Salter's
transcript of this MS. Taken together, the three MSS. of the Proclamation make the order of events in Chester quite clear.

MS. 'A' represents both the situation pre-1532, and the first two stages
of change, (*a*) between 1532 and 1540—*the deletions*; and (*b*) 1540—*the
insertions*. MS. 'C' represents the third change, probably between 1558
and 1575—*the omissions*. MS. 'B' is a late copy of 'A', *c.* 1630, incorporat-
ing the insertions and indicating the deletions, but in modernized spelling.

The Pre-Reformation Banns, transcribed here as C. 2, show one stage
of change. When this and the copies of the Proclamation are compared
with the Banns of 1600 (pp. 132–5 above), the whole unhappy history
of the plays' last days is finally revealed.

      [   ] The p(ro)clamac(i)on for the plaies   [?]
      [   ] newly made by Will(ia)m Newhall   [1]
      [   ] Pentice the first yere of his entre   [?]

Fforasm[2]e as of old tyme not only for the augmentac(i)on & incres[3]
faith of o[4]auyo(r) ih(es)u Crist & to exort the mynd(es) of the co(m)mon people [5]
doctryne th[6]f but also for the co(m)men welth & p(ro)sp(er)itie of this Citie a pla[7]
& div(er)se sto[8] of the bible begynnyng with the creac(i)on & fall of lucifer & endy [9]
iugement of th[10] world to be declared & plaied in the witson weke was devised & [11]

Collations of the words and phrases missing through damage to the MS.

(A.) (Salter, *MDC*, p. 33)	MS. B.	MS. C.
		—
1. ( )	clarke of the	
2. fforasmoche	For as much as	For as myche as
3. incre( )	Increse of the holy and Catholick	increse of the holy and catholyk
4. o( )uyor	our sauiour	our saviyo^r
5. ( )f	to good devotion & holsome	to gud devoc(i)on and holsam
6. th( )f	therof	therof
7. pla( )	play & declaration of	play & declarac(i)on
8. storiez	storyes	stories
9. ( )	ending w(i)th the generall	endyng w^t the gen(er)all
10. e	the	the
11. ma( )	made by one S(i)r	—

[13]omtyme   dissolued

henry ffr(a)unc[12] /\monk of this /\monestry who obteyned & gate of Clement then beyng [14]
daies of p(ar)[15]n & of the Busshop(pe) of Chest(e)r at that tyme beyng xlv daiez of p(ar)don g[16]
thensforth [17] eu(er)y p(er)son resortyng in pecible man(er) with gode devoc(i)on to here & se the [18].
frome tyme to tyme asoft as they shalbe plaied within this Citie and ~~that eu(er)y p(er)son~~ [19]
~~disturbyng the same plaiez in eny man(er) wise to suche tyme as he or they be acursed therof~~ [20]
~~p(e)p(e) Clem[21] bulles unto suche tyme as he or they be absolued therof~~ / which plaiez were [22]
to the hon(or) of god by john arneway then mair of this citie of Chest(e)r & his brether(e)n & holl(e).co(mi)nal[23]
therof to be br[? gh ? 24] forthe declared & plaid at the Cost(es) & charges of the craft(es)men & occupac(i)ons of [25]

12. ( )	frances
13. somtyme	somtyme
14. ( )	for 'beyng', *bushop* of rome a 1000
15. par( )	p(ar)don
16. g( )	graunted from
17. to	& that
18. sai( )	sayd playes
19. ( )	or p(er)sons
20. sai( )	sayd
21. Clement( )	Clemants
22. de(.)	deuised
23. cominalte	cominalty
24. brog( )	brought
25. ( )	the

{ lines 9–11 in brackets }

{ lines 6–11 omitted }

deuised
comynaltie
braught
the

342

said Cit[26] whiche hitherunto haue frome tyme to tyme used & p(er)formed the same accordi[27]

Wherfore Maist(er) mair in the kynges name straitly chargeth & co(m)maundeth that eu(er)y p(er)son & [28]

of what asta[29] degre or condic(i)on so eu(er) he [30] they be resortyng to the said plaiez do use th[31]

pecible with[32]akyng eny assault affrey or other disturbans wherby the same [33]

shalbe disturbed & that no man(er) p(er)son or p(er)sons who so eu(er) he or they be do use or we[34]

unlaufull wepons within the p(re)cynct of the said Citie duryng the tyme of the said p[35]

not only upon payn of cursyng by the auctorite of the said Pope Clement bull (ce) but als [36] opon

payn of enprisonment of their bodiez & makyng fyne to the kyng at maist(er) mairs pleasure

[37] god saue the kyng & m(aiste)r mair etc.

p(er) me W. Newhall fact(um) temp(or)e Will(ielm)o
Sneyde drap(er) s(ecun)do temp(or)e sui maioral(itatis)

Citty	Citie
Accordingly	Accordingly
& p(er)sons	& p(er)sons
estate	astate
or	or
themselues	theym selff
w(it)hout making	without making
playes	playes
weare	weyre
playes	playes
also	—
(last eight words omitted)	/and
line 20 in brackets	lines 19 & 20 omitted.

26. Citee
27. accordi( )
28. ( )
29. astate
30. ( )
31. th( )
32. with(out m)akyng
33. ( )
34. we( )
35. p( )
36. also
37. and

343

B. Copy of the Proclamation in B.M. MS. Harl. 2013. f. 1ˣ

The Proclamation for Whits(u)ne playes made by W(illia)m Newall clarke of the pentice. 24 H 8. W(illia)m Snead 2ⁿᵈ year maior.

For as much as oulde tyme not only for the augmentation and Increese of the holy & Catholick faith of our Sauiour Jesu Crist & to exort the mindes of comon people to good devotion & holsome doctrine thereof but also for the comonwelth & p(ro)sperity of this Citty a play & declaration of diuers storyes of the bible begening w(i)th the Creation & fall of lucifer & ending w(i)th the generall judgment of the world to be declared & played in the whitsune weeke was deuised & made by one S(i)r henry frances somtyme Moonck of this monastrey disolued who obtayning & gat of clemant then bushop of rome a 1000 dayes of p(ar)don & of the bushop of Chester at that tyme 40 dayes of p(ar)don granted from thensforth tyme to tyme as oft as the (*sic*) shall be played within the sayd citty [& that euery p(er)son or p(er)sons distur-bing the sayd playes in any maner wise to be accused by the Authority of the sayd pope Clemants bulles untill such tyme as he or they be absoloued therof] w(hi)ch playes were deuised to the honor of god by John Arnway then maior of this citty of Chester his bretheren & whole cominalty therof to be brought forth declared & played at the cost & charges of the craftesmen & occupations of the sayd Citty w(hi)ch hitherunto haue from tyme to tyme used & p(er)formed the same. Accordingly wherfore Mʳ Maior in the Kings name stratly chargeth & comandeth that euery p(er)son & p(er)sons of what estate degree or condition so euer he or they be resorting to the sayd playes do use themselues peaciblie w(it)hout making any asault affray or other disturbance wherby the same playes shall be disturbed & that no maner of p(er)son or p(er)sons who so euer he or they be do use or weare any unlawfull weapons within the p(re)cinct of the sayd citty during the tyme of the sayd playes [not only upon payn of cursing by Authority of the sayd pope Clemants bulles but also] upon payne of imprisonment of theire bodyes and making fine to the King at Mʳ mairs pleasure.

344

C (1) Randle Holme's copy of the Proclamation (post-1540), transcribed from B.M. MS. MS. Harl. 2150. f. 86.

Ffor as myche as of old tyme not only for the Augmentac(i)on & incresse of the holy and catholyk ffaith of our saviyᵒʳ cryst Jh(es)u and to exhort the myndes of the comen peple to gud deuoc(i)on and holsam doctryne therof but Also for the comen welth and p(ro)speritie of this Citie A play and declarac(i)on of many and dyuers stories of the bible begynnyng wᵗ the creac(i)on & fall of lucifer & endyng wᵗ the gen(er)all jugement of the world to be declared and playde now in the whisun (sic) weke. whiche playes were deuised to the honoʳ of god by John Arneway sometyme Maire of this Citie of Chester & his bretheryn & holl comynaltie therof to be braught forth declared and plaid at the costys of the craftys men and occupac(i)ons of the said Citie whiche herunto from tyme to tyme usyd and p(er)fo(r)med the same. Accordingly wherfore mʳ mair in the kinges name straitly chargith and comaundyth that any p(er)son and p(er)sons of what astate degree or condic(i)on so eu(er) he or they be resorting to the said playes do use theym self peccably without making any Assault Afrey or other disturbans wherby the same playes shalbe disturbed & that no man(er) p(er)son or p(er)sons who euer he or they be do use or weyre eny unlaufull w(ea)pons wᵗin the p(re)cinct of the said Citie duryng the tyme of the said playes Apon peyne of imprisonyment of theire bodies and making fyne to the king at and

Maisteres Maires pleasure ʌ god saue the kyng, Mʳ maist(er) Mayer, etc.

345

APPENDIX D

C (2) Randle Holme's copy of the Pre-Reformation Banns noting deletions made, presumably post-1531; transcribed from B.M. MS.
Harl. 2150. ff. 86–88b.†

Lordinges Royall and Reuerentt
Louely ladies that here be hentt
Sou(ver)eigne Citizins hether am I sent
A message for to say.

I pray you all that be p(re)sent
That you will here w^t good intent
And lett your eares to be lent
Hertfull (*sic* ?harkful) I you pray.

Our wurshipffull mair of this Citie
With all this Royall co(mmon)altie
Solem pagens ordent hath he
At the Ff(east) of whytsonday tyde.

How eu(er)y craft in his decree
bryng forth their playes Solemplye
I shall declare you brefely
Yf ye will abyde a while.

Then follows the list of companies, starting with the tanners.
The list specifies (f. 88) that

The wurshipffull wyffys of this towne
Ffynd of our lady thassumpcon

and concludes with the ten stanzas printed below

Sou(ver)eigne syres to you I say
And to all this ffeyre cuntrie
That played shalbe this godely play
In the whitson weke

That is brefely for to sey
Uppon monday tuysday and wennysday
Whoo lust to see theym he may
And non of theym to seke

Erazed in the
booke
Also maister Maire of this Citie
W^t all his bretheryn accordingly
A Solempne p(ro)cession ordent hath he
To be done to the best.

346

Appon the day of corpus (ch)r(ist)i
The blessed Sacrament caried shalbe
And A play sett forth by the clergye*
In hono^r of the fest.

Many torches there may you see
Marchuntys and craftys of this Citie
By order passing in theire Degree
A goodly sight that day.

They come from saynt maries on the hill
The churche of saynt Johns untill
And there the sacrament live (*sic* ?leave) they will
The south (*sic* ?sooth) as I you say

Whoo so comyth these playes to see
With good deuoc(i)on merelye
Hertely welcome shall he be
And haue right good chere

Sur John Aneway was maire of this Citie
When these playes were begon truly
God grant us merely
And see theym many a yere

Now haue I done that lyeth in me
To p(ro)cure this solempnitie
That these playes contynued may be
And well sett fourth Alway

erazed
Jh(es)u crist that syttys on hee
And his blessyd mother marie
Saue all this goodely company
And kepe you nyght and day

I would like to acknowledge the help received in preparing the Chester documents from the archivist at the Town Hall, Miss Mary Finch.

* It will be seen that when these Banns were written there were *two* religious plays in Chester—a single, unspecified play performed by the clergy on Corpus Christi Day and the cyclic plays performed at Whitsun by the guilds. The same Banns served for the announcement of both originally, but the inference to be drawn from the erasure marks is that the former was suppressed shortly after the break with Rome.

† Extracts from the Post Reformation Banns are printed in Ch. IV, pp. 133–5 above.

APPENDIX E

A LIST OF STREET PAGEANT THEATRES

tabulated to illustrate the development of Pageant devices into conventions suitable for stage purposes, and giving the principal source of information about each.

Date	Place	Occasion	Devices	Station	Source
1207	London	Reception of Emperor Otho.	1. Citizens adorn themselves	Processional Riding	Matt. Westminster
1236	London	Marriage of Henry III & Eleanor of Provence	1. & 2. Streets decorated with coloured cloths, garlands, torches etc.	Processional Riding	Matt. Paris
1298	London	Edward I's victorious return from Falkirk	1. 2 & 3. Animals,—in trade symbolism	Processional Riding	Stow
1313	Paris	Visit of Ed. II & the King of Navarre	1. 2 & 4. Excerpts from 'mystères'	Procession with halts?	Godefroy de Paris
1313	London	Birth of Ed. III	1. 2 & 5. A ship,—in trade symbolism 6. Heraldic decoration	Processional Riding	Walsingham
1377	London	Richard II's coronation	1, 2, 6 & 7. Conduit used as platform stage 8. Music, singing,—anthems 9. Castle structure 10. Angel offers crown mechanically 11. Mimed direct address	Riding & a halt before one platform—the Great Conduit	Walsingham
1389	Paris	Reception of Isabella of Bavaria	1, 2a (tapestry with stories) 3a (in romance symbolism), 6, 7, 7a (gate arches) 8, 9, 10, 11 12. Mock Battle, Ric. I, v. Saracens 13. An Interior represented by draped curtains 14. Artificial tree	Procession with halts to view performances a. 1st Porte St. Denis b. Fountain Rue St. Denis c. Steps of Trinity Church d. 2nd Porte St. Denis e. Steps of St. James Chapel Porte du Chastelet	Froissart

1392	London	Richard II restores civic liberties	1, 2*a*, 3*a*, 7, 7*a*, 8, 9, 10, 11 14 & 15 allegory,—Scriptural 16 God represented 17 Speeches,—in Latin 10 & 18 Two level stage representing Heaven & Earth. 6	Procession with performances 1. Gt. Conduit 2. Little Conduit 3. Temple Bar	Ric. Maydiston
1399	Saragosa	Don Martin I's coronation			De Milá
1414	Saragosa	Don Fernando de Antequerra's coronation	8, 9 &		W. M. Shoemaker Gesta Hen. V.
1415	London	Henry V's victorious return from Agincourt	19. A disc is made to revolve mechanically 1, 2, 3*a*, 6, 7, 7*a*, 8*a*, Roundels & Minstrelsy 9, 11, 15, 17, & 20. Giants	Procession with performances 1 & 4 Drawbridge 5 Tun in Cornhill 6 Cross in Cheapside	
1431	Paris	Henry VI's French Coronation	1, 2, 3*b* (Hunting Scene) 4 4*a* (Miracle Floats) 5*a* (in romance allegory) 6*a* (Historical allegory) 7, 7*a*, 8, 8*a*, 11 12*a* (Wildmen and Women) 21 The Nine Worthies	Procession with performances 4, *b, c, d, e,* & *f.* *g.* Steps of the church of the Holy Innocents	Monstrelet
1432	London	Henry VI's return	1, 2, 3*a*, 6, 7, 7*a*, 8*a*, 9, 14*a* (in trade symbolism) 14*b* (in historical allegory) 14*a* (in scriptural allegory) 15, 15*a* (moral) 15*b* (historical) 16. 17*a* (in English) 22. Liberal Sciences 23. Colour Symbolism 24. Single authorship	Procession with performances 7. London Bridge South 4, 5, 1, 6, & 2 8. Standard in Cornhill	Lydgate
1445	London	Reception of Margaret of Anjou	1, 2, 4, 5, 6, 7, 8*a*, 9, 15, 16, 17*a*, & 24	7, 4, 5, 1, 6	Lydgate

After 1445, with the exception of recourse to mythological allegory of neo-classical inspiration, tradition governs both the subject-matter used and the methods of representing it. Similarly the sites chosen from which to present the pageants remain the same, with the addition of the Conduit in Gracechurch St. in the sixteenth century. The best printed list of all the English Pageants, Provincial as well as Metropolitan, is provided in R. Withington's *English Pageantry*, Vol. I.

APPENDIX F

Lists of specimen items extracted from French and
English Expense Accounts relating to the medieval
religious stage.

Extracts, from printed sources, relating to expenses incurred in performances of religious plays for comparison with the full account of expenses for the Pageant on London Bridge, 1464, listed in Appendix B.

List 1

Specimen items from the expense accounts of the *Mystère des Trois
Doms*, performed at Romans, May 1509, extracted from M. Giraud's
printed transcript of the treasurer's accounts.

Et Tornefol vi liv. iij quarts coste par compte fet .	iijfl. ijs. ixd.
Plus ocre jaune	vjs.
Plus feruza (*i.e. ceruse—white lead*) xv liv. . .	vjfl. iijs.
Plus espongues xij liv.	ivfl. vjs.
Plus follies de fert blanches cc monte . .	xvjfl. iijs.
Plus follies dor fauces troys grosses, monte . .	vfl. iijs.
Plus orpiment (i.e. sulphur paint) vi liv. . . .	jfl. vjs.
Plus vermelhon vi liv.	ijfl. ijs.
Plus or fin c. monte.	xvifl.
Plus or paty vi cc.	vijfl. vjs.
Plus argent j c.	xs.
Plus pour plusieurs pos et houles (*i.e. bowls*) de terra .	vs. vd.
Plus pour cordes et fils de Polmart . . .	ijs vijd.
Plus pour j liv. et demi syes (*i.e. soies de porc—pig bristles*) pour faire les pinseaux (*i.e. paint-brushes*)	js. vjd.
Plus troys liv. inde (*i.e. indigo*) que vallent . .	iijfl. ixs.
Plus sinople j once	ijs.
Plus asur iv onces	jfl.

Other items listed include

Large quantities of nut and olive oil—presumably to mix with paint.
Sulphur and gunpowder.
Paper of various sorts and colours.
Glue and alum.
Images.
Actors' hand properties.
Drinks and refreshments for workmen.

APPENDIX F

For discussion of this play and its production, see Ch. IV, pp. 164–166 and Ch. VIII, pp. 302–306 above.

List 2

Items from the expense accounts of Guilds performing religious plays at Coventry, York and Canterbury.

(a) *Coventry:* Extracts from Sharp's *Dissertation* which, in regard to these records, has become source after the destruction of the originals in the bombing of 1940.

The Smiths' Company

1451	It(em) payd for vj skynnys of whitled' (*white leather*) to godds g(ar)ment	xviijᵈ
1477	It(em) for Assadyn*; silv(er) papur & gold papur, gold foyle & grene ffoyle	ijˢ jᵈ
1480	P(aid) for a quart of red wyn for pilat	ijᵈ
1499	It(em) payde for colours and gold foyle & sylv(er) foyle for ij myttyrs.	
1501	It(em) p(ai)d to the p(a)ynt(er) for his warkemonchipe	xxjˢ vijᵈ
,,	It(e)m for v ʒardes off blowe bokeram	ijˢ xjᵈ
1554	Payd for a bysschops taberd of scarlet that we bowght in the trente (*Trinity*) church	xˢ†

The Cappers' Company

1543	P(ai)d for a lace ‡ of Irone to compas (th)e beame	xjᵈ
1553	P(ai)d to (th)e carpent(er) for tendyng on (th)e pageant	xijᵈ
1565	It(em) for a hoke of Iren	xvjd
,,	It(em) payd for reprasyons (*repairs*) of the pagyand, tymber, nayles & iren	vijˢ viijᵈ
,,	It(em) payd for rosshes & small corde	iijᵈ
,,	P(ai)d for canvas	vjᵈ

The Drapers' Company

1538	It(e)m payd for kepyng the wynde (*windlass*)	vjᵈ
1543	Payd for a new roppe for the wynd	xviijᵈ
1557	Paid for a peyre of gloves for god	ijᵈ

* Tinsel: Ben Jonson uses it in this sense, spelt arsedine, *B.F.* II.2.
† This entry indicates the source of many actors' costumes after the Reformation.
‡ i..e a cross-beam for the windlass (lit. wind-lace).

APPENDIX F

(b) *York:* Extracts from Davies' *York Records.*

Corpus Christi Plays

1397   Pro clavis ferri ad emendacionem pagine   . v^d
        (For iron bolts to mend the pageant)

,,   Roberto Paton pro factura pagine in opere car-
          pentario per duos dies   .   . ij^d
        (To Robert Paton for two days' work as a car-
        penter on the pageant)

St. George's Day Show

1554   Item, payd to Mr. Thornton for sylver paper for
        skottchons and for oyle and varmolon
        (*vermilion*) to the same   .   . iij^s iij^d

,,   Item, payd for vj yerdes of canves to the pagyant $iiij^s$

,,   Item, payd to William Paynter for payntyng the
        canves and pagyant   .   .   . xvj^d

(c) *Canterbury:* Specimen extracts from Chambers' *Med. Stage, ii.*

St. Thomas' Day Pageant

1504/5   Paied to Sampson Carpenter and his man hewyng and
        squeryng of tymber for the Pagent.

,,   For gunpowder.

,,   For forgyng and makyng the knyghtes harnes (*armour*).

1505–37   Paied to hym that turned the vyce (*windlass*).

,,   Paied for wyre for the vyce of the Angell.

,,   For a new leder bag for the blode.

,,   For wasshyng of the albe and other clothys abowte the
        Auter (*altar*) and settyng on agayn the apparell.

I must emphasize that both of these lists, French and English, are not
direct copies of complete accounts, but only of specimen items in such
accounts selected and set out here to give some idea of both the variety of
materials used on the medieval religious stage and the colourful nature
of the product presented to audiences.

Comparison may usefully be made here with Tudor Revels Accounts
some of which have survived and are now in the P.R.O. For details see
Chambers, *Eliz. Stage*, iv, pp. 131 *et seq.*

APPENDIX G

A Transcript of the Title-page of
Thomas Preston's play
CAMBISES

The play was entered in the Stationers' Register in 1569 by John Alde. Two editions were printed during the sixteenth century, the first by John Alde and the second by his son Edward Alde, but neither of them is dated.

The Dramatis Personae number thirty-eight characters, and the division of parts shows that a company of six men and two boys was thought sufficient to handle them all.

The full text of the second edition is printed by J. Q. Adams in *Chief Pre-Shakespearean Dramas*, Boston, 1925.

A LAMENTABLE TRAGEDIE

MIXED FULL OF PLESANT MIRTH, CONTAINING

THE LIFE OF CAMBISES, KING OF PERCIA

FROM THE BEGINNING OF HIS KINGDOME, VNTO

HIS DEATH, HIS

ONE GOOD DEEDE OF EXECUTION, AFTER THAT MANY

WICKED DEEDES AND TYRANNOUS MURDERS,

COMMITTED

BY AND THROUGH HIM, AND LAST OF ALL, HIS

ODIOUS DEATH BY GODS IUSTICE APPOINTED.

DONE IN SUCH ORDERS AS FOLLOWETH.

BY THOMAS PRESTON.

353

DRAMATIS PERSONAE

CAMBISES, King of Persia.
SMIRDIS, brother of the king.
SISAMNES, the judge.
OTIAN, his son.
PRAXASPES, a councellor.
YOUNG CHILD, his son.
LORDS,
KNIGHTS, } in attendance on the king.
QUEEN, wife of Cambises.
WAITING-MAID, attending the queen.
WIFE OF PRAXASPES.

SHAME.
AMBIDEXTER.
COUNCELL.
ATTENDANCE.
DILIGENCE.
PREPARATION.

SMALL HABILITY.
COMMONS CRY.
COMMONS COMPLAINT.
TRIALL.
PROOF.
EXECUTION.
CRUELTY.
MURDER.

HUF,
RUF, } ruffianly soldiers.
SNUF,
MERETRIX, their companion.
HOB,
LOB, } clownish countrymen.
MARION-MAY-BE-GOOD, Hob's
     wife.
VENUS.
CUPID.

THE SCENE: Persia.

THE DIUISION OF THE PARTS

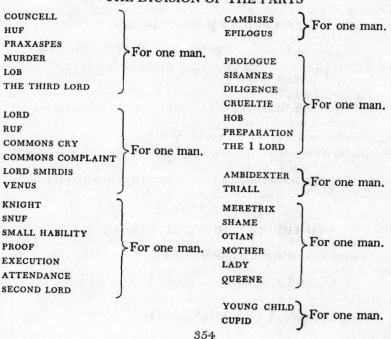

COUNCELL
HUF
PRAXASPES
MURDER
LOB
THE THIRD LORD
} For one man.

LORD
RUF
COMMONS CRY
COMMONS COMPLAINT
LORD SMIRDIS
VENUS
} For one man.

KNIGHT
SNUF
SMALL HABILITY
PROOF
EXECUTION
ATTENDANCE
SECOND LORD
} For one man.

CAMBISES
EPILOGUS
} For one man.

PROLOGUE
SISAMNES
DILIGENCE
CRUELTIE
HOB
PREPARATION
THE 1 LORD
} For one man.

AMBIDEXTER
TRIALL
} For one man.

MERETRIX
SHAME
OTIAN
MOTHER
LADY
QUEENE
} For one man.

YOUNG CHILD
CUPID
} For one man.

354

APPENDIX H

Plays for Queen Elizabeth I at Oxford, 1566

The description of the arrangements for these entertainments by John Bereblock, an eyewitness, has long been available in print, but in Latin.* L. B. Campbell in *Scenes and Machines on the English Stage* (1923) commented on this account but did not supply the translation on which the commentary was based. Judging from the conclusions she drew from it I can only think it was inaccurate. F. S. Boas likewise quoted Bereblock's Latin at length in *University Drama in the Tudor Age* (1914) and supplemented this account with extracts from another eyewitness record, the Twyne MS.: he even referred, in passing, to a free translation by Mr. Durand (P.M.L.A., Vol. xx, 1905, pp. 502–528), but did not remedy its defects by supplying an accurate one himself.

I am myself convinced that it is impossible to visualize the arrangements without the aid of an accurate translation of the Latin. In attempting to supply one now I would like to record the help I have received from Mr. Dacre Balsdon and Mrs. Dora Pym in regard to the text, and to the Librarian at Christ Church, Mr. W. G. Hiscock, in regard to the topography of the College in 1566: for an understanding of the latter is vital to any success with the former.

The Queen was housed in the Old Deanery which forms the east block of Tom Quad. The area, some forty feet square, separating this block from the southern block of the Quadrangle containing the Hall (which lies at right angles to the Old Deanery) has been modified twice since 1566, and virtually nothing is known of its physical appearance at that time. However, it is still possible to see the door cut high in the wall of the Old Deanery and at the same level above the ground as the Great Hall. This door has long since been blocked in. It is thus possible to see where the Queen came from to attend the plays. This knowledge is vital when attempting to reconstruct the arrangements from Bereblock's Latin description. Here is the relevant extract, verbatim:

'Nocte adveniente, spectacula apparatissima data sunt, quae non nullis, qui eadem otiosi tota die expectarant, pro mercedis cumulo claritate sua fuerunt. Nihilque jam pretiosius vel magnificentius excogitari potuit illorum apparatione atque instructione.

'Primo ibi ab ingenti solido pariete patefacto aditu, proscenium insigne fuit, ponsque ab eo ligneus pensilis, subliciis impositus, parvo et perpolito tractu per transversos gradus ad magnam Collegii aulam

* See Notes and Sources, Ch. VII, note 49, p. 384 below.

protrahitur; festa fronde coelato pictoque umbraculo exornatur, ut per eum, sine motu et perturbatione prementis vulgi, Regina posset, quasi aequabili gressu, ad praeparata spectacula contendere.

'Erat aula laqueari aurato, et picto arcuatoque introrsus tecto, granditate ac superbia sua veteris Romani palatii amplitudinem, et magnificentia imaginem antiquitatis diceres imitari. Parte illius superiori, qua occidentem respicit, theatrum excitatur magnum et erectum, gradibusque multis excelsum. Juxta omnes parietes podia et pegmata extructa sunt, subsellia eisdem superiora fuerunt multorum fastigiorum, unde viri illustres ac matronae suspicerentur, et populus circum cira ludos prospicere potuit. Lucernae, lichni, candelaeque ardentes clarissimam ibi lucem fecerunt.

'Tot luminaribus, ramulis ac orbibus divisis, totque passim funalibus inaequali splendore, incertam praebentibus lucem, splendebat locus, ut et instar diei micare, et spectaculorum claritatem adjuvare candore summo visa sint. Ex utroque scenae latere comoedis ac personatis magnifica palatia aedesque apparatissimae extruuntur. Sublime fixa sella fuit, pulvinaribus ac tapetiis ornata aureoque umbraculo operata. Reginae destinatus locus erat.'

The first paragraph offers no particular difficulty in translation:

'At nightfall sumptuous spectacles were presented which by their excellence amply rewarded those who had been eagerly awaiting them through the idle moments of the day. No cost or care had been spared in the preparation of their equipment and arrangement.'

It is in the second paragraph that trouble starts. This centres on the words *aditu, proscenium* and *pons . . . pensilis*. Bereblock says: 'First there was a magnificent *proscenium*, an entrance having been cut in the great solid wall . . .' His use of *paries* instead of *murus* for wall indicates clearly that the wall in question was that of a building—i.e. her lodgings in the Old Deanery—and this we can still see. The word *proscenium* means literally 'a platform' and hence 'a stage' in the Roman sense. * It does not indicate the presence of 'a proscenium-arch' as Miss Campbell appears to have thought. In determining what exactly Bereblock was describing we are assisted by two fragments of evidence, one internal to his text and one external. First, Bereblock's description moves in a logical progression via a paragraph of general introduction to the more particularized subject of the Queen's approach to the Hall, thence to the appearance of the Hall and so to the stage. The latter is described specifically by the Latin word *scena* and, more generally, as *theatrum*. I can only think he intended the word *proscenium* to describe another platform external to the Hall. This is partly confirmed by evidence from a new source brought to my notice by Mr. Hiscock: Bodl. MS. Top. e.9, which details sums of money paid

* De Witt uses the word in this sense on his famous drawing of the Swan Theatre. See Vol. II, 1576–1660, Pt. 1, Plate VIII.

to workmen on this occasion. One item is payment for taking down the stage, scaffolds, bridge and a porch. What is this porch—so clearly an independent item—if not Bereblock's *proscenium?* As an assumption it at least has the advantage of giving sense to Bereblock's Latin syntax. If this is so, we may visualize the Queen stepping out from her lodgings through a newly cut door on to a specially prepared platform from which she could be seen but not jostled by the *'vulgus'*, the crowds that invariably gather to watch royalty. 'From this "porch" or platform (*ab eo*) hangs a wooden bridge (*pons ligneus pensilis*) that is supported on posts (*subliciis impositus*) and prolonged (*protrahitur*) by a small highly polished extension (*parvo et perpolito tractu*) "over" or more literally "at right angles to" the steps (*per transversos gradus*) leading up to the Great Hall of the College.'

This may be expressed diagrammatically in groundplan as follows:

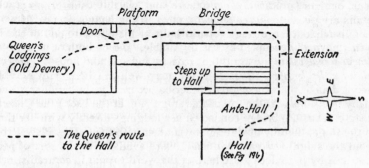

FIGURE 19a.

It is thus reasonably clear how she obtained access to the plays (*ad praeparata spectacula*) with leisurely gait (*quasi aequabili gressu*) without being jostled or disturbed by (*sine motu et perturbatione*) the dense crowd (*prementis vulgi*). Bereblock then takes us inside the Hall which, he tells us, 'was panelled in gold and painted within the arch of the roof: and you would admit that, in its dimensions, it resembled the scale and grandeur of an ancient Roman palace, not to say the splendour of antiquity itself.'

Here it should be noted that it is the Hall and not the stage that is likened to a Roman palace, and that in the most general terms.*

The next major difficulty is presented by the two words *theatrum* and *scena*, taken in conjunction with the phrase *parte illius superiori, qua occidentem respicit.* The question that arises is whether *scena* and *theatrum* are used synonymously, or whether deliberately to indicate different objects. If the latter, then there is at least no doubt that *scena* means stage

* Miss Campbell appears to have taken this passage to indicate the use of a Serlian (or at least neo-Terentian) proscenium-arched stage.

in our sense of that word, the acting area: but *theatrum* is ambiguous. It can mean stage; it can mean auditorium; it can mean both at once. The phrase *parte illius superiori, qua occidentem respicit* is equally ambiguous. Literally it means, 'in the upper part of it (i.e. the Hall), which looks back on the west'. The word *superus*, in the context of place, usually indicates a raised area; in classical Latin, a tribunal or rostrum. In the case of a college hall *superus* can surely mean only upper in the sense of the high table end. At Christ Church this is the west end of the Hall—just as the altar in the Cathedral is 'at the east end'. It is there, then, at the west end of the Hall, that the *theatrum*, 'large and raised, is erected' (*excitatur magnum et erectum*). The fact that Bereblock then goes on to describe the seating arrangements in the next sentence, saying that 'scaffolds and benches' (*podia et pegmata*) had been built 'adjoining all the walls' (*juxta omnes parietes*), inclines me to believe that the *theatrum*, raised by many steps, or tiers (*gradibusque multis excelsum*), was the auditorium of which details are given (*podia et pegmata*, etc.) in the next sentence. If so, we may visualize a large stage (*scena*) built at the opposite end of the Hall to that normally occupied by the high table, 'and on both of its sides' (*ex utroque scenae latere*) 'magnificent palaces and splendid houses' (*magnifica palatia aedesque apparatissimae*). We may well ask here why Bereblock uses a double plural except to describe accurately the familiar scene of 'many mansions'. At the top of this stage (i.e. at the back) the Queen sat in state. Thus the bridge connected her lodgings directly with her throne on the stage, thereby obviating any contact with the public. Places 'round about the stage' (*circum circa ludos*) were available to the sort of people described by Bereblock's use here of the word *populus* in contradistinction to *viri illustres ac matronae*. The latter are said to have occupied the scaffolds and benches adjacent to the walls, the higher portions of which were divided into separate seats, or boxes (*multorum fastigiorum*).

It only remains now to supply a diagram of these arrangements in the Hall and provide a coherent translation of the whole passage:

'At nightfall sumptuous spectacles were presented which by their excellence amply rewarded those who had been eagerly awaiting them through the idle moments of the day. Nothing more costly and magnificent could be devised than the equipment and arrangement of these shows.

'First there was a magnificent platform approached by an entrance cut in the great solid wall (*of her lodgings*): from the platform a wooden suspension bridge supported on posts and prolonged by a small highly polished extension over the steps up to the Great Hall of the College. The bridge was covered with an awning embossed and painted with festive leaves, so that the Queen could make her way easily to the spectacles prepared for her without being jostled or disturbed by the dense crowd (*below*).

'The Hall was panelled in gold and painted within the arch of the roof: and you would admit that in its dimensions it resembled the scale and

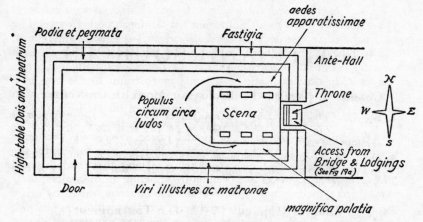

FIGURE 19b.   The dimensions of the stage are not provided, but it
probably occupied a larger area than suggested in this diagram.

grandeur of an ancient Roman palace, not to say the splendour of antiquity itself. In the west end of the Hall a large raised auditorium had
been built, rising in many tiers with rostrums and scaffolds adjoining all
the walls. The upper seats on these scaffolds were partitioned into many
boxes in which illustrious spectators of both sexes could be seen. Space
was available round about the stage for other people (? *commoners and
undergraduates*) to view the plays. Lamps, torches and candles were
burning to illuminate the Hall. With so many lamps arranged in branches
and circles and so many flickering candles here and there offering varied
light, the whole place was bright as day and added brilliance to the plays.
On both sides of the stage splendid palaces and stately houses were
erected for the actors. Raised on high was set a throne covered with arras
and a cloth of estate. This was for the Queen's use.'

NOTES AND SOURCES

Chapter I, pages 3–12. Prologue: Monkish Darkness

1. See G. Cohen, *Le Livre du conduite et compte des Dépenses pour le Mystère de la Passion Joué à Mons en 1501*, Paris, 1925; also A-T de Giradot, *Mystère des Actes des Apôtres (Bourges)*, Paris, 1854.

2. Of quite outstanding usefulness in this respect is the unique bibliography of Royal Entries supplied by G. R. Kernodle, *From Art to Theatre*, Chicago, 1944.

Chapter II, pages 13–14. The Tournament

1. This subject is discussed at length by C. du Fresne, Sieur Du Cange, 'Des armes à outrance, etc.', edited by C. Leber in *Collections des meilleurs dissertations, notices et traités particuliers relatifs à l'histoire de France* (Paris, 1828), iii, 2. See also J. Strutt, *The Sports and Pastimes of the People of England* (ed. W. Hone, London, 1830), pp. 129–133; N. Denholm-Young, 'The Tournament in the Thirteenth Century', *Studies in Mediaeval History presented to F. M. Powicke* (1948), p. 241, n. 1.

2. 'Ars enim belandi, si non praeluditur cum necessaria fuerit, non habetur.' C. du Fresne, Sieur Du Cange, 'L'Origine et de l'usage des tournois', edited by M. Petitot in *Collection complète des mémoires relatifs à l'histoire de France* (Paris, 1824), iii, 109, quoting Cassiodorus, I, 1, ep. 40. For the political significance of early Tournaments see Denholm-Young, *The Tournament*, p. 240.

3. 'Non potest athleta magnos spiritus ad certamen afferre, qui nunquam suggillatus est. Ille qui sanguinem suum vidit, cuius dentes crepuerunt sub pugno, ille qui supplantus adversarium toto tulit corpore, nec proiecit animum proiectus, qui quoties cecidit contumacior surrexit cum magna spe descendit ad pugnam.' C. du Fresne, Sieur Du Cange, *L'Origine des tournois*, p. 119.

4. See C. Von Hefele, *Histoire des Conciles* (Paris, 1869–73), vii, pp. 209, 239, 308, 507, etc. Pope Alexander III in the Lateran Council of 1179 said of them: 'Those detestable assemblies of a market day or festival which are generally called tournaments. . . . And if anyone shall there meet his death, no matter if he has time to repent, even so the Church denies him burial rites.' See also Denholm-Young, *The Tournament*, p. 243.

5. See du Fresne, Sieur Du Cange, *L'Origine des tournois*, p. 127.

6. 'Qu'entre Pentescote e quaresme/Pristrent cheval(i)ers cent e treis/ Estre chevals, estre harneis.' P. Meyer, *L'Histoire de Guillaume le Maréchal, Compte de Striguil et de Pembroke, Régent d'Angleterre de 1216 à 1219, poème Français* (Paris, 1891–1901), 3 vols., I, p. 125. In a des-

cription of a similar Tournament in the reign of Henry I between Normans and English at Mt. St. Michel and at which three nephews of King Henry I were present, it is said that '. . . either side entered *Pesle-mesle* together'. A. Favyn, *The Theater of Honour and Knighthood* (London, 1623), ii, 488.

7. Matthew Paris, *Chronica Majora* (Rolls Ed.), ii, 407: 'Eodem tempore (1194) rex Ricardus in Angliam transiens statuit per loca certa Torneamenta fieri, hac fortasse inductus ratione, ut milites regni undique concurrentes vires suas flexis in girum fraenis experirentur; ut, si bellum adversus Crucis inimicos vel etiam finitimos movere decreverint, agiliores ad praelium et exercitatiores redderentur.' See also Roger Wendover, *Flores Historiarum* (ed. Henry Coxe, 1841), iii, 85; Denholm-Young, *The Tournament*, p. 241, n. i.

8.
> 'Celui en costé sez Maisieres,
> Apele-on Jehan de Rosieres.
> Cil-là sont de delà la mer,
> Einglois; si fouit moult à amer;
> Chevalier preu, saige et honeste;
> Si sont venu véoir la feste.'

Les Tournois de Chauvenci, ed. P. I. J. Delmotte (Valenciennes, 1835), lines 363–8.

9. For Tournaments in the Middle East, see *Notes & Queries* (3rd series), vi, 288; C. du Fresne, 'Des Cottes d'Armes', ed. C. Leber in *Collection des meilleurs dissertations* (Paris, 1828), iii, 306–308; also *Gestes des Chiprois*, ed. G. Raynaud, Geneva, 1887.

10. *A Perambulation of Kent* (London, 1590), p. 448. See *B.M. MS. Harl. 293, No. 123*: 'Hoc est breve Dño Regis R.I. Missum Dño. Cantuariensi. de Concessione Torneamenta in Anglia.' Also *B.M. MS. Harl. 69, f. 62*:

11. Denholm-Young, *The Tournament*, pp. 245 et seq.

12. *Ibid.*, pp. 257–264.

13. *Archaeologia*, xvii, 297, note a. The original is to be found in *B.M. MS. Rawlinson, 277* and a printed transcript in *Statutes of the Realm* (ed. 1810). For the equivalent French Ordinance see A. Favyn *THK*, ii, 491.

14. See Ruth Clyne, 'The Influence of Romances on Tournaments of the Middle Ages', *Speculum*, 1945, xx, pp. 204–211. Also, Denholm-Young, *The Tournament*, p. 254.

15. Specimens of this procedure may be found in the 'Pas de la Bergière' (see p. 22 above); the 'Pas d'Armes de l'Arbre de Charlemagne' in Olivier de la Marche, *Mémoires* (ed. Henri Beaume, Paris, 1883), i, 290; the 'Pas d'Armes de l'Arbre d'or', in *B.M. MS. Harl. 69, f. 128* & *B.M. MS. Lansdowne 285*, f. 26.

16.
> 'En loges, après en salles,
> Et en fueillies grans comme hales,
> Dressa-on tables et trétians.

16. (*cont.*)

> Don mangier ne fas autre conte;
> Et tant i ot fait à devise,
> Et de viande et de servise.
> Pou mangerent, assez chanterent
> Après mangier, en piez leverent.
> Tument tables, tument tretel.
> Trompent flaiot, tabors, fretel
> Estoient bien en lor saison.
> Lors comança une chanson
> Madame de Chini première
> Por ce qu'estoit chief et banière,
> Et raliance de la feste,
> Qui tant parest riche et honeste.
> De chanter chaseuns cuers s'avance:
> "Mal déhait ait qui ne vient en la dance."
> Qui dont véist dances venir,
> Bachelers par les mains tenir,
> Bel li samblast et bel li fust
> Sans contredit et sans refust,
> N'i a celui que ne fes joie.'

Les Tournois de Chauvenci, ed. cit., lines 1317–1349.

17. Apart from the somewhat sketchy accounts given by the various Chroniclers, most of the information concerning English Tournaments is to be found in 'The Book of Certaine Triumphs' (*B.M. MS. Harl. 69*) and in *B.M. MS. Lansdowne 285* which contain a variety of documents relating to Tournaments and the Court of Chivalry.

18. See Denholm-Young, *The Tournament*, pp. 265–267. See also R. S. Loomis, 'Edward I, Arthurian Enthusiast', *Speculum*, 1953, xxviii, pp. 114–127.

19. 'Et disoient li Alemant, li Thiois, li Flamenc, et li Englés que li princes de Galles estoit la fleur de toute la chevalerie du monde.'Froissart, *Œuvres* (ed. Kervyn de Lettenhove, Brussels, 1867–77), vii, 227.

20. 'Il avoit fait cryer unes grandes festes de joustes à la mi-aoust à estre en la bonne cité de Londres, et l'avoit fair cryer et asavoir par deçà la mer, en Flandres, en Haynau, en Braibant et en France.' *Ibid.*, iv, pp. 123, 124. See also Chambers, *Med. Stage*, i, p. 392, n. 3.

21. Holinshed, *Chronicles of England* (London, 1807), ii, 627. In 1308, Giles of Argentine held the field against all comers at Stepney as 'King of the Greenwood': Denholm-Young, *The Tournament*, p. 267. It is significant that the dress of the defendants is not mentioned. I think one may reasonably infer that this omission implies that the usual practice of continental Tournaments was here followed, that is, the defendants wore armour devoid of attempted disguise.

22. John Stow, *Survey of London* (ed. C. L. Kingsford, Oxford, 1908), ii, 29. Cf. 'Le Pas d'Armes du Chateau de la Joyeuse Garde', described by M. V. de la Colombière in *Le Vrai Théâtre d'honneur* (Paris, 1648), i, 81, for a continental example.

23. *B.M. MS. Harl. 69: B.M. MS. Lansdowne, 285; College of Arms MS. L5.*

24. *B.N. MS. Français, 2692.* Cf. *B.M. MS. Lansdowne, 285,* ff. 15–41b.

25. *B.M. MS. Lansdowne, 285,* f. 10. For continental examples of this procedure see Favyn, *THK.,* ii, 465; also Plate X.

26. T. Comte de Quatrebarbes, *Œuvres Complètes du Roi René* (Angers, 1845), ii, pp. 49–99, an edition of Codex Colbert 4369 written on vellum and bound in 4to, dated 1449, 3rd June.

27.
> 'A Tharascon, en ung lieu moult faitis,
> On trouvera pour jouster unes lices
> Appartenans à tieulx plaisans delices,
> Et à ung bout, chascun bien le verra,
> Une gente pastourelle serra
> Soubx ung arbre gardant ses brebiettes,
> Laquelle ara, car bien lui affera,
> Ses chosettes propres et joliettes.
> Deux escuz de jouste à l'arbre atachiez
> Seront: l'un blanc, signifiant léesse,
> Qui ne sera d'autre couleur tachiez;
> Et l'autre noir, signifiant noblesse
> De deux gentilz escuiers pastoureaux,
> Tendans ainsi que serviteurs loyaulx
> De la pastourelle grace aquerir.
> Qui plus avant en voudroit enquerir,
> Cellui du blanc est bien d'amours content,
> Et l'autre mal; si ne voise ferir.
> L'un des escuz qui le cas bien n'entent.
> Quinconques vueille aux pastoureaux jouster,
> S'il est content d'amours et de sa dame
> A l'escu noir puet aler sans douter,
> Comme cellui qui vray servant se clame.
> Et d'ung baston le touchier sans nul blame,
> Le mal content doit l'escu blanc touchier.'

Quatrebarbes, *op. cit.,* p. 52, lines 77–101.

28.
> 'Là véissiez venir la pastourelle,
> Le chevalier premier juge à sa dextre,
> Le roy d'armes d'autre part à senestre,
> Qui devoyent des querelles jugier;
> Et les brebis aloyent à sequestre
> Pour non elle trop forment eslongier.
> Tout homme estoit à cheval bien monté,
> Exceptez deux conduisans les brebis.
> ....
> La bergiere chevauchoit haquenée
> Moult noblement de harnois aornée
> D'ung fin drap d'or figuré cramoysi,
> Et à cheval estoit menée ainsi
> Par la bride de deux gens jouvenceaux
> Alans à pié, gentils hommes aussi,
> Bien desguisez en habis pastoureaulx.'

Ibid., pp. 55–56, lines 199–206, 210–216. For full discussion of the growth of the Pastoral ideal see J. Huizinga, *op. cit.*

29.   'La bergiere son propre lieu avoit
       Si gracieux que homme faire savoit,
       D'arbres, de fleurs et de gente verdure
       Si hautement paré qu'estre devoit;
       Et là se mit attendant l'aventure.

       Le pursuyvant les deux escuz pendi
       A ung arbre prez de la pastourelle.
       ....
       Et sa holette environ d'une toise,
       Dont la ferrure estoit de fin argent.
       Son barrillet d'argent avoit aussi
       A son costé pour moullier sa bouchette;
       Sa pennetiere elle portoit ainsi
       Que les autres, qui moult estoit doucette.'
  Ibid., pp. 57–58, lines 236–242, 263–268.

30.   'Ainsi estoit l'un tousiours attendant.
       L'un l'escu blanc avoit, l'autre le noir;
       Et au premier econtre eulx contedant
       L'un ou l'autre sailloit de son manoir.'
  Ibid., p. 58, lines 285–288.

31.   'Verge et bouquet gagnay à brief parler,
       Et ung baisier lequel je tins moult chier.'
  Ibid., p. 64, lines 467–468.

32. *Ibid.*, p. 82.

33. Olivier de la Marche, 'Traité d'un Tournoy tenu à Gand par Claude de Vauldray, seigneur de l'aigle, l'an 1469' ed. B. Prost, in *Traités du Duel Judiciaire, etc.* from Bibliothèque de Valenciennes MSS. 581 and 601 (Paris, 1872), p. 55.

34. 'Vray est que ledit entrepreneur, pour sa première bonne adventure, se partist, n'a pas gramment, du riche royaume d'Enfance, et entra en ung pays gasté, maigre et stérile, que on appelle Jonesse. Et fut longtamps vaucrant et errant ycelluy païs, sans estre repeu que de pensées, cuidiers ou d'espérance; qui fut la pasture qui plus le soustint et conforta en iceluy voyaige, ouquel ne trouva aventure que à compter face, jusques ad ce qu'il se trouva en la grant plaine de Plaisance, qui siet entre le chasteau de Beaulté et la noble montaigne de Grâce, que l'on dist Bonne Renommée.' *Ibid.*, pp. 58, 59.

35. 'qui le mena à toute paine en l'ermitage de Bel Acœil, qui est scituée au hault de la montaigne de Grâce, et le médicina et aléga.' *Ibid.*, p. 59.

36. *Ibid.*, p. 60. Also see Plates I, No. 1, and XXII, No 32.

37. *Ibid.*, pp. 68, 71, 72.

38. W. W. Skeat, *The Flower and the Leaf, Chaucerian and Other Pieces* (1897), pp. 361–379.

39. *Ibid.*, p. 367, lines 206 *et seq.*

40. See Ch. II, pp. 36–38 above, and Appendix A.

41. Cf. Skeat, *op. cit.*, line 502:
> 'Tho nine, crowned, be very exemplair
> Of all honour longing to chivalry,
> And those, certain, be called the Nine Worthy.'

42. See Plates II, VII and IX.

43. See lines 504–511. The Conqueror's symbol; Livy cited in line 533.

44. Woodbind was the symbol for
> '. . . such as never were
> To love untrew in word, ne thought, ne dede.'

See Skeat, *op. cit.*, line 485.

45. Use, here, of the word 'disgysing' is curious. I take it to mean disguise in the literal sense and to confirm Miss Welford's hypothesis. See *CM*, pp. 41 and 124. Also, Ch. V, p. 180 and Chapter VI, pp. 195–207 above.

46. See *C.A. MS. 1st M. 13*. ff. 51 *et seq*. The Tournament held to mark the creation of Prince Henry as Duke of York is described in B.M. MS. Cot. Jul. B. XII. ff. 91 *et seq.*; it has been transcribed and printed by J. Gairdner, *Letters and Papers illustrative of the reigns of Ric. III and Hen. VII*, i. pp. 388 *et seq*.

47. *B.M. MS. Harl. 69*, f. 4b.

48. *B.M. MS. Cot. Jul. B. XII*, f. 91. See n.46 above.

49. *Ibid.*

50. G. A. Bergenroth, *Calendar of State Papers (Spain and England, 1495–1509)*, 1862, p. 231. Letter, dated 16.vi.1500, from de Puebla to Miguel Parez Almazaa.

51. *B.M. MS. Cot. Jul. B. XII*, ff. 99b–101b. See n.46 above.

52. *B.M. MS. Harl. 69*, f. 5b.

53. *B.M. MS. Harl. 69*, f. 25: printed in *Ant. Rep. (ed. cit.)* i, 153. See Fig. 5, p. 38 above.

54. *Ed. cit.*, p. 324. See Notes to Illustrations, Frontispiece, p. 391 below.

55. '*The Knight's Tale*', lines 1880 *et seq*. Chaucer had had practical experience in preparing lists for Richard II. See C. Spurgeon, *Chaucer Criticism*, i, p. 10.

56. *B.N. MS. Français 2692*. See Plate VIII.

57. *Survey*, i, 268.

58. *Ibid.*, i, 257.

59. *B.M. MS. Lansdowne 285*, ff. 36b–38b. See also the account given by Olivier de la Marche, *Mémoires*, iii, pp. 48–54: 'En descendant du hourt avoit trois hourtz deçà et delà desdits degrez. Au premier estoient chevaliers, au second estoient escuyers, et au troisieme les archiers de la couronne.' He describes the Lord Mayor's scaffold as 'non pas si hault que la maison du Roy'.

60. See Favyn, *THK*, ii, pp. 462, 463.

61. William Nevill, *The Castle of Pleasure* (ed. R. Cornelius for E.E.T.S., London, 1930), p. 81, lines 162–172.

62. *C.A. MS. 1st M. 13*, ff. 52 and 52b. See also f. 57b, quoted Ch. III. note 8, p. 368 below.

63. 'Description of the Trial by Combate, As in Queen Elizabeth's Reign, Anno. 1671.' Printed in *Ant. Rep., ed. cit.*, i, pp. 181–183. The quotation is given here in modern spelling.

64. See J. Strutt, *The Sports & Pastimes of the People of England* (ed. W. Hone), London, 1830, pp. 111 *et seq.*

65. Stow, *Survey*, i, p. 94.

66. For the sorts of tradesmen involved in the provision of equipment for Tournaments see *Archaeologia*, XVII, pp. 297–307 ('Roll of Purchases made for the Tournament in Windsor Park, 1278'). For a full account of the Herald's duties, see Sir John Ferne, *The Blazon of Gentrie*, London, 1586, p. 152.

67. *B.M. MS. Harl. 69*, f. 1b.

68. *B.N. MS. Français, 21809*, f. 103b.

69. *B.M. MS. Cot. Vesp. C. XIV*, f. 94.

70. *C.A. MS. 1st M. 13*, f. 10b.

71. *Ibid.*, f. 52b.

72. See Olivier de la Marche, *Mémoires*, i, p. 292 and ii, p. 118.

73. Quatrebarbes, *op. cit.*, p. lxxvi: M.V. de la Colombière, *Le Vrai Theatre d'Honneur* (Paris, 1648), i, 81. This *Pas d'Armes* was held in 1448 at Saumur.

74. This was held at Bruges in 1468 as part of the celebrations to mark the wedding of Margaret, sister to Edward IV, to the Duke of Burgundy. It is described in *B.M. MS. Harl. 69*, f. 12. See also *B.M. MS. Lansdowne 285*, f. 26. A tree is said to have decorated a Tournament as early as the year 1263. This was held at Nordhausen. The tree had gold leaves which were distributed as prizes. See Du Cange, 'Des Armes à outrance, etc.', *ed. cit.*, iii. 17.

75. *C.A. MS. 1st M. 13*, f. 51.

76. *B.M. MS. Cot. Vit. A. XVI*, f. 198.

77. *C.A. MS. 1st M. 13*, ff. 56b and 57.

78. *Ibid.*, f. 52.

79. *Ibid.*, f. 57b.

80. See G. R. Kernodle, *From Art to Theatre* (Chicago, 1944), pp. 70 *et seq.* Also Plates XIV and XV.

81. Du Cange, 'Des cottes d'Armes, etc.', *ed. cit.*, iii, 295.

82. See M. C. Linthicum, *Costume in Elizabethan Drama*, Oxford, 1936, p. 16, and Sir John Ferne, *The Blazon of Gentrie*, London, 1586, pp. 163–170.

83. The individual's identification devices were extended to his household and account for the wearing of livery. Long usage made the custom familiar throughout society and therefore just as useful as an aid to the dramatist. One of the more curious uses to which livery-colours were put in the Tournament was advertisement.

A fine English example is preserved in the proclamation of Jousts to celebrate the marriage of Edward IV's second son, Richard Duke of York, to the Lady Anne Mowbray in January, 1477. Shields were used as posters and hung on the palace gates at Westminster, on London Bridge and on the Standard in Cheapside. At each site there were three shields. All three were quartered blue and tawny, that is, in the livery-colours of the Duke of Norfolk, the bride's father. In the first Quarter of each was a letter of the alphabet in gold and a jewel. The first bore the letter 'A' and a diamond. Beneath this, those wishing to take part in the 'Just-Royal' were to subscribe their names. The other two bore the letters 'E' and 'M' with a ruby and an emerald respectively. These were for subscribers to the tilt and joust with swords. The manuscript gives no explanation of the significance, if any, of these particular letters and jewels: but it has been suggested to me by Rouge-Croix that since these devices were later to be presented as prizes, the letters in fact are the first initial of the ladies who initiated the Tournament. The letter 'A' for the Just-Royal (the most important combat), with its diamond (the most valued of stones), would therefore indicate the emprise of the Lady Anne who would herself present the prize and lead off the dance.

In what detail these identification devices were absorbed into the theatre it is hard to say. The essential point to grasp is that colours had acquired far more significance in the fifteenth and sixteenth centuries than the mere shades or tints of particular primaries which is all they represent for us today. Of their theatrical effectiveness to an audience versed in these conventions, I think it is sufficient to instance the Tournament scene in *Pericles* (Act. II, Scene 2).

84. See Sir William St. John Hope and E. G. Cuthbert Atchley, *English Liturgical Colours*, 1918.

Chapter III, pages 51–58. Pageant Theatres of the Streets

1. *B.M. MS. Cot. Jul. B. XII*, f. 15b. A transcript of this section of the MS (Hen. VII's first Progress, ff. 8b *et seq.*) which is reasonably accurate may be found in Leland, *Collectanea*, (ed. 1770) iv. pp. 185 *et seq.*

2. Descriptions of these entries may be found in the following sources. Entry of the Emperor Otho: Matthew Westminster, *The Flowers of History* (in trans., Rd. C. D. Yonge, 1853), ii, 106: Wedding of Henry III: Matthew Paris, *Chronica Majora* (Rolls Ed.), iii, pp. 336–338. Entry of Edward I (1274): Matthew Westminster, *op. cit.*, ii, 468.

3. Stow, *Survey*, i, 95. See Chambers, *Med. Stage*, ii, 167. The *Chro. Dun.* which Stow cites as his authority (*Annals*, p. 207) and which Chambers states he is unable to identify is the Chronicle of Dunmow, *B.M. MS. Harl. 530*, ff. 2–13. For more detailed accounts of thirteenth-century entries see R. Withington, 'The Early Royal Entry', *P.M.L.A.*, xxxii, No. 4 (1917).

4. See Thomas Walsingham, *Historia Anglicana* (ed. H. T. Riley, 1863), i, pp. 331, 332.

5. Stow, *Survey, ed. cit.*, p. 17. Also Figs. 7 and 8 and Plate XXXI, No. 50.

6. *Bodl. MS. Ash. 793*, ff. 128–129.

7. *B.M. MS. Cot. Vit. A. XVI*, f. 192b.

8. *C.A. MS. 1st M. 13*, f. 104b. There is a link here with Tournaments. At the Jousts for Katherine of Arragon, 'th'excellent nombre of co(m)mons that were su(m)what touched and spokyn of in the first day of Justs were now also in their forsaid stag(e)s, wyndowes and batilments right plentifull.' *Ibid.*, f. 57b.

9. I am not myself sure when these organized 'standinges' replaced processional ridings. The change possibly coincided with the growth in the number of stages used.

10. For the London Entry of the Emperor Charles V in 1522, between the Conduit in Cornhill and the Great Conduit, 'ther dyd stand a pageaunte off an ylonde betokenyng the Ile of englonde compassede all abowte w^t water made in silver and byce lyke to waves off the see'. Cf. Shakespeare, *Ric. II*, II, i, 45.

11. *Bodl. MS. Ash. 793*, f. 128b.

12. See G. M. Trevelyan, *English Social History*, 1944, pp. 31 *et seq*.

13. See C. M. Clode, *Early History of the Merchant Taylors' Company*, London, 1888, pp. 35 and 292. R. Withington in his *English Pageantry* argues that this tableau was the work of the Grocers' Company on the grounds that the Grocers symbolize their trade in later pageants by the use of trees (see Chambers, *Med. Stage*, ii, pp. 163 and 173). He has failed to notice, however, that whereas the Grocers quite naturally make use of orchard trees on later occasions, on this, the uncultivated trees of the forest are most in evidence. If, too, we are to take the use of trees to indicate that the Grocers were responsible, we might equally assume from the presence of wild animals that the Skinners devised it, since animals later become their usual symbol. In 1619, for example, for the institution of Sir William Cockayn, a member of the Company of Skinners, as Lord Mayor of London, the dramatist Thomas Middleton was employed to write the show *The Triumphs of Love and Antiquity*, and there describes the setting for the first pageant as, 'a Wilderness, most gracefully and artfully furnish't with diverse kindes of beasts bearing the Furre, proper to the Fraternity . . .' (1st Ed., London 1619, sig. B2).

14. *Bodl. MS. Ash. 793*, f. 129. See also Withington, *EP*, i, pp. 129, 130.

15. *B.M. MS. Cot. Jul. B. XII*, f. 19.

16. *Ibid.*, ff. 20b and 21.

17. *P.Q.E.*, i, 76.

18. Fabyan, *Chronicles of England* (for Pyson, 1516, fol.), Sig. BB.V. Lydgate's own account is printed in *Minor Poems* (ed. MacCracken for E.E.T.S.), ii, pp. 643–644.

19. *B.M. MS. Cot. Jul. B. XII*, f. 20.

20. *Ibid.*, f. 11.

21. *Ibid.*, f. 16. The use of the word 'triumphe' here is interesting. See p. 52 above.

22. *Ibid.*, f. 16b.

23. Hall's *Chronicle* (ed. London, 1809), p. 423. On the whole subject of British historical primitivism, see E. A. Greenlaw, *Studies in Spenser's Historical Allegory*, Baltimore, 1932, and T. D. Kendrick, *British Antiquity*, London, 1950. Also C. L. Kingsford, *Chronicles of London*, Oxford, 1905.

24. *Ibid.*, p. 428.

25. See Appendix B. Lydgate's own account is printed in *MP* (see note 18 above), ii, pp. 630–648, 'King Henry VI's Triumphal Entry into London 21 Feb. 1432'. Another account by John Carpenter, the Town Clerk, is printed in *Munimenta Gildhallae* (ed. H. T. Riley, 3 vols., Rolls series, 1859–62), iii, pp. 457–464.

26. *MP*, lines 72–96, p. 633.

27. *Ibid.*, lines 139–154, p. 635.

28. *Ibid.*, lines 181–203, pp. 636, 637. See Ch. II, p. 47 above.

29. *Ibid.*, lines 271–306, pp. 639–641.

30. Printed by J. Leland, *Collectanea* (ed. 1774, 6 vols.), iv, 314, 315.

31. *P.Q.E.*, i, pp. 91, 92.

32. *B.M. MS. Cot. Jul. B. XII*, f. 19.

33. *Ibid.*, f. 16.

34. *B.M. MS. Cot. Vit. A. XVI*, f. 194.

35. *B.M. MS. Cot. Jul. B. XII*, f. 18b.

36. Robert Yarrington, *Two Lamantable Tragedies*, ed. H. A. Bullen in, *A Collection of Old Plays*, p. 7. See also on this subject, H. H. Adams, *English Domestic or Homiletic Tragedy*, Columbia, 1943.

37. In the seventeenth century choice of theme was so directly governed by appropriateness and compliment that Masks became too topical to warrant revival.

38. See Withington, *EP*, i, pp. 149, 176 and 180–185.

39. Jonson, *Works*, vii, pp. 90, 91.

40. *P.J.I.*, i, 341. For Dekker's and Jonson's respective contributions see Jonson *Works*, vii, pp. 77–79; Thomas Dekker, *The Dramatic Works*, ed. F. Bowers, ii, pp. 229–309; R. Withington, *EP*, 1. pp. 222–226; and G. Wickham, 'Contribution de Ben Jonson et de Dekker aux fêtes du couronnement de Jacques 1er', in *Les Fêtes de la Rennaissance*. I, ed. J. Jacquot for Editions du Centre National de la Recherche Scientifique, Paris, 1956, pp. 279–283.

41. *Works*, vii, 89.

42. *Ibid.*, vii, 90.

43. *MP*, *op. cit.*, p. 633, lines 92–95.

44. *EP*, i, 177, quoting *Corpus Christi Coll. Cantab. MS. 298.*

45. *P.J.I.*, i, 348.

46. Entry of Charles V, London, 1522. See *EP*, i, 178.

47. *C.A. MS. 1st M. 13*, ff. 45 and 45b.

48. *C.A. MS. 1st M. 13*, ff. 33b and 34. See also *B.M. MS. Cot. Vit. A. XVI*, f. 184.

49. *Works*, vii, 83.

50. S. Harrison, *Arches of Triumph*, London, 1604, in fol. Harrison, who describes himself as 'architect and joiner', designed, engraved and published the arches and wrote his own descriptive text.

51. *P.J.I.*, i, 349.

52. *Ibid.*, i, 357.

53. This and the following two quotations are taken from 'A Calendar of Dramatic Records in the books of the Livery Companies of London', *Collections*, Vol. III, ed. F. P. Wilson for Malone Soc., 1954.

54. 'Troia-Nova Triumphans', printed as an Appendix by W. Fairholt, in *Lord Mayor's Pageants*, 2 vols. for Percy Soc., 1844. See p. 15.

55. *House Book*, City of York, VI, ff. 15–18, printed in *A Volume of English Miscellanies* (ed. James Raine, jr., for Surtees Soc., 1890), lxxxv, pp. 53–58.

56. *Ibid.*, p. 57.

57. *MP*, ii, pp. 641–643.

58. *Leland Collectanea, ed. cit.*, iv, 314.

59. Harrison, *Arches of Triumph*, sig. F.

60. All the sixteenth-century examples cited here are discussed by Withington, *EP*, i, pp. 170–221.

61. *MP*, ii, 642.

62. *B.M. MS. Cot. Nero. C. IX*, ff. 174 and 175.

63. *C.A. MS. 1st M. 13*, f. 8.

64. *Chroniques, ed. cit.*, xiv. 10.

65. *C.A. MS. 1st M. 13*, f. 34.

66. *Chroniques, ed. cit.*, xiv, 8.

67. See W. H. Shoemaker, *The Multiple Stage in Spain during the 15th and 16th Centuries* (Princeton, 1935).

68. *B.M. MS. Cot. Vesp. B. II.*, ff. 9 and 9b.

69. This, and the other two quotations above, are taken from *House Book*, City of York, VI, ff. 15 *et seq.*, *ed. cit.*, pp. 53–58.

70. *B.M. MS. Cot. Jul. B. XII*, f. 20b.

71. *C.A. MS. 1st M. 13*, ff. 39b and 40.

72. *Ant. Rep.*, ii, pp. 233 and 237.

73. Leland, *Collectanea, ed. cit.*, iv, 318 and 319.

74. *Ibid.*

75. Withington, *EP*, i, 212. He gives as his source, *Documents relative to the Reception at Edinburgh of the Kings & Queens of Scotland* (Bannatyn Club, Edinburgh, 1822).

76. Harrison, *Arches of Triumph*, sig. H.

77. See Arden Shakespeare, *A. & C.*, IV, xiv, p. 160. Also p. 395 below.

78. *C.A. MS. 1st M.* 13, ff. 34 and 35. Lime and stone are expressly mentioned as part of the illusion created by 'tregetoures' in Chaucer's *Frankleyn's Tale* (see Ch. VI, p. 212 above): and enjoined by Shakespeare for the costume of Wall in *M.N.D.*, V, 1, 132 and 162.

79. See Appendix B.

80. *C.A. MS. 1st M.* 13, f. 35.

81. Jonson, *Works*, vii, 102. For the preceding quotation see Harrison, *Arches of Triumph*, sig. I, and *Works*, p. 95. For the following quotation see *Works*, p. 100.

82. Tablets with verses were given to Richard II and his Queen in 1392. If this was not standard practice, we may well ask how the Herald obtained the text of the Worcester Pageants prepared in 1486 but which were not, in the event, performed: see *B.M. MS. Cot. Jul. B. XII*, f. 13b. In the sixteenth century it became usual to print the text of a pageant reception for circulation after the event as was the practice with Masks and many plays.

83. Froissart, *Chroniques*, *ed. cit.*, xiv, 9.

84. *C.A. MS. 1st M. 13*, f. 48.

85. See *B.M. MS. Cot. Jul. B. XII*, f. 17b: *C.A. MS. 1st M. 13*, f. 33b.

86. A full description is given by T. Godefroy, *Le Ceremonial de France*, Paris, 1619, pp. 55–58.

87. Leland *Collectanea*, *ed. cit.*, iv, 289. See Plate XIV.

88. Froissart, *Chroniques*, *ed. cit.*, xiv, 11.

89. See p. 83 above. Also Withington, *EP*, i, 133.

90. *House Book*, City of York, *ed. cit.*, p. 56.

91. *C.A. MS. 1st M. 13*, f. 32b.

92. *MP*, ii, pp. 634–636. See pp. 48 and 77 above.

93. T. Godefroy, *op. cit.*, p. 56.

94. Leland *Collectanea*, *ed. cit.*, iv, 220.

95. *C.A. MS. 1st M. 13*, f. 89b.

96. *B.M. MS. Cot. Jul. B. XII*, f. 20.

97. *Guildhall MS. 3313*, II, f. 32.

98. *Ant. Rep.*, ii, 238.

99. Leland, *op. cit.*, iv, 317.

100. *P.J.I.*, i, 369. This is the source of all the quotations from Dekker's account which follow in the course of the next few pages. The source for the quotations from Ben Jonson's account is *Works*, vii, pp. 80–109. Since my examples are only a few of the many provided, this general reference should prove more helpful than a multiplicity of *op. cits.* and *ibids*.

101. T. Godefroy, *op. cit.*, p. 56.

102. *C.A. MS. 1st M. 13*, f. 40b.

103. See Froissart, *Chroniques, ed. cit.*, xiv, 11, and *C.A. MS. 1st M. 13*, f. 65.

104. Thomas Churchyard, *A Discourse of the Queen's Majesty's Entertainment in Suffolk and Norfolk*, London, 1578. 4to. Sig. C, iv.

105. *Ibid.*, sig. C. For the *Pas d'Armes* of the *Chateau de la Joyeuse-Garde* at Saumur in 1448, Roi Réné prescribes, *'deux estafiers turcs, habillez à leur mode'* and again, *'un nain vestu à la turque'*.

106. See George Whetstone, *Promos and Cassandra*, Pt. 11, Act I, Scenes 4–6. Shakespeare, *Love's Labour's Lost*, V, ii, 522 *et seq.* Also Tiddy, *The Mummers' Play* (1923), p. 98. For the attacks, on Munday, see Fairholt, *op. cit.*, pp. 22–37.

107. Churchyard, *op. cit.*, sig. E, iijb.

108. Anthony Munday, *The Fishmonger's Pageant*, 1616 (*ed. cit.*), pp. 11, 25 and 26.

109. *'Troia-Nova Triumphans'*, printed by W. Fairholt, *op. cit.*, Appendix, p. 11.

110. *P.J.I.*, i, 340.

111. *Works*, vii, 91.

Chapter IV, pages 112–116. Miracle Plays

1. The orthodox view of the naïve nature of mediaeval stagecraft stems from the statements made by David Rogers (son of Robert Rogers Archdeacon of Chester, who died in 1595) and Sir William Dugdale who wrote about the Coventry plays in his *Antiquities of Warwickshire*, published in 1656. F. M. Salter has demonstrated that David Rogers' account of the Chester plays in *A Breviarye, or Some few Collections of the City of Chester* is not trustworthy (see *MDC*, pp. 54 *et seq.*). Hardin Craig has shown that Dugdale's statement is equally fallacious: see *ERD*, pp. 238–240. Also Ch. IV, pp. 169–174 above.

2. Gardiner, *Mysteries' End*, p. 73, quoting York *House Books*, Vol. XXXIV, fol. 106. The word 'to' in the phrase 'thoghe it was plawsible to yeares ago' makes no sense to me. Since the Creed Play at York was substituted for the Miracle Cycle every ten years, ought we not to read '10' instead of 'to' in this passage? See p. 383, n. 14 below.

3. See Salter, *MDC*, pp. 51–53 and Gardiner, *op. cit.*, pp. 79–83. The documents in the suit were transcribed and printed by Canon R. H. Morris, *Chester during the Plantagenet and Tudor Periods*, 1893, pp. 319–322.

4. A document in *Liber actorm̄ coram comij regys* in the Diocesan Registry at York found and printed by Gardiner, *op. cit.*, p. 78. Quoted by Hardin Craig, *ERD*, p. 360.

5. See Gardiner, *op. cit.*, pp. 54–57.

6. See Chambers, *Med. Stage*, ii, pp. 221, 224 and 446–450. Also Gardiner, *op. cit.*, p. 52. Both base their views on passages in J. S. Brewer's, *Letters and Papers of the Reign of Hen. VIII* (ed. 1862–1918, 18 vols.).

7. Bale tells us this himself: *Scriptores*, i, 702. See also Cromwell's accounts, printed by Brewer, *op. cit.*, xiv, Pt. 2, pp. 337–339. See also Vol. II, 1576-1660, Pt. 1, p. 352, n. 15.

8. See Ch. VIII, pp. 293–295 above. Also Gardiner, *op. cit.*, pp. 29–45.

9. See Salter, *MDC*, pp. 35 *et seq.* Gardiner, *op. cit.*, pp. 54 *et seq.*

10. If we date the start of the attack on the Miracle Plays *c.* 1530 and the last performances as taking place within the period 1575 to 1585, this means that suppression took a full fifty years to effect. The determination of the municipalities to retain the plays must be measured by the number of performances which were actually given during this period. Gardiner suggests that the communal nature of the old plays made them more attractive to the inhabitants of provincial towns than visits from professional players (*op. cit.*, pp. 91–93). Concerning the attitude of the citizens of York who, according to the Mayor in 1568, 'were muche desyreous to have Corpuscrysty play this yere', see R. Davies, *York Records of the Fifteenth Century*, 1843, pp. 260–272. In Coventry, Thomas Massye tried vainly to revive the plays as late as 1603: see Ch. VIII, p. 299 above.

11. See Chambers, *Med. Stage*, ii, Ch. XX. The opening paragraph in particular and this chapter in general have been paraphrased so often by subsequent historians that the largely speculative nature of Chambers' enquiries has been translated into narrow dogma which, by virtue of the source, appears to possess an unimpeachable orthodoxy.

12. See n. 11 above and in particular Allardyce Nicoll, *Mimes, Masks and Miracles*, 1931, pp. 175–179.

13. If the Chester tradition is accepted (for refutation of it see pp. 20–25 above) translation into English took place *c.* 1328. Chambers accepts this view (*Med. Stage*, ii, pp. 352–354) but is unable to substantiate it factually. The first text in English known to him (and it is still the earliest) is the *Shrewsbury MS. Mus. iii, 42* containing fragments of a *Pastores*, *Quem quaeritis* and *Perigrine*, which was dated by Professor Skeat (who discovered it) as of the early fifteenth century. Chambers describes it as 'transitional between the liturgical play and the miracle-play proper' (*Med. Stage*, ii, p. 427; see also pp. 87–90, and Hardin Craig, *ERD*, pp. 199–240). I find it impossible myself to reconcile this statement with Chambers' views either on the translation of the Chester Cycle or of the translation of the plays in general. A way of getting at the truth in this matter seems to me to be by comparison with the history of the Street Pageant Theatres. See Ch. IV, pp. 122–123 above.

14. The first specific record of the performance of plays in conjunction with the Corpus Christi Festival in England comes from Beverley, Yorks., and is dated 1377. See A. F. Leach, 'Some English Plays and Players, 1220–1548', in *An English Miscellany presented to Dr. F. J. Furnivall*, O.U.P., 1901.

15. See Hardin Craig, *ERD*, pp. 94–96: Gardiner, *op. cit.*, pp. 7–19.

16. The first out-of-door performance of something approaching a full cycle of plays of which record survives is that at Cividale in N. Italy, 1298. It is to be noted that the performance took place, 'die vii exeunte

Maio, videlicet in die Pentecostes et in aliis duobus sequentibus diebus'. See Chambers, *Med. Stage*, ii, p. 77: also, pp. 138 *et seq.* above.

17. See Chambers, *Med. Stage*, ii, p. 87. This is a subject which deserves more detailed treatment. Leach (*op. cit.*) drew attention fifty years ago to the part likely to have been played by the secular clergy in developing the Miracle Plays. He listed the secular clerks of the Universities, secular canons and vicars choral of the collegiate churches, the parish clerks, the mendicant friars and the town clerks and clergy of the grammar schools as persons who might be thought of in this context as doing more than cloistered monks to propagate the cult of Miracle Plays.

18. See *Coventry Leet Book*, ed. Harris for E.E.T.S., i, 555: Also p. 293 above.

19. See pp. 136 *et seq.* above.

20. See R. Lebègue, *La Tragédie religieuse*, Paris, 1929; Chambers, *Med. Stage*, ii, pp. 1–67: Karl Young, *The Drama of the Mediaeval Church, ed. cit.*, pp. 397 *et seq.*

21. See Gardiner, *op. cit.*, pp. 11–16.

22. Craig, *ERD*, p. 128, citing *Historia Monasterii Sancti Petri Gloucestriae*: Rolls Series, *Chronicles and Memorials*, ii, 44.

23. Craig, *ERD*, p. 133. See p. 347 above.

24. See Ch. III, pp. 85 *et seq.* above.

25. See Ch. III, pp. 53 *et seq.* above.

26. The first persons in modern times to collect together and print any substantial number of documents relating to the Chester Plays were Dr. Hermann Deimling and Canon R. H. Morris. Deimling edited the surviving MSS. of the plays for E.E.T.S., 1893. Morris, in *Chester in the Plantagenet and Tudor Periods* (?1893), printed his own transcriptions of many MSS. relating to performances and attempted a reconstruction of them, pp. 303–330.

Chambers, when compiling his two-volume *The Mediaeval Stage* in 1903, appears to have accepted Morris's transcriptions as accurate without checking them for himself. By the same token, subsequent historians have copied Chambers' observations on the Chester Plays (*op. cit.*), ii, pp. 348–356 and 407–409 and given his errors the blessing of authority by repetition. They are to be found in every book on the mediaeval drama printed between 1903 and 1956. F. M. Salter seems to have been the first person to look at the original MSS. since Morris transcribed them. The errors which he found, and the new construction he put upon the documents in consequence, are printed in *Mediaeval Drama in Chester* (1955), pp. 29–80 and 115–128.

My own quotations from the documents are given in my own transcription, and copies of the most controversial ones are reproduced in full in Appendix D of this volume.

27. *MDC*, p. 33. See Morris, *Chester*, p. 317, who incidentally contradicts himself on p. 204, where he states that Wm. Newhall succeeded Rauff Wryne as Clerk of the Pentice in 1543. See *MDC*, p. 115, n. 3.

28. The Proclamations, which I label henceforward as A, B and C, are to be found in the following MSS.:

A. Chester Town Hall: 'Book Containing Fragments of Assembly Orders.'

B. *Ibid.* Also *B.M. MS. Harl. 2013*, f. 1*.

C. *B.M. MS. Harl. 2150*, f. 86.

In respect of B., I can find no trace of the '[in R]udio' noted by Chambers, *Med. Stage*, ii, p. 349 n. i, and by Salter *MDC*, p. 116, n. 3. I suspect that Chambers took it from Deimling without checking the MS., and that Salter has followed him. See Appendix D, pp. 340–345 above.

29. The Banns are to be found in the following MSS.:

1. Pre-Reformation: *BM. MS. Harl. 2150*, ff. 86–88b. This is a copy made by Randle Holme, of an original now lost. However, the copyist was a very punctilious scribe, since he has indicated by the marginal note 'Erazed in the booke' what part of the original was deleted post 1532–47. The deletions relate to Corpus Christi and the Virgin Mary.

2. Post-Reformation: *B.M. MS. Harl. 2013*, f. 1. Also in other MSS. containing the Chester Plays: *Harl. 1944, Bodl. 175* and *Huntington Lib. MS. HM 2*.

See F. M. Salter, 'The Banns of the Chester Plays', in *Review of English Studies*, xv (1939). Also Appendix D, pp. 346–347 above.

30. See Salter, *MDC*, pp. 39 *et seq.*

31. G. Ormerod in his *History of the County Palatine and City of Chester*, 3 vols., 1882, quotes from Leycester's own transcript, made in 1644, of the original charter given by Earl Hugh Lupus on his establishment of the Benedictine Convent of St. Werburgh, 1093 A.D. See Vol. I, pp. 12–14.

32. A résumé is given by R. H. Morris, *Chester*, p. 123.

33. *Ibid.*, p. 134, n. 1.

34. *Ibid.*, pp. 323–330. Davies, *York Records*, pp. 274–276.

35. *Chester*, p. 119.

36. *Ibid.*, pp. 142–146.

37. *Med. Stage*, ii, p. 77.

38. See Lucy Toulmin-Smith, *York Mystery Plays*, 1885, pp. xxxi and xxxii.

39. See Chambers, *Med. Stage*, ii, p. 118.

40. *Ibid.*, ii, p. 344.

41. *Ibid.*, ii, pp. 371–373, 377–379. Also Hardin Craig, *ERD*, pp. 127–140 and 265–280.

42. *English Works*, ed. F. D. Matthew for E.E.T.S., p. 429.

43. G. M. Trevelyan, *History of England* (ed. 1948), pp. 233–236.

44. See Owst, *op. cit.*, Ch. VIII, pp. 471–547, 'The Sermon and Drama', for a general discussion of this subject.

45. See Trevelyan, *English Social History*, pp. 8–14, and Owst, *op. cit.*, pp. 287 *et seq.*

46. See Hardin Craig, *ERD*, pp. 269–275: also p. 347, note* above.

47. Davies, *op. cit.*, p. 230. It would also accord with the extraordinary lists from York, one dated 1415 and the other slightly later, of no less than 57 scriptural subjects allotted to separate crafts. Initially, each guild would have a separate subject since it walked as a composite unit in the procession. For the purposes of dramatic performances, however, they would combine with one another in order to bring their respective subjects into line with the requirements of a self-contained play. See Davies, *op. cit.*, pp. 233–235 and 273; Toulmin-Smith, *York Mystery Plays*, pp. xxx–xxxvi.

48. See *Coventry Leet Book*, ed. Harris for E.E.T.S., 1907, i, pp. 556–564; and Salter, *MDC*, pp. 54–80.

49. Where, in some late sixteenth- and early seventeenth-century paintings the costume is not contemporary dress it is not historically accurate either. It is employed to give better colour contrast or for some other essentially visual and pictorial reason.

50. *ERD*, pp. 251 *et seq.*

51. *Ibid.*, pp. 270 *et seq.*

52. This is a most useful example of how Protestantism can obscure academic judgement. See T. Sharp, *A Dissertation on the Coventry Mysteries*, Coventry, 1825, p. 54.

53. See Chambers, *Med. Stage*, ii, pp. 17 *et seq.*

54. It is important not to attribute too sophisticated a mentality to the authors, however, some of whom may not have been all that learned in geography and history themselves.

55. See Chambers, *Med. Stage*, ii, pp. 14, 19, 21 and 306–315.

56. *Ibid.*, ii, pp. 79 *et seq.*

57. *Ibid.*, ii, pp. 315–321.

58. *Ibid.*, ii, pp. 80 and 85.

59. *Ibid.*, ii, pp. 79 and 85.

60. At Beverley Minster in 1220 when the Resurrection play was acted in the church yard of the Minster, some boys 'went on to the vaults and galleries on the top of the Church, to get, I suppose, through the lofty windows . . . a better view of the persons and gestures of the players, and to hear the dialogue more easily, like Zacheus when he climbed up the sycamore tree.' See A. F. Leach, 'Some English Plays and Players', in *An English Miscellany presented to F. J. Furnivall*, 1901, p. 206.

61. See *EES*, III, pp. 178–88.

62. Conditions in France and Germany parallel those in England, and the evidence is far more detailed.

63. See pp. 168–169 above and p. 384 note 39 below.

64. See Chambers, *Med. Stage*, ii, Appendix W, pp. 329–406.

65. R. Davies, *York Records*, p. 231.

66. *Med. Stage*, ii, p. 380.

67. Hall's *Chronicle*, ed. cit., p. 493. Also p. 640, for the entry of the Emperor Charles V to London, 1522.

68. M. Giraud, *Composition, mise en scène et réprésentation du Mystère des Trois Doms joué à Romans les 27, 28 et 29 mai, aux fêtes de Pentecôte de l'an 1509*, Lyon, 1848. See p. 32.

69. *Ibid.*, see pp. 33–39.

70. *Ibid.*, p. 23.

71. *Ibid.*, p. 24.

72. *Ibid.*, 'Paye le dit jour Amyen Grégoyre pour plussieurs ferrements de fert pour les tours et tornelles et autres angins pour les dites feyntes . . . v. fl. vjs.'

    'Paye . . . Amyen Grégoyre pour vj barres fort longues pour la grant trabuchet (*i.e. trebuchet = winch*), et troys fautures (*i.e. ceintures = belts*), pour les troys angels auesques les clauettes (*= linch pins*) quantouyeres pour desandre de paradis que pessa tout ansamble xxxix liv: et pour ce lui ay delivre la sōme de . . . iij. fl: iijs.'

    'Paye . . . Grégoire pour deux grans bojons (*i.e. boulons = bolts*) pour fere vyrer la gorge danfert pessa troys liv:, monte . . . iijs.'

73. *Ibid.*, pp. 33–39.

74. See Salter, *MDC*, pp. 54–80. Also Sharp, *Dissertation*; D. Penn, *The Staging of the 'Miracles de Nostre Dame'*, N.Y., 1933: G. Frank, *Mediaeval French Drama*, 1954, pp. 160–172. See Appendix F above.

75. F. J. Furnivall, *The Digby Plays*, ed. for E.E.T.S., 1896, from *Bodl. MS. Digby 133*.

76. *Ibid.*, p. xi.

77. *Ibid.*, pp. 67, 89, 93.

78. *Ibid.*, pp. 113 and 131.

79. See Chambers, *Med. Stage*, ii, Appendix W.

80. *Ibid.* See p. 384, note 39 below.

81. See Craig, *ERD*, pp. 239–241.

82. Other plays suggest by their very nature that the street was used: notably *Balam and Balak* and the *Entry into Jerusalem* in several Cycles. My point, however, is that it is improper to use what is clearly an exceptional stage direction as an example of regular practice.

    Ladders were used by the Drapers of Coventry in 1557 and 1566 (Sharp, *Dissertation*, p. 74) and by the Coopers of Chester in 1572 (Salter, *MDC*, p. 73).

83. *MDC*, pp. 54–80. I cannot accept myself his assessment of the value of 1*d* in those days. Cf. Appendix B and Appendix F above.

84. Sharp, *Dissertation*, pp. 64 and 78 respectively.

85. See Salter, *MDC*, p. 61, and Appendix B above.

86. Sharp, *Dissertation*, pp. 18–20.

87. Smiths' Company accounts for 1584: 'Itm̄ payde to Cookeson for makynge of a whele to the skaffolde . . . viij^d: Itm̄ payde for a Iron pynne and a Cotter for the skaffolde whele . . . iiij^d.' (Sharp, *Dissertation*, p. 38; see also p. 20.)

88. See Salter, *MDC*, pp. 23 and 68; *Coventry Leet Book*, ed. Harris for E.E.T.S. i, 300; and L. Toulmin Smith, *York Mystery Plays*, p. xxxii.

89. See *York Mystery Plays*, pp. xxxii–xxxvi; also Davies *York Records*, pp. 241 *et seq.*

90. *B.M. MS. Harl. 1948*, f. 48. See Salter, *MDC*, p. 56, quoting *B.M. MS. Harl. 1944*, ff. 21b and 22. There are several discrepancies between these two MS. accounts. The most notable is that where, in the latter, the carts are said to have 'stoode upon 6 wheles', in the former they are 'upon 4 wheeles'.

Chapter V, pages 180–186. Tudor Theatres and Entertainers

1. 'The Mask of Augurs', *Works*, vii, 631.

2. F. Mandet, *Histoire de la langue Romane (Roman Provençal)*, (Paris, 1840), pp. 172 *et seq.* See also A. Nicoll, *Masks, Mimes and Miracles*, 1931, Ch. III: Chambers, *Med. Stage*, i, Chs. I, II and III, and ii, Appendix B, pp. 230–266. For the principal itineraries see Raimon de Loi, *Trails of the Troubadours* (New York, 1926); also H. J. Chaytor, *The Troubadours in England*, 1923; and J. Audian, *Les Troubadours e l'Angleterre* (Paris, 1927).

3. For the influence of Provençal upon the English language see Warton *HEP*, *ed. cit.*, p. 226; and Audian, *op. cit.*, pp. 20 *et seq.*

4. I am indebted to Professor William Beare for the information that in doing this they were repeating the practice of their predecessors in Greece, Homer being the chief among them. The musical accompaniment of the lyre or harp was intended to supply *rhythmic* rather than *melodic* assistance. The 'recitative' of opera and oratorio is probably a direct survival. See Chambers, *Med. Stage*, i, pp. 74–75.

5. Warton, *HEP*, p. 63.

6. G. R. Owst, *Literature and Pulpit*, p. 13, quoting *B.M. MS. Roy. 17c. viii*, f. 2b.

7. *B. Text, Passus XIII*, lines 224 *et seq.*

8. *Chronica Majora* (Rolls Ed.) iii, pp. 336–338.

9. Mandet, *op. cit.*, p. 178.

10. *Ibid.*, pp. 181–188.

11. *HEP*, p. 65; also Nicoll, *op. cit.*, p. 165.

12. See Chambers, *Med. Stage*, ii, App. E, citing the Bursars' Rolls of Durham Priory.

13. See Chambers, *Med. Stage*, ii, pp. 240–258.

14. H. Bradshaw, *The Holy Lyfe and History of Saynt Werburge*, ed. Carl Horstmann for E.E.T.S., 1887, p. 61.

15. *Ibid.*, p. 64. These two extracts should be compared with the account of the 'gestes' recited at this feast in lines 1695–1729. The stories chanted by the minstrels are very similar to those represented in the tapestries.

16. See Ch. VIII, pp. 263 *et seq.* above.

17. See Ch. VI, p. 198 above. This is as true in the case of Sword, Morris and other Folk Dances of country revels as it is of more sophisticated courtly ones. See Chambers, *Med. Stage*, i, Chs. VIII–X.

18. Froissart, *Chroniques, ed. cit.*, vi, 392

19. The original (in Latin) is printed in *Archaeologia*, xxxi, pp. 37, 43, 44, 120, 122: also Chambers, *Med. Stage*, i, 392, notes 2 and 3.

20. *B.N. MS Français 2,692.* See Plate IX and Fig. 6, p. 46 above.

21. Holinshed, *Chronicles of England* (ed. London, 1807) ii, 627. See Ch. II, p. 20 above.

Chapter VI, pages 191–197. Mummings and Disguisings

1. 'A mumming for the Goldsmiths of London' in *The Minor Poems of John Lydgate*, ed. H. N. McCracken for E.E.T.S., 1934, 2 vols, ii, p. 698, referred to as *MP*.

2. *MP*, ii, 695.

3. *Ibid.*, ii, 682.

4. See Welsford, *CM*, pp. 17 and 20–36; also *O.E.D.* sub 'mum'; Chambers, *Med. Stage*, i, p. 396, ii, p. 2.

5. Lydgate, *Troy Book*, ed. H. Bergen for E.E.T.S., 1906, 2 vols., ii, p. 169. Miss Welsford is the only person so far to have attempted an explanation of the letters 'M' or 'μ' which are to be found in the margins of the Lydgate MSS. in question (Trin. Coll., Camb., R.3.20). She suggests that these may indicate the points at which the disguised persons acted and supports this argument, withal advising caution, by comparing this usage with that of the word 'Marche', found by M. Luzel in the margin of an ancient Breton Mystery Play. (Luzel 'Sainte Tryphine et le roi Arthur', Quimperlé, 1863, p. xxiv. See Welsford, *CM*, pp. 58–59.) To this most interesting suggestion I think should be added the fact that the various changes of figure in Folk Dancing are still organized in this manner.

6. See Warton, *HEP*, p. 377; Welsford, *CM*, pp. 60–61; J. W. Cunliffe, *Early English Classical Tragedies* (1912), p. xviii; Chambers, *Med. Stage*, ii, p. 162, n. 1.

7. See Ch. III, pp. 64–68 and 73–74 above.

8. *MP*, ii, pp. 672 and 691.

9. *Ibid.*, pp. 675, 668 and 433 respectively.

10. Leland, *Collectanea*, pp. 255, 256 (1489). *Ibid.*, p. 235 (1487). On Twelfth Night, 1493, '. . . in Westm̄ Halle . . . theyre was a playe, wᵗ a pageant of St. George wᵗʰ a castle, and also xij lords̄, knights̄, and Esquyers wᵗʰ xij ladies dysguysed w̄ch dyd daunce . . .' (*B.M. Add. MS. 6113*, f. 169).

11. *Survey*, 1, 97.

12. See Ch. II, p. 20 above.

13. See Shakespeare, *L.L.L.*, V, ii; also Ch. III, p. 110 and Ch. VI, p. 201 above.

14. *CM*, p. 40.

15. *Ibid.*, p. 54.

16. *MP*, ii, 672.

17. *Ibid.*, 668.

18. *Ibid.*, pp. 698–701.

19. *Ibid.*, pp. 695–698; *CM*, pp. 54–55. According to Stow, William East-field was himself a Mercer and Mayor in 1429–30 and again in 1437–8. See *Survey*, ii, 173.

20. See St. Luke v, 1–11 and St. John xxi, 1–15; also W. Oakshott, *The Sequence of Mediaeval Art*, 1950, Plate 24.

21. *Henry V, Letter Book 1*, f. 223. Quoted by H. T. Riley, in *Memorials of London and London Life* (1868), p. 669; also by Chambers, *Med. Stage*, 1, p. 394, n. 3; and Welsford, *CM*, p. 38. There is also an Act of Parliament of 1512, 'Acte against disguysed persons wearing of visours', quoted by Chambers, *Med. Stage*, i, pp. 393, 394; Welsford, *CM*, p. 37. The use of the word 'enterlude' at this date is remarkable. See Ch. VII, pp. 234–236 above.

22. The Mayor of Bristol's Register or Calendar, 18 Ed. IV., now known as Ricart's Calendar; quoted in *Notes and Queries*, 2nd S., xii, 498.

23. See H. C. Gardiner, *Mysteries' End*, New Haven, 1946, pp. 16–17.

24. *MP*, ii, p. 675 and p. 682 respectively.

25. *Ibid.*, p. 433 and p. 691 respectively. See E. P. Hammond, *English verse between Chaucer and Surrey*, 1927, pp. 113–8.

26. See Ch. V, p. 186 and Ch. VIII, pp. 263 *et seq.* above.

27. See Chambers, *Med. Stage*, ii, 161.

28. See pp. 218–221 above.

29. *C.A. MS. 1st M. 13*, ff. 53 and 53b.

30. *Ibid.*, f. 53b.

31. See Ch. VIII, pp. 278 *et seq.* above.

32. See W. Mead, *The Mediaeval Feast*, 1934. Also *CM*, pp. 42–47.

33. S. Bentley, *Excerpta Historica* (London, 1831), p. 277, quoting *Hil. Brevia Retourab. 1, Ed. 2*, vol. 93a. See *B.M. Add. MS. 4569*.P, f. 307, for the next reign when strenuous efforts were also made to collect cloth for hangings. 'Majori villa Sandwyci. A writ to him to provide Sailcloth, quantumcumq̅z̅ poterit invenire in ballira sua. To hang the halles with against the kings coronation.

Norf. Suff. The like ⎫ Ib juxt'
Glouc.   The like ⎭

34. *MP*, pp. 623–624. See also John Russell, *Boke of Nurture*, ed. from *BM. MS. Harl. 40411* by F. J. Furnivall for E.E.T.S., 1868, pp. 51–54. This custom persisted into the sixteenth century. Of the many and elaborate subtilties presented at the feast following the enthronement of Archbishop Warham in 1504, one is of particular interest, illustrating yet again the intimate connection between the several forms of pageantry: 'A Subtiltie, a kyng syttyng in a Chayre with many Lordes about hym, and certayne Knyghtes with other people standyng at the Barre, and before them two knyghtes rydyng on horsebacke in whyte harness, runnyng with speares at a Tylt as men of armes.' A somewhat curious device for an Archbishop when one recalls the Papal attitude to Tournaments in earlier times. See *C.A. MS. 2nd M. 16*, ff. 150–152.

35. Chaucer, *The Frankleyn's Tale*, lines 1136 *et seq.*

36. See B. de Montfauçon *Monuments Français* (Paris, 1729), iii, 64; also Ch. V, pp. 185–186 above.

37. See Ch. III, pp. 93 and 104 above.

38. Welsford, *CM*, p. 44, quoting 'Le livre des fais et bonnes moers du sage roy Charles', Pt. 3, Ch. XL, ed. Buchon, in *Choix de Chroniques et Mémoires*, p. 301.

39. *MP*, p. 683, lines 38–46.

40. See Ch. VI, p. 197 above, and Ch. VIII, note 21, p. 386 below. S. Anglo in "The Court Festivals of Hen. VII," *Bulletin of the John Rylands Library, Manchester*, Vol. 43 (Sept. 1960) No. 1, pp. 12–45 provides the fullest transcript yet made of these and other payments for entertainments during the reign of Hen. VII.

41. The accounts covering the years 1491–1505, were first noticed by J. P. Collier in 1823 and printed in his *Annals of the Stage*. The B.M. *MS.* 7099, ff. 22 *et seq.*, is clearly a later copy of that 'in the Chapter-house, Westminster' which Collier claims to have used. See Chambers, *Eliz. Stage*, iv, pp. 133 *et seq.* for the present location of this and other accounts relating to early Tudor Revels. Also S. Anglo, *op. cit.* Collier includes a further Disguising on 23rd Dec. for which Jakes Hautes received another £10.

42. *C.A. MS. 1st M. 13*, ff. 57–58. See Ch. II, pp. 43 and 44 above.

43. *B.M. MS. Harl. 69*, f. 4b.

44. Hall's *Chronicle*, ed. 1809, p. 518. The description of the jousts is given, pp. 516–518; that of the evening festivities, pp. 518–519. All my quotations on pp. 217 and 218 above are taken from this source.

45. *Ibid.*, p. 526. On this famous passage, see Withington, *EP*, i, pp. 121–123; and Welsford, *CM*, pp. 130 *et seq.*

46. *Ibid.*, pp. 722 *et seq.* The description both of the banqueting hall and of that in which the entertainment was given is very detailed and supplies an image of an environment that is sumptuous and seeking to be artistic too. All the quotations on pp. 219–221 are taken from this source. For the Venetion Secretary's account see J. S. Brewer, *The Reign of Henry VIII*, ii, pp. 150–154. His description of the auditorium is singularly detailed. See Plates XXIV and XXVII.

47. *C.A. MS. 1st M. 13*, f. 53.

48. See Chambers, *Eliz. Stage*, i, pp. 27 *et seq.*

49. See Ch. VIII, pp. 278 *et seq.* above.

50. Leland, *Collectanea*, iv, 262. See also Brewer, *Reign of Hen. VIII*, ii. 152.

51. Stow, *Survey*, ii, 116. See also *Notes & Queries*, I, iv. 254.

52. B. Prost, *Relation du Tournois de Nozeroy*, Paris, 1878, p. 249: '. . . au chateau de Noseroy en une sale basse, s'est treuvée faicte une lice tendue de toile, pour couvre à la salle raze. En laquelle salle, ait esté allumées environ cinq douzaines de torches, à heure de huit en nuit; en laquelle se sont treuvez messeigneurs les Juges, en ung chaffault bien tapissé, comme il est de costume en tel cas; et emprès d'icellcy ung aultre, qui estoit semblablement richment tapissé, là où estoit madame la princesse d'Oranges, accompaignée de plusieurs dames et damoiselles.'

53. *B.M. MS. Vit. A. XVI*, f. 198, collated with *C.A. MS. 1st M. 13*, f. 52.

54. The passages for comparison both come from *C.A. MS. 1st M. 13*. The respective folios are 52b and 57b.

55. *Ibid.*, f. 52b.

56. *Ibid.*, f. 59.

57. 'Ceremonies and Services at Court in the time of King Henry the Seventh', printed in *Ant. Rep. ed. cit.*, i. pp. 296–341. See p. 313: also Plates X and XXIII, No. 33, and Ch. VIII, p. 276 above.

58. These torchbearers have their origins in the early mumming. See Plate No. XXIII, No. 33.

59. *C.A. MS. 1st M. 13*, f. 55. See also J. S. Brewer, *Letters and Papers of Henry VIII*, 4. ii, No. 3104, p. 1396 for a similar device in 1527.

60. See Welsford, *CM*, pp. 149, 150.

61. The text is printed by H. A. Evans, *English Masques*, 1900. It is discussed by Welsford, *CM*, pp. 171 *et seq.*

62. Albert Feuillerat, *Documents relating to the Revels at Court in the time of King Edward VI and Queen Mary*, 1914, p. 59.

63. Welsford, *CM*, p. 163 citing J. Nichols, *PQE.*, iii pp. 309 f.

64. C. F. Menestrier, *Traité des Tournois, etc.*, Lyons, 1669, Sig. vi.

65. See Introduction, pp. xxxiv–xxxvii above.

Chapter VII, pages 230–231. Morals and Interludes

1. M. Sepet, 'Les Prophètes du Christ', in *Bibl. de l'Ecole des Chartes*, 28th year, vol. iii. Also Chambers, *Med. Stage*, ii, pp. 52 *et seq.*

2. Chambers, *Med. Stage*, ii, p. 52; G. R. Owst, *Literature and Pulpit*, p. 472.

3. *Sarum Breviary*, i, cxxxv.

4. The last two lines of the Digby play of St. Mary Magdalene read:
> 'Now, clerkys with voice cler,
> Te Deum laudamus lett us syng.'

(Ed. F. J. Furnival, for E.E.T.S., p. 136.)

5. See Owst, *op. cit.*, pp. 123–134.

6. See Toulmin Smith, *York Plays*, pp. xxviii–xxxi; R. Davies, *York Records*, pp. 172 and 265–273; Hardin Craig, *ERD*, pp. 337–341; Leach, *op. cit.*, pp. 220–226; Sharp, *Dissertation*, pp. 9, 10 and 12.

7. Chambers, *Med. Stage*, ii, p. 151.

8. Owst, *op. cit.*, p. 149. The whole of his Ch. IV, 'Fiction and Instruction in the Sermon Exempla', is of vital concern to any student of this subject in relation to mediaeval and Elizabethan drama.

9. *Ibid.*, p. 152.

10. *Ibid.*, pp. 68 *et seq.*

11. On the subject of 'all the Knights of Christ and his whole army, namely, the apostles, martyrs and all holy men' fighting against 'the Devil and his ministers', see the sermons of John Bromyard, quoted by Owst, *op. cit.*, p. 393. Also, Langland, *Piers Plowman*, B.V. 594 *et seq.*, and Plate XIV.

12. An excellent example is the Chester play of 'The Sacrifice of Isaac', where the 'Expositor' rounds off the scriptural narrative with an explanation:

> 'Lordinges, this significacion
> of this deed of devotion,
> and you will, you wit mon,
> may turne you to much good.

> This deed you se done in this place
> In example of Ihesu done yt was,
> that for to wyn mankinde grace
> was sacrifised on the rode.'

Abraham is said to represent 'the father of heaven and Isaac, Ihesu that was obedyent aye'. The whole play reads like a lecture with acted illustrations. See the *Chester Plays*, ed. cit., pp. 63–83.

13. See the *Digby Plays* of the Conversion of St. Paul and St. Mary Magdalen, *ed. cit.*; also *Le Mystère des Trois Doms, ed. cit.*

14. See n. 6 above, and Ch. IV. pp. 114–115 above.

15. See Leach, *op. cit.*, pp. 225–228; Hardin Craig, *ERD*, pp. 269–276 and 313–314; F. J. Furnivall, *The Digby Plays*, for E.E.T.S., p. 1–23; Sharp, *Dissertation*, pp. 9 and 10, for Saint Plays at Coventry.

16. *Med. Stage*, ii, p. 183; Welsford, *CM*, p. 46.

17. See Irving Ribner, 'Morality Roots of the Tudor History Play', in *Tulane Studies in English*, Vol. iv, New Orleans, U.S.A., 1954, pp. 21–43.

18. See A. P. Rossiter, *Woodstock, A Moral History*, 1946; E. N. S. Thompson, *The English Moral Play* (New Haven), 1910; H. H. Adams, *English Domestic or Homiletic Tragedy, 1575–1643* (Columbia), 1943.

19. *Chronicle*, ed. cit., p. 719.

20. Chambers was surely mistaken in thinking that the play was twenty years old. Hall's point is that Wolsey's anger was so great that he did not hesitate to imprison a person who had held a responsible office for twenty years. See *Med. Stage*, ii, p. 219.

21. *Chronicle, ed. cit.*, p. 735.

22. 'That the shift from religious questions to political questions should have been one of the first new movements in the morality plays is natural, for in early sixteenth-century England religion and politics were closely intertwined. The new Tudor doctrines of absolutism and passive obedience had strong religious foundations. Religious interests under the Reformation, moreover, found their manifestations in partisan political interest to such an extent that the two at times became indistinguishable.' (Irving Ribner, 'Morality Roots of the Tudor History Play', in *Tulane Studies in English*, Vol. iv, New Orleans, U.S.A., 1954, p. 23.)

23. *Chronicle, ed. cit.*, p. 784.

24. See H. C. Gardiner, *Mysteries' End*, New Haven, 1946, pp. 46–64; and Chambers, *Med. Stage*, ii, pp. 217–226.

25. J. P. Collier, *Annals of the Stage*, 1831, vol. i, pp. 130–132.

26. See Gardiner, *op. cit.*, p. 53, note 30; and Chambers, *Med. Stage*, ii, p. 223.

27. See Chambers, *Med. Stage*, ii, p. 220; and Collier, *op. cit.*, i, p. 128.

28. *Med. Stage*, ii, p. 221.

29. *Epistle Exhortatorye of an Inglyshe Christian*, 1544, written under the pseudonym of Henry Stalbridge.

30. See Chambers, *Med. Stage*, ii, pp. 222 and 447.

31. Chambers, *Eliz. Stage*, i, pp. 243–4, quoting Calendar of Letters and State Papers, relating to English Affairs, principally in the Archives of Simancas, ed. M. A. S. Hume, 4 vols., 1892–99, i, 62. Despite Elizabeth's apology, the practice did not cease immediately.

32. Chambers, *Med. Stage*, ii, p. 222; and Collier *op. cit.*, i, p. 130.

33. *Staple of News*, the third Intermeane after the third Act, lines 46–49.

34. See T. H. Vail Motter, *The School Drama in England*, 1929.

35. See F. S. Boas, *University Drama in the Tudor Age*, 1914. L. B. Campbell, *Scenes and Machines on the English Stage*, 1923.

36. See Chambers, *Med. Stage*, ii, pp. 199–226.

37. Ed. by J. Manly in *Specimens of the Pre-Shakespearean Drama*, 1897, pp. 239–276, from the MS. in the Library of Trinity College, Dublin. See also Appendix G (pp. 353–354 above) which gives the cast list of *Cambises*, broken down to show which actors double which parts. The date of performance was 1561.

38. See Chambers, *Eliz. Stage*, i, p. 242, and *Med. Stage*, ii, p. 222.

39. At Leconfield, Leicester, Halsted, and Winchester there is record of plays being given in churches until the Reformation. In 1542 Bishop Bonner published an injunction against plays in chapels and churches

largely because of their controversial nature. See Gardiner, *op. cit.*, p. 54. In Elizabeth's reign, however, when the scholars of King's College, Cambridge, played Plautus in the chapel on a Sunday night for the Queen to watch, no one appears to have thought the event either impious or untoward. See Vol. II, 1576–1660, Pt. 1, pp. 177–182.

40. Hall's *Chronicle*, *ed. cit.*, p. 735.

41. *Ibid.*, p. 519.

42. Collier, *op. cit.*, i, pp. 135 and 141–142. This subject is discussed at greater length in Vol. II, 1576–1660, Pt. 1, pp. 276 *et seq.*

43. W. W. Greg, *Henslowe Papers*, 1907, p. 116. The date is March 10th, 1598. See also p. 113 n., App. I, Art. 1. See also Vol. II, 1576–1660, Pt. 1, pp. 310 *et seq.*

44. See Salter, *MDC*, pp. 57, 61–62 and 124.

45. See Chambers, *Eliz. Stage*, iii, pp. 21–28.

46. *Ibid.*, iii, pp. 24 *et seq.* See Vol. II, 1577–1660, Pt. 1, pp. 183–6.

47. Campbell, *op cit.*, p. 87, Boas, *op. cit.*, p. 17.

48. *Ibid.*, p. 91 and p. 104 respectively.

49. They are discussed extensively by F. S. Boas, *University Drama in the Tudor Age*, 1913, pp. 89–108; but both the performances themselves and Dr. Boas' very full treatment of them seem to have suffered an unwarranted neglect in general histories of the Elizabethan drama.

The fullest account of the visit to Cambridge was written in English by the University Registrary, Matthew Stokys; that of the visit to Oxford by John Bereblock in Latin. Both of these are printed in J. Nicholls, *P.Q.E.*, ed. 1788, i, 233–258 and i, 357–383, respectively. The best account in English of the visit to Oxford is *Twyne MS. xvii*, pp. 160–169 (*not ff.* 160–169 as stated by Boas). See Appendix H above. Leslie Hotson in a more recent review of the arrangements at Cambridge (*Shakespeare's Wooden 'O'*, 1959, pp. 161–3) faults Chambers for a misconception in his reconstruction (*Eliz. Stage*, i. 226) but supplies no evidence to support his own gloss that the houses were 'at the ends of the stage'.

50. Nicholls, *P.Q.E.*, *ed. cit.*, i, 245.

51. *Ibid.*, 246.

52. *Ibid.*, i, 247.

53. *Ibid.*, i, 362–363.

54. See Campbell, *op. cit.*, pp. 93–98. Also Boas, *op. cit.*, pp. 109–132.

55. See J. W. Cunliffe, *Early English Classical Tragedies*, 1912.

56. Ed. for Malone Soc. by A. Brown and F. P. Wilson, 1957.

Chapter VIII, page 262. Players and Commerce

1. See W. Beare, *The Roman Stage*, 1955.

2. See Chambers, *Med. Stage*, i, pp. 8 *et seq.*; also H. C. Gardiner, *op. cit.*, p. 1.

3. *Med. Stage*, i, pp. 89–115; Welsford, *CM*, Chs. I–III inclusive.

4. *Med. Stage*, i, pp. 97 *et seq.*; R. Withington, *EP*, i, pp. 4–72.

5. See *Med. Stage*, i, p. 244.

6. *Ibid.*, i, Chs. VII–XVII inclusive.

7. *Ibid.*, i, p. 58.

8. *Ibid.*, ii, pp. 262–263.

9. *Literature and Pulpit*, p. 12. Langland thinks of them in just these terms: 'Ac japer and janglers: Judas children' (*Piers Plowman*, A, Prologue 55; B, Prologue 35).

10. See Owst, *Literature and Pulpit*, p. 11.

11. See Craig, *ERD*, p. 19.

12. See H. C. Gardiner, *op. cit.*, pp. 1–19.

13. *House of Fame*, line 1260. See also Ch. VI, n. 35, p. 381 above.

14. 'Account Roll of Selby Abbey', in *Yorkshire Archaeological Journal* (1900), Vol. XC, pp. 408–419. See especially pp. 411–415.

15. Chambers, *Med. Stage*, ii, p. 247.

16. *Ibid.*, ii, p. 250.

17. See Appendix C, pp. 332–339 above.

18. Chambers, *Med. Stage*, ii, p. 247.

19. *Ibid.*, ii, p. 251.

20. See Appendix C.

21. I have been able to establish that the following MSS. or printed transcripts concerning entertainments at the Burgundian, French and English Courts were the work of contemporary Heralds: the *Mémoires* of Olivier de la Marche (see *ed. cit.*); *Bib. Nat. MS. Français* 21809; *B.M. MS. Cotton Nero C. IX*; *College of Arms MS. 1st M. 13*; *BM. MSS. Cot. Vesp. C. XII*, f. 236 *et seq.*; *Cot. Jul. B. XII*. See also Leland, *Collectanea*; Grosse, *Antiquarian Repertory*; Chaytour, *op. cit.*, p. 10; and C. L. Kingsford, *English Historical Literature in the 15th century* (1913), Appendix XV, 'The Record of Bluemantle Pursuivant, 1417–1472', pp. 37–388. I must emphasize, however, that efforts to establish the connection between Heralds and Court Entertainments during the fifteenth and sixteenth centuries are at present frustrated by the difficulties which surround consultation of the MSS. in the College of Arms. No Catalogue exists and 'searching' is not permitted in the Library. It is through the good offices of Sir Anthony Wagner, Garter Principal King of Arms, that I have been able to unearth as much material as appears in these pages from this source.

22. *Account Roll of Selby Abbey, ed. cit.*, p. 410. (See n. 14 above.)

23. See R. Davies, *York Records*, p. 277; also the important evidence from Gloucester cited by Chambers, *Med. Stage*, ii, p. 189, n. 5.

24. The transcript printed in J. T. Murray's *English Dramatic Companies*, 1910, ii, 214, is inaccurate in some details. The reading printed in my text is taken directly from the MS. Account Book at the Council House.

25. This year and the next were busy ones theatrically in Bristol. Besides Leicester's actors, Lord Sheffield's Company, Lord Charles Howard's, Lord Berkeley's, the Earl of Bath's and the Earl of Derby's Players visited the City. All of them presented their plays in the Guildhall and received, as fee in reward from the Mayor, xs or xiij^s iiij^d.

26. *Dulwich College MSS., Alleyn Papers*; Vol. I, Article 11, in the transcription of W. W. Greg, *Henslowe Papers*, 1907, pp. 35, 36. C. W. Hodges (*The Globe Restored*, 1953, p. 98) prints part of this letter translated into modern spelling and punctuation but without either acknowledging the fact or citing Greg's transcript.

27. Chambers, *Med. Stage*, ii, pp. 240–244.

28. See Appendix B, p. 330 above.

29. *C.A. MS. 1st M 13*, f. 64b.

30. On this subject see E. K. Chambers, *The English Folk Play*, 1933; also R. J. E. Tiddy, *The Mummers' Play*, 1923; and C. J. Sharp, *The Sword Dances of Northern England*, n.d.

31. Chambers, *Eliz. Stage*, i, p. 73.

32. *Ibid.*, i, p. 71. Also, *Med. Stage*, i, p. 404, n. 5.

33. *H.O.*, pp. 112, 113.

34. *Ant. Rep.*, i, pp. 306, 307.

35. See Chambers, *Eliz. Stage*, i, p. 57.

36. *B.M. MS. Lansdowne 83*, f. 158. An anonymous report on the working of the office drawn up *c.* 1573 and printed by Chambers, *op. cit.*, pp. 1 and 2.

37. (ed. 1622), p. 204.

38. E. C. Batten, *The Registers of Richard Fox while Bishop of Bath and Wells* (1889), p. 10.

39. See especially the King's Secretary's instructions to the Corporation of York for the reception of Richard III in 1483 printed by Withington, *EP*, i, p. 155.

40. Chambers, *Eliz. Stage*, i, pp. 27–70.

41. See Chambers, *Eliz. Stage*, i, p. 33.

42. See *H.O.* and *B.M. MS. Harl. 642*.

43. *B.M. MS. Cot. Vesp. C. XIV*, f. 95b.

44. *Ibid.*, f. 94.

45. *H.O.*, pp. 109–133 and *Ant. Rep.*, i, pp. 313 *et seq.*

46. *C.A. MS. 1st M. 13*, f. 7b.

47. *Ibid.*, f. 56b.

48. *B.M. Add. MS. 7099*, f. 3: Bentley, *op. cit.*, p. 89. See also *Eliz. Stage*, iv. pp. 132–135.

49. *C.A. MS. 1st M. 13*, f. 11.

50. In September 1500 he was paid both 'opon his bill' and 'for ij myny-strelles'.

51. *B.M. MS. Lansdowne, 83*, f. 158.

52. *Ant. Rep.*, i, pp. 296–340. See also p. 276 above.

53. *H.O.*, pp. 109–133; a printed transcript of *B.M. MS. Harl. 642*, ff. 198–217. The style of *H.O.* is that of straightforward instruction. The account from the retiring usher (see p. 276 above) is punctuated with passages in *oratio recta*, e.g. '. . . in all my sesson in the gret chambre . . .' etc. (*Ant. Rep., ed. cit.*, i, p. 312).

54. *H.O.*, p. 110 (*Ant. Rep.*, i, p. 299).

55. *Ibid.*, p. 116 (*Ant. Rep.* i, p. 299).

56. *Ant. Rep.*, i, p. 313. The cupboard, similar to that described in this passage and *not* a tableau, is represented in the plate that G. R. Kernodle takes to be a pageant structure at Binche in 1549 (*op. cit.*, p. 96).

57. *Ibid.*, p. 314.

58. E. C. Batten, *op. cit.*, p. 62, footnote*, says erroneously that this abstract is in the P.R.O. He probably refers to J. Gairdner's *Letters and Papers illustrative of the reigns of Ric. III and Hen. VII* (London, 1858), which is a Rolls Office publication. Gairdner prints an abstract (pp. 404–417), transcribed from *B.M. MS. Cot. Vesp. C. XIV*, ff. 94–103b. This MS. is not in Fox's hand throughout, but has many marginal annotations and alterations in his hand.

59. Bacon, *op. cit.*, p. 204.

60. *C.A. MS. 1st M.13*, fols. 1–11. This is the earliest of them all. Of the others, *B.M. MS. Cot. Vit. C. XI*, ff. 117–126b, follows it most nearly.

61. *B.M. MS. Cot. Vesp. C.XIV*, f. 94.

62. *Ibid.*, f. 99.

63. *Guildhall MS. 3313*, f. 39.

64. *Repertory*, I, f. 62; see Withington, *EP*, i, 165, n. 1. The latter is mistaken in supposing there to have been a show in 1499.

65. *B.M. MS. Cot. Vit. A. XVI*, f. 183b.

66. *Repertory*, I, f. 61b.

67. *Bridge House Rentals*, Vol. 4 (1484–1509), f. 227b.

68. *Ibid.*, Vols. 3 and 4. See Appendix B, pp. 321–324 above.

69. Harrison, *Arches of Triumph*, sig. B.

70. *Ibid.*, sig. K; see also *P.J.I.*, i, p. 376.

71. This was normal practice where the Miracle Plays were concerned; see p. 298 above. Stow says that in his lifetime pageant gear for the Lord Mayor's Show and Midsummer Watch was stowed in Leadenhall: see *Survey*, ii. p. 159. This is confirmed in the records of the Mercers Company, 1544: see Malone Soc. *Collections III*, p. 35.

72. *Guildhall MS. 3313*, f. 39.

73. *City Journal 10*, f. 190b. For a provincial example of the same procedure, see the arrangements for Richard III's reception in York, 1483, *EP*, i, p. 156, n. 3.

74. Bentley, *op. cit.*, p. 126.

75. *City Journal XXVI*, f. 77b. See also *Letter Book BB*, f. 200.

76. This and the following figures are taken from E. B. Jupp, *The Carpenters Company* (1848), Appendix A, List 5, pp. 294, 295; J. F. Firth, *Historical Memoranda* (1848), p. 102; and C. Welch, *The History of the Worshipful Company of Pewterers of the City of London* (1902), II, p. 46. See also *P.J.I.*, i, pp. 331–336. The deductions from these figures are my own.

77. *Ed. cit.*, i, pp. 287, 292, 319 and 417. See also T. Sharp, *Dissertation*, p. 80.

78. *Leet Book*, i, p. 556.

79. *Ibid.*, ii, pp. 707, 708; Sharp, *Dissertation*, p. 43.

80. See L. T. Smith, *York Mysteries*, p. xxxviii.

81. Leach, *op. cit.*, pp. 211, 212.

82. F. M. Salter, *MDC*, p. 63.

83. L. T. Smith, *op. cit.*, p. xxxix.

84. *Ibid.*, pp. xxxv–xlii; *Coventry Leet Book*, i, p. 555.

85. *Leet Book*, i, p. 312.

86. Leach, *op. cit.*, pp. 216, 217.

87. Salter, *MDC*, pp. 58, 59; L. T. Smith, *York Mysteries*, p. xxxvi; Leach, *op. cit.*, p. 224.

88. *Leet Book*, ii, p. 709; Sharp, *Dissertation*, p. 44.

89. Leach, *op. cit.*, p. 209.

90. L. T. Smith, *op. cit.*, p. xxxvii.

91. Salter, *MDC*, pp. 77 *et seq.*; Sharp, *Dissertation*, p. 78; see also Appendices B, C and Ch. VIII, pp. 267–270 above.

92. See Sharp, *Dissertation*, pp. 75–77.

93. *Ibid.*, pp. 68–73 and 217; Hardin Craig, *ERD*, pp. 163–166 and 295. I am not sure whether the Robert Crowe who wrote the play of the *Golden Fleece* is this man or his father. If this man, may he be the original of Shakespeare's Holofernes?

94. F. S. Salter, *MDC*, pp. 74, 75; Sharp, *Dissertation*, pp. 16–21.

95. L. T. Smith, *op. cit.*, p. xlii, citing *Council Book V*, 28th April.

96. Sharp, *Dissertation*, pp. 21 and 49, 50.

97. *Ibid.*, pp. 21 and 48.

98. F. M. Salter, *MDC*, p. 77, and Sharp, *Dissertation*, pp. 29 and 49. See also p. 46, note * above.

99. L. T. Smith, *op. cit.*, p. xli, citing *House Book $\overline{T}$*, f. 146. Sharp, *Dissertation*, p. 22, citing an order of the Smiths Company, 13 Hen. VII.

100. Leach, *op. cit.*, p. 225; Chambers, *Med. Stage*, ii, pp. 377–379.

101. Leach, *op. cit.*, pp. 215 and 226; Chambers, *Med. Stage*, ii, pp. 338–341; Sharp, *Dissertation*, p. 40.

102. See Leach, *op. cit.*, p. 221; and Chambers, *Med. Stage*, ii, p. 341.

Chapter IX, pages 307–321. Audiences and Critics

1. On the quarrel between Ben Jonson and Inigo Jones on the matter of whose name should take precedence on the title-page of a Mask see Introduction, p. xxvii above; also Vol. II, 1576–1660, Pt. 1, pp. 272–4.

2. St. Francis was born in 1182 and his Order was founded in 1209; St. Dominic was born *c.* 1170. St. Dominic's Order of Friars Preachers grew from 16 founder members in 1216 to 12,000 preachers in 1337 according to the census of Benedict XII. The influence of these Dominicans in the courts and universities of Europe was matched by that of St. Francis' and St. Bernard's followers among poor and illiterate folk.

3. See Chambers, *Med. Stage*, ii, pp. 75–97.

4. Lydgate, *The Fall of Princes*, ed. H. Bergen, for E.E.T.S., 1924, I, p. 7.

5. Lydgate, *Troy Book*, ed. H. Bergen, for E.E.T.S. 1906, II, p. 168.

6. See N. Coghill, 'The Basis of Shakespearean Comedy', in *Essays and Studies*, ed. G. Rostrevor Hamilton, 1950.

NOTES TO ILLUSTRATIONS

Some of these illustrations depict actual stages, actors, settings and costumes used in the performance of plays or other dramatic entertainments of the period. Others illustrate unfamiliar entertainments of a quasi-dramatic kind. Others again illustrate the pictorial conventions regularly used for the visual representation of subject matter that was also treated dramatically.

In making my selection, my object has been to illustrate as fully as possible the elements of dramatic spectacle in the Middle Ages, in terms of both the stage conventions themselves and the visual relationship between the spectators and these conventions in the theatres of worship and of social recreation.

Wherever possible I have included cross references to verbal descriptions in the text of the convention depicted in the illustration. In one respect, however, they still fail to do justice to their begetters: the colour is lacking. An attempt is made to remedy this defect in Appendices B and F.

FRONTISPIECE

These beautiful miniatures, which illustrate so clearly how a 'scaffold high' was constructed, should be compared with those illustrated in the well-known Fouquet miniature of the Martyrdom of St. Apollonia; cf. also Plates VIII and IX and Fig. 3, p. 32 above.

It happens that Olivier de la Marche's instructions to the illustrator of his poem have survived. The description of Atropos' scaffold reads as follows:

'The scene of this picture shall be laid in a great sandy place. An inclosed lists shall be there, and in the midst on one side there shall be a platform richly ornamented. And on this shall be a chair all of gold, where the Goddess of Death shall be sitting, with a crown of gold on her head. And she shall be covered with a cloak thrown over her in the fashion of Spain, which cloak shall be made of various colours, and especially of earth-colour. And the said mantle shall be dotted with worms after the manner of embroidery. And on the chair shall be written in letters of azure, in a conspicuous place, "Atropos, Goddess of Death". And she shall hold in her right hand a silver dart, and the point shall be red. Round this dart shall be written "Defiance". The lists shall be black, and on one of the sides shall be banners of gold. . . .'

PLATE I. No. 1

Two Wild Men. The origin and development of this popular *Pageant* figure is discussed by R. Withington, *EP*, i, pp. 72–77: see especially p. 73, n. 5.

In the Victoria and Albert Museum there is a fine Swiss tapestry of the mid-fifteenth century (approx. 7 ft. × 3 ft.) depicting a 'wild woman' and a wild man with fantastic animals (see Ch. II, pp. 24–25 above); also an English silver-gilt perfume case of the mid-fourteenth century depicting, in coloured enamel, a knight slaying a wild man. Cf. Plate XXII, No. 32, and pp. 24–5 and 42 above.

Two painted panels by Albrecht Dürer, now in the Alte Pinakothek, Munich.

PLATE II. No. 2
Parading the Lists Prior to a Tilt. The ornate pavilions are fine examples of the kind that were normally used functionally as 'changing rooms', but which came to be used as scenic emblems in their own right. Three French Knights held the lists against all comers from foreign countries, especially England, for thirty days at St. Inglevert, a village on the frontier between France and England which, in 1390, lay between Calais and Boulogne.

An illumination representing the Jousts of St. Inglevert (*c.* 1480) in Froissart's Chronicle. (*B.M. MS. Harl. 4379,* f. 23b.)

PLATE II. No. 3
Jousting at Barriers: an incident in *Le Pas d'Armes de Sandricourt,* 16.x.1493. This is one of several illuminations in a manuscript which provides an eye-witness account of the ceremonies by Orleans Herald.

B.N. MS. Français 21809, fol. 107.

PLATE III. No. 4
Jousting at Barriers, France, 1565. This is No. 5 in the series of eight magnificent Valois tapestries woven in Brussels to commemorate the Valois-Medici festivities at the Tuilleries, 1565, on the instructions of Catherine de Medici and which are now hung in the Uffizi, Florence. Valuable articles on the history, portraiture and subject-matter of these tapestries by J. Ehrmann and P. Francastel are printed in *Les Fêtes de la Renaissance,* ed. J. Jacquot for Le Centre National de la Recherche Scientifique, Paris, 1956, pp. 93–105.

Uffizi Gallery, Florence.

PLATE IV. No. 5
Allegorical treatment of the Tournament in fourteenth-century *Pas d'Armes.* Reliefs carved on French ivory mirror cases. (4 ins. × 4 ins.)

In the *Collezione Carrand,* The Bargello, Florence.

PLATE V. No. 6
Jousting, or Running, at the Ring: an incident in the *Pas d'Armes de Sandricourt,* 1493.

See Plate II, No. 3.

PLATE VI. No. 7
Jousting at the Quintain, which here takes the form of a dragon with a long lead weight attached to its tail. Note the two-storied auditorium in which princely spectators are standing, not sitting.

Detail from Valois tapestry No. 3, 1565. See Note to Plate III and Ch. II, p. 38 above.

PLATE VI. No. 8

A *Pas d'Armes*, taking the form of the siege of an elephant and castle, 1565.

> Detail from Valois tapestry No. 2. See Note to Plate III and Fig. 1, p. 29 above. Uffizi Gallery, Florence.

PLATE VII. No. 9

Heralds issuing a Challenge. This Plate and No. 10 are both taken from *B.M. MS. Cot. Jul. E. IV.*, a lavishly illustrated book, usually known as *The Pageants of the Earl of Warwick*. Although the illuminations are not coloured, they provide a counterpart to King René's *Le Livre des Tournois* (see Note to Plate VIII) as the best pictorial record of English Tournament ceremonial in the latter half of the fifteenth century.

This drawing shows by means of a formalized mountain, a formalized audience-chamber and an heraldic tabard how news of an intended Tournament was passed between nations. See Ch. II, p. 40 above. Cf. Plate XII.

> *B.M. MS. Cot. Jul. E. IV. f.* 7.

PLATE VII. No. 10

Tilting, with lances splintering on impact. Although the artist's control of perspective leaves much to be desired, the separate 'boxes' for minstrels, heralds and other spectators can be clearly distinguished.

> *B.M. MS. Cot. Jul. E. IV. f.* 15b.

PLATE VIII. No. 11

A Tournament, Lists and Auditorium. This and the next two illustrations are three of the many glorious illuminations by René, King of Anjou and Sicily, in his *Le Livre des Tournois*. The original is in a magnificent state of preservation in *Le Grand Réserve* of the Bibliothèque National, Paris. There are several MS. copies of it, and the magazine *Verve* brought out a facsimile of many of the illuminations together with a transcript of the text as a supplement, Vol. IV, No. 16, 1946.

This illumination is particularly valuable in showing the method of construction employed. It should be compared with Plate IX, which shows these same timber scaffolds covered with gaily coloured cloths and heraldic blazons. Cf. Frontispiece.

> *B.N. MS Français 2692*, ff. xxxivb and xxxv.

PLATE IX. No. 12

Spectators and Combatants at a Tournament of the pesle-mesle sort. The King of Arms is depicted in the centre of the lists and the pursuivants, musicians and attendant squires and armourers round the edge. In the central 'box' are the Judges in scarlet robes, identifiable by their blazons, and waited on by a Herald. Cf. Plate VIII and Note.

> *B.N. MS. Français 2692*, ff. lxxiib and lxxiij.

PLATE X. No. 13

Prize-giving after a Tournament: an elaborate ceremony in which the judges, heralds, minstrels and ladies were all involved. This illumination, remarkable for its beautiful portraiture, shows the ornately mounted jewel which formed the prize and also illustrates the method of lighting the hall (which is hung with dark green cloth). See Ch. II, pp. 21–22 above. Also Note to Plate VIII.

B.N. MS. Français 2692, f. lxxivb.

PLATE XI

The Formalized Interior, represented by a suspended curtain drawn open to reveal the scene. See also Fig. 11, p. 154, above.

No. 14. French stained glass, late twelfth century. The suspended lamp serves as a further symbol to suggest an interior scene.

Chartres Cathedral.

No. 15. English alabaster relief, early fifteenth century.

Victoria and Albert Museum.

PLATE XII

Formalized Mountains.

No. 16. The temptation of Christ in 'the wilderness'. Carved in stone by Thomas Boudin, 1612, in the north ambulatory of Chartres Cathedral.

No. 17. Apollo and the Muses (represented as instrumentalists) on Parnassus, as represented in one of the Valois-Medici tapestries, 1565. See Plate III, No. 4.

Valois Tapestry, No. 1.

These illustrations should be compared with the verbal descriptions of scenic mountains. See pp. 44, 70, 91, 170 and 209 above. Also Plate VII, No. 9.

PLATE XIII. No. 18

The Ship of Honour, erected on La Porte St. Denis in Paris as the first pageant-theatre in the celebrations to mark the wedding of Mary Tudor to Louis XII of France in 1514. This and the next three illustrations are reproduced from *B.M. MS. Cot. Vesp. B. II*, which is an official account in French of these festivities and the accompanying ceremonial, probably written by a herald and certainly by an eye-witness.

The ship, its cargo, passengers and their significance are described on fols. 3b and 4. The illumination is on f. 4b. The survival of this convention into the seventeenth century is illustrated in Plate XIX, No. 25.

These illustrations should be compared with verbal descriptions of ships used scenically indoors and out in 1313, 1389, 1430 and 1501. See pp. 44, 54, 92, 201, 209 and 213 above.

B.M. MS. Cot. Vesp. B. II, f. 4b.

PLATE XIII. No. 19

The Fountain of Grace, the second of the pageant stages erected in Paris, 1514, to celebrate the marriage of Mary Tudor to Louis XII of France. Cf. Plate XXVIII, No. 41. See also pp. 43, 90, 95 and 244–5 above.

B.M. MS. Cot. Vesp. B. II. Descriptive text, ff. 5 and 5b. Illumination, f. 6.

PLATE XIV. No. 20

Double Pageant Stage erected at the Chatelet in Paris as the sixth pageant theatre for Mary Tudor, 1514. Justice and Verity sit enthroned on the upper stage. Phoebus, Diana, Concord, Minerva and Stella Maris, all holding their appropriate identification symbols, stand on the lower stage. The flanking figures are images. See Plate XIII, No. 18, and Ch. III, pp. 81–88 above.

> *B.M. MS. Cot. Vesp. B. II.* Descriptive text, ff. 11b–12b. Illumination, f. 11.

PLATE XV. No. 21

Double Pageant Stage erected in front of the Church of the Holy Innocents. This is the only definitive illustration known to me of medieval stage machinery in action. The rosebud grew up out of the rose-bush, opened its petals to reveal the girl—symbolizing Mary Tudor—and then continued its ascent to the height of the upper stage. The lily on the upper stage opened similarly to reveal the youth—symbolizing the King of France. Bride and bridegroom are thus united on the upper stage symbolizing the garden of France between the four Cardinal Virtues. The wall and turrets symbolize Paris, at the gate of which Peace sits in triumph over Discord. See notes to Plates XIII, No. 18, and XIV, No. 20.

> *B.M. MS. Cot. Vesp. B. II.* Descriptive text, ff. 9 and 9b. Illumination, f. 10.

PLATE XVI. No. 22

The Tree of Genealogy as represented on a pageant stage in France. It was erected at the Chatelet, Paris, in 1517 for the coronation of Louis XII's daughter, Queen Claude, and should therefore be compared with the double stage on the same spot illustrated in Plate XIV. See Ch. III, pp. 72 *et seq.* above.

> *B.M. MS. Cot. Titus. A. XVII.* Descriptive text, f. 39b. Illumination, f. 40.

PLATE XVII. No. 23

Pageant Arch erected in Cornhill for Katherine of Aragon's reception into London, 1501, reconstructed from the minutely detailed description given by an eye-witness herald. It was called the Pageant of the Moon and in it, Raphael, King Alphonso and the prophet Job read the Princess's horoscope in a much more optimistic vein than fate was to admit of fulfilment. This arch should be compared with those erected for James I's coronation in 1603, for which Jonson, Dekker and Middleton were responsible. See Stephen Harrison, *Arches of Triumph*; also J. Jacquot, *Les Fêtes de la Renaissance*, and C. W. Hodges, *The Globe Restored*, for reproductions of Harrison's original engravings.

> *C.A. MS. 1st M. 13*, ff. 37, 37b.

PLATE XVIII. No. 24

Artificial Animals in the procession for the Archduchess Isabella's entry into Brussels, 1615. Mr. James Laver, discussing them in the Faber Gallery reproduction (p. 8), supposes them to have been real camels, one of them being fitted out with a horn to represent a unicorn. This seems highly improbable. In the first place they are too large; in the second, the skirts seem designed to conceal the 'porters' carrying these spectacularly large beasts; and thirdly the means of constructing such beasts artificially are known to us. See Ch. III, pp. 88 n*, 99 and 102 and Ch. VIII, p. 224 above; also Vol. II, 1576–1660, Pt. 1, Plates XIII, XXV and XXVI.

> Detail from the picture by Denis van Alsloot in the Victoria and Albert Museum.

PLATE XIX. No. 25

Pageant Cars: the Ship of Charles V, the Car of Apollo and the Car of Diana in the Brussels 'Triumph' for the Archduchess Isabella, 1615.

Quite apart from the lavish and artistic decoration of the pageant-waggons, these cars illustrate for us several points of medieval stage-craft that are otherwise difficult to visualize.

Chief among them are: (1) The Pageant Cloth (Car of the Muses) which screens the cart wheels from view while serving a decorative function of its own. (2) The arbour, decorated with gold stars on a blue ground to indicate night, should be compared with Circe's in Plate XXVII. (3) The ship (made in 1558, stored for nearly sixty years and newly refurnished) is 'carried' by 'porters' concealed within the sea horses and sea elephants, and should be compared with Plate XIII, No. 18.

> Detail from the picture by Denis van Alsloot in the Victoria and Albert Museum.

It is reproduced in colour in *Isabella's Triumph*, ed. James Laver for the Faber Gallery, 1947.

PLATE XX. Nos. 26 and 27

The Clock Tower in St. Mark's Square, Venice, was built by Gianpaolo Ranieri of Reggio Emilia and completed in 1499.

No. 27 shows the group of figures situated above the clock face and below the bell, bellmen (wild Moors) and the Lion of St. Mark. Figures of a Madonna and Child are seated in a niche under a canopy, while the Magi, led by an angel, pass before them.

Normally the doors on either side of the niche contain very large figures representing the hour and minutes of the day: but on Ascension Day these are replaced by the figures of the Magi and angel who, at every hour, come out through the door on the left of the picture and process past the Virgin and Child. As they do so, the angel raises its trumpet and the kings raise their turbans and offer their gifts. They disappear again through the door on the right.

No. 26 shows the figures themselves, which are three-quarters life size, carved in wood and beautifully painted. The little wheel and lever on the left-hand side of each figure is the mechanism which, on engaging with a raised mounting on the floor to the left of the Virgin, causes the body to incline forward at the waist. This, in turn, causes the arm to rise to the turban-crown and to doff it as the figure passes in front of the Virgin.

A superb English example of such clock-mechanism is that in Wells Cathedral. See Ch. IV, pp. 166–7 above, and Plates XXIX–XXXI below.

PLATE XXI. No. 28

Pageant Car of the Nativity in the Brussels 'Triumph' for the Archduchess Isabella, 1615. The floor of the tableau-stage is a clear 6 ft. off the ground and, taking the height of the actors to be no less than 5 ft., the whole structure must be thought of as between 15 and 20 ft. high. This gable roof could certainly conceal a winch mechanism if it were required.

The picture serves to show how ludicrous a double stage of this sort would be (as described by David Rogers, son of Archdeacon Rogers) with the area at present used for actors screened off to serve as a dressing-room and the stage giddily perched at what is now roof level. See Ch. IV, pp. 173–4 above.

> Detail from the picture by Denis van Alsloot in the Victoria and Albert Museum.

It is reproduced in colour in *Isabella's Triumph*, ed. James Laver for Faber Gallery, 1947.

PLATE XXI. No. 29

Hell-mouth and Devils as depicted in stained glass. See Plate XXXII, No. 52.

> Window XV, King's College, Cambridge.

PLATE XXI. No. 30

A Devil fighting an angel in the streets of Brussels, 1615. The picture illustrates vividly how both the physical reality of supernatural beings and the contemporary nature of their dress survived into the seventeenth century as stage conventions in North-Western Europe.

> Detail from the picture by Denis van Alsloot in the Victoria and Albert Museum. See Nos. 24, 25 and 28 above.

PLATE XXII. No. 31

Minstrels: an early fourteenth-century troupe, some disguised as animals, from the MS. *Le Roman de Fauvel* by Gervais de Bus with additions by Chaillon de Perstain.

> *B.N. MS. Français 146*, f. 36b.

Some of these correspond with the kind of costumes which the Royal Wardrobe had to provide for Edward III in 1347–49. See Ch. V, pp. 188–9 above.

PLATE XXII. No. 32

Wild Men dancing at the French Court, 1393. The dancers' garments caught fire when torches were dropped on them and the 'mommerie', according to Froissart, ended in disaster. This miniature, despite the rather arbitrary perspective, illustrates the normal lay-out of the banqueting hall or chamber for social recreation. Besides the musicians in their gallery and the dais and cloth of estate, the cupboard bearing precious plate and the tapestry on the walls are to be noted. See Note to Plate I, and Ch. VI, pp. 212–16 and 221–3 above.

> *B.M. MS. Harl. 4380*, f. 1.

PLATE XXIII. No. 33

Minstrels and Torchbearers with a Fool, providing entertainment for their patron at dinner, Flanders, *c.* 1500.

> *B.M. Add. MS. 24098*, f. 19b.

PLATE XXIII. No. 34

A Court Fool, c. 1480, from Olivier de la Marche's *Le Chevalier Délibéré*.

> *Bib. de l'Arsenal, MS. 5*, 117.

PLATE XXIV. Nos. 35 and 36

These two engravings depict the Cortile of the Pitti Palace, Florence, roofed over with red satin for the *Sbarra* and *Naumachia*, two of the principal festivities marking the wedding of Christine of Lorraine and the Grand Duke of Tuscanny in 1589. They were first identified by L. Magagnato, *Teatri italiani del cinquecento*, 1954.

No. 35 represents the empty courtyard with a 'barrier' in the middle and a 'castle' or 'battlement' standing out from a 'painted cloth' representing a 'city' and suspended against the far wall.

No. 36 depicts the 'sea battle' in progress. The 'castle' and 'city' defended by 'Turks' are now beseiged by 'Christians' whose ships are engaging with the 'Turkish' fleet, and afloat on water specially pumped into the courtyard for the occasion. The cloth should be compared with that behind Circe's arbour in Plate XXVII: see also Vol. II, 1576–1660, pp. 265 and 341–8.

On this spectacle see J. Jacquot, 'Les Fêtes de Florence (1589): quelques aspects de leur mise en scène', *Theatre Research*. III (1961) No. 3, pp. 157–176, especially pp. 162–5. Also A. M. Nagler, 'Theater Der Medici', *Maske und Kothurn*, IV (1958) No. 2/3, pp. 168–198.

PLATE XXV. No. 37

John Lydgate, with St. James on his right, presents his book (The *Secreta Secretorum*) to Thomas Montacute, Earl of Salisbury (omitted here).

The likeness would seem to be a good one; for when this portrait is compared with that in *B.M. MS. Harl. 2278* (showing Lydgate presenting his *Life of St. Edmund* to Henry VI.) f. 6., the resemblance is striking.

PLATE XXV. No. 38

The Execution of Mary Queen of Scots, in the great hall of Fotheringay Castle, 8th February 1587. This pen-and-ink sketch was made by Robert Beale, Clerk to the Council, who carried the death warrant to Fotheringay and read it aloud there. It is preserved among his papers, now in the British Museum, and depicts: (1) the entry of the queen (on the left), (2) her preparation and (3) her execution.

This railed, raised stage corresponds closely with the descriptions Professor Hotson discovered in the records of the Office of Works concerning preparations for stage plays in the hall at night. See *The First Night of Twelfth Night*. See also Ch. VII., pp. 247–252 above, and Vol. II, 1576–1660, Pt. 1, Plate XXXII.

PLATE XXVI. No. 39

A Comedy of Low Life performed on a village green in the Low Countries, *c.* 1550. The actors' tiring-house consists of a pole frame from which four curtains are suspended, admitting easy entrance and exit to the 'platea' or 'apron stage'. It is to be remarked that a comparatively small minority of the population are spending their leisure in watching the play. Cf. Vol. II, 1576–1660, Pt. 1, Plate XI.

In the extreme right of the picture, a procession may be seen wending its way towards the church. The banners and images carried by laymen are particularly interesting. See Ch. IV, pp. 147–8 and p. 174 above.

'La Kermesse', a painted panel by Peter Breughel, now in the Musée Calvet at Avignon.

PLATE XXVII. No. 40

A Ballet at the French Court. The French Ballet of the sixteenth century was a courtly entertainment of song, words, spectacle and dance equivalent to the English Disguising.

The plate shows the seating and scenic arrangements for the '*Ballet Comique de la royne, faict aux nopces de monsieur le Duc de Joyeuse et madamoyselle de Vaudremont sa sœur par Balthasar di Beauioyeulx, valet de chambre du Roy, et de la Reine sa mère*', which was published under that title in Paris, 1582.

The scenic units represent Circe's garden, a fountain, a sky-palace and an arbour. Spectators are seated at floor level, but stand in the scaffolds along the walls.

The arches of the 'garden' were constructed in perspective with a scenic cloth behind the centre one. The balustrade around it was ornamented in gold and silver, and animals can be seen parading within. The whole unit was lit by oil lamps. Immediately in front of the garden on the left of the picture is the fountain. See Plate XXVIII, No. 42: also Ch. VII, p. 244 above.

Ed. cit., sig. A. iv.

PLATE XXVIII

No. 41. *Detail of an Arbour* for the Ballet Comique de la Reine, *ed. cit.*, sig. I, iii. The trees were artificial, being made of the usual painted fabrics (see Ch. VII, p. 244 above). This unit is illustrated in position in Plate XXVII.

See Note to Plate XXVII.

No. 42. *Detail of a Fountain* for the Ballet Comique de la Reine, *ed. cit.*, sig. D. ij. The fountain was set on wheels and carried the orchestra, dressed as Tritons. The Tritons are shown in another engraving, sig. D. iv.

See Note to Plate XXVII: also Ch. VII, p. 244 above.

PLATE XXIX. No. 43

'*Quem quaeritis in sepulchro, O Christicolae?*' An English alabaster relief of the three Marys at the Christ's tomb on Easter morning. Note the crowned angels and the formalized trees beside the empty tomb.

Victoria and Albert Museum.

PLATE XXIX. No. 44

The Virgin and Mary Magdalen: plaster cast of stone carving. The two figures illustrated are reproduced from a cast in the Musée de Chaillot: the cast itself is taken from the fourteenth-century frieze in the South ambulatory of Nostre-Dame, Paris. This frieze, representing a series of scenes from the Life of Christ in dramatic tableaux, was repainted by Viollet-le-Duc in bright colours. The cast is not painted and the plate omits the figures that separate the Virgin from Mary Magdalen in the original frieze.

PLATE XXX. No. 45

Shepherds receiving news of the Nativity from an angel: carving in stone, c. 1250, on the tympanum of the Portail-Royal.

Chartres Cathedral.

PLATE XXX. No. 46

The cutting off of Malchus' ear: English alabaster relief of the early fifteenth century.

Victoria and Albert Museum.

PLATE XXXI. Nos. 47–50

English Alabaster Reliefs of scriptural scenes as visualized in the early fifteenth century and therefore representative of the costumes and groupings of identical scenes in the Miracle Cycles. See W. L. Hildburgh, *English Alabaster Carvings as records of the medieval religious drama.* Soc. of Antiquaries, 1949.

No. 47. *Christ before Herod.* The turban is as much a concession to the fact that Herod was not a Christian as to any geographical considerations.

No. 48. *The Deposition from the Cross.*

No. 49. *The Resurrection.*

No. 50. *The Ascension.* The formalized cloud on which Christ is standing bears so close a resemblance to descriptions of the cloud machines by which stage ascensions were effected from 1377 onwards that it is hard to believe this relief does not take its inspiration from the religious stage. In it may be seen the prototype of the 'glory' so familiar in seventeenth-century theatres of neo-classical design. See Ch. III, pp. 94–97 and Ch. IV, pp. 166–168 above.

Victoria and Albert Museum.

PLATE XXXII. No. 51

Christ in Glory: a vast mosaic in the dome of the central apse of the Romanesque Cathedral at Monreale, Palermo, Sicily.

PLATE XXXII. No. 52

The Last Judgement as depicted in one of the great frescoes which used to surround the Campo Santo at Pisa. This one, attributed to Orcagna (1308–1368) along with most of the others, was destroyed by shelling during the Second World War.

Of the many possible versions of the Doom all over Europe I have chosen this one because it illustrates two points concerning Hell of major importance to its representation on the stage. First, Hell mouth, though ghoulish in itself, was only the gateway to a house or castle itself containing many mansions, or rather, torture chambers. Secondly, the tortures inflicted upon the damned were no laughing matter. Compare the disembowelled men in the top left-hand corner of this picture with the stage directions of the Bourges *Actes des Apôtres*, described in the text, Ch. I, p. 4 above. See also Ch. IV, p. 152 above.

LIST OF MANUSCRIPTS

I. BIBLIOTHEQUE NATIONALE, PARIS

BIBL: ROI. 51
Mystère de St. Martin.
Author: Andrieu de la Vigne.

——   8069
Codex membranaceus.

FRANÇAIS   90
Fêtes données à la reine de Hongroie 1502.
Author: Bretagne Herald.

——   902
La Resurection du Sauveur.
Twelfth century. Anglo-Norman Verse.

——   2,692
Le Livre des Tournois du Roi René.
Le Grand Réserve.

——   138
L'histoire de la Toison d'or.
Author: William, Bishop of Tournay.

——   837 and 1553
Songs of the Trouvères and Jongleurs.

——   24,432
Le Pas Salhadin.
A late fourteenth century copy of an original of the thirteenth century.

——   146
Le Roman de Fauvel.

——   1,436
Matters relating to Tournaments.

——   21,809
Matters relating to Tournaments.

——   819 and 820
Miracles de Nôtre Dame par personages.

——   143
Illuminated MS. concerning the representation of Gods and Goddesses. Early fourteenth century. *Le Grand Réserve.*

——   12,536
Valenciennes Passion Play. Author: Hubert Cailleau. 1547. *Le Grand Réserve.*

II. BODLEIAN LIBRARY

ASHMOLE   793
The Pageants of 1392 for Richard II.

TWYNE   XVII
Queen Elizabeth I's visit to Oxford, 1566.

E. MUSEO. 94

Ricardi Maydiston de concordia inter Regem Ric. II et ciritatem London.

TOP. e.9.

Payments to workmen in Christchurch, 1566.

III. BRITISH MUSEUM

ADDITIONAL 4569. P

Divers Writs.

—— 6113

The marriage of Charles, Duke of Burgundy with Princess Margaret, daughter of King Edward IV.

COTTON, JULIUS B. II.

A London Chronicle, containing Lydgate's verses for Henry VI's entry into London.

—— JULIUS B. XII.

Henry VII's first Progress, ceremonies at Court, etc.

—— JULIUS E. IV. The Pageants of the Earl of Warwick; illuminated.

—— NERO C. IX.

The Marriage of Charles, Duke of Burgundy with Princess Margaret.

—— TITUS A. XII.

Le sacre couronnement, triomphe, et entrée à Paris de Madame Claude de France, fille de Louis XII roy de France et de Anne héritière de Bretagne, épouse de Francis I. Illuminated. (1517)

—— TITUS C. I.

Matters relating to Tournaments.

—— VESPASIAN A. XXV.

Machyn's Diary.

—— VESPASIAN B. II.

De la reception et entrée de la illustrissime dame et princesse Marie d'Angleterre (fille de Hen. VII) dans la ville de Paris le 6 Nov.re 1514 avec belles peintures.

—— VESPASIAN B. IV.

Henry VII's Welsh Progress—in Latin Verse.

—— VESPASIAN C. XIV. (1)

Matters relating to Katherine of Aragon's reception in England.

—— VITELLIUS A. XVI.

A Chronicle of London; containing a description of the Pageants for Prince Arthur's wedding to Katherine of Aragon.

—— VITELLIUS C. XI.

Two abstracts for the reception of Katherine of Aragon and fragments from the official record of the reception. All late copies.

HARLEIAN 69

The Book of Certain Triumphs.

—— 293

Matters relating to Tournaments.

—— 530

The Chronicle of Dunmow.

—— 642

Liber Niger; and Ordinances for Henry VII's Household. Late Copy.

—— 1,039

Coats of Arms. Officers at Henry V's coronation.

—— 1,944

The Breviarye of Chester, compiled by David Rogers.

—— 1,948

A shorter copy.

—— 2,013

The Chester Cycle. George Bellin's copy of the Banns and Plays, 1600.

—— 2,054

Chester, Smiths' Company Accounts, 1554–78.

—— 2,104

Matters relating to Chester.

—— 2,150

The Chester Cycle. Proclamation and Banns, c. 1540.

—— 4,379

Froissart's Chronicle (Vol. IV). Illuminated.

—— 6,018

A record of books loaned from the Cottonian Library to various persons including Inigo Jones.

—— 7,021 (22)

A catalogue of Certain Combats granted by the Kings of England.

LANSDOWNE 285

Various Challenges, Tournaments, etc.

IV. COLLEGE OF ARMS

L. 5   The challenge of Anthony Woodville.

1st M. 6   Documents relating to Tournaments, including the original drawings of which those in B.M. MS. Harl. 69 are copies.

1st M. 13   The official account of Katherine of Aragon's reception in England, 1501.

1st M. 16   Miscellaneous Heraldic Documents, fourteenth, fifteenth and sixteenth centuries.

V. CORPORATION OF LONDON RECORDS

BRIDGE HOUSE RENTAL BOOKS

Vol. I, 1404–1421 (paper); Vol. II, 1423–1460 (paper); Vol. III, 1460–1484 (vellum); Vol. IV, 1484–1509 (vellum).

The annual accounts of the Bridgemasters, including the rental of occupiers and vacancies belonging to the Bridge in divers London parishes, toll charges, etc.

LIST OF MANUSCRIPTS

CITY JOURNAL. Being the MS. records of the Court of Common Council.
REPERTORIES. Being the MS. records of the Court of Aldermen.

VI. CHESTER, TOWN HALL
Book containing fragments of Assembly Orders.
Assembly Book, 1529–1624.

VII. BEVERLEY, TOWN HALL
Account Rolls of Obedientiaries of Selby Abbey.

VIII. BRISTOL, COUNCIL HOUSE
Ricart's Calendar.
Treasurer's Accounts for 1577–78.

NOTE ON THE MSS & PRINTED RECORDS RELATING TO THE RECEPTION OF KATHERINE OF ARAGON INTO LONDON, 1499–1501.

The festivities associated with this event are incomparably better documented than any others in the fifteenth or early sixteenth century. No less than eleven MSS survive and these are supplemented by Bacon's *Life of Henry VII* and many of the letters which passed between the English and Spanish Courts.

Three of the MSS are abstracts; probably minutes of Privy Council deliberations, defining the nature of the planned festivities and allocating responsibility for their execution. Three more contain the reaction of the City Livery Companies to these instructions. Another contains an eye witness account of much that actually took place. The remaining four are more or less official histories. The difference in the standpoint of the various writers is itself helpful.

C.A. *MS. 1st M. 13*. ff. 1–11. An abstract of plans for the reception, written when it was still imagined that Katherine would land at Gravesend. This dates it between 1499 and 1500. The MSS does not appear to have been printed or referred to previously.

B.M. *MS Cot. Vit. C. XI* ff. 112b–126, & B.M. *MS Cot. Vesp. C. XIV.* ff. 94–103b. Both are abstracts of preparations, the latter probably the final draft actually put into practice with only minor modifications. They have been transcribed and printed by J. Gairdner, *Memorials of Henry VII*, 1858, ii. pp. 103 *et seq.*, and i. pp. 404 *et seq.* respectively.

Of the histories, more or less official, unquestionably the fullest is C.A. *MS 1st M. 13*, ff 27–67. It was written by someone having access to information at source, almost certainly Richmond King-at-Arms. It was printed first by Leland (*Collectanea*, ed. London, 1770, v. pp. 352–382) in a condensed form, and, subsequently, more or less in full by F. Grosse for *Ant. Rep.* ii, pp. 284–333. S. Anglo, 'The Court Festivals of Henry VII,' *Bulletin of the John Rylands Library*, Vol. 43 (1960) No. 1, p. 12 still refers his readers to the latter but has evidently not consulted the original MS. Since Grosse's transcription is very inaccurate—words and at times whole lines are omitted—the quotations and references given here are from the original MS. only.

B.M. *MS. Harl. 69*, ff 28b–46, albeit in erratic order, follows C.A. MS 1st M. 13, but the account of the street-pageants is omitted.

Guildhall MS. 3313. ff 29b–45b deals principally with the Pageants, the emphasis being laid upon the part played by the City. The MS has been transcribed and published by A. J. Thomas and I. D. Thornley, *The Great Chronicle of London*, London, 1938.

The last of the histories is an MS which, in the nineteenth century, was said to be in the Advocate's Library in Edinburgh, now the National Library of Scotland, but I have not myself either seen it or verified its continued existence.

There remain the three MSS at Guildhall which give details of the City of London's preparations.

Repertory, Vol. 1, ff 61b and 62. This corresponds with the first of the Abstracts in this list (C.A. *MS 1st M. 13* ff. 1–11) and gives details of the initial plans in 1499.

City Journal, Vol. f. 190b give facts about the financing of the pageants of 1501.

Bridge House Rentals, Vol. 4 (1484–1509) ff. 224b and 227b. This only concerns the Pageant on London Bridge itself. Many of the letters on the subject which passed between Spain and England are printed by G. A. Bergenroth, *Calender of Letters, Despatches and State Papers relating to the negotiating between Spain and England, 1495–1509*, ed. in. trans. London, 1862.

LIST OF
PRINTED BOOKS

ADAMS, H. H. *English Domestic or Homiletic Tragedy, 1575 to 1642.* Columbia University Press, 1943.

ADAMS, J. C. *The Globe Playhouse.* Harvard University Press, 1942.

ADAMS, J. Q. *Shakespearean Playhouses.* Cambridge, Massachusetts, n.d.

—— *Chief Pre-Shakespearean Dramas.* Boston, 1924.

ANGLO, S. 'The Court Festivals of Henry VII', *Bulletin of the John Rylands Library*, Vol. 43 (1960) No. 1, pp. 12–45.

ANTIQUARIAN REPERTORY. See Grose, F.

ARCHAEOLOGIA. See Society of Antiquaries.

AUDIAU, J. *Les Troubadours et l'Angleterre.* Paris, 1927.

AUSTIN, Thomas. *Two 15th Century Cookery Books.* (Ed. for E.E.T.S.), 1888.

BACON, Francis. *A Complete History of England.* London, 1622, fol.

—— *Essays.* (Ed. S. H. Reynolds), Oxford, 1890.

BAKER, H. C. *The Dignity of Man, Studies in the Persistence of an Idea*, 1947, and *The Wars of Truth*, 1952.

BALFOUR, Sir John. *Heraldic Tracts.* Edinburgh, 1837.

BAPST, G. *Essai sur l'Histoire du Théâtre.* Paris, 1893.

BATTEN, E. C. *The Register of Richard Fox while Bishop of Bath and Wells.* London, 1889.

BEARE, W. *The Roman Stage.* Revised ed., 1955.

BEAUJOYEUX, Balthasar de. *Balet Comique de la royne, faict aux nopces de monsieur le Duc de Joyeuse et mademoyselle de Vaudemont sa sœur.* Paris, 1582, 4to.

BEIJER, A. 'The Study of Theatre History in Universities', in *Universities and the Théâtre.* Ed. D. G. James, 1952.

BENTLEY, Samuel. *Excerpta Historica.* London, 1831.

BERGENROTH, G. A. *Calendar of Letters, Despatches and State Papers relating to the Negotiations between Spain and England, 1495–1509.* Ed. in trans: London, 1862.

BEVINGTON, D. *From Mankind to Marlowe*, Harvard, 1962.

BLOCK, K. S. *Ludus Coventriae or the Plaie called Corpus Christi.* Ed. for E.E.T.S. from *B.M. MS. Cot. Vesp. D. VIII*, 1922.

BLOUNT, T. *Glossographia.* 1st Ed. 1656; 2nd Ed. 1661.

BOAS, F. S. *University Drama in the Tudor Age.* Oxford, 1914.

BREWER, J. S. *The Reign of Henry VIII*, 2 vols., 1884.

—— *Calendar of Letters and Papers, Foreign and Domestic of the Reign of Henry VIII*, Vols. 1–4 (1509–1530); Vol. 1 ed. 1920; vols. 2–4 ed. 1864–76.

BROTANEK, R. *Die Englischen Maskenspiele.* Vienna, 1902.

BROUCHARD, C. *Origines du Théâtre de Lyon.* Lyons 1875.

CAMPBELL, L. B. *Scenes and Machines on the English Stage during the Renaissance: a classical revival.* Cambridge, 1923.

CAMPBELL, Rev. W. *Materials for a History of the Reign of Henry VII.* Rolls Series, 2 vols., London, 1873–77.

CARYSFOOT, Wm. Earl of. *The Pageants of Richard Beauchamp, Earl of Warwick.* Oxford, 1908 (Fac. of MS. Cot. Jul. E. iv).

CHAMBERS, Sir E. K. *The Medieval Stage.* 2 vols., Oxford, 1903.

—— *The Elizabethan Stage.* 4 vols., Oxford, 1923.

—— *Notes on the History of the Revels Office under the Tudors.* London, 1906.

—— *The English Folk Play.* 1933.

CHARTIER, Alain de. *Les Chroniques du feu roi Charles VII.* Paris, 1528, fol.

CHASSANG, A. *Des essais dramatiques imités de l'antiquité au XIVe et XVe Siècle.* Paris, 1852.

CHAYTOR, H. J. *The Troubadours in England.* Cambridge, 1923.

CHURCHYARD, Thomas. *A Discourse of the Queens Majesty's Entertainment in Suffolk and Norfolk.* London, 1578, 4to.

CLARKE, S. W. *The Miracle Play in England.* n.d. (?1900).

CLAREMONT, Francesca. *Catherine of Aragon.* 1939.

CLEDAT, L. *Le Théâtre en France au Moyen Age.* Paris, 1896, 8vo.

CLEMEN, W. H. *The Development of Shakespeare's Imagery,* 1951.

CLEPHAN, R. C. *The Tournament, its Periods and Phases.* London, 1919.

CLODE, C. M. *Early History of the Merchant Taylors Company.* London, 1888, 4to.

—— *Memorials of the Guild of Merchant Taylors.* London, 1875.

CLYNE, Ruth H. 'The Influence of Romances on Tournaments of the Middle Ages'. *Speculum,* 1945, xx. 204–11.

COCHERIS, H. *Entrées de Marie d'Angleterre femme de Louis XII à Abbeville et à Paris.* Paris, 1859, 8vo.

COGHILL, N. 'The Basis of Shakespearean Comedy', in *Essays and Studies, 1950.* Ed. G. Rosstrevor-Hamilton.

—— 'Comic Form in *Measure for Measure*', in *Shakespeare Survey 8.* Ed. A. Nicoll, 1955.

—— *The Masque of Hope.* O.U.P., 1948.

COHEN, Gustave. *Histoire de la Mise en scène dans le Théâtre réligieux français du moyen âge.* Paris, 1906, 8vo.

—— *Le Livre du conduite et compte des Dépenses pour le Mystère de la Passion joué à Mons en 1501.* Paris, 1925.

—— *Etudes d'histoire du théâtre en France.* Paris, 1956.

COLLIER, J. P. *Annals of the Stage.* 1831.

COMYNS, Sir John. *Digest of the Laws of England.* London, 1762–67, fol.

COULTON, G. G. *The Chronicles of European Chivalry.* London, 1930.

CRAIG, H. *English Religious Drama.* 1955.

—— *Two Coventry Corpus Christi Plays.* For E.E.T.S. 2nd ed., 1957.

CRIPPS-DAY, F. H. *History of the Tournament in England and France,* 1918.

CUNLIFFE, J. W. *Early English Classical Tragedies.* Oxford, 1912.

CUNNINGHAM, P. *Extracts from the Accounts of the Revels at Court.* Shakespeare Society, London, 1842.

DAVIES, R. *York Records of the Fifteenth Century,* 1843.

DEIMLING, H. *The Chester Cycle.* Ed. for E.E.T.S., 1893.

DELMOTTE, P. I. M. J. *Les Tournois de Chavenci, décrits par Jacques Bretex, 1285.* Valenciennes, 1835, 8vo.

DENHOLM-YOUNG, N. 'The Tournament in the Thirteenth Century'. *Studies in Mediaeval History presented to F. M. Powicke,* 1948, pp. 240–268.

DEVON, F. *Issues of the Exchequer, Hen. III to Hen. VI.* London, 1837.

DE LA COLOMBIERE, M. V. *Le Vrai théâtre d'honneur.* Paris, 1648, fol.

DONALDSON, E. T. *Piers Plowman and the authors of the C Text.* Yale, 1949.

DORAN, Dr. *The History of the Court Fools.* London, 1858.

DU FRESNE, C. Sieur du Cange. 'L'Origine et l'usage des tournois'. Ed. M. Petitot, in *Collection complète des mémoires rélatifs à l'histoire de France.* Paris, 1824, 8vo.

—— { 'Des armes à outrance, des joutes . . .'
—— { 'Des cottes d'Armes et de l'origine des couleurs.'
Ed. C. Leber, in *Collection des meilleurs dissertations, notices, et traités particuliers rélatif à l'histoire de France.* Paris, 1828, 8vo.

DIX, Dom G. *The Shape of the Liturgy.* 1946.

ENCYCLOPEDIE ALPINA ILLUSTREE. *La Cathédrale de Chartres.* Paris, 1942.

ENGLAND, G. and POLLARD, A. W. *The Townley Plays.* For E.E.T.S., 1897. 2nd ed. 1907.

EVANS, H. A. *English Masques.* London, 1900.

EVANS, J. and SERGEANTSON, M. S. *English Mediaeval Lapidaries.* E.E.T.S., London, 1933.

EVANS, J. *Dress in Mediaeval France.* 1952.

FABYAN, R. *Chronicle.* For Pynson, 1516. Ed. H. Ellis, 1871.

FAIRHOLT, F. W. *The Civic Garland: A Collection of Songs from London Pageants.* Percy Society, London, 1845.

—— *Lord Mayors' Pageants: Being Collections towards a History of These Annual Celebrations. Vol. I: History of Lord Mayors' Pageants. Vol. II: Reprints of Lord Mayors' Pageants.* 2 vols., Percy Society, London, 1843–44.

—— '*MISCELLANEA GRAPHICA.*' London, 1857, fol.

—— '*BROADSIDES—Henry VIII to Elizabeth, 1519–1603, Nos. 1–107.*' Privately bound and presented to the Society of Antiquaries.

FARMER, J. S. *The Dramatic Writings of John Bale, Bishop of Ossory.* London, 1907.

FAVAL, E. *Mimes Français du XIIIᵉ Siècle.* Paris, 1910.

FAVYN, A. *A Theatre of Honour and Knighthood.* London, 1623.

FERNE, J. *The Blazon of Gentrie.* London, 1586, 4to.

FERRARI, Guglio. *La Scènographia.* Milan, 1902.

FEUILLERAT, A. *Documents Relating to the Office of the Revels in the Time of Elizabeth.* Louvain, 1908.

—— *Documents Relating to the Revels at Court in the Time of King Edward VI and Queen Mary.* Louvain, 1914.

FIRTH, J. F. *Historical Memoranda.* London, 1848.

FITCH, R. *The Norwich Grocers' Play.* Norwich, 1856.

FLORIO, J. *Vocabolario, italiano e inglese.* 1611, fol.

FOURNIER, E. *Le Théâtre français avant le Renaissance, 1450–1550*. Paris, n.d.

FRANK, G. *The Mediaeval French Drama*. 1954.

FROISSART, Sir John. *Chroniques de Froissart*. Ed. Kervyn de Lettenhove. 29 vols., Brussels, 1872.

FRONING, R. *Das Drama des Mittelalters*. Stuttgart, 1891.

FURNIVALL, F. J. *The Digby Plays*. Ed. for E.E.T.S., 1896, from *Bodl. MS. Digby 133*.

FURNIVALL, F. J. and POLLARD, A. W. *The Macro Plays*. E.E.T.S., 1904.

GAIRDNER, J. *The Paston Letters*. 6 vols. Ed. London, 1904.

—— *Letters and Papers Illustrative of the Reigns of Ric. III and Hen. VII*. 2 vols., Rolls Series, London, 1861–63.

—— *Calendar of Letters and Papers, Foreign and Domestic, Hen. VIII*. Vols. 5–13 (1531- 1538). Ed. 188–93.

GARDINER, H. C. *Mysteries' End*. New Haven, 1946.

GERAUD, H. *Paris sous Phillipe-le-bel*. Paris, 1837, 4to.

GIRADOT, A-T de. *Mystère des Actes des Apôtres (Bourges)*. Paris, 1854.

GIRAUD, M. *Composition, mise en scène et réprésentation du Mystère des Trois Doms joué à Romans les 27, 28 et 29 mai, aux fêtes de Pentecôte de l'an 1509*. Lyons, 1848, 8vo.

GLODEFROY F. *Dictionnaire de l'ancienne langue Française du IXe siècle*. 10 vols., Paris, 1881–1902.

GODEFROY de PARIS. *Chronique Métrique*. (Ed. J. A. Buchon). Paris, 1827. 8vo. (Suivie de la Teille de Paris en 1313).

GODEFROY, Theodore (Advocat au Parlement de Paris). *Le Cérémonial de France*. Paris, 1619, 4to.

GOLDWELL, Henry. *Brief declaration of the shows performed before the Queen's Majesty and the French Ambassadors*. 1581.

GORDON, D. J. 'Ben Jonson's Haddington Masque', in *M.L.R.*, Vol. XLII, No. 2 (April, 1947).

GOTCH, J. A. *Inigo Jones*. London, 1928.

GRAVES, T. S. *The Court and the London Theatres during the reign of Elizabeth*. London, 1913.

GREG, W. W. *Henslowe Papers*. 1907.

—— *The Assumption of the Virgin*. Oxford, 1915.

—— *The Play of Antichrist at Chester*. 1935.

—— *A Bibliography of the English Printed Drama to the Restoration*, 4 vols. Bibliographical Society, 1939–59.

—— *A List of English Plays written before 1643 and printed before 1700*. Bibliographical Society, 1900.

—— *A List of Masques, Pageants, etc., supplementary to a List of English Plays*. Bibliographical Society, 1902.

GREENLAW, E. A. *Studies in Spenser's Historical Allegory*. Baltimore, 1932 (Johns Hopkins Monographs in Literary History, Vol. 2).

GREGORY, William. *Chronicle of London*. (Ed. J. Gairdner), Camden Society, 1876.

GROSE, F. *The Antiquarian Repertory*. 4 vols., London, 1775. 2nd Ed., 4 vols., London, 1807.

HALL, Edward. *Chronicle*. London, 1548, fol.   Ed. Sir H. Ellis, London, 1809. 4to.

HARRIS, M. D. *Coventry Leet Book.* 2 vols. Ed. for E.E.T.S., 1907–9.

HARRISON, Stephen. *The arches of triumph erected in honour of K. James I at his maiesties entrance and passage through his honourable citty of London 15, March 1603. invented and published by S. Harrison and graven by W. Kip.* London, 1604, fol.

HARROD, H. *Norfolk Archaeology.* London, 1859.

HAWES, Stephen. *The Pastime of Pleasure.* Reprinted from the ed. of 1555. Percy Society (Vol. XVIII), 1845. Ed. W. E. Mead, for E.E.T.S., 1928.

HEFELE, C. J. Von. *Histoires des Conciles.* Paris, 1869–73.

HODGES, C. W. *The Globe Restored.* 1953.

—— 'Unworthy Scaffolds', in *Shakespeare Survey 3.* Ed. A. Nicoll, 1950.

HOLINSHED, R. *Chronicles of England.* London, 1586, fol. Ed. London, 1807–8.

HOLSBOER, S. Wilma. *L'Histoire de la Mise en Scène dans le théâtre Français 1600–1657.* Paris, 1933.

HONE, William. *Ancient Mysteries Described.* 1823.

HOPE, Sir William St. John and ATCHLEY, E. G. C. F. *English Liturgical Colours.* S.P.C.K., 1918.

HOTSON, L. *The First Night of Twelfth Night.* 1954.

HUIZINGA, J. *The Waning of the Middle Ages.* 1924.

HENRI. II. *C'est l'ordre qui a été tenu à la nouvelle et joyeuse entrée que très haut et très excellent et très puissant prince le Roy très chrétien Henri deuxieme a faite en sa bonne ville et cité de Paris le 16 Juin 1549.* Paris, 1549.

HILDBURGH, W. L. *English alabaster carvings as records of the mediaeval religious drama*, London, for Soc. of Antiquaries, 1949.

HISTOIRE LITTERAIRE DES TROUBADOURS. Paris 1774, 8vo.

HOUSEHOLD ORDINANCES. *See* SOCIETY OF ANTIQUARIES.

HOUSEHOLD, Royal. *Statutes for the ordering of* . . . London, 1505, 4to.

JACQUOT, J. *Les Fêtes de la Rennaissance.* I and II, Paris, 1956 and 1956–60.

JONSON, Ben. *Complete Works.* Ed. C. Herford and P. Simpson, 11 vols., 1925–52.

JUBINAL, Achille. *Jongleurs et Trouvères.* (Ed. from *B.N. MSS. Français 837 and 1553*), Paris, 1835, 8vo.

—— *La Resurrection du Saueur; Fragment d'un Mystère.* (Ed. from *B.N. MS. Français, 902*), Paris, 1834, 8vo.

—— *Mystères Inédits.* Paris, 1837, 8vo.

—— *Nouveau recueil de contes.* Paris, 1839–42, 8vo.

JUPP, E. B. *The Carpenters' Company.* London, 1848. 2nd ed. with supplement, 1887.

KEITH, W. G. 'The Art of Scenic Decoration' in *The Builder.* Vol. CVII (1914).

KENDRICK, T. D. *British Antiquity.* London, 1950.

KERNODLE, G. R. *From Art to Theatre.* Chicago, 1944.

KINGSFORD, C. L. *Chronicles of London.* Oxford, 1905.

—— *Henry V.* London, 1911. *See* STOW, John.

KIP, W. *See* HARRISON, Stephen.

KITTO, H. D. F. *Form and Meaning in Drama.* 1956.

LA MARCHE, Olivier de. *Les Mémoires.* Lyons, 1561, fol. Brussels, 1616, 4to. Ed. Henri Beaune et J. d'Arbaumont, 4 vols., Paris, 1883–88, 8vo.

—— *Le Chevalier Délibéré*. Ed. F. Lippman for Bibliographical Society, 1898.

LAMBARD, William. *A Perambulation of Kent*. 2nd ed., London, 1596, 8vo.

LANGLOIS, E. H. *Discours sur les déguisemens monstrueux dans le cours du Moyen Age*. Rouen, 1833, 8vo.

LA RUE, Abbé de. *Essais historiques sur les bardes, les jongleurs et les trouvères normands et anglo-normands*. Caen, 1834, 8vo.

LAWRENCE, W. J. *The Elizabethan Playhouse and Other Studies*. 2 vols., Stratford, 1912–13.

—— *The Physical Conditions of the Elizabethan Public Playhouse*. Cambridge, 1927.

LEACH, A. F. 'Some English Plays and Players, 1220–1548', in *An English Miscellany presented to Dr. F. J. Furnivall*, 1901.

LEBÈGUE, R. *La Tragédie religieuse*. Paris, 1929.

LECLERC, H. *Les Origines italiennes de l'architecture théâtrale moderne*. Paris, 1946.

LELAND, J. *De rebus Britannicis collectanea cum T. Hearnii praefatione notis et indice ad editionem primam*. Ed. 2a, 6 vols, 1774.

LIBER ALBUS. Compiled by John Carpenter (Common Clerk) and Richard Whitington (Mayor) of London. Translated from the Latin and Anglo-Norman and edited by H. T. Riley. London, 1861.

LINDSAY, Sir David. *Works*. Ed. D. Hamar for S.T.S., 4 vols., 1931–36.

LINTHICUM, M. C. *Costume in Elizabethan Drama*. Oxford, 1936.

LOOMIS, L. H. 'Secular Dramatics in the Royal Palace, Paris, 1378, 1389, and Chaucer's "Tregetoures",' *Speculum*, 1958, xxxiii.

LOOMIS, R. S. 'Edward I, Arthurian Enthusiast', *Speculum*, 1953, xxviii.

LUDUS COVENTRIAE or the Plaie called Corpus Christi. See BLOCK, K. S.

LYDGATE, John. *Minor Poems*. 2 vols., ed. H. N. MacCracken, E.E.T.S., London, 1934.

—— *The Fall of Princes*. Ed. H. Bergen, E.E.T.S., London, 1924–27.

—— *Troy Book*. Ed. H. Bergen, E.E.T.S., London, 1906–35.

MACHYN, H. *Diary*. (Ed. from *B.M. MS. Cot. Vit. F. v.*), for Camden Society by J. G. Nichols, Vol. XVII.

MAGNIN, Charles. *Fragment d'un Comique*. (Ed. from *MS. Bibl. Roy. 8069*), Paris, 1840, 8vo.

—— *Les Origines du théâtre moderne*. Paris, 1838, 8vo.

MÂLE, E. *L'Art religieux de la Fin du Moyen Âge en France*, Paris, 1922.

MANDET, Francisque. *Histoire de la Langue Romane (Roman Provençal)*. Paris, 1840, 8vo.

MANLY, J. M. *Specimens of the Pre-Shakespearean Drama*. Boston, 1897.

MATTINGLEY, G. *Catherine of Aragon*. London, 1942.

MAYDISTON, Richard. *De Concordia inter Ric. II et civitates London*. Ed. Thomas Wright, Camden Society, London, 1838.

MEAD, W. *The Mediaeval Feast*. London, 1934.

MEDICI TAPESTRIES. *The Marriage of Henry of Valois to Catherine de Medici*. Uffizi Galleries, Florence. Cat. Nos. 472–474 and 492, See JACQUOT, J.

MENESTRIER, Claude François. *Traité des tournois, joustes, carrousels, et autres spectacles publics*. Lyon, 1669, 4to.

MEYER, Paul. *L'Histoire de Guillaume le Marechal, Compte de Striguil et de Pembroke, Regent d'Angleterre de 1216 à 1219, poème Français.* 3 vols., Paris, 1891–1901.

MIDDLETON, Thomas. *The Triumphs of Love and Antiquity.* London, 1619, 4to.

MONSTRELET. *Chroniques.* Ed. Metayer, Paris, 1595, fol.

MORRIS, R. H. *Chester during the Plantagenet and Tudor Periods.* 1893.

MURRAY, J. T. *English Dramatic Companies,* 1910.

NAPIER, Mrs. A. (Robina). *A Noble Boke of Cookry.* Transcribed and edited, London, 1882.

NEVILL, William. *The Castle of Pleasure.* Ed. Roberta Cornelius for E.E.T.S., London, 1930.

NICHOLL, J. *Some Account of the Worshipful Company of Ironmongers.* 2nd ed., London, 1866.

NICHOLS, J. *The Progresses and Public Processions of Queen Elizabeth.* 3 vols., London, 1788–1804. 2nd Ed. 1823.

—— *The Progresses, Processions and Magnificent Festivities of King James the First.* 4 vols., London, 1828.

NICHOLS, J. G. *The Fishmongers' Pageant on Lord Mayor's Day 1616 devised by Anthony Munday.* Ed. Nichols, London, 1844, fol.

NICOLAS, H. *Proceedings and Ordinances of the Privy Council, 1386–1542.* 7 vols., London, 1834–37.

NICOLL, A. *Masks, Mimes and Miracles.* London, 1931.

—— *Stuart Masques and the Renaissance Stage.* New York, 1938.

NOBLE, The Rev. M. *A History of the College of Arms.* London, 1804.

NORRIS, Edwin. *The Ancient Cornish Drama.* 2 vols., 1859.

ORMEROD, G. *History of the County Palatine and City of Chester.* 3 vols., 2nd ed., 1882.

OWST, G. R. *Preaching in Mediaeval England.* 1927.

—— *Literature and Pulpit in Mediaeval England.* 1933.

PARIS, Matthew. *Historia.* Ed. 1589, Tigur.

—— *Chronica Majora.* Rolls Ed., 1872–83.

PENN, D. *The Staging of the 'Miracles de Nostre Dame'.* New York, 1933.

PETIT de JULLEVILLE, L. *Les Mystères.* 2 vols., Paris, 1880.

POLLARD, A. W. *English Miracle Plays, Moralities and Interludes.* 1927.

PORTAL, F. *Des couleurs symboliques.* Paris, 1837, 8vo.

PROSSER, E. *Drama and Religion in the English Mystery Plays,* Stanford, 1961.

PROST, B. *Traités du duel Judiciares, Relation de Pas d'Armes et Tournois.* Paris, 1872, 8vo. Another Ed., illustrated but with a new title page entitled: *Traicté de la forme et devis comme on faict les tournois.* Paris, 1878, 8vo.

QUATREBARBES, Th. Comte de. *Œuvres complètes du Roi René.* Angers, 1845.

RAINE, J. (the younger). *A Volume of English Miscellanies.* Ed. for Surtees Society, 1890.

REYHER, P. *Les Masques Anglais.* Paris, 1909.

REYNOLDS, G. F. *Some Principles of Elizabethan Staging*. Modern Philology, II (April, 1905); III (June, 1905).

RIBNER, I. 'Morality Roots of the Tudor History Play' in *Tulane Studies in English*, Vol. IV, New Orleans, 1954, pp. 21–43.

RILEY, H. T. *Memorials of London and London Life*. London, 1868.

—— *Munimenta Gildhallae*. 3 vols. in 4. Rolls Series, 1859–62.

ROBBINS, E. W. *Dramatic Characterization in Printed Commentaries on Terence, 1473–1600*. Illinois, 1951.

ROSSITER, A. P. *Woodstock, A Moral History*. 1946.

—— *English Drama from Early Times to the Elizabethans*. London, 1950.

—— 'Ambivalence: the Dialectic of the Histories', in *Talking of Shakespeare*. Ed. J. Garrett, 1954.

RUSSELL, John. *The Boke of Nurture*. Ed. F. J. Furnivall (from *MS. Harl. 4011*). London, 1868.

SALTER, F. M. *Mediaeval Drama in Chester*. Toronto, 1955.

—— 'The Banns of the Chester Plays', reprinted from the *Review of English Studies*, Vol. XVI, No. 62, April, 1940.

SCHRADE, L. *La Représentation d'Edipo Tiranno au Teatro Olimpico, Vicence, 1585*, Paris, 1960.

SFORZA, Constanzo. *Le nozze di C. Sforza e Camilla d'Aragona celebrate a Pesaro nel maggio 1475*. (Reprint of 1475 Vincenza ed.), public. a cura di T. de Marinis, Rome, 1946.

SHAPIRO, I. A. 'The Bankside Theatres: Early Engravings', in *Shakespeare Survey*, i, ed. A. Nicoll, 1948.

SHARP, T. *A Dissertation on the Pageants or Dramatic Mysteries anciently performed at Coventry*. Coventry, 1825.

SHOEMAKER, W. H. *The Multiple Stage in Spain during the 15th and 16th Centuries*. Princeton, 1935.

SKEAT, W. W. 'The Flower and the Leaf', in *Chaucerian and Other Pieces*. Oxford, 1897, pp. 361–379.

SOUTHERN, R. *The Open Stage*, 1952.

—— *Changeable Scenery, its Origin and Development in the British Theatre*. 1954.

—— *The Mediaeval Theatre in the Round*. 1957.

SPURGEON, C. *Five Hundred Years of Chaucer Criticism*. 3 vols., Cambridge, 1925.

STOW, John. *Survey of London*. Ed. C. L. Kingsford, 2 vols., Oxford, 1908.

STRUTT, Joseph. *The Sports and Pastimes of the People of England*. 1st Ed., London, 1801; ed. William Hone, London, 1830.

SOCIETY OF ANTIQUARIES. *Archaeologia*. Vol. XVII, London, 1814. Household Ordinances, *A Collection of Ordinances and Regulations for the Government of the Royal Household*. Ed. 1790.

THOMPSON, E. N. S. *The English Moral Play* (New Haven) 1910.

THORNDIKE, A. H. *Shakespeare's Theater*. 1916.

TIDDY, R. J. E. *The Mummer's Play*. Oxford, 1923.

TILLYARD, E. M. *Shakespeare's History Plays*. 1944.

TOULMIN-SMITH, L. *English Guilds*. Ed. for E.E.T.S., 1870.

—— *York Mystery Plays*. 1885.

TREBUTIEN, G. S. *Le Pas Salhadin*. (Ed. from *B.N. MS. Fr. 24432*, ff. 29b–33b.) Paris, 1836, 8vo.

TREVELYAN, G. M. *English Social History*. London, 1944.

UNWIN, George. *The Guilds and Companies of London*. London, 1908.

VAIL MOTTER, T. H. *The School Drama in England*. 1929.
VARDAC, N. *Stage to Screen*. Harvard, 1949.
VELLEY, l'abbé P. F. *Histoire de France*. Paris, 1799, 12mo.
VERVE. René d'Anjou. *Traité de la Forme et Devis d'un Tournoi*. Vol. IV, No. 16 (April, 1946).
VIDAL, A. *Les Vieilles Corporations de Paris. La Chapelle St. Julien-des-ménestriers et les ménestrals à Paris*. Paris, 1878, 4to.
VIGENERE, Blaise de. *La Somptueuse et magnifique Entrée du très-chrestien Roy Henry III . . . en la Cité de Mantoüe*. Paris, 1574, 4to.
VULSON, Marc de. *Le vray théâtre d'Honneur et de Chevalerie*. 2 vols., Paris, 1648.

WALLACE, C. W. *The Evolution of the English Drama up to Shakespeare*. London, 1912.
WALSINGHAM, T. *Chronica Monasterii S. Albani*. 7 vols. in 12. Rolls Series, 1863–76.
—— *Historia Anglicana*. Ed. H. T. Riley, London, 1863, 8vo.
WARTON, T. *History of English Poetry*. (A full reprint—text and notes—of ed. London, 1778–81.) London, 1840, 8vo.
WEDGEWOOD, C. V. *Seventeenth Century English Literature*. Oxford, 1950.
WELCH, C. *The History of the Worshipful Company of Pewterers of the City of London*. 2 vols., London, 1902.
WELSFORD, E. *The Court Masque*. Cambridge, 1927.
—— *The Fool, his Social and Literary History*. London, 1935.
WENDOVER, Roger. *Flores Historiarum*. 4 vols, ed. Henry Coxe, 1841.
WESTMINSTER, Matthew. *The Flowers of History*. Ed. in trans. by C. D. Younge, London, 1853.
WHETSTONE, George. *The (first and) seconde part of the Famous Historie of Promos and Cassandra*. London, 1578, 4to.
—— *The Rocke of Regard*. London, 1576, 8vo.
WILLARD FARNHAM. *The Mediaeval Heritage of Elizabethan Tragedy*, 1936, and *Shakespeare's Tragic Frontier*, 1950.
WILSON, F. P. *A Calendar of the Dramatic Records in the Books of the Livery Companies of London 1485–1640*. Ed. for Malone Society, Collections III.
WITHINGTON, Robert. *English Pageantry. An Historical Outline*. 2 vols., Harvard University Press, 1918–20.
—— 'The Early Royal Entry', in *P.M.L.A.*, Vol. XXXII, No. 4 (1917).
WRIGHT, J. G. *Anglo-Norman Resurrection Play*. Paris, 1931.
WRIGHT, T. *The Tournament of Totenham and the Fest*. London, 1836, 4to.
WARBURG INSTITUTE, University of London. *The Mediterranean Tradition in England*. (O.U.P.) 1945.

YOUNG, K. *The Drama of the Mediaeval Church*. 2 vols., 1933.
YORKSHIRE ARCHAEOLOGICAL JOURNAL. 'Account Roll of Selby Abbey, 1397–98', in Vol. XV. (1900), pp. 408–9.

INDEX

PLATE I

No. 1. *Two Wild Men*; painted panels

PLATE II

No. 2. *Tilting*; manuscript illumination

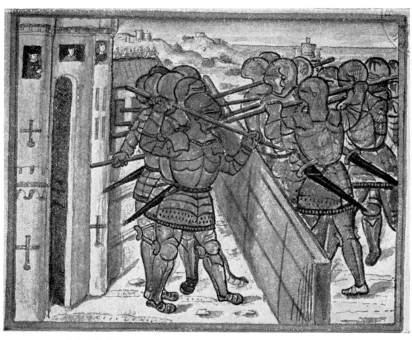

No. 3. *Jousting at Barriers*; manuscript illumination

PLATE III

No. 4. *Jousting at Barriers*; tapestry

PLATE IV

No. 5. *A Pas d'Armes*; carved ivory mirror cases

PLATE V

No. 6. *Jousting at the Ring*; manuscript illumination

PLATE VI

No. 7. *Jousting at the Quintain*; detail from tapestry

No. 8. *A Pas d'Armes, the Elephant and Castle*; detail from tapestry

PLATE VII

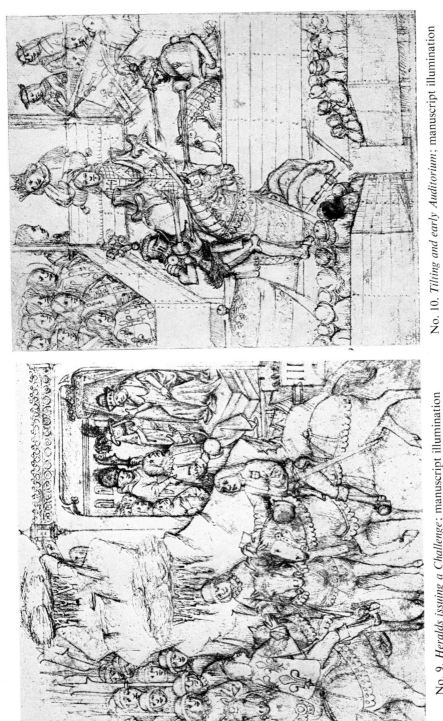

No. 10. *Tilting and early Auditorium*; manuscript illumination

No. 9. *Heralds issuing a Challenge*; manuscript illumination

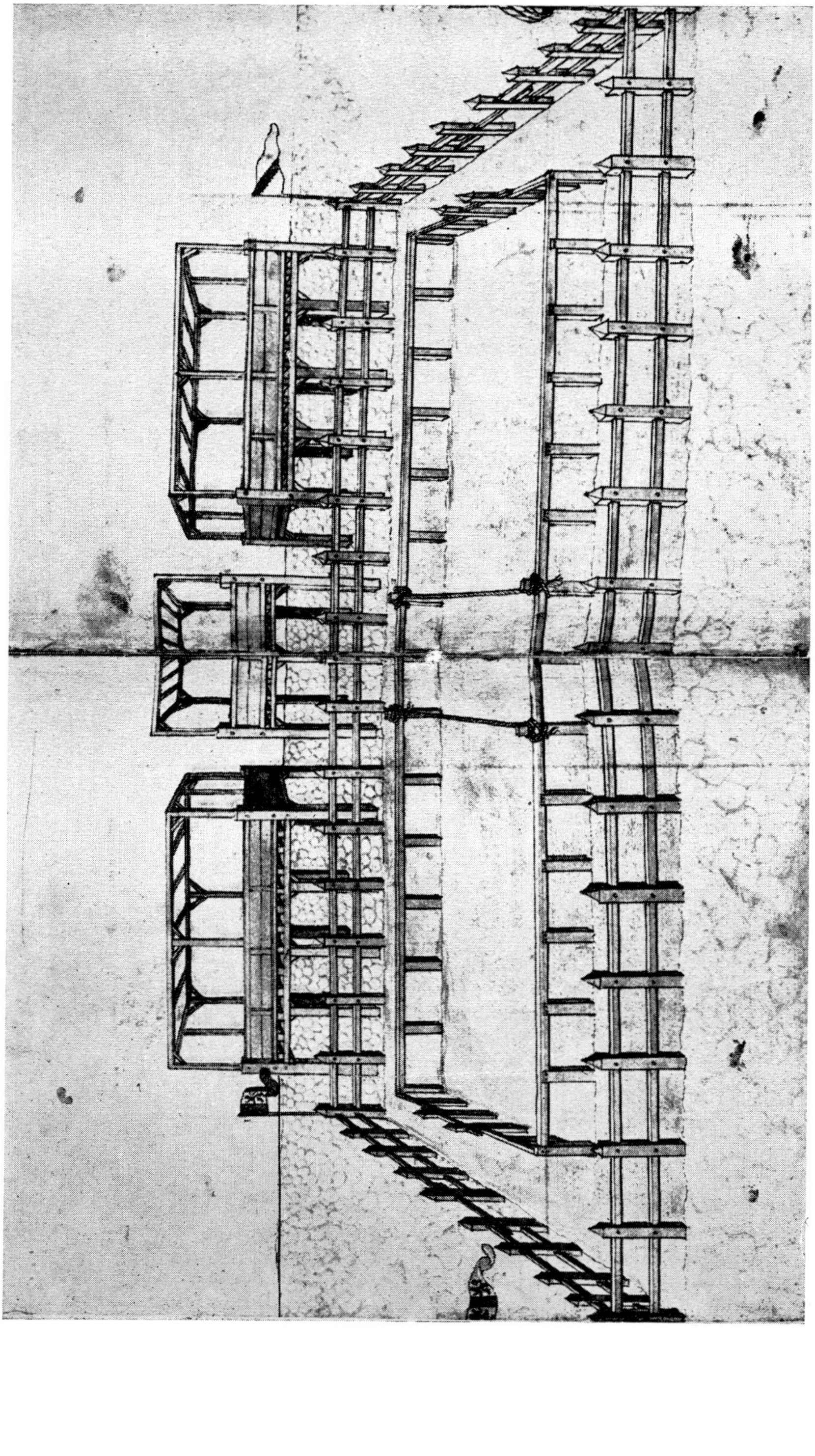

PLATE VIII

No. 11. *A Tournament, Lists and Auditorium;* manuscript illumination

PLATE IX

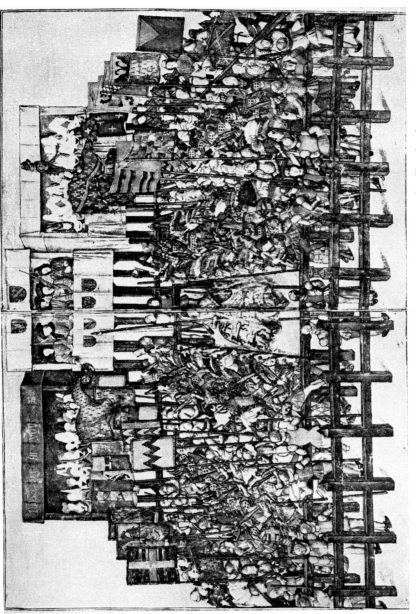

No. 12. *A Tournament, Spectators and Combatants*; manuscript illumination

PLATE X

No. 13. *A Tournament, Prize-giving*; manuscript illumination

PLATE XI

No. 15. *A Formalized Interior*; alabaster relief

No. 14. *A Formalized Interior*; stained glass

PLATE XII

No. 17. *A Formalized Mountain*; detail from tapestry

No. 16. *A Formalized Mountain*; carving in stone

PLATE XIII

No. 19. *A Formalized Fountain with Virtues*; manuscript illumination

No. 18. *A Formalized Ship*; manuscript illumination

PLATE XIV

No. 20. *Double Pageant Stage with Virtues*; manuscript illumination

PLATE XV

No. 21. *Double Pageant Stage with Mechanical Flowers*; manuscript illumination

PLATE XVI

No. 22. *Genealogical Tree and seated Virtues*; manuscript illumination

PLATE XVII

No. 23. *Pageant Archway*; reconstructed drawing

PLATE XVIII

No. 24. *Pageant Animals*; detail from painted panel

PLATE XIX

No. 25. *Pageant Cars*; detail from painted panel

PLATE XX

No. 26. *Mechanical Figures of Angel and Magi designed for a Clock*; St. Mark's Square, Venice

No. 27. *The Clock with Figures in position*; St. Mark's Square, Venice

PLATE XXI

28. *Pageant Car of the Nativity*; detail from
    painted panel

No. 29. *Hell-mouth and Devils*;
      stained glass

30. *Angel and Devil in Combat*; detail from
    painted panel

PLATE XXII

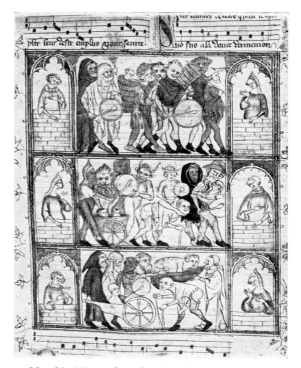

No. 31. *Minstrels, a fourteenth-century troupe*;
manuscript illumination

No. 32. *A Mumming of Wildmen, their costumes having caught fire*; manuscript
illumination

PLATE XXIII

No. 34. *Fool's Costume;* manuscript illumination

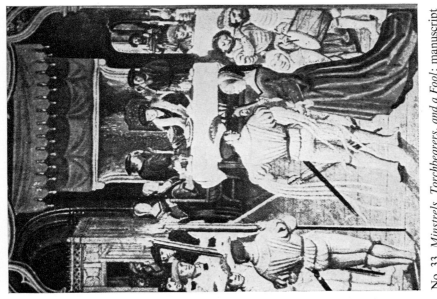

No. 33. *Minstrels, Torchbearers, and a Fool;* manuscript illumination

PLATE XXIV

No. 35. *Banquet Hall prepared for a Disguising*; engraving

No. 36. *The same, with the Disguising in progress*; engraving

PLATE XXV

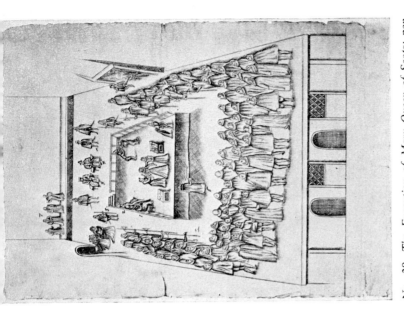

No. 38. *The Execution of Mary Queen of Scots*; pen drawing

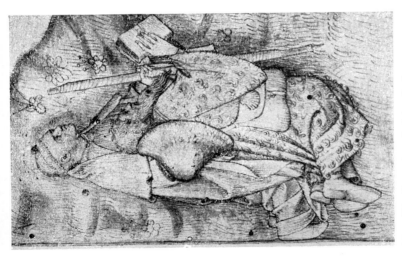

No. 37. *Portrait of John Lydgate*; manuscript illumination

PLATE XXVI

No. 39. *Outdoor, Peasant Stage*; oil painting

PLATE XXVII

No. 40. *A Ballet at the French Court*; engraving

PLATE XXVIII

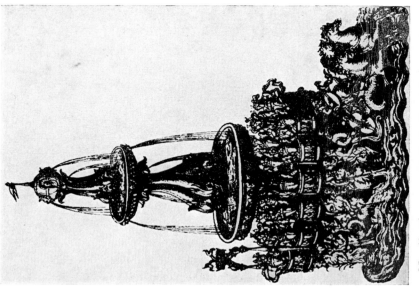

No. 42. *The same, detail of a Fountain*; engraving

No. 41. *The same, detail of an Arbour*; engraving

PLATE XXIX

No. 44. *The Virgin and Mary Magdalen*; stone carving

No. 43. *The three Marys at the Sepulchre*; alabaster relief

PLATE XXX

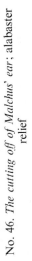

No. 46. *The cutting off of Malchus' ear*; alabaster relief

No. 45. *Shepherds led by an Angel*; carving in stone

PLATE XXXI

No. 47. *Christ before Herod*; alabaster relief

No. 48. *The Deposition from the Cross*; alabaster relief

No. 49. *The Resurrection*; alabaster relief

No. 50. *The Ascension*; alabaster relief

PLATE XXXII

No. 51. *Christ in Glory*; mosaic

No. 52. *Last Judgement*; fresco